THE
ORDEAL OF CIVILIZATION

PL. I. CEREMONY OF MEDIEVAL HOMAGE

THE ORDEAL OF CIVILIZATION

A SKETCH OF THE DEVELOPMENT AND WORLD-WIDE DIFFUSION OF OUR PRESENT-DAY INSTITUTIONS AND IDEAS

BY

JAMES HARVEY ROBINSON

AUTHOR OF "THE MIND IN THE MAKING"
"THE NEW HISTORY" "THE HISTORY OF WESTERN EUROPE"
"THE HUMANIZING OF KNOWLEDGE" ETC.

Profusely Illustrated

HARPER & BROTHERS PUBLISHERS
NEW YORK AND LONDON
MCMXXVI

THE ORDEAL OF CIVILIZATION

Copyright, 1926, by
HARPER & BROTHERS
Printed in the U. S. A.

K-A

CONTENTS

CONTENTS

CONTENTS

[vii]

CONTENTS

PUBLISHER'S NOTE

To Messrs. Ginn & Company both the Author and the Publishers of "The Ordeal of Civilization" are indebted for their coöperation in the labor involved in the preparation and manufacture of the book for the general public. A large part of the material, both text and illustrations, of this volume is taken from *Mediaeval and Modern Times,* by permission of Ginn & Company.

LIST OF PLATES

[xi]

LIST OF PLATES

THE
ORDEAL OF CIVILIZATION

THE
ORDEAL OF CIVILIZATION

CHAPTER I

GETTING UNDER WAY

The Living Past." Meaning of the "Middle Ages." The Mighty Roman Empire. Weaknesses of the Roman Imperial Government. The Rise of the Christian Church.

"The Living Past"

MANY years ago the writer became dissatisfied with what passed for *history*. He sympathized with the harsh judgments which Voltaire, Herbert Spencer, Buckle, John Richard Green, and many others had heaped upon those who pretended to give their contemporaries some idea of the past. Instead of illuminating man's career as a skillful biographer unfolds the story of his hero, our historical manuals have commonly been little more than arid and unprofitable chronicles, relieved here and there by some casual anecdote. And even intelligent people still express their distaste for history by saying that they have no knack for remembering dates—as if this were the main point in studying the past.

Without having as yet met with that ingenious expression of Mr. F. S. Marvin's, *The Living Past*, the writer became increasingly conscious of the fundamental fact that it is the past that makes the present, and that what goes before is the key to what comes after.

In order at the very start to make plain the nature and variety of our abject dependence upon the past, we have only to consider our language, our customs, our knowledge, our views of this world and the next, our tastes and the means of gratifying them. "On every hand the past controls us, for the most part unconsciously and without protest on our part. We are in the main its willing adherents. The imagination of the most radically minded cannot transcend any great part of the ideas and customs transmitted to him. When once we grasp this truth we shall, according to our mood, humbly congratulate ourselves that, poor pygmies that we are, we are permitted to stand on the giant's shoulders and enjoy an outlook that would be quite hidden from us if we had to trust to our own short legs; or we may resentfully chafe at our bonds and, like Prometheus, vainly strive to wrest ourselves from the rock of the past in our eagerness to bring relief to the suffering children of men." [1]

As Goethe says, gloomily:

> Es erben sich Gesetz' und Rechte
> Wie eine ew'ge Krankheit fort.

Whether we are tempted to curse the past as a sort of chronic disease, or bless it as the giver of all good things, we are inevitably its offspring; it makes us its own long before we know enough to defend ourselves. It is almost all that we have, and to understand it is to understand ourselves, our possibilities of achievement, our frustrations and perplexities.

Only gradually did the writer come to conceive of history as something far more vital than the record of bygone events and the description of extinct institutions. He then saw that if history was to fulfill its chief function and become an essential explanation of how our own civilization came to take the form it has, and present the problems that it does, a fresh selection from the records of the past would have to be made. Much that had been included in historical manuals would of necessity be left out as irrelevant or unimportant. Only those considerations would properly find a place which clearly served to forward the main purpose of seeing more and more distinctly how this, our present Western civilization, in which we have been born and are now immersed, has come about. We shall discover that, in spite of the drag of the past, our era is in many ways a novel human adventure, the outcome of which no man can foresee.

This volume is not merely a sketch of the history of western Europe, but rather the background of contemporaneous ways of doing and thinking not only in Europe, but in North and South America, Australasia, latterly, even in India, Japan, western Asia, and Africa. For during the past two or three centuries the knowledge and devices of western Europe have

---

[1] *The New History* (1912), p. 256, by the present author.

disseminated themselves over the whole globe, as no other civilization in the history of mankind has done. This is because modern science and invention generated incidentally their own unprecedented and varied means of world-wide penetration, through previously unheard-of methods of effective and rapid intercommunication and transportation. Down to the nineteenth century fleet-footed, tireless runners, camels, asses, and horses, oars and sails, were the only known ways of carrying news or goods. Then came steam, electricity, gasoline, submarine cables thousands of miles long, lastly the ether itself.

But before we go farther let us come into the clear as to what is to be meant by civilization in its fullest sense.

It includes all those discoveries and inventions, all their accompanying knowledge, ideals, joys, and scruples, which are the peculiar prerogative of men as distinguished from their fellow animals. There was a time, mayhap a million years ago, when all the human race led the life of a wild creature. Naked and houseless and speechless men wandered about, like a bear or a gorilla, in a precarious search for their daily food. Such sticks and stones as came to hand were their only weapons against their foes, human and otherwise. There are no such simple people any more, nor have there been in historic times. While we are all born absolutely uncivilized, every human being to-day, even the savage Australian, the Bushman, and the Eskimo, grows up among those who know how to talk, make a fire, erect shelters, according to their circumstances, fabricate tools and weapons and articles of adornment. The young have everywhere to master rules of conduct and alien ideas of safe and unsafe, right and wrong.

While all portions of the human race are now highly civilized compared with mankind in the beginning, we are apt to think of civilization in those very exceptionally elaborate and sophisticated forms in which it has miraculously developed here and there during the past five or six thousand years. Higher civilization is naturally far more precarious than its lower forms. It flames up from the smoldering, undying fire, and then subsides, as has happened so often—in Ancient Egypt, Mesopotamia, India, China, Greece, Italy, Peru, and Central America. All higher civilizations, with their art and literature, their aggressive states, their codes of law, their temples and palaces, have so far proved episodal and fleeting. In some cases the dust of the desert or the creepers of the jungle have given them decent burial; in others the collapse was not complete and the traditions of knowledge and skill were feebly perpetuated and formed the germs of a new blossoming.

Men have hitherto ill understood themselves and their world. They have not only suffered from blank ignorance, but from tremendous and grotesque misapprehensions in regard to their nature and surroundings. Whether they can ever learn enough to control the fluctuations of civilization no one can say. So far it has certainly been drift rather than mastery. The best knowledge of man and his world which is now scattered about in the heads and books of those who have taken the most pains to inform themselves is incalculably greater than ever before in man's history. It is this knowledge, called "science," and its applications which constitute the distinctive trait of our present civilization.

Its steady progress is by no means assured. The accumulation of knowledge, invention and criticism has been going on uninterruptedly since, let us say, the twelfth century—that is, for seven hundred years. Slow and halting at first, it now proceeds with stupendous rapidity, in certain ranges. Should this revision and enrichment of human ideas continue without a serious setback for several hundred years to come, it would be the first instance of such steady advance in man's history. But what are to be the effects of binding the peoples of the whole earth together, of giving every man and woman a vote, of the assumption that the people at large constitute the court of last resort?—to mention only two or three of our innovations. All of these and many others are unprecedented experiments and adventures. Will democracy continue to generate great combinations of ignorance and reaction—of which some impressive examples have already appeared—to perpetuate race, religious and economic prejudice and jealousy? Will they successfully oppose and check the progress and diffusion of scientific discovery? Will they succeed in maintaining outworn and hampering notions of human relationship and duty?

We do not have to attempt to answer these questions. I am merely justifying the title of this volume. I am urging that no single thing would do more to weaken the dangers which threaten our civilization and impede its advance and expansion than a knowledge of history in the sense in which the word is used here. And so it seems fair to call this book *The Ordeal of Civilization,* since it is essentially an explanation of the origin of the most comprehensive and momentous of all human trials and experiments.

Meaning of the "Middle Ages"

The development of our present civilization began with the first inventions and findings-out of mankind, of which no records remain. The further the tale can be carried back the more impressive becomes the fact that civilization and knowledge are matters of accumulation, extending through hundreds of thousands of years and confined to no country or people or age. The history of European culture cannot be limited to Europe itself. It did not originate there, and seems to have been imported at various times from various quarters. Such familiar things as our alphabet and numerals, our week with its seven days dedicated to gods, our day of rest, our division of time into hours, these all come from Asia. The achievements of the Greeks were based on what had long been going on in Egypt and the eastern Mediterranean region. The refinements of civilization in the first great state of western Europe, the Roman Empire, were almost entirely of Greek origin.

Fortunately we can take up the story with the decline and break-up of the Roman Empire. Professor Breasted has in his *Conquest of Civilization* admirably explained our previously contracted debts to the past.

It is impossible to divide the past into distinct, clearly defined periods and prove that one age ended and another began in a particular year, such as 476, or 1453, or 1789. Men do not and cannot change their habits and ways of doing things all at once, no matter what happens. It is true that a single event, such as an important battle which results in the loss of a nation's independence, may produce an abrupt change in the government. This in turn may either encourage or discourage trade and manufacture, and modify the language and alter the interests of a people. But these deeper changes take place only very gradually. After a battle or a revolution the farmer will sow and reap in his old way; the artisan will take up his familiar tasks, and the merchant his buying and selling. The scholar will study and write as he formerly did, and the household will go on under the new government just as it did under the old. So a change in government affects the habits of a people but slowly in any case, and it may leave them quite unaltered.

This tendency of mankind to do, in general, this year what it did last, in spite of changes in some one department of life,— such as substituting a president for a king, traveling by rail instead of on horseback, or getting the news from a newspaper instead of from a neighbor,—results in what is called the *unity* or *continuity of history*. The truth that no sudden change has ever taken place in all the customs of a people, and that it cannot, in the nature of things, take place, is perhaps the most fundamental lesson that history teaches. Nations retain their old customs while they adopt new ones, and a small portion of a nation may advance while the greater part of it stays behind.

We cannot, therefore, hope to fix any year or event which may properly be taken as the beginning of that long period which followed the break-up of the Roman Empire in western Europe and which is commonly called the "Middle Ages." Beyond the northern and eastern boundaries of the Roman Empire, which embraced the whole civilized world from the Euphrates to Britain, mysterious peoples moved about whose history before they came into occasional contact with the Romans is practically unknown.

These Germans, or "barbarians," as the Romans called them, were destined to put an end to the Roman Empire in western Europe. They had first begun to make trouble about a hundred years before Christ, when a great army of them was defeated by the Roman general Marius. Julius Cæsar narrates in polished Latin, familiar to all who begin the study of that language, how fifty years later he drove back other bands. Five hundred years elapsed, however, before German chieftains succeeded in founding kingdoms within the boundaries of the Empire. With their establishment the Roman government in western Europe may be said to have come to an end and the Middle Ages to have begun.

Yet it would be a great mistake to suppose that this means that the Roman civilization suddenly disappeared at this time. Long before the German conquest, art and literature had begun to decline toward the level that they reached in the Middle Ages. Many of the ideas and conditions which prevailed after the coming of the barbarians were common enough before. Even the ignorance and strange ideas which we associate particularly with the Middle Ages are to be found in the later Roman Empire.

The word "Medieval" falls very differently upon different ears. To many it is a term of reproach or detraction, suggesting stupid holdovers from the "Dark Ages." To those, on the other hand, who are loyal to the Roman Catholic Church, it recalls "the age of faith," of saints, knights, and devout expeditions to regain the holy sepulcher. To a small class of artists and men of letters the cathedrals and troubadours represent loveliness and heroism which have been lost in a world of present business and heartless science. There are plenty of excuses for these divergent estimates and emotions. This volume contains no attacks on the period, nor is there any effort to defend the ancient ways. For the writer is averse to such procedure. He can record Saint Bernard's hot denunciation of the stuff of which crusaders were made, without remaining untouched by the Canticle of the Sun. The worldly lives of many thirteenth-century bishops do not make their cathedral churches the less marvelous.

The Middle Ages embrace, roughly, a thousand years of startling change which separates Theodoric the Great from

[9]

Henry VIII, Boethius from Rabelais. The period falls into two parts: the Early Middle Ages, when for five centuries things went for a time from bad to worse in the matter of increasing ignorance and disorder, with but slight premonitions of betterment. Then followed the Later Middle Ages, especially from about the year 1100, when a great revival of civilization began which still stirs the admiration of those who are out of harmony with the latter days.

For our purposes the chief importance of the Middle Ages lies in the fact that we do not inherit our civilization directly from the Roman Empire, as it inherited its civilization from the Greeks. The intervening medieval period emphasized habits of thought and institutions which have deeply affected modern men and women even down to the present day. We shall have opportunity to observe many instances of this in the following account of the break-up of the Roman Empire, the Germanic invasions and succeeding age of turmoil, the subsequent rise of towns, the spread of trade, the rôle of the Church, the revival of higher education, the substitution of the kingly state for the feudal baronies,—in all these and many other respects the Middle Ages will be seen to form in a peculiar and intimate sense the background of our prevailing civilization. Without some knowledge of medieval culture no sure grasp on conditions to-day is possible. Whether it be a question of perpetuating its moral, religious, and artistic ideals, or of supplanting them, they underlie the great issues of modern times. For each stage in man's development is at once an indispensable prerequisite and an unavoidable obstacle to those who would press forward in human knowledge and social adjustments.

The Mighty Roman Empire

Before we begin our study of the history of western civilization since the break-up of the Roman Empire we must stop to consider briefly the way in which Europeans were living before the barbarian leaders succeeded in establishing their kingdoms.

At the opening of the fifth century there were no separate, independent states in western Europe such as we find on the map to-day. The whole area now occupied by England, France, Spain, and Italy formed at that time only a part of the vast realms ruled over by the Roman emperor and his host of officials. As for Germany, most of it was still familiar only to the half-savage tribes who inhabited it. The Romans had tried in vain to conquer this part of Europe, but finally had to content themselves with keeping the German hordes out of the Empire by means of fortifications and guards along the Rhine and Danube rivers.

ROMAN AQUEDUCT NEAR NÎMES

This structure was built by the Romans about A.D. 20 to supply the Roman colony of Nemausus (now called Nîmes) in southern France with water from two excellent springs twenty-five miles distant. It is nearly 900 feet long and 160 feet high, and carried the water over the valley of the river Gard. The channel for the water is at the very top, and one can still walk through it. The miles of aqueduct on either side of this bridge have almost disappeared

The Roman Empire, which embraced southern and western Europe, western Asia, and even the northern portion of Africa, included the most diverse peoples and races. Egyptians, Arabs, Jews, Greeks, Italians, Gauls, Britons, Iberians,—all alike were under the sovereign rule of "Rome." One great state embraced the nomad shepherds who spread their tents on the borders of Sahara, the mountaineers in the fastnesses of Wales, and the citizens of Athens, Alexandria, and Rome, heirs to all the luxury and learning of the ages. Whether one lived in York or Jerusalem, Memphis or Vienna, he paid his taxes into the same treasury, he was tried by the same law, and looked to the same armies for protection.

At first it seems incredible that this huge Empire, which included African and Asiatic peoples as well as the most various races of Europe in all stages of civilization, could have held together for five centuries instead of falling to pieces, as might have been expected, long before the barbarians came in sufficient strength to establish their own kingdoms in its midst.

When, however, we consider the bonds of union which held the state together, it is easy to understand why the Empire endured so long. These were (1) the wonderfully organized government with its officials in every part of the realm, watching everything and allowing nothing to escape them; (2) the worship of the head of the Empire, the emperor; (3) the hardy legions of soldiers who had made Rome's conquests and could be used to put down revolt and keep out the barbarians; (4) the Roman law in force everywhere; (5) the admirable roads, which enabled the soldiers to march quickly from place to place; and, lastly, (6) the Roman colonies and the teachers sent out by the government, for through them the same ideas and ways of doing things were carried to even the most distant parts of the Empire.

Let us first glance at the government and the emperor. His decrees were dispatched throughout the length and breadth of the Roman dominions; whatsoever he approved became law, according to the well-known principle of the Roman constitution. While the cities were permitted some freedom in the management of their own affairs, the emperor and his innumerable officials kept an eye upon even the humblest citizen. The Roman government, besides maintaining order, settling law cases, and defending the boundaries, assumed many other responsibilities. It watched the grain dealers, butchers, and bakers, and saw to it that they properly supplied the public and never deserted their occupation. In some cases it forced the son to follow the profession of his father. If it could have had its way, it would have had every one belong to a definite class of society, and his children after him. It kept the unruly poorer classes in the towns quiet by furnishing them with bread, and sometimes with wine, meat, and clothes. It provided amusement for them by expensive entertainments, such as races and gladiatorial combats. In a word, the Roman government was not only wonderfully organized, so that its power was felt throughout its whole extent, but it attempted to regulate almost every interest in life.

Every one was required to join in the worship of the emperor because he stood for the majesty and glory of the Roman dominion. The inhabitants of each province might revere their particular gods, undisturbed by the government, but all were obliged, as good citizens, to join in the official sacrifices to the head of the State, as if he were a god. The early Christians were persecuted, not only because their religion was different from that of their fellows, but because they refused to reverence the images of the emperor, and openly prophesied the downfall of the Roman State. Their religion seemed incompatible with good citizenship, since it forbade them to show the usual respect for the government.

As there was one government, so there was one law for all the civilized world. The same principles of reason, justice, and humanity were believed to hold whether the Roman citizen lived upon the Euphrates or the Thames. The law of the Roman Empire is its chief legacy to posterity. Its provisions are still in force in many of the states of Europe to-day, and it is one of the subjects of study in our American universities. Wives and children were protected from the cruelty of the head of the house, who, in earlier centuries, had been privileged to treat the members of his family as slaves. The law held that it was better that a guilty person should escape than that an innocent person should be condemned. It conceived mankind, not as a group of nations and tribes, each with its own laws, but as one people included in one great empire and subject to a single system of law based upon fairness and reason.

Magnificent roads were constructed, which enabled the messengers of the government and its armies to reach every part of the Empire with what at that time seemed incredible speed. These highways made trade comparatively easy and encouraged merchants and travelers to visit the most distant portions of the realm. Everywhere they found the same coins and the same system of weights and measures.

Colonies were sent out to the confines of the Empire, and the remains of great public buildings, of theaters and bridges, of sumptuous villas and baths at places like Trèves, Cologne,

ROMAN BRIDGE AT ST. CHAMAS

This Roman bridge with its handsome portals, at St. Chamas in southern France, was built in the time of the Emperor Augustus; that is, about the beginning of the Christian era

Bath, and Salzburg, indicate how thoroughly the influence and civilization of Rome penetrated to the utmost parts of the territory subject to her rule.

The government encouraged education by supporting at least three teachers in every town of any considerable importance. They taught rhetoric and oratory and explained the works of the great Latin and Greek writers, so that an educated man was pretty sure to find, even in the outlying parts of the great Empire, other educated men with much the same interests and ideas as his own. Everywhere men felt themselves to be not

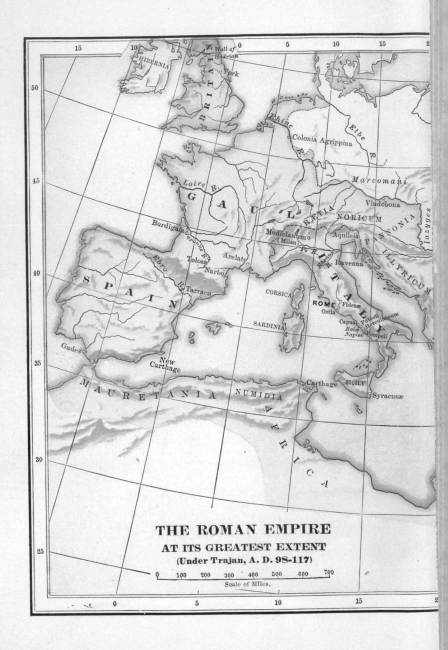

THE ROMAN EMPIRE

AT ITS GREATEST EXTENT

(Under Trajan, A. D. 98-117)

Scale of Miles.

0 100 200 300 400 500 600 700

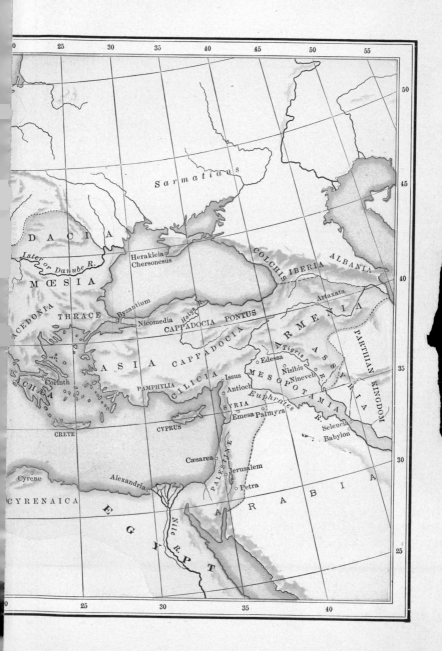

mere natives of this or that country but citizens of the Roman world.

During the four centuries from the first emperor, Augustus, to the barbarian invasions we hear of no attempt on the part of its subjects to overthrow the Empire or to withdraw from it. The Roman State, it was universally believed, was to endure

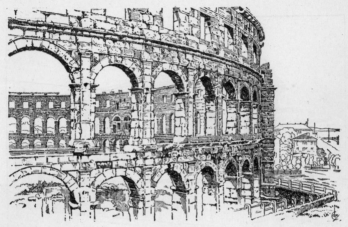

ROMAN AMPHITHEATER AT POLA

Every large Roman town had a vast arena, or amphitheater, in which thousands of spectators could be seated to watch the public fights between professional swordsmen (gladiators) and between men and wild beasts. The emperors and rich men paid the expenses of these combats. The greatest of these arenas was the Coliseum at Rome. The one here represented shows that a Roman town of perhaps 40,000 inhabitants was supplied with an amphitheater holding no less than 20,000 spectators, who must have assembled from all the region around. The seats have disappeared; only the outside walls remain

forever. Had a rebellious nation succeeded in throwing off the rule of the emperor and in establishing its independence, it would simply have placed itself outside the civilized world.

The Weaknesses of the Roman Imperial Government

Just why the Roman government, long so powerful and so universally respected, finally became unable longer to defend

its borders, and gave way before the scattered attacks of the
German peoples, who never combined in any general alliance
against it, is a very difficult question to answer satisfactorily.
We know very little about the times, because the accounts that
have come down to us give us no reasons why things happened
as they did, and the best we can do is to see what were the
conditions in the Empire when the Germans invaded it.

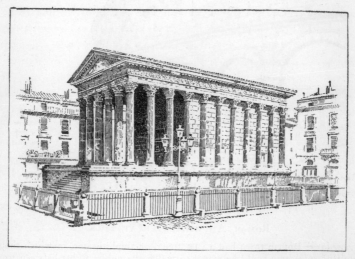

ROMAN TEMPLE AT NÎMES

This beautiful temple at Nîmes, France, was probably built about the year
one of the Christian era. It was situated in the forum with other public
buildings which have now disappeared. After the break-up of the Roman
Empire it was used as a Christian church, then as a town hall, then as a
warehouse, and finally as a stable. In 1824 it was restored to its original
condition as we now find it

The Roman government was in some respects astonishingly
strong and well organized, but there was no satisfactory way
of choosing a new emperor. No candidate could secure the
election unless he was supported by the army, and the soldiers
in the various parts of the Empire often proposed different
men for whom they were willing to fight. Civil war would
then follow, which would come to a close only when one candi-

date succeeded in getting the better of all his rivals. This brought about frequent disorders, which did their part in weakening the Empire.

It required a great deal of money to support the luxurious palaces of the emperors at Rome and Constantinople with their innumerable officials and servants, and to supply "bread and circuses" for the populace of the towns. All sorts of taxes and exactions were consequently devised by ingenious officials to make up the necessary revenue. The crushing burden of the great land tax, the emperor's chief source of income, was greatly increased by the bad way in which it was collected. The government made a group of the richer citizens in each of the towns permanently responsible for the whole amount due each year from all the landowners within their district. It was their business to collect the taxes and make up any deficiency, it mattered not from what cause.

This responsibility, together with the weight of the taxes themselves, ruined so many landowners that the government was forced to decree that no one should desert his estates in order to escape the exactions. Only the very rich could stand the drain on their resources. The middle class sank into poverty and despair, and in this way the Empire lost just that prosperous class of citizens who should have been the leaders in business enterprises.

The sad plight of the poorer laboring classes was largely due to the institution of slavery which prevailed everywhere in ancient times. When the Romans conquered a new region they were in the habit, in accordance with the customs of war, of reducing a considerable part of the inhabitants to slavery. In this way the number of slaves was constantly increased. There were millions of them. A single rich landholder might own hundreds and even thousands, and it was a poor man that did not have several at least. For six or seven centuries before the barbarian invasions every kind of labor fell largely into their hands in both country and town.

Land was the only highly esteemed form of wealth in the Roman Empire, in spite of the heavy taxes imposed upon it.

Without large holdings of land no one could hope to enjoy a high social position or an honorable office under the government. Consequently the land came gradually into the hands of the rich and ambitious, and the small landed proprietor disappeared. Great estates called "villas" covered Italy, Gaul, and Britain.

These villas were cultivated and managed by armies of slaves, who not only tilled the land, but supplied their master, his household, and themselves with much that was needed on

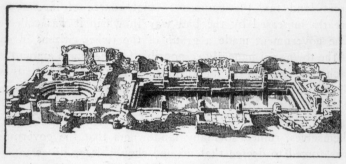

ROMAN BATHS AT BATH

There are hot springs at Bath, England, and here the Roman colonists in Britain developed a fashionable watering place. In recent years the soil and rubbish which had through the centuries collected over the old Roman buildings has been removed and we can get some idea of how they were arranged. The picture represents a model of a part of the ruins. To the right is a great quadrangular pool, 83 by 40 feet in size, and to the left a circular bath. Over the whole, a fine hall was built, with recesses on either side of the big pool where one might sit and talk with his friends

the plantation. The workmen among them made the tools, garments, and other manufactured articles necessary for the whole community, or "family," as it was called. Slaves cooked the food, waited on the proprietor, wrote his letters, read to him, and entertained him in other ways. Although a villa might be as extensive as a large village, all its members were under the absolute control of the proprietor of the estate.

Quite naturally, free men scorned to work with their hands or even to carry on retail business, for these occupations were associated in their minds with the despised slave.

Each great household where articles of luxury were in demand relied upon its own host of skillful slaves to produce them. Moreover, the owners of slaves frequently hired them out to those who needed workmen, or permitted them to work

ROMAN GATE AT TRÈVES

Colonia Augusta Treverorum (now called Trier or Trèves) was one of the chief Roman colonies on the German boundaries of the Empire. The Roman emperors often resided there, and the remains of their palace are still to be seen. The great gate here represented was designed to protect the entrance of the town, which was surrounded with a wall, for the Romans were in constant danger of attack from the neighboring German tribes. One can also see at Trèves the remains of a vast amphitheater in which on two occasions Constantine had several thousand German prisoners cast to be killed by wild animals for the amusement of the spectators

for wages, and in this way left little for the free man to do even if he was willing to work.

A notable improvement in the condition of slaves took place during the centuries immediately preceding the barbarian invasions. Their owners abandoned the horrible subterranean prisons in which the farm hands had once been miserably huddled at night. The law, moreover, protected the slave from some of the worst forms of abuse; first and foremost, it deprived his master of the right to kill him.

Slaves began to decrease in numbers before the German invasions. In the first place, the supply had been cut off after the Roman armies ceased to conquer new territory. In the second place, masters began to free their slaves on a large scale,—for what reasons we do not know. When a slave was freed he was called a *freedman,* but he was by no means in the position of one who had been born free. It was true that he was no longer a mere thing that could be bought and sold, but he had still to serve his former master,—who had now become his *patron,*—for a certain number of days in the year. He was obliged to pay him a part of his earnings and could not marry without his patron's consent.

But, as the condition of the slaves improved, and many of them became freedmen, the state of the poor free man only became worse. In the towns, if he tried to earn his living, he was forced to mingle with those slaves who were permitted to work for wages and with the freedmen, and he naturally tended to sink to their level.

In the country the free agricultural laborers became *coloni,* a curious intermediate class, neither slave nor really free. They were bound to the particular bit of land which some great proprietor permitted them to cultivate, and remained attached to it if it changed hands. Like the later medieval serf, they could not be deprived of their fields so long as they paid the owner a certain part of their crop and worked for him during a period fixed by the customs of the estate upon which they lived. This system made it impossible for the farmer to become really independent, or for his son to become better off than he.

When a country is prosperous the population tends to increase. In the Roman Empire, even as early as Augustus, a falling off in numbers was apparent, which was bound to weaken the State. War, plague, the evil results of slavery, and the outrageous taxation all combined to hasten the depopu-

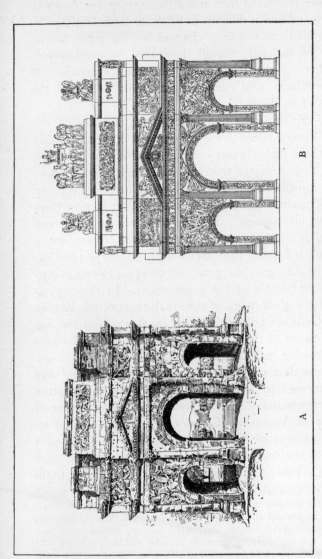

A · B

A Roman Triumphal Arch

A, Roman triumphal arch at Orange, France, as it now looks; B, original appearance of arch. The Romans were accustomed to build huge and handsome arches to commemorate important victories. There were naturally a number at Rome; of those built in the chief cities of the Empire, several still remain. The one pictured above was built at the Roman colony of Arausio, on the river Rhône, to celebrate a victory over the Gauls in A.D. 21. The sculptures represent the fight between the Roman soldiers and the Gauls, and the captives that the Romans took. Modern cities have erected similar arches; e.g. Paris, Berlin, London, and New York lation; for when it is hard to make a living, men are deterred from marrying and find it difficult to bring up large families.

Underneath all these unhappy changes lay the great fact of the depletion of the soil through ignorance or carelessness. "The exhaustion of the Roman soil and the devastation of the Roman provinces shed enough light for us to behold the dread outlines of its doom." [1]

In order to replenish the population great numbers of the neighboring German tribes were encouraged to settle within the Empire, where they became *coloni*. Constantine is said to have called in three hundred thousand of a single people. Barbarians were enlisted in the Roman legions to help keep out their fellow Germans. Julius Cæsar was the first to give them a place among his soldiers. This custom became more and more common, until, finally, whole armies were German, entire tribes being enlisted under their own chiefs. Some of the Germans rose to be distinguished generals; others attained important positions as officials of the government. In this way it came about that a great many of the inhabitants of the Roman Empire were Germans before the great invasions, and the line dividing the citizens of the Roman Empire and the barbarians was already growing indistinct.

As the Empire declined in strength and prosperity and was gradually permeated by the barbarians, its art and literature fell far below the standard of the great writers and artists of the golden age of Augustus. Cicero's clear style had lost its charm for the readers of the fourth and fifth centuries, and a flowery kind of rhetoric took its place. No more great men of letters arose. Few of those who understand and enjoy Latin

---

[1] Professor V. G. Simkhovitch. See his admirable "Rome's Fall Reconsidered" in a little volume called *Toward the Understanding of Jesus.* "Go to the ruins of ancient and rich civilizations in Asia Minor, northern Africa or elsewhere. Look at the unpeopled valleys, at the dead and buried cities, and you can decipher there the promise and the prophecy that the law of soil exhaustion held in store for all of us. It is but the story of an abandoned farm on a gigantic scale. Depleted of humus by constant cropping, land could no longer reward labor and support life; so the people abandoned it." *Op. cit.,* 137-138.

literature to-day would think of reading any of the poetry or prose written in the later centuries of the Roman Empire.

During the three hundred years before the invasions those who studied at all did not ordinarily take the trouble to read the best books of the earlier Greek and Roman writers, but relied upon mere collections of quotations, and got their information from textbooks.

These textbooks the Middle Ages inherited and continued to use. The great Greek writers were forgotten altogether, and only a few of the better known Latin authors like Cicero, Virgil, and Ovid continued to be copied and read.

The Rise of the Christian Church

We have still to consider the most important thing that happened in the Roman Empire on the eve of its break-up, and that is the establishment of the Christian Church. The common people among the Greeks and Romans had always believed in a great many gods and had held that the souls of men continued after death to exist in the lower regions, but they thought of the life to come as a dreary existence much less interesting than that in this world. Many of the philosophers, however, had come to believe in a great and good God who ruled all things and whom it was man's duty to obey. Plato and Cicero, for example, held that good men would be rewarded in the next world and bad men punished.

Christianity brought with it hope for all kinds of weary and discouraged men and women. It proclaimed that God was their father, that he had sent his son to save them, and that if they believed in Christ and tried their best to lead a good life, their sins would be forgiven them, and after death they would find everlasting happiness in heaven.

The first Christians looked for the speedy return of Christ before their own generation should pass away. Since all were filled with enthusiasm for the Gospel and eagerly awaited the last day, they did not feel the need for much organization. But as time went on the Christian communities greatly increased in size, and many persons joined them who had little or none of the original earnestness and religion. It became necessary to develop a regular system of church government in order to control the sinful and expel those who brought disgrace upon their religion by notoriously bad conduct.

Gradually the followers of Christ came to believe in a "Catholic"—that is, a universal—Church which embraced all the groups of true believers in Christ, wherever they might be. To this one universal Church all must belong who hoped to be saved.[1]

A sharp distinction was already made between the officers of the Church, who were called the *clergy,* and the people, or *laity.* To the clergy was committed the government of the Church as well as the teaching of its members. In each of the Roman cities was a bishop, and at the head of the country communities, a priest, who had derived his name from the original elders mentioned in the New Testament.[2] It was natural that the bishops in the chief towns of the Roman provinces should be especially influential in church affairs. They came to be called archbishops, and might summon the bishops of the province to a council to decide important matters.

In 311 the Roman emperor Galerius issued a decree placing the Christian religion upon the same legal footing as the worship of the Roman gods. His successor, Constantine, the first Christian emperor, strictly enforced this edict. Constantine's successors soon forbade the worship of the old pagan gods and began to issue laws which gave the Christian clergy important privileges.

In the last book of the Theodosian Code,—a great collection of the laws of the Empire, which was completed in 438,—all the emperors' decrees are to be found which relate to the

[1] "Whoever separates himself from the Church," writes St. Cyprian (died 258), "is separated from the promises of the Church. . . . He is an alien, he is profane, he is an enemy; he can no longer have God for his father who has not the Church for his mother. If anyone could escape who was outside the Ark of Noah, so also may he escape who shall be outside the bounds of the Church."

[2] Our word "priest" comes from the Latin word *presbyter*, meaning "elder."

Christian Church and the clergy. We find that the clergy, in view of their holy duties, were exempted from certain burdensome government offices and from some of the taxes which the laity had to pay. They were also permitted to receive bequests. The emperors themselves built churches and helped the Church in many ways. Their example was followed by rulers and private individuals all through the Middle Ages, so that the Church became incredibly wealthy and enjoyed a far greater income than any state of Europe. The clergy were permitted to try certain law cases, and they themselves had the privilege of being tried in their own Church courts for minor criminal offenses.

The Theodosian Code makes it *unlawful* for any one to differ from the beliefs of the Catholic Church. Those who dared to disagree with the teachings of the Church were called *heretics*. If heretics ventured to come together, their meetings were to be broken up and the teachers heavily fined. Houses in which the doctrines of the heretics were taught were to be confiscated by the government. The books containing their teachings were to be sought out with the utmost care and burned under the eyes of the magistrate; and if any one was convicted of concealing a heretical book, he was to suffer capital punishment.

It is clear, then, that very soon after the Christian Church was recognized by the Roman government it induced the emperors to grant the clergy particular favors, to destroy the pagan temples and prohibit pagan worship, and, finally, to persecute all those who ventured to disagree with the orthodox teachings of the Church.

We shall find that the governments in the Middle Ages, following the example of the Roman emperors, continued to grant the clergy special privileges and to persecute heretics, often in a very cruel manner.

In these provisions of the Theodosian Code the later medieval Church is not merely foreshadowed, but—except for the papacy—is firmly established. The imperial government in the West was soon overthrown by the barbarian conquerors, but the Catholic Church converted and ruled these conquerors.

When the officers of the Empire deserted their posts, the bishops stayed to meet the oncoming invader. They continued to represent the old civilization and ideas of order. It was the Church that kept the Latin language alive among those who knew only a rude German dialect. It was the Church that maintained some little education even in the times of greatest ignorance, for without the ability to read Latin the priests could not have performed the religious services and the bishops could not have carried on their correspondence with one another.

A distinction should be made between the Christian Church and Christianity, between a highly organized and potent institution, much resembling a state in its governmental powers, and, on the other hand, the religion which it was the business of the Church to administer, expound, and defend. The Church was much more novel in its nature and later in its origin than the beliefs that had become interwoven into the Christian faith and doctrine. The Church, as it was to persist during the Middle Ages and down to the present, was mainly a product of the later Roman Empire, although organized before its recognition by Constantine and its first great council at Nicæa in 325. The Christian religion was Jewish in origin and the sacred writings of the Jews were accepted by the Christians as their holy book, the Word of God. In the Old Testament they could carry back their faith to the very beginnings of things—man's creation and fall, and the promise of a redeemer to come in the fullness of time. They interpreted various passages in the Jewish writings as clear forecasts of the Church, and regarded themselves as the divinely elected successors of the chosen people, who had been God's appointed vehicle for his truth until on an evil day, in wicked blindness they failed to recognize his son as the promised messiah, and put him to a cruel death.

Gradually a small collection of Christian writings—the four gospels, the Acts of the Apostles and some of Paul's letters, together with a few other brief treatises—were sifted out as especially authoritative and gathered into a supplement to the Old Testament. The name New Testament is first mentioned by Tertullian about the year 200. The history of the New Testament is complicated and obscure. Doubts were long harbored in regard to the propriety of including Hebrews, James, Revelation, and several of the letters which follow Paul's epistles, but in 393 a council at Hippo enumerates the books as they now stand. As Harnack says, the formation of the New Testament was rather one of exclusion than of mere collection, and a number of highly edifying early Christian works, as well as the inferior ones, were rejected.

The New Testament was originally in Greek, and the words *kyrie eleison* (Lord, have mercy) lingering in the Catholic ritual remind one of this. One of its parts, the fourth gospel, opens with an invocation of the mystical Greek doctrine of the Word, or Logos. "In the beginning was the Word, and the Word was with God, and the Word was God." Paul, the first great Christian theologian, had some familiarity with Hellenic speculations. The later Church fathers, notably Augustine, were deeply affected by Greek thought, especially a revived and distorted Platonism that prevailed in their time. Several of the broader-minded of the fathers freely acknowledged that Christianity was not new except as bringing together in final and inspired form the insight and beliefs which had been expressed by earlier sages and seekers after God.

Modern scholars and critics regard the Bible as an anthology embracing contributions from many hands during at least a thousand years. Assuming that the latest writings in the Old Testament belong to the days of Alexander the Great [1] and that Paul's letters to the Galatians and to the Christians of Salonika—the earliest portions of the New Testament—should be dated between A.D. 46-48, it is obvious that there is a gap of about three centuries in the anthology. This can be filled

---

[1] There is a longer and a shorter Old Testament. When the Greek Jews at Alexandria prepared a Greek translation of their sacred writings they included certain later books, not included in the Hebrew canon. While the Roman Catholic Church regards the so-called Apocrypha as on an equal footing with the rest of the Bible, the Protestant reformers assigned these works an inferior position, and they rarely appear any longer in our English Bible.

in to some extent by surviving religious works not included in the Bible. They show that the teachings of Jesus were less unique than is usually supposed and that they can often be paralleled by those of his spiritual contemporaries.

In short, when Christianity is viewed historically and critically it is found to possess a continuity, like all other human interests. Many of its teachings can be traced back to quite primitive beginnings; the Jewish religion was deeply affected by Mesopotamian and Persian beliefs, and Christianity by the current conceptions of the centuries during which it was taking form. An English writer has said most truly that "the religion of a given race at a given time is relative to the whole mental attitude of that time. It is impossible to separate the religious phenomena from the other phenomena, in the same way that you can separate a vein of silver from the rock in which it is imbedded. . . . We may concentrate our attention chiefly upon them, but they will still remain a part of the whole complex life of the time, and they cannot be understood except in relation to that life." [1] It must be obvious that no really new religion could ever be introduced among men. It must take account of their prepossessions and make terms with their longings and state of knowledge if it is to prevail and not remain a mere temporary freak. This process of borrowing and lending which has gone on through the religious history of man is technically called *syncretism*. It is accepted as a premise by all competent modern scholars.

The old idea that Christianity met and conquered "paganism," as we find it described in Homer or Virgil, is a gross misapprehension. Juvenal, writing about the year 200, declares that no child longer believes in Charon and his single punt transporting untold thousands across the Stygian river filled with black frogs. Doubtless the simple old notions still held among the "pagans" or country jakes, as the Christians named them. It was not, however, the old Greek and Roman gods against which they had to make way, but a number of new

[1] Hatch, *The Influence of Greek Ideas and Usages upon the Christian Church*, p. 3.

religions which often promised similar rewards to their faithful adherents. Stoicism was for the intelligent, but, as Cumont points out, few could delight in doubt or relish philosophic subtleties. Scientific interest was declining and the discoveries of former times were being forgotten. "Since the intellect was unable to formulate a consistent rule of life, faith alone could supply it, and the multitudes gravitated toward the temples, where the truths taught to men in earlier days by the Oriental gods were revealed." [1] Some taught redemption at the shrines of Isis or the Great Mother or in the caves of Mithra—the god of the legions. Manichæism coming from Persia strangely resembled Christianity and the Christians deemed it a base imitation of their faith.

Among the Christians themselves there was great divergence of opinion in regard to "the Truth." Peter and Paul found it hard to come to terms, as one can see by reading the letter to the Galatians. The dubious treatises called II Peter and Jude are full of denunciation of false teachers engaged in bringing in privily destructive "heresies." These disturbers are described bitterly as "creatures without reason, born mere animals to be taken and destroyed, railing in matters whereof they are ignorant." Just as the Romans, according to Tertullian's *Apology,* accused the Christians of elaborate uncleannesses, so the writer of II Peter accuses those who differed from him of walking after the flesh in the lust of defilement and despising dominion. Thus did that Christian tolerance begin which was to continue through the wars of religion in the sixteenth century and well beyond them.

As time went on and the Roman government put its power into the balance, "orthodoxy" emerged and was enforced with extraordinary success during the Middle Ages by the might of the ecclesiastical organization, supported by the secular rulers. Of all this plenty of illustration will come as we proceed.

[1] Cumont, *Oriental Religions in Roman Paganism,* p. 34.

CHAPTER II

THE GERMAN INVASIONS AND THE BREAK-UP OF THE ROMAN EMPIRE

Founding of Kingdoms by German Chiefs. The Kingdom of the Franks. The Results of the Barbarian Invasions. The Perpetuation of the Roman Empire in Eastern Europe

Founding of Kingdoms by German Chiefs

PREVIOUS to the year 375 the attempts of the Germans to penetrate into the Roman Empire appear to have been due to their love of adventure, their hope of plundering their civilized neighbors, or the need of new lands for their increasing numbers. And the Romans, by means of their armies, their walls, and their guards, had up to this time succeeded in preventing the barbarians from violently occupying Roman territory. But suddenly a new force appeared in the rear of the Germans which thrust some of them across the northern boundary of the Empire. The Huns, a Mongolian folk from central Asia, swept down upon the Goths, who were a German tribe settled on the lower Danube, and forced a part of them to seek shelter across the river, within the limits of the Empire.

Here they soon fell out with the Roman officials, and a great battle was fought at Adrianople in 378 in which the Goths defeated and slew the Roman emperor, Valens. The Germans had now not only broken through the boundaries of the Empire, but they had also learned that they could defeat the Roman legions. The battle of Adrianople may therefore be said to mark the beginning of the conquest of the western part of the Empire by the Germans. For some years, however, after the battle of Adrianople the various bands of West Goths—or *Visigoths*, as they are often called—were induced to accept the terms of peace offered by the emperor's officials, and some of the Goths agreed to serve as soldiers in the Roman armies.

Among the Germans who succeeded in getting an important position in the Roman army was Alaric, but he appears to have become dissatisfied with the treatment he received from the emperor. He therefore collected an army, of which his countrymen, the West Goths, formed a considerable part, and set out for Italy, and finally decided to march on Rome itself. The Eternal City fell into his hands in 410 and was plundered by his followers.

Although Alaric did not destroy the city, or even seriously damage it, the fact that Rome had fallen into the hands of an invading army was considered a portentous event. The pagans explained it on the ground that the old gods were angry because so many people had deserted them and become Christians. St. Augustine, in his famous book, *The City of God,* took much pains to prove that the Roman gods had never been able on previous occasions to prevent disaster to their worshipers, and that Christianity could not be held responsible for the troubles of the time.

Alaric died before he could find a satisfactory spot for his people to settle upon permanently. After his death the West Goths wandered into Gaul, and then into Spain. Here they came upon the Vandals, another German tribe, who had crossed the Rhine four years before Alaric had captured Rome. For three years they had devastated Gaul and then had moved down into Spain. For a time after the arrival in Spain of the West Goths, there was war between them and the Vandals. The West Goths seem to have got the best of their rivals, for the Vandals determined to move on across the Strait of Gibraltar into northern Africa, where they established a kingdom and conquered the neighboring islands in the Mediterranean.

Having rid themselves of the Vandals, the West Goths took possession of a great part of the Spanish peninsula, and this they added to their conquests across the Pyrenees in Gaul, so that their kingdom extended from the river L o i r e to the Strait of Gibraltar.

It is unnecessary to follow the confused history of the movements of the innumerable bands of restless barbarians who wandered about Europe during the fifth century. Scarcely any part of western Europe was left unmolested; even Britain was conquered by German tribes, the Angles and Saxons.

To add to the universal c o n f u s i o n caused by the influx of the German tribes, the Huns (the Mongolian people who had first pushed the West Goths into the Empire) now began to fill all western Europe with terror.

ROMAN MAUSOLEUM AT ST. RÉMY

The Roman town of Glanum (now called St. Rémy) in southern France was destroyed by the West Goths in 480. Little remains of the town except a triumphal arch and the great monument pictured here. Above the main arches is the inscription, SEX. L. M. IVLIEI. C. F. PARENTIBUS. SVEIS, which seems to mean "Sextus Julius and [his brothers] Lucius and Marcus, sons of Gaius, to their parents" surrendered, only to be treacherously slain a few days later by Theodoric's own hand (493).

Theodoric put the name of the emperor at Constantinople on the coins which he issued, and did everything in his power to gain the emperor's approval of the new German kingdom. Nevertheless, although he desired that the emperor should

CHURCH OF SANT' APOLLINARE NUOVO

This church was erected at Ravenna by Theodoric. Although the outside has been changed, the interior, here represented, remains much the same as it was originally. The twenty-four marble columns were brought from Constantinople. The walls are adorned with *mosaics;* that is, pictures made by piecing together small squares of brightly colored marbles or glass

sanction his usurpation, Theodoric had no idea of being really subordinate to Constantinople.

The invaders took one-third of the land for themselves, but this seems to have been done without causing any serious disorder. Theodoric greatly admired the Roman laws and institutions and did his best to preserve them. The old offices and titles were retained, and Goth and Roman lived under the same Roman law. Order was maintained and learning encouraged.

In Ravenna, which Theodoric chose for his capital, beautiful buildings still exist that date from his reign.[1]

While Theodoric had been establishing his kingdom in Italy in this enlightened way, Gaul, which we now call France, was coming under the control of the most powerful of all the barbarian peoples, the *Franks*, who were to play a more important rôle in the formation of modern Europe than any of the other German races (see next section).

Besides the kingdom of the East Goths in Italy and of the Franks in Gaul, the West Goths had their kingdom in Spain, the Burgundians had established themselves on the Rhône River, and the Vandals in Africa. Royal alliances were concluded between the various reigning houses, and for the first time in the history of Europe we see something like a family of nations, living each within its own boundaries and dealing with one another as independent powers. It seemed for a few years as if the new German kings who had divided up the western portion of the Empire among themselves would succeed in keeping order and in preventing the loss of such civilization as remained.

But no such good fortune was in store for western Europe, which was now only at the beginning of the turmoil which was to leave it almost completely barbarized, for there was little to encourage the reading or writing of books, the study of science, or attention to art, in a time of constant warfare and danger.

Theodoric had a distinguished Roman counselor named Cassiodorus (d. 575), to whose letters we owe a great part of our knowledge of this period, and who busied himself in his old age

[1] The headpiece of this chapter represents the tomb of Theodoric. Emperors and rich men were accustomed in Roman times to build handsome tombs for themselves. Theodoric followed their example and erected this two-storied building at Ravenna to serve as his mausoleum. The dome consists of a single great piece of rock 36 feet in diameter, weighing 500 tons, brought from across the Adriatic. Theodoric was a heretic in the eyes of the Catholic Church (he was an Arian—the Unitarian of that day), and not long after his death his remains were taken out of his tomb and scattered to the winds, and the building converted into a church. The picture represents the tomb as it probably looked originally; it has been somewhat altered in modern times, but is well preserved.

MAP OF EUROPE IN THE TIME OF THEODORIC

It will be noticed that Theodoric's kingdom of the East Goths included a considerable part of what we call Austria to-day, and that the West Gothic kingdom extended into southern France. The Vandals held northern Africa and the adjacent islands. The Burgundians lay in between the East Goths and the Franks. The Lombards, who were later to move down into Italy, were in Theodoric's time east of the Bavarians, after whom modern Bavaria is named. Some of the Saxons invaded England, but many remained in Germany, as indicated on the map. The Eastern Empire, which was all that remained of the Roman Empire, included the Balkan Peninsula, Asia Minor, and the eastern portion of the Mediterranean. The Britons in Wales, the Picts in Scotland, and the Scots in Ireland were Celts, consequently modern Welsh, Gaelic, and Irish are closely related and belong to the Celtic group of languages

Under their able chief, Attila, this savage people invaded Gaul. But the Romans and the German inhabitants joined together against the invaders and defeated them in the battle of Châlons, in 451. After this rebuff in Gaul, Attila turned to Italy. But the danger there was averted by a Roman embassy, headed by Pope Leo the Great, who induced Attila to give up his plan of marching upon Rome. Within a year he died and with him perished the power of the Huns, who never troubled Europe again.

The year 476 has commonly been taken as the date of the "fall" of the Western Empire and of the beginning of the Middle Ages. What happened in that year was this. During the last centuries of the Roman Empire there were often two (sometimes more) emperors who shared the responsibility of governing the vast Roman realms. One commonly resided in Italy, the other at Constantinople (see below, p. 48). Most of the Roman emperors in the West had proved weak and indolent rulers. So the barbarians wandered hither and thither pretty much at their pleasure, and the German troops in the service of the Empire became accustomed to set up and depose emperors to suit their own special interest, very much in the same way that a boss in an American city often succeeds in securing the election of a mayor who will carry out his wishes. Finally in 476, Odoacer, the most powerful among the rival German generals in Italy, banished the last of the emperors of the West and ruled in his stead.[1]

It was not, however, given to Odoacer to establish an enduring German kingdom on Italian soil, for he was conquered by the great Theodoric, the king of the East Goths (or Ostrogoths). Theodoric had spent ten years of his early youth in Constantinople and had thus become familiar with Roman life and was on friendly terms with the emperor of the East.

The struggle between Theodoric and Odoacer lasted for several years, but Odoacer was finally shut up in Ravenna and

---

[1] The common misapprehensions in regard to the events of 476 are discussed by the author in *The New History*, pp. 154 ff.

surrendered, only to be treacherously slain a few days later by Theodoric's own hand (493).

Theodoric put the name of the emperor at Constantinople on the coins which he issued, and did everything in his power to gain the emperor's approval of the new German kingdom. Nevertheless, although he desired that the emperor should

CHURCH OF SANT' APOLLINARE NUOVO

This church was erected at Ravenna by Theodoric. Although the outside has been changed, the interior, here represented, remains much the same as it was originally. The twenty-four marble columns were brought from Constantinople. The walls are adorned with *mosaics;* that is, pictures made by piecing together small squares of brightly colored marbles or glass

sanction his usurpation, Theodoric had no idea of being really subordinate to Constantinople.

The invaders took one-third of the land for themselves, but this seems to have been done without causing any serious disorder. Theodoric greatly admired the Roman laws and institutions and did his best to preserve them. The old offices and titles were retained, and Goth and Roman lived under the same Roman law. Order was maintained and learning encouraged.

in preparing textbooks of the "liberal" arts and sciences,—grammar, arithmetic, logic, geometry, rhetoric, music, and astronomy. His treatment of these seven important subjects, to which he devotes a few pages each, seems to us very absurd and enables us to estimate the low plane to which learning had fallen in Italy in the sixth century. Yet these and similar works were regarded as standard treatises and used as textbooks all through the early Middle Ages, while the really great Greek and Roman writers of an earlier period were forgotten.

Between the time of Theodoric and that of Charlemagne three hundred years elapsed, during which scarcely a person was to be found who could write out, even in the worst of Latin, an account of the events of his day. Everything conspired to discourage education. The great centers of learning—Carthage, Rome, Alexandria, Milan—had all been partially destroyed by the invaders. The libraries which had been kept in the temples of the pagan gods were often burned, along with the temples themselves, by Christian enthusiasts, who were not sorry to see the heathen books disappear with the heathen religion. Shortly after Theodoric's death the emperor at Constantinople withdrew the support which the Roman government had been accustomed to grant to public teachers, and closed the great school at Athens. The only important historian of the sixth century was the half-illiterate Gregory, bishop of Tours (d. 594), whose whole work is evidence of the sad state of affairs. He at least heartily appreciated his own ignorance and exclaims, in bad Latin, "Woe to our time, for the study of books has perished from among us."

The year after Theodoric's death one of the greatest of the emperors of the East, Justinian (527-565), came to the throne at Constantinople. He undertook to regain for the Empire the provinces in Africa and Italy that had been occupied by the Vandals and East Goths. His general, Belisarius, overthrew the Vandal kingdom in northern Africa in 534, but it was a more difficult task to destroy the Gothic rule in Italy. However, in spite of a brave resistance, the Goths were so completely defeated in 553 that they agreed to leave Italy with all their movable possessions. What became of the remnants of the race we do not know.

The destruction of the Gothic kingdom was a disaster for Italy, for the Goths would have helped defend it against later and far more barbarous invaders. Immediately after the death of Justinian the country was overrun by the Lombards, the last of the great German peoples to establish themselves within the bounds of the former Roman Empire. They were a savage race, a considerable part of which was still pagan. The newcomers first occupied the region north of the Po, which has ever since been called "Lombardy" after them, and then extended their conquests southward. Instead of settling themselves with the moderation and wise statesmanship of the East Goths, the Lombards moved about the peninsula pillaging and massacring. The Lombards were unable, however, to conquer all of Italy. Rome, Ravenna, and southern Italy continued to be held by the "Roman" emperors who succeeded Justinian at Constantinople. As time went on, the Lombards lost their wildness and adopted the habits and religion of the people among whom they lived. Their kingdom lasted over two hundred years, until it was conquered by Charlemagne (see below, p. 86).

The Kingdom of the Franks

The various kingdoms established by the German chieftains were not very permanent, as we have seen. The Franks, however, succeeded in conquering more territory than any other people and in founding an empire far more important than the kingdoms of the West and East Goths, the Vandals, or the Lombards. We must now see how this was accomplished.

When the Franks are first heard of in history they were settled along the lower Rhine, from Cologne to the North Sea. Their method of getting a foothold in the Empire was essentially different from that which the Goths, Lombards, and Vandals had adopted. Instead of severing their connection with Germany and becoming an island in the sea of the Empire, they conquered by degrees the territory about them. However far they might extend their control, they remained in constant touch with their fellow barbarians behind them. In this way they retained the warlike vigor that was lost by the races who were completely surrounded by the comforts of Roman civilization.

In the early part of the fifth century they had occupied the district which forms to-day the kingdom of Belgium, as well as the regions east of it. In 486, seven years before Theodoric founded his I t a l i a n kingdom, they went forth under their first great king, Clovis (a name that later grew into Louis), and defeated the Roman general who opposed them. They extended their control over Gaul as far south as the Loire, which at that time formed the northern boundary of the kingdom of the West Goths. Clovis next enlarged his empire on the east by the conquest of the Alemanni, a German people living in the region of the Black Forest.

The battle in which the Alemanni were defeated (496) is in one respect important above all the other battles of Clovis. Although still a pagan himself, his wife had b e e n converted to Christianity. In the midst of the battle, according to Gregory of Tours, seeing his troops giving way, he called upon Jesus Christ and pledged himself to be bap-

FRANKISH WARRIOR

It is very hard to find illustrations for a chapter on the barbarian invasions, for this period of disorder was not one in which pictures were being painted or buildings erected. From the slight descriptions we have of the costume worn by the Frankish soldiers, we infer that it was something like that represented here. We know that they wore their hair in long braids and carried weapons similar to those in the picture. We may confidently infer that they had no trousers; nor guns, tanks, and poisonous gases to kill the inhabitants of the Roman Empire

tized in his name if he would help the Franks to victory over
their enemies. When he won the battle he kept his word and
was baptized, together with three thousand of his warriors.

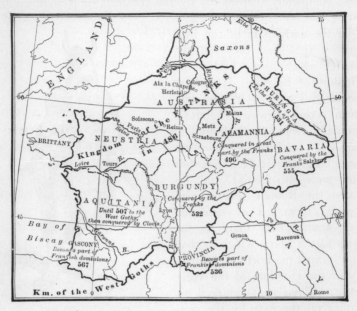

THE DOMINIONS OF THE FRANKS UNDER THE MEROVINGIANS

This map shows how the Frankish kingdom grew up. Clovis while still
a young man defeated the Roman general Syagrius in 486, near Soissons,
and so added the region around Paris to his possessions. He added Ale-
mannia on the east in 496. In 507 he made Paris his capital and conquered
Aquitania, previously held by the West Goths. He also made a beginning
in adding the kingdom of the Burgundians to his realms. He died in 511.
His successors in the next half century completed the conquest of Burgundy
and added the old Roman "province" (Provincia), Bavaria, and Gascony.
There were many divisions of the Frankish realms after the time of Clovis,
and the eastern and western portions, called Austrasia and Neustria, were
often ruled by different branches of the *Merovingians,* as Clovis's family
was called from his mythical ancestor *Meroveus*

It is from Bishop Gregory of Tours, mentioned above, that
most of our knowledge of Clovis and his successors is derived.
In Gregory's famous *History of the Franks* the cruel and

unscrupulous Clovis appears as God's chosen instrument for the support of the Christian faith. Certainly Clovis quickly learned to combine his own interests with those of the "orthodox" Christian Church, and, later, an alliance between the popes and the Frankish kings was destined to have a great influence upon the history of western Europe.

To the south of Clovis's new possessions in Gaul lay the kingdom of the West Goths; to the southeast that of another German people, the Burgundians. Clovis speedily extended his power to the Pyrenees, and forced the West Goths to confine themselves to the Spanish portion of their realm, while the Burgundians soon fell completely under the rule of the Franks. Clovis, by a series of murders, brought portions of the Frankish nation itself, which had previously been independent of him, under his scepter.

When Clovis died in 511 at Paris, which he had made his residence, his four sons divided his possessions among them. Wars between rival brothers, interspersed with the most horrible murders, fill the annals of the Frankish kingdom for over a hundred years after the death of Clovis. Yet the nation —which was one day to become the French—continued to develop in spite of the unscrupulous deeds of its rulers.

The Frankish kings who followed Clovis succeeded in extending their power over pretty nearly all the territory that is included to-day in France, Belgium, and the Netherlands, as well as over a goodly portion of modern Germany. Half a century after the death of Clovis, their dominions extended from the Bay of Biscay on the west to a point east of Salzburg.

The Results of the Barbarian Invasions

As one looks back over the German invasions it is natural to ask upon what terms the newcomers lived among the old inhabitants of the Empire, how far they adopted the customs of those among whom they settled, and how far they clung to their own habits? These questions cannot be answered very satisfactorily. So little is known of this confused period of which we have been speaking that it is impossible to follow closely the mingling of the new peoples with the old.

The reader should be on his guard, however, against the confident but generally ill-founded enthusiasts who picture the German invasions as a divine punishment meted out to the sinful and decadent Roman Empire. The idea of the moral superiority of the Germans can be traced back to Tacitus. Salvian, a Christian priest, writing on *God's Government* a generation after Alaric's attack on Rome, contends that the Romans, once a virtuous and heroic people, had sunk into wickedness and corruption. In spite of their civilization they were far inferior to the untutored but sturdy barbarian. The Romans oppressed one another in intolerable ways, while the Germans, at least those of the same race and kin, followed the gospel admonition to love one another. Many Romans, he declares, preferred to enjoy real freedom under barbarian rule rather than the slavery of a Roman freeman.

These old ideas have in recent decades taken a new form in the theory of the inherent superiority of the Germanic or Nordic people. This was eloquently presented to his patriotic audiences by the German philosopher Fichte during the Napoleonic wars. He maintained that the Germans had a particular mission in the "realization of absolute Truth," and British historians—for example, Freeman—felt that freedom had emerged from the forests of Germany.[1] The World War, directed on the part of Great Britain and the United States against autocracy and militarism as represented by Germany, tended to popularize some reservations. The British Parliament might have a remote Germanic origin, but still more Teutonic were the Kaiser and the German army.

This is not the place to discuss the question of race superiority. The inclination, nay, obligation, to boast of one's own people is well nigh universal. It is as common among the Caribbeans and Eskimos as in France or the United States. From an historical and ethnological standpoint generalizations

---

[1] More recent instances of Nordic enthusiasts are Stewart Chamberlain, Lothrop Stoddard, and Madison Grant.

about race are hazardous in the extreme. It is an observable fact that all civilized peoples are made up of a great number of strains due to migrations and invasions. Nevertheless, certain physical characteristics can be distinguished, such as the color of the eyes, the shape of the skull, the tint and character of the hair, height, bodily proportions, etc. These reappear in all sorts of combinations as the centuries go on. A very rough classification of mankind can therefore be made on the basis of physical traits.

The fundamental question is whether or no these bodily peculiarities, and the classification based on them, have any decisive and permanent connection with intellectual or artistic capacity, military energy, economic and governmental ingenuity, religious insight, and the "love of freedom"? When the question is fairly presented to one as to whether light or dark hair, a round or a long head, a red, white, black, or yellow skin, determines one's ability to write a poem, solve a mathematical problem, improve a machine gun or commune with God, or merely just take on the culture in which one happens to be born,—when this question is thus bluntly put few would feel that it could be answered with assurance, and among these few there would be found no fairly qualified historian, anthropologist, biologist, or psychologist. All these realize that the problem is exceedingly difficult. Race, in the sense of bodily characteristics, is a matter of biology; culture, on the other hand, is something artificial and cumulative which seems to be readily acquired to an astonishing degree by all kinds of people regardless of their physical peculiarities.

All peoples are mongrel as the result, first, of human restlessness and migrations, historic and prehistoric, and, secondly, the fact that men and women of whatsoever "race" can mate and have offspring in which the physical traits of both parents have an *equal* chance of perpetuation. These inexorable circumstances are constantly neglected by popular prejudice. The "Romans" of the fifth century were just the inhabitants of the Roman Empire. The West Gothic or East Gothic or Frankish kingdoms included "Romans" for the most part, with the addition of the followers of Alaric, Theodoric, or Clovis, most miscellaneous in themselves. We are apt to see in the United States, a "melting pot" *par excellence,* which we may regard, in our ignorance, as a rather novel and singular thing. But melting pots have been the rule everywhere and always.

It would therefore be best to confine the word "racial" to physical characteristics. These assuredly play a great part in the sentiments, habits, and institutions of mankind, if not in their natural capacity to assimilate or forward culture. An eminent anthropologist, Edward Sapir, states the whole case fairly enough: "The reasonable man will feel about all the race talk that it is an exceedingly muddled affair. He will adopt for his practical policy the maxim, Let race alone. That is, he will try to act as though, for cultural purposes, race did not exist. He will do his level best to act courteously to individuals of all races and he will pay them all the compliment of assuming that they are essentially similar in potentiality to himself and his like." In short, one familiar with recent scientific studies of mankind will not allow his estimate of individuals to be affected by primitive race prejudices parading as grandiose generalizations about the genius of Nordic and the Latin peoples, the Jew, the yellow man, and the black man.

Turning back to the effects of the influx of Germans into the Roman Empire and the setting up of kingdoms by Teutonic chieftains, a few things at least are fairly clear.

In the first place, we must avoid exaggerating the numbers in the various bodies of invaders. The writers of the time indicate that the West Goths, when they were first admitted to the Empire before the battle of Adrianople, amounted to four or five hundred thousand persons, including men, women, and children. This is the largest band reported, and it must have been greatly reduced before the West Goths, after long wanderings and many battles, finally settled in Spain and southern Gaul. The Burgundians, when they appear for the first time on the banks of the Rhine, are reported to have had eighty thousand warriors among them. When Clovis and his army were baptized, Gregory of Tours speaks of "over three thousand" soldiers who became Christians upon that occasion. This would seem to indicate that this was the entire army of the Frankish king at this time.

Undoubtedly these figures are very meager and unreliable. But the readiness with which the Germans appear to have adopted the language and customs of the Romans would tend to prove that the invaders formed but a small minority of the population. Since hundreds of thousands of barbarians had been absorbed during the previous five centuries, the invasions of the fifth century can hardly have made an abrupt change in the character of the population.

The barbarians within the old Empire were soon speaking the same conversational Latin which was everywhere used by the Romans about them. This was much simpler than the elaborate and complicated Latin language used in books, which we find so much difficulty in learning nowadays. The speech of the common people was gradually diverging more and more, in the various countries of southern Europe, from the written Latin, and finally grew into French, Spanish, Italian, and Portuguese. But the barbarians did not produce this change, for it had begun before they came and would have gone on without them. They did no more than contribute a few convenient words to the new languages.

The northern Franks, who did not penetrate far into the Empire, and the Germans who remained in what is now Germany and in Scandinavia, had of course no reason for giving up their native tongues; the Angles and Saxons in Britain also kept theirs. These Germanic languages in time became Dutch, English, German, Danish, Swedish, etc. Of this matter something will be said later.

The Germans and the older inhabitants of the Roman Empire appear to have had no dislike for one another, except when there was a difference in religion.[1] Where there was no

---

[1] The West and East Goths and the Burgundians were heretics in the eyes of the Catholic Church, for they had been taught their Christianity by Arian missionaries who disagreed with the Catholic Church on certain points.

religious barrier the two races intermarried freely from the first. The Frankish kings did not hesitate to appoint Romans to important positions in the government and in the army, just as the Romans had long been in the habit of employing the barbarians as generals and officials.[1] In only one respect were the two races distinguished for a time—each had its particular law.

The West Goths were probably the first to write down their ancient laws, using the Latin language for the purpose. Their example was followed by the Franks, the Burgundians, and later by the Lombards and other peoples. These codes make up the "Laws of the Barbarians," which form our most important source of knowledge of the habits and ideas of the Germans at the time of the invasions. For several centuries following the barbarian conquests, the members of the various German tribes appear to have been judged by the laws of the particular people to which they belonged. The older inhabitants of the Empire, on the contrary, continued to have their lawsuits decided according to the Roman law.

The German laws did not provide for trials, either in the Roman or the modern sense of the word. There was no attempt to gather and weigh evidence and base the decision upon it. Such a mode of procedure was far too elaborate for the simple-minded Germans. Instead of a regular trial, one of the parties to the case was designated to prove that his side of the case was right by one of the following methods, developed under the influence of Christianity:

1. He might solemnly swear that he was telling the truth and get as many other persons of his own class as the court required, to swear that they believed that he was telling the truth. This was called *compurgation*. It was believed that God would punish those who swore falsely.

2. On the other hand, the parties to the case, or persons representing them, might meet in combat, on the supposition

---

[1] See the present writer's *The New History*, Section VI, on "The Fall of Rome."

that Heaven would grant victory to the right. This was the so-called *wager of battle*.

3. Lastly, one or other of the parties might be required to submit to the *ordeal* in one of its various forms: He might plunge his arm into hot water, or carry a bit of hot iron for some distance, and if at the end of three days he showed no ill effects, the case was decided in his favor. Or he might be ordered to walk over hot plowshares, and if he was not burned, it was assumed that God had intervened by a miracle to establish the right. This method of trial is but one example of the rude civilization which displaced the refined and elaborate organization of the Romans.

The account which has been given of the conditions in the Roman Empire, and of the manner in which the barbarians occupied its western part, serve to explain why the following centuries—known as the early Middle Ages—were a time of ignorance and disorder. The Germans, no doubt, varied a good deal in their habits and character. The Goths differed from the Lombards, and the Franks from the Vandals; but they were all alike in knowing nothing of the art, literature, and science which had been developed by the Greeks and adopted by the Romans. The invaders were ignorant, simple, vigorous people, with no taste for anything except fighting, eating, and drinking. Such was the disorder that their coming produced that the declining civilization of the Empire was pretty nearly submerged. The libraries, buildings, and works of art were destroyed or neglected, and there was no one to see that they were restored. So the western world fell back into a condition similar to that in which it had been before the Romans conquered and civilized it.

The loss was, however, temporary. The great heritage of skill and invention which had been slowly accumulated in Egypt, western Asia, and Greece, which formed the basis of the civilization which the Romans had adopted and spread abroad throughout their great Empire, did not wholly perish.

It is true that the break-up of the Roman Empire and the centuries of turmoil which followed set everything back, but we shall see how the barbarian nations gradually developed into our modern European states, how universities were established in which the books of the Greeks and Romans were again studied. Architects arose in time to imitate the old buildings and build a new kind of their own quite as imposing as those of the Romans, and men of science carried discoveries far beyond anything known to the wisest of the Greeks and Romans.

The Perpetuation of the Roman Empire in Eastern Europe

Although the Roman Empire nominally remained one in law, government, and culture until the Germans came in sufficient force to conquer the western portions of it, a tendency may nevertheless be noticed some time before the barbarian conquest for the eastern and western portions to drift apart. Constantine, who established his supremacy only after a long struggle with his rivals, hoped to strengthen the vast state by creating a second capital, which should lie far to the east and dominate a region very remote from Rome. Constantinople was accordingly founded in 330 on the confines of Europe and Asia.[1]

Thereafter there were often two emperors, one in the west and one in the east, but they were supposed to govern one empire conjointly and in "unanimity." New laws were to be accepted by both. The writers of the time do not speak of two states but continue to refer to "the Commonwealth" (*Res publica*), as if the administration were still in the hands of one ruler. Indeed, the idea of one government for all civilized mankind did not disappear but continued to influence men during the whole of the Middle Ages.

Although it was in the eastern part of the Empire that the barbarians first got a permanent foothold, the emperors at Constantinople were able to keep a portion of the old possessions

---

[1] Constantine built his new capital on the site of an old town, Byzantium, which he renamed after himself, Constantinople—that is, Constantine City. The adjective "Byzantine" applied to the eastern part of the Roman Empire is of course derived from the older name "Byzantium."

of the Empire under their rule for centuries after the Germans had completely conquered the West. When at last the eastern capital of the Empire fell, it was not into the hands of the Germans, but into those of the Turks, who have held it ever since 1453.

There will be no room in this volume to follow the history of the Eastern Empire, although it should not be ignored in studying the development of Western civilization. Its language and civilization had always been Greek, and owing to this and the influence of the Orient, its civilization offers a marked contrast to that of the Latin West, which was adopted by the Germans. Learning never died out in the East as it did in the West, nor did art reach so low an ebb. For some centuries after the break-up of the Roman Empire in the West, the capital of the Eastern Empire enjoyed the distinction of being the largest and most wealthy city of Europe. Within its walls could be found a refinement and civilization which had almost disappeared in the West; and its beautiful buildings, its parks and paved streets, filled travelers from the West with astonishment.

CHAPTER III

RISE OF THE PAPACY AND OF THE MONKS

Increasing Importance of the Christian Church. Origin of the Power of the Popes. Gregory the Great. Monks and Monasteries. Missionary Work of the Monks. Mohammed and His Religion. Conquests of the Mohammedans; the Caliphate

Increasing Importance of the Christian Church

BESIDES the emperors at Constantinople and the various German kings, there grew up in Europe a line of rulers far more powerful than any of these, namely, the *popes*. We must now consider the Christian Church and see how the popes gained their great influence.

We have already seen how marvelously the Christian communities founded by the apostles and their fellow missionaries multiplied until, by the middle of the third century, writers like St. Cyprian came to conceive of a "Catholic," or all-embracing, Church. We have seen how Emperor Constantine favored Christianity, and how his successors worked in the interest of the new religion; how carefully the Theodosian Code safeguarded the Church and the "orthodox" or officially sanctioned Christian clergy, and how harshly those were treated who ventured to hold another view of Christianity from that sanctioned by the government.

We must now follow this most powerful and permanent of all the institutions of the later Roman Empire into the Middle Ages. We must stop first to consider how the Western, or Latin, portion of Christendom, which gradually fell apart from the Eastern, or Greek, region, came to form a separate institution under the popes, the longest and mightiest line of rulers that the world has ever seen. We shall see how a peculiar class of Christians, the monks, appeared; how they joined hands with the clergy; how the monks and the clergy met the barbarians, subdued and civilized them, and then ruled them for centuries.

One great source of the Church's strength lay in the general fear of death and judgment to come, which Christianity had brought with it. The educated Greeks and Romans of the classical period usually thought of the next life, when they thought of it at all, as a very uninteresting existence compared with that on this earth. One who committed some great crime might suffer for it after death with pains similar to those of the hell in which the Christians believed. But the great part of humanity were supposed to lead in the next world a shadowy existence, neither sad nor glad. Religion was mainly an affair of this life; the gods were worshiped with a view to securing happiness and success in this world.

Since no great satisfaction could be expected in the next life, it was naturally thought wise to make the most of this one. The possibility of pleasure ends—so the Roman poet Horace urges—when we join the shades below, as we all must do soon. Let us, therefore, take advantage of every harmless pleasure and improve our brief opportunity to enjoy the good things of earth. We should, however, be reasonable and temperate, avoiding all excess, for that endangers happiness. Above all, we should not worry uselessly about the future, which is in the hands of the gods and beyond our control.

The Stoics believed in a beneficent God, the maker of all things, whose works it was man's privilege to appreciate and revere. They also taught the brotherhood of man. The Epicureans held that the world, man, and the gods themselves were the result of a fortuitous concourse of atoms, destined to dissolve sooner or later. They denied that the soul survived death and heartily deprecated all anxiety about a life to come or the vengeance of the gods, who took no note of mankind and their deeds, by way either of aid or of punishment.

Christianity, and various "mysteries" imported from western Asia and Egypt, opposed this view of life with an entirely different one. It constantly emphasized man's existence after death, which it declared to be infinitely more important than his brief sojourn on earth. Under the influence of the Church this conception of life, in its orthodox Christian form, prevailed, and was taught to the barbarians.

The "other-worldliness" became so intense that thousands gave up their ordinary occupations altogether and devoted their entire attention to preparation for the next life. They shut themselves in lonely cells; and, not satisfied with giving up most of their natural pleasures, they inflicted bodily suffering upon themselves by hunger, cold, and other discomforts. They trusted that in this way they might avoid some of the sins into which they were apt to fall, and that, by self-inflicted punishment in this world, they might perchance escape some of that reserved for them in the next.

The barbarians were taught that their fate in the next world depended largely upon the Church. Its ministers never wearied of presenting the alternative which faced every man so soon as this short earthly existence should be over,—the alternative between eternal bliss in heaven and perpetual, unspeakable torment in hell. Only those who had been duly baptized could hope to reach heaven; but baptism washed away only past sins and did not prevent constant relapse into new ones. These, unless their guilt was removed through the Church, would surely drag the soul down to hell.

The divine power of the Church was, furthermore, established in the eyes of the people by the wonderful works which Christian saints were constantly performing. They healed the sick, made the blind to see and the lame to walk. They called down God's wrath upon those who opposed the Church and invoked terrible punishments upon those who treated her holy rites with contempt. To the reader of to-day, the frequency of the miracles narrated by medieval writers seems astonishing. The lives of the saints, of which hundreds and hundreds have been preserved, contain little else than accounts of them, and no one appears to have doubted their everyday occurrence.

A word should be said of the early Christian church buildings. The Romans were accustomed to build near their market places a species of public hall, in which townspeople could meet one another to transact business, and in which the judges could hear cases, and public officials attend to their duties. These buildings were called _basilicas_. There were several magnificent ones in Rome itself, and there was doubtless at least one to be found in every town of considerable size. The roofs of these spacious halls were usually supported by long rows of columns; sometimes there were two rows on each side, forming aisles. When, after Constantine had given his approval to Christianity, large, fine churches began to be built they were constructed like these familiar public halls and, like them, were called basilicas.

During the sixteen hundred years that have passed since Constantine's time naturally almost all the churches of his day have disappeared or been greatly altered. But the beautiful church of Santa Maria Maggiore in Rome (p. 54) was built only a hundred years later, and gives us an excellent notion of a Christian basilica with its fine rows of columns and its handsome mosaic decorations. In general, the churches were plain and unattractive on the outside. A later chapter will explain how the basilica grew into the Gothic cathedral, which was as beautiful outside as inside.

The importance of the Church for the student of medieval history does not lie, however, exclusively in its religious functions, vital as they were, but also in its remarkable relations to the government. From the days of Constantine on, the Catholic Church had usually enjoyed the hearty support and protection of the government. But so long as the Roman Empire remained strong and active there was no chance for the clergy to free themselves from the control of the emperor, even if they had been disposed to do so. He made such laws for the Church as he saw fit, and the clergy did not complain. The government was, indeed, indispensable to them. It undertook

SANTA MARIA MAGGIORE

This beautiful church at Rome was built shortly after Constantine's time, and the interior, here shown, with its stately columns above which are fine mosaics, is still nearly as it was in the time of St. Augustine, fifteen hundred years ago. The ceiling is of the sixteenth century

to root out paganism by destroying the heathen shrines and preventing heathen sacrifices, and it punished severely those who refused to accept the teachings sanctioned by the Church.

But as the great Empire began to fall apart, there was a growing tendency among the churchmen in the West to resent the interference of the new rulers whom they did not respect. Consequently they managed gradually to free themselves in large part from the control of the government. They then proceeded to assume themselves many of the duties of government, which the weak and disorderly states into which the Roman Empire fell were unable to perform properly.

INCREASING IMPORTANCE OF THE CHRISTIAN CHURCH

One of the bishops of Rome (Pope Gelasius I, d. 496) briefly stated the principle upon which the Church rested its claims, as follows: "Two powers govern the world, the priestly and the kingly. The first is assuredly the superior, for the priest is responsible to God for the conduct of even the emperors themselves." Since no one denied that the eternal interests of mankind, which were under the care of the Church, were infinitely more important than those merely worldly matters which the State regulated, it was natural for the clergy to hold that, in case of conflict, the Church and its officers, rather than the king, should have the last word.

Gradually, as we have said, the Church began to undertake the duties which the Roman government had previously performed and which our governments perform to-day, such as keeping order, the management of public education, the trial of lawsuits, etc. There were no well-organized states in western Europe for many centuries after the break-up of the Roman Empire. The authority of the various barbarian kings was seldom sufficient to keep their realms in order. There were always many powerful landholders scattered throughout the kingdom who did pretty much what they pleased and settled their grudges against their fellows by neighborhood wars. Fighting was the main business as well as the chief amusement of this class. The king was unable to maintain peace and protect the oppressed, however anxious he may have been to do so.

Under these circumstances it naturally fell to the Church to keep order, when it could, by either threats or persuasion; to see that contracts were kept, the wills of the dead carried out, and marriage obligations observed. It took the defenseless widow and orphan under its protection and dispensed charity; it promoted education at a time when few laymen, however rich and noble, were able even to read. These conditions serve to explain why the Church was finally able so greatly to extend the powers which it had enjoyed under the Roman Empire, and why it undertook duties which seem to us to belong to the State rather than to a religious organization.

RISE OF THE PAPACY AND OF THE MONKS

Origin of the Power of the Popes

We must now turn to a consideration of the origin and growth of the supremacy of the popes, who, by raising themselves to the headship of the Western Church, became in many respects more powerful than any of the kings and princes with whom they frequently found themselves in bitter conflict.

While we cannot discover in the Theodosian Code any recognition of the supreme headship of the bishop of Rome, there is little doubt that he and his flock had almost from the very first enjoyed a leading place among the Christian communities. The Roman Church was the only one in the West which could claim the distinction of having been organized by the immediate followers of Christ,—"the two most glorious apostles, Peter and Paul."

The New Testament speaks repeatedly of Paul's presence in Rome. As for Peter, there had been from early times a tradition, accepted throughout the Christian Church, that he was the first bishop of Rome. This belief appears in the works of Christian writers before the close of the second century. There is, certainly, no conflicting tradition, no rival claimant. The belief itself, whether or not it corresponds with actual events, is a fact of the greatest historical importance. Peter enjoyed a preëminence among the other apostles and was singled out by Christ upon several occasions. In a passage of the New Testament which has affected history more profoundly than the edicts of the most powerful monarch, Christ says: "And I say also unto thee, That thou art Peter, and upon this rock I will build my church;[1] and the gates of hell shall

---

[1] Matt. xvi, 18-19. Two other passages in the New Testament were held to substantiate the divinely ordained headship of Peter and his successors: Luke xxii, 32, where Christ says to Peter, "Strengthen thy brethren," and John xxi, 15-17, where Jesus said to him, "Feed my sheep." Of course the word *ecclesia* (French, *église*) as used in the New Testament by those who supposed that the consummation of all things was not far distant, had a different meaning from that it acquired as time went on. "Church" is perhaps derived circuitously from *kurios*, meaning lord or authority. *Ecclesia* in the beginning meant simply a meeting or assembly of the brethren.

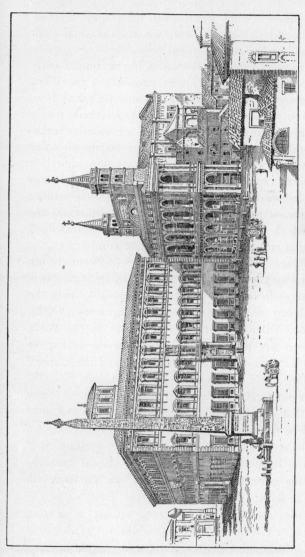

THE LATERAN PALACE AS IT NOW LOOKS

When Constantine became a Christian he turned over to the Roman bishops a great palace which had formerly belonged to the wealthy Roman family of the Laterani, hence the name Lateran, applied to both the palace and to the church which Constantine built for the popes close to the palace. Here the popes carried on their business for a thousand years, but during the past few centuries they have resided in the Vatican. The church of the Lateran claims to be "the mother and head of all the churches of the city and of the world"—*Omnium urbis et orbis ecclesiarum mater et caput*, as the Latin inscription runs on the present church. An earthquake, successive fires, and great alterations have left little or nothing of the original structure not prevail against it. And I will give unto thee the keys of the kingdom of heaven: and whatsoever thou shalt bind on earth shall be bound in heaven; and whatsoever thou shalt loose on earth shall be loosed in heaven."

Thus it was natural that the Roman Church should early have been looked upon as the "mother church" in the West. Its doctrines were considered the purest, since they had been handed down from its exalted founders. When there was a difference of opinion in regard to the truth of a particular teaching, it was natural that all should turn to the bishop of Rome for his view. Moreover, the majesty of Rome, the capital of the world, helped to exalt its bishop above his fellows. It was long, however, before all the other bishops, especially those in the large cities, were ready to accept unconditionally the authority of the bishop of Rome, although they acknowledged his leading position and that of the Roman community.

We know comparatively little of the bishops of Rome during the first three or four centuries of the Church's existence. It is only with the accession of Leo the Great (440-461) that the history of the papacy may, in one sense, be said to have begun. At his suggestion, Valentinian III, the emperor in the West, issued a decree in 445 declaring the power of the bishop of Rome supreme, by reason of Peter's headship, and the majesty of the city of Rome. He commanded that the bishops throughout the West should receive as law all that the bishop of Rome approved, and that any bishop refusing to answer a summons to Rome should be forced to obey by the imperial governor.

But a council at Chalcedon, six years later, declared that new Rome on the Bosporus (Constantinople) should have the same power in the government of the Church as old Rome on the Tiber. This decree was, however, never accepted in the Western, or Latin, Church, which was gradually separating from the Eastern, or Greek, Church, whose natural head was at Constantinople. Although there were times of trouble to come when for years the claims of Pope Leo appeared an empty boast, still his emphatic assertion of the supremacy of the

Roman bishop was a great step toward bringing the Western Church under a single head.

The name "pope" (Latin, *papa*, "father") was originally and quite naturally given to all bishops, and even to priests. It began to be especially applied to the bishops of Rome, perhaps as early as the sixth century, but was not apparently confined

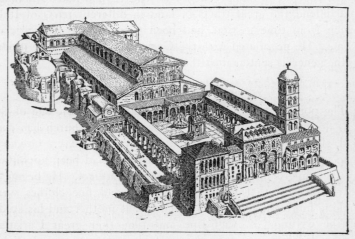

THE ANCIENT BASILICA OF ST. PETER

Of the churches built by Constantine in Rome that in honor of St. Peter was, next to the Lateran, the most important. It was constructed on the site of Nero's circus, where St. Peter was believed to have been crucified. It retained its original appearance, as here represented, for twelve hundred years, and then the popes (who had given up the Lateran as their residence and come to live in the Vatican palace close to St. Peter's) determined to build the new and grander church one sees to-day. Constantine and the popes made constant use in their buildings of columns and stones taken from the older Roman buildings, which were in this way demolished

to them until two or three hundred years later. Gregory VII (d. 1085) was the first to declare explicitly that the title should be used only for the bishop of Rome.

Not long after the death of Leo the Great, Odoacer put an end to the Western line of emperors. Then Theodoric and his East Goths settled in Italy, only to be followed by still less desirable intruders, the Lombards. During this tumultuous period the people of Rome, and even of all Italy, came to regard the pope as their natural leader. The Eastern emperor was far away, and his officers, who managed to hold a portion of central Italy around Rome and Ravenna, were glad to accept the aid and counsel of the pope. In Rome the pope watched over the elections of the city officials and directed the manner in which the public money should be spent. He had to manage and defend the great tracts of land in different parts of Italy which from time to time had been given to the bishopric of Rome. He negotiated with the Germans and even gave orders to the generals sent against them.

Gregory the Great

The pontificate of Gregory the Great (590-604), one of the half dozen most distinguished heads that the Church has ever had, shows how great a part the papacy could play. Gregory, who was the son of a rich Roman senator, had been appointed by the emperor to the honorable office of prefect. He began to fear, however, that his proud position and fine clothes were making him vain and worldly. His pious mother and his study of the writings of Augustine and the other great Christian writers led him, upon the death of his father, to spend all his handsome fortune in founding seven monasteries. One of these he established in his own house, and he subjected himself to such severe discipline that his health never entirely recovered from it.

When Gregory was chosen pope (in 590) and most reluctantly left his monastery, ancient Rome, the capital of the Empire, was already transforming itself into medieval Rome, the capital of Christendom. The temples of the gods had furnished materials for the many Christian churches. The tombs of the apostles Peter and Paul were soon to become the center of religious attraction and the goal of pilgrimages from every part of western Europe. Just as Gregory assumed office a great plague was raging in the city. In true medieval fashion he arranged a solemn procession in order to obtain from heaven a cessation of the pest. Then the Archangel Michael was seen over the tomb of Hadrian sheathing his fiery sword as a sign that the wrath of the Lord had been turned away. With Gregory we leave behind us the Rome of Cæsar and Trajan and enter upon that of the popes.

Gregory enjoyed an unrivaled reputation during the Middle Ages as a writer. His works show, however, how much less

HADRIAN'S TOMB

The Roman emperor Hadrian (d. 138) built a great circular tomb at Rome, on the west bank of the Tiber, for himself and his successors. It was 240 feet across, perhaps 165 feet high, covered with marble and adorned with statues. When Rome was besieged by the Germans in 537, the inhabitants used the tomb for a fortress and threw down the statues on the heads of the barbarians. Since the time when Gregory the Great saw the Archangel Michael sheathing his sword over Hadrian's tomb it has been called the Castle of the Holy Angel

cultivated his period was than that of his predecessors. His most popular book was his *Dialogues,* a collection of accounts of miracles and popular legends. It is hard to believe that it could have been composed by the greatest man of the time and that it was written for adults.[1] In his commentary on Job,

[1] He is reckoned, along with Augustine, Ambrose, and Jerome, as one of the four great Latin "fathers" of the Church.

Gregory warns the reader that he need not be surprised to find mistakes in Latin grammar, since in dealing with so holy a work as the Bible a writer should not stop to make sure whether his cases and tenses are right.

Gregory's letters show clearly what the papacy was coming to mean for Europe when in the hands of a really great man. While he assumed the humble title of "Servant of the servants of God," which the popes still use, Gregory was a statesman whose influence extended far and wide. It devolved upon him to govern the city of Rome,—as it did upon his successors down to the year 1870,—for the Eastern emperor's control had become merely nominal. He had also to keep the Lombards out of central Italy, which they failed to conquer largely on account of the valiant defense of the popes. These duties were functions of the state, and in assuming them Gregory may be said to have founded the "temporal" power of the popes.

Monks and Monasteries

Beyond the borders of Italy, Gregory was in constant communication with the emperor and the Frankish and Burgundian rulers. Everywhere he used his influence to have good clergymen chosen as bishops, and everywhere he watched over the interests of the monasteries. But his chief importance in the history of the papacy is due to the missionary enterprises he undertook, through which the great countries that were one day to be called England, France, and Germany were brought under the sway of the Roman Church and its head, the pope.

As Gregory had himself been a devoted monk, it was natural that he should rely chiefly upon the monks in his great work of converting the heathen. Consequently, before considering his missionary achievements, we must glance at the origin and character of the monks, who are so conspicuous throughout the Middle Ages.

It would be difficult to overestimate the influence that the monks and other religious orders exercised for centuries in Europe. The proud annals of the Benedictines, Franciscans,

Dominicans, and Jesuits contain many a distinguished name. Eminent philosophers, scientists, historians, artists, poets, and statesmen may be found in their ranks. Among those whose achievements we shall mention later are "The Venerable Bede," Boniface, Thomas Aquinas, Roger Bacon, Fra Angelico, Luther, Erasmus—all these, and many others who have been leaders in various branches of human activity, were, or had been, members of religious orders.

The life in a monastery appealed to many different kinds of people. The monastic life was safe and peaceful, as well as holy. The monastery was the natural refuge not only of the religiously minded, but of those of a studious or thoughtful disposition who disliked the career of a soldier and were disinclined to face the dangers and uncertainties of the times. Even the rude and unscrupulous warriors hesitated to destroy the property or disturb the life of those who were believed to enjoy special favor. The monastery furnished, too, a refuge for the friendless, an asylum for the disgraced, and food and shelter for the indolent, who would otherwise have had to earn their living. There were, therefore, many different motives which led people to enter monasteries. Kings and nobles, for the good of their souls, readily gave land upon which to found colonies of monks, and there were plenty of remote spots in the mountains and forests to invite those who wished to escape from the world and its temptations, its dangers and disappointments, or its cares.

Monastic communities first developed on a large scale in Egypt in the fourth century. The idea, however, was quickly taken up in Europe. At the time that the Germans were winning their first great victory at Adrianople, St. Jerome was busily engaged in writing letters to men and women whom he hoped to induce to become monks or hermits. In the sixth century monasteries multiplied so rapidly in western Europe that it became necessary to establish definite rules for these communities which proposed to desert the ordinary ways of the world and lead a holy life apart. Accordingly St. Benedict drew up, about the year 526, a sort of constitution for the monastery of Monte Cassino,[1] in southern Italy, of which he was the head. This was so sagacious, and so well met the needs of the monastic life, that it was rapidly accepted by the other monasteries and gradually became the "rule" according to which all the Western monks lived.[2]

The Rule of St. Benedict is as important as any constitution that was ever drawn up for a state. It is for the most part very wise and sensible. It provided that, since not every one is fitted for the monk's life, the candidate for admission to the monastery should pass through a period of probation, called the *novitiate*, before he was permitted to take the solemn, final vows. The brethren were to elect the head of the monastery, the abbot, as he was called. Along with frequent prayer and meditation, the monks were to do the necessary cooking and washing for the monastery and raise the necessary vegetables and grain. They were also to read and teach. Those who were incapacitated for outdoor work were assigned lighter tasks, such as copying books.

The monk had to take the three vows of obedience, poverty, and chastity. He was to obey the abbot without question in all matters that did not involve his committing a sin. He pledged himself to perpetual and absolute poverty, and everything he used was the property of the convent. He was not permitted to own anything whatsoever—not even such innocent things as a book or a pen. Along with the vows of obedience and poverty, he was also required to pledge himself never to marry. For not only was the single life considered more holy than the married, but the monastic organization would have been impos-

[1] This was situated on a lofty hill, lying some ninety miles south of Rome. Benedict selected a site formerly occupied by a temple to Apollo, of which the columns may still be seen in one of the courts of the present building. The monastery was destroyed by the Lombards not long after its foundation and later by the Mohammedans, so none of the present buildings go back to the time of Benedict.

[2] Benedict did not introduce monasticism in the West, as is sometimes supposed, nor did he even found an *order* in the proper sense of the word, under a single head, like the later Franciscans and Dominicans. Nevertheless, the monks who lived under his rule are ordinarily spoken of as belonging to the Benedictine order.

sible unless the monks remained single. Aside from these restrictions, the monks were commanded to live reasonable and natural lives and not to destroy their health, as some earlier ones had done, by undue fasting in the supposed interest of their souls.

The influence of the Benedictine monks upon Europe is incalculable. From their numbers no less than twenty-four popes and forty-six hundred bishops and archbishops have been chosen. They boast almost sixteen thousand writers, some of great distinction. Their monasteries furnished retreats during the Middle Ages, where the scholar might study and write in spite of the prevailing disorder of the times.

The copying of books, as has been said, was a natural occupation of the monks. Doubtless their work was often done carelessly, with little heart and less understanding. But, with the great loss of manuscripts due to the destruction of libraries and the general lack of interest in books, it was most essential that new copies should be made. Even poor and incorrect ones were better than none. Almost all the books written by the Romans disappeared altogether during the Middle Ages, but from time to time a monk would copy out the poems of Virgil, Horace, or Ovid, or the speeches of Cicero. In this way some of the chief works of the Latin writers have continued to exist down to the present day.

The monks regarded good hard work as a great aid to salvation. They set the example of careful cultivation of the lands about their monasteries and in this way introduced better farming methods into the regions where they settled. They entertained travelers at a time when there were few or no inns and so increased the intercourse between the various parts of Europe.

The Benedictine monks were ardent and faithful supporters of the papacy. The Church, which owes much to them, extended to them many of the privileges enjoyed by the clergy. Indeed, the monks were reckoned as clergymen and were called the "regular" clergy, because they lived according to a *regula,* or rule, to distinguish them from the "secular" clergy, who continued to live in the world (*saeculum*) and did not take the monastic vows described above.

The home which the monks constructed for themselves was called a monastery or abbey. This was arranged to meet their particular needs and was usually at a considerable distance from any town, in order to insure solitude and quiet.[1] It was modeled upon the general plan of the Roman country house. The buildings were arranged around a court. On all four sides

CLOISTERS OF HEILIGENKREUZ

This picture of the cloister in the German monastery of Heiligenkreuz is chosen to show how the more ordinary monastery courts looked, with their pleasant sunny gardens

of this was a covered walk, called the *cloister*, which made it possible to reach all the buildings without exposing one's self to either the rain or the hot sun. Not only the Benedictines but all the orders which sprang up in later centuries arranged their homes in much the same way.

On the north side of the court was the *church*, which always faced west. As time went on and certain groups of monks were given a great deal of property, they constructed very

---

[1] Later monasteries were sometimes built in towns, or just outside the walls.

beautiful churches for their monasteries. Westminster Abbey was originally the church of a monastery lying outside the city of London, and there are in Great Britain many picturesque remains of ruined abbey churches which attract the attention of every traveler.

On the west side of the court were storerooms for provisions; on the south side, opposite the church, was the "refec-

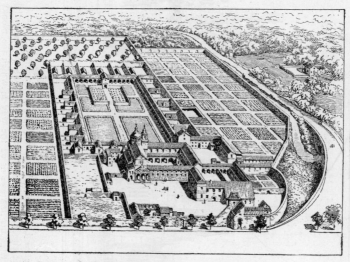

MONASTERY OF VAL DI CRISTO

This monastery in southern Spain has two cloisters; the main one lies to the left. One can see how the buildings were surrounded by vegetable gardens and an orchard which supplied the monks with food. Compare picture of another monastery (p. 98)

tory," or dining room, and a sitting room that could be warmed in cold weather. In the cloister near the dining room was a "lavatory" where the monk could wash his hands before meals. To the east of the court was the "dormitory," where the monks slept. This always adjoined the church, for the Rule required that the monks should hold services seven times a day. One of these services, called vigils, came well before daybreak, and it was convenient when you were summoned in the dark-

Melrose Abbey

The monastery at Melrose, Scotland, was founded in the eleventh century, but the church of which we here see the ruins was not built until about 1450. Sir Walter Scott in one of his well-known novels, *The Monastery*, describes his impressions of the way in which the monks lived

ness out of your warm bed to be able to go down a short passage that led from the dormitory into the choir of the church, where the service was held.

The Benedictine Rule provided that the monks should so far as possible have everything for their support on their own land. So outside the group of buildings around the cloister would be found the garden, the orchard, the mill, a fish pond, and fields for raising grain. There were also a hospital for the sick and a guest house for pilgrims or poor people who happened to come along. In the greater monasteries there were also quarters where a king or nobleman might spend a few nights in comfort.

Missionary Work of the Monks

The first great undertaking of the monks was the conversion of those German peoples who had not yet been won over to Christianity. These the monks made not merely Christians, but also dutiful subjects of the pope. In this way the strength of the Roman Catholic Church was greatly increased. The first people to engage the attention of the monks were the heathen German tribes who had conquered the once Christian Britain.

The islands which are now known as the kingdom of Great Britain and Ireland were, at the opening of the Christian era, occupied by several Celtic peoples of whose customs and religion we know almost nothing. Julius Cæsar commenced the conquest of the islands (55 B.C.); but the Romans never succeeded in establishing their power beyond the wall which they built, from the Clyde to the Firth of Forth, to keep out the wild tribes of the North. Even south of the wall the country was not completely Romanized, and the Celtic tongue has survived down to the present day in Wales.

At the opening of the fifth century the barbarian invasions forced Rome to withdraw its legions from Britain in order to protect its frontiers on the Continent. The island was thus left to be conquered gradually by the Germans, mainly Saxons and Angles, who came across the North Sea from the region south of Denmark. Almost all record of what went on during the two centuries following the departure of the Romans has disap-

[69]

peared. No one knows the fate of the original Celtic inhabitants of England. It was formerly supposed that they were all killed or driven to the mountain districts of Wales, but this seems unlikely. More probably they were gradually lost among the dominating Germans with whom they merged into one people. The Saxon and Angle chieftains established small kingdoms, of which there were seven or eight at the time when Gregory the Great became pope.

ST. MARTIN'S, CANTERBURY

A church built during the period when the Romans were occupying England had been used by Bertha, the Christian wife of the king of Kent. Augustine found this on his arrival in Canterbury and is said to have baptized the king there. It has been rebuilt and added to in later times, but there are many Roman bricks in the walls, and the lower parts of the church as we now see it may go back to the Roman period

Gregory, while still a simple monk, had been struck with the beauty of some Angles whom he saw one day in the slave market at Rome. When he learned who they were he was grieved that such handsome beings should still belong to the kingdom of the Prince of Darkness, and he wished to go as a missionary to their people, but permission was refused him. So when he became pope he sent forty monks to England under the leadership of a prior, named Augustine (who must not be confused with the church father of that name). The heathen king of Kent, in whose territory Augustine and his monks landed with fear and trembling (597), had a Christian wife, the daughter of a Frankish king. Through her influence the monks were kindly received and were given an ancient church at Canterbury, dating from the Roman occupation before the German invasions. Here they established a monastery, and from this center the conversion, first of Kent and then of the whole island, was gradually accomplished. Canterbury has always maintained its early preëminence and may still be considered the religious capital of England.[1]

England thus became a part of the ever-growing territory embraced in the Roman Catholic Church and remained for nearly a thousand years as faithful to the pope as any other Catholic country.

The conversion of England by the missionaries from Rome was followed by a period of general enthusiasm for Rome and its literature and culture. The English monasteries became centers of learning unrivaled perhaps in the rest of Europe. A constant intercourse was maintained with Rome. Masons and glassmakers were brought across the Channel to replace the wooden churches of Britain by stone edifices in the style of the Romans. The young English clergy were taught Latin and sometimes Greek. Copies of the ancient classics were brought from the Continent and copied. The most distinguished writer of the seventh and early eighth centuries in Europe was the English monk Bæda (often called "The Venerable Bede," 673-735), from whose admirable history of the Church in England most of our information about the period is derived.

In 718 St. Boniface, an English monk, was sent by the pope as a missionary to the Germans. After four years spent in

---

[1] In Ireland the Christian faith had survived the German invasions of Britain, and Irish missionaries were crossing to northern Britain when the Roman missionaries arrived. For some time there was a bitter rivalry between these two groups, who differed especially in their attitude toward the headship of the bishop of Rome. In the end the Roman missionaries, with the support of the king of Northumbria, prevailed (Council of Whitby, 664), and the Irish missionaries sadly withdrew.

reconnoitering the field of his future labors, he visited Rome and was made a missionary bishop, taking the same oath of obedience to the pope that the bishops in the immediate vicinity of Rome were accustomed to take. Indeed, absolute subordination to the pope was a part of his religion, and he became a powerful agent in extending the papal power.

Boniface succeeded in converting many of the more remote German tribes who still clung to their old pagan beliefs. His energetic methods are illustrated by the story of how he cut down the sacred oak of the old German god, Odin, at Fritzlar, in Hesse, and used the wood to build a chapel, around which a monastery soon grew up. In 732 Boniface was raised to the dignity of Archbishop of Mainz and proceeded to establish in the newly converted region a number of German bishoprics, Salzburg, Regensburg, Würzburg, and others; this gives us some idea of the geographical extent of his labors.

Mohammed and His Religion

Just at the time that Gregory the Great was doing so much to strengthen the power and influence of the popes in Rome, a young Arab caravan leader in far away Mecca was meditating upon the mysteries of life and devising a religion which was destined to spread with astounding rapidity into Asia, Africa, and Europe and to become a great rival to Christianity. And to-day the millions who believe in Mohammed as God's greatest prophet are probably equal in number to those who are faithful to the pope, as the head of the Catholic Church.

Before the time of Mohammed the Arabs had played no great part in the world's history. The scattered tribes were constantly at war with one another, and each tribe worshiped its own gods, when it worshiped at all. Mecca was considered a sacred spot, however, and the fighting was stopped four months each year so that all could peacefully visit the *Kaaba*, a sort of temple full of idols and containing in particular a black stone, about as long as a man's hand, which was regarded as specially worthy of reverence.

MOHAMMED AND HIS RELIGION

Mohammed was poor and earned a living by conducting caravans across the desert. He was so fortunate as to find a rich widow in Mecca, named Kadijah, who gave him employment and later fell in love with him and became his wife. She was his first convert and kept up his courage when few of his fellow townsmen in Mecca were inclined to pay any attention to his new religious teachings.

As Mohammed traveled back and forth across the desert with his trains of camels heavily laden with merchandise he had plenty of time to think, and he became convinced that God was sending him messages which it was his duty to reveal to mankind. He met many Jews and Christians, of whom there were great numbers in Arabia, and from them he got some ideas of the Old and New Testaments. But when he tried to convince people that he was God's prophet, and that the Angel Gabriel had appeared to him in his dreams and told him of a new religion, he was treated with scorn.

Finally, he discovered that his enemies in Mecca were planning to kill him, and he fled to the neighboring town of Medina, where he had friends. His flight, which took place in the year 622, is called the *Hejira* by the Arabs. It was taken by his followers as the beginning of a new era—the year one, as the Mohammedans reckon time.

A war followed between the people of Mecca and those who had joined Mohammed in and about Medina. It was eight years before his followers became numerous enough to enable him to march upon Mecca and take it with a victorious army. Before his death in 632 he had gained the support of all the Arab chiefs, and his new religion, which he called *Islam* (submission to God), was accepted throughout the whole Arabian peninsula.

Mohammed probably could neither write nor read well, but when he fell into trances from time to time he would repeat to his eager listeners the words which he heard from heaven, and they in turn wrote them down. These sayings, which were collected into a volume shortly after his death, form the *Koran*, the Mohammedan Bible. This contains the chief beliefs of the

new religion as well as the laws under which all good Mohammedans were to live. It has been translated into English several times. Parts of it are very beautiful and interesting,
while other portions are dull and stupid to an Occidental reader.

The Koran follows the Jewish and Christian religions in proclaiming one God, "the Lord of the worlds, the merciful and
compassionate." Mohammed believed that there had been
great prophets before him,—Abraham, Moses, and Jesus
among others,—but that he himself was the last and greatest
of God's messengers, who brought the final and highest form
of religion to mankind. He destroyed all the idols in the
Kaaba at Mecca and forbade his followers to make any images
whatsoever—but he left the black stone.

Besides serving the one God, the Mohammedan was to honor
his parents, aid the poor, protect the orphan, keep his contracts,
give full measure, and weigh with a just balance. He was not
to walk proudly on the earth, or to be wasteful, "for the wasteful were ever the devil's brothers." He was to avoid, moreover,
all strong drink, and this command has saved Mohammed's
faithful followers from the terrible degradation which alcohol
has made so common in our Western world.

Besides obeying these and other commands the Mohammedan who would be saved must do five things: First, he must
recite daily the simple creed, "There is no god but God, and
Mohammed is his prophet." Secondly, he must pray five times
a day—just before sunrise, just after noon, before and after
sunset, and when the day has closed. It is not uncommon
to see in well-furnished houses in this country the so-called
"prayer rugs" brought from Mohammedan countries. These
are spread down on the ground or the flat roof of the Oriental
house, and on them the worshiper kneels to pray, turning his
face toward Mecca and bowing his head to the ground. The
pattern of the rug indicates the place where the bowed head is
to be placed. Thirdly, the Mohammedan must fast during the
whole month of *ramadan;* he may neither eat nor drink from
sunrise to sunset, for this is the month in which God sent
Gabriel down from the seventh heaven to bring the Koran,

which he revealed, paragraph by paragraph, to Mohammed. Fourthly, the Mohammedan must give alms to the poor, and, fifthly, he must, if he can, make a pilgrimage to Mecca at least once during his lifetime. Tens of thousands of pilgrims flock to Mecca every year. They enter the great courtyard surrounding the Kaaba, which is a plain, almost cubical, building, supposed to have been built in the first place by Abraham. The sacred black stone is fixed in the outside wall at the southeast corner, and the pilgrims must circle the building seven times, kissing the black stone each time as they pass it.

The Koran announces a day of judgment when the heavens shall be opened and the mountains be powdered and become like flying dust. Then all men shall receive their reward. Those who have refused to accept Islam shall be banished to hell to be burned and tormented forever. "They shall not taste therein coolness or drink, save scalding water and running sores," and the scalding water they shall drink like thirsty camels.

Those, on the other hand, who have obeyed the Koran, especially those who die fighting for Islam, shall find themselves in a garden of delight. They shall recline in rich brocades upon soft cushions and rugs and be served by surpassingly beautiful maidens, with eyes like hidden pearls. Wine may be drunk there, but "their heads shall not ache with it, neither shall they be confused." They shall be content with their past life and shall hear no foolish words; and there shall be no sin but only the greeting, "Peace, peace."

The religion of Mohammed was much simpler than that of the medieval Christian Church; it did not provide for a priesthood or for any great number of ceremonies. The Mohammedan mosque or temple is a house of prayer and a place for reading the Koran; no altars or images or pictures of any kind are permitted in it. The mosques are often very beautiful buildings, especially in great Mohammedan cities, such as Jerusa'em, Damascus, Cairo, and Constantinople. They have great courts surrounded by covered colonnades and are adorned with beautiful marbles and mosaics and delightful windows with bright stained glass. The walls are adorned with passages from

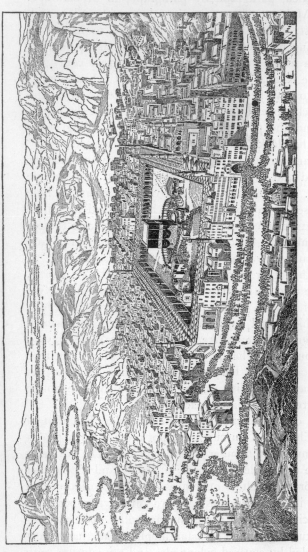

MECCA AND ITS MOSQUE

Mecca is situated in a barren, rocky region. The sacred building, called the Kaaba, lies in a vast court surrounded by a colonnade with minarets. Into the court the pilgrims are making their way to walk around the Kaaba seven times and kiss the black stone, embedded in the corner of the building, to the left, as we see it. The Kaaba is covered with a great cloth sent each year by the Egyptian government. The old weather-beaten cover is torn up and sold to the pilgrims for relics. The only entrance to the Kaaba is a little door seven feet from the ground, just under the edge of the cloth the Koran, and the floors covered with rich rugs. They have one or more minarets from which the *muezzin,* or call to prayer, is heard five times a day.

The Mohammedans, like other Eastern peoples, have been very particular to keep the women by themselves in a separate part of the house, called the *harem,* or women's quarters. They might not go out without the master's permission and even then not without wearing a veil; no man was ever to see a respectable woman's face, except her father, brother, or husband. But in recent years the status of women is rapidly changing as the result of Western ideas. The Koran permits a man to have as many as four wives, but in practice only men of the richer classes had more than one. For a woman to attempt to escape from the harem was a crime punishable with death.

Slaves are very common in Mohammedan countries, but once they are freed they are as good as any one else and may then hold the highest places in the government.

Conquests of the Mohammedans; the Caliphate

Mohammed had occupied the position of pope and king combined, and his successors, who took the title of *caliph* (which means "successor" or "representative"), were regarded as the absolute rulers of the Mohammedans. Their word was law in both religious and worldly matters. Mohammed's father-in-law was the first caliph. His successor, Omar (634-644), led the Arabs forth to conquest, and in a few years Syria, Egypt, and the great empire of Persia came under their dominion. The capital of the caliphate was later transferred from Medina to Damascus, which occupied a far better position for governing the new realms. Although the Mohammedans were constantly fighting among themselves, they succeeded in extending their territory so as to include Asia Minor and the northern coast of Africa. A great part of the people whom they conquered accepted the new religion of the prophet.

Something over a hundred years after Mohammed's death a new line of caliphs came into power and established (762) a new capital on the river Tigris near the site of ancient Babylon.

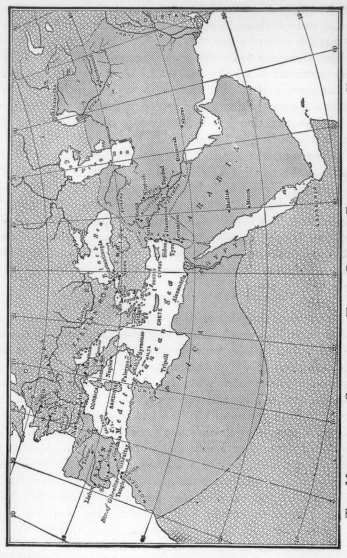

The Mohammedan Conquests at Their Greatest Extent, about the Year 750

This new city of Bagdad became famous for its wealth, magnificence, and learning. It was five miles across and at one time is supposed to have had two millions of inhabitants. In the ninth century it was probably the richest and most splendid city in the world.

The most entertaining example of Arabic literature which has been translated into English is the *Thousand and One Nights*, or *The Arabian Nights' Entertainments*, as it is commonly called. These include the story of "Sindbad the Sailor," "Aladdin and the Lamp," "Ali Baba and the Forty Thieves," and other famous tales. The great collection was got together in Egypt, perhaps in the fifteenth century, but many of the stories are very much older and were translated by the Arabs from the Persian, when the caliphs of Bagdad were at the height of their power. Some of these stories give one a lively idea of Mohammedan manners and customs.

The Mohammedans made two or three attempts to cross over from Asia into Europe and take Constantinople, the capital of the Eastern Empire, but failed. It was more than eight hundred years after Mohammed's death that the Turks, converts to Mohammedanism, succeeded in this, and Constantinople is still a Mohammedan city. Long before the Turks captured Constantinople, however, the Arabs at the other end of the caliph's empire had succeeded in crossing the Strait of Gibraltar from Africa and possessing themselves of Spain.

The kingdom of the West Goths was in no condition to defend itself when a few Arabs and a much larger number of Berbers, inhabitants of northern Africa, ventured to invade Spain. Some of the Spanish towns held out for a time, but the invaders found allies in the numerous Jews, who had been shamefully treated by their Christian countrymen. As for the innumerable serfs who worked on the great estates of the aristocracy, a change of landlords made very little difference to them. In 711 the Arabs and Berbers gained a great battle, and the peninsula was gradually overrun by new immigrants from Africa.

GIRALDA

This tower, called the Giralda, was originally the great minaret of the chief mosque at Seville. It was built, 1184-1196, out of Roman and West Gothic materials, and many Roman inscriptions are to be seen on the stones used for the walls. Originally the tower was lower than it now is. All the upper part, including the story where the bells hang, was rebuilt by the Christians after they drove the Moors out of the city

In seven years the Mohammedans were masters of almost the whole region south of the Pyrenees. They then began to cross into Gaul. For some years the Duke of Aquitaine kept them in check; but in 732 they collected a large army, defeated the duke near Bordeaux, advanced to Poitiers, and then set out for Tours. Here they met the army of the Franks which Charles the Hammer (Martel), the king's chief minister, had brought together to meet the new danger. We know very little indeed of this famous battle of Tours, except that the Mohammedans were repulsed and that they never again made any serious attempt to conquer western Europe beyond the Pyrenees. They retired to Spain and there developed a great and prosperous kingdom, far in advance of the Christian kingdoms to the north of them.

Some of the buildings which they erected soon a f t e r their arrival still stand. Among these is the mosque at Cordova with its forest of columns and arches.[1]

[1] This great mosque, which the Mohammedan rulers built at Cordova on the site of a Christian church of the West Goths, was second in size only to the Kaaba at Mecca. It was begun about 785 and gradually enlarged and beautified during the following two

[80]

Pl. II. Interior of the Great Mosque of Cordova

PL. III. COURT OF THE LIONS IN THE ALHAMBRA

They also erected a great tower at Seville, the Giralda, reproduced by the architects of the already destroyed Madison Square Garden in New York. The Mohammedans built beautiful palaces and laid out charming gardens. One of these palaces, the Alhambra, built at Granada some centuries after their arrival in Spain, is a marvel of lovely detail. They also founded a great university at Cordova, to which Christians from the north sometimes went in search of knowledge.

Historians commonly regard it as a matter of great good luck that Charles the Hammer and his barbarous soldiers succeeded in defeating and driving back the Mohammedans at Tours. But had they been permitted to settle in southern France they might have developed science and art far more rapidly than did the Franks. It is difficult to say whether it was a good thing or a bad thing that the Moors, as the Mohammedans in Spain were called, did not get control of a portion of Gaul.

---

centuries, with the hope that it would rival Mecca as a place of pilgrimage. The part represented in the illustration was built by Caliph Al-Hakim, who came to the throne in 961. The beautiful holy of holies (the entrance of which may be seen in the background) is richly adorned with magnificent mosaics. The whole mosque is 570 by 425 feet; that is, about the size of St. Peter's in Rome.

CHAPTER IV

CONDITIONS IN CHARLEMAGNE'S TIME

Charlemagne and His Conquests. Reëstablishment of a Line of "Roman" Emperors in the West. Charlemagne's Contributions to Order and Education

Charlemagne and His Conquests

WE have seen how the kings of the Franks, Clovis and his successors, conquered a large territory, including western Germany and what is called France to-day. As time went on, the king's chief minister, who was called the Mayor of the Palace, got almost all the power into his hands and really ruled in the place of the king. Charles Martel, who defeated the Mohammedans at Tours in 732, was the Mayor of the Palace of the western Frankish king. His son, Pippin the Short, finally determined to do away altogether with the old line of kings and put himself in their place. Before taking the decisive step, however, he consulted the pope. To Pippin's question whether it was right that the old line of kings should continue to reign when they no longer had any power, the pope replied: "It seems better that he who has the power in the State should be king, and be called king, rather than he who is falsely called king." With this sanction, then (752), the Frankish counts and dukes, in accordance with the old German ceremony, raised Pippin on their shields, in somewhat the way college boys nowadays carry off a successful football player on their shoulders. He was then anointed king by St. Boniface, the apostle to the Germans, of whom we have spoken, and received the blessing of the pope.[1]

It would hardly be necessary to mention this change of dynasty in so short a history as this, were it not that the calling in of the pope brought about a revolution in the ideas of kingship. The kings of the German tribes had hitherto usually been successful warriors who held their office with the consent of the people, or at least of the nobles. Their election was

---

[1] The old line of kings which was displaced by Pippin are known as the Merovingians. Pippin and his successors are called the Carolingian line.

not a matter that concerned the Church at all. But when, after asking the pope's opinion, Pippin had the holy oil poured on his head,—in accordance with an ancient religious custom of the Jews,—first by Bishop Boniface and later by the pope himself, he seemed to ask the Church to approve his usurpation. As Gibbon puts it, "A German chieftain was transformed into the Lord's anointed." The pope threatened with God's anger any one who should attempt to supplant the consecrated family of Pippin.

It thus became a *religious* duty to obey the king and his successors. He came to be regarded by the Church, when he had received its approval, as God's representative on earth. Here we have the beginning of the later theory of kings "by the grace of God," against whom it was a sin to revolt, however bad they might be. We shall see presently how Pippin's famous son Charlemagne received his crown from the hands of the pope.

Charlemagne, who became king of all the Frankish realms in 771, is the first historical personage among the German peoples of whom we have any satisfactory knowledge.[1] Compared with him, Theodoric, Clovis, Charles Martel, Pippin, and the rest are but shadowy figures. The chronicles tell us something of their deeds, but we can make only the vaguest inferences in regard to their appearance or character.

Charlemagne's looks, as described by his secretary, so exactly correspond with the character of the king as exhibited in his reign that they are worthy of attention. He was tall and stoutly built; his face was round, his eyes were large and keen, his nose somewhat above the common size, his expression bright and cheerful. The good proportions and grace of his body prevented the observer from noticing that his neck was rather short and his person somewhat too stout. His voice was clear, but rather weak for his big body. He delighted in riding and

---

[1] "Charlemagne" is the French form for the Latin *Carolus Magnus* (Charles the Great). We must never forget, however, that Charlemagne was a *German*, and he talked a German language, namely Frankish, and that his favorite palaces at Aix-la-Chapelle, Ingelheim, and Nimwegen were in German regions.

hunting, and was an expert swimmer. His excellent health and his physical endurance can alone explain the astonishing swiftness with which he moved about his vast realm and conducted innumerable campaigns against his enemies in widely distant regions in rapid succession.

Charles was an educated man for his time, and one who knew how to appreciate and encourage scholarship. While at dinner he had some one read to him; he delighted especially in history, and in St. Augustine's *City of God*. He tried to learn writing, which was a very unusual accomplishment at that time for any but churchmen, but began too late in life and got no farther than signing his name. He called learned men to his court and did much toward reëstablishing a regular system of schools. He was also constantly occupied with buildings and other public works calculated to adorn his kingdom. He himself planned the remarkable cathedral at Aix-la-Chapelle and showed the greatest interest in its furnishings. He commenced two palaces, one near Mainz and the other at Nimwegen, in Holland, and had a long bridge constructed across the Rhine at Mainz.

The impression which his reign made upon men's minds continued to grow after his death. He became the hero of a whole series of romantic adventures which were as firmly believed for centuries as his real deeds. In the fancy of an old monk in the monastery of St. Gall, writing of Charlemagne not long after his death, the king of the Franks swept over Europe surrounded by countless legions of soldiers who formed a very sea of bristling steel. Knights of superhuman valor formed his court and became the models of knighthood for the following centuries. Distorted but imposing, the Charlemagne of poetry meets us all through the Middle Ages.

A study of Charlemagne's reign will make clear that he was a truly remarkable person, one of the greatest figures in the world's records and deservedly the hero of the Middle Ages.

It was Charlemagne's ideal to bring all the German peoples together into one great Christian empire, and he was wonderfully successful in attaining his end. Only a small portion of what is now called Germany was included in the kingdom ruled over by Charlemagne's father, Pippin the Short. Frisia and Bavaria had been Christianized, and their rulers had been induced by the efforts of Charlemagne's predecessors and of the missionaries, especially Boniface, to recognize the overlordship of the Franks. Between these two half-independent countries lay the unconquered Saxons. They were as yet pagans and appear still to have clung to much the same institutions as those under which they had lived when the Roman historian Tacitus .described them seven centuries earlier.

The Saxons occupied the region beginning somewhat east of Cologne and extending to the Elbe, and north to where the great cities of Bremen and Hamburg are now situated. They had no towns or roads and were consequently very difficult to conquer, as they could retreat, with their few possessions, into the forests or swamps as soon as they found themselves unable to meet an invader in the open field. Charlemagne never undertook, during his long military career, any other task half so serious as the subjugation of the Saxons, which occupied many years.

Nowhere do we find a more striking example of the influence of the Church than in the reliance that Charlemagne placed upon it in his dealings with the Saxons. He deemed it quite as essential that after a rebellion they should promise to honor the Church and be baptized, as that they should pledge themselves to remain true and faithful subjects of the king. He was in quite as much haste to found bishoprics and monasteries as to build fortresses. The law for the newly conquered Saxon lands issued some time between 775 and 790 provides the same death penalty for him who "shall have shown himself unfaithful to the lord king" and him who "shall scorn to come to baptism and shall wish to remain a pagan."

Charlemagne believed the Christianizing of the Saxons so important a part of his duty that he decreed that any one should suffer death who broke into a church and carried off anything by force. No one, under penalty of heavy fines, was to make vows in the pagan fashion, at trees or springs, or partake of any heathen feasts in honor of the demons (as the Christians termed the heathen gods), or fail to present infants for baptism before they were a year old.

These provisions are characteristic of the theory of the Middle Ages according to which the government and the Church went hand in hand in ordering and governing the life of the people. Disloyalty to the Church was regarded by the State as quite as serious a crime as treason against itself. While the claims of the two institutions sometimes conflicted, there was no question in the minds either of the king's officials or of the clergy that both the civil and ecclesiastical governments were absolutely necessary; neither of them ever dreamed that they could get along without the other.

Before the Frankish conquest the Saxons had no towns. Now, around the seat of a bishop, or about a monastery, men began to collect, and towns and cities grew up. Of these the chief was Bremen, which is still one of the most important ports of Germany.

Summoned by the pope to protect him from his old enemies the Lombards, Charlemagne invaded Lombardy in 773 with a great army and took Pavia, the capital, after a long siege. The Lombard king was forced to become a monk, and his treasure was divided among the Frankish soldiers. Charlemagne then took the extremely important step, in 774, of having himself recognized by all the Lombard dukes and counts as king of the Lombards.

So far we have spoken only of the relations of Charlemagne with the Germans, for even the Lombard kingdom was established by the Germans. He had, however, other peoples to deal with, especially the Slavs on the east (who were one day to build up the kingdoms of Poland and Bohemia and the vast Russian empire) and, on the opposite boundary of his dominion, the Moors in Spain. Against these it was necessary to protect his realms, and the second part of Charlemagne's reign was devoted to what may be called his foreign policy. A single campaign in 789 seems to have sufficed to subdue the Slavs, who lay to the north and east of the Saxons, and to force the

Bohemians to acknowledge the supremacy of the Frankish king and pay tribute to him.

The necessity of protecting the Frankish realms against any new uprising of these non-German nations led to the establishment, on the confines of the kingdom, of *marches,* that is, districts under the military control of counts of the march, or *margraves.*[1] Their business was to prevent any invasion of the interior of the kingdom. Much depended upon the efficiency of these men; in many cases they founded powerful families and later helped to break up the empire by establishing themselves as practically independent rulers.

At an assembly that Charlemagne held in 777, ambassadors appeared before him from certain dissatisfied Mohammedans in Spain. They had fallen out with the emir of Cordova[2] and now offered to become the faithful subjects of Charlemagne if he would come to their aid. In consequence of this embassy he undertook his first expedition to Spain in the following year. After some years of war the district north of the Ebro was conquered by the Franks, and Charlemagne established there the Spanish march. In this way he began that gradual expulsion of the Mohammedans from the peninsula, which was to be carried on by slowly extending conquests until 1492, when Granada, the last Mohammedan stronghold, fell.

Reëstablishment of a Line of "Roman" Emperors in the West

But the most famous of all the achievements of Charlemagne was his reëstablishment of a line of so-called Roman emperors in the year 800. It came about in this wise. Charlemagne went to Rome in that year to settle a dispute between Pope Leo III and his enemies. To celebrate the satisfactory settlement of

[1] The king of Prussia had, among other titles, that of Margrave of Brandenburg. The German word *Mark* is often used for "march" on maps of Germany. In English and French the title is "Marquis."

[2] The Mohammedan caliphate broke up in the eighth century, and the ruler of Spain first assumed the title of emir (about 756) and later (929) that of caliph. The latter title had originally been enjoyed only by the head of the whole Arab empire, who had his capital at Damascus, and later at Bagdad.

the dispute, the pope held a solemn service on Christmas Day in St. Peter's. As Charlemagne was kneeling before the altar during this service, the pope approached him and set a crown upon his head, saluting him, amid the acclamations of those present, as "Emperor of the Romans."

The reasons for this extraordinary act, which Charlemagne insisted took him completely by surprise, are given in one of the Frankish histories, the *Chronicles of Lorsch,* as follows: "The name of Emperor had ceased among the Greeks, for they were under the reign of a woman [the Empress Irene], wherefore it seemed good both to Leo, the apostolic pope, and to the bishops who were in council with him, and to all Christian men, that they should name Charles, King of the Franks, as Emperor. For he held Rome itself, where the ancient Cæsars had always dwelt, in addition to all his other possessions in Italy, Gaul, and Germany. Wherefore, as God had granted him all these dominions, it seemed just to all that he should take the title of Emperor, too, when it was offered to him at the wish of all Christendom."

Charlemagne appears to have accepted gracefully the honor thus thrust upon him. Even if he had no right to the imperial title, it had a certain appropriateness under the circumstances. Before his coronation by the pope he was only king of the Franks and of the Lombards; but his conquests seemed to give him a right to a higher title which should include all his outlying realms.

The empire thus reëstablished in the West was considered to be a continuation of the Roman Empire founded by Augustus. Charlemagne was reckoned the immediate successor of the emperor at Constantinople, Constantine VI, whom Irene had deposed and blinded. Yet, it is hardly necessary to say that the position of the new emperor had little in common with that of Augustus or Constantine. In the first place, the Eastern emperors continued to reign in Constantinople for centuries, quite regardless of Charlemagne and his successors. In the second place, the German kings who wore the imperial crown after

Charlemagne were generally too weak really to rule over Germany and northern Italy, to say nothing of the rest of western Europe. Nevertheless, the Western Empire, which in the twelfth century came to be called the *Holy Roman Empire,* endured for over a thousand years. It came to an end only in 1806, when Napoleon reconstructed southern Germany and the last of the old line of emperors laid down the crown.

The assumption of the title of emperor was destined to make the German rulers a great deal of trouble. It constantly led them into unsuccessful efforts to keep control over Italy, which really lay outside their natural boundaries. Then the circumstances under which Charlemagne was crowned made it possible for the popes to claim, later, that it was they who had transferred the imperial power from the old eastern line of emperors to Charlemagne and his family, and that this was a proof of their right to dispose of the crown as they pleased. The difficulties which arose necessitated many a weary journey to Rome for the emperors, and many unfortunate conflicts between them and the popes.

Charlemagne's Contributions to Order and Education

The task of properly governing his vast dominions taxed even the highly gifted and untiring Charlemagne; it was quite beyond the power of his successors. The same difficulties continued to exist that had confronted Charles Martel and Pippin—above all, a scanty royal revenue and overpowerful officials, who were apt to neglect the interests and commands of their sovereign.

Charlemagne's income, like that of all medieval rulers, came chiefly from his royal estates, as there was no system of general taxation such as had existed under the Roman Empire. He consequently took the greatest care that his numerous plantations should be well cultivated, and that not even a turnip or an egg which was due him should be withheld. An elaborate set of regulations for his farms is preserved, which sheds much light upon the times.

The officials upon whom the Frankish kings were forced to rely chiefly were the counts, the "hand and voice of the king" wherever he could not be in person. They were expected to maintain order, see that justice was done in their district, and raise troops when the king needed them. On the frontier were the counts of the march, or margraves (marquises), already mentioned. These titles, together with that of duke, still exist as titles of nobility in Europe, although they are rarely associated with any governmental duties except in cases where their holders have the right to sit in the upper House of Parliament.

Charlemagne held assemblies of the nobles and bishops of his realm each spring or summer, at which the interests of the empire were considered. With the sanction of his advisers he issued an extraordinary series of laws, called *capitularies,* a number of which have been preserved. With the bishops and abbots he discussed the needs of the Church, and, above all, the necessity of better schools for both the clergy and the laity. The reforms which he sought to introduce give us an opportunity of learning the condition in which Europe found itself after four hundred years of disorder.

Charlemagne was the first important king since Theodoric to pay any attention to book learning. About 650 the supply of papyrus—a kind of paper that the Greeks and Romans used—had been cut off, owing to the conquest of Egypt by the Arabs, and as our kind of paper had not yet been introduced from China, there was only the very expensive parchment to write upon. While this had the advantage of being more durable than papyrus, its high cost discouraged the copying of books. The eighth century—that immediately preceding Charlemagne's coronation—is commonly regarded as the most ignorant, the darkest, and the most barbarous period of the Middle Ages.

Yet, in spite of this dark picture, there was promise for the future. It was evident, even before Charlemagne's time, that Europe was not to continue indefinitely in the path of ignorance. Latin could not be forgotten, for that was the language of the Church, and all its official communications were in that tongue. Consequently it was absolutely necessary that the Church should maintain some sort of education in order that there might be persons who knew enough to write a Latin letter

AN EXAMPLE OF THE STYLE OF WRITING USED IN THE BOOKS OF CHARLEMAGNE'S TIME[1]

and conduct the church services. Some of those who learned Latin must have used it to read the old books written by the Romans. Then the textbooks of the later Roman Empire con-

[1] These lines are taken from a manuscript written in 825. The part here given is addressed to the bishops and warns them of the terrible results of disobeying the rules of the Church. Perhaps the scribe did not fully understand what he was doing, for he has made some of those mistakes which Charlemagne was so anxious to avoid. Then there are some abbreviations which make the lines difficult to read. They ought probably to have run as follows: . . . *mereamini. Scit namque prudentia vestra, quam terribili anathematis censura feriuntur qui praesumptiose contra statuta universalium conciliorum venire audeant. Quapropter et vos diligentius ammonemus, ut omni intentione illud horribile execrationis judicium* . . .

It is interesting to note how nearly the form of the letters resembles that used by the early printers six hundred and fifty years later. One can see the old Roman letters used as capitals and a modification of these appearing as "lower case."

tinued to be used, and these, poor as they were, contained something about grammar, arithmetic, geometry, astronomy, and other subjects.

It seemed to Charlemagne that it was the duty of the Church not only to look after the education of its own officers but to provide the opportunity of at least an elementary education for the people at large. In accordance with this conviction, he issued (789) an order to the clergy to gather together the children of both freemen and serfs in their neighborhood and establish schools "in which the boys may learn to read."

It would be impossible to say how many of the abbots and bishops established schools in accordance with Charlemagne's recommendations. It is certain that famous centers of learning existed in monasteries at Tours, Fulda, Corbie, Orléans, and other places during his reign. Charlemagne further promoted the cause of education by the establishment of the famous "School of the palace" for the instruction of his own children and the sons of his nobles. He placed the Englishman Alcuin at the head of the school, and called distinguished men from Italy and elsewhere as teachers. The best known of these was the historian Paulus Diaconus, who wrote a history of the Lombards, to which we owe most of what we know about them.

Charlemagne appears to have been particularly impressed with the constant danger of mistakes in copying books, a task frequently turned over to ignorant and careless persons. He thought it very important that the religious books should be carefully copied. It should be noted that he made no attempt to revive the learning of Greece and Rome. He deemed it quite sufficient if the churchmen would learn their Latin well enough to read the church services and the Bible intelligently.

The hopeful beginning that was made under Charlemagne in the revival of education was destined to prove disappointing in its immediate results. It is true that the ninth century produced a few noteworthy men who have left works which indicate acuteness and mental training. But the break-up of Charlemagne's empire, the struggles between his descendants, the coming of new barbarians, and the disorder caused by the unruly feudal lords, who were not inclined to recognize any master, all combined to keep Europe back for at least two centuries more. Indeed, the tenth and the first half of the eleventh century seem, at first sight, little better than the seventh and the eighth. Yet ignorance and disorder never were quite so prevalent after, as they were before, Charlemagne.

CHAPTER V

FEUDS AND FEUDALISM

The Disruption of Charlemagne's Empire. The Medieval Castle. The Serfs and the Manor. The Feudal System. Neighborhood Warfare in the Middle Ages

The Disruption of Charlemagne's Empire

ALTHOUGH feuds and feudalism have nothing in common etymologically, being derived from different Germanic roots, they were so closely connected historically for several centuries after Charlemagne's day that they summarize no inconsiderable part of medieval history.

It was a matter of great importance to Europe whether Charlemagne's extensive empire held together or fell apart after his death in 814. He does not seem to have had any expectation that it would hold together, because some years before his death he arranged that it should be divided among his three sons. But as two of these died before he did, it fell into the hands of the only surviving son, Louis, who succeeded his august father as king of all the various parts of the Frankish domains and was later crowned emperor.

Louis, called the "pious," proved a feeble ruler. He tried all sorts of ways of dividing the empire peaceably among his rebellious and unruly sons, but he did not succeed, and after his death they, and their sons as well, continued to fight over

the question of how much each should have. It is not necessary to speak of the various temporary arrangements that were
made. Finally, it was agreed in 870, by the Treaty of Mersen,
that there should be three states, a West Frankish kingdom, an
East Frankish kingdom, and a kingdom of Italy. The West
Frankish realm corresponded roughly with the present boundaries of France and Belgium. Its people talked dialects derived
from the spoken Latin, which the Romans had introduced after

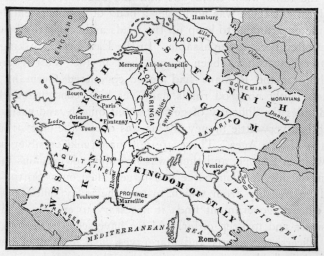

MAP OF TREATY OF MERSEN

This map shows the division of Charlemagne's empire made
in 870 by his descendants in the Treaty of Mersen

Cæsar's army conquered Gaul. The East Frankish kingdom
included the rest of Charlemagne's empire outside of Italy and
was German in language.

Each of the three realms established by the Treaty of Mersen
was destined finally to grow into one of the powerful modern
states which we see on the map of Europe to-day, but hundreds
of years elapsed before the kings grew strong enough to control their subjects, and the Treaty of Mersen was followed by
several centuries of constant disorder and local warfare. Let us

consider the difficulties which stood in the way of creating large and powerful states.

In the first place, a king found it very hard to get rapidly from one part of his realms to another in order to put down rebellions, for the remarkable roads which the Romans had so carefully constructed to enable their armies to move about had fallen into disrepair.

To have good roads one must be constantly working on them, for the rains wash them out and the floods carry away the bridges. As there was no longer a body of engineers employed by the government to keep up the roads and repair the bridges, they often became impassable. In the East Frankish kingdom matters must have been worse than in the West Frankish realm, for the Romans had never conquered Germany and consequently no good roads had ever been constructed there.

Besides the difficulty of getting about quickly and easily, the king had very little money. This was one of the chief troubles of the Middle Ages. There are not many gold or silver mines in western Europe, and there was no supply of precious metals from outside, for commerce had largely died out. So the king had no treasury from which to pay the many officials which an efficient government finds it necessary to employ to do its business and to keep order. As we have seen, he had to give his officers, the counts and margraves, *land* instead of *money*, and their land was so extensive that they tended to become rulers themselves within their own possessions.

Of course the king had not money enough to support a standing army, which would have enabled him to put down the constant rebellions of his distant officers and of the powerful and restless nobility whose chief interest in life consisted in fighting.

In addition to the weakness and poverty of the kings there was another trouble,—and that the worst of all,—namely, the constant new invasions from all directions which kept all three parts of Charlemagne's empire, and England besides, in a constant state of terror and disaster. These invasions were almost as bad as those which had occurred before Charlemagne's time; they prevented western Europe from becoming peaceful and

[96]

prosperous and serve to explain the dark period of two hundred years which followed the break-up of Charlemagne's empire.

We know how the Mohammedans had got possession of northern Africa and then conquered Spain, and how Charles Martel had frustrated their attempt to add Gaul to their possessions. But this rebuff did not end their attacks on southern Europe. They got control of the island of Sicily shortly after Charlemagne's death, and then began to terrorize Italy and

AMPHITHEATER AT ARLES IN THE MIDDLE AGES

The great Roman amphitheater at Arles (built probably in the first or second century) is about fifteen hundred feet in circumference. During the eighth century, when the Mohammedans were invading southern France, it was converted into a fortress. Many of the inhabitants settled inside its walls, and towers were constructed, which still stand. The picture shows it before the dwellings were removed, about 1830

southern France. Even Rome itself suffered from them. The accompanying picture shows how the people of Arles, in southern France, built their houses inside the old Roman amphitheater in order to protect themselves from these Mohammedan invaders.

On the east the German rulers had constantly to contend with the Slavs. Charlemagne had defeated them in his time, as mentioned above, but they continued to make much trouble for two centuries at least. Then there were also the Hun-

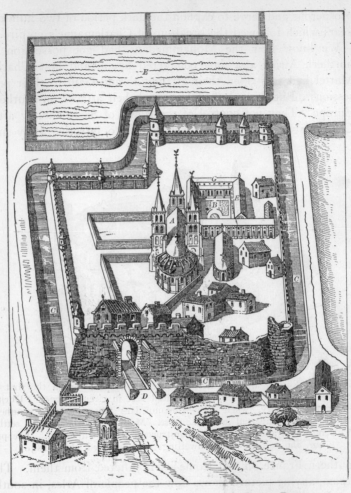

MONASTERY OF ST. GERMAIN DES PRÈS, PARIS

This famous monastery, now in the midst of Paris, was formerly outside of the walls when the town was much smaller, and was fortified as shown in the picture, with a moat (*C*) and drawbridge (*D*). One can see the abbey church (*A*), which still stands; the cloister (*B*); the refectory, or dining room (*E*); and the long dormitory (*G*). It was common in the age of disorder to fortify monasteries and sometimes even churches, as nothing was so sacred as to protect it from the danger of attack garians, a savage race from Asia, who ravaged Germany and northern Italy and whose wild horsemen penetrated even into the West Frankish kingdom. Finally, they were driven back eastward and settled in the country now named after them—Hungary.

And lastly there came the Northmen, bold and adventurous pirates from the shores of Denmark, Sweden, and Norway. These skillful and daring seamen not only attacked the towns on the coast of the West Frankish kingdom but made their way up the rivers, plundering and burning the villages and towns as far inland as Paris. In England we shall find them, under the name of Danes, invading the country and forcing Alfred the Great to recognize them as the masters of northern England.[1]

So there was danger always and everywhere. If rival nobles were not fighting one another, there were foreign invaders of some kind devastating the country, bent on robbing, maltreating, and enslaving the people whom they found in towns and villages and monasteries. No wonder that strong castles had to be built and the towns surrounded by walls; even the monasteries, which were not of course respected by pagan invaders, were in some cases protected by fortifications.

In the absence of a powerful king with a well-organized army at his back, each district was left to look out for itself. Doubtless many counts, margraves, bishops, and other great landed proprietors who were gradually becoming independent princes earned the loyalty of the people about them by taking the lead in defending the country against its invaders and by establishing fortresses as places of refuge when the community was hard pressed. These conditions serve to explain why such government as continued to exist during the centuries following the death of Charlemagne was necessarily carried on mainly, not by the king and his officers, but by the great landholders.

[1] These Scandinavian pirates are often called *vikings*, from their habit of leaving their long boats in the *vik*, which meant, in their language, "bay" or "inlet."

The Medieval Castle

As one travels through England, France, or Germany to-day he often comes upon the picturesque ruins of a medieval castle perched upon some rocky cliff and overlooking the surrounding country for miles. As he looks at the thick walls often surrounded by a deep, wide trench once filled with water, and observes the great towers with their tiny windows, he cannot

A MEDIEVAL CASTLE NEAR KLAGENFURT, AUSTRIA

It was not uncommon in mountainous regions to have fortresses perched so high on rocky eminences that it was practically impossible to capture them

but wonder why so many of these forts were built, and why people lived in them. It is clear that they were never intended to be dwelling places for the peaceful households of private citizens; they look rather like the fortified palace of a ruler.

Obviously, whoever lived there was in constant expectation of being attacked by an army, for otherwise he would never have gone to the trouble and expense of shutting himself up in those dreary, cold, stone rooms, behind walls from ten to twenty feet thick. We can picture the great hall of the castle crowded with the armed followers of the master of the house, ready to fight for him when he wished to make war on a neighbor; or if he himself were attacked, they would rush to the little windows and shoot arrows at those who tried to approach, or pour lighted pitch or melted lead down on their enemies if they were so bold as to get close enough to the walls.

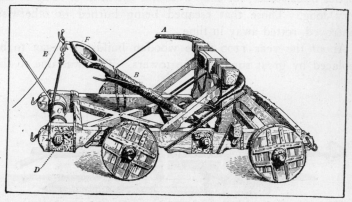

MACHINE FOR HURLING STONES

This was a medieval device for throwing stones and bolts of iron, which were often heated red hot before they were fired. It consisted of a great bow (*A*) and the beam (*B*), which was drawn back by the windlass (*C*) turned by a crank applied at the point (*D*). Then a stone was put in the pocket (*F*) and the trigger pulled by means of the string (*E*). This let the beam fly up with a bang against the bumper, and the missile went sailing against the wall or over it among the defenders of the castle

The Romans had been accustomed to build walls around their camps, and a walled camp was called *castrum;* and in such names as Rochester, Winchester, Gloucester, Worcester, we have reminders of the fact that these towns were once fortresses. These Roman camps, however, were all *government* fortifications and did not belong to private individuals.

But as the Roman Empire grew weaker and the disorder caused by the incoming barbarians became greater, the various counts and dukes and even other larger landowners began to build forts for themselves, at first nothing more than a great round mound of earth surrounded by a deep ditch and a wall made of stakes interwoven with twigs. On the top of the mound was a wooden fortress, surrounded by a fence or palisade, similar to the one at the foot of the mound. This was the type of "castle" that prevailed for several centuries after Charlemagne's death. There are no remains of these wooden castles in existence, for they were not the kind of thing to last very long. Those that escaped being burned or otherwise destroyed, rotted away in time.

About the year 1100 these wooden buildings began to be replaced by great square stone towers. This was due to the

MEDIEVAL BATTERING-RAM

This is a simple kind of a battering ram which was trundled up to the walls of a besieged castle and then swung back and forth by a group of soldiers, with the hope of making a breach. The men were often protected by a covering over the ram

fact that the methods of attacking castles had so changed that wood was no longer a sufficient protection. The Romans when they besieged a walled town were accustomed to hurl great stones and heavy-pointed stakes at the walls and over them. They had ingenious machines for this purpose, and they also had ways of protecting their soldiers when they crept up to the walls with their battering-rams and pickaxes in the hope of making a breach and so getting into the town. But the German barbarians who overran the Roman Empire were unaccustomed to these machines, which therefore had fallen into disuse. But the practice of taking towns by means of them

MOVABLE TOWER

This attacking tower was rolled up to the wall of the besieged town after
the moat had been filled up at the proper point. The soldiers then swarmed
up the outside and over a bridge onto the wall. Skins of animals were hung
on the side to prevent the tower from being set on fire

was kept up in the Eastern Empire, and during the Crusades, which began about 1100, they were introduced once more into western Europe, and this is the reason why stone castles began to be built about that time.

A square tower can, however, be more easily attacked than a round tower, which has no corners, so a century later round towers became the rule and continued to be used until about the year 1500, when gunpowder and cannon had become so common that even the strongest castle could no longer be defended, for it could not withstand the force of cannon balls. The accompanying pictures give an idea of the stone castles built from about 1100 to 1450 or 1500.

TOWER OF BEAUGENCY

This square donjon not far from Orléans, France, is one of the very earliest square towers that survive. It is a translation into stone of the wooden donjons that prevailed up to that time. It was built about 1100 just after the beginning of the First Crusade. It is about 76 by 66 feet in size and 115 feet high

As we have no remains or good pictures of the early wooden castles on a mound, we must get our notions of the arrangement of a castle from the later stone fortresses, many of which can still be found in Europe. When the castle was not on a steep rocky hill, which made it very hard to approach, a deep ditch was constructed outside the walls, called the *moat*. This was filled with water and crossed by a bridge, which could be drawn up when the castle was attacked, leaving no way of getting across. The doorway was further protected by a grating of heavy planks, called the *portcullis,* which could be quickly dropped down to close the entrance. Inside the castle was the great *donjon,* or chief tower, which had several stories, although one would not suspect it from its plain exterior. There was sometimes also a fine hall, as at Couçy, and handsome rooms for the use of the lord and his family, but sometimes they lived in the donjon. There were buildings for storing supplies and arms, and usually a chapel.

The Serfs and the Manor

Obviously the owner of the castle had to obtain supplies to support his family and servants and armed men. He could not have done this had he not possessed extensive tracts of land. A great part of western Europe in the time of Charlemagne appears to have been divided into great estates or plantations.

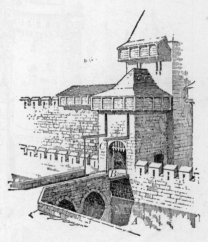

FORTIFIED GATE OF A MEDIEVAL CASTLE

Here one can see the way in which the entrance to a castle was protected: the moat (*A*); the drawbridge (*B*); the portcullis (*C*)

These medieval estates were called *vils,* or *manors,* and closely resembled the Roman *villas* described in an earlier chapter.[1] The peasants who tilled the soil were called *villains,* a word derived from *vil.* A portion of the estate was reserved by the lord for his own use; the rest of the plowed land was divided up among the peasants, usually in long strips, of which each peasant had several scattered about the manor.

[1] See above, p. 18.

Coucy le Château

This castle of Coucy le Château was built by a vassal of the king of France in the thirteenth century. It is at the end of a hill and protected on all sides but one by steep cliffs. One can see the moat (*A*) and the double drawbridge and towers which protected the portal. The round donjon is probably the largest in the world, 100 feet in diameter and 210 feet high. At the base its walls are 34 feet thick. At the end of the inner court (*C*) was the residence of the lord (*D*). To the left of the court was a great hall, and to the right the quarters of the garrison

THE SERFS AND THE MANOR

The peasants were generally serfs (not unlike the Roman *coloni*) who did not own their fields, but could not, on the other hand, be deprived of them so long as they worked for the lord and paid him certain dues. They were attached to the land and went with it when it changed hands. The serfs were required to till those fields which the lord reserved for himself and to gather in his crops. They might not marry

PIERREFONDS

This castle of Pierrefonds, not very far from Paris, was built by the brother of the king of France, about 1400. It has been very carefully restored in modern times and gives one a good idea of the way in which the feudal lords of that late period lived. Within the walls is a handsome central courtyard and magnificent apartments

without their lord's permission. Their wives and daughters helped with the indoor work of the manor house. In the women's buildings the women serfs engaged in spinning, weaving, sewing, baking, and brewing, thus producing clothes, food, and drink for the whole community.

We get our clearest ideas of the position of the serfs from the ancient descriptions of manors, which give an exact account of what each member of a particular community owed to the

[107]

lord. For example, we find that the abbot of Peterborough held a manor upon which Hugh Miller and seventeen other serfs, mentioned by name, were required to work for him three days in each week during the whole year, except one week at Christmas, one at Easter, and one at Whitsuntide. Each serf was to give the lord abbot one bushel of wheat and eighteen sheaves of oats, three hens, and one cock yearly, and five eggs at Easter. If he sold his horse for more than ten shillings, he was to give the said abbot fourpence. Five other serfs, mentioned by name, held but half as much land as Hugh and his companions, by paying and doing in all respects half as much service.

One of the most remarkable characteristics of the manor was its independence of the rest of the world. It produced nearly everything that its members needed, and might almost have continued to exist indefinitely without communication with those who lived beyond its bounds. Little or no money was necessary, for the peasants paid what was due to the lord in the form of labor and farm products. They also rendered the needful help to one another and found little occasion for buying and selling.

There was almost no opportunity to better one's condition, and life must have gone on for generation after generation in a weary routine. And the life was not merely monotonous, it was wretched. The food was coarse and there was little variety, as the peasants did not even take pains to raise fresh vegetables. The houses usually had but one room, which was ill-lighted by a single little unglazed window and had no chimney.

The increased use of money in the twelfth and thirteenth centuries, which came with the awakening of trade and industry, tended to break up the manor. The old habit of trading one thing for another without the intervention of money began to disappear. As time went on, neither the lord nor the serf was satisfied with the old system, which had answered well enough in the time of Charlemagne. The serfs, on the one hand, began to obtain money by the sale of their products in the markets of neighboring towns. They finally found it more profitable to pay the lord a certain sum instead of working for him, for they could then turn their whole attention to their own farms.

The landlords, on the other hand, found it to their advantage to accept money in place of the services of their tenants. With this money the landlord could hire laborers to cultivate his fields and could buy the luxuries which were brought to his notice as commerce increased. So it came about that the lords, especially in France and England, gradually gave up their control over the peasants, and there was no longer very much difference between the serf and the freeman who paid a regular rent for his land. A serf might also gain his liberty by running away from his manor to a town. If he remained undiscovered, or was unclaimed by his lord, for a year and a day, he became a freeman.

The slow extinction of serfdom in western Europe appears to have begun as early as the twelfth century. A very general emancipation had taken place in England and France during the thirteenth and fourteenth centuries, though there were still some serfs in France when the revolution came in 1789. Germany was far more backward in this respect. We find the peasants revolting against their hard lot in Luther's time (1524-1525), and it was not until the nineteenth century that the serfs were freed in central and southern Europe and Russia.

The Feudal System

These manors served to support their lords and left them free to busy themselves fighting with other landowners in the same position as themselves.

Landholders who had large estates and could spare a portion of them were accustomed to grant some of their manors to another person on condition that the one receiving the land should swear to be true to the giver, should fight for him on certain occasions, and should lend him aid when particular difficulties arose. It was in this way that the relation of *lord* and *vassal* originated. The vassal who received the land pledged himself to be true to his lord, and the lord, on the other hand, not only let his vassal have the land but agreed to protect him when it was necessary. These arrangements between vassals and lords constituted what is called the *feudal system*.

The feudal system, or feudalism, was not established by any decree of a king or in virtue of any general agreement between all the landowners. It grew up gradually and irregularly without any conscious plan on any one's part, simply because it seemed convenient and natural under the circumstances. The owner of vast estates found it to his advantage to parcel them out among vassals, that is to say, men who agreed to accompany him to war, guard his castle upon occasion, and assist him when he was put to any unusually great expense. Land granted upon the terms mentioned was called a *fief*. One who held a fief might himself become a lord by granting a portion of his fief to a vassal upon terms similar to those upon which he held his lands of his lord, or *suzerain*. The vassal of a vassal was called a *subvassal*.

There was still another way in which the number of vassals was increased. The owners of small estates were usually in a defenseless condition, unable to protect themselves against the attacks of the great nobles. They consequently often deemed it wise to put their land into the hands of a neighboring lord and receive it back from him as a fief. They thus became his vassals and could call upon him for protection.

The one proposing to become a vassal knelt before the lord and rendered him homage [1] by placing his hands between those of the lord and declaring himself the lord's "man" for such and such a fief. Thereupon the lord—with no conscious irony—gave his vassal the kiss of peace and raised him from his kneeling posture. Then the vassal swore an oath of fidelity upon the Bible, or some holy relic, solemnly binding himself to fulfill all his duties toward his lord. This act of rendering homage by placing the hands in those of the lord and taking the oath of fidelity was the first and most essential duty of the vassal. For a vassal to refuse to do homage for his fief when it changed hands amounted to a declaration of revolt and independence.

[1] "Homage" is derived from the Latin word *homo*, meaning "man."

The obligations of the vassal varied greatly. He was expected to join his lord when there was a military expedition on foot, although it was generally the case that the vassal need not serve at his own expense for more than forty days. The rules in regard to the length of time during which a vassal might be called upon to guard the castle of his lord varied almost infinitely.

The conditions upon which fiefs were granted might be dictated either by interest or occasionally by mere fancy. Sometimes the most fantastic and seemingly absurd obligations were imposed. We hear of vassals holding on condition of attending the lord at supper with a tall candle, or furnishing him with a great yule log at Christmas. Perhaps the most extraordinary instance upon record is that of a lord in Guienne who solemnly declared upon oath, when questioned by the commissioners of Edward I, that he held his fief of the king upon the following terms: When the

CEREMONY OF HOMAGE

This is a modern picture of the way in which the ceremony of homage took place. The new vassal is putting his hands between those of his lord. To the left are retainers in their chain armor, and back of the lord and his lady is the jester, or court fool, whose business it is to amuse his master when he needs entertainment

lord king came through his estate he was to accompany him to a certain oak. There he must have waiting a cart loaded with wood and drawn by two cows without any tails. When the oak was reached, fire was to be applied to the cart and the whole burned up, "unless mayhap the cows make their escape."

Besides the military service due from the vassal to his lord, he was expected to attend the lord's court when summoned. There he sat with other vassals to hear and pronounce upon those cases in which his fellow vassals were involved. Moreover he had to give the lord the benefit of his advice when required, and attend him upon solemn occasions.

Under certain circumstances vassals had to make money payments to their lord; as, for instance, when the lord was put to extra expense by the necessity of knighting his eldest son or providing a dowry for his daughter, or when he was captured by an enemy and was held for ransom. Lastly, the vassal might have to entertain his lord should he be passing his castle. There are amusingly detailed accounts in some of the feudal contracts of exactly how often the lord might come, how many followers he might bring, and what he should have to eat.

There were fiefs of all kinds and of all grades of importance, from that of a duke or count, who held directly of the king and exercised the powers of a practically independent prince, down to the holding of the simple knight, whose bit of land, cultivated by peasants or serfs, was barely sufficient to enable him to support himself and provide the horse upon which he rode to perform his military service for his lord.

It is essential to observe that the fief was not granted for a certain number of years, or simply for the life of the grantee, to go back at his death to the owner. On the contrary, it became *hereditary* in the family of the vassal and passed down to the eldest son from one generation to another. So long as the vassal remained faithful to his lord and performed the stipulated services, and his successors did homage and continued to meet the conditions upon which the fief had originally been granted, neither the lord nor his heirs could rightfully regain possession of the land.

The result was that little was left to the original owner of the fief except the services and dues to which the *practical* owner, the vassal, had agreed in receiving it. In short, the fief came really to belong to the vassal, and only the shadow of ownership remained in the hands of the lord. Nowadays the owner of land either makes some use of it himself or leases it for a definite period at a fixed money rent. But in the Middle Ages most of the land was held by those who neither really owned it nor paid a regular rent for it, and yet who could not be deprived of it by the nominal owner or his successors.

Obviously the great vassals who held directly of the king became almost independent of him as soon as their fiefs were granted to them and their descendants. Their vassals, since they had not done homage to the king himself, often paid little attention to his commands. From the ninth to the thirteenth century, the king of France or the king of Germany did not rule over a great realm occupied by subjects who owed him obedience as their lawful sovereign, paid him taxes, and were bound to fight under his banner as the head of the State. As a feudal landlord himself, the king had a right to demand fidelity and certain services from those who were his vassals. But the great mass of the people over whom he nominally ruled, whether they belonged to the nobility or not, owed little to the king directly, because they lived upon the lands of other feudal lords more or less independent of him.

Neighborhood Warfare in the Middle Ages

One has only to read a chronicle of the time to discover that brute force governed almost everything outside of the Church. The feudal obligations were not fulfilled except when the lord was sufficiently powerful to enforce them. The oath of fidelity was constantly broken, and faith was violated by both vassal and lord.

It often happened that a vassal was discontented with his lord and transferred his allegiance to another. This he had a right to do under certain circumstances, as, for instance, when his lord refused to see that justice was done him in his court. But such changes were generally made merely for the sake of the advantages which the faithless vassal hoped to gain. The records of the time are full of accounts of refusal to do homage, which was the commonest way in which a vassal revolted from his lord. So soon as a vassal felt himself strong enough to face his lord's displeasure, or when the lord was a helpless child, the vassal was apt to declare his independence by refusing to recognize as his lord the one from whom he had received his land.

We may say that war, in all its forms, was the law of the feudal world. War formed the chief occupation of the restless nobles who held the land and were supposed to govern it. An enterprising vassal was likely to make war upon each of the lords to whom he had done homage; secondly, upon the bishops and abbots with whom he was brought into contact, and whose control he particularly disliked; thirdly, upon his fellow vassals; and lastly, upon his own vassals. The feudal bonds, instead of offering a guarantee of peace and concord, appear to have been a constant cause of violent conflict. Every one was bent upon profiting by the permanent or temporary weakness of his neighbor. This chronic fighting extended even to members of the same family; the son, anxious to enjoy a part of his heritage immediately, warred against his father, younger brothers against older, and nephews against uncles who might seek to deprive them of their rights.

In theory, the lord could force his vassals to settle their disputes in an orderly manner before his court; but often he was neither able nor inclined to bring about a peaceful adjustment, and he would frequently have found it hard to enforce the decisions of his own court. So the vassals were left to fight out their quarrels among themselves, and they found their chief interest in life in so doing. War was practically sanctioned by law. This is shown by two striking examples. The great French code of laws of the thirteenth century and the Golden Bull, a most important body of laws drawn up for Germany in 1356, did not prohibit neighborhood war, but merely provided that it should be conducted in what was considered a decent and gentlemanly way.

Justs and tourneys were military exercises—play wars—to fill out the tiresome periods which occasionally intervened between real wars. They were, in fact, diminutive battles in which whole troops of hostile nobles sometimes took part. These rough plays called down the condemnation of the popes and even of the kings. The latter, however, were much too fond of the sport themselves not to forget promptly their own prohibitions.

The horrors of this constant fighting led the Church to try to check it. About the year 1000 several Church councils in southern France decreed that the fighters were not to attack churches or monasteries, churchmen, pilgrims, merchants, and women, and that they must leave the peasant and his cattle and plow alone. Then Church councils began to issue what was known as the "Truce of God," which provided that all warfare was to stop during Lent and various other holy days as well as on Thursday, Friday, Saturday, and Sunday of every week. During the truce no one was to attack any one else. Those besieging castles were to refrain from any assaults during the period of peace, and people were to be allowed to go quietly to and fro on their business without being disturbed by soldiers.

If any one failed to observe the truce, he was to be excommunicated by the Church—if he fell sick no Christian should dare to visit him, and on his deathbed he was not to receive the comfort of a priest, and his soul was consigned to hell if he had refused to repent and mend his ways. It is hard to say how much good the Truce of God accomplished. Some of the bishops and even the heads of great monasteries liked fighting pretty well themselves. It is certain that many disorderly lords paid little attention to the truce, and found three days a week altogether too short a time for plaguing their neighbors.

Yet we must not infer that the idea of a State ceased to exist altogether during the centuries of confusion that followed the break-up of Charlemagne's empire, or that kingdoms fell entirely apart into little local governments independent of each other. In the first place, a king always retained some of his ancient majesty. He might be weak and without the means to enforce his rights and to compel his more powerful subjects to meet their obligations toward him. Yet he was, after all, the *king*, solemnly anointed by the Church as God's representative on earth. He was always something more than a feudal lord. The kings were destined to get the upper hand before many

[115]

centuries in England, France, and Spain, and finally in Italy and Germany, and to destroy the castles behind whose walls their haughty nobles had long defied the royal power.

This brief resumé of what passed for "government" in the earlier Middle Ages is essential to the understanding of the development of modern kingdoms and of very recent republics. Government is still an unsolved problem which may be worked out in quite different ways from what any one now can anticipate. As yet we have not discovered any way in which large numbers of human beings can manage their common affairs satisfactorily, without many reminders of the traditional weaknesses, inefficiency, and corruption of "government" as it has been handed down to us.

CHAPTER VI

POPES AND EMPERORS

Origin of the Holy Roman Empire. The Church and Its Property. Powers Claimed by the Popes. Gregory VII and Emperor Henry IV. The Hohenstaufen Emperors and the Popes

The Origin of the Holy Roman Empire

ONE of the problems that face a historical writer is that of ordering his narrative. There is no foreordained way of doing this. He has to show the development of various important institutions, ideas, preoccupations, and enthusiasms. This invites a topical ordering. But he has also to keep his eye on the general chronology or succession of events so as to bring together contemporaneous happenings. Otherwise he will confuse and irritate his readers by dragging them back over and over again to see how this, that, and the other human interest got under way, loomed large, and mayhap later faded away or was supplanted by other interests. In order to give various essential topics their due and at the same time not outrun more than is unavoidable the order of events, the following plan has been adopted here in the treatment of the period from Charlemagne to Emperor Charles V—full seven centuries. First comes the outward history of central Europe, especially the strangely intermingled tales of Germany and Italy and the struggles between German kings and Roman popes. This will carry us to the middle of the thirteenth century, when the general trend of affairs in both Germany and Italy had become so opposed to national unification that there will be no surprise that this was postponed until the nineteenth century. Next we shall glance at the Crusades, which both illustrate the international enterprises of the twelfth and thirteenth centuries and furnish some explanation of the broadening of the Western outlook and the increase of knowledge. Then follow chapters which attempt to sketch the general state of business, thought, and art in the twelfth and especially the thirteenth century, merging into the so-called Italian Renaissance and the period of rapid geographical discovery. It will be noted that so far medieval France and England have not had their quota of attention. The story of the disentangling of these two neighboring lands and the establishment of independent kingdoms under potent rulers like Louis XI and Henry VII carries our story back to the early Middle Ages only for the moment, and when the chapter is done we are ready to understand the conditions and events in the days of Francis I, Henry VIII, Leo X, Erasmus, and Luther.

Charlemagne's successors in the German part of his empire found it quite as hard as did the kings of the western, or French, kingdom to keep control of their vassals. Germany, like France, was divided up into big and little fiefs, and the dukes and counts were continually waging war upon each other and upon their king. The general causes of this chronic disorder in the Middle Ages have been described in a previous chapter.

The first German ruler whom we need to notice here was Otto the Great, who came to the throne in the year 936. He got as many of the great fiefs as possible into the hands of his relatives in the illusive hope that they would be faithful to him. He put an end forever to the invasions of the Hungarians who had been ravaging Germany. He defeated them in a great battle near Augsburg and drove them out of his realms. As has already been said, they finally settled in eastern Europe and laid the foundations of what became the Hungarian monarchy of succeeding centuries.

But the most noteworthy of Otto's acts was his interference in Italian affairs, which led to his winning once more for the German kings the imperial crown that Charlemagne had worn. We have seen how Charlemagne's successors divided up his realms into three parts by the Treaty of Mersen in 870 (see above, p. 95). One of these parts was the kingdom of Italy. We know but little of what went on in Italy for some time after the Treaty of Mersen. There was incessant warfare, and the disorder was increased by the attacks of the Mohammedans. Various powerful nobles were able to win the crown for short periods. Three at least of these Italian kings were crowned "emperor" by the pope. Then for a generation there was no emperor in the west, until Otto the Great ag̲ ̲ ̲ured the title.

It would seem as if Otto had quite enough troubl̲ ̲ ̲ne, but he thought that it would make him and his re̲ ̲ ̲re glorious if he added northern Italy to his realms. ̲ ̲ ̲ı he crossed the Alps, married the widow of one of t̲ ̲ ̲n kings, and, without being formally crowned, v̲ ̲ ̲ acknowledged as king of Italy. He had to hasten bac̲ ̲ many to put down a revolt organized by his own son, ̲ ̲ years later he was called to Rome by the pope to protect̲ from the attacks of his enemies. Otto accepted the invitat̲ and the grateful pope in return crowned him emperor, Charlemagne's successor (962).

The coronation of Otto was a very important event in German history; for, from this time on, the German kings, instead of confining their attention to keeping their own kingdom in order, were constantly distracted by the necessity of keeping hold on their Italian kingdom, which lay on the other side of a great range of mountains. Worse than that, they felt that they must see to it that a pope friendly to them was elected, and this greatly added to their difficulties.

The succeeding German emperors had usually to make several costly and troublesome journeys to Rome,—a first one to be crowned, and then others either to depose a hostile pope or to protect a friendly one from the oppression of neighboring lords. These excursions were very distracting, especially to a ruler who left behind him in Germany a rebellious nobility that always took advantage of his absence to revolt.

Otto's successors dropped their old title of king of the East Franks as soon as they had been duly crowned by the pope at Rome, and assumed the magnificent and all-embracing designation, "Emperor Ever August of the Romans." [1] Their "Holy Roman Empire," as it came to be called later, which was to endure, in name at least, for more than eight centuries, was obviously even less like that of the ancient Romans than was Charlemagne's. As *kings* in Germany and Italy they had practically all the powers that they enjoyed as *emperors*. The title of emperor was of course a proud one, but it gave the German kings no additional power except the fatal right that they claimed of taking part in the election of the pope. We shall find that, instead of making themselves feared at home and building up a great state, the German emperors wasted their strength in a long struggle with the popes, who proved themselves in the end far stronger, and eventually reduced the empire to a mere shadow.

The Church and Its Property

In order to understand the long struggle between the emperors and the popes, we must stop to consider the condition of the Church in the early Middle Ages. It seemed to be losing all its strength and dignity and to be falling apart, just as Charlemagne's empire had dissolved into feudal bits. This was chiefly due to the vast estates of the clergy. Kings, princes, and rich landowners had long considered it meritorious to make donations to bishoprics and monasteries, so that a very considerable portion of the land in western Europe had come into the hands of churchmen.

[1] Henry II (1002-1024) and his successors, not venturing to assume the title of emperor till crowned at Rome, but anxious to claim Rome as attached to the German crown, began to call themselves, before their coronation, King of the Romans.

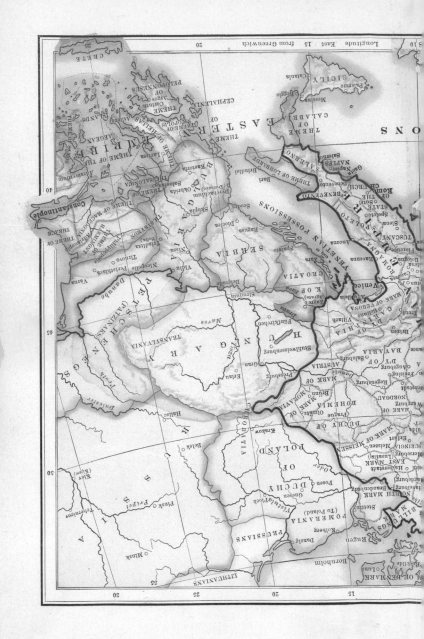

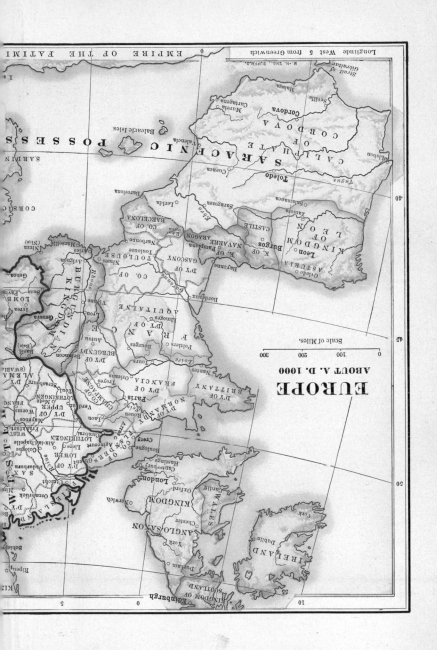

A king, or other landed proprietor, might grant fiefs to churchmen as well as to laymen. The bishops became the vassals of the king or of other feudal lords by doing homage for a fief and swearing fidelity, just as any other vassal would do. An abbot would sometimes secure for his monastery the protection of a neighboring lord by giving up his land and receiving it back again as a fief.

One great difference, however, existed between the Church lands and the ordinary fiefs. According to the law of the Church, the bishops and abbots could not marry and so could have no children to whom they might transmit their property. Consequently, when a landholding churchman died, some one had to be chosen in his place who should enjoy his property and perform his duties. The rule of the Church had been, from time immemorial, that the clergy of the diocese should choose the bishop, their choice being ratified by the people. As for the abbots, they were, according to the Rule of St. Benedict, to be chosen by the members of the monastery.

In spite of these rules, the bishops and abbots had come, in the tenth and eleventh centuries, to be selected, to all intents and purposes, by the various kings and feudal lords. It is true that the outward forms of a regular election were usually permitted; but the feudal lord made it clear whom he wished chosen, and if the wrong person was elected, he simply refused to hand over to him the lands attached to the bishopric or abbey. The lord could in this way control the choice of the prelates, for in order to become a real bishop or abbot, one had not only to be elected, he had also to be solemnly "invested" with the appropriate powers of a bishop or abbot and with his lands.

When a bishop or abbot had been duly chosen, the feudal lord proceeded to the *investiture*. The new bishop or abbot first became the "man" of the lord by doing him homage, and then the lord transferred to him the lands and rights attached to the office. No careful distinction appears to have been made between the property and the religious powers. The lord often conferred both by bestowing upon a bishop the ring and the crosier (see headpiece to Chapter VIII, p. 152), the emblems of religious authority. It seemed shocking enough that the lord, who was often a rough soldier, should dictate the selection of the bishops; but it was still more shocking that he should assume to confer religious powers with religious emblems. Yet even worse things might happen, since sometimes the lord, for his greater convenience, had himself made bishop.

The Church itself theoretically looked at the property attached to a church office as a mere incident and considered the religious prerogatives the main thing. And since the clergy alone could rightly confer these, it was natural that they should claim the right to bestow the lands (":temporalities") attached to them, upon whomsoever they pleased without consulting any layman whatever.

Against this claim the king might urge that a simple minister of the Gospel, or a holy monk, was by no means necessarily fitted to manage the interests of a feudal state, such as the great archbishoprics and bishoprics, and even the abbeys, had become in Germany and elsewhere in the eleventh century.

In short, the situation in which the bishops found themselves was a very complicated one. (1) As an officer of the Church, the bishop saw to it that parish priests were properly selected and ordained, he tried certain cases in his court, and performed the Church ceremonies. (2) He managed the lands which belonged to the bishopric, which might, or might not, be fiefs. (3) As a vassal of those who had granted lands to the bishopric upon feudal terms, he owed the usual feudal dues, including the duty of furnishing troops to his lord. (4) Lastly, in Germany, the king had found it convenient, from about the beginning of the eleventh century, to confer upon the bishops in many cases the authority of a count in the districts about them. In this way they might have the right to collect tolls, coin money, and perform other important governmental duties. When a prelate took office he was invested with all these various functions at once, both spiritual and governmental.

To forbid the king to take part in the investiture was, consequently, to rob him not only of his feudal rights but also of his authority over many of his government officials, since bishops, and sometimes even abbots, were counts in all but name. He therefore found it necessary to take care who got possession of the important church offices.

Still another danger threatened the wealth and resources of the Church. During the tenth and eleventh centuries the rule of the Church prohibiting the clergy from marrying appears to have been widely neglected in Italy, Germany, France, and England. To the stricter critics of the time this appeared a terrible degradation of the clergy, who, they felt, should be unencumbered by family cares and should devote themselves wholly to the service of God. The question, too, had another side. It was obvious that the property of the Church would soon be dispersed if the clergy were allowed legally to marry, since they would wish to provide for their children. Just as the feudal lands had become hereditary, so the Church lands would become hereditary unless the clergy were forced to remain unmarried.

Besides the feudalizing of its property and the marriage of the clergy, there was a third great and constant source of weakness and corruption in the Church, at this period, namely, the temptation to buy and sell Church offices. Had the duties and responsibilities of the bishops, abbots, and priests always been heavy, and their income slight, there would have been little tendency to bribe those who could bestow the offices. But the incomes of bishoprics and abbeys were usually considerable, and sometimes very great, while the religious duties attached to the office of bishop or abbot, however serious in the eyes of the pious, might easily be neglected by the unscrupulous. The revenue from a great landed estate and the high rank that went with the office were enough to induce the members of the noblest families to vie with each other in securing Church positions. The king or prince who possessed the right of investiture was sure of finding some one willing to pay something for important benefices.

The sin of buying or selling Church offices was recognized as a most serious one. It was called "simony," a name derived from Simon the Magician, who, according to the account in the Acts of the Apostles, offered money to the Apostle Peter if he would give him the power of conferring the Holy Spirit upon those upon whom he should lay his hands. As the apostle denounced this first simonist,—"Thy silver perish with thee, because thou hast thought to obtain the gift of God with money" (Acts viii, 20),—so the Church has continued ever since to denounce those who propose to purchase its sacred powers.

Doubtless very few bought positions in the Church with the view of obtaining the "gift of God," that is to say, the religious office. It was the revenue and the honor that were chiefly coveted. Moreover, when a king or lord accepted a gift from one for whom he procured a benefice, he did not regard himself as selling the office; he merely shared its advantages. No transaction took place in the Middle Ages without accompanying gifts and fees of various kinds.

The evil of simony was, nevertheless, very demoralizing, for it spread downward and infected the whole body of the clergy. A bishop who had made a large outlay in obtaining his office naturally expected something from the priests, whom it was his duty to appoint. Then the priest, in turn, was tempted to exact too much for baptizing and marrying his parishioners, and for burying the dead.

So it seemed, at the opening of the eleventh century, as if the Church was to be dragged down by its property into the anarchy of feudalism described in a preceding chapter.

The popes had therefore many difficulties to overcome in the gigantic task which they undertook of making the Church a great international monarchy, like the Roman Empire, with its capital at Rome: The control exercised by kings and feudal lords in the selection of Church officials had to be done away with. Simony with its degrading effects had to be abolished. The marriage of the clergy had to be checked, for fear that the property and wealth of the Church would go to their families and so be lost to the Church.

[124]

The first great step toward the freeing of the Church from the control of the kings and feudal lords was taken by Pope Nicholas II. In 1059 he issued a remarkable decree which took the election of the head of the Church once for all out of the hands of both the emperor and the people of Rome, and placed it definitely and forever in the hands of the *cardinals,* who represented the Roman clergy.[1] Obviously the object of this decree was to prevent all interference, whether of the distant emperor, of the local nobility, or of the Roman mob. The college of cardinals still exists and still elects the pope.

The reform party which directed the policy of the popes had, it hoped, freed the head of the Church from the control of worldly men by putting his election in the hands of the Roman clergy. It now proposed to emancipate the Church as a whole from the base entanglements of earth: first, by strictly forbidding the married clergy to perform religious functions and by exhorting their flocks to refuse to attend their ministrations; and secondly, by depriving the kings and feudal lords of their influence over the choice of the bishops and abbots, since this influence was deemed the chief cause of worldliness among the prelates. Naturally these last measures met with far more general opposition than the new way of electing the pope. The magnitude of the task which the popes had undertaken first became fully apparent when the celebrated Gregory VII ascended the papal throne, in 1073.

Powers Claimed by the Popes

Among the writings of Gregory VII there is a very brief statement, called the *Dictatus,* of the powers which he believed

[1] The word "cardinal" (Latin, *cardinalis,* "principal") was applied to the priests of the various parishes in Rome, to the several deacons connected with the Lateran,—which was the cathedral church of the Roman bishopric,—and, lastly, to six or seven suburban bishops who officiated in turn in the Lateran. The title became a very distinguished one and was sought by ambitious foreign prelates and ecclesiastical statesmen, like Wolsey, Richelieu, and Mazarin. If their official titles were examined, it would be found that each was nominally a cardinal bishop, priest, or deacon of some Roman Church. The number of cardinals varied until fixed, in 1586, at six bishops, fifty priests, and fourteen deacons.

the popes to possess. Its chief claims are the following: The pope enjoys a unique title; he is the only *universal* bishop and may depose and reinstate other bishops or transfer them from place to place. No council of the Church may be regarded as speaking for Christendom without his consent. The Roman Church has never erred, nor will it err to all eternity. No one may be considered a Catholic Christian who does not agree with the Roman Church. No book is authoritative unless it has received the papal sanction.

Gregory does not stop with asserting the pope's complete supremacy over the Church. He says that "the pope is the only person whose feet are kissed by all princes"; that he may depose emperors and "absolve subjects from allegiance to an unjust ruler." No one shall dare to condemn one who appeals to the pope. No one may annul a decree of the pope, though the pope may declare null and void the decrees of all other earthly powers; and no one may pass judgment upon his acts.

Immediately upon his election as pope, Gregory began to put into practice his high conception of the rôle that the religious head of Christendom should play. He dispatched legates throughout Europe, and from this time on these legates became a powerful instrument of the Church's government. He warned the kings of France and England and the youthful German ruler, Henry IV, to forsake their evil ways, to be upright and just, and to obey his admonitions. He explained, kindly but firmly, to William the Conqueror that the papal and kingly powers are both established by God as the greatest among the authorities of the world, just as the sun and moon are the greatest of the heavenly bodies. But the papal power is obviously superior to the kingly, for it is responsible for it; at the Last Day Gregory would have, he urged, to render an account of the king as one of the flock intrusted to his care. The king of France was warned to give up his practice of simony, lest he be excommunicated and his subjects freed from their oath of allegiance. All these acts of Gregory appear to have been dictated not by worldly ambition but by a fervent conviction of their righteousness and his obsessive responsibility for all men.

Gregory VII and Emperor Henry IV

Obviously Gregory's plan of reform included all the states of western Europe, but conditions were such that the most striking conflict took place between him and the emperor. The trouble came about in this way. Henry IV's father had died in 1056, leaving only his good wife Agnes and their little son of six years to maintain the hard-fought prerogatives of the German king in the midst of ambitious vassals whom even the strong Otto the Great had found it difficult to control.

In 1065 the fifteen-year-old lad, Henry IV, was declared of age, and his lifelong difficulties began with a great rebellion of the Saxons. They accused the young king of having built castles in their land and of filling them with rough soldiers who preyed upon the people. Pope Gregory felt it his duty to interfere. To him the Saxons appeared a people oppressed by a heedless youth guided by evil counselors. But Henry continued to associate with counselors whom the pope had excommunicated and went on filling important bishoprics in Germany and Italy, regardless of the pope's prohibitions.

The popes who immediately preceded Gregory had more than once forbidden the churchmen to receive investiture from laymen. Gregory reissued this prohibition in 1075, just as the trouble with Henry had begun. Investiture was, as we have seen, the legal transfer by the king, or other lord, to a newly chosen Church official, of the lands and rights attached to the office. In forbidding lay investiture Gregory attempted nothing less than a revolution. The bishops and abbots were often officers of government, exercising in Germany and Italy powers similar in all respects to those of the counts. The king not only relied upon them for advice and assistance in carrying on his government, but they were among his chief allies in his constant struggles with his vassals.

Gregory dispatched three envoys to Henry (end of 1075) with a fatherly letter in which he reproached the king for his wicked conduct. But he evidently had little expectation that mere expostulation would have any effect upon Henry, for he gave his legates instructions to use threats, if necessary. The legates were to tell the king that his crimes were so numerous, so horrible, and so well known, that he merited not only excommunication but the permanent loss of all his royal honors.

The violence of the legates' language not only kindled the wrath of the king but also gained for him friends among the bishops. A council which Henry summoned at Worms (in 1076) was attended by more than two-thirds of all the German bishops. Here Pope Gregory was declared deposed, and many terrible charges of immorality brought against him. The bishops publicly proclaimed that he had ceased to be their pope. It appears very surprising, at first sight, that the king should have received the prompt support of the German churchmen against the head of the Church. But it must be remembered that the prelates really owed their offices to the king and not to the pope.

Gregory's reply to Henry and the German bishops who had deposed him was speedy and decisive. "Incline thine ear to us, O Peter, chief of the apostles. As thy representative, and by thy favor, has the power been granted especially to me by God of binding and loosing in heaven and earth. On the strength of this, for the honor and glory of thy Church, in the name of Almighty God, Father, Son, and Holy Ghost, I withdraw, through thy power and authority, from Henry the King, son of Henry the Emperor, who has risen against thy Church with unheard-of insolence, the rule over the whole kingdom of the Germans and over Italy. I absolve all Christians from the bonds of the oath which they have sworn, or may swear, to him; and I forbid anyone to serve him as king."

For a time after the pope had deposed him everything went against Henry. Instead of resenting the pope's interference, the discontented Saxons, and many other of Henry's vassals, believed that there was now an excellent opportunity to get rid of Henry and choose a more agreeable ruler. The pope was even invited to come to Augsburg to consult with the princes as to whether Henry should continue to be king or another ruler should be chosen in his stead. It looked as if the pope was, in truth, to control the civil government.

Henry decided to anticipate the arrival of the pope. He hastened across the Alps in midwinter and appeared as an humble suppliant before the castle of Canossa,[1] whither the pope had come on his way to Augsburg. For three days the German king presented himself before the closed door, barefoot and in the coarse garments of a pilgrim and a penitent, and even then Gregory was induced only by the expostulations of his influential companions to admit the humiliated ruler. The spectacle of this mighty prince of distinguished appearance, humiliated and in tears before the little man who humbly styled himself the "servant of the servants of God," has always been regarded as most completely typifying the power of the Church and the potency of her curses, against which even the most exalted of the earth found no weapon of defense except abject penitence.

The pardon which Henry received at Canossa did not satisfy the German princes. They therefore proceeded to elect another ruler, and the next three or four years was a period of bloody struggles between the adherents of the rival kings. Gregory remained neutral until 1080, when he again "bound with the chain of anathema" Henry, "the so-called king," and all his followers. He declared him deprived of his royal power and dignity and forbade all Christians to obey him.

The new excommunication had precisely the opposite effect from the first one; it seemed to increase rather than decrease Henry's friends. The German clergy again deposed Gregory VII. Henry's rival for the throne fell in battle, and Henry betook himself to Italy with the double purpose of installing a pope of his own choice and winning the imperial crown. Gregory held out for no less than two years; but at last Rome fell into Henry's hands, and Gregory withdrew and soon after died.

---

[1] The castle of Canossa belonged to Gregory VII's ally and admirer, the Countess of Tuscany. It was destroyed by the neighboring town of Reggio about two centuries after Gregory's time, and only the ivy-clad ruins, represented in the headpiece of this chapter, remain.

His last words were, "I have loved justice and hated iniquity, therefore I die in exile."

The death of Gregory did not, however, put an end to Henry's difficulties. He spent the remaining twenty years of his life in trying to maintain his rights as king of Germany and Italy against his rebellious subjects on both sides of the Alps. In Germany his chief enemies were the Saxons and his discontented vassals. In Italy the pope was now actively engaged as a temporal ruler, in building up a little state of his own, and he was always ready to encourage the vivacious Lombard cities in their opposition to the German emperors.

All his life long Henry was turning from one enemy to another. Finally, his discontented German vassals induced his son, whom he had had crowned as his successor, to revolt against his father. Thereupon followed more civil war, more treason, and a miserable abdication. In 1106 death put an end to one of the saddest reigns that history records.

The achievement of the reign of Henry IV's son, Henry V (1106-1125), which chiefly interests us was the adjustment of the question of investitures. Pope Paschal II, while willing to recognize those bishops already chosen by the king, provided they were good men, proposed that thereafter Gregory's decrees against investiture by laymen should be carried out. The clergy should no longer do homage by laying their hands, consecrated to the service of the altar, in the bloodstained hands of the nobles. Henry V, on the other hand, declared that unless the clergy took the oath of fealty the bishops would not be given the lands, towns, castles, tolls, and privileges attached to the bishoprics.

After a succession of troubles a compromise was at last reached in the Concordat of Worms (1122), which put an end to the controversy over investitures in Germany. The emperor promised to permit the Church freely to elect the bishops and abbots and renounced his old claim to invest with the religious emblems of the ring and the crosier. But the elections were to be held in the presence of the king, and he was permitted, in a separate ceremony, to invest the new bishop or abbot with his

fiefs and his governmental powers by a touch of the scepter. In this way the religious powers of the bishop were obviously conferred by the churchmen who elected him; and although the king might still practically invalidate an election by refusing to hand over the lands, nevertheless the direct appointment of the bishops and abbots was taken out of his hands. As for the emperor's control over the papacy, too many popes, since the advent of Henry IV, had been generally recognized as properly elected without the sanction of the emperor, for any one to believe any longer that his sanction was necessary.

The Hohenstaufen Emperors and the Popes

A generation after the matter of investitures had been arranged by the Concordat of Worms the most famous of medieval German emperors, next to Charlemagne, came to the throne. This was Frederick I (1152-1190), commonly called Barbarossa, from his red beard. He belonged to the family of Hohenstaufen, so called from their castle in southern Germany. Frederick's ambition was to restore the Roman Empire to its old glory and influence. He regarded himself as the successor of the Cæsars, as well as of Charlemagne and Otto the Great. He believed his office to be quite as truly established by God himself as the papacy. When he informed the pope that he had been recognized as emperor by the German nobles, he too took occasion to state quite clearly that the headship of the empire had been "bestowed upon him by God" and he did not ask the pope's sanction as his predecessors had done.

In his lifelong attempt to maintain what he thought to be his rights as emperor he met, quite naturally, with the three old difficulties. He had constantly to be fighting his rivals and rebellious vassals in Germany; he had to face the opposition of the popes, who never forgot the claims that Gregory VII had made to control the emperor as well as other rulers. Lastly, in trying to keep hold of northern Italy, which he believed to belong to his empire, he spent a great deal of time with but slight results.

[131]

One of the greatest differences between the early Middle Ages and Frederick's time was the development of town life. Up to this period we have heard only of popes, emperors, kings, bishops, and feudal lords. From now on we shall have to take the towns and their citizens into account. No nation makes much progress without towns; for only when people get together in considerable numbers do they begin to build fine buildings,

RUINS OF BARBAROSSA'S PALACE AT GELNHAUSEN

Frederick Barbarossa erected a handsome palace at Gelnhausen (not far east of Frankfurt). It was destroyed by the Swedes during the Thirty Years' War, but even what now remains is imposing, especially the arcade represented in the picture

establish universities and libraries, make inventions and carry on trade, which brings them into contact with other people in their own country and in foreign lands. (See below, Chapter IX, for medieval town life.)

The towns had never decayed altogether in Italy, and by the time of Frederick Barbarossa they had begun to flourish once more, especially in Lombardy. Each of such towns as Milan, Verona, and Cremona were practically independent states. Their government was in the hands of the richer citizens, and

the poorer people were not given any voice in city affairs. Compared with a modern city they were very disorderly, for sometimes the poor revolted against the rich, and often the nobles, who had moved in from the country and built fortified palaces in the towns, fought among themselves. And then the various towns were always fighting one another.

ITALIAN TOWNS IN THE TWELFTH CENTURY

But in spite of all the warfare and disorder, the Italian cities became wealthy and, as we shall see later, were centers of learning and art similar to the ancient cities of Greece, such as Athens and Corinth. They were able to combine in a union known as the Lombard League to oppose Frederick, for they hated the idea of paying taxes to a German king from across the Alps. Frederick made several expeditions to Italy, but he

BAPTISTRY, CATHEDRAL, AND LEANING TOWER, PISA

Pisa was once a Roman colony with handsome buildings, all of which have disappeared. In the eleventh century it became an important commercial city. It took a considerable part in the Crusades, and its inhabitants were enriched by trade. The cathedral is a basilica, erected after the Pisans won a great naval battle over the Mohammedans in 1118, not long before the time of Frederick Barbarossa. It was consecrated in 1063. The circular baptistry in the foreground was begun in 1153, but was not completed for more than a century. The bell tower, which, owing to the sinking of the foundations, has become celebrated as the Leaning Tower, was begun in 1174, although not completed until much later only succeeded, after a vast amount of trouble, in getting them to recognize him as a sort of overlord. He was forced to leave them to manage their own affairs and go their own way. They could, of course, always rely upon the pope, when it came to fighting the emperor, for he was quite as anxious as the towns to keep Frederick out of Italy.

So Frederick failed in his great plans for restoring the Roman Empire; he only succeeded in adding a new difficulty for his descendants. In spite of his lack of success in conquering the Lombard cities, Frederick tried to secure *southern* Italy for his descendants. He arranged that his son should marry Constance, the heiress of Naples and Sicily. This made fresh trouble for the Hohenstaufen rulers, because the pope, as feudal lord of Naples and Sicily, was horrified at the idea of the emperor's controlling the territory to the south of the papal possessions as well as that to the north.

After some forty years of fighting in Germany and Italy Frederick Barbarossa decided to undertake a crusade to the Holy Land and lost his life on the way thither. His son was carried off by Italian fever while trying to put down a rebellion in southern Italy, leaving the fate of the Hohenstaufen family in the hands of his infant son and heir, the famous Frederick II. It would take much too long to try to tell of all the attempts of rival German princes to get themselves made king of Germany and of the constant interference of the popes who sided now with this one and now with that. It happened that one of the greatest of all the popes, Innocent III, was ruling during Frederick II's early years. After trying to settle the terrible disorder in Germany he decided that Frederick should be made emperor, hoping to control him so that he would not become the dangerous enemy of the papacy that his father and grandfather had been. As a young man Frederick made all the promises that Innocent demanded, but he caused later popes infinite anxiety.

Frederick II (1212-1250) is reported to have been nearsighted, bald, and wholly insignificant in person; but he exhibited the most extraordinary energy and ability in the organization of his kingdom of Sicily, in which he was far more interested than in Germany. He drew up an elaborate code of laws for his southern realms and may be said to have founded the first modern well-regulated state, in which the king was indisputably supreme. He had been brought up in Sicily and was much influenced by the Mohammedan culture which prevailed there. He appears to have rejected many of the opinions of the time. His enemies asserted that he was not even a Christian, and that he declared that Moses, Christ, and Mohammed were all alike impostors.

We cannot stop to relate the romantic and absorbing story of his long struggle with the popes. They speedily discovered that he was bent upon establishing a powerful state to the south of them, and upon extending his control over the Lombard cities in such a manner that the papal possessions would be held as in a vise. This, they felt, must never be permitted. Consequently almost every measure that Frederick adopted aroused their suspicion and opposition, and they made every effort to destroy him and his house.

His chance of success in the conflict with the head of the Church was gravely affected by a promise which he had made before Innocent III's death to undertake a crusade. He was so busily engaged with his endless enterprises that he kept deferring the expedition, in spite of the papal admonitions, until at last the pope lost patience and excommunicated him. While excommunicated, he at last started for the East. He met with signal success and actually brought Jerusalem, the Holy City, once more into Christian hands, and was himself recognized as king of Jerusalem.

Frederick's conduct continued, however, to give offense to the popes. He was denounced in solemn councils, and at last deposed by one of the popes. After Frederick died (1250) his sons maintained themselves for a few years in the Sicilian kingdom; but they finally gave way before a French army, led by the brother of St. Louis, Charles of Anjou, upon whom the pope bestowed the southern realms of the Hohenstaufens.

THE HOHENSTAUFEN EMPERORS AND THE POPES

With Frederick's death the medieval German empire may be said to have come to an end. It is true that after a period of "fist law," as the Germans call it, a new king, Rudolf of Hapsburg, was elected in Germany in 1273. The German kings continued to call themselves emperors. Few of them, however, took the trouble to go to Rome to be crowned by the pope. No serious effort was ever made to reconquer the Italian territory for which Otto the Great, Frederick Barbarossa, and his son and grandson had made such serious sacrifices. Germany was hopelessly divided and its king was no real king. He had no capital and no well-organized government.

By the middle of the thirteenth century it becomes apparent that neither Germany nor Italy was to be easily converted into a strong single kingdom like England and France. The map of Germany shows a confused group of duchies, counties, archbishoprics, bishoprics, abbacies, and free towns, each one of which asserted its practical independence of the weak king and emperor.

In northern Italy each town, including a certain district about its walls, had become an independent state, dealing with its neighbors as with independent powers. The Italian towns were destined to make important contributions to our modern culture during the fourteenth and fifteenth centuries. Venice and Florence, in spite of their small size, came to be reckoned among the most important states of Europe. In the central part of the peninsula the pope maintained more or less control over his possessions, but he often failed to subdue the towns within his realms. To the south Naples remained for some time under the French dynasty, which the pope had called in, while the island of Sicily drifted into Spanish hands.

CHAPTER VII

THE CRUSADES

Origin of the Crusades. The First Crusade. The Hospitalers and Templers. The Second and Later Crusades. Some Results of the Crusades

Origin of the Crusades

OF all the events of the Middle Ages, the most romantic and fascinating are the Crusades, the military expeditions to Syria and Palestine, undertaken by devout and adventurous kings and knights with the hope of permanently reclaiming the Holy Land from the infidel Turks. All through the twelfth and thirteenth centuries each generation beheld at least one great army of crusaders gathering from all parts of the West and starting toward the Orient. Each year witnessed the departure of small bands of pilgrims or of solitary soldiers of the cross.

For two hundred years there was a continuous stream of Europeans of every rank and station—kings and princes, powerful nobles, simple knights, common soldiers, ecclesiastics, monks, townspeople, and even peasants—from England, France, Germany, Spain, and Italy, making their way into western Asia. If they escaped the countless dangers which beset them on the journey, they either settled in this distant land and devoted themselves to war or commerce, or returned home, bringing with them tales of great cities and new peoples, of skill, knowledge, and luxury unknown in the West.

Our sources of information in regard to the Crusades are so abundant and so rich in picturesque incidents that writers have often yielded to the temptation to give more space to these expeditions than their consequences really justify. They were, after all, only the earliest of the great foreign enterprises which have been undertaken from time to time by the western European peoples. While their influence upon the European countries was doubtless very important,—like that of the later conquest of India by the English and the colonization of America,—the details of the campaigns in the East scarcely belong to our story.

Syria had been overrun by the Arabs in the seventh century, shortly after the death of Mohammed, and the Holy City of Jerusalem had fallen into the hands of the infidels. The Arab, however, shared the veneration of the Christian for the places associated with the life of Christ and, in general, permitted the Christian pilgrims who found their way thither to worship unmolested. But with the coming of a new and ruder people, the Seljuk Turks, in the eleventh century, the pilgrims began to bring home news of great hardships. Moreover, the eastern emperor was defeated by the Turks in 1071 and lost Asia Minor. The presence of the Turks, who had taken possession of the fortress of Nicæa, just across from Constantinople, was of course a standing menace to the Eastern Empire. When the energetic Emperor Alexius (1081-1118) ascended the throne he endeavored to expel the infidel. Finding himself unequal to the task, he appealed for assistance to the head of Christendom, Pope Urban II. The first great impetus to the Crusades was the call issued by Urban at the celebrated Church council which met in 1095 at Clermont in France.

In an address, which produced more remarkable immediate results than any other which history records, the pope exhorted knights and soldiers of all ranks to give up their usual wicked business of destroying their Christian brethren in private warfare and turn, instead, to the succor of their fellow Christians in the East. He warned them that the insolent Turks would, if unchecked, extend their sway still more widely over the faithful servants of the Lord. Urban urged, besides, that France was too poor to support all its people, while the Holy Land flowed with milk and honey. "Enter upon the road to the Holy Sepulcher; wrest the land from the wicked race and subject it to yourselves." When the pope had finished, all who were present exclaimed, with one accord, "It is the will of God." This, the pope declared, should be the rallying cry of the crusaders, who were to wear a cross upon their bosoms as they went forth, and upon their backs as they returned, as a holy sign of their sacred mission.

The Crusades are ordinarily represented as the most striking examples of the simple faith and religious enthusiasm of the Middle Ages. They appealed, however, to many different kinds of men. The devout, the romantic, and the adventurous were by no means the only classes that were attracted. Syria held out inducements to the discontented noble who might hope to gain a principality in the East, to the merchant who was looking for new enterprises, to the merely restless who wished to avoid his responsibilities at home, and even to the criminal who enlisted with a view of escaping the results of his past offenses.

It is noteworthy that Urban appeals especially to those who had been "contending against their brethren and relatives," and urges those "who have hitherto been robbers now to become soldiers of Christ." And the conduct of many of the crusaders indicates that the pope found a ready hearing among this class. Yet other motives than a love of adventure and the hope of conquest impelled many who took their way eastward. Great numbers, doubtless, went to Jerusalem "through devotion alone, and not for the sake of honor or gain," with the sole object of freeing the Holy Sepulcher from the hands of the infidel.

To such as these the pope promised that the journey itself should take the place of all penance for sin. The faithful crusader, like the faithful Mohammedan, was assured of immediate entrance into heaven if he died repentant. Later, the Church exhibited its extraordinary authority by what would seem to us an unjust interference with business contracts. It freed those who "with a pure heart" entered upon the journey from the payment of interest upon their debts, and permitted them to mortgage property against the wishes of their feudal lords. The crusaders' wives and children and property were taken under the immediate protection of the Church, and he who troubled them incurred excommunication. These various considerations help to explain the great popularity of under-takings that, at first sight, would seem to have promised only hardships and disappointment.

The Council of Clermont met in November. Before spring (1096) those who set forth to preach the Crusade,—above all, the famous Peter the Hermit, who was formerly given credit for having begun the whole crusading movement,—had collected, in France and along the Rhine, an extraordinary army of the common folk. Peasants, workmen, vagabonds, and even women and children answered the summons, all blindly intent upon rescuing the Holy Sepulcher, two thousand miles away. They were confident that the Lord would sustain them during the weary leagues of the journey, and that, when they reached the Holy Land, he would grant them a prompt victory over the infidel.

This great host was got under way in several divisions under the leadership of Peter the Hermit, and of Walter the Penni-less and other humble knights. Many of the crusaders were slaughtered by the Hungarians, who rose to protect themselves from the depredations of this motley horde in its passage through their country. Part of them got as far as Nicæa, only to be slaughtered by the Turks. This is but an example, on a large scale, of what was going on continually for a century or so after this first great catastrophe. Individual pilgrims and adventurers, and sometimes considerable bodies of crusaders, were constantly falling a prey to every form of disaster—starvation, slavery, disease, and death—in their persistent endeavors to reach the far away Holy Land.

The First Crusade

The most conspicuous figures of the long period of the Cru-sades were not, however, to be found among the lowly followers of Peter the Hermit, but were the knights, in their long coats of flexible armor. A year after the summons issued at Clermont great armies of fighting men had been collected in the West under distinguished leaders—the pope speaks of three hundred thousand soldiers. Of the various divisions which were to meet in Constantinople, the following were the most important: the volunteers from Provence under the papal legate and Count Raymond of Toulouse; inhabitants of Germany, particularly of Lorraine, under Godfrey of Bouillon and his brother Baldwin, both destined to be rulers of Jerusalem; and lastly, an army of French and of the Normans of southern Italy under Bohemond and Tancred.

KNIGHT OF THE FIRST CRUSADE

In the time of the Crusades knights wore a coat of interwoven iron rings, called a hauberk, to protect themselves. The habit of using the rigid iron plates, of which later armor was constructed, did not come in until the Crusades were over

The distinguished noblemen who have been mentioned were not actually in command of real armies. Each crusader undertook the expedition on his own account and was only obedient to any one's orders so long as he pleased. The knights and men naturally grouped themselves around the more noted leaders, but considered themselves free to change chiefs when they pleased. The leaders themselves reserved the right to look out for their own special interests rather than sacrifice themselves to the good of the expedition.

Upon the arrival of the crusaders at Constantinople it quickly became clear that they had not much more in common with the "Greeks" [1] than with the Turks. Emperor Alexius ordered his soldiers to attack Godfrey's army, encamped in the

[1] The people of the Eastern Empire were called Greeks because the Greek language continued to be used in Constantinople.

suburbs of his capital, because their chief at first refused to take the oath of feudal homage to him. The emperor's daughter Anna, in her history of the times, gives a sad picture of the outrageous conduct of the crusaders. They, on the other hand, denounced the Greeks as traitors, cowards, and liars.

The eastern emperor had hoped to use his western allies to reconquer Asia Minor and force back the Turks. The leading knights, on the contrary, dreamed of carving out principalities for themselves in the former dominions of the emperor, and proposed to control them by right of conquest. Later we find both Greeks and western Christians shamelessly allying themselves with the Mohammedans against each other. The relations of the eastern and western enemies of the Turks were well

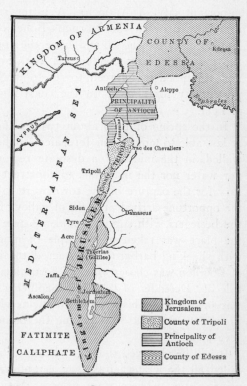

MAP OF THE CRUSADERS' STATES IN SYRIA

illustrated when the crusaders besieged their first town, Nicæa. When it was just ready to surrender, the Greeks arranged with the enemy to have their troops admitted first. They then closed the gates against their western confederates and invited them to move on.

[143]

The first real allies that the crusaders met with were the Christian Armenians, who gave them aid after their terrible march through Asia Minor. With their help Baldwin got possession of Edessa, of which he made himself prince. The chiefs induced the great body of the crusaders to postpone the march on Jerusalem, and a year was spent in taking the rich and important city of Antioch. A bitter strife then broke out, especially between the Norman Bohemond and the count of Toulouse, as to who should have the conquered town. After the most unworthy conduct on both sides, Bohemond won, and Raymond was forced to set to work to conquer another principality for himself on the coast about Tripoli (see map p. 143).

In the spring of 1099 about twenty thousand warriors were at last able to move upon Jerusalem. They found the city well walled, in the midst of a desolate region where neither food nor water nor the materials to construct the apparatus necessary for the capture of the town were to be found. However, the opportune arrival at Jaffa of galleys from Genoa furnished the besiegers with supplies, and, in spite of all the difficulties, the place was taken in a couple of months. The crusaders, with shocking barbarity, massacred the inhabitants. Godfrey of Bouillon was chosen ruler of Jerusalem and took the modest title of "Defender of the Holy Sepulcher." He soon died and was succeeded by his brother Baldwin, who left Edessa in 1100 to take up the task of extending the bounds of the kingdom of Jerusalem.

It will be observed that the "Franks," as the Mohammedans called all the western folk, had established the centers of four principalities. These were Edessa, Antioch, the region about Tripoli conquered by Raymond, and the kingdom of Jerusalem. The last was speedily increased by Baldwin; with the help of the mariners from Venice and Genoa, he succeeded in getting possession of Acre, Sidon, and a number of other less important coast towns.

The news of these Christian victories quickly reached the West, and in 1101 tens of thousands of new crusaders started eastward. Most of them were lost or dispersed in passing through Asia Minor, and few reached their destination. The original conquerors were consequently left to hold the land against the Saracens and to organize their conquests as best they could. This was a very difficult task—too difficult to accomplish under the circumstances.

The permanent hold of the Franks upon the eastern borders of the Mediterranean depended upon the strength of the colonies which their various princes were able to establish. It is impossible to learn how many pilgrims from the West made their permanent homes in the new Latin principalities. Certainly the greater part of those who visited Palestine returned home after fulfilling the vow they had made—to kneel at the Holy Sepulcher.

Still the princes could rely upon a certain number of soldiers who would be willing to stay and fight the Mohammedans. The Turks, moreover, were so busy fighting one another that they showed less energy than might have been expected in attempting to drive the Franks from the narrow strip of territory—some five hundred miles long and fifty wide—which they had conquered.

The Hospitalers and Templars

A noteworthy outcome of the crusading movement was the foundation of several curious orders, of which the Hospitalers and the Templars were the most important. These orders combined the two dominant interests of the time, those of the monk and of the soldier. They permitted a man to be both at once; the knight might wear a monkish cowl over his coat of armor.

The Hospitalers grew out of a monastic association that was formed before the First Crusade for the succor of the poor and sick among the pilgrims. Later the society admitted knights to its membership and became a military order, at the same time continuing its care for the sick. This charitable association, like the earlier monasteries, received generous gifts of land in western Europe and built and controlled many fortified monasteries in the Holy Land itself. After the evacuation of Syria in the thirteenth century, the Hospitalers moved their headquarters to the island of Rhodes, and later to Malta. The order still exists, and it is considered a distinction to this day to have the privilege of wearing its emblem, the cross of Malta.

COSTUME OF THE
HOSPITALERS

The Hospitaler here represented bears the peculiar Maltese cross on his bosom. His crucifix indicates his religious character, but his sword and the armor which he wears beneath his long gown enabled him to fight as well as pray and succor the wounded

Before the Hospitalers were transformed into a military order, a little group of French knights banded together in 1119 to defend pilgrims on their way to Jerusalem from the attacks of the infidel. They were assigned quarters in the king's palace at Jerusalem, on the site of the former Temple of Solomon; hence the name "Templars," which they were destined to render famous. The "poor soldiers of the Temple" were enthusiastically approved by the Church. They wore a white cloak adorned with a red cross, and were under a very strict monastic rule which bound them by the vows of obedience, poverty, and celibacy. The fame of the order spread throughout Europe, and the most exalted, even dukes and princes, were ready to renounce the world and serve Christ under its black and white banner, with the legend *Non nobis, Domine.*

The order was aristocratic from the first, and it soon became incredibly rich and independent. It had its collectors in all parts of Europe, who dispatched the "alms" they received to the Grand Master at Jerusalem. Towns, churches, and estates were given to the order, as well as vast sums of money. The king of Aragon proposed to bestow upon it a third of his kingdom. The pope showered privileges upon the Templars. They were exempted from tithes and taxes and were brought under his immediate jurisdiction; they were released from feudal obligations, and bishops were forbidden to excommunicate them for any cause.

No wonder they grew insolent and aroused the jealousy and hate of princes and prelates alike. Even Innocent III violently upbraided them for admitting to their order wicked men who then enjoyed all the privileges of churchmen. Early in the fourteenth century, through the combined efforts of the pope and Philip the Fair of France, the order was brought to a terrible end. Its members were accused of the most abominable practices,—such as heresy, the worship of idols, and the systematic insulting of Christ and his religion. Many distinguished Templars were burned for heresy; others perished miserably in dungeons. The once powerful order was abolished and its property confiscated.

The Second and Later Crusades

Fifty years after the preaching of the First Crusade, the fall of Edessa (1144), an important outpost of the Christians in the East, led to a second great expedition. This was forwarded by no less a person than St. Bernard, who went about using his unrivaled eloquence to induce volunteers to take the cross. In a fierce hymn of battle he cried to the Knights Templars: "The Christian who slays the unbeliever in the Holy War is sure of his reward, the more sure if he himself be slain. The Christian glories in the death of the infidel, because Christ is glorified." The king of France readily consented to take the cross, but the emperor, Conrad III, appears to have yielded only after St. Bernard had preached before him and given a vivid picture of the terrors of the Judgment Day.

In regard to the less distinguished recruits, a historian of the time tells us that so many thieves and robbers hastened to take the cross that every one felt that such enthusiasm could only be the work of God himself. St. Bernard himself, the chief promoter of the expedition, gives a most unflattering description of the "soldiers of Christ." "In that countless multitude you will find few except the utterly wicked and impious, the sacrilegious, homicides, and perjurers, whose departure is a double gain. Europe rejoices to lose them and Palestine to gain them; they are useful in both ways, in their absence from here and their presence there." It is unnecessary to describe the movements and fate of these crusaders; suffice it to say that, from a military standpoint, the so-called Second Crusade was a miserable failure.

KRAK DES CHEVALIERS, RESTORED

This is an example of the strong castles that the crusaders built in Syria. It was completed in the form here represented about the year 1200 and lies halfway between Antioch and Damascus. It will be noticed that there was a fortress within a fortress. The castle is now in ruins (see headpiece of this chapter)

In the year 1187, forty years later, Jerusalem was recaptured by Saladin, the most heroic and distinguished of all the Mohammedan rulers of that period. The loss of the Holy City led to the most famous of all the military expeditions to the Holy Land, in which Frederick Barbarossa, Richard the Lion-Hearted of England, and his political rival, Philip Augustus of France, all took part (see below, p. 239). The accounts of the enterprise show that while the several Christian leaders hated one another heartily enough, the Christians and Mohammedans were coming to respect one another. We find examples of the most courtly relations between the representatives of the opposing religions. In 1192 Richard of England concluded a truce with Saladin by the terms of which the Christian pilgrims were allowed to visit the places in safety and comfort.

At the opening of the thirteenth century the crusading enterprises took a surprising turn. In the so-called Fourth Crusade under the influence of the wily Venetians, an ill-assorted combination of French nobles, Norman adventurers (those who had conquered southern Italy), Genoese merchants, as well as the Venetians themselves, managed to capture Constantinople in 1204. They then divided up the little that remained at that time of the Eastern Roman Empire into duchies and principalities and made Count Baldwin of Flanders "Latin Emperor." This situation did not last long and soon the line of Greek emperors was restored. But it served to increase for a time the intercourse between the West and the East. It was just at this period that the books of Aristotle, which had been cherished in Constantinople but lost in the West, began to be mentioned in Paris, later to become the chief inspiration of Western universities in the whole range of learning.

Later crusading expeditions were directed against the Moslem power in Egypt. Those of Frederick II of Hohenstaufen and of Saint Louis of France, romantic as they were, need not detain us. Jerusalem was lost in 1244 only to be regained during the World War by a Christian power. Although there was continued discussion of the possibility of recovering the holy sepulcher, the Crusades may be said to have come to an end before the end of the thirteenth century.

Some Results of the Crusades

For one class at least, the Holy Land had great and permanent charm, namely, the Italian merchants, especially those from Genoa, Venice, and Pisa. It was through their early interest and by means of supplies from their ships, that the conquest of the Holy Land had been rendered possible. The merchants always made sure that they were well paid for their services. When they aided in the successful siege of a town they arranged that a definite quarter should be assigned to them in the captured place, where they might have their market, docks, church, and all that was necessary for a permanent center for their business. This district belonged to the town from which the merchants came. Venice even sent governors to live in the quarters assigned to its citizens in the kingdom of Jerusalem. Marseille also had independent quarters in Jerusalem, and Genoa had its share in the county of Tripoli.

This new commerce had a most important influence in bringing the West into permanent relations with the Orient. Eastern products from India and elsewhere—silks, spices, camphor, musk, pearls, and ivory—were brought by the Mohammedans from the East to the commercial towns of Palestine and Syria; then, through the Italian merchants, they found their way into France and Germany, suggesting ideas of luxury hitherto scarcely dreamed of by the still half-barbarous Franks.

Moreover, the Crusades had a great effect upon the methods of warfare, for the soldiers from the West learned from the Greeks about the old Roman methods of constructing machines for attacking castles and walled towns. This led, as has been pointed out in a previous chapter, to the construction in western Europe of stone castles, first with square towers and later with round ones, the remains of which are so common in Germany, France, and England. The Crusades also produced heraldry, or the science of coats of arms. These were the badges that single knights or groups of knights adopted in order to distinguish themselves from other people. Some of the terms used in heraldry, such as *gules* for red, and *azur* for blue, are of Arabic origin.

Some of the results of the Crusades upon western Europe must already be obvious, even from this very brief account. Thousands and thousands of Frenchmen, Germans, and Englishmen had traveled to the Orient by land and by sea. Most of them came from hamlets or castles where they could never have learned much of the great world beyond the confines of their native village or province. They suddenly found themselves in great cities and in the midst of unfamiliar peoples and customs. This could not fail to make them think and give them new ideas to carry home. The Crusade took the place of a liberal education. The crusaders came into contact with those who knew more than they did, above all the Arabs, and brought back with them new notions of comfort and luxury.

Yet in attempting to estimate the debt of the West to the Crusades it should be remembered that many of the new things may well have come from Constantinople, or through the Mohammedans of Sicily and Spain, quite independently of the armed incursions into Syria. Moreover, during the twelfth and thirteenth centuries towns were rapidly growing up in Europe, trade and manufactures were extending, and the universities were being founded. It would be absurd to suppose that without the Crusades this progress would not have taken place. So we may conclude that the distant expeditions and the contact with strange and more highly civilized peoples did no more than hasten the improvement which was already perceptible before Urban made his ever-memorable address at Clermont. It should be added that during the thirteenth century the intercourse between western Europe and the far East was made possible by the creation of the vast Mongol empire extending from the Baltic to the Pacific Ocean. Various Europeans visited the Mongol court, and some of the Chinese inventions, especially paper, printing, the use of the compass and gunpowder, may have had an effect, now hard to trace, on similar discoveries in western Europe.

CHAPTER VIII

THE MEDIEVAL CHURCH AT ITS HEIGHT

Organization and Powers of the Church. The Heretics and the Inquisition. The Franciscans and Dominicans

Organization and Powers of the Church

IN the preceding pages it has been necessary to refer constantly to the Church and the clergy. Indeed, without them medieval history would become almost a blank, for the Church was incomparably the most important institution of the time, its officers were the soul of nearly every great enterprise, and to its writers we owe a great part of our knowledge of what would otherwise have passed into oblivion. We have already learned something of the rise of the Church and of its head, the pope, as well as the mode of life and the work of the monks as they spread over Europe. We have also watched the long struggle between the emperors and the popes in which the emperors were finally worsted. We may now consider the Medieval Church as a completed institution at the height of its power in the twelfth and thirteenth centuries.

We have already had abundant proofs that the Medieval

Church was very different from our modern churches, whether Catholic or Protestant.

1. In the first place, every one was required to belong to it, just as we all must belong to some country to-day. One was not born into the Church, it is true, but he was ordinarily baptized into it when he was a mere infant. All western Europe formed a single religious association, from which it was a crime to revolt. To refuse allegiance to the Church, or to question its authority or teachings, was regarded as treason against God and was punishable with death.

2. The Medieval Church did not rely for its support, as churches usually must to-day, upon the voluntary contributions of its members. It enjoyed, in addition to the revenue from its vast tracts of lands and a great variety of fees, the income from a regular tax, the *tithe*. Those upon whom this fell were forced to pay it, just as we all must now pay taxes imposed by the government.

3. It is clear, moreover, that the Medieval Church was not merely a religious body, as churches are to-day. Of course it maintained places of worship, conducted devotional exercises, and cultivated the religious life; but it did far more. It was, in a way, a *State,* for it had an elaborate system of law, and its own courts, in which it tried many cases which are now settled in our ordinary courts.[1] One may get some idea of the business of the Church courts from the fact that the Church claimed the right to try all cases in which a clergyman was involved, or any one connected with the Church or under its special protection, such as monks, students, crusaders, widows, orphans, and the helpless. Then all cases where the rites of the Church, or its prohibitions, were involved came ordinarily before the Church courts, as, for example, those concerning marriage, wills, sworn contracts, usury, blasphemy, sorcery, heresy, and so forth. The

---

[1] The law of the Church was known as the *canon law.* It was taught in most of the universities and practiced by a great number of lawyers. It was based upon the "canons," or rules, enacted by the various Church councils, from that of Nicæa down, and, above all, upon the decrees and decisions of the popes.

[153].

Church even had its prisons, to which it might sentence offenders for life.

4. The Church not only performed the functions of a State; it had the organization of a State. Unlike the Protestant ministers of to-day, all churchmen and religious associations of medieval Europe were under one supreme head, the pope, who made laws for all and controlled every Church officer, wherever he might be, whether in Italy or Germany, Spain or Ireland. The whole Church had one official language, Latin, in which all communications were written and in which its services were everywhere conducted.

The Medieval Church may therefore properly be called a monarchy in its government. The pope was its all-powerful and absolute head. He was the supreme lawgiver. He might set aside or repeal any law of the Church, no matter how ancient, so long as he did not believe it to be ordained by the Scriptures or by Nature. He might, for good reasons, make exceptions to all merely human laws; as, for instance, permit cousins to marry, or free a monk from his vows. Such exceptions were known as *dispensations*.

The pope was not merely the supreme lawgiver; he was the supreme judge. Any one, whether clergyman or layman, in any part of Europe could appeal to him at any stage in the trial of a large class of cases. Obviously this system had serious drawbacks. Grave injustice might be done by carrying to Rome a case which ought to have been settled in Edinburgh or Cologne, where the facts were best known. The rich, moreover, always had the advantage, as they alone could afford to appeal suits to so distant a court.

The control of the pope over all parts of the Christian Church was exercised by his *legates*. These papal ambassadors were intrusted with great powers. Their haughty mien sometimes offended the prelates and rulers to whom they brought home the authority of the pope,—as, for instance, when the legate Pandulf grandly absolved all the subjects of King John of England, before his very face, from their oath of fealty to him (see below, pp. 240 ff.).

ORGANIZATION AND POWERS OF THE CHURCH

The task assumed by the pope of governing the whole western world naturally made it necessary to create a large body of officials at Rome in order to transact all the multiform business and prepare and transmit the innumerable legal documents.[1] The cardinals and the pope's officials constituted what was called the papal *curia,* or court.

To carry on his government and meet the expenses of palace and retinue, the pope had need of a vast income. This he secured from various sources. Heavy fees were exacted from those who brought cases to his court for decision. The archbishops, bishops, and abbots were expected to make generous contributions when the pope confirmed their election. In the thirteenth century the pope himself began to fill many benefices throughout Europe, and customarily received half the first year's revenues from those whom he appointed. For several centuries before the Protestants finally threw off their allegiance to the popes, there was widespread complaint on the part of both clergy and laymen that the fees and taxes levied by the Roman *curia* were excessive.

Next in order below the head of the Church were the archbishops and bishops. An archbishop was a bishop whose power extended beyond the boundaries of his own diocese and who exercised a certain control over all the bishops within his province.

There is perhaps no class of persons in medieval times whose position it is so necessary to understand as that of the bishops. They were regarded as the successors of the apostles, whose powers were held to be divinely transmitted to them. Their insignia of office, the miter and crosier, are familiar to every one.[2] They represented the Church Universal in their respective dioceses, under the supreme headship of their "elder brother,"

---

[1] Many of the edicts, decisions, and orders of the popes were called *bulls,* from the seal (Latin, *bulla*) attached to them.

[2] The headpiece of this chapter represents an English bishop ordaining a priest and is taken from a manuscript of Henry II's time. The bishop is wearing his miter and holds his pastoral staff, the crosier, in his left hand while he raises his right, in blessing, over the priest's head.

the bishop of Rome, the successor of the chief of the apostles. Each bishop had his especial church, which was called a cathedral, and usually surpassed the other churches of the diocese in size and beauty.

In addition to the oversight of his diocese, it was the bishop's business to look after the lands and other possessions which belonged to the bishopric. Lastly, the bishop was usually a feudal lord, with the obligations which that implied. He might have vassals and subvassals, and often was himself a vassal, not only of the king but also of some neighboring lord.

CANTERBURY CATHEDRAL

The bishop's church was called a cathedral, because in it stood the bishop's chair, or throne (Latin, *cathedra*). It was therefore much more imposing ordinarily than the parish churches, although sometimes the abbey churches belonging to rich monasteries vied with the bishop's church in beauty

The lowest division of the Church was the parish. At the head of the parish was the parish priest, who conducted services in the parish church and absolved, baptized, married, and buried his parishioners. The priests were supposed to be supported by the lands belonging to the parish church and by the tithes. But both of these sources of income were often in the hands of laymen or of a neighboring monastery, while the poor priest received the merest pittance, scarcely sufficient to keep soul and body together.

The clergy were set apart from the laity in several ways. The higher orders—bishop, priest, deacon, and subdeacon—were required to remain unmarried, and in this way were freed from the cares and interests of family life. The Church held, moreover, that the higher clergy, when they had been properly ordained, received through their ordination a mysterious imprint, the "indelible character," so that they could never become simple laymen again, even if they ceased to perform their duties altogether. Above all, the clergy alone could administer the *sacraments* upon which the salvation of every individual soul depended.

The punishment for sin imposed by the priest was called *penance*. This took a great variety of forms. It might consist in fasting, repeating prayers, visiting holy places, or abstaining from one's ordinary amusements. A journey to the Holy Land was regarded as taking the place of all other penance. Instead, however, of requiring the penitent actually to perform the fasts, pilgrimages, or other sacrifices imposed as penance by the priest, the Church early began to permit him to change his penance into a contribution, to be applied to some pious enterprise, like building a church or bridge, or caring for the poor and sick.

The influence of the clergy was greatly increased by the fact that they alone were educated. For six or seven centuries after the overthrow of the Roman government in the west, very few outside of the clergy ever dreamed of studying, or even of learning to read and write. Even in the thirteenth century an offender who wished to prove that he belonged to the clergy, in order that he might be tried by a Church court, had only to show that he could read a single line; for it was assumed by the judges that no one unconnected with the Church could read at all.

It was therefore inevitable that all the teachers were clergymen, that almost all the books were written by priests and monks, and that the clergy was the ruling power in all intellectual, artistic, and literary matters—the chief guardians and promoters of civilization. Moreover, the civil government was forced to rely upon churchmen to write out the public documents and proclamations. The priests and monks held the pen for the king. Representatives of the clergy sat in the king's councils and acted as his ministers; in fact, the conduct of the government largely devolved upon them.

The offices in the Church were open to all ranks of men, and many of the popes themselves sprang from the humblest classes. The Church thus constantly recruited its ranks with fresh blood. No one held an office simply because his father had held it before him, as was the case in the civil government.

No wonder that the churchmen were by far the most powerful class in the Middle Ages. They controlled great wealth; they alone were educated; they held the keys of the kingdom of heaven and without their aid no one could hope to enter in. By excommunication they could cast out the enemies of the Church and could forbid all men to associate with them, since they were accursed. By means of the *interdict* they could suspend all religious ceremonies in a whole city or country by closing the church doors and prohibiting all public services.

The Heretics and the Inquisition

Nevertheless, in spite of the power and wonderful organization of the Church, a few people began to revolt against it as early as the time of Gregory VII; and the number of these rebels continued to increase as time went on. Popular leaders arose who declared that no one ought any longer to rely upon the Church for his salvation; that all its elaborate ceremonies were worse than useless; that its Masses, holy water, and relics were mere money-getting devices of a sinful priesthood and helped no one to heaven.

Those who questioned the teachings of the Church and proposed to cast off its authority were, according to the accepted view of the time, guilty of the supreme crime of heresy. Heretics were of two sorts. One class merely rejected the practices and some of the doctrines of the Roman Catholic Church while they remained Christians and endeavored to imitate as nearly as possible the simple life of Christ and the apostles.

Among those who continued to accept the Christian faith but refused to obey the clergy, the most important sect was that of the Waldensians, which took its rise about 1175. These were followers of Peter Waldo of Lyon, who gave up all their property and lived a life of apostolic poverty. They went about preaching the Gospel and explaining the Scriptures, which they translated from Latin into the language of the people. They made many converts, and before the end of the twelfth century there were great numbers of them scattered throughout western Europe.

On the other hand, there were popular leaders who taught that the Christian religion itself was false. They held, with the Manichæans of the late Roman Empire, that there were two principles in the universe, the good and the evil, which were forever fighting for the victory. They asserted that the Jehovah of the Old Testament was really the evil power, and that it was, therefore, the evil power whom the Catholic Church worshiped. These heretics were commonly called Albigensians, a name derived from the town of Albi in southern France, where they were very numerous.

It is difficult for us who live in a religiously tolerant age to understand the universal and deep-rooted horror of heresy which long prevailed in Europe. But we must recollect that to the orthodox believer in the Church nothing could exceed the guilt of one who committed treason against God by rejecting the religion which had been handed down in the Roman Church from the immediate followers of his Son. Moreover, doubt and unbelief were not merely sin; they were revolt against the most powerful social institution of the time, which, in spite of the sins of some of its officials, continued to be venerated by people at large throughout western Europe. The story of the Albigensians and Waldensians, and the efforts of the Church to suppress them by persuasion, by fire and sword, and by the stern court of the Inquisition, form a terrible chapter in medieval history.

[159]

In southern France there were many adherents of both the Albigensians and the Waldensians, especially in the county of Toulouse. At the beginning of the thirteenth century there was in this region an open contempt for the Church, and bold heretical murmurings were heard even among the higher classes.

Against the people of this flourishing land Pope Innocent III preached a crusade in 1208. An army marched from northern France into the doomed region and, after one of the most atrocious and bloody wars upon record, suppressed the heresy by wholesale slaughter. At the same time, the war checked the civilization and destroyed the prosperity of the most enlightened portion of France.

The most permanent defense of the Church against heresy was the establishment, under the headship of the pope, of a system of courts designed to ferret out secret cases of unbelief and bring the offenders to punishment. These courts which devoted their whole attention to the discovery and conviction of heretics were called the Holy Inquisition, which gradually took form after the Albigensian crusade. The unfairness of the trials and the cruel treatment to which those suspected of heresy were subjected, through long imprisonment or torture,—inflicted with the hope of forcing them to confess their crime or to implicate others,—have rendered the name of the Inquisition infamous.

Without by any means sympathizing with the methods employed, it may be remarked that the inquisitors were usually earnest and upright men, and the methods of procedure of the Inquisition were not more cruel than those used in the secular courts of the period.

The assertion of the suspected person that he was not a heretic did not receive any attention, for it was assumed that he would naturally deny his guilt, as would any other criminal. A person's belief had, therefore, to be judged by outward acts. Consequently one might fall into the hands of the Inquisition by mere accidental conversation with a heretic, by some unintentional neglect to show due respect toward the Church rites, or by the malicious testimony of one's neighbors. This is really the most terrible aspect of the Inquisition and its procedure.

If the suspected person confessed his guilt and abjured his heresy, he was forgiven and received back into the Church; but a penance of life imprisonment was imposed upon him as a fitting means of wiping away the unspeakable sin of which he had been guilty. If he persisted in his heresy, he was "relaxed to the secular arms"; that is to say, the Church, whose law forbade it to shed blood, handed over the convicted person to the civil power, which burned him alive without further trial.

The Franciscans and Dominicans

We may now turn to that far more cheerful and effective method of meeting the opponents of the Church, which may be said to have been discovered by St. Francis of Assisi. His teachings and the example of his beautiful life probably did far more to secure continued allegiance to the Church than all the harsh devices of the Inquisition.

We have seen how the Waldensians tried to better the world by living simple lives and preaching the Gospel. Owing to the disfavor of the Church authorities, who declared their teachings erroneous and dangerous, they were prevented from publicly carrying on their missionary work. Yet all conscientious men agreed with the Waldensians that the world was in a sad plight, owing to the negligence and the misdeeds of the clergy. St. Francis and St. Dominic strove to meet the needs of their time by inventing a new kind of clergyman, the begging brother, or "mendicant friar" (from the Latin *frater*, "brother"). He was to do just what the bishops and parish priests often failed to do—namely, lead a holy life of self-sacrifice, defend the Church's beliefs against the attacks of the heretics, and awaken the people to a new religious life.

There is no more lovely and fascinating figure in all history than St. Francis. He was born (probably in 1182) at Assisi, a little town in central Italy. He was the son of a well-to-do merchant, and during his early life he lived a very gay life, spending his father's money freely. He read the French romances of the time and dreamed of imitating the brave knights whose adventures they described. Although his companions were wild and reckless, there was a delicacy and chivalry in Francis's own make-up which made him hate all things coarse and heartless. When later he voluntarily became a beggar, his ragged cloak still covered a true poet and knight.

The contrast between his own life of luxury and the sad state of the poor early afflicted him. When he was about twenty, after a long and serious illness which made a break in his gay life and gave him time to think, he suddenly lost his love for the old pleasures and began to consort with the destitute, above all with lepers. His father does not appear to have had any fondness whatever for beggars, and the relations between him and his son grew more and more strained. When finally he threatened to disinherit the young man, Francis cheerfully agreed to surrender all right to his inheritance. Stripping off his clothes and giving them back to his father, he accepted the worn-out garment of a gardener and became a homeless hermit, busying himself in repairing the dilapidated chapels near Assisi.

He soon began to preach in a simple way, and before long a rich fellow townsman resolved to follow Francis's example—sell his all and give to the poor. Others soon joined them, and these joyous converts, free of worldly burdens, went barefoot and penniless about central Italy preaching the Gospel instead of shutting themselves up in a monastery.

When, with a dozen followers, Francis appealed to the pope in 1210 for his approval, Innocent III hesitated. He did not believe that any one could lead a life of absolute poverty. Then might not these ragged, ill-kempt vagabonds appear to condemn the Church by adopting a life so different from that of the rich and comfortable clergy? Yet if he disapproved the friars, he would seem to disapprove at the same time Christ's directions to his apostles. He finally decided to authorize the brethren to continue their missions.

Seven years later, when Francis's followers had greatly increased in number, missionary work was begun on a large scale, and brethren were dispatched to Germany, Hungary, France, Spain, and even to Syria. It was not long before an English chronicler was telling with wonder of the arrival in his country of these barefoot men, in their patched gowns and with ropes about their waists, who, with Christian faith, took no thought for the morrow, believing that their Heavenly Father knew what things they had need of.

As time went on, the success of their missionary work led the pope to bestow many privileges upon them. It grieved Francis, however, to think of his little band of companions being converted into a great and powerful order. He foresaw that they would soon cease to lead their simple, holy life, and would become ambitious and perhaps rich. "I, little Brother Francis," he writes, "desire to follow the life and the poverty of Jesus Christ, persevering therein until the end; and I beg you all and exhort you to persevere always in this most holy life of poverty, and take good care never to depart from it upon the advice and teachings of any one whomsoever."

After the death of St. Francis (1226) many of the order, which now numbered several thousand members, wished to maintain the simple rule of absolute poverty; others, including the new head of the order, believed that much good might be done with the wealth which people were anxious to give them. They argued that the individual friars might still remain absolutely possessionless, even if the order had beautiful churches and comfortable monasteries. So a stately church was forthwith constructed (1228-1253) at Assisi to receive the remains of their humble founder, who in his lifetime had chosen a deserted hovel for his home; and a great chest was set up in the church to receive the offerings of those who desired to give.

St. Dominic (b. 1170), the Spanish founder of the other great mendicant order, was not a simple layman like Francis. He was a churchman and took a regular course of instruction in theology for ten years in a Spanish university. He then (1208) accompanied his bishop to southern France on the eve of the Albigensian crusade and was deeply shocked to see the prevalence of heresy. His host at Toulouse happened to be an Albigensian, and Dominic spent the night in converting him. He then and there determined to devote his life to fighting heresy.

By 1214 a few sympathetic spirits from various parts of Europe had joined Dominic, and they asked Innocent III to sanction their new order. The pope again hesitated, but is said to have dreamed a dream in which he saw the great Roman Church of the Lateran tottering and ready to fall had not

CHURCH OF ST. FRANCIS AT ASSISI

Assisi is situated on a high hill, and the monastery of the Franciscans is built out on a promontory. The monastery has *two* churches, one above the other. The lower church, in which are the remains of St. Francis, was begun in 1228 and contains pictures of the life and miracles of the saint

Dominic supported it on his shoulders. He interpreted this as meaning that the new organization might sometime become a great aid to the papacy, and gave it his approval. As soon as possible Dominic sent forth his followers, of whom there were but sixteen, to evangelize the world, just as the Franciscans were undertaking their first missionary journeys. By 1221 the Dominican order was thoroughly organized and had sixty monasteries scattered over western Europe.

THE FRANCISCANS AND DOMINICANS

"Wandering on foot over the face of Europe, under burning suns or chilling blasts, rejecting alms in money but receiving thankfully whatever coarse food might be set before the wayfarer, enduring hunger in silent resignation, taking no thought for the morrow, but busied eternally in the work of snatching souls from Satan and lifting men up from the sordid cares of daily life" (Henry C. Lea)—in this way did the early Franciscans and Dominicans win the love and veneration of the people.[1]

The Dominicans were called the "Preaching Friars" and were carefully trained in theology in order the better to refute the arguments of the heretics. The pope delegated to them especially the task of conducting the Inquisition. They early began to extend their influence over the universities, and the most distinguished two theologians and teachers of the thirteenth century, Albertus Magnus and Thomas Aquinas, were Dominicans. Among the Franciscans, on the other hand, there was always a considerable party who were suspicious of learning and who showed a greater desire to remain absolutely poor than did the Dominicans. Yet as a whole the Franciscans, like the Dominicans, accepted the wealth that came to them, and they too contributed distinguished scholars to the universities.

The inevitable conflicts between this mighty ecclesiastical state—the Church—and the secular rulers were in no way confined to the troubles between popes and emperors already described. The issues between Church and State during the fourteenth and fifteenth centuries, which were prominent in France and England as well as Germany, will be discussed as a preliminary to the defection of northern Germany and England from the Holy Roman Apostolic Church. This took place in the early sixteenth century and is usually called "The Reformation" (see below, Chapter XIII).

[1] Called respectively gray friars and black friars in England.

CHAPTER IX

MEDIEVAL TOWNS — THEIR BUSINESS AND BUILDINGS

The Towns and Guilds. Business in the Later Middle Ages. Gothic Architecture. The Italian Cities of the Renaissance

The Towns and Guilds

IN discussing the Middle Ages we have hitherto dealt mainly with kings and emperors, and with the popes and the Church of which they were the chief rulers; we have also described the monks and monasteries, the warlike feudal lords and their castles, and the hard-working serfs who farmed the manors; but nothing has been said about the people who lived in the towns.

Towns have, however, in human development, always been the chief centers of progress and enlightenment, for the simple reason that people must live close together in large numbers before they can escape the bondage of the soil, develop business on a large scale, carry on trade with foreign countries, establish good schools and universities, erect noble public buildings, encourage art and literature, erect libraries and museums and art galleries. One does not find these in the country, for the people outside the towns are too scattered and usually too poor to have the things that are common enough in large cities.

One of the chief peculiarities of the early Middle Ages, from the break-up of the Roman Empire to the time of Gregory VII, let us say, was the absence of large and flourishing towns in western Europe, and this fact alone would serve to explain why there was so little progress.

The Roman towns were decreasing in population before the German inroads. The confusion which followed the invasions hastened their decline, and a great number of them disappeared altogether. Those which survived and such new towns as sprang up were, to judge from the chronicles, of very little importance during the early Middle Ages. We may assume, therefore, that during the long period from Theodoric to Frederick Barbarossa by far the greater part of the population of England, Germany, and northern and central France were living in the country, on the great estates belonging to the feudal lords, abbots, and bishops.[1]

It is hardly necessary to point out that the gradual reappearance of town life in western Europe is of the greatest interest to the student of history. The cities had been the centers of Greek and Roman civilization, and in our own time they dominate the life, culture, and business enterprise of the world. Were they to disappear, our whole existence, even in the country, would necessarily undergo a profound change and tend to become primitive again, like that of the age of Charlemagne.

A great part of the medieval towns, of which we begin to have some scanty records about the year 1000, appear to have originated on the manors of feudal lords or about a monastery or castle. The French name for town, *ville,* is derived from "vill," the name of the manor, and we use this old Roman word (*villa*) when we call a town Jackson*ville* or Harris*ville*. The need of protection was probably the usual reason for establishing a town with walls about it, so that the townspeople and the neighboring country people might find safety within it when attacked by neighboring feudal lords.

The way in which a medieval town was built seems to justify this conclusion. It was generally crowded and compact, compared with its more luxurious Roman predecessors. Aside from the market place there were few or no open spaces. There

---

[1] In Italy and southern France town life was doubtless more general than in northern Europe. This was a hold-over from the Roman Empire.

were no amphitheaters or public baths as in the Roman cities. The streets were often mere alleys over which the jutting stories of the high houses almost met. The high, thick wall that surrounded it prevented its extending easily and rapidly as our cities do nowadays.

A CASTLE WITH A VILLAGE BELOW IT

A village was pretty sure to grow up near the castle of a powerful lord and might gradually become a large town

All towns outside of Italy were small in the eleventh and twelfth centuries, and, like the manors on which they had grown up, they had little commerce as yet with the outside world. They produced almost all that their inhabitants needed except the farm products which came from the neighboring country. There was likely to be little expansion so long as the town remained under the absolute control of the lord or monastery upon whose land it was situated. The townspeople were scarcely more than serfs, in spite of the fact that they lived within a wall and were traders and artisans instead of farmers. They had to pay irritating dues to their lord, just as if they still formed a farming community.

With the increase of trade (see following section) came the longing for greater freedom. For when new and attractive commodities began to be brought from the East and the South, the people of the towns were encouraged to make things which they could exchange at some neighboring fair for the products of distant lands. But no sooner did the townsmen begin to engage in manufacturing and to enter into relations with the outside world than they became conscious that they were subject to the exactions and restrictions of the manorial lords, which rendered progress impossible.

Consequently, during the twelfth century there were many insurrections of the towns against their lords and a general demand that the lords should grant the townsmen *charters* in which the rights of both parties should be definitely stated. These charters were written contracts between the lord and the town government, which served at once as the certificate of birth of the town and as its constitution. The old dues and services which the townspeople owed as serfs (see above, pp. 105 ff.) were either abolished or changed into money payments.

As a visible sign of their freedom, many of the towns had a belfry, a high building with a watchtower, where a guard was kept day and night in order that the bell might be rung in case of approaching danger.[1] Connected with it was an assembly hall, where those who governed the town held their meetings, and a prison. Not until the fourteenth century did the wonderful town halls begin to be erected, which, with the exception of the cathedrals and other churches, are usually the most remarkable buildings which the traveler sees to-day in the old commercial cities of Europe.

The tradesmen in the medieval towns were at once manufacturers and merchants; that is, they made, as well as offered

---

[1] At the beginning of this chapter there is a sketch of the town of Siegen in Germany, as it formerly looked, with its walls and towers.

STREET IN QUIMPER, FRANCE

None of the thoroughfares in even the oldest European towns look just as
they did in the twelfth and thirteenth centuries, but here and there, as in
this town of Brittany, one can still get some idea of the narrow, cramped
streets and overhanging houses and the beautiful cathedral crowded in
among them

for sale, the articles which they kept in their shops. Those who belonged to a particular trade—the bakers, the butchers, the sword makers, the armorers, etc.—formed unions or guilds to protect their special interests. The oldest statutes of a guild in Paris are those of the candle makers, which go back to 1061. The number of trades differed greatly in different towns, but the guilds all had the same object—to prevent any one from practicing a trade who had not been duly admitted to the union and so to reduce competition—"the closed shop."

A young man had to spend several years in learning his trade. During this time he lived in the house of a "master workman" as an "apprentice," but received no remuneration. He then became a "journeyman" and could earn wages, although he was still allowed to work only for master workmen and not directly for the public. A simple trade might be learned in three years, but to become a goldsmith one must be an apprentice for ten years. The number of apprentices that a master workman might employ was strictly limited, in order that the journeymen might not become too numerous.

The way in which each trade was to be practiced was carefully regulated, as well as the time that should be spent in work each day. The system of guilds may have discouraged enterprise but they maintained uniform standards everywhere. Had it not been for these unions, the defenseless, isolated workmen, serfs as they had formerly been, would have found it impossible to secure freedom and municipal independence from the feudal lords who had formerly been their masters.

Business in the Later Middle Ages

The chief reason for the growth of the towns and their increasing prosperity was a great development of trade throughout western Europe. Commerce had pretty much disappeared with the decline of the Roman roads and the general disorganization produced by the barbarian invasions. In the early Middle Ages there was no one to mend the ancient Roman roads. The great network of highways from Persia to Britain fell apart when independent nobles or poor local communities took the place of a world empire. All trade languished, for there was little demand for those articles of luxury which the Roman communities in the North had been accustomed to obtain from the South, and there was but little money to buy what we should consider the comforts of life; even the nobility lived uncomfortably enough in their dreary and rudely furnished castles.

In Italy, however, trade does not seem to have altogether ceased. Venice, Genoa, Amalfi, and other towns appear to have developed a considerable Mediterranean commerce even before the Crusades. Their merchants, as we have seen, supplied the destitute crusaders with the material necessary for the conquest of Jerusalem. The passion for pilgrimages offered inducements to the Italian merchants for extending their operations to the Orient, whither they transported the pilgrims and returned with the products of the East. The Italian cities established trading stations in the East and carried on a direct traffic with the caravans which brought to the shores of the Mediterranean the products of Arabia, Persia, India, and the remote Spice Islands. The southern French towns and Barcelona entered also into commercial relations with the Mohammedans in northern Africa.

This progress in the South could not but stir the lethargy of western Europe. When commerce began to revive, it encouraged a revolution in industry. So long as the manor system prevailed and each man—the farmer, miller, and blacksmith—was occupied in producing only what he and the other people on the estate needed, there was nothing to send abroad and nothing to exchange for luxuries. But when merchants began to come with tempting articles, the members of a community were encouraged to produce a surplus of goods above what they themselves needed, and to sell or exchange this surplus for commodities coming from a distance. Merchants and artisans gradually directed their energies toward the production of what others might buy, as well as of what was needed by the little group to which they belonged.

The romances of the twelfth century indicate that the West was astonished and delighted by the luxuries of the East—the rich fabrics, Oriental carpets, precious stones, perfumes, drugs, silks; the porcelains from China, spices from India, and cotton from Egypt. Venice introduced the silk industry from the East and the manufacture of those glass articles which the traveler may still buy in the Venetian shops. The West learned how to make silk and velvet as well as light and gauzy cotton and linen fabrics. The Eastern dyes were introduced, and Paris was soon imitating the tapestries of the Saracens. In exchange for those luxuries which they were unable to produce, the Flemish towns sent their woolen cloths to the East, and Italy its wines.

The Northern merchants dealt mainly with Venice and brought their wares across the Brenner Pass and down the Rhine, or sent them by sea to be exchanged in Flanders (see map). By the thirteenth century important centers of trade had come into being, some of which are still among the great commercial towns of the world. Hamburg, Lübeck, and Bremen carried on active trade with the countries on the Baltic and with England. Augsburg and Nuremberg, in southern Germany, became important on account of their situation on the line of trade between Italy and the North. Bruges and Ghent sent their manufactures everywhere. English commerce was relatively unimportant as yet compared with that of the great ports of the Mediterranean.

It was very difficult indeed to carry on business on a large scale in the Middle Ages, for various reasons. In the first place, as has been said, there was little money, and money is essential to easy buying and selling, unless people confine themselves merely to exchanging one article for another. There were few gold and silver mines in western Europe and consequently the kings and feudal lords could not supply enough coin. Moreover, the coins were crude, with such rough, irregular edges that many people yielded to the temptation to pare off a little of the precious metal before they passed the money on. "Clipping," as this was called, was harshly punished, but that did not stop the practice, which continued for hundreds of years. Nowadays our coins are perfectly round and usually have "milled" edges, so that no one would think of trying to appropriate bits of them as they pass through his hands.

It was universally believed that everything had a "just" price, which was merely enough to cover the cost of the materials used in its manufacture and to remunerate the maker for the work he had put into it. It was considered theoretically outrageous to ask more than the just price, no matter how anxious the purchaser might be to obtain the article.

MEDIEVAL COINS

The two upper coins reproduce the face and reverse of a silver penny of William the Conqueror's reign, and below is a silver groat of Edward III. The same irregularities in outline, it may be noted, are to be observed in Greek and Roman coins

Every manufacturer was required to keep a shop in which he offered at retail all that he made. Those who lived near a town were permitted to sell their products in the market place within the walls on condition that they sold directly to the consumers. They might not dispose of their whole stock to one dealer, for fear that if he had all there was of a commodity he might raise the price above the just one. These ideas made wholesale trade very difficult. But those most concerned probably found ways of compromising with the theories of the righteous.

Akin to these prejudices against wholesale business was that against interest. Money was believed to be a dead and sterile thing, and no one had a right to demand any return for lending it. Interest was considered wicked, since it was exacted by those who took advantage of the embarrassment of others. "Usury," as the taking of even the most moderate and reasonable rate of interest was then called, was strenuously forbidden by the laws of the Church. We find Church councils ordering that impenitent usurers should be refused Christian burial and have their wills annulled. So money lending, which is necessary to all great commercial and industrial undertakings, was left to the Jews, from whom Christian conduct was not expected.

This ill-starred people played a most important part in the economic development of Europe, but they were terribly maltreated by the Christians, who held them guilty of the supreme crime of putting Christ to death. The active persecution of the Jews did not, however, become common before the thirteenth century, when they first began to be required to wear a peculiar cap, or badge, which made them easily recognized and exposed them to constant insult. Later they were sometimes shut up in a particular quarter of the city, called the Jewry. As they were excluded from the guilds, they not unnaturally turned to the business of money lending, which no Christian might practice. Undoubtedly this occupation had much to do in causing their unpopularity. The kings permitted them to make loans, often at a most exorbitant rate; Philip Augustus allowed them to exact forty-six per cent, but reserved the right to extort their gains from them when the royal treasury was empty. In England the usual rate was a penny a pound for each week.

In the thirteenth century the Italians—Lombards, as the English called them [1]—began to go into a sort of banking business and greatly extended the employment of bills of exchange. They lent for nothing, but exacted damages for all delay in repayment. This appeared reasonable and right even to those

[1] There is a Lombard Street in the center of old London where one still finds banks.

who condemned ordinary interest. A history of free thought in business might be written as well as of freedom in religious ideas!

Another serious disadvantage which the medieval merchant had to face was the payment of an infinite number of tolls and duties which were demanded by the lords through whose domains his road passed. Not only were duties exacted on the highways, bridges, and at the fords, but those barons who were so fortunate as to have castles on a navigable river blocked the stream in such a way that the merchant could not bring his vessel through without a payment for the privilege.

The charges were usually small, but the way in which they were collected and the repeated delays must have been a serious source of irritation and loss to the merchants. For example, a certain monastery lying between Paris and the sea required that those hastening to town with fresh fish should stop and let the monks pick out what they thought worth three pence, with little regard to the condition in which they left the goods. When a boat laden with wine passed up the Seine to Paris, the agent of the lord of Poissy could have three casks broached, and, after trying them all, he could take a measure from the one he liked best. At the markets all sorts of dues had to be paid, such, for example, as fees for using the lord's scales or his measuring rod. Besides this, the great variety of coinage which existed in feudal Europe caused infinite perplexity and delay.

Commerce by sea had its own particular trials, by no means confined to the hazards of wind and wave, rock and shoal. Pirates were numerous in the North Sea. They were often organized and sometimes led by men of high rank, who appear to have regarded the business as no disgrace. The coasts were dangerous and lighthouses and beacons were few. Moreover, natural dangers were increased by false signals which wreckers used to lure ships to shore in order to plunder them.

With a view to mitigating these manifold perils, the towns early began to form unions for mutual defense. The most famous of these was that of the German cities, called the Hanseatic League. Lübeck was always the leader, but among the seventy towns which at one time and another were included in the confederation, we find Cologne, Brunswick, Danzig, and other centers of great importance. The union purchased and controlled settlements in London,—the so-called Steelyard near London Bridge,—at Wisby, Bergen, and the far-off Novgorod in Russia. They managed to monopolize nearly the whole trade on the Baltic and North Sea, through either treaties or the influence that they were able to bring to bear.[1]

The League made war on the pirates and did much to reduce the dangers of traffic. Instead of dispatching separate and defenseless merchantmen, their ships sailed out in fleets under the protection of a man-of-war. On one occasion the League undertook a successful war against the king of Denmark, who had interfered with their interests. At another time it declared war on England and brought her to terms. For two hundred years before the discovery of America, the League played a great part in the commercial affairs of western Europe; but it had begun to decline even before the discovery of new routes to the East and West Indies revolutionized trade.

It should be observed that, during the thirteenth, fourteenth, and fifteenth centuries, trade was not carried on between *nations*, but by the various *towns*, like Venice, Lübeck, Ghent, Bruges, Cologne. A merchant did not act or trade as an independent individual but as a member of a particular merchant guild, and he enjoyed the protection of his town and of the treaties it arranged. If a merchant from a certain town failed to pay a debt, a fellow townsman might be seized if found in the town where the debt was due. At the period of which we have been speaking, an inhabitant of London was considered as much of a foreigner in Bristol as was the merchant from Cologne or Antwerp. Only gradually did the towns merge into the nations to which their people belonged.

The increasing wealth of the merchants could not fail to raise them to a position of importance which earlier tradesmen had not enjoyed. They began to build fine houses and to buy the various comforts and luxuries which were finding their way into

[1] The ships of the Hanseatic League were very small (see below, p. 363).

western Europe. They wanted their sons to be educated, and so it came about that other people besides clergymen began to learn how to read and write. As early as the fourteenth century many of the books appear to have been written with a view of meeting the tastes and needs of the business class.

Representatives of the towns were summoned to the councils of the kings—into the English Parliament and the French Estates General about the year 1300, for the monarch was obliged to ask their advice when he demanded their money to carry on his government and his wars (see below, pp. 243 ff.). The rise of the business class alongside of the older orders of the clergy and nobility is one of the most momentous changes of the thirteenth century.

Gothic Architecture

Almost all the medieval buildings have disappeared in the ancient towns of Europe. The stone town walls, no longer adequate or needed for protection in our times, have been removed, and their place taken by broad and handsome avenues. The old houses have been torn down in order to widen and straighten the streets and permit the construction of modern dwellings. Here and there one can still find a walled town, but they are few in number and are merely curiosities.

Of the buildings erected in towns during the Middle Ages only the churches remain, but these fill the beholder with wonder and admiration. It seems impossible that the cities of the twelfth and thirteenth centuries, which were neither very large nor very rich, could possibly have found money enough to pay for them. It has been estimated that the bishop's church at Paris (Notre Dame) would cost at least five millions of dollars to reproduce, and there are a number of other cathedrals in France, England, Italy, Spain, and Germany which must have been almost as costly. No modern buildings equal them in beauty and grandeur, and they are the most striking memorial of the religious spirit, the power of the bishops, and the town pride of the Middle Ages.

[178]

PL. IV. FAÇADE OF THE CATHEDRAL AT REIMS

PL. V. ROSE WINDOW OF REIMS CATHEDRAL

The construction of a cathedral sometimes extended over two or three centuries, and much of the money for it must have been gathered penny by penny. It should be remembered that every one belonged in those days to the one great Catholic Church, so that the building of a new church was a matter of interest to the whole community—to men of every rank, from the bishop himself to the workman and the peasant.

ROMANESQUE CHURCH OF CHÂTEL-MONTAGNE IN THE
DEPARTMENT OF ALLIER, FRANCE

This is a pure Romanesque building with no alterations in a later style, such as are common. Heavy as the walls are, they are reënforced by buttresses along the sides. All of the arches are round, none of them pointed

Up to the twelfth century churches were built in what is called the *Romanesque,* or Roman-like, style because they resembled the solid old basilicas referred to in an earlier chapter (see p. 53, above). These Romanesque churches usually had *stone* ceilings, and it was necessary to make the walls very thick and solid to support them. There was a main aisle in the center, called the *nave,* and a narrower aisle on either side, separated from the nave by massive stone pillars, which helped to hold up the heavy ceiling. These pillars were connected by round arches of stone above them. The tops of the windows were round, and the ceiling was constructed of round vaults, somewhat like a stone bridge, so the *round* arches form one of the striking features of the Romanesque style which distinguishes it from the Gothic style, that followed it. The windows had to be small in order that the walls should not be weakened, so the Romanesque churches are rather dark inside.

FIGURES ON NOTRE DAME, PARIS

Such grotesque figures as these are very common adornments of Gothic buildings. They are often used for spouts to carry off the rain and are called gargoyles, that is, "throats" (compare our words "gargle" and "gurgle"). The two here represented are perched on a parapet of one of the church's towers

The architects of France were not satisfied, however, with this method of building, and in the twelfth century they invented a new and wonderful way of constructing churches and other buildings which enabled them to do away with the heavy walls and put high, wide, graceful windows in their place. This new style of architecture is known as the *Gothic*,[1] and its underlying principles can readily be understood from a little study of the accompanying diagram, which shows how a Gothic cathedral is supported, not by heavy walls, but by *buttresses*.

The architects discovered in the first place that the concave stone ceiling, which is known as the *vaulting* (*A*), could be

[1] The inappropriate name "Gothic" was given to the beautiful churches of the North by Italian architects of the sixteenth century, who did not like them and preferred to build in the style of the ancient Romans. The Italians with their "classical" tastes assumed that only German barbarians—whom they carelessly called Goths—could admire a Gothic cathedral.

supported by *ribs* (*B*). These could in turn be brought together and supported on top of pillars which rested on the floor of the church. So far so good! But the builders knew well enough that the pillars and ribs would be pushed over by the weight and outward "thrust" of the stone vaulting if they were not firmly supported from the outside. Instead of erecting heavy walls to insure this support they had recourse to buttresses (*D*), which they built quite outside the walls of the church, and connected them by means of "flying" buttresses (*C*) with the points where the pillars and ribs had the most tendency to push outward. *In this way a vaulted stone ceiling could be supported without the use of a massive wall.* This ingenious use of buttresses instead of walls is the fundamental principle of Gothic architecture, and it was discovered for the first time by the architects in the medieval towns.

The wall, no longer essential for supporting the ceiling, was used only to

CROSS SECTION OF AMIENS
CATHEDRAL

It will be noticed that there is a row of rather low windows opening under the roof of the aisle. These constitute the so-called *triforium* (*E*). Above them is the *clerestory* (*F*), the windows of which open between the flying buttresses. So it came about that the walls of a Gothic church were in fact mainly windows. The Egyptians were the first to invent the clerestory inclose the building, and windows could be built as high and wide as pleased the architect. By the use of *pointed* instead of *round* arches it was possible to give great variety to the windows and vaulting. So pointed arches came into general use, and the Gothic is often called the "pointed" style on this account, although the use of the ribs and buttresses is the chief peculiarity of that form of architecture, not the pointed arch.

The light from the huge windows (those at Beauvais are fifty to fifty-five feet high) would have been too intense had it not been softened by the stained glass, set in exquisite stone tracery, of varied and graceful design. The stained glass of the medieval cathedral, especially in France, where the glass workers brought their art to the greatest perfection, was one of its chief glories. By far the greater part of this old glass has of course been destroyed, but it is still so highly prized that every bit of it is now carefully preserved, for it has never since been equaled. A window set with odd bits of it pieced together like crazy patchwork is more beautiful, in its rich and jewel-like coloring, than the finest modern work.

FLYING BUTTRESSES OF NOTRE DAME, PARIS

The size of the buttresses and the height of the clerestory windows of a great cathedral are well shown here

Pl. vi. Interior of Exeter Cathedral

PL. VII. NORTH PORCH OF CHARTRES CATHEDRAL

GOTHIC ARCHITECTURE

As the skill of the architects increased they became bolder and bolder and erected churches that were marvels of lightness and delicacy of ornament, without sacrificing dignity or beauty of proportion. The façade of Reims cathedral was one of the most famous examples of the best work of the thirteenth century, with its multitude of sculptured figures and its gigantic rose window, filled with exquisite stained glass of great brilliancy. The interior of Exeter cathedral, although by no means so spacious as a number of the French churches, affords an

GROTESQUE HEADS, REIMS CATHEDRAL

Here and there about a Gothic cathedral the stone carvers were accustomed to place grotesque and comical figures and faces. During the process of restoring the cathedral at Reims a number of these heads were brought together, and the photograph was taken upon which the illustration is based

excellent example of the beauty and impressiveness of a Gothic interior. The porch before the north entrance of Chartres cathedral is a magnificent example of fourteenth-century work.

One of the charms of a Gothic building is the profusion of carving—statues of saints and rulers and scenes from the Bible, cut in stone. The same kind of stone was used for both constructing the building and making the statues, so they harmonize perfectly. Here and there the Gothic stone carvers would introduce amusing faces or comical animals.

In the fourteenth and fifteenth centuries Gothic buildings other than churches were built. The most striking and important of these were the guild halls, erected by the rich corporations of merchants, and the town halls of important cities. But the Gothic style has always seemed specially appropriate for churches. Its lofty aisles and open floor spaces, its soaring arches leading the eye toward heaven, and its glowing windows suggesting the glories of paradise, may well have fostered the faith of the medieval Christian.

EVE AND THE SERPENT, REIMS

The Italian Cities of the Renaissance

We have been speaking so far of the town life in northern Europe in the twelfth and thirteenth centuries. We must now see how the Italian towns in the following two centuries reached a degree of prosperity and refinement undreamed of north of the Alps. Within their walls learning and art made such extraordinary progress that a special name is often given to the period when they flourished—the *Renaissance*,[1] or new birth. The Italian towns, like those of ancient Greece, were each a little state with its own peculiar life and institutions. Some of them, like Rome, Milan, and Pisa, had been important in Roman times; others, like Venice, Florence, and Genoa, did not become conspicuous until about the time of the Crusades.

The map of Italy at the beginning of the fourteenth century was still divided into three zones, as it had been in the time of the Hohenstaufens.[2] To the south lay the kingdom of Naples.

---

[1] This word, although originally French, has come into such common use that it is quite permissible to pronounce it as if it were English,—*re-nā'sens.*

[2] See map above, p. 133.

Then came the states of the Church, extending diagonally across the peninsula. To the north and west lay the group of city-states to which we now turn our attention.

Of these none was more celebrated than Venice, which in the history of Europe ranks in importance with Paris and London. This singular town was built upon a group of sandy islets lying

A SCENE IN VENICE

Boats, called gondolas, took the place of carriages in Venice; one might reach any point in the city by some one of the numerous canals, which take the place of streets. There are also narrow lanes along the canals, crossing them here and there by bridges, so one can wander about the town on foot

in the Adriatic Sea, about two miles from the mainland. It was protected from the waves by a long, narrow sand bar similar to those which fringe the Atlantic coast from New Jersey southward. Such a situation would not ordinarily have been deliberately chosen as the site of a great city; but it was a good place for fishermen, and its very desolation and inaccessibility recommended it to those settlers who fled from their homes on the mainland during the barbarian invasions. As time went

[185]

on, the location proved to have its advantages commercially, and even before the Crusades Venice had begun to engage in foreign trade. Its enterprises carried it eastward, and it early acquired possessions across the Adriatic and in the Orient. The

ST. MARK'S AND THE DOGE'S PALACE IN VENICE

One sees the façade of St. Mark's to the left, and that of the doge's palace beyond. The church, modeled after one in Constantinople, was planned before the First Crusade and is adorned with numerous colored marble columns and slabs brought from the East. The interior is covered with mosaics, some of which go back to the twelfth and the thirteenth centuries. The façade is also adorned with brilliant mosaics. St. Mark's "is unique among the buildings of the world in respect to its unparalleled richness of material and decoration." The doge's palace contained the government offices and the magnificent halls in which the senate and Council of Ten met. The palace was begun about 1300, and the façade we see in the picture was commenced about a hundred years later. It shows the influence of the Gothic style, which penetrated into northern Italy

influence of this intercourse with the East is plainly shown in the celebrated church of St. Mark, whose domes and decorations suggest Constantinople rather than Italy.

It was not until early in the fifteenth century that Venice found it to her interest to extend her sway upon the Italian

[186]

mainland. She doubtless believed it dangerous to permit her rival, Milan, to get possession of the Alpine passes through which her goods found their way north. It may be, too, that she preferred to draw her food supplies from the neighborhood instead of transporting them across the Adriatic from her eastern possessions. Moreover, all the Italian cities except Venice already controlled a larger or smaller area of country about them.

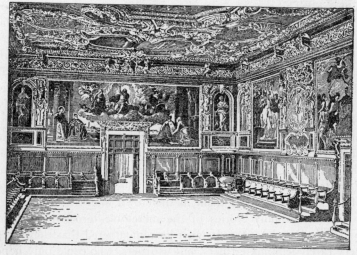

SENATE CHAMBER IN THE DOGE'S PALACE

This is an example of the magnificent decoration of the rooms used by the Venetian government. It was adorned by celebrated painters in the sixteenth century, when Venice became famous for its artists

In the fifteenth century Venice reached the height of its prosperity. It had a population of two hundred thousand, which was very large for those days. It had three hundred seagoing vessels which went to and fro in the Mediterranean, carrying wares from the East to the West. It had a war fleet of forty-five galleys, manned by eleven thousand marines ready to fight the battles of the republic, and had agents in every important city of Europe. But when the route to India by sea was discovered (see below, pp. 221 ff.), Venice could no longer keep control of the trade with the East, and while it remained an important city, it no longer enjoyed its former influence and power.

Although Venice was called a republic, it was really governed by a very small group of persons. In 1311, after a rebellion, the famous Council of Ten was created as a sort of committee of public safety. The whole government, domestic and foreign, was placed in its hands, in conjunction with the senate and the *doge* (that is, duke), the nominal head of the republic. The government, thus concentrated in the hands of a very few, was carried on with great secrecy, so that public discussion, such as prevailed in Florence and led to innumerable revolutions there, was unheard of in Venice. The Venetian merchant was such a busy person that he was quite willing that the State should exercise its functions without his interference.

Venice often came to blows with other rival cities, especially Genoa, but its citizens lived quietly at home under the government of its senate, the Council of Ten, and the doge. The other Italian towns were not only fighting one another much of the time, but their government was often in the hands of *despots*, somewhat like the old Greek tyrants, who got control of towns and managed them in their own interest.

There are many stories of the incredible ferocity exhibited by the Italian despots. It must be remembered that they were very rarely legitimate rulers, but usurpers, who could only hope to retain their power so long as they could keep their subjects in check and defend themselves against equally illegitimate usurpers in the neighboring cities. This situation developed a high degree of sagacity, and many of the despots found it to their interest to govern well and even to give dignity to their rule by patronizing artists and men of letters. But the despot usually made many bitter enemies and was almost necessarily suspicious of treason on the part of those about him. He was ever conscious that at any moment he might fall a victim to the dagger or the poison cup.

The Italian towns carried on their wars among themselves largely by means of hired troops. When a military expedition was proposed, a bargain was made with one of the professional leaders (*condottieri*), who provided the necessary force. As the soldiers had no more interest in the conflict than did those whom they opposed, who were likewise hired for the occasion, the fight was not usually very bloody; for the object of each side was to capture the other without unnecessarily rough treatment.

It sometimes happened that the leader who had conquered a town for his employer appropriated the fruits of the victory for himself. This occurred in the case of Milan in 1450. The old line of despots (the Visconti) having died out, the citizens hired a certain captain, named Francesco Sforza, to assist them in a war against Venice, whose possessions

TOMB OF AN ITALIAN DESPOT

The family of the Visconti maintained themselves many years as despots of Milan. Gian Galeazzo Visconti began in 1396 a magnificent Carthusian monastery not far from Milan, one of the most beautiful structures in Italy. Here, long after his death, a monument was erected to him as founder of the monastery. The monument was begun about 1500 but not completed for several decades

now extended almost to those of Milan. When Sforza had repelled the Venetians, the Milanese found it impossible to get rid of him, and he and his successors became rulers over the town.

An excellent notion of the position and policy of the Italian despots may be derived from a little treatise called *The Prince*, written by the distinguished Florentine historian, Machiavelli (1469-1527). The writer appears to have intended his book as a practical manual for the despots of his time. It is a cold-blooded discussion of the ways in which a usurper may best retain his control over a town after he has once got possession of it. The author even takes up the questions as to how far princes should consider their promises when it is inconvenient to keep them, and how many of the inhabitants the despot may wisely kill. Machiavelli concludes that the Italian princes who have not observed their engagements overscrupulously, and who have boldly put their political adversaries out of the way, have fared better than their more conscientious rivals.

The history of Florence, perhaps the most important of the Italian cities, differs in many ways from that of Venice and of the despotisms of which Milan was an example. Florence was a republic, and all classes claimed the right to interest themselves in the government. This led to constant changes in the constitution and frequent struggles between the different political parties. When one party got the upper hand it generally expelled its chief opponents from the city. Exile was a terrible punishment to a Florentine, for Florence was not merely his native city—it was his *country*, and loved and honored as such.

By the middle of the fifteenth century Florence had come under the control of the great family of the Medici, whose members played the rôle of very enlightened political bosses. By quietly watching the elections and secretly controlling the selection of city officials, they governed without letting it be suspected that the people had lost their power. The most distinguished member of the House of Medici was Lorenzo the Magnificent (d. 1492); under his rule Florence reached the height of its glory in art and literature.

As one wanders about Florence to-day, he is impressed with the contradictions of the Renaissance period. The streets are

PL. VIII. GHIBERTI'S DOORS AT FLORENCE

PL. IX. HOLY FAMILY, BY ANDREA DEL SARTO

lined with the palaces of the noble families to whose rivalries much of the continual disturbance was due. The lower stories of these buildings are constructed of great stones, like fortresses, and their windows are barred like those of a prison; yet within they were often furnished with the greatest taste and luxury. For in spite of the disorder, against which the rich protected themselves by making their houses half strongholds, the beautiful churches, noble public buildings, and works of art which now fill the museums indicate that mankind has never, perhaps, reached a higher degree of perfection in the arts of peace than amidst the turmoil of this restless town.

THE PALACE OF THE MEDICI IN FLORENCE

This was erected about 1435 by Cosimo de' Medici, and in it Lorenzo the Magnificent conducted the government of Florence and entertained the men of letters and artists with whom he liked best to associate. It shows how fortresslike the lower portions of a Florentine palace were, in order to protect the owner from attack

During the same period in which Venice and Florence became leaders in wealth and refinement, Rome, the capital of the popes, likewise underwent a great change. After the popes returned from their seventy years' residence in France and Avignon (see below, p. 280) they found the town in a dilapidated state. For years they were able to do little to restore it, as there was a long period during which the papacy was weakened by the existence of a rival line of popes who

CATHEDRAL AND BELL TOWER
AT FLORENCE

The church was begun in 1296 and completed in 1436. The great dome built by the architect Brunelleschi has made his name famous. It is 300 feet high. The façade is modern but after an old design. The bell tower, or campanile, was begun by the celebrated painter Giotto about 1335 and completed about fifty years later. It is richly adorned with sculpture and colored marbles and is considered the finest structure of the kind in the world

continued to live at Avignon. When the "great schism" was over (see below, p. 281) and all the European nations once more acknowledged the pope at Rome (1417), it became possible to improve the city and revive some of its ancient glory. Architects, painters, and men of letters were called in and handsomely paid by the popes to erect and adorn magnificent buildings and to collect a great library in the Vatican palace.

The ancient basilica of St. Peter's (see above, p. 59) no longer satisfied the aspirations of the popes. It was gradually torn down, and after many changes of plan the present celebrated church with its vast dome and imposing approach took its place. The old palace of the Lateran, where the government of the popes had been carried on for a thousand years, had been deserted after the return from Avignon, and the new palace of the Vatican

PL. X. PORTRAIT BY JAN VAN EYCK

PL. XI. MELANCHOLIA, BY ALBRECHT DURER

was gradually constructed to the right of St. Peter's. It has thousands of rooms great and small, some of them adorned by the most distinguished of the Italian painters, and others filled with ancient statuary.

St. Peter's and the Vatican Palace

This is the largest church in the world. It is about 700 feet long, including the portico, and 435 feet high, from the pavement to the cross on the dome. The reconstruction was begun as early as 1450 but it proceeded very slowly. Several great architects, Bramante, Raphael, Michael Angelo, and others were intrusted with the work. After many changes of plan the new church was finally in condition to consecrate in 1626. The construction of the vast palace of the popes, which one sees to the right of the church, was carried on during the same period. It is said to have no less than eleven thousand rooms. Some of them are used for museums and others are celebrated for the frescoes which adorn their walls, by Raphael, Michael Angelo, and other of Italy's greatest artists

As one visits Venice, Florence, and Rome to-day he may still see, almost perfectly preserved, many of the finest of the buildings, paintings, and monuments which belong to the period we have been discussing.

CHAPTER X

BOOKS AND KNOWLEDGE IN THE MIDDLE AGES

How the Modern Languages Originated. The Troubadours and Chivalry. Medieval Science. Medieval Universities and Studies. Beginnings of Modern Inventions. The Art of the Renaissance. European Exploration of the Globe

How the Modern Languages Originated

WE should leave the Middle Ages with a very imperfect notion of the background of modern civilization if we did not stop to consider what people were thinking about during that period, what they had to read, what they believed about the world in which they lived and the important discoveries they were making.

To begin with, the Middle Ages differed from our own time in the very general use then made of Latin, in both writing and speaking. The language of the Roman Empire continued to be used in the thirteenth century, and long after; all books that made any claim to learning were written in Latin; the professors in the universities lectured in Latin, learned friends wrote to one another in Latin, and state papers, treaties, and legal documents were drawn up in the same language. The ability of every educated person to make use of Latin, as well as of his native tongue, was a great advantage at a time when there were many obstacles to intercourse among the various nations. It helps to explain, for example, the remarkable way in which the pope kept in touch with all the clergymen of western Christendom, and the ease with which students, friars, and merchants could wander from one country to another. There is no more interesting or important revolution than that by which the languages of the people in the various European countries gradually pushed aside the ancient tongue and took its place, so that even scholars scarcely ever think now of writing books in Latin.

In order to understand how it came about that two languages, the Latin and the native speech, were both commonly used in all the countries of western Europe all through the

Middle Ages,[1] we must glance at the origin of the modern languages. These all fall into two quite distinct groups, the *Germanic* and the *Romance*.

Those German peoples who had continued to live outside of the Roman Empire, or who, during the invasions, had not settled far enough within its bounds to be led, as were the Franks in Gaul, to adopt the tongue of those they had conquered, naturally adhered to the language they had always used; namely, the particular Germanic tongue which their forefathers had spoken for untold generations. From the various languages used by the German barbarians, modern German, English, Dutch, Swedish, Norwegian, Danish, and Icelandic are derived.

The second group of languages developed within the territory which had formed a part of the Roman Empire, and includes modern French, Italian, Spanish, and Portuguese. It has now been clearly proved, by a very minute study of the old forms of words, that these Romance languages were one and all derived from the *spoken* Latin, employed by the soldiers, merchants, and people at large. This differed considerably from the elaborate and elegant written Latin which was used, for example, by Cicero and Cæsar. It was undoubtedly much simpler in its grammar and varied a good deal in different regions; a Gaul, for instance, could not pronounce the words like a Roman. Moreover, in conversation people did not always use the same words as those employed in books. For example, a horse was commonly spoken of as *caballus,* whereas a writer would use the word *equus;* it is from *caballus* that the word for "horse" in Spanish, Italian, and French is derived (*caballo, cavallo, cheval*).

---

[1] In Germany the books published annually in the German language did not exceed those in Latin until after 1690.

It has been a common situation to have the priests and scholars using some ancient, revered, "classical" tongue instead of that of the people at large. China, India, Egypt, Assyria, and ancient Judea offer examples. The Greeks and our modern nations form *exceptions* rather than follow the rule in employing the same language whatever the theme in hand or the social position of the speaker.

As time went on the spoken language diverged farther and farther from the written. Latin is a troublesome speech on account of its complicated inflections and grammatical rules, which can be mastered only after a great deal of study. The people of the more remote Roman provinces and the incoming barbarians naturally paid very little attention to the niceties of syntax and found easy ways of saying what they wished.[1]

Yet several centuries elapsed after the German invasions before there was anything written in the language used in conversation. So long as the uneducated could understand the correct Latin of the books when they heard it read or spoken, there was no necessity of writing anything in their familiar daily speech. But by the time Charlemagne came to the throne the gulf between the spoken and the written language had become so great that he advised that sermons should be given thereafter in the language of the people, who, apparently, could no longer follow the Latin.

Although little was written in any German language before Charlemagne's time, there is no doubt that the Germans possessed an unwritten literature, which was passed down by word of mouth for several centuries before any of it was written out.

The oldest form of English is commonly called Anglo-Saxon and is so different from the language which we use that, in order to be read, it must be learned like a foreign language. We hear of an English poet, as early as Bede's time, a century before Charlemagne. A manuscript of an Anglo-Saxon epic, called *Beowulf,* has been preserved which belongs perhaps to the close of the eighth century. The interest which King Alfred displayed in the English language has already been mentioned. This old form of our language prevailed until after the Norman Conquest; the *Anglo-Saxon Chronicle,* which does not close until 1154, is written in pure Anglo-Saxon. Here is an example:

---

[1] Even the monks and others who wrote Latin in the Middle Ages often did not know enough to follow strictly the rules of the language. Moreover, they introduced many new words to meet the new conditions and the needs of the time, such as *imprisonare,* "to imprison"; *utlagare,* "to outlaw"; *baptizare,* "to baptize"; *foresta,* "forest"; *feudum,* "fief," etc.

HOW THE MODERN LANGUAGES ORIGINATED

"Here on thissum geare Willelm cyng geaf Rodberde eorle thone eorldom on Northymbraland. Da komon tha landes menn togeanes him & hine ofslogen, & ix hund manna mid him." [1] In modern English this reads: "In this year King William gave the Earl Robert the earldom of Northumberland. Then came the men of the country against him and slew him, and nine hundred men with him."

By the middle of the thirteenth century, two hundred years after the Norman Conquest, English begins to look somewhat familiar:

> And Aaron held up his hond
> To the water and the more lond;
> Tho cam thor up schwilc froschkes here
> The dede al folc Egipte dere;
> Summe woren wilde, and summe tame,
> And tho hem deden the moste schame;
> In huse, in drinc, in metes, in bed,
> It cropen and maden hem for-dred. . . .

> And Aaron held up his hand
> To the water and the greater land;
> Then came there up such host of frogs
> That did all Egypt's folk harm;
> Some were wild, and some were tame,
> And those caused them the most shame;
> In house, in drink, in meats, in bed,
> They crept and made them in great dread. . . .

Chaucer (about 1340-1400) was the first great English writer whose works are now read with pleasure, although one is sometimes puzzled by his spelling and certain words which are no longer used. This is the way one of his tales opens:

> A poure wydow somdel stope in age,
> Was whilom dwellyng in a narwe cotage,
> Bisyde a grove, stondyng in a dale.
> This wydwe of wichh I tele yow my tale,
> Syn thilke day that sche was last a wif,
> In pacience ladde a ful symple lyf.

[1] In writing Anglo-Saxon two old letters are used for *th*, one (þ) for the sound in "thin" and the other (ð) for that in "father." The use of these old letters serves to make the language look more different from that of to-day than it is.

In the Middle Ages, however, French, not English, was the most important of the national languages of western Europe. In France a vast literature was produced in the language of the people during the twelfth and thirteenth centuries which profoundly affected the books written in Italy, Spain, Germany, and England.

Two quite different languages had gradually developed in France from the spoken Latin of the Roman Empire. To the north, French was spoken; to the south, Provençal.[1]

Very little in the ancient French language written before the year 1100 has been preserved. The West Franks undoubtedly began much earlier to sing of their heroes, of the great deeds of Clovis and Charles Martel. These famous rulers were, however, completely overshadowed later by Charlemagne, who became the unrivaled hero of medieval poetry and romance. It was believed that he had reigned for a hundred and twenty-five years, and the most marvelous exploits were attributed to him and his knights. He was supposed, for instance, to have led a crusade to Jerusalem. Such themes as these—more legend than history—were woven into long epics, which were the first written literature of the Frankish people. These poems, combined with the stories of adventure, developed a spirit of patriotic enthusiasm among the French which made them regard "fair France" as the especial care of Providence.

The famous *Song of Roland*, the chief character of which was one of Charlemagne's captains, was written a little before the First Crusade. In the latter part of the twelfth century the romances of King Arthur and his Knights of the Round Table began to appear. These enjoyed great popularity in all western Europe for centuries, and they are by no means forgotten yet. Arthur, of whose historical existence no one can be

---

[1] Of course there was no sharp line of demarcation between the people who used the one language or the other, nor was Provençal confined to southern France. The language of Catalonia, beyond the Pyrenees, was essentially the same as that of Provence. French was called *langue d'oïl*, and the southern language *langue d'oc*, each after the word used for "yes" (*oui*).

quite sure, was supposed to have been king of Britain shortly after the Saxons gained a foothold in the island.[1]

In other long poems of the time, Alexander the Great, Cæsar, and other ancient worthies appear as heroes. The absolute disregard of historical facts and the tendency to represent the warriors of Troy and Rome as medieval knights show the inability of the medieval mind to understand that the past could have been different from the present. All these romances are full of picturesque adventures and present a vivid picture of the valor and loyalty of the true knight, as well as of his ruthlessness and contempt for human life.

Besides the long and elaborate epics, like *Roland,* and the romances in verse and prose, there were numberless short stories in verse (the *fabliaux*), which usually dealt with the incidents of everyday life, especially with the comical ones. Then there were the fables, the most famous of which are the stories of Reynard the Fox, which were satires upon the customs of the time, particularly the weaknesses of the priests and monks.

The Troubadours and Chivalry

Turning now to southern France, the beautiful songs of the *troubadours,* which were the glory of the Provençal tongue, reveal a gay and polished society at the courts of the numerous feudal princes. The rulers not merely protected and encouraged the poets—they aspired to be poets themselves and to enter the ranks of the troubadours, as the composers of these elegant verses were called. These songs were always sung to an accompaniment of some instrument, usually the lute. The troubadours traveled from court to court, not only in France, but north into Germany and south into Italy, carrying with them the southern French poetry and customs. We have few examples of Provençal before the year 1100, but from that

[1] Malory's *Mort d'Arthur,* a collection of the stories of the Round Table made in the fifteenth century for English readers, is the best place to turn for these famous stories.

time on, for two centuries, countless songs were written, and many of the troubadours enjoyed an international reputation. The terrible Albigensian crusade brought misery and death into the sprightly circles which had gathered about the Count of Toulouse and other rulers who had treated the heretics too leniently (see above, p. 160).

For the student of history, the chief interest of the long poems of northern France and the songs of the South lies in the insight that they give into the ideals and aspirations of this feudal period. These are usually summed up in the term *chivalry,* or *knighthood,* of which a word may properly be said here, since we should know little of it were it not for the literature of which we have been speaking. The knights play the chief rôle in all the medieval romances; and, since many of the troubadours belonged to the knightly class, they naturally have much to say of it in their songs.

Chivalry was not a formal institution established at any particular moment. Like feudalism, with which it was closely connected, it had no founder, but appeared spontaneously throughout western Europe to meet the ideas and desires of the period. When the youth of good family had been carefully trained to ride his horse, use his sword, and manage his hawk in the hunt, he was made a *knight* by a ceremony in which the Church took part, although the knighthood was actually conferred by an older knight.

The knight was a Christian soldier, and he and his fellows were supposed to form, in a way, a separate order, with high ideals of the conduct befitting their class. Knighthood was not, however, membership in an association with officers and a definite constitution. It was an ideal, half-imaginary society—a society to which even those who enjoyed the title of king or duke were proud to belong. One was not born a knight as he might be born a duke or count, and could become one only through the ceremony mentioned above. Although most knights belonged to the nobility, one might be a noble and still not belong to the knightly order, and, on the other hand, one who was baseborn might be raised to knighthood on account of some valorous deed.

The knight must, in the first place, be a Christian and must obey and defend the Church on all occasions. He must respect all forms of weakness and defend the helpless wherever he might find them. He must fight the infidel Mohammedans ceaselessly, pitilessly, and never give way before the enemy. He must perform all his feudal duties, be faithful in all things to his lord, never lie or violate his plighted word. He must be generous and give freely and ungrudgingly to the needy. He must be faithful to his lady and be ready to defend her and her honor at all costs. Everywhere he must be the champion of the right against injustice and oppression. In short, chivalry was the Christianized profession of arms.

In the stories of King Arthur and his Knights of the Round Table there is a picture of the ideal knight. The dead Lancelot is addressed by one of his sorrowing companions as follows: "Thou wert the courtliest knight that ever bare shield, and thou wert the truest friend to thy lover that ever bestrode horse, and thou wert the truest lover among sinful men that ever loved woman, and thou wert the kindest man that ever struck with sword, and thou wert the goodliest person that ever came among the crowd of knights, and thou wert the meekest man and the gentlest that ever ate in hall among ladies, and thou wert the sternest knight to thy mortal foe that ever put spear in breast."

The Germans also made their contribution to the literature of chivalry. The German poets of the thirteenth century are called *Minnesingers*. Like the troubadours, whom they greatly admired, they usually sang of love, hence their name (German, *Minne*). The most famous of the minnesingers was Walther von der Vogelweide (d. about 1228), whose songs are full of enthusiasm for his German fatherland. Wolfram von Eschenbach (d. about 1225) in his story of *Parsifal* gives the long and sad adventures of a knight in search of the Holy Grail—the sacred vessel which had held the blood of Christ, which only a person perfectly pure in thought, word, and deed could hope to behold.

Medieval Science

So long as all books had to be copied by hand, there were, of course, but few of them compared with those of modern times. The literature of which we have been speaking was not in general *read*, but was only *listened to*, as it was sung or recited by those who made it their profession. Wherever the wandering troubadour or minnesinger appeared he was sure of a delighted audience for his songs and stories, both serious and light. People unfamiliar with Latin could, however, learn little of the past, for there were no translations of the great classics of Greece and Rome, of Homer, Plato, Cicero, or Livy. All that they could know of ancient history was derived from the fantastic romances referred to above, which had for their theme the quite preposterous deeds ascribed to Alexander the Great, Æneas, and Cæsar. As for their own history, the epics relating to the earlier course of events in France and the rest of Europe were hopelessly confused. For example, the writers attributed to Charlemagne a great part of the acts of the Frankish kings from Clovis to Pippin.

Of what we should call scientific books there were practically none. It is true that there was a kind of encyclopedia in verse which gave a great deal of misinformation about things in general. Every one continued to believe, as the Greeks and Romans had done, in strange animals like the unicorn, the dragon, and the phenix, and in still stranger habits of real animals. A single example will suffice to show what passed for zoölogy in the thirteenth century.

"There is a little beast made like a lizard and such is its nature that it will extinguish fire should it fall into it. The beast is so cold and of such a quality that fire is not able to burn it, nor will trouble happen in the place where it shall be." This beast signifies the holy man who lives by faith, who "will never have hurt from fire nor will hell burn him. . . . This beast we name also by another name, salamander. It is accustomed to mount into apple-trees, poisons the apples, and in a well where it falls it poisons the water."

"The eagle [we are told by a learned writer of the time of Henry II], on account of its great heat, mixeth very cold stones with its eggs when it sitteth on them, so that the heat shall not destroy them. In the same way our words, when we speak with undue heat, should later be tempered with discretion, so that we may conciliate in the end those whom we offended by the beginning of our speech."

It will be noticed that the habits of the animals were supposed to have some moral or religious meaning and carry with them a lesson for mankind. It may be added that this and similar stories were centuries old and are found in the encyclopedias of the Romans. The most improbable things were repeated from generation to generation without its occurring to any one to inquire if there was any truth in them. Even the most learned men of the time believed in astrology and in the miraculous virtues of herbs and gems. For instance, Albertus Magnus, one of the most distinguished thinkers of the thirteenth century, says that a sapphire will drive away boils and that the diamond can be softened in the blood of a stag, which will work best if the stag has been fed on wine and parsley.

From the Roman and early Christian writers the Middle Ages got the idea of strange races of men and manlike creatures of various kinds. We find the following in an encyclopedia of the thirteenth century: "Satyrs be somewhat like men, and have crooked noses, and horns in the forehead, and are like to goats in their feet. St. Anthony saw such an one in the wilderness. . . . These wonderful beasts be divers; for some of them be called Cynocephali, for they have heads as hounds, and seem beasts rather than men; and some be called Cyclops, and have that name because each of them hath but one eye, and that in the middle of the forehead; and some be all headless and noseless and their eyes be in the shoulder; and some have plain faces without nostrils, and the nether lips of them stretch so that they veil therewith their faces when they be in the heat of the sun. Also in Scythia be some with so great and large ears, that they spread their ears and cover all their bodies with them, and these be called Panchios. . . .

"And others there be in Ethiopia, and each of them have only one foot, so great and so large that they beshadow themselves with the foot when they lie gasping on the ground in strong heat of the sun; and yet they be so swift that they be likened to hounds in swiftness of running, and therefore among the Greeks they be called Cynopodes. Also some have the soles of their feet turned backward behind the legs, and in each foot eight toes, and such go about and sojourn in the desert of Lybia."

Two old subjects of study were revived and received great attention in Europe from the thirteenth century onward until recent times. These were *astrology* and *alchemy*.

Astrology was based on the belief that the planets influence the make-up of men and consequently their fate. Following an idea of the Greek philosophers, especially Aristotle, it was believed that all things were compounded of "the four elements" earth, air, fire, and water. Each person was a particular mixture of these four elements, and the position of the planets at the time of his birth was supposed to influence his mixture or "temperament."

By knowing a person's temperament one could judge what he ought to do in order to be successful in life, and what he should avoid. For example, if one were born under the influence of Venus he should be on his guard against violent love and should choose for a trade something connected with dress or adornment; if he were born under Mars he might make armor or horseshoes or become a successful soldier. Many common words are really astrological terms, such as "ill-starred," "disastrous," "jovial," "saturnine," "mercurial," (derived from the names of the planets). Astrology was taught in the universities because it was supposed to be necessary for physicians to choose times when the stars were favorable for particular kinds of medical treatment.

Alchemy was chemistry directed toward the discovery of a method of turning the baser metals, like lead and copper, into gold and silver; also of a panacea for all diseases. The alchemists, even if they did not succeed in their chief aims, learned a great deal incidentally in their laboratories, and finally our modern chemistry emerged from alchemy. Like astrology, alchemy goes back to ancient times, and the people of the thirteenth century got most of their ideas through the Mohammedans, who had in turn got theirs from the Greek books on the subjects.

Medieval Universities and Studies

All European countries now have excellent schools, colleges, and universities. These had their beginning in the later Middle Ages. With the incoming of the barbarous Germans and the break-up of the Roman Empire, education largely disappeared in western Europe and for hundreds of years there was nothing, outside of Italy and Spain, corresponding to our universities and colleges. Some of the schools which the bishops and abbots had established in accordance with Charlemagne's commands (see above, pp. 90 ff.) were, it is true, maintained all through the dark and disorderly times which followed his death. But the little that we know of the instruction offered in them would indicate that it was very elementary.

About the year 1100 an ardent young man named Abelard started out from his home in Brittany to visit all the places where he might hope to receive instruction in logic and philosophy, in which, like all his learned contemporaries, he was especially interested. He reports that he found teachers in several of the French towns, particularly in Paris, who were attracting large numbers of students to listen to their lectures upon logic, rhetoric, and theology. Abelard soon showed his superiority to his teachers by defeating them—according to his own story—several times in debate. So he began lecturing on his own account, and such was his success that thousands of students flocked to hear him.

Abelard did not found the University of Paris, as has sometimes been supposed, but he did a great deal to make the discussions of theological problems popular, and by his attractive method of teaching he greatly increased the number of those who wished to study.

Before the end of the twelfth century the teachers had become so numerous in Paris that they formed a union, or guild, for the advancement of their interests. This union of professors was called by the usual name for corporations in the Middle Ages, _universitas;_ hence our word "university." The king and the pope both favored the university and granted the teachers and students many of the privileges of the clergy, a class to which they were regarded as belonging, because learning had for so many centuries been confined to the clergy.

About the time that we find the beginnings of a university or guild of professors at Paris, another great institution of learning was growing up at Bologna. Here the chief attention was given, not to theology, as at Paris, but to the study of the law, both Roman and church (canon) law. Students began to stream to Bologna in greater and greater numbers. In order to protect themselves in a town where they were regarded as strangers, they also organized themselves into unions, which became so powerful that they were able to force the professors to obey the rules which they laid down.

The University of Oxford was founded in the time of Henry II, probably by English students and masters who had become discontented at Paris for some reason. The University of Cambridge, as well as numerous universities in France, Italy, and Spain, were founded in the thirteenth century. The German universities were established somewhat later, most of them in the latter half of the fourteenth and in the fifteenth centuries. The northern institutions generally took the great mother university on the Seine as their model, while those in southern Europe usually adopted the methods of Bologna.

When, after some years of study, a student was examined by the professors, he was, if successful, admitted to the corporation of teachers and became a _master_ himself. What we call a _degree_ to-day was originally, in the medieval universities, nothing more than the right to teach; but in the thirteenth century many who did not care to become professors in our sense of the word began to desire the honorable title of *master* or *doctor* (which is only the Latin word for "teacher").[1]

The students in the medieval universities were of all ages, from thirteen to forty, and even older. There were no university buildings, and in Paris the lectures were given in the Latin Quarter, in Straw Street, so called from the straw strewn on the floors of the hired rooms where the lecturer explained the textbook, with the students squatting on the floor before him. There were no laboratories, for there was no experimentation. All that was required was a copy of the textbook. This the lecturer explained sentence by sentence, and the students listened and sometimes took notes.

The most striking peculiarity of the instruction in the medieval university was the supreme deference paid to Aristotle. Most of the courses of lectures were devoted to the explanation of some one of his numerous treatises—his *Physics,* his *Metaphysics,* his treatises on logic, his *Ethics,* his minor works upon the soul, heaven and earth, etc. Only his logical treatises had been known to Abelard, as all his other works had been forgotten in western Europe. But early in the thirteenth century all his comprehensive contributions to science reached the West, either from Constantinople or through the Arabs, who had brought them to Spain. The Latin translations were bad and obscure, and the lecturer had enough to do to give some meaning to them, to explain what the Arab philosophers had said of them, and to reconcile them to the teachings of Christianity.

Aristotle was, of course, a pagan. He was uncertain whether the soul continued to exist after death; he had never heard of the Bible and knew nothing of the salvation of man through Christ. One would have supposed that he would have been promptly rejected with horror by the ardent Christian believers of the Middle Ages. But the teachers of the thirteenth cen-

---

[1] The origin of the bachelor's degree, which comes at the end of our college course nowadays, may be explained as follows: The bachelor in the thirteenth century was a student who had passed part of his examinations in the course in "arts," as the college course was then called, and was permitted to teach certain elementary subjects before he became a full-fledged master. So the A.B. was inferior to the A.M. then as now.

tury were fascinated by his logic and astonished at his learning. The great Dominican theologians of the time, Albertus Magnus (d. 1280) and Thomas Aquinas (d. 1274), did not hesitate to prepare elaborate commentaries upon all his works. He was called "The Philosopher"; and so fully were scholars convinced that it had pleased God to permit Aristotle to say the last word upon each and every branch of knowledge that they humbly accepted him, along with the Bible, the church fathers, and the canon and Roman law, as one of the unquestioned authorities which together formed a complete and final guide for humanity in conduct and in every branch of science.

The term "scholasticism" is commonly given to the beliefs and method of discussion of the medieval professors. To those who later outgrew the fondness for logic and the supreme respect for Aristotle, scholasticism, with its neglect of Greek and Roman literature, came to seem an arid and profitless plan of education. Yet, if we turn over the pages of the wonderful works of Thomas Aquinas, we see that the scholastic philosopher might be a person of extraordinary insight and learning, ready to recognize all the objections to his position and able to express himself with great clearness and cogency. The training in logic, if it did not increase the sum of human knowledge, accustomed the student to make careful distinctions and present his arguments in a fatally convincing way.

No attention was given to the great subject of history in the medieval universities, nor was Greek taught. Latin had to be learned in order to carry on the work at all, but little time was given to the Roman classics. The new modern languages were considered entirely unworthy of the learned. It must, of course, be remembered that none of the books which we consider the great classics in English, French, Italian, or Spanish had as yet been written.

Although the medieval professors paid the greatest respect to the Greek philosopher Aristotle and made Latin translations of his works the basis of the college course, very few of them could read any Greek and none of them knew much about Homer or Plato or the Greek tragedians and historians. In the fourteenth century Petrarch (1304-1374) set the example in Italy of carefully collecting all the writings of the Romans, which he greatly admired. He made an unsuccessful effort to learn Greek, for he found that Cicero and other Roman writers were constantly referring with enthusiasm to the Greek books to which they owed so much.[1]

Petrarch had not the patience or opportunity to master Greek, but twenty years after his death a learned Greek prelate from Constantinople, named Chrysoloras, came to Florence and found pupils eager to learn his language so that they could read the Greek books. Soon Italian scholars were going to Constantinople to carry on their studies, just as the Romans in Cicero's time had gone to Athens. They brought back copies of all the ancient writers that they could find, and by 1430 Greek books were once more known in the West, after a thousand years of neglect.

In this way western Europe caught up with ancient times; scholars could once more know all that the Greeks and Romans had known and could read in the original the works of Homer, Sophocles, Herodotus, Plato, Aristotle, Demosthenes, and other philosophers, historians, orators, and tragedians. Those who devoted their lives to a study of the literature of Greece and Rome were called *Humanists*. The name is derived from the Latin word *humanitas*, which means "culture," in Matthew Arnold's sense. In time the colleges gave up the exclusive study of Aristotle and substituted a study of the Greek and Latin literature, and in this way what is known as our "classical" course of study originated.

Beginnings of Modern Inventions

So long, however, as intellectual men confined themselves to studying the old books of Greece and Rome they were not likely to advance beyond what the Greeks and Romans had known. In order to explain modern discoveries and inventions

---

[1] The writer, in his early days, with the collaboration of his friend, Henry W. Rolfe, translated a number of Petrarch's letters which were published under the title *Petrarch, the First Modern Scholar*. The second corrected and enlarged edition appeared in 1914 (Putnam).

we have to take account of those who began to suspect that Aristotle was ignorant and mistaken upon many important matters, and who set to work to examine things about them with the hope of finding out more than any one had ever known before.

Even in the thirteenth century there were a few scholars who criticized the habit of relying upon Aristotle for all knowledge. The most notorious faultfinder was Roger Bacon, an English Franciscan monk (d. about 1290), who declared that even if Aristotle were very wise he had only planted the tree of knowledge and that this had "not as yet put forth all its branches nor produced all its fruits." If we could continue to live for endless centuries we mortals could never hope to reach full and complete knowledge of all the things which are to be known. No one knows enough of nature completely to describe the peculiarities of a single fly and "give the reason for its color and why it has just so many feet, no more and no less." Bacon held that truth could be reached a hundred thousand times better by experiments with real things than by poring over the bad Latin translations of Aristotle. "If I had my way," he declared, "I should burn all the books of Aristotle [in their Latin version], for the study of them can only lead to a loss of time, produce error and increase ignorance."

Roger Bacon declared that if men would only study common things instead of reading the books of the ancients, science would outdo the wonders which people of his day thought could be produced by magic. He said that in time men would be able to fly, would have carriages which needed no horses to draw them and ships which would move swiftly without oars, and that bridges could be built without piers to support them.

All this and much more has come true, but inventors and modern scientists owe but little to the books of the Greeks and Romans, which the scholastic philosophers and the Humanists relied upon. Although the Greek philosophers devoted considerable attention to natural science, they were not much inclined to make long and careful experiments or to invent anything like the microscope or telescope to help them. They knew very little indeed about the laws of nature and were sadly mistaken upon many points. Aristotle thought that the sun and all the stars revolved about the earth and that the heavenly bodies were perfect and unchangeable. He believed that heavy bodies fell faster than light ones and that all earthly things were made of the four elements—earth, air, water, and fire. The Greeks and Romans knew nothing of the compass, or gunpowder, or the printing press, or the uses to which steam can be put. Indeed, they had scarcely anything that we should call a machine.[1]

The thirteenth century witnessed certain new achievements in the history of Europe. The compass began to be utilized in a way to encourage bolder and bolder ventures out upon the ocean. The properties of the lens were discovered, and before the end of the century spectacles are mentioned. The lens

EFFECTS OF CANNON ON A MEDIEVAL CASTLE

made the later telescope, microscope, spectroscope, and camera possible, upon which so much of our modern science depends. The Arabic numerals began to take the place of the awkward Roman system of using letters. One cannot well divide XLVIII by VIII, but he can easily divide 48 by 8. Roger Bacon knew of the explosive nature of a compound of sulphur, saltpeter, and charcoal, and a generation after his death gunpowder began to be used a little for guns and artillery. A

---

[1] They had some practical devices, like the derrick, and many ingenious playthings, which are described by Hero of Alexandria.

document is still preserved referring to the making of brass cannon and balls in Florence in the year 1326. By 1350 powder works were in existence in at least three German towns, and French and English books refer now and then to its use.[1]

At least a hundred and fifty years elapsed, however, before gunpowder really began to supplant the old ways of fighting with bows and arrows and axes and lances. By the year 1500 it was becoming clear that the old stone castles were insufficient protection against cannon, and a new type of unprotected castle began to be erected as residences of the kings and the nobility. Gunpowder has done away with armor, bows and arrows, spears and javelins, castles, and walled towns. Whether such fearfully destructive compounds as have recently been discovered will induce the nations to give up war altogether as too dangerous and terrible a thing to resort to under any circumstances is as yet an unsettled question!

The inventions of the compass, of the lens, and of gunpowder have helped to revolutionize the world. To these may be added the printing press, which has so facilitated and encouraged reading that it is nowadays rare to find anybody in western Europe or North America who cannot read.

The Italian classical scholars of the fifteenth century succeeded, as we have seen, in arousing a new interest in the books of the Greeks as well as of the Romans. They carefully collected every ancient work that they could lay hands on, made copies of it, edited it, and, if it was in Greek, translated it into Latin. While they were in the midst of this work certain patient experimenters in Germany and Holland were turning their attention to a new way of multiplying books rapidly and cheaply by the use of lead type and a press.

The Greeks and Romans and the people of the Middle Ages knew no other method of obtaining a new copy of a book

---

[1] Paper, printing (with blocks, appropriate to the Chinese method of writing), gunpowder for military purposes, and the compass for navigation, were known hundreds of years earlier in China. See the admirable volume of the lamented student of Chinese culture, Thomas Francis Carter, *The Invention of Printing in China and Its Spread Westward.*

except by writing it out laboriously by hand. The professional copyists were incredibly dexterous with their quills, as may be seen in pages from a Bible of the thirteenth century which are reproduced in their original size.[1] The letters are as clear, small, and almost as regular as if they had been printed. The whole volume containing the Old and New Testaments is not as large as this book. After the scribe had finished his work the volume was often turned over to the *illuminator,* who would put in bright illuminated initials and sometimes page borders, which were delightful in design and color.[2] Books designed to be used in the church services were adorned with pictures as well as with ornamented initials and decorative borders.

The written books were, in short, often both compact and beautiful, but they were never cheap or easily produced in great numbers. When Cosimo, the grandfather of Lorenzo the Magnificent, wished to form a library just before the invention of printing, he applied to a contractor who engaged forty-five

[1] Between pp. 214 and 215 are reproductions, exactly the size of the original, of two pages in a manuscript Bible of the thirteenth century (in Latin) belonging to the library of Columbia University. The first of the two was chosen to illustrate the minuteness and perfection of the best work; the second to show irregularities and mistakes due to negligence or lack of skill in the copyists.

The first of the two pages is taken from 1 Maccabees i, 56-ii, 65 (a portion of the Scriptures not usually included in the Protestant Bibles). It begins, ". . . ditis fugitivorum locis. Die quintadecima mensis Caslev, quinto et quadragesimo et centesimo anno aedificavit rex Antiochus abominandum idolum desolationis super altare Dei; et per universas civitates Juda in circitu aedificaverunt aras et ante januas domorum, et in plateis incendebant thura, et sacrificabant et libros legis Dei com[busserunt]." The scribes used a good many abbreviations, as was the custom of the time, and what is transcribed here fills five lines of the manuscript. For some time the printed books perpetuated the abbreviations of the scribes.

The second less perfect page here reproduced is from the prophet Amos, iii, 9-vii, 16. It begins, "vinearum vestrarum: oliveta vestra et ficeta vestra comedit eruca et non redistis ad me, dicit Dominus."

[2] The word "miniature," which is often applied to them, is derived from *minium,* that is, vermilion, which was one of the favorite colors. Later the word came—in the waywardness of etymology—to be applied to anything *small.*

Page from a Copy of the Bible Made in the Thirteenth Century, Showing Perfection of the Best Work
(see note, p. 213)

ANOTHER PAGE FROM THE SAME VOLUME FROM WHICH THE PAGE OPPOSITE IS TAKEN, SHOWING IMPERFECTIONS AND MISTAKES OF POOR COPYISTS

copyists. By working hard for nearly two years they were able to produce only two hundred volumes for the new library.

Moreover, it was impossible before the invention of printing to have two copies of the same work exactly alike. Even with the greatest care a scribe could not avoid making some mistakes, and a careless copyist was sure to make a great many. The universities required their students to report immediately

CLOSING LINES OF THE PSALTER OF 1459 (MUCH REDUCED)

The closing lines (that is, the so-called *colophon*) of the second edition of the Psalter, which are here reproduced, are substantially the same as those of the first edition. They may be translated as follows: "The present volume of the Psalms, which is adorned with handsome capitals and is clearly divided by means of rubrics, was produced not by writing with a pen but by an ingenious invention of printed characters; and was completed to the glory of God and the honor of St. James by John Fust, a citizen of Mainz, and Peter Schoifher of Gernsheim, in the year of our Lord 1459, on the 29th of August"

any mistakes discovered in their textbooks, in order that the error might not be reproduced in another copy and so lead to a misunderstanding of the author. With the invention of printing it became possible to produce in a short time a great many copies of a given book which were exactly alike. Consequently, if sufficient care was taken to see that the types were properly set, the whole edition, not simply a single copy, might be relied upon as correct.

[216]

After the supply of papyrus—the paper of the Egyptians, Greeks, and Romans—was cut off from Europe by the conquest of Egypt by the Mohammedans the people of the Middle Ages used *parchment,* made from the skin of lambs and goats. This was so expensive that printing would have been of but little use, even if it had been thought of, before paper was introduced into Europe by the Mohammedans.[1] Paper began to become common in the thirteenth and fourteenth centuries and was already replacing parchment before the invention of printing.

AN OLD-FASHIONED PRINTING OFFICE

Until the nineteenth century printing was carried on with very little machinery. The type was inked by hand, then the paper laid on and the form slipped under a wooden press operated by hand by means of a lever

The earliest book of any considerable size to be printed was the Bible, which appears to have been completed at Mainz in the year 1456. A year later the famous Mainz Psalter was finished, the first dated book. There are, however, earlier examples of little books printed with engraved blocks (like those of the Chinese), and even with movable types. In the German towns, where the art spread rapidly, the printers adhered to the style of letters which the scribe had found it convenient to make with his quill—the so-called *Gothic,* or black letter. In Italy, however, where the first printing press was set up in 1466, a type was soon adopted which resembled the letters used in ancient Roman inscriptions. This was quite similar to the style of letter commonly used to-day.

[1] The Arabs derived their knowledge of paper-making from the Chinese, who antedated its use in western Europe by at least a thousand years.

The Italians also invented the compressed *italic* type, which enabled them to get a great many words on a page. The early printers generally did their work conscientiously, and the very first book printed is in most respects as well done as any later book.

By the year 1500, after printing had been used less than half a century, there appear to have been at least forty printing presses to be found in various towns of Germany, France, Italy, the Netherlands, and England. These presses had, it is estimated, already printed eight millions of volumes. So there was no longer any danger of the old books being again lost, and the encouragement to write and publish new books was greatly increased. From that date our sources for history become far more voluminous than those which exist for the previous history of the world; we are much better informed in regard to events and conditions since 1500 than we ever can be respecting those of the earlier periods.

The Art of the Renaissance

We have already described briefly the work of the medieval architects and referred to the beautiful carvings that adorned the Gothic cathedrals and to the pictures of saints and angels in stained glass which filled the great church windows. But in the fourteenth and fifteenth centuries art developed in a most astonishing manner in Italy and set new standards for all of western Europe.

Florence was the great center of artistic activity during the fifteenth century. The greatest sculptors and almost all of the most famous painters and architects of the time either were natives of Florence or did their best work there. During the first half of the century sculpture again took the lead. The bronze doors of the baptistery at Florence by Ghiberti, which were completed in 1452, are among the finest products of Renaissance sculpture.[1]

[1] Opposite the cathedral at Florence stands the ancient baptistery. Its northern bronze doors, with ten scenes from the Bible, surrounded by a very lovely border of foliage, birds, and animals, were completed by Lorenzo Ghiberti in 1452, after many years of labor. Michael Angelo declared them worthy to be the gates of heaven.

THE ART OF THE RENAISSANCE

Florence reached the height of its preëminence as an art center during the reign of Lorenzo the Magnificent, who was a devoted patron of all the arts. With his death (1492), this preëminence passed to Rome, which was fast becoming one of the great capitals of Europe. The art-loving popes, Julius II and Leo X, took pains to secure the services of the most distinguished artists and architects of the time in the building and adornment of St. Peter's and the Vatican; that is, the papal church and palace (see above, pp. 192 ff.).

During the sixteenth century the art of the Renaissance reached its highest development. Among all the great artists of this period three stand out in heroic proportions—Leonardo da Vinci, Michael Angelo, and Raphael. The first two, not only practiced, but achieved distinction in, the three arts of architecture, sculpture, and painting.[1] It is impossible to give in a few lines any idea of the beauty and significance of the work of these great geniuses. Both Raphael and Michael Angelo left behind them so many and such magnificent frescoes and paintings, and in the case of Michael Angelo statues as well, that it is easy to appreciate their importance. Leonardo, on the other hand, left but little completed work. His influence on the art of his time, which was probably greater than that of either of the others, came from his many-sidedness, his originality, and his unflagging interest in the discovery and application of new methods. He was almost more experimenter than artist.

While Florence could no longer boast of being the art center of Italy, it still produced great artists, among whom Andrea del Sarto may be especially mentioned. But the most important center of artistic activity outside of Rome in the sixteenth century was Venice. The distinguishing characteristic of the Venetian pictures is their glowing color. This is strikingly exemplified in the paintings of Titian, the most famous of all the Venetian painters.

It was natural that artists from the northern countries should be attracted by the renown of the Italian masters and, after learning all that Italy could teach them, should return home to

[1] Leonardo was engineer and inventor as well.

practice their art in their own particular fashion. About a century after painting began to develop in Italy two Flemish brothers, Van Eyck by name, showed that they were not only able to paint quite as excellent pictures as the Italians of their day, but they also discovered a new way of mixing their colors superior to that employed in Italy. Later, when painting had reached its height in Italy, Albrecht Dürer (1471-1528) and Hans Holbein the Younger in Germany vied with even Raphael and Michael Angelo in the mastery of their art. Dürer is especially celebrated for his wonderful woodcuts and copper-plate engravings, in which field he has perhaps never been excelled.

When, in the seventeenth century, painting had declined south of the Alps, Dutch and Flemish masters—above all, Rubens (1577-1640) and Rembrandt—developed a new and admirable school of painting. To Van Dyck (1599-1641), another Flemish master, we owe many noble portraits of historically important persons. Spain gave to the world in the seventeenth century a painter whom some would rank higher than even the greatest artists of Italy, namely, Velasquez (1599-1660). His genius, like that of Van Dyck, is especially conspicuous in his marvelous portraits.

European Exploration of the Globe

One of the most astonishing peculiarities of our age is the way in which all the world has been brought together. Western merchants, explorers, soldiers and missionaries, Western religion, science, and political ideas, are spreading over the whole globe. Modern methods of rapid intercommunication invite a unification of all the peoples of the earth.

The business and commerce of the medieval towns was on what would seem to us a pitifully small scale. There were no great factories, such as have grown up in recent times with the use of steam and machinery, and the ships which sailed the Mediterranean and the North Sea were small and held only a tiny cargo compared with modern merchant vessels. The gradual growth of a world commerce began with the sea voy-

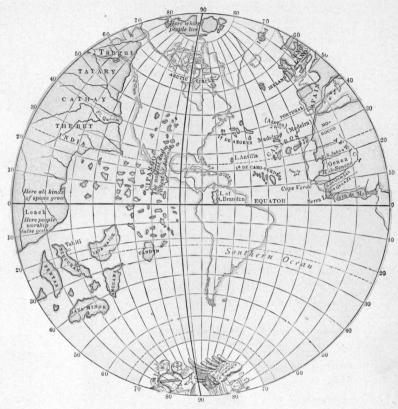

A MAP OF THE GLOBE IN THE TIME OF COLUMBUS

In 1492 a German mariner, Behaim, made a globe which is still preserved in Nuremberg. He did not know of the existence of the American continents or of the vast Pacific Ocean. It will be noticed that he places Japan (Cipango) where Mexico lies. In the reproduction many names are omitted and the outlines of North and South America are sketched in so as to make clear the misconceptions of Columbus's time

ages of the fifteenth century, which led to the exploration by Europeans of the whole globe, most of which was entirely unknown to the Venetian merchants and those who carried on the trade of the Hanseatic League. The Greeks and Romans knew little about the world beyond southern Europe, northern Africa, and western Asia, and much that they knew was forgotten during the Middle Ages. The Crusades took many Europeans as far east as Egypt and Syria.

About 1260 two Venetian merchants, the Polo brothers, visited China and were received kindly at Pekin by the emperor of the Mongols. On a second journey they were accompanied by Marco Polo, the son of one of the brothers. When they got safely back to Venice in 1295, after a journey of twenty years, Marco dictated an account of his experiences which filled his readers with wonder. Nothing stimulated the interest of the West more than his fabulous description of the abundance of gold in Zipangu (Japan) and of the spice markets of the Moluccas and Ceylon.

About the year 1318 Venice and Genoa opened up direct communication by sea with the towns of the Netherlands. Their fleets, which touched at the port of Lisbon, aroused the commercial enterprise of the Portuguese, who soon began to undertake extended maritime expeditions. By the middle of the fourteenth century they had discovered the Canary Islands, Madeira, and the Azores. Before this time no one had ventured along the coast of Africa beyond the arid region of Sahara. The country was forbidding, there were no ports, and mariners were, moreover, discouraged by the general belief that the torrid region was uninhabitable. In 1445, however, some adventurous sailors came within sight of a headland beyond the desert and, struck by its luxuriant growth of tropical trees, they called it Cape Verde (the green cape). Its discovery put an end once for all to the idea that there were only parched deserts to the south.

For a generation longer the Portuguese continued to venture farther and farther along the African coast, in the hope of finding it coming to an end, so they might make their way by sea

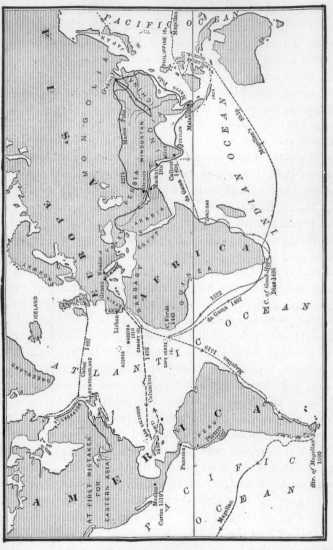

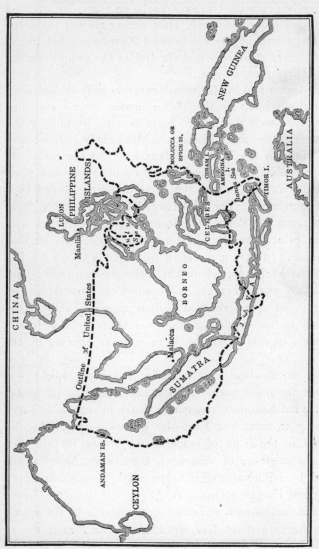

THE MALAY ARCHIPELAGO

The outline of the United States has been drawn in to make clear the vast extent of the region explored by the Portuguese at the opening of the sixteenth century. It is not far from two thousand miles from Ceylon to Malacca Strait, and as far from there on to the Spice Islands as from Denver, Colorado, to Richmond, Virginia to India. At last, in 1486, Diaz rounded the Cape of Good Hope. Twelve years later (1498) Vasco da Gama, spurred on by Columbus's great discovery, after sailing around the Cape of Good Hope and northward beyond Zanzibar, aided by an Arab pilot steered straight across the Indian Ocean and reached Calicut, in Hindustan, by sea.

Vasco da Gama and his fellow adventurers were looked upon with natural suspicion by the Mohammedan spice merchants, who knew very well that their object was to establish *direct* trade between the Spice Islands (Moluccas) and western Europe. Hitherto the Mohammedans had had the monopoly of the spice trade between the Moluccas and the eastern ports of the Mediterranean, where the products were handed over to Italian merchants. The Mohammedans were unable, however, to prevent the Portuguese from concluding treaties with the Indian princes and establishing trading stations at Goa and elsewhere. In 1512 a successor to Vasco da Gama reached Java and the Moluccas, where the Portuguese speedily built a fortress. By 1515 Portugal had become the greatest among sea powers; and spices reached Lisbon regularly without the intervention of the Mohammedan merchants or the Italian towns, which, especially Venice, were mortally afflicted by the change.

There is no doubt that the desire to obtain spices was at this time the main reason for the exploration of the globe. This motive led European navigators to try in succession every possible way to reach the East—by going around Africa, by sailing west in the hope of reaching the Indies (before they knew of the existence of America), then, after America was discovered, by sailing around it to the north or south, and even sailing around Europe to the north.

It is hard for us to understand this enthusiasm for spices, for which we care much less nowadays. One former use of spices was to preserve food, which could not then as now be carried rapidly, while still fresh, from place to place; nor did our conveniences then exist for keeping it by the use of ice.

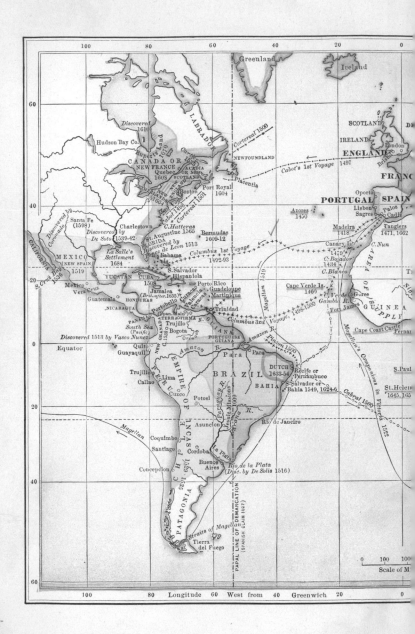

Greenland

Iceland

SCOTLAND

IRELAND

ENGLAND   London

Cortereal 1500

NEWFOUNDLAND

Cabot's 1st Voyage 1497

FRANC

Discovered 1610

Hudson Bay Co.

Rupert's Land

LABRADOR

CANADA OR
NEW FRANCE
Quebec
1608

ACADIA
OR NOVA
SCOTIA

Placentia

Oporto

PORTUGAL SPAIN

Azores
1450

Lisbon
Sagres

Palos
Cadiz

Boston   Port Royal
1604

Cortereal 1501

Madeira
1418

Tangiers
1471, 1662

Santa Fe
(1598)

Discovered by
Coronado

Charlestown
Discovered by
De Soto 1539-42

C.Hatteras

FLORIDA
St.Augustine 1566
Discovered by
Ponce de Leon 1513

Bermudas
1609-12

Canary Is.
1479

C.Nun

Columbus 1st Voyage
1492-93

C.Bojador
1434

C.Blanco

MEXICO
(NEW SPAIN)

La Salle's
Settlement
1684

Bahama

S.Cruz Isl.

CALIFORNIA

Discovered by
Coronado

YUCATAN
1506

CUBA

S.Salvador
Hispaniola

Porto Rico
Guadeloupe
Martinique

Cape Verde Is.
1460

Goree

Verde
Gambia R.

Fort James

GUINEA

Mexico
Vera Cruz

Jamaica
(Brit. after 1655)
(Span. 1509)

Guatemala

HONDURAS

NICARAGUA

Portobello
TERRA FIRMA

Trinidad

Cape Coast Castle

Fernan

S.Paul

Discovered 1513 by Vasco Nunez

South Sea
(Pacific)

NEW GRANADA

Trujillo
Bogota

Orinoco R.

GUIANA
PORTUGUESE
GUIANA

Columbus 3rd Voyage, 1498-1500

St.Helena
1645, 165

Equator

Quito
Guayaquil

Amazon R.

Para
Para

Pinzon 1500

Cabral 1500

Trujillo
Lima
Callao

EMPIRE OF INCAS

Cuzco

BRAZIL

BAHIA

Recife or
Pernambuco

Salvador or
Bahia 1549, 1624-6

DUTCH
1633-54

Magellan's Companions in Vittoria 1522

Potosi

Asuncion

Jesuit Missions
1609

Rio de Janeiro

Magellan

Coquimbo
Santiago

Cordoba

Rio de la Plata
(Disc. by De Solis 1516)

Concepcion

Buenos
Aires

PATAGONIA

Straits of Magellan

Tierra
del Fuego

PAPAL LINE OF DEMARCATION
(SPANISH CLAIM 1527)

0   100   100

Scale of M

100   80   Longitude   60   West from   40   Greenwich   20   0

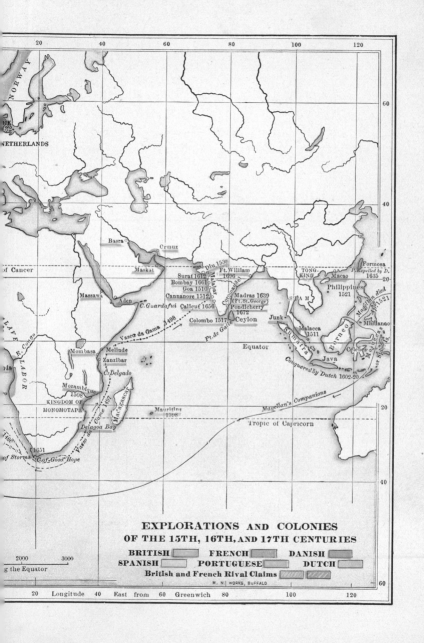

EXPLORATIONS AND COLONIES
OF THE 15TH, 16TH, AND 17TH CENTURIES

BRITISH ☐ FRENCH ☐ DANISH ☐
SPANISH ☐ PORTUGUESE ☐ DUTCH ☐
British and French Rival Claims ☐ ☐

M. N. WORKS, BUFFALO

Moreover, spice served to make even tainted food more palatable than it would otherwise have been.

It inevitably occurred to thoughtful men that the East Indies could be reached by sailing *westward*. All intelligent people knew, all through the Middle Ages, that the earth was a globe. The chief authority upon the form and size of the earth continued to be the ancient astronomer Ptolemy, who had lived about A.D. 150. He had reckoned the earth to be about one-sixth smaller than it is; and as Marco Polo had given an exaggerated idea of the distance which he and his companions had traveled eastward, and as no one suspected the existence of the American continents, it was supposed that it could not be a very long journey from Europe across the Atlantic to Japan.

In 1492, as we all know, a Genoese navigator, Columbus (b. 1451), who had had much experience on the sea, got together three little ships and undertook the journey westward to Zipangu,—the land of gold,—which he hoped to reach in five weeks. In about a month from the time he left the Canary Islands he came upon land, the island of San Salvador, and believed himself to be in the East Indies. Going on from there he discovered the island of Cuba, which he believed to be the mainland of Asia, and then Haiti, which he mistook for the longed-for Zipangu. Although he made three later expeditions and sailed down the coast of South America as far as the Orinoco, he died without realizing that he had not been exploring the coast of Asia.

After the bold enterprises of Vasco da Gama and Columbus, an expedition headed by the Portuguese Magellan succeeded in circumnavigating the globe. There was now no reason why the new lands should not become more and more familiar to the European nations. The coast of North America was explored principally by English navigators, who for over a century pressed northward, still in the vain hope of finding a northwest passage to the Spice Islands.

Cortes began the Spanish conquests in the western world by undertaking the subjugation of the Aztec empire in Mexico in 1519. A few years later Pizarro established the Spanish power in Peru. Spain now superseded Portugal as a maritime power, and her importance in the sixteenth century is to be attributed largely to the wealth which came to her from her possessions in the New World—mainly gold and silver.

By the end of the century the Spanish Main—that is, the northern coast of South America—was much frequented by adventurous seamen, who combined in about equal parts the occupations of merchant, slaver, and pirate. Many of these hailed from English ports, and it is to them that England owes the beginning of her commercial greatness.

It is hardly necessary to say that Europeans exhibited an utter disregard for the rights of the people with whom they came in contact and often treated them with contemptuous cruelty. The exploration of the globe and the conquest by European nations of peoples beyond the sea led finally to the vast colonization of modern times, which has caused many wars but has served to spread European ideas throughout the world.

CHAPTER XI

THE DEVELOPMENT OF ENGLAND AND FRANCE

Conquest of England by the Normans. Henry II and the Plantagenets. The Great Charter and the Beginnings of the English Parliament. Wales and Scotland. The Hundred Years' War. The New Monarchy in England. The Crafty Louis XI of France

Conquest of England by the Normans

TWO great powers of modern times have so far been neglected in this narrative—France and England. Their political history was intermingled for three centuries, from the Norman conquest down to the end of the Hundred Years' War. In the latter half of the fifteenth century they were finally disentangled and went their own way, each destined to play a very great part in world history. Much that has been said of the conditions in central Europe apply to them. The characteristic medieval institutions of feudalism, serfdom, and the papal monarchy may be illustrated quite as well in English and French experience as in that of Germany or Italy. Nevertheless, these two western countries outgrew the medieval organizations rather more promptly than central and southern Europe, and passed into the stage of unified monarchical states, later to become exponents of democratic institutions, and so-called free government. The following review of English and French political history will necessarily carry us back once more to the early Middle Ages, but it will at the same time, form an excellent introduction to the general nature and relations of the European governments as they stood at the opening of the eventful sixteenth century.

English history has of course a particular interest for English-speaking people. From England the United States and the vast British Empire have inherited their language and habits of thought, much of their literature, and many of their laws and institutions. In this volume it will not, however, be possible to study England except in so far as it has played a part in the general development of the world. This it has greatly influenced by its commerce and industry and colonies, as well as by the example it was the first to set in modern times of permitting the people to share with the king in the government.

The conquest of the island of Britain by the German Angles and Saxons has already been spoken of, as well as the conversion of these pagans to Christianity by Augustine and his monks.[1] The several kingdoms founded by the German invaders were brought under the overlordship of the southern kingdom of Wessex by King Egbert, a contemporary of Charlemagne.

But no sooner had the long-continued invasions of the Germans come to an end and the country been partially unified than the Northmen (or Danes, as the English called them), who were ravaging France, began to make incursions into England. Before long they had conquered a large district north of the Thames and were making permanent settlements. They were defeated, however, in a great battle by Alfred the Great, the first English king of whom we have any satisfactory knowledge. He forced the Danes to accept Christianity, and established, as the boundary between their settlements and his own kingdom of Wessex, a line running from London across the island to Chester.

But Danes kept coming, and the Danish invasions continued for more than a century after Alfred's death (901). Sometimes they were bought off by a money payment called the *Danegeld,* which was levied on the people of England like any other tax. But finally a Danish king (Cnut) succeeded in making himself king of England in 1017. This Danish dynasty maintained itself, however, for only a few years. Then a last weak Saxon king, Edward the Confessor, reigned for twenty years.

Upon his death one of the greatest events in all English history occurred. The most powerful of the vassals of the king

[1] See above, pp. 70 f.

of France crossed the English Channel, conquered England, and made himself king. This was William, Duke of Normandy.

We have seen how Charlemagne's empire broke up, and how the feudal lords became so powerful that it was difficult for the king to control them. The West Frankish kingdom, which we shall hereafter call France, was divided up among a great many dukes and counts, who built strong castles, gathered armies and fought against one another, and were the terror alike of priest, merchant, and peasant.

In the tenth century certain great fiefs of the French king, like Normandy, Brittany, Flanders, and Burgundy, developed into little nations, each under its line of able rulers. Each had its own particular customs and culture, some traces of which may still be noted by the traveler in France. These feudal states were created by certain families of nobles who possessed exceptional energy or statesmanship. By conquest, purchase, or marriage they increased the number of their fiefs, and they insured their control over their vassals by promptly destroying the castles of those who refused to meet their obligations.

Of these French subnations none was more important or interesting than Normandy. The Northmen had for many years been the scourge of those who lived near the North Sea before one of their leaders, Rollo (or Hrolf), agreed in 911 to accept from the West Frankish king a district on the coast, north of Brittany, where he and his followers might peacefully settle. Rollo assumed the title of Duke of the Normans, and introduced the Christian religion among his people. For a considerable time the newcomers kept up their Scandinavian habits and language. Gradually, however, they appropriated such culture as their neighbors possessed, and by the twelfth century their capital, Rouen, was one of the most enlightened cities of Europe. Normandy became a source of infinite perplexity to the French kings when, in 1066, Duke William added England to his possessions and the title of "the Conqueror" to his name; for he thereby became so powerful that his overlord, the king of France, could hardly hope to control the Norman dukes any longer.

William of Normandy claimed that he was entitled to the English crown, but we are somewhat in the dark as to the alleged basis of his claim. There is a story that he had visited the court of Edward the Confessor and had become his vassal on condition that, should Edward die childless, he was to declare William his successor. However this may be, Harold of Wessex assumed the English crown upon Edward's death and paid no attention to William's demand that he should surrender it.

William thereupon appealed to the pope, promising that if he came into possession of England, he would see that the English clergy submitted to the authority of the Roman bishop. Consequently the pope, Alexander II, condemned Harold and blessed in advance any expedition that William might undertake to secure his rights. The conquest of England therefore took on the character of a sort of holy war, and as the expedition had been well advertised, many adventurers flocked to William's standard. During the spring and summer of 1066 ships were building in the various Norman harbors for the purpose of carrying William's army across the Channel.

Harold, the English king, was in a very unfavorable position to defend his crown. In the first place, while he was expecting William's coming, he was called to the north of England to repel a last invasion of the fierce Norsemen, who had again landed in England and were devastating the coast towns. He was able to put them to flight, but, as he was celebrating his victory by a banquet, news reached him that William had actually landed with his Normans in southern England. It was autumn now and the peasants, who formed a large part of Harold's forces, had gone home to harvest their crops, so he had to hurry south with an insufficient army.

The English occupied the hill of Senlac, west of Hastings, and awaited the coming of the enemy. They had few horses and fought on foot with their battle-axes. The Normans had horses, which they had brought across in their ships, and were supplied with bows and arrows. The English fought bravely and repulsed the Normans as they tried to press up the hillside.

But at last they were thrown into confusion, and King Harold was killed by a Norman arrow which pierced his eye.

William thus destroyed the English army in this famous battle of Hastings, and the rightful English king was dead. But the Norman duke was not satisfied to take possession of England as a conqueror merely. In a few weeks he managed to induce a number of influential nobles and several bishops to agree to accept him as king, and London opened its gates to him. On Christmas Day, 1066, he was chosen king by an assembly in Westminster Abbey (where Harold had been elected a year before) and was duly crowned.

In the Norman town of Bayeux a strip of embroidery is preserved some two hundred and thirty feet long and eighteen inches wide. If it was not made by Queen Matilda, William's wife, and her ladies, as some have sup-

ABBAYE AUX DAMES, CAEN

William the Conqueror married a lady, Matilda, who was remotely related to him. This was against the rules of the Church, and he took pains to get the pope's sanction for his marriage. But he and his queen were afraid that they might have committed a sin in marrying, so William built a monastery for men and Matilda a nunnery for women as a penance. The churches of these monasteries still stand in the Norman city of Caen. William was buried in his church. The picture represents the interior of Matilda's church and is a good example of what the English called the Norman style of architecture

[231]

posed, it belongs at any rate to the time of the Norman conquest of England, which it pictures with much detail. It tells the story of the preparations and the landing of the Normans with their horses from their ships on the English coast, the starting for the battlefield of Hastings, and the battle of Hastings, in actual progress; the English are on their hill, trying to drive back the invaders. While the ladies could not draw very well, historians think that they are able to enrich their ideas of the time from this embroidery.

We cannot trace the history of the opposition and the revolts of the great nobles which William had to meet within the next few years. His position was rendered doubly difficult by troubles which he encountered on the Continent as Duke of Normandy. Suffice it to say, that he succeeded in maintaining himself against all his enemies.

William's policy in England exhibited profound statesmanship. He introduced the Norman feudalism to which he was accustomed, but took good care that it should not weaken his power. The English who had refused to join him before the battle of Hastings were declared to have forfeited their lands, but were permitted to keep them upon condition of receiving them back from the king as his vassals. The lands of those who actually fought against him at Hastings, or in later rebellions, including the great estates of Harold's family, were seized and distributed among his faithful followers, both Norman and English, though naturally the Normans among them far outnumbered the English.

William declared that he did not propose to change the English customs but to govern as Edward the Confessor, the last Saxon king, had done. He maintained the Witenagemot, a council made up of bishops and nobles, whose advice the Saxon kings had sought in all important matters. But he was a man of too much force to submit to the control of his barons. He avoided giving to any one person a great many estates in a single region, so that no one should become inconveniently powerful. Finally, in order to secure the support of the smaller landholders and to prevent combinations against him among the greater ones, he required every landowner in England to take an oath of fidelity *directly* to him, instead of having only a few great landowners as vassals, who had their own subvassals under their own control, as in France.

We read in the *Anglo-Saxon Chronicle* (1086): "He came, on the first day of August, to Salisbury, and there came to him his wise men and all the land-owning men of property there were over all England, whosoever men they were; and all bowed down to him and became his men, and swore oaths of fealty to him that they would be faithful to him against all other men."

It is clear that the Norman Conquest was not a simple change of kings, but that a new element was added to the English people. We cannot tell how many Normans actually emigrated across the Channel, but they evidently came in considerable numbers, and their influence upon the English habits and government was very great. A century after William's conquest the whole body of the nobility, the bishops, abbots, and government officials, had become practically all Norman. Besides these, the architects who built the castles and fortresses, the cathedrals and abbeys, came from Normandy. Merchants from the Norman cities of Rouen and Caen settled in London and other English cities, and weavers from Flanders in various towns and even in the country. For a short time these newcomers remained a separate people, but by the year 1200 they had become for the most part indistinguishable from the great mass of English people amongst whom they had settled. They had nevertheless made the people of England more energetic, active-minded, and varied in their occupations and interests than they had been before the conquest.

Henry II and the Plantagenets

William the Conqueror was followed by his sons, William Rufus and Henry I. Upon the death of the latter the country went through a disastrous period of civil war, for some of the nobility supported the Conqueror's grandson Stephen, and some his granddaughter Matilda. After the death of Stephen, when Henry II, Matilda's son,[1] was finally recognized in 1154 by all as king, he found the kingdom in a melancholy state. The nobles had taken advantage of the prevalent disorder to erect castles without royal permission and to establish themselves as independent rulers, and many disorderly hired soldiers had been brought over from the Continent to support the rivals for the throne.

NORMAN GATEWAY AT BRISTOL, ENGLAND

This beautiful gateway was originally the entrance to a monastery, begun in 1142. It is one of the finest examples of the Norman style of building to be seen in England

Henry II (1154-1189) at once adopted vigorous measures. He destroyed the illegally erected fortresses, sent off the foreign soldiers, and deprived many earls who had been created by Stephen and Matilda of their titles. Henry's task was a difficult one. He had need of all his tireless energy and quickness of mind to restore order in England and at the same time rule the wide realms on the Continent which he had either inherited or gained through his marriage with a French heiress.

In order to avoid all excuse for the private warfare which was such a persistent evil on the Continent, he undertook to improve and reform the law courts. He arranged that his judges should make regular circuits throughout the country, so that they might try cases on the spot at least once a year. We find, too, the beginning of our grand jury in a body of men in each neighborhood who were to

[1] See genealogical table below, p. 238.

be duly sworn in, from time to time, and should then bring accusations against such malefactors as had come to their knowledge.

As for the "petty" or smaller jury of twelve, which actually tried the accused, its origin and history are obscure. Henry II's juries left the verdict for Heaven to pronounce in the ordeal; but a century later we find the jury of twelve itself rendering verdicts. The plan of delegating to twelve men the duty of deciding on the guilt or innocence of a suspected person was very different from the earlier systems. It resembled neither the Roman trial, where the judges made the decision, nor the medieval compurgation and ordeals (see above, pp. 46 f.). The decisions of Henry's judges were mainly drawn from old English custom, instead of from Roman law as in France, and they became the basis of the *common law* which is still used in all English-speaking countries.

Henry's reign was embittered by the famous struggle with Thomas

CHOIR OF CANTERBURY CATHEDRAL

The choir of Canterbury Cathedral was destroyed by fire four years after Thomas Becket was murdered there. The picture shows how it was rebuilt under Henry II during the years 1175-1184. The two lower rows of arches are the round kind that had been used up to that time, while the upper row shows how the pointed arch was coming in

Becket, which illustrates admirably the peculiar dependence of the monarchs of his day upon the churchmen. Becket was born in London and became a cleric, but he grew up in the service of the king and was able to aid Henry in gaining the throne. Thereupon the new king made him his chancellor. Becket proved an excellent minister and defended the king's interest even against the Church. He was fond of hunting and of war and maintained a brilliant court from the revenues of the numerous church positions which he held. It appeared to Henry that there could be no better head for the English clergy than his sagacious and worldly chancellor. He therefore determined to make him Archbishop of Canterbury.

In securing the election of Becket as Archbishop of Canterbury, Henry intended to insure his own complete control of the Church. He proposed to punish churchmen who committed crimes, like other offenders, to make the bishops meet all the feudal obligations, and to prevent appeals to the pope. Becket, however, immediately gave up his gay life and opposed every effort of the king to reduce the independence of the Church. After a haughty assertion of the supremacy of the Church over the king's government, Thomas fled from the wrathful and disappointed monarch to France and the protection of the pope.

In spite of a patched-up reconciliation with the king, Becket proceeded to excommunicate some of the great English prelates and, as Henry believed, was conspiring to rob his son of the crown. In a fit of anger, Henry exclaimed among his followers, "Is there no one to avenge me of this miserable churchman?" Unfortunately certain knights took the rash expression literally, and Becket was murdered in his own cathedral of Canterbury, whither he had returned. The king really had no wish to resort to violence, and his remorse when he heard of the bloody deed, and his terror at the consequences, were most genuine. The pope proposed to excommunicate him. Henry, however, made peace with the papal legates by the solemn assertion that he had never wished the death of Thomas and by promising to return to Canterbury all the property which he had confis-

THE PLANTAGENET POSSESSIONS IN ENGLAND AND FRANCE

cated, to send money to aid in the capture of the Holy Sepulcher at Jerusalem, and to undertake a crusade himself.

Although Henry II was one of the most important kings in English history, he spent a great part of his time across the Channel in his French possessions. A glance at the accompanying map will show that rather more than half of his realms lay across the English Channel. He controlled more territory in France than the French king himself. As great-grandson of William the Conqueror, he inherited the duchy of Normandy and the suzerainty over Brittany. His mother, Matilda, had married the count of Anjou and Maine, so that Henry II inherited these fiefs along with those which had belonged to William the Conqueror. Lastly, he had himself married Eleanor, heiress of the dukes of Guienne, and in this way doubled the extent of his French lands.[1] Henry II and his successors are known as the Plantagenets, owing to the habit that his father, the count of Anjou, had of wearing a bit of broom (*planta genista*) in his helmet.

So it came about that the French kings beheld a new State, under an able and energetic ruler, developing within their borders and including more than half the territory over which they were supposed to rule. A few years before Henry II died,

[1] William the Conqueror, king of England (1066–1087)

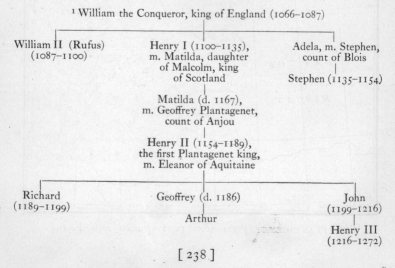

William II (Rufus)
(1087–1100)

Henry I (1100–1135),
m. Matilda, daughter
of Malcolm, king
of Scotland

Adela, m. Stephen,
count of Blois

Stephen (1135–1154)

Matilda (d. 1167),
m. Geoffrey Plantagenet,
count of Anjou

Henry II (1154–1189),
the first Plantagenet king,
m. Eleanor of Aquitaine

Richard
(1189–1199)

Geoffrey (d. 1186)

Arthur

John
(1199–1216)

Henry III
(1216–1272)

an ambitious monarch, Philip Augustus (1180-1223), ascended the French throne, and made it the chief business of his life to get control of his feudal vassals, above all, the Plantagenets.

Henry divided his French possessions among his three sons, Geoffrey, Richard, and John; but father and sons were engaged in constant disputes with one another, as none of them were easy people to get along with. Philip Augustus took advantage of these constant conflicts of the brothers among themselves and with their father. These quarrels were most fortunate for the French king, for had the Plantagenets held together they might have annihilated the royal house of France, whose narrow dominions their own possessions closed in on the west and south.

So long as Henry II lived there was little chance of expelling the Plantagenets from France; but with the accession of his reckless son, Richard the Lion-Hearted, the prospects of the French king brightened wonderfully. Richard is one of the most famous of medieval knights, but he was a very poor ruler. He left his kingdom to take care of itself while he went upon a crusade to the Holy Land (see above, p. 148). He persuaded Philip Augustus to join him; but Richard was too overbearing and masterful, and Philip too ambitious, to make it possible for them to agree for long. The king of France, who was physically delicate, was taken ill on the way and was glad of the excuse to return home and brew trouble for his powerful vassal. When Richard himself returned, after several years of romantic but fruitless adventure, he found himself involved in a war with Philip Augustus, in the midst of which he died (1199).

Richard's younger brother, John, who enjoys the reputation of being the most despicable of English kings, speedily gave Philip a good excuse for seizing a great part of the Plantagenet lands. John was suspected of conniving at the brutal murder of his nephew Arthur (the son of Geoffrey [1]). He was also guilty of the less serious offense of carrying off and marrying a lady betrothed to one of his own vassals. Philip Augustus, as

---

[1] Geoffrey, John's next older brother, who would naturally have succeeded Richard, died in 1186.

John's suzerain, summoned him to appear at the French court to answer the latter charge. Upon John's refusal to appear or to do homage for his continental possessions, Philip caused his court to issue a decree confiscating almost all of the Plantagenet lands, leaving to the English king only the southwest corner of France.

Philip found little difficulty in possessing himself of Normandy itself, which showed no disinclination to accept him in place of the Plantagenets. Six years after Richard's death the English kings had lost all their continental fiefs except Guienne. It should be observed that Philip, unlike his ancestors, was no longer merely *suzerain* of the new conquests, but made himself duke of Normandy, and count of Anjou, of Maine, etc. The boundaries of his domain—that is, the lands which he himself controlled directly as feudal lord—now extended to the sea.

St. Louis, Philip's successor, arranged with John's successor in 1258 that the English king should do him homage for Guienne, Gascony, and Poitou and should surrender every claim on all the rest of the former possessions of the Plantagenets. So it came about that the English kings continued to hold a portion of France for several hundred years.

John not only lost Normandy and other territories which had belonged to the earlier Norman kings but he actually consented to become the pope's vassal, receive England as a fief from the papacy, and pay tribute to Rome. This strange proceeding came about in this wise: The monks of Canterbury had (1205) ventured to choose an archbishop—who was at the same time their abbot—without consulting King John. Their appointee hastened off to Rome to gain the pope's confirmation, while the irritated John forced the monks to hold another election and make his treasurer archbishop. The pope at that time was no less a person than Innocent III, one of the most salient of medieval rulers.[1] Innocent rejected both the men who had been elected, sent for a new deputation of monks from Canterbury, and bade them choose Stephen Langton, a man of great ability.

[1] See above, p. 135.

John then angrily drove the monks of Canterbury out of the kingdom.

Innocent replied by placing England under the *interdict;* that is to say, he ordered the clergy to close all the churches and suspend all public services—a very terrible thing to the people of the time. John was excommunicated, and the pope threatened that unless the king submitted to his wishes he would depose him and give his crown to Philip Augustus of France. As Philip made haste to collect an army for the conquest of England, John humbly submitted to the pope in 1213. He went so far as to hand England over to Innocent III and receive it back as a fief, thus becoming the vassal of the pope. He agreed also to send a yearly tribute to Rome.

The Great Charter and the Beginnings of the English Parliament

We must now turn to the most important event in John's reign—the drawing up of the Great Charter of English liberties.

When, in 1213, John proposed to lead his English vassals across the water in order to attempt to reconquer his lost possessions in France, they refused to accompany him on the ground that their feudal obligations did not bind them to fight outside of their country. Moreover, they showed a lively discontent with John's tyranny and his neglect of those limits of the kingly power which several of the earlier Norman kings had solemnly recognized. In 1214 a number of the barons met and took a solemn oath that they would compel the king, by arms if necessary, to sign a charter containing the things which, according to English traditions, a king might *not* do. As John would not agree to this, it proved necessary to get together an army and march against him. The insurgent nobles met him at Runnymede, not far from London. Here on the 15th of June, 1215, they forced him to swear to observe what they believed to be the rights of his subjects, which they had carefully written out.

The Great Charter is perhaps the most famous document in the history of government; its provisions furnish a brief and comprehensive statement of the burning governmental questions of that period. The nobles, who concluded this treaty with a tyrannous ruler, saw that it was to their interest to have the rights of the common freeman safeguarded as well as their own. The king promises to observe the rights of his vassals, and the vassals in turn agree to observe the rights of their men. The towns are not to be oppressed. The merchant is not to be deprived of his goods for small offenses, nor the farmer of his wagon and implements. The king is to impose no tax, besides the three stated feudal aids,[1] except with the consent of the great council of the nation. This is to include the prelates and greater barons and all who hold directly of the king.

There is no more notable clause in the Charter than that which provides that no freeman is to be arrested, or imprisoned, or deprived of his property, unless he be immediately sent before a court of his peers for trial. To realize the importance of this, we must recollect that in France, down to 1789,—nearly six hundred years later,—the king exercised such unlimited powers that he could order the arrest of any one he pleased, and could imprison him for any length of time without bringing him to trial, or even informing him of the nature of his offense. The Great Charter provided further that the king should permit merchants to move about freely and should observe the privileges of the various towns; nor were his officers longer to be allowed to exercise despotic powers over those under them.

The Charter closes with the promise that "the church of England shall be free, and that the men in our kingdom shall have and hold all the aforesaid liberties, rights, concessions, well, peacefully, freely, quietly, fully and completely for themselves and for their heirs, from us and our heirs in all things and places forever."

It must be remembered, however, that the Great Charter was no democratic document. The English aristocracy which

---

[1] These were payments made when the lord knighted his eldest son, gave his eldest daughter in marriage, or had been captured and was waiting to be ransomed.

forced the Charter on their perverse king naturally had their own special interests in mind. The nobles, churchmen, merchants, and other *freemen* made up only about a sixth of the population, and the Charter has little or nothing to say of the serfs, or villains, who formed the great mass of the English people at the time. They could still be victimized as before by their master, the lord of the manor.

In spite of his solemn confirmation of the Charter, John, with his accustomed treachery, made an unsuccessful attempt to break his promises; but neither he nor his successors ever succeeded in getting rid of the document. Later there were times when the English kings evaded its provisions and tried to rule as absolute monarchs. But the people—a term which tended steadily to become more and more comprehensive—always sooner or later bethought them of the Charter, which thus continued to form a barrier against permanent despotism in England.

During the long reign of John's son, Henry III (1216-1272), England began to construct her Parliament, an institution which has not only played a most important rôle in English history, but has also served as the model for similar bodies in almost every civilized state in the world.

The Great Council of the Norman kings, like the older Witenagemot of Saxon times, was a meeting of nobles, bishops, and abbots, which the king summoned from time to time to give him advice and aid, and to sanction important governmental undertakings. During Henry's reign its meetings became more frequent and its discussions more vigorous than before, and the name *Parliament* began to be applied to it.

In 1265 a famous Parliament was held, where a most important new class of members—the *commons*—were present, who were destined to give it its future greatness. In addition to the nobles and prelates, two simple knights were summoned from each county and two citizens from each of the more flourishing towns to attend and take part in the discussions.

Edward I, the next king, definitely adopted this innovation. He doubtless called in the representatives of the towns because the townspeople were becoming rich and he wished to have an opportunity to ask them to make grants of money to meet the expenses of the government. He also wished to obtain the approval of all classes when he determined upon important measures affecting the whole realm. Ever since the so-called "Model Parliament" of 1295, the commons, or representatives of the people, have always been included along with the clergy and nobility when the national assembly of England has been summoned.

The Parliament early took the stand that the king must agree to "redress of grievances" before they would grant him any money. This meant that the king had to promise to remedy any acts of himself or his officials of which Parliament complained before it would agree to let him raise the taxes. Instead of following the king about and meeting wherever he might happen to be, Parliament from the time of Edward I began to hold its sessions in the city of Westminster, now a part of London, where it still continues to meet.

Under Edward's successor, Edward II, Parliament solemnly declared in 1322 that important matters relating to the king and his heirs, the state of the realm and of the people should be considered and determined upon by the king "with the assent of the prelates, earls and barons, and the commonalty (that is, commons) of the realm." Five years later Parliament showed its power by deposing the inefficient king, Edward II, and declared his son, Edward III, the rightful ruler of England.

The new king, who was carrying on an expensive war with France, needed much money and consequently summoned Parliament every year, and, in order to encourage its members to grant him money, he gratified Parliament by asking their advice and listening to their petitions. He passed no new law without adding "by and with the advice and consent of the lords spiritual and temporal and of the commons."

At this time the separation of the two houses of Parliament took place, and ever since the "lords spiritual and temporal"—that is, the bishops and higher nobles—have sat by themselves in the House of Lords, and a House of Commons, including the country gentlemen (knights) and the representatives elected by the more important towns, have met by themselves. Parliament thus made up is really a modern, not a medieval, institution, and we shall hear much of it later.

Wales and Scotland

The English kings who preceded Edward I (1272-1307) had ruled over only a portion of the island of Great Britain. To the west of their kingdom lay the mountainous district of Wales, inhabited by that remnant of the original Britons which the German invaders had been unable to conquer. To the north of England was the kingdom of Scotland, which was quite independent except for an occasional recognition by the Scotch kings of the English kings as their feudal superiors. Edward I, however, succeeded in conquering Wales permanently and Scotland temporarily.

For centuries a border warfare had been carried on between the English and the Welsh. William the Conqueror had found it necessary to establish a chain of fortresses on the Welsh frontier, and Chester, Shrewsbury, and Monmouth became the outposts of the Normans. While the raids of the Welsh constantly provoked the English kings to invade Wales, no permanent conquest was possible, for the enemy retreated into the mountains about Snowden, and the English soldiers were left to starve in the wild regions into which they had ventured. The Welsh were encouraged in their long and successful resistance against the English by the songs of their *bards,* who promised that their people would sometime reconquer the whole of England, which they had possessed before the coming of the Angles and Saxons.

When Edward I came to the throne he demanded that Llewellyn, prince of Wales, as the head of the Welsh clans was called, should do him homage. Llewellyn, who was a man of ability and energy, refused the king's summons, and Edward marched into Wales. Two campaigns were necessary before the Welsh finally succumbed. Llewellyn was killed (1282), and with him expired the independence of the Welsh people.

[245]

Edward divided the country into shires and introduced English laws and customs, and his policy of conciliation was so successful that there was but a single rising in the country for a whole century. He later presented his son to the Welsh as their prince, and from that time down to the present the title of "Prince of Wales" has usually been conferred upon the heir to the English throne.

The conquest of Scotland proved a far more difficult matter than that of Wales.

CONWAY CASTLE

Edward built this fine castle in 1284 on the north coast of Wales, to keep the Welsh in check. Its walls are 12 to 15 feet in thickness. There were buildings inside, including a great banqueting hall 130 feet long

At the time when the Angles and Saxons conquered Britain, some of them wandered north as far as the Firth of Forth and occupied the so-called Lowlands of Scotland. The mountainous region to the north, known as the Highlands, continued to be held by wild tribes related to the Welsh and Irish and talking a language similar to theirs, namely Gaelic. There was constant warfare between the older inhabitants themselves and between them and the newcomers from Germany, but both Highlands and Lowlands were finally united under a line of Scottish kings, who moved their residence down to Edinburgh, which, with its fortress, became their chief town.

It was natural that the language of the Scotch Lowlands should be English, but in the mountains the Highlanders to this day continue to talk the ancient Gaelic of their forefathers.

It was not until the time of Edward I that the long series of troubles between England and Scotland began. The death of the last representative old line of Scotch kings in 1290 was followed by the appearance of a number of claimants to the crown. In order to avoid civil war, Edward was asked to decide who should be king. He agreed to make the decision on condition that the one whom he selected should hold Scotland as a *fief* from the English king. This arrangement was adopted, and the crown was given to John Baliol. But Edward unwisely made demands upon the Scots which aroused their anger, and their king renounced his homage to the king of England. The Scotch, moreover, formed an alliance with Edward's enemy, Philip the Fair of France; thenceforth, in all the difficulties between England and France, the English kings had always to reckon with the disaffected Scotch, who were glad to aid England's enemies.

Edward marched in person against the Scotch (1296) and speedily put down what he regarded as a rebellion. He declared that Baliol had forfeited his fief through treason, and that consequently the English king had become the real ruler of Scotland. He emphasized his claim by carrying off the famous Stone of Scone (now in Westminster Abbey), upon which the kings of Scotland had been crowned for ages. Continued resistance led Edward to attempt to incorporate Scotland with England in the same way that he had treated Wales. This was the beginning of three hundred years of intermittent war between England and Scotland, which ended only when a Scotch king, James VI, succeeded to the English throne in 1603 as James I.

That Scotland was able to maintain her independence was mainly due to Robert Bruce, a national hero who succeeded in bringing both the nobility and the people under his leadership. Edward I died, old and worn out, in 1307, when on his way north to put down a rising under Bruce, and left the task of dealing with the Scotch to his incompetent son, Edward II.

The Scotch acknowledged Bruce as their king and decisively defeated Edward II in the battle of Bannockburn (1314), the most famous conflict in Scottish history. Nevertheless, the English refused to acknowledge the independence of Scotland until forced to do so in 1328.

In the course of their struggles with England the Scotch people of the Lowlands had become more closely welded together, and the independence of Scotland, although it caused much bloodshed, first and last, served to develop certain permanent differences between the little Scotch nation and the rest of the English race. No Scotchman to the present day likes to be mistaken for an Englishman. The peculiarities of the language and habits of the people north of the Tweed have been made familiar by the novels of Sir Walter Scott and Robert L. Stevenson and by the poems of Robert Burns.

The Hundred Years' War

England and France were both becoming strong states in the early fourteenth century. The king in both of these countries had got the better of the feudal lords, and a parliament had been established in France as well as in England, in which the townspeople as well as the clergy and nobility were represented. But both countries were set back by a long series of conflicts known as the Hundred Years' War, which was especially disastrous to France. The trouble arose as follows:

It will be remembered that King John of England had lost all the French possessions of the Plantagenets except the duchy of Guienne. For this he had to do homage to the king of France and become his vassal. This arrangement lasted for many years, but in the time of Edward III the old French line of kings died out, and Edward declared that he himself was the rightful ruler of all France because his mother, Isabella, was a sister of the last king of the old line.

The French lawyers, however, decided that Edward had no claim to the French throne and that a very distant relative of the last king was the legal heir to the crown (Philip VI). Edward, nevertheless, maintained that he was rightfully king of

France.[1] He added the French emblem of the lilies (fleurs-de-lis) to the lions on the English coat of arms. In 1346 he landed in Normandy with an English army, devastated the country, and marched up the Seine toward Paris. He met the troops of Philip at Crécy, where a celebrated battle was fought, in which the English with their long bows and well-directed arrows put to rout the French knights. Ten years later the English made another incursion into France and again defeated the French cavalry. The French king (John II) was himself captured and carried off to London.

The French Parliament, commonly called the Estates General, came together to consider the unhappy state of affairs. The members from the towns were more numerous than the representatives of the clergy and nobility. A great list of reforms was drawn up. These provided among other things

[1] The French kings during the fourteenth and fifteenth centuries:

Louis IX (St. Louis) (1226–1270)

Philip III (1270–1285)

Philip IV, the Fair (1285–1314) — Charles of Valois, ancestor of the house of Valois

Louis X (1314–1316); Isabella, m. Edward II; Philip V (1316–1322); Charles IV (1322–1328)

daughter; John (1316), an infant who died when but a few days old; Edward III of England; daughters; daughter

Philip VI (1328–1350)

John II (1350–1364)

Charles V (1364–1380); Philip, founder of the powerful house of Burgundy

Charles VI (1380–1422)

Charles VII (1422–1461)

Louis XI (1461–1483)

Charles VIII (1483–1498)

that the Estates General should meet regularly even when the king failed to summon them, and that the collection and expenditure of the public revenue should be no longer entirely under the control of the king but should be supervised by the representatives of the people. The city of Paris rose in support of the revolutionary Estates, but the violence of its allies discredited rather than helped the movement, and France was soon glad to accept the unrestricted rule of its king once more.

ROYAL ARMS OF EDWARD III

On the upper left-hand quarter and the lower right-hand are the lilies as represented in heraldry

The history of the French Estates General forms a curious contrast to that of the English Parliament, which was laying the foundation of its later power during this very period. While the French king occasionally summoned the Estates when he needed money, he did so only in order that their approbation of new taxes might make it easier to collect them. He never admitted that he had not the right to levy taxes if he wished without consulting his subjects.

In England, on the other hand, the kings ever since the time of Edward I had repeatedly agreed that no new taxes should be imposed without the consent of Parliament. Edward II, as we have seen, had gone farther and accepted the representatives of the people as his advisers in all important matters touching the welfare of the realm. While the French Estates gradually sank into insignificance, the English Parliament soon learned to grant no money until the king had redressed the grievances which it pointed out, and thus it insured its influence over the king's policy.

Edward III found it impossible, however, to conquer France, and the successor of the French king, John II, managed before

Edward died in 1377 to get back almost all the lands that the English had occupied.

For a generation after the death of Edward III the war with France was almost discontinued. France had suffered a great deal more than England. In the first place, all the fighting had been done on her side of the Channel, and in the second place, the soldiers, who found themselves without occupation, wandered about in bands maltreating and plundering the people. In one of his letters, Petrarch, who visited France at this period, tells us that he could not believe that this was the same kingdom which he had once seen so rich and flourishing. "Nothing presented itself to my eyes but fearful solitude and extreme poverty, uncultivated land and houses in ruins. Even about Paris there were everywhere signs of fire and destruction. The streets were deserted; the roads overgrown with weeds."

The horrors of war had been increased by the deadly bubonic plague which appeared in Europe early in 1348. In April it had reached Florence; by August it was devastating France and Germany; it then spread over England from the southwest northward, attacking every part of the country during the year 1349. This disease, like other terrible epidemics, such as smallpox and cholera, came from Asia. Those who were stricken with it usually died in two or three days. It is impossible to tell what proportion of the population perished. Reports of the time say that in one district of France only onetenth of the people survived, in another but one-sixteenth; and that for a long time five hundred bodies were carried from the great hospital of Paris every day. A careful estimate shows that in England toward one-half of the population died. At the Abbey of Newenham only the abbot and two monks were left alive out of twenty-six. There were constant complaints that certain lands were no longer of any value to their lords because the tenants were all dead.

In England the growing discontent among the farming classes may be ascribed partly to the results of the great pestilence and partly to the new taxes which were levied in order to prolong the disastrous war with France. Up to this time the majority of those who cultivated the land belonged to some particular manor, paid stated dues to their lord, and performed definite services for him. Hitherto there had been relatively few farm hands who might be hired and who sought employment anywhere that they could get it. The black death, by greatly decreasing the number of laborers, raised wages and served to increase the importance of the unattached laborer. Consequently he not only demanded higher wages than ever before but readily deserted one employer when another offered him more money.

This appeared very shocking to those who were accustomed to the traditional rates of payment; and the government undertook to keep down wages by prohibiting laborers from asking more than had been customary during the years that preceded the pestilence. Every laborer, when offered work at the established wages, was ordered to accept it on pain of imprisonment. The first "Statute of Laborers" was issued in 1351; but apparently it was not obeyed and similar laws were enacted from time to time for a century.

The old manor system was breaking up. Many of the laboring class in the country no longer held land as serfs, but moved from place to place and made a living by working for wages. The villain, as the serf was called in England, began to regard the dues which he had been accustomed to pay to his lord as unjust. A petition to Parliament in 1377 asserts that the villains are refusing to pay their customary services to their lords or to acknowledge the obligations which they owe as serfs.

In 1381 the peasants rose in revolt against the taxes levied on them to carry on the hopeless war with France. They burned some of the houses of the nobles and of the rich ecclesiastics, and took particular pains to see that the registers were destroyed which were kept by the various lords enumerating the obligations of their serfs.

Although the peasants met with little success, serfdom decayed rapidly. It became more and more common for the serf to pay his dues to the lord in money instead of working for him, and in this way he lost one of the chief characteristics of a serf. The landlord then either hired men to cultivate the fields which he reserved for his own use, or rented the land to tenants. These tenants were not in a position to force their fellow tenants on the manor to pay the full dues which had formerly been exacted by the lord. Sixty or seventy years after the Peasants' War the English rural population had in one way or another become free men, and serfs had practically disappeared.

The war between England and France almost ceased for nearly forty years after the death of Edward III. It was renewed in 1415, and the English king won another great victory at Agincourt, similar to that gained at Crécy. Once more the English bowmen slaughtered great numbers of French knights. Fifteen years later the English had succeeded in conquering all of France north of the Loire River; but a considerable region to the south still continued to be held by King Charles VII of France. He was weak and indolent and was doing nothing to check the English victories. The English were engaged in besieging the great town of Orléans when help and encouragement came to the French from a most unexpected quarter. A peasant girl put on a soldier's armor, mounted a horse, and led the faint-hearted French troops to victory.

To her family and her companions Joan of Arc seemed only "a good girl, simple and pleasant in her ways," but she brooded much over the disasters that had overtaken her country, and a "great pity on the fair realm of France" filled her heart. She saw visions and heard voices that bade her go forth to the help of the king and lead him to Reims to be crowned.

The modern student of abnormal psychology may well suspect that behind these voices and patriotic ambitions lay a deep desire on Joan's part to be a man and consort with men instead of sheep and women. She longed to be a soldier and ride bravely on her horse. This explanation makes against the ugly aspersions cast upon her by Voltaire and more recent scandal mongers, for which there is no historical foundation.

It was with the greatest difficulty that she got anybody to believe in her mission or to help her to get an audience with her sovereign. But her own firm faith in her divine guidance triumphed over all doubts and obstacles. She was at last accepted as a God-sent champion and placed at the head of some troops dispatched to the relief of Orléans. This city, which was the key to southern France, had been besieged by the English for some months and was on the point of surrender. Joan, who rode at the head of her troops, clothed in armor like a man, had now become the idol of the soldiers and of the people. Under the guidance and inspiration of her courage, sound sense, and burning enthusiasm, Orléans was relieved and the English completely routed. The Maid of Orléans, as she was henceforth called, was now free to conduct the king to Reims, where he was crowned in the cathedral (July 17, 1429).

The Maid now felt that her mission was accomplished and begged permission to return to her home and her brothers and sisters. To this the king would not consent, and she continued to fight his battles with success. But the other leaders were jealous of her, and even her friends, the soldiers, were sensitive to the taunt of being led by a woman. During the defense of Compiègne in May, 1430, she was allowed to fall into the hands of the Duke of Burgundy, who sold her to the English. They were not satisfied with simply holding as prisoner that strange maiden who had so discomfited them; they wished to discredit everything that she had done, and so declared, and undoubtedly believed, that she was a witch who had been helped by the devil. She was tried by a court of clergymen, found guilty, and burned at Rouen in 1431. Her bravery and noble constancy affected even her executioners, and an English soldier who had come to triumph over her death was heard to exclaim: "We are lost—we have burned a saint." The English cause in France was indeed lost, for her spirit and example had given new courage and vigor to the French armies.[1]

[1] Bernard Shaw in the scholarly and amusing introduction to his play of *Saint Joan* gives an excellent idea of the attitude and procedure of those who tried Joan.

THE NEW MONARCHY IN ENGLAND

The English Parliament became more and more reluctant to grant funds when there were no more victories gained. From this time on the English lost ground steadily. They were expelled from Normandy in 1450. Three years later, the last vestige of their possessions in southern France passed into the hands of the French king. The Hundred Years' War was over, and although England still retained Calais, the great question whether she should extend her sway upon the Continent was finally settled.

The New Monarchy in England

The close of the Hundred Years' War was followed in England by the Wars of the Roses, between the rival houses which were struggling for the crown. The badge of the house of Lancaster was a red rose, and that of York was a white one.[1] Each party was supported by a group of the wealthy and powerful nobles whose conspiracies, treasons, murders, and executions fill the annals of England during the period which we have been discussing.

The nobles no longer owed their power as they had in previous centuries to *vassals* who were bound to follow them to

[1] Descent of the rival houses of Lancaster and York:

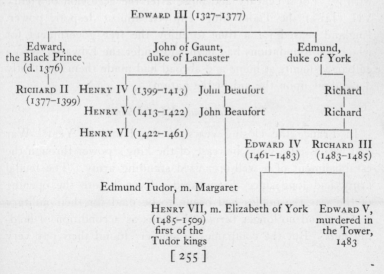

EDWARD III (1327–1377)

Edward, the Black Prince (d. 1376)

John of Gaunt, duke of Lancaster

Edmund, duke of York

RICHARD II (1377–1399)

HENRY IV (1399–1413)   John Beaufort

Richard

HENRY V (1413–1422)   John Beaufort

Richard

HENRY VI (1422–1461)

EDWARD IV (1461–1483)   RICHARD III (1483–1485)

Edmund Tudor, m. Margaret

HENRY VII, m. Elizabeth of York (1485–1509) first of the Tudor kings

EDWARD V, murdered in the Tower, 1483

war. Like the king, they relied upon *hired soldiers*. It was easy to find plenty of restless fellows who were willing to become the retainers of a nobleman if he would agree to clothe them and keep open house, where they might eat and drink their fill. Their master was to help them when they got into trouble, and they on their part were expected to intimidate, misuse, and even murder at need those who opposed the interests of their chief.

It is needless to speak of the several battles and the many skirmishes of the miserable Wars of the Roses. These lasted from 1435, when the Duke of York set seriously to work to displace the weak-minded Lancastrian king (Henry VI), until the accession of Henry VII, of the house of Tudor, thirty years later.

The Wars of the Roses had important results. Nearly all the powerful families of England had been drawn into the war, and a great part of the nobility, whom the kings had formerly feared, had perished on the battlefield or lost their heads in the ruthless executions carried out by each party after it gained a victory. This left the king far more powerful than ever before. He could now control Parliament, even if he could not do away with it. For a century and more after the accession of Henry VII (1485) the Tudor kings enjoyed almost despotic power. England ceased for a time to enjoy the free government for which the foundations had been laid under the Edwards, whose embarrassments at home and abroad had made them constantly dependent upon the aid of the nation.

The Crafty Louis XI of France

In France the closing years of the Hundred Years' War had witnessed a great increase of the king's power through the establishment of a well-organized standing army. The feudal army had long since disappeared. Even before the opening of the war the nobles had begun to be paid for their military services and no longer furnished troops as a condition of holding fiefs. But the companies of soldiers found their pay very uncertain, and plundered their countrymen as well as the enemy.

As the war drew to a close, the lawless troopers became a terrible scourge to the country and were known as *flayers,* on account of the horrible way in which they tortured the peasants in the hope of extracting money from them. In 1439 the Estates General approved a plan devised by the king, for putting an end to this evil. Thereafter no one was to raise a company without the permission of the king, who was to name the captains and fix the number of the soldiers.

The Estates agreed that the king should use a certain tax, called the *taille,* to support the troops necessary for the protection of the frontier. This was a fatal concession, for the king now had an army and the right to collect what he chose to consider a permanent tax, the amount of which he later greatly increased; he was not dependent, as was the

LOUIS XI OF FRANCE

English king, upon the grants made for brief periods by the representatives of the nation.

Before the king of France could hope to establish a compact, well-organized state it was necessary for him to reduce the power of his vassals, some of whom were almost his equal in strength. The older feudal families had many of them succumbed to the attacks and the diplomacy of the kings of the thirteenth century, especially of St. Louis. But he and his successors had raised up fresh rivals by granting whole provinces to their younger sons. In this way new and powerful lines of feudal nobles were established, such, for example, as the houses of Orléans, Anjou, Bourbon, and, above all, Burgundy. The process of reducing the power of the nobles had, it is true, been begun. They had been forbidden to coin money, to maintain armies, and to tax their subjects, and the powers of the king's judges had been extended over all the realm. But the task of consolidating France was reserved for the son of Charles VII, the shrewd and treacherous Louis XI (1461-1483).

The most powerful and dangerous of Louis XI's vassals were the dukes of Burgundy, and they gave him a great deal of trouble. Of Burgundy something will be said in a later chapter. Louis XI had himself made heir to a number of provinces in central and southern France,—Anjou, Maine, Provence, etc.,—which by the death of their possessors came under the king's immediate control (1481). He humiliated in various ways the vassals who in his early days had combined against him. The Duke of Alençon he imprisoned; the rebellious Duke of Nemours he caused to be executed in the most cruel manner. Louis's aims were worthy, but his means were generally despicable. It sometimes seemed as if he gloried in being the most rascally among rascals, the most treacherous among the traitors.

Both England and France emerged from the troubles and desolations of the Hundred Years' War stronger than ever before. In both countries the kings had overcome the menace of the old feudalism by destroying the power of the great families. The royal government was becoming constantly more powerful. Commerce and industry increased the people's wealth and supplied the monarchs with the revenue necessary to maintain government officials and a sufficient army to keep order throughout their realms. They were no longer forced to rely upon the uncertain fidelity of their vassals. In short, England and France were both becoming modern states.

CHAPTER XII

EMPEROR CHARLES V AND HIS VAST REALMS

Maximilian the Matchmaker. How Italy Became the Battleground of the European Powers. Condition of Germany in Charles V's Day

Maximilian the Matchmaker

POLITICAL history has to do with governmental policy. Hitherto, it has been concerned largely with rulers, their lust for territory and their consequent wars. Until recently kingship was a sort of private possession, transmitted hereditarily and deeply affected by marriages and the claims growing out of relationships. So political history is ofttimes grotesque and wearisome, full of seemingly irrelevant and casual circumstances, which diminish its dignity by reducing the serious matter of government to mean squabbles between unworthy rivals. There was little new in the matchmaking of the Emperor Maximilian, but it illustrates the melancholy antecedents of government as we now know it. The diplomats before the World War were the successors of the matchmakers of the sixteenth century. Whether international relations are to be redeemed from the scandalous precedents of the past remains to be seen.

In the year 1500 a baby was born in the town of Ghent who was destined before he reached the age of twenty to rule, as Emperor Charles V, over more of Europe than any one since Charlemagne. He owed his vast empire not to any conquests of his own but to an extraordinary series of royal marriages which made him heir to a great part of western Europe. These marriages had been arranged by his grandfather, Maximilian I. Maximilian belonged to the House of Hapsburg, and in order to understand European history since 1500 we must take note of Maximilian and the Hapsburg line.

The German kings had failed to create a strong kingdom such as those over which Louis XI of France and Henry VII of England ruled. Their fine title of emperor had made them a great deal of trouble and done them no good, as we have seen.[1] Their attempts to keep Italy as well as Germany under their rule, and the alliance of the mighty bishop of Rome with their enemies had well-nigh ruined them. Their position was further weakened by the fact that their office was not strictly hereditary. Although the emperors were often succeeded by their sons, each new emperor had to be *elected,* and those great vassals who controlled the election naturally took care to bind the candidate by solemn promises not to interfere with their privileges and independence. The result was that, after the downfall of the Hohenstaufens, Germany fell apart into a great number of practically independent states, of which none were very large and some were extremely small.

After an interregnum, Rudolf of Hapsburg had been chosen emperor in 1273. The original seat of the Hapsburgs, who were destined to play such a great part in European affairs, through the World War, was in northern Switzerland, where the vestiges of their original castle may still be seen. Rudolf was the first prominent member of the family; he established its position and influence by seizing the duchies of Austria and Styria, which became, under his successors, the nucleus of the extensive Austrian possessions.

About a century and a half after the death of Rudolf, the German princes began regularly to choose as their emperor the ruler of the Austrian possessions, so that the imperial title became, to all intents and purposes, hereditary in the Hapsburg line. The Hapsburgs were, however, far more interested in adding to their family domains than in advancing the interests of the German Empire as a whole. Indeed, the Holy Roman Empire was nearly defunct and, in the memorable words of Voltaire, it had ceased to be either holy, or Roman, or an empire.

Maximilian, while still a very young man, married Mary of Burgundy, the heiress to the Burgundian realms, which included what we now call Holland and Belgium and portions of eastern France. In this way the House of Austria got a hold on the shores of the North Sea. Mary died in 1482 and

[1] See above, chapter VI.

her lands were inherited by her infant son, Philip. Maximilian's next matrimonial move was to arrange a marriage between his son Philip and Joanna, the heiress to the Spanish kingdoms, and this makes it necessary for us to turn a moment to Spain, of which little or nothing has been said since we saw how the kingdom of the Visigoths was overthrown by the Mohammedan invaders, over seven hundred years before Maximilian's time.

The Mohammedan conquest served to make the history of Spain very different from that of the other states of Europe. One of its first and most important results was the conversion of a great part of the inhabitants to Mohammedanism. During the tenth century, which was so dark a period in the rest of Europe, the Arab civilization in Spain reached its highest development. The various elements in the population, Carthaginian, Roman, Gothic, Arab, and Berber, appear to have been thoroughly amalgamated. Agriculture, industry, commerce, art, and the sciences made rapid progress. Cordova, with its half million of inhabitants, its stately palaces, its university, its three thousand mosques and three hundred public baths, was perhaps unrivaled at that period in the whole world. There were thousands of students at the University of Cordova at a time when, in the North, only clergymen had mastered even the simple arts of reading and writing. This brilliant civilization lasted, however, for hardly more than a hundred years. By the middle of the eleventh century the caliphate of Cordova had fallen to pieces, and shortly afterward the country was overrun by new invaders from Africa.

But the Christians were destined to reconquer the peninsula. As early as the year 1000 several small Christian kingdoms—Castile, Aragon, and Navarre—had come into existence in the northern part of Spain. Castile, in particular, began to push back the Mohammedans and, in 1085, reconquered Toledo from them. Aragon also widened its bounds by incorporating Barcelona and conquering the territory watered by the Ebro. By 1250 the long war of the Christians against the Mohammedans, which fills the medieval annals of Spain, had been so successfully prosecuted that Castile extended to the south coast and included the great towns of Cordova and Seville. The Christian kingdom of Portugal was already as large as it is to-day.

The Moors, as the Spanish Mohammedans were called, maintained themselves for two centuries more in the mountainous kingdom of Granada, in the southern part of the peninsula. During this period Castile, which was the largest of the Spanish kingdoms and embraced all the central part of the peninsula, was too much occupied by internal feuds and struggles over the crown to wage successful war against the Moorish kingdom to the south.

The first Spanish monarch whose name need be mentioned here was Queen Isabella of Castile, who, in 1469, concluded an all-important marriage with Ferdinand, the heir of the crown of Aragon. It is with this union of Castile and Aragon that the great importance of Christian Spain in European history begins. For the next hundred years Spain was to enjoy more military power than any other European state.

Ferdinand and Isabella undertook to complete the conquest of the peninsula, and in 1492, after a long siege, the city of Granada fell into their hands, and therewith the last vestige of Moorish domination disappeared.[1]

In the same year that the conquest of the peninsula was completed, the discoveries of Columbus, made under the auspices of Queen Isabella, opened up sources of undreamed-of wealth beyond the seas. The transient greatness of Spain in the sixteenth century is largely to be attributed to the riches which poured in from her American possessions. The shameless and cruel looting of the Mexican and Peruvian cities by Cortes and Pizarro, and the products of the silver mines of the New

[1] No one can gaze upon the great castle and palace of the Alhambra, which was built for the Moorish kings, without realizing what a high degree of culture the Moors had attained. Its beautiful and impressive arcades, its magnificent courts, and the delicate tracery of its arches represent the highest achievement of Arabic architecture (see above, pp. 80 f.).

World, enabled Spain to assume, for a time, a position in Europe which her internal strength and normal resources would never have permitted.

Unfortunately, the most industrious, skillful, and thrifty among the inhabitants of Spain, that is, the Moors and the Jews, who well-nigh supported the whole kingdom with the products of their toil, were bitterly persecuted by the Christians. So anxious was Isabella to rid her kingdom of the infidels that she revived the court of the Inquisition.[1] For several decades its tribunals arrested and condemned innumerable persons who were suspected of heresy, and thousands were burned at the stake during this period. These wholesale executions have served to associate Spain especially with the horrors of the Inquisition. Finally, in 1609, a century after Isabella's death, the Moors were driven out of the country altogether. The persecution diminished or disheartened the most useful and enterprising portion of the Spanish people, and permanently crippled the country.

It was no wonder that the daughter and heiress of Ferdinand and Isabella seemed to Maximilian an admirable match for his son Philip. Philip died, however, in 1506,—six years after his eldest son Charles was born,—and his poor wife, Joanna, became insane with grief and was thus incapacitated for ruling. So Charles could look forward to an unprecedented accumulation of glorious titles as soon as his grandfathers, Maximilian of Austria and Ferdinand of Aragon, should pass away.[2] He was soon to be duke of Brabant, margrave of Antwerp, count of Holland, archduke of Austria, count of Tyrol, king of Cas-

[1] See above, pp. 158 ff.

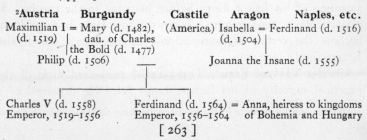

[2] Austria   Burgundy   Castile   Aragon   Naples, etc.

Austria	Burgundy	Castile	Aragon	Naples, etc.
Maximilian I = Mary (d. 1482),		(America) Isabella = Ferdinand (d. 1516)		
(d. 1519) dau. of Charles		(d. 1504)		
the Bold (d. 1477)				
Philip (d. 1506)		Joanna the Insane (d. 1555)		
Charles V (d. 1558)		Ferdinand (d. 1564) = Anna, heiress to kingdoms		
Emperor, 1519–1556		Emperor, 1556–1564 of Bohemia and Hungary		

tile, Aragon, and Naples,[1] and of the vast Spanish possessions in America—to mention a few of his more important titles.

Ferdinand died in 1516, and Charles, now a lad of sixteen, who had been born and reared in the Netherlands, was much bewildered when he first landed in his Spanish dominions. The Burgundian advisers whom he brought with him were distasteful to the haughty Spaniards, to whom, of course, they were foreigners; suspicion and opposition awaited him in each of his several Spanish kingdoms, for he found by no means a united Spain. Each kingdom demanded special recognition of its rights and proposed important reforms before it would acknowledge Charles as its king.

It seemed as if the boy would have his hands full in asserting his authority as the first "king of Spain"; nevertheless, a still more imposing title and still more perplexing responsibilities were to fall upon his shoulders before he was twenty years old. It had long been Maximilian's ambition that his grandson should succeed him upon the imperial throne. After his death, in 1519, the electors finally chose Charles as emperor—the fifth of that name—instead of the rival candidate, Francis I of France. By this election the king of Spain, who had not yet been in Germany and who never learned its language, became its ruler at a critical juncture, when the teachings of Luther (see next chapter) were adding a new kind of trouble to the old disorders.

How Italy Became the Battleground of the European Powers

In order to understand the Europe of Charles V and the constant wars which occupied him all his life, we must turn back and review the questions which had been engaging the attention of his fellow kings before he came to the throne. It is particularly necessary to see clearly how Italy had suddenly become the center of commotion—the battlefield for Spain, France, and Germany.

Charles VIII of France (1483-1498) possessed little of the practical sagacity of his father, Louis XI. He dreamed of a

[1] Naples and Sicily were in the hands of the king of Aragon at this time.

mighty expedition against the Turks and of the conquest of Constantinople. As the first step he determined to lead an army into Italy and assert his claim, inherited from his father, to the kingdom of Naples, which was in the hands of the House of Aragon.[1] While Italy had everything to lose by permitting a powerful foreign monarch to get a foothold in the South, there was no probability that the various little states in which the peninsula was divided would lay aside their animosities and combine against the invader. On the contrary, Charles VIII was urged by some of the Italians themselves to come.

Had Lorenzo the Magnificent still been alive, he might have organized a league to oppose the French king, but he had died in 1492, two years before Charles started. Lorenzo's sons failed to maintain the influence over the people of Florence which their father had enjoyed; and the leadership of the city fell into the hands of the Dominican friar, Savonarola, whose fervid preaching attracted and held for a time the attention of the fickle Florentine populace. He believed himself to be a prophet and proclaimed that God was about to scourge Italy for its iniquities.

When Savonarola heard of the French invasion, it appeared to him that this was indeed the looked-for scourge of God, which might afflict, but would also purify, the Church. As Charles approached Florence, the people rose in revolt against the Medici, sacked their palaces, and drove out the three sons of Lorenzo. Savonarola became the chief figure in the new republic which was established.[2] Charles was admitted into

---

[1] It will be remembered that the popes, in their long struggle with Frederick II and the Hohenstaufens, finally called in Charles of Anjou, the brother of St. Louis, and gave to him both Naples and Sicily. Sicily revolted in 1282 and was united with the kingdom of Aragon, which still held it when Charles V came to the Spanish throne. Naples also was conquered by the king of Aragon, and was in his family when Charles VIII undertook his Italian expedition. Louis XI, although he claimed the right of the French to rule in Naples, had prudently refused to attempt to oust the Aragonese usurpers, as he had quite enough to do at home.

[2] The fate of Savonarola was a tragic one. He lost the confidence of the Florentines and was regarded as a nuisance by the pope. Three years after Charles VIII's visit he was accused of heresy and executed.

Florence, but his ugly, insignificant figure disappointed the Florentines. They soon made it clear to him that they did not regard him in any sense as a conqueror, and would oppose a prolonged occupation by the French. So, after a week's stay, the French army left Florence and proceeded on its southward journey.

The next power with which Charles had to deal was the pope, who ruled over the states of the Church. The pope was greatly perturbed when he realized that the French army was upon him. He naturally dreaded to have a foreign power in control of southern Italy just as his predecessors had dreaded the efforts of the Hohenstaufens to add Naples to their empire. He was unable, however, to oppose the French and they proceeded on their way.

The success of the French king seemed marvelous, for even Naples speedily fell into his hands. But he and his troops were demoralized by the wines and other pleasures [1] of the South, and meanwhile his enemies at last began to form a combination against him. Ferdinand of Aragon was fearful lest he might lose Sicily, and Emperor Maximilian objected to having the French control Italy. Charles's situation became so dangerous that he thought himself fortunate, at the close of 1495, to escape, with the loss of only a single battle, from the country he had hoped to conquer.

The results of Charles VIII's expedition appear at first sight trivial; in reality they were momentous. In the first place, it was now clear to Europe that the Italians had no real national feeling, however much they might despise the "barbarians" who lived north of the Alps. From this time down to the latter half of the nineteenth century, Italy was dominated by foreign

[1] An incident of a certain class of the pleasures was the black pox, or "French disease." This later received the name of syphilis from a character which appears in a medical poem of Hieronymus Fracastorius, an Italian physician who died in 1553. Henry VIII and Ulrich of Hutten suffered from the malady, and Ulrich, with forced facetiousness, has much to say on the subject. Shakespeare uses "the pox" as a current curse of his time.

nations, especially Spain and Austria. In the second place, the French learned to admire the art and culture of Italy. The nobles began to change their feudal castles, which since the invention of gunpowder were no longer impregnable, into luxurious palaces and country houses. The new scholarship of

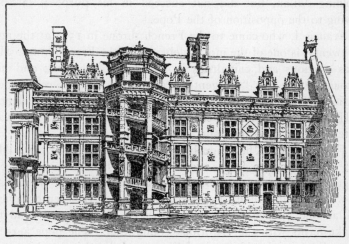

COURT OF THE PALACE AT BLOIS

The expedition of Charles VIII to Italy called the attention of French architects to the novel Renaissance style used there. As cannon had by this time begun to render the old kind of castles with thick walls and towers useless as a means of defense, the French kings began to construct magnificent palaces of which several still exist. Charles VIII's successor, Louis XII, began a handsome structure at Blois, on the Loire River, and Francis I added a wing, the inner side of which is here reproduced. Its magnificent open staircase and wide, high windows have little in common with the old donjons of feudal times

Italy also took root and flourished not only in France but in England and Germany as well, and Greek began to be studied outside of Italy. Consequently, just as Italy was becoming, politically, the victim of foreign aggressions, it was also losing, never to regain, that intellectual leadership which it had enjoyed since the revival of interest in Latin and Greek literature.

It would be wearisome and unprofitable to follow the attempts of the French to get a foothold in Milan. Suffice it to say that Charles VIII soon died and that his successor Louis XII laid claim to the duchy of Milan in the north as well as to Naples in the south. But he concluded to sell his claim to Naples to Ferdinand of Aragon and centered his attention on holding Milan, but did not succeed in his purpose, largely owing to the opposition of the Pope.

Francis I, who came to the French throne in 1515 at the age of twenty, is one of the most celebrated of the French kings. He was gracious and chivalrous in his ideas of conduct, and his proudest title was "the gentleman king." Like his contemporaries, Pope Leo X, son of Lorenzo de' Medici, and Henry VIII of England, he helped artists and men of letters and was interested in fine buildings.

Francis opened his reign by a very astonishing victory. He led his troops into Italy, over a pass which had hitherto been regarded as impracticable for cavalry, and defeated the Swiss —who were in Milan's pay—at Marignano. He then occupied Milan and opened negotiations with Leo X, who was glad to make terms with the victorious young king. The pope agreed that Francis should retain Milan, and Francis on his part acceded to Leo's plan for turning over Florence once more to the Medici, of which family the pope himself was a member. This was done, and some years later this memorable republic became the grand duchy of Tuscany, governed by a line of petty princes under whom its former glories were never renewed.

Friendly relations existed at first between the two young sovereigns, Francis I and Charles V, but there were several circumstances which led to an almost incessant series of wars between them. France was clamped in between the northern and southern possessions of Charles, and had at that time no natural boundaries. Moreover, there was a standing dispute over portions of the Burgundian realms, for both Charles and Francis claimed the *duchy* of Burgundy and also the neighboring *county* of Burgundy—commonly called Franche-Comté.

Charles also believed that, through his grandfather, Maximilian, he was entitled to Milan, which the French kings had set their hearts upon retaining. For a generation the rivals fought over these and other matters, and the wars between Charles and Francis were but the prelude to a conflict lasting over two centuries between France and the overgrown power of the House of Hapsburg.

In the impending struggle it was natural that both monarchs should try to gain the aid of the king of England, whose friendship was of the greatest importance to each of them, and who was by no means loath to take a hand in European affairs. Henry VIII had succeeded his father, Henry VII, in 1509 at the age of eighteen. Like Francis, he was good-looking, and in his early years made a very happy impression upon those who came in contact with him. He gained much popularity by condemning to death the two men who had been most active in extorting the "benevolences" which his father had been wont to require of unwilling givers. With a small but important class, his learning brought him credit. He married, for his first wife, an aunt of Charles V, Catherine of Aragon, and chose as his chief adviser Thomas Wolsey, whose career and sudden downfall were to be strangely associated with the fate of the unfortunate Spanish princess.[1]

In 1520 Charles V started for Germany to receive the imperial crown at Aix-la-Chapelle. On his way he landed in England with the purpose of keeping Henry from forming an alliance with Francis. He judged the best means to be that of freely bribing Wolsey, who had been made a cardinal by Leo X, and who was at the time all-powerful with Henry. Charles therefore bestowed on the cardinal a large annuity in addition to one which he had granted him somewhat earlier. He then set sail for the Netherlands, where he was duly crowned king of the Romans. From there he proceeded, for the first time, to Germany, where he summoned his first diet at Worms.

[1] See below, pp. 309 f.

Condition of Germany in Charles V's Day

Until the close of the World War Germany meant to us the German federation, one of the four largest of the European states. It was a compact federation, made up of twenty-two monarchies and three little city-republics. Each member of the union managed its local affairs quite independent of any other member, but left all questions of national importance to be settled by the central government at Berlin. This federation was, however, less than half a century old.

In the time of Charles V there was no such Germany as this, but only what the French called the "Germanies"; that is, two or three hundred states, which differed greatly from one another in size and character. This one had a duke, that a count, at its head, while others were ruled over by archbishops, bishops, or abbots. There were many cities, like Nuremberg, Frankfurt, and Cologne, which were just as independent as the electorate of Brandenburg—later to become the kingdom of Prussia— or the great duchies of Bavaria, Württemberg, and Saxony. Lastly there were the knights, whose possessions might consist of no more than a single strong castle with a wretched village lying at its foot.

As for the emperor, he no longer had any power to control his vassals. He could boast of unlimited pretensions and great traditions, but he had neither money nor soldiers. At the time of Luther's birth the poverty-stricken Frederick III (Maximilian's father) might have been seen picking up a free meal at a monastery or riding behind a slow but economical ox team. The real power in Germany lay in the hands of the more important vassals.

First and foremost among these were the seven *electors,* so called because since the thirteenth century they had enjoyed the right to elect the emperor. Three of them were archbishops—kings in all but name of considerable territories on the Rhine, namely, the electorates of Mainz, Trèves, and Cologne. Near them, to the south, was the region ruled over by the elector of the Palatinate; to the northeast were the territories of the electors of Brandenburg and of Saxony; the king of Bohemia made the seventh of the group.

Beside these states, the dominions of other rulers scarcely less important than the electors appear on the map. Some of these territories, like Württemberg, Bavaria, Hesse, and Baden, are familiar to us to-day as members of the German "Reich," but all of them have been much enlarged since the sixteenth century by the absorption of the little states that formerly lay within and about them.

The towns, which had grown up since the great economic revolution that had brought in commerce and the use of money in the thirteenth century, were centers of culture in the north of Europe, just as those of Italy were in the south. Nuremberg, the most beautiful of the old German cities, still possesses a great many of the extraordinary buildings and works of art which it produced in the sixteenth century. Some of the towns were immediate vassals of the emperor and were consequently independent of the particular prince within whose territory they were situated. These were called *free*, or *imperial*, cities and must be reckoned among the states of Germany.

THE WALLS OF ROTHENBURG

One town in Germany, Rothenburg, on the little river Tauber, once a free imperial city, retains its old walls and towers intact and many of its old houses. It gives the visitor an excellent idea of how the smaller imperial towns looked two or three hundred years ago

[271]

The knights, who ruled over the smallest of the German territories, had earlier formed a very important class, but the introduction of gunpowder and new methods of fighting put them at a disadvantage, for they clung to their medieval traditions. Their tiny realms were often too small to support them, and they frequently turned to robbery for a living and proved a great nuisance to the merchants and townspeople whom they plundered now and then.

It is clear that these states, little and big, all tangled up with one another, would be sure to have disputes among themselves which would have to be settled in some way. The emperor was not powerful enough to keep order, and the result was that each ruler had to defend himself if attacked. Neighborhood war was permitted by law if only some courteous preliminaries were observed. For instance, a prince or town was required to give warning three days in advance before attacking another member of the empire.

Germany had a national assembly, called the *diet*, which met at irregular intervals, now in one town and now in another, for Germany had no capital city. The towns were not permitted to send delegates until 1487, long after the townspeople were represented in France and England. The restless knights and other minor nobles were not represented at all and consequently did not always consider the decisions of the diet binding upon them.

It was this diet that Charles V summoned to meet him on the Rhine, in the ancient town of Worms, when he made his first visit to Germany in 1520. The most important business of the assembly proved to be the consideration of the case of a university professor, Martin Luther, who was accused of writing heretical books, and who had in reality begun what proved to be the first successful revolt against the seemingly all-powerful Medieval Church.

CHAPTER XIII

THE BREAK-UP OF THE MEDIEVAL CHURCH: PROTESTANTS *vs.* CATHOLICS

Church and State. Long-standing Question of Church Reform. Martin Luther's Revolt Against the Papacy. The Diet at Worms, 1520–1521. The Protestant Reformation in Germany. Zwingli and Calvin. How England Fell Away from the Papacy. England Becomes Protestant

Church and State

BY far the most important event during the reign of Charles V was the secession of a considerable portion of western Europe from the papal monarchy. The Medieval Church, which was described in a previous chapter, was in this way broken up, and *Protestant* churches appeared in various European countries which declared themselves entirely independent of the pope and rejected a number of the religious beliefs and practices which the Christian Church had previously maintained.

With the exception of England all those countries that lay within the ancient bounds of the Roman Empire—Italy, France, Spain, Portugal, as well as southern Germany and Austria—continued to be faithful to the pope and the Roman Catholic Church. On the other hand, the rulers of the northern German states, of England, Holland, Denmark, Norway, and Sweden, sooner or later became Protestants. In this way Europe was divided into two great religious parties, and this led to terrible wars and cruel persecutions which fill the annals of the sixteenth and seventeenth centuries.

While there can be no doubt that conflicting views of Christianity played a great part in the Protestant Revolt, there were underlying political and economic considerations of a perfectly worldly nature that entered into the decision of the various European rulers to espouse the new or cling to the old beliefs. In short, the Medieval Church was in many ways so secular an institution, so enmeshed in the ordinary affairs of government, that its disruption involved all sorts of questions other than the theory and practice of salvation. This will become apparent enough—shockingly so—as we proceed.

The final, if partial, disruption of the papal monarchy in the first half of the sixteenth century was the culmination of a long series of struggles to reform the Church or futile attempts to overthrow it in its existing form. In order to understand the attitude of the European princes toward the ecclesiastical organization as a serious rival against which they had to protect themselves we must review the curious relations, friendly and hostile, which had existed between Church and State in the two centuries preceding the so-called "Reformation." At the same time we can take note of the earlier religious leaders who had much in common with Luther and Calvin but who came too early to gain the sympathy of the rulers of their time. For after all it was the rulers alone, not the reformers or their followers, who were in a position to withdraw from the ancient and revered international ecclesiastical State of which all western European countries were members down to the opening of the sixteenth century.

We have seen that the Medieval Church was a single great institution with its head, the pope, at Rome and its officers in all the countries of western Europe. It had its laws, law courts, taxes, and even prisons, like the various kings and other rulers. In general, the kings were ready to punish every one who revolted against the Church. Moreover, the State depended upon the churchmen in many ways. It was the churchmen who wrote out the documents which the king required; they took care of the schools, aided the poor, and protected the weak. They tried, by issuing the Truce of God, to discourage neighborhood warfare, which the kings were unable to stop.

But as the period of disorder drew to an end and the kings and other rulers began to get the better of the feudal lords and established peace in their realms, they began to think that the Church had become too powerful and too rich. Certain difficulties arose of which the following were the most important:

1. Should the king or the pope have the advantage of selecting the bishops and the abbots of rich monasteries? Naturally

both were anxious to place their friends and supporters in these influential positions. Moreover, the pope could claim a considerable contribution from those whom he appointed, and the king naturally grudged him the money.

2. How far might the king venture to tax the lands and other property of the Church? Was this vast amount of wealth to go on increasing and yet make no contribution to the support of the government? The churchmen usually maintained that they needed all their money to carry on the Church services, keep up the churches and monasteries, take care of the schools and aid the poor, for the State left them to bear all these necessary burdens. The law of the Church permitted the churchmen to make voluntary gifts to the king when there was urgent necessity.

3. Then there was trouble over the cases to be tried in the Church courts and the claim of churchmen to be tried only by clergymen (so-called "benefit of clergy"). Worst of all was the habit of appealing cases to Rome, for the pope would often decide the matter in exactly the opposite way from which the king's court had decided it.

4. Lastly, there was the question of how far the pope as head of the Christian Church had a right to interfere with the government of a particular state, when he did not approve of the way in which a king was acting. The powers of the pope were very great, every one admitted, but even the most devout Catholics differed somewhat as to just how great they were.

We have seen some illustrations of these troubles in the chapter on the Popes and Emperors. A famous conflict between the king of France, Philip the Fair, and Pope Boniface VIII, about the year 1300, had important results. Philip and Edward I of England, who were reigning at the same time, had got into the habit of taxing the churchmen as they did their other subjects.

It was natural after a monarch had squeezed all that he could out of the Jews and the towns, and had exacted every possible feudal due, that he should turn to the rich estates of the clergy, in spite of their claim that their property was dedicated to

God and owed the king nothing. The extensive enterprises of Edward I led him in 1296 to demand one-fifth of the personal property of the clergy. Philip the Fair exacted one-hundredth and then one-fiftieth of the possessions of clergy and laity alike.

Against this impartial system Boniface protested in the harsh bull, *Clericis laicos* (1296). He claimed that the civil governments had always been exceedingly hostile to the clergy, and that the rulers were now exhibiting this hostility by imposing heavy burdens upon the Church, forgetting that they had no control over the clergy and their possessions. The pope, therefore, forbade all churchmen, including the monks, to pay, without his consent, to a king or ruler any part of the Church's revenue or possessions upon any pretext whatsoever. He likewise forbade the kings and princes under pain of excommunication to presume to exact any such payments.

It happened that just as the pope was prohibiting the clergy from contributing to the taxes, Philip the Fair had forbidden the exportation of all gold and silver from the country. In that way he cut off an important source of the pope's revenue, for the church of France could obviously no longer send anything to Rome. The pope was forced to give up his extreme claims. He explained the following year that he had not meant to interfere with the payment on the clergy's part of customary feudal dues nor with their loans of money to the king.

In spite of this setback, the pope never seemed more completely the recognized head of the western world than during the first great jubilee, in the year 1300, when Boniface called together all Christendom to celebrate the opening of the new century by a great religious festival at Rome. It is reported that two millions of people, coming from all parts of Europe, visited the churches of Rome, and that in spite of widening the streets, many were crushed in the crowd. So great was the influx of money into the papal treasury that two assistants were kept busy with rakes collecting the offerings which were deposited at the tomb of St. Peter.

Boniface was, however, very soon to realize that even if western Christendom regarded Rome as its religious center, the rulers would not accept him as their political head. When he dispatched an obnoxious prelate to Philip the Fair, ordering him to free a certain nobleman whom he was holding prisoner, the king declared the confident language of the papal envoy to be high treason and sent one of his lawyers to the pope to demand that the messenger be punished.

Philip was surrounded by a body of lawyers, and it would seem that they, rather than the king, were the real rulers of France. They had, through their study of Roman law, learned to admire the absolute power exercised by the Roman emperor. To them the civil government was supreme, and they urged the king to punish what they regarded as the insolent conduct of the pope. Before taking any action against the head of the Church, Philip called together the Estates General (1302), including not only the clergy and the nobility but the people of the towns as well. The Estates General, after hearing a statement of the case from one of Philip's lawyers, agreed to support their monarch.

Nogaret, one of the chief legal advisers of the king, undertook to face the pope. He collected a little troop of soldiers in Italy and marched against Boniface, who was sojourning at Anagni, where his predecessors had excommunicated two emperors, Frederick Barbarossa and Frederick II. As Boniface, in his turn, was preparing solemnly to proclaim the king of France an outcast from the Church, Nogaret penetrated into the papal palace with his soldiers and heaped insults upon the helpless but defiant old man. The townspeople forced Nogaret to leave the next day, but Boniface's spirit was broken and he soon died at Rome (1303).

King Philip now proposed to have no more trouble with popes. He arranged in 1305 to have the Archbishop of Bordeaux chosen head of the Church, with the understanding that he should transfer the papacy to France. The new pope accordingly summoned the cardinals to meet him at Lyon, where he was crowned under the title of "Clement V." He remained in France during his whole pontificate, moving from one rich abbey to another.

At Philip's command he reluctantly undertook a sort of trial of the deceased Boniface VIII, who was accused by the king's lawyers of all sorts of abominable crimes. Then, to please the king, Clement brought the Templars to trial; [1] the order was abolished, and its possessions in France, for which the king had longed, were confiscated. Obviously it proved very advantageous to the king to have a pope within his realm. Clement V died in 1314. His successors took up their residence in the town of Avignon, just outside the French frontier of those days. There they built a sumptuous palace in which successive popes lived in great splendor for sixty years.

The prolonged exile of the popes from Rome, lasting from 1305 to 1377, is commonly called the Babylonian Captivity [2] of the Church, on account of the woes attributed to it. The popes of this period were for the most part good and earnest men; but they were all Frenchmen, and the proximity of their court to France led to the natural suspicion that they were controlled by the French kings. This, together with their luxurious court, brought them into discredit with the other nations.

At Avignon the popes were naturally deprived of some of the revenue which they had enjoyed from their Italian possessions when they lived at Rome. This deficiency had to be made up by increased taxation, especially as the expenses of the splendid papal court were very heavy. The papacy was, consequently, rendered unpopular by the methods employed to raise money.

The papal exactions met with the greatest opposition in England because the popes were thought to favor France, with which country the English were at war. A law was passed by Parliament in 1352, ordering that all who procured a Church office from the pope should be outlawed, since they were enemies of the king and his realm. This and similar laws failed, however, to prevent the pope from filling English benefices.

[1] See above, p. 147.
[2] The name recalled, of course, the long exile of the Jews from their land.

The English king was unable to keep the money of his realm from flowing to Avignon, and at the meeting of the English Parliament held in 1376 a report was made that the taxes levied by the pope in England were five times those of the king.

Long-standing Question of Church Reform

The most famous and conspicuous critic of the pope at this time was John Wycliffe, a teacher at Oxford. He was born about 1320, but we know little of him before 1366, when Urban V demanded that England should pay the tribute promised by King John when he became the pope's vassal. Parliament declared that John had no right to bind the people without their consent, and Wycliffe began his career of opposition to the papacy by trying to prove that John's agreement was void. About ten years later we find the pope issuing bulls against the teachings of Wycliffe, who had begun to assert that the state might appropriate the property of the Church, if it was misused, and that the pope had no authority except as he acted according to the Gospels. Soon Wycliffe went further and boldly attacked the papacy itself, as well as many of the Church institutions.

Wycliffe's anxiety to teach the people led him to have the Bible translated into English. He also prepared a great number of sermons and tracts in English. He is the father of English prose, for we have little in English before his time, except poetry.

Wycliffe and his "simple priests" were charged with encouraging the discontent and disorder which culminated in the Peasants' War.[1] Whether this charge was true or not, it caused many of his followers to fall away from him. But in spite of this and the denunciations of the Church, Wycliffe was not seriously interfered with and died peaceably in 1384. Wycliffe is remarkable as being the first distinguished scholar and reformer to repudiate the headship of the pope and those practices of the Church of Rome which a hundred and fifty

[1] See above, pp. 251 f.

years after his death were attacked by Luther in his successful revolt against the Medieval Church.

Pope Gregory XI moved back from Avignon to Rome in 1377. His French cardinals found the neglected ancient seat of the papacy dilapidated and distasteful. On Gregory's death a year later they chose a simple Italian monk, Urban VI, to succeed him. Urban proved a highly unmanageable person and proposed to reduce the cardinals to a simple and holy life. So they, for the most part, returned to Avignon and selected a new pope more to their taste, Clement VII, on the ground that the election of Urban was invalid, owing to the intimidation which they claimed had been exercised by a Roman mob. This created the *Great Schism,* which was to last for some forty years. There had been plenty of anti-popes in former times, but never such an enduring doubt as to who was really God's appointed head of the Church. Urban created new cardinals pledged to Rome, and on his death they selected a successor. So there were two colleges of cardinals, each claiming the divine right to choose the ruler of Christendom. The Italian states naturally supported the Roman line; France that at Avignon; England, hostile to France, the Roman line; Scotland, hostile to England, the French line.

This stirred up the great question whether there was not some authority superior to even the popes themselves, to settle the distressing and demoralizing conflict. The answer was found in the belief that a general council of Christendom, inspired by the Holy Spirit, was superior to the papacy. Many such councils had been held, the earlier ones in the East before the separation of the Western Latin Church and the Eastern in 1054, when Hildebrand (soon to be Gregory VII), was beginning to dream of his Dictatus. Later councils were held in Rome. After a vast amount of discussion a council was called at Pisa in 1409, where the two existing popes were deposed and a new one elected. But the deposed rivals had their following and the result was that there were now three popes instead of two claiming the headship of the Church.

Finally the memorable Council of Constance met in 1414. It continued its sessions until 1417. Hus, a Bohemian leader, who had been greatly affected by the works of Wycliffe, appeared before the Council to defend his views. He was condemned as an impenitent heretic by the Council and burned, as was the rule of the day, by the city authorities of Constance (1415). But the Hussites of Bohemia continued to be a strong and aggressive power for years, much dreaded by the orthodox Germans, who hated them on both racial and religious grounds. The Council boldly asserted its superiority to the pope and provided that regular meetings of general councils should be held every ten years. It made feeble attempts to reform the chief recognized abuses in the Church. Its main result was the "healing" of the Schism, for it chose a new pope, Martin V, and managed to dispose of the rival lines.

All the discussion and criticism that this Council, and another later held at Basel, aroused did much to prepare the German princes for the final revolt from the papal monarchy which occurred a century later. The German diets held from time to time usually alluded to the Council of Constance and drew up long lists of grievances against the papal régime. After the long periods of exile and schism the popes, settled once more in Rome, pursued a policy of worldly aggrandization. Alexander VI (of the house of Borgia), Julius II, with his military aspirations, and Leo X (of the house of Medici) were what passed for popes in the days when the Protestant Revolt was brewing. It was no sudden thing begun by Luther; the only wonder is that it was so long delayed, considering the elaborate preparations of the previous century.

The Germans, while good Catholics, were suspicious of the popes, whom they regarded as Italians, bent upon getting as much money as possible out of the simple people north of the Alps. The revenue flowing to the popes from Germany was very large. The great German prelates, like the archbishops of Mainz, Trèves, and Cologne, were each expected to contribute no less than ten thousand gold guldens to the papal treasury upon having their election confirmed by the church authorities at Rome. The pope enjoyed the right to fill many important church offices in Germany, and frequently appointed Italians, who drew the revenue without performing the duties attached to the office. A single person frequently held several church offices. For example, early in the sixteenth century, the archbishop of Mainz was at the same time archbishop of Magdeburg and bishop of Halberstadt. There were instances in which a single person had accumulated over a score of benefices.

It is impossible to exaggerate the impression of widespread discontent with the condition of the Church which one meets in the writings of the early sixteenth century. The whole German people, from the rulers down to the humblest tiller of the fields, felt themselves unjustly used. The clergy were denounced as both immoral and inefficient. While the begging friars—the Franciscans, Dominicans, and Augustinians[1]—were scorned by many, they, rather than the ordinary priests, appear to have carried on the real religious work.

At first, however, no one thought of withdrawing from the Church or of attempting to destroy the power of the pope. All that the Germans wanted was that the money which flowed toward Rome should be kept at home, and that the clergy should be upright, earnest men who should conscientiously perform their religious duties.

Among the critics of the Church in the early days of Charles V's reign the most famous and influential was Erasmus (1469?-1536). He was a Dutchman by birth, but spent his life in various other countries—France, England, Italy, and Germany. He was a citizen of the world and in correspondence with literary men everywhere, so that his letters give us an excellent idea of the feeling of the times. He was greatly interested in the Greek and Latin authors, but his main purpose in life was to better the religious conditions. He was well aware of the bad reputation of many of the clergymen of the time and he especially disliked the monks, for when he was a

---

[1] The Augustinian order, to which Luther belonged, was organized in the thirteenth century, a little later than the Dominican and the Franciscan.

PL. XII. EMPEROR CHARLES V, BY TITIAN

PL. XIII. ERASMUS, BY HOLBEIN

boy he had been forced into a monastery, much against his will.

It seemed to Erasmus that if everybody could read the Bible, especially the New Testament, for himself, it would bring about a great change for the better. He wanted to have the Gospels and the letters of Paul translated into the language of the people so that men and women who did not know Latin could read them and be helped by them.

Erasmus believed that the two arch enemies of true religion were (1) paganism, into which many of the more enthusiastic Italian Humanists fell in their admiration for the Greek and Latin writers; and (2) the popular confidence in outward acts and ceremonies, like visiting the graves of saints, the mere repetition of prayers, and so forth. He claimed that the Church had become careless and had permitted the simple teachings of Christ to be buried under myriads of dogmas introduced by the theologians. "The essence of our religion," he says, "is peace and harmony. These can only exist where there are few dogmas and each individual is left to form his own opinion upon many matters."

In a little book called *The Praise of Folly*, Erasmus has much to say of the weaknesses of the monks and theologians, and of the foolish people who thought that religion consisted simply in pilgrimages, the worship of relics, and the procuring of indulgences. Scarcely one of the abuses which Luther later attacked escaped Erasmus's pen. The book is a mixture of the lightest humor and the bitterest earnestness. As one turns its pages one is sometimes tempted to think Luther half right when he declared Erasmus "a regular jester who makes sport of everything, even of religion and Christ himself."

Yet there was in this humorist a deep seriousness that cannot be ignored. Erasmus believed, however, that revolt from the pope and the Church would produce a great disturbance and result in more harm than good. He preferred to trust in the slower but surer effects of education and knowledge. Superstitions and the undue regard for the outward forms of religion would, he argued, be outgrown and quietly disappear as mankind became more enlightened.

He believed, moreover, that the time was favorable for reform. As he looked about him he beheld intelligent rulers on the thrones of Europe, men interested in books and art and ready to help scholars and writers. There were Henry VIII of England and Francis I of France. Then the pope himself, Leo X, the son of Lorenzo the Magnificent, was a friend and admirer of Erasmus and doubtless sympathized with many of his views. The youthful Charles V had advisers who believed Erasmus to be quite right and were ready to work toward a reform of the Church. Charles was a devout Catholic, but he too agreed that there were many evils to be remedied. So it seemed to Erasmus that the prospects were excellent for a peaceful reform; but, instead of its coming, his latter years were embittered by Luther's revolt and all the ill-feeling and dissensions that it created.

Martin Luther's Revolt Against the Papacy

Martin Luther was born in 1483. He was the son of a poor miner, and he often spoke in later life of the poverty and superstition in which his boyhood was spent. His father, however, was determined that his son should be a lawyer, and so Martin was sent to the University of Erfurt. After he finished his college course and was about to take up the study of the law he suddenly decided to become a monk. He summoned his college friends for a last evening together, and the next morning he led them to the gate of a monastery, bade them and the world farewell, and became a begging friar.

He was much worried about his soul and feared that nothing he could do would save him from hell. He finally found comfort in the thought that in order to be saved he had only to believe sincerely that God would save him, and that he could not possibly save himself by trying to be good. He gained the respect of the head of the monastery, and when Frederick the Wise of Saxony was looking about for teachers in his new university at Wittenberg, Luther was recommended as a good person to teach Aristotle; so he became a professor.

As time went on Luther began to be suspicious of some of the things that were taught in the university. He finally decided that Aristotle was after all only an ancient heathen who knew nothing about Christianity and that the students had no business to study his ethical works. He urged them to rely instead upon the Bible, especially the letters of St. Paul, and upon the writings of St. Augustine, who closely followed Paul in many respects.

Luther's main point was that man, through Adam's sin, had become so corrupt that he could, of himself, do nothing pleasing to God. He could only hope to be saved through *faith* in God's promise to save those who should repent. Consequently "good works," such as attending church, going on pilgrimages, repeating prayers, and visiting relics of the saints, could do nothing for a sinner if he was not already "justified by faith," that is, made acceptable to God by his faith in God's promises. If he was "justified," then he might properly go about his daily duties, for they would be pleasing to God without what the Church was accustomed to regard as "good works."

Luther's teachings did not attract much attention until the year 1517, when he was thirty-four years old. Then something occurred to give him considerable prominence.

The fact has already been mentioned that the popes had undertaken the rebuilding of St. Peter's, the great central church of Christendom. The cost of the enterprise was very great, and in order to collect contributions for the purpose, Pope Leo X arranged for an extensive distribution of *indulgences* in Germany.

In order to understand the nature of indulgences and Luther's opposition to them, we must consider the teaching of the Catholic Church in regard to the forgiveness of sin. The Church taught that if one died after committing a deadly ("mortal") sin which he had not repented and confessed, his soul would certainly be lost. If he sincerely repented and confessed his sin to a priest, God would forgive him and his soul would be saved, but he would not thereby escape punishment. This punishment might consist in fasting, saying certain prayers, going on a pilgrimage, or doing some other "good work." It was assumed, however, that most men committed so many sins that even if they died repentant, they had to pass through a long period in purgatory, where they would be purified by suffering before they could enter heaven.

Now an indulgence was a pardon, issued usually by the pope himself, which freed the person to whom it was granted *from a part or all of his suffering in purgatory*. It did not forgive his sins or in any way take the place of true repentance and confession; it only reduced the punishment which a truly contrite sinner would otherwise have had to endure, either in this world or in purgatory, before he could be admitted to heaven.[1]

The contribution to the Church which was made in return for indulgences varied greatly; the rich were required to give a considerable sum, while the very poor were to receive these pardons gratis. The representatives of the pope were naturally anxious to collect all the money possible, and did their best to induce every one to secure an indulgence, either for himself or for his deceased friends in purgatory. In their zeal they made many claims for the indulgences, to which no thoughtful churchman or even layman could listen without misgivings.

In October, 1517, Tetzel, a Dominican monk, began preaching indulgences in the neighborhood of Wittenberg, and making claims for them which appeared to Luther wholly irreconcilable with the deepest truths of Christianity as he understood and taught them. He therefore, in accordance with the custom of the time, wrote out a series of controversial statements in regard to indulgences. These *theses,* as they were called, he posted on the church door and invited any one interested in the matter

---

[1] It has been a common mistake of Protestants to suppose that the indulgence was forgiveness granted beforehand for sins to be committed in the future. There is absolutely no foundation for this idea. A person proposing to sin could not possibly be contrite in the eyes of the Church, and even if he secured an indulgence, it would, according to the theologians, have been quite worthless.

to enter into a discussion with him on the subject, which he believed was very ill-understood.

In posting these theses, Luther did not intend to attack the Church, and had no expectation of creating a sensation. The theses were in Latin and addressed, therefore, only to learned men. It turned out, however, that every one, high and low, learned and unlearned, was ready to discuss the perplexing theme of the nature of indulgences. The theses were promptly translated into German, printed, and scattered abroad throughout the land. In these *ninety-five theses* Luther declared that the indulgence was very unimportant and that the poor man would better spend his money for the needs of his household. The truly repentant, he argued, do not flee punishment, but bear it willingly in sign of their sorrow. Faith in God, not the procuring of pardons, brings forgiveness, and every Christian who feels true sorrow for his sins will receive full remission of the punishment as well as of the guilt. Could the pope know how his agents misled the people, he would rather have St. Peter's burn to ashes than build it up with money gained under false pretenses. Then, Luther adds, there is danger that the common man will ask awkward questions. For example, "If the pope releases souls from purgatory for money, why not for charity's sake?" or, "Since the pope is rich as Crœsus, why does he not build St. Peter's with his own money, instead of taking that of the poor man?"

Luther now began to read church history and reached the conclusion that the influence of the popes had not been very great until the times of Gregory VII (see above, pp. 125 ff.), and therefore that they had not enjoyed their supremacy over the Church for more than four hundred years before his own birth. He was mistaken in this conclusion, but he had hit upon a line of argument that has been urged by Protestants ever since. They assert that the power of the Medieval Church and of the papacy developed gradually, especially during the Middle Ages, and that the apostles knew nothing of masses, indulgences, pilgrimages, purgatory, or the headship of the bishop of Rome.

The publication of Luther's theses brought him many sympathizers in Germany. Some were attracted by his protests against the ways in which the popes raised money, and others liked him for attacking Aristotle and the scholastic theologians. Erasmus's publisher at Basel agreed to print Luther's books, of which he sent copies to Italy, France, England, and Spain, and in this way the Wittenberg monk began before long to be widely known outside of Germany as well as within it.

But Erasmus himself, the mighty sovereign of the men of letters, refused to take sides in the controversy. He asserted that he had not read more than a dozen pages of Luther's writings. Although he admitted that "the monarchy of the Roman high priest was, in its existing condition, the pest of Christendom," he believed that a direct attack upon it would do no good. Luther, he urged, would better be discreet and trust that as mankind became more intelligent they would outgrow their false ideas.

To Erasmus, man was capable of progress; educate him and extend his knowledge, and he would grow better and better. He was, moreover, a free agent, with, on the whole, upright tendencies. To Luther, on the other hand, man was utterly corrupt, and incapable of a single righteous wish or deed. His will was enslaved to evil, and his only hope lay in the recognition of his absolute inability to better himself, and in an absolute reliance upon God's mercy. By *faith*, and not by doing "good works," could he be saved.

Erasmus was willing to wait until every one agreed that the Church should be reformed. Luther had no patience with an institution which seemed to him to be leading souls to destruction by inducing men to rely upon their good works. Both men realized that they could never agree. For a time they expressed respect for each other, but at last they became involved in a bitter controversy in which they gave up all pretense to friendship. Erasmus declared that Luther, by scorning good works and declaring that no one could do right, had made his followers indifferent to their conduct, and that those who accepted

Luther's teachings straightway became pert, rude fellows, who would not take off their hats to him on the street.

By 1520, Luther, who gave way at times to his naturally violent disposition, had become threatening and abusive and suggested that the German rulers should punish the churchmen and force them to reform their conduct. "We punish thieves with the gallows, bandits with the sword, heretics with fire; why should we not, with far greater propriety, attack with every kind of weapon these very masters of perdition, the cardinals and popes?" "The die is cast," he writes to a friend; "I despise Rome's wrath as I do her favor; I will have no reconciliation or intercourse with her in all time to come. Let her condemn and burn my writings. I will, if fire can be found, publicly condemn and burn the whole papal law."

Luther had gained the support of a celebrated German knight, Ulrich von Hutten, who was an ardent enemy of the popes. He and Luther vied with one another during the year 1520 in attacking the pope and his representatives. They both possessed a fine command of the German language, and they were fired by a common hatred of Rome. Hutten had little or none of Luther's religious fervor, but he was a born fighter and he could not find colors dark enough in which to picture to his countrymen the greed of the papal curia, which he described as a vast den, to which everything was dragged which could be filched from the Germans.

Of Luther's popular pamphlets, the first really famous one was his *Address to the German Nobility*, in which he calls upon the rulers of Germany, especially the knights, to reform the abuses themselves, since he believed that it was vain to wait for the Church to do so. He explains that there are three walls behind which the papacy had been wont to take refuge when any one proposed to remedy its abuses. There was, first, the claim that the clergy formed a separate class, superior even to the civil rulers, who were not permitted to punish a churchman, no matter how bad he was. Secondly, the pope claimed to be superior even to the great assemblies of the Church, called general councils, so that even the representatives of the Church itself might not correct him. And, lastly, the pope assumed the sole right, when questions of belief arose, to interpret with authority the meaning of the Scriptures; consequently he could not be refuted by arguments from the Bible.

Luther undertook to cast down these defenses by denying, to begin with, that there was anything especially sacred about a clergyman except the duties which he had been designated to perform. If he did not attend to his work, it should be possible to deprive him of his office at any moment, just as one would turn off an incompetent tailor or farmer, and in that case he should become a simple layman again. Luther claimed, moreover, that it was the right and duty of the civil government to punish a churchman who does wrong just as if he were the humblest layman. When this first wall was destroyed the others would fall easily enough, for the dominant position of the clergy was the very cornerstone of the Medieval Church.

The *Address to the German Nobility* closes with a long list of evils which must be done away with before Germany can become prosperous. Luther saw that his view of religion really implied a social revolution. He advocated reducing the monasteries to a tenth of their number and permitting those monks who were disappointed in the good they got from living in them freely to leave. He would not have the monasteries prisons, but hospitals and refuges for the soul-sick. He points out the evils of pilgrimages and of the numerous church holidays, which interfered with daily work. The clergy, he urged, should be permitted to marry and have families like other citizens. The universities should be reformed, and "the accursed heathen, Aristotle," should be cast out from them.

It should be noted that Luther appeals to the authorities not in the name of religion primarily, but in that of public order and prosperity. He says that the money of the Germans flies "feather-light" over the Alps to Italy, but it immediately becomes like lead when there is a question of its coming back. He showed himself a master of vigorous language, and his denunciations of the clergy and the Church resounded like a trumpet call in the ears of his countrymen.[1]

Luther had long expected to be excommunicated. But it was not until late in 1520 that John Eck, a personal enemy of his, arrived in Germany with a papal bull condemning many of Luther's assertions as heretical and giving him sixty days in which to recant. Should he fail to return to his senses within that time, he and all who adhered to or favored him were to be excommunicated, and any place which harbored him should fall under the interdict. Now, since the highest power in Christendom had pronounced Luther a heretic, he should unhesitatingly have been delivered up by the German authorities. But no one thought of arresting him.

The bull irritated the German princes; whether they liked Luther or not, they decidedly disliked to have the pope issuing commands to them. Then it appeared to them very unfair that Luther's personal enemy should have been intrusted with the publication of the bull. Even the princes and universities that were most friendly to the pope published the bull with great reluctance. In many cases the bull was ignored altogether. Luther's own sovereign, the elector of Saxony, while no convert to the new views, was anxious that Luther's case should be fairly considered, and continued to protect him. One mighty prince, however, the young Emperor Charles V, promptly and willingly published the bull; not, however, as emperor, but as ruler of the Austrian dominions and of the Netherlands. Luther's works were publicly burned at Louvain, Mainz, and Cologne, the strongholds of the old theology.

The Wittenberg professor felt driven to oppose himself to both pope and emperor. "Hard it is," he exclaimed, "to be forced to contradict all the prelates and princes, but

[1] Luther had said little of the doctrines of the Church in his *Address to the German Nobility*, but within three or four months he issued a second work, in which he sought to overthrow the whole system of the sacraments, as it had been taught by the theologians. Four of the seven sacraments—ordination, marriage, confirmation, and extreme unction—he rejected altogether. He revised the conception of the Mass, or the Lord's Supper. The priest was, in his eyes, only a *minister*, in the Protestant sense of the word, one of whose chief functions was preaching.

there is no other way to escape hell and God's anger." Late in 1520 he summoned his students to witness what he called "a pious, religious spectacle." He had a fire built outside the walls of Wittenberg and cast into it Leo X's bull condemning

Bulla contra Erro
res Martini Lutheri
et sequarium.

THE PAPAL BULL DIRECTED AGAINST LUTHER, 1521

This is a much-reduced reproduction of the title-page of the pope's bull "against the errors of Martin Luther and his followers" as it was printed and distributed in Germany. The coat of arms with its "balls" is that of the Medici family to which Leo X belonged

him, and a copy of the Church canon, together with a volume of scholastic theology which he specially disliked.

Yet Luther dreaded disorder. He was certainly sometimes reckless and violent in his writings and often said that bloodshed could not be avoided when it should please God to visit

his judgments upon the stiff-necked and perverse generation of
"Romanists," as the Germans contemptuously called the supporters of the pope. Yet he always discouraged hasty reform.
He was reluctant to make changes, except in belief. He held
that so long as an institution did not actually mislead, it did
no harm. He was, in short, no fanatic at heart.

The Diet at Worms, 1520–1521

The pope's chief representative in Germany, named Aleander, wrote as follows to Leo X about this time: "I am pretty
familiar with the history of this German nation. I know their
past heresies, councils, and schisms, but never were affairs so
serious before. Compared with present conditions, the struggle
between Henry IV and Gregory VII was as violets and roses.
. . . These mad dogs are now well equipped with knowledge
and arms; they boast that they are no longer ignorant brutes
like their predecessors; they claim that Italy has lost the
monopoly of the sciences and that the Tiber now flows into
the Rhine. Nine-tenths of the Germans are shouting 'Luther,'
and the other tenth goes so far at least as 'Death to the Roman
curia.' "

Among the enemies of Luther and his supporters none was
more important than the young emperor. It was toward the
end of the year 1520 that Charles came to Germany for the
first time. After being crowned King of the Romans at Aix-
la-Chapelle, he assumed, with the pope's consent, the title of
emperor elect, as his grandfather Maximilian had done. He
then moved on to the town of Worms, where he was to hold
his first diet and face the German situation.

Although scarcely more than a boy in years, Charles had
already begun to take life very seriously. He had decided that
Spain, not Germany, was to be the bulwark and citadel of all
his realms. Like the more enlightened of his Spanish subjects,
he realized the need of reforming the Church, but he had no
sympathy whatever with any change of religious belief. He
proposed to live and die a devout Catholic of the old type, such
as his orthodox ancestors had been. He felt, moreover, that he

must maintain the same religion in all parts of his heterogeneous dominions. If he should permit the Germans to declare
their independence of the Church, the next step would be for
them to claim that they had a right to regulate their government regardless of their emperor.

Upon arriving at Worms the case of Luther was at once
forced upon Charles's attention by Aleander, the papal representative, who was indefatigable in urging him to outlaw the
heretic without further delay. While Charles seemed convinced
of Luther's guilt, he could not proceed against him without
serious danger. The monk had become a sort of national hero
and had the support of the powerful elector of Saxony. Other
princes, who had ordinarily no wish to protect a heretic, felt
that Luther's denunciation of the evils in the Church and of
the actions of the pope was very gratifying. After much discussion it was finally arranged, to the great disgust of the
zealous Aleander, that Luther should be summoned to Worms
and be given an opportunity to face the German nation and
the emperor, and to declare plainly whether he was the author
of the heretical books ascribed to him, and whether he still
adhered to the doctrines which the pope had condemned.

The emperor accordingly wrote the "honorable and respected"
Luther a very polite letter, desiring him to appear at Worms
and granting him a safe-conduct thither.

It was not, however, proposed to give Luther an opportunity
to defend his beliefs before the diet. When he appeared he
was simply asked if a pile of his Latin and German works
were really his, and, if so, whether he revoked what he had
said in them. To the first question the monk replied in a low
voice that he had written these and more. As to the second
question, which involved the welfare of the soul and the Word
of God, he asked that he might have a little while to consider.

The following day, in a Latin address which he repeated in
German, he admitted that he had been over-violent in his
attacks upon his opponents; but he said that no one could deny
that, through the popes' decrees, the consciences of faithful
Christians had been tormented, and their goods and posses-

sions, especially in Germany, devoured. Should he recant those things which he had said against the popes' conduct, he would only strengthen the papal tyranny and give an opportunity for new usurpations. If, however, adequate arguments against his position could be found in the Scriptures, he would gladly and promptly recant.

There was now nothing for the emperor to do but to outlaw Luther, who had denied the binding character of the commands of the head of the Church. Aleander was accordingly assigned the agreeable duty of drafting the famous Edict of Worms.

This document declared Luther an outlaw on the following grounds: that he questioned the recognized number and character of the sacraments, impeached the regulations in regard to the marriage of the clergy, scorned and vilified the pope, despised the priesthood and stirred up the laity to dip their hands in the blood of the clergy, denied free will, taught licentiousness, despised authority, advocated a brutish existence, and was a menace to Church and State alike. Every one was forbidden to give the heretic food, drink, or shelter, and required to seize him and deliver him to the emperor.

Moreover, the decree provides that "no one shall dare to buy, sell, read, preserve, copy, print, or cause to be copied or printed, any books of the aforesaid Martin Luther, condemned by our holy father the pope, as aforesaid, or any other writings in German or Latin hitherto composed by him, since they are foul, noxious, suspected, and written by a notorious and stiff-necked heretic. Neither shall any one dare to affirm his opinions, or proclaim, defend, or advance them in any other way that human ingenuity can invent,—notwithstanding that he may have put some good into his writings in order to deceive the simple man."

"I am becoming ashamed of my fatherland," Hutten cried when he read the Edict of Worms. So general was the disapproval of the edict that few were willing to pay any attention to it. Charles V immediately left Germany, and for nearly ten years was occupied outside it with the government of Spain and a succession of wars.

AETHERNA IPSE SVAE MENTIS SIMVLACHRA LVTHERVS
EXPRIMIT·AT VVLT·VS CERA LVCAE OCCIDVOS
·M·D·X·X·

LUTHER AS A MONK, BY CRANACH, 1520

None of the portraits of Luther are very satisfactory. His friend Cranach was not, like Holbein the Younger, a great portrait painter. This cut shows the reformer when his revolt against the Church was just beginning. He was thirty-seven years old and still in the dress of an Augustinian friar, which he soon abandoned

PORTRAIT OF FREDERICK THE WISE, BY ALBRECHT DÜRER

Frederick the Wise, elector of Saxony, was very proud of the university
that he founded at Wittenberg, and, while he was a devout Catholic and
seems hardly to have understood what Luther stood for, he protected his
professor and did not propose to have him tried for heresy by the Church.
The portrait is a fine example of the work of the artist who distinguished
himself as both a painter and an engraver

The Protestant Reformation in Germany

As Luther neared Eisenach upon his way home from Worms he was kidnapped by his friends and conducted to the Wartburg, a castle belonging to the elector of Saxony. Here he was concealed until any danger from the action of the emperor or diet should pass by. His chief occupation during several months of hiding was to begin a new translation of the Bible into German. He had finished the New Testament before he left the Wartburg in March, 1522.

Up to this time, German editions of the Scriptures, while not uncommon, had been poor and obscure. Luther's task was a difficult one. He was anxious above all that the Bible should be put into language that would seem perfectly clear and natural to the common folk. So he went about asking the mothers and children and the laborers questions which might draw out the expression that he was looking for. It sometimes took him two or three weeks to find the right word. But so well did he do his work that his Bible may be regarded as a great landmark in the history of the German language. It was the first book of any importance written in modern German, and it has furnished an imperishable standard for the language.

Previous to 1518 there had been very few books or pamphlets printed in German. The translation of the Bible into language so simple that even the unlearned might read it was only one of the signs of a general effort to awaken the minds of the common people. Luther's friends and enemies also commenced to write for the great German public in its own language. The common man began to raise his voice, to the scandal of the learned.

Hundreds of pamphlets, satires, and cartoons have come down to us which indicate that the religious and other questions of the day were often treated in somewhat the same spirit in which our comic papers deal with political problems and discussions now. We find, for instance, a correspondence between Leo X and the devil, and a witty dialogue between a well-known knight, Franz von Sickingen, and St. Peter at the gate of heaven.

Hitherto there had been a great deal of talk of reform, but as yet nothing had actually been done. There was no sharp line drawn between the different classes of reformers. All agreed that something should be done to better the Church; few realized how divergent were the real ends in view. The rulers listened to Luther because they were glad of an excuse to get control of the church property and keep money from flowing to Rome. The peasants listened because he put the Bible in their hands and they found nothing there that proved that they ought to go on paying the old dues to their lords.

While Luther was quietly living in the Wartburg, translating the Bible, people began to put his teachings into practice. The monks and nuns left their monasteries in his own town of Wittenberg. Some of them married, which seemed a very wicked thing to all those who held to the old beliefs. The students and citizens tore down the images of the saints in the churches and opposed the celebration of the Mass, the chief Catholic ceremony.

Luther did not approve of these sudden and violent changes and left his hiding place to protest. He preached a series of sermons in Wittenberg in which he urged that all alterations in religious services and practices should be introduced by the *government* and not by the *people*. He said, however, that those who wished might leave their monasteries and that those who chose to stay should give up begging and earn their living like other people. He predicted that if no one gave any money to the Church, popes, bishops, monks, and nuns would in two years vanish away like smoke.

But his counsel was not heeded. First, the German knights organized a movement to put the new ideas in practice. Franz von Sickingen and Ulrich von Hutten, admirers of Luther, attacked the archbishop of Trèves and proclaimed that they were going to free his subjects from "the heavy unchristian yoke of the 'parsons' and lead them to evangelical liberty." But the German princes sided with the archbishop and battered down Franz von Sickingen's castle with cannon, and the aggrieved Franz was fatally injured by a falling beam. Twenty other castles of the knights were destroyed and this put an end to their revolt; but Luther and his teachings were naturally blamed as the real reason for the uprising.

The conservative party, who were frankly afraid of Luther, received a new and terrible proof, as it seemed to them, of the noxious influence of his teachings. In 1525 the serfs rose, in the name of "God's justice," to avenge their wrongs and establish their rights. Luther was not responsible for the civil war which followed, though he had certainly helped to stir up discontent. He had asserted, for example, that the German feudal lords were hangmen, who knew only how to swindle the poor man. "Such fellows were formerly called rascals, but now must we call them 'Christian and revered princes.'" Yet in spite of his harsh talk about the princes, Luther really relied upon them to forward his movement, and he justly claimed that he had greatly increased their power by attacking the authority of the pope and subjecting the clergy in all things to the government.

Some of the demands of the peasants were perfectly reasonable. The most popular expression of their needs was the dignified "Twelve Articles." In these they claimed that the Bible did not sanction any of the dues which the lords demanded of them, and that, since they were Christians like their lords, they should no longer be held as serfs. They were willing to pay all the old and well-established dues, but they asked to be properly remunerated for extra services demanded by the lord. They thought too that each community should have the right freely to choose its own pastor and to dismiss him if he proved negligent or inefficient.

There were, however, leaders who were more violent and who proposed to kill the "godless" priests and nobles. Hundreds of castles and monasteries were destroyed by the frantic peasantry, and some of the nobility were murdered with shocking cruelty. Luther tried to induce the peasants, with whom, as the son of a peasant, he was at first inclined to sympathize, to remain quiet; but when his warnings proved vain, he turned against them. He declared that they were guilty of the most fearful crimes, for which they deserved death of both body and soul many times over. They had broken their allegiance, they had wantonly plundered and robbed castles and monasteries, and lastly, they had tried to cloak their dreadful sins with excuses from the Gospels. He therefore urged the government to put down the insurrection without pity.

Luther's advice was followed with terrible literalness by the German rulers, and the nobility took fearful revenge on the peasants. In the summer of 1525 their chief leader was defeated and killed, and it is estimated that ten thousand peasants were put to death, many with the utmost cruelty. Few of the rulers or landlords introduced any reforms, and the misfortunes due to the destruction of property and to the despair of the peasants cannot be imagined. The people concluded that the new gospel was not for them, and talked of Luther as Dr. Lügner, that is, "liar." The old exactions of the lords of the manors were in no way lightened, and the situation of the serfs for centuries following the great revolt was worse rather than better.

Charles V was occupied at this time by his quarrels with Francis I and was in no position to return to Germany and undertake to enforce the Edict of Worms against Luther and his followers. Germany, as we have seen, was divided up into hundreds of practically independent countries, and the various electors, princes, towns, and knights naturally could not agree as to what would best be done in the matter of reforming the Church. It became apparent not long after the Peasant War that some of the rulers were going to accept Luther's idea that they need no longer obey the pope and that they were free to proceed to regulate the property and affairs of the churchmen in their respective domains without regard to the pope's wishes. Other princes and towns agreed that they would remain faithful to the pope if certain reforms were introduced, especially if the papal taxation were reduced. Southern Germany decided for the pope and remains Catholic down to the present day. Many of the northern rulers, on the other hand, adopted the new teachings, and finally all of them fell away from the papacy and became Protestant.

Since there was no one powerful enough to decide the great question for the whole of Germany, the diet which met at Speyer in 1526 determined that pending the summoning of a Church council each ruler should "so live, reign, and conduct himself as he would be willing to answer before God and His Imperial Majesty." For the moment, then, the various German governments were left to determine the religion of their subjects.

Yet everybody still hoped that one religion might ultimately be agreed upon. Luther trusted that all Christians would sometime accept the new gospel. He was willing that the bishops should be retained, and even that the pope should still be regarded as a sort of presiding officer in the Church. As for his enemies, they were equally confident that the heretics would in time be suppressed, as they had always been in the past, and that harmony would thus be restored. Neither party was right; for the decision of the diet of Speyer was destined to become a permanent arrangement, and Germany remained divided between different religious faiths.

New sects opposed to the old Church had also begun to appear. Zwingli, a Swiss reformer, was gaining many followers, and the Anabaptists were rousing Luther's apprehensions by their radical plans for doing away with the Catholic religion altogether. The emperor, finding himself again free for a time to attend to German affairs, commanded the diet, which again met at Speyer in 1529, to order the enforcement of the Edict of Worms against the heretics. No one was to preach against the Mass, and no one was to be prevented from attending it freely.

This meant that the "Evangelical" princes would be forced to restore the most characteristic of the Catholic ceremonies. As they formed only a minority in the diet, all that they could do was to draw up a *protest,* signed by John Frederick, elector of Saxony, Philip of Hesse, and fourteen of the imperial towns

(Strasbourg, Nuremberg, Ulm, etc). In this they claimed that the majority had no right to abrogate the edict of the former diet of Speyer, which had been passed unanimously, and which all had solemnly pledged themselves to observe. They therefore appealed to the emperor and a future council against the tyranny of the majority. Those who signed this appeal were called from their action *Protestants*. Thus originated the name which came to be generally applied to Christians who do not accept the rule and teachings of the Roman Catholic Church.

Ever since the diet at Worms the emperor had resided in Spain, busied with a succession of wars carried on with the king of France. It will be remembered that both Charles and Francis claimed Milan and the duchy of Burgundy, and they sometimes drew the pope into their conflicts. But in 1530 the emperor found himself at peace for the moment and came to Germany to hold a brilliant diet of his German subjects at Augsburg in the hope of settling the religious problem, which, however, he understood very imperfectly. He ordered the Protestants to draw up a statement of exactly what they believed, which should serve as a basis for discussion. Melanchthon, Luther's most famous friend and colleague, who was noted for his great learning and moderation, was intrusted with this delicate task.

The *Augsburg Confession,* as his declaration was called, is a historical document of great importance for the student of the Protestant revolt. Melanchthon's gentle disposition led him to make the differences between his belief and that of the old Church seem as few and slight as possible. He showed—quite rightly—that both parties held the same fundamental views of Christianity. But he defended the Protestants' rejection of a number of the practices of the Roman Catholics, such as the celibacy of the clergy and the observance of fast days. There was little or nothing in the Augsburg Confession concerning the organization of the Church.

Certain theologians who had been loud in their denunciations of Luther were ordered by the emperor to prepare a refutation of the Protestant views. The statement of the Catholics admitted that a number of Melanchthon's positions were perfectly orthodox; but the portion of the Augsburg Confession which dealt with the practical reforms advocated by the Protestants was rejected altogether.

Charles V declared the Catholic statement to be "Christian and judicious" and commanded the Protestants to accept it. They were to cease troubling the Catholics and were to give back all the monasteries and church property which they had seized. The emperor agreed, however, to urge the pope to call a Church council to meet within a year. This, he hoped, would be able to settle all differences and reform the Church according to the views of the Catholics.

It is unnecessary to follow in detail the progress of Protestantism in Germany during the quarter of a century succeeding the diet of Augsburg. Enough has been said to show the character of the revolt and the divergent views taken by the German princes and people. For ten years after the emperor left Augsburg he was kept busy in southern Europe by new wars; and in order to secure the assistance of the Protestants, he was forced to let them go their own way. Meanwhile the number of rulers who accepted Luther's teachings gradually increased. Finally, there was a brief war between Charles V and the Protestant princes, but there was little fighting done. Charles brought his Spanish soldiers into Germany and captured both John Frederick of Saxony and his ally, Philip of Hesse, the chief leaders of the Lutheran cause, whom he kept prisoners for several years.

This episode did not, however, check the progress of Protestantism. The king of France promised them help against his enemy, the emperor, and Charles was forced to agree to a peace with the Protestants.

In 1555 the religious Peace of Augsburg was ratified. Its provisions are memorable. Each German prince and each town and knight immediately under the emperor was to be at liberty to make a choice between the beliefs of the venerable Catholic Church and those embodied in the Augsburg Confession. If, however, an ecclesiastical prince—an archbishop, bishop, or abbot—declared himself a Protestant, he must surrender his possessions to the Church. Every German was either to conform to the religious practices of his particular state or emigrate from it. Every one was supposed to be either a Catholic or a Lutheran, and no provision was made for any other belief.

This religious peace in no way established freedom of conscience, except for the rulers. Their power, it must be noted, was greatly increased, inasmuch as they were given the control of religious as well as of secular matters. This arrangement which permitted the ruler to determine the religion of his realm was more natural in those days than it would be in ours. The Church and the civil government had been closely associated with one another for centuries. No one as yet dreamed that every individual might safely be left quite free to believe what he would and to practice any religious rites which afforded him help and comfort.

Zwingli and Calvin

For at least a century after Luther's death the great issue between Catholics and Protestants dominates the history of all the countries with which we have to do, except Italy and Spain, where Protestantism never took permanent root. In Switzerland, England, France, and Holland the revolt against the Medieval Church produced discord, wars, and profound changes, which must be understood in order to follow the later development of these countries.

We turn first to Switzerland, lying in the midst of the great chain of the Alps which extends from the Mediterranean to Vienna. During the Middle Ages the region destined to be included in the Swiss Confederation formed a part of the Holy Roman Empire and was scarcely distinguishable from the rest of southern Germany. As early as the thirteenth century the three "forest" cantons on the shores of the winding lake of Lucerne formed a union to protect their liberties against the encroachments of their neighbors, the Hapsburgs. It was about this tiny nucleus that Switzerland gradually consolidated.

Lucerne and the free towns of Zurich and Bern soon joined the Swiss league. By brave fighting the Swiss were able to frustrate the renewed efforts of the Hapsburgs to subjugate them.

Various districts in the neighborhood joined the Swiss union in succession, and even the region lying on the Italian slopes of the Alps was brought under its control. Gradually the bonds between the members of the union and the Empire were broken. In 1499 the cantons were finally freed from the jurisdiction of the emperor and Switzerland became a practically independent country. Although the original union had been made up of German-speaking people, considerable districts had been annexed in which Italian or French was spoken.[1] The Swiss did not, therefore, form a compact, well-defined nation, and consequently for some centuries their confederation was weak and ill-organized.

In Switzerland the first leader of the revolt against the Church was a young priest named Zwingli, who was a year younger than Luther. He lived in the famous monastery of Einsiedeln, near the Lake of Zurich, which was the center of pilgrimages on account of a wonder-working image. "Here," he says, "I began to preach the Gospel of Christ in the year 1516, before any one in my locality had so much as heard the name of Luther."

Three years later he was called to an influential position as preacher in the cathedral of Zurich, and there his great work really commenced. He then began to denounce the abuses in the Church as well as the shameless traffic in soldiers, which he had long regarded as a blot upon his country's honor.[2]

But the original cantons about the Lake of Lucerne, which feared that they might lose the great influence that, in spite of their small size, they had hitherto enjoyed, were ready to

[1] This condition has not changed; all Swiss laws are still proclaimed in three languages.

[2] Switzerland had made a business, ever since the time when Charles VIII of France invaded Italy, of supplying troops of mercenaries to fight for other countries, especially for France and the pope, and Swiss guards may still be seen in the pope's palace.

fight for the old faith. The first armed collision between the
Swiss Protestants and Catholics took place at Kappel in 1531,
and Zwingli fell in the battle. The various cantons and towns
never came to an agreement in religious matters, and Switzerland is still part Catholic and part Protestant.

Far more important than Zwingli's teachings, especially for
England and America, was the work of Calvin (1509-1564),

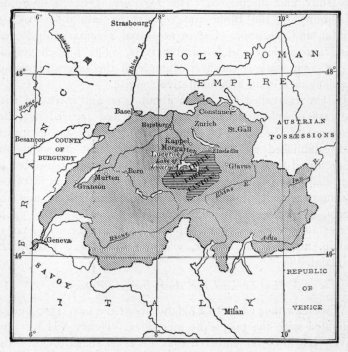

THE SWISS CONFEDERATION IN THE SIXTEENTH CENTURY

which was carried on in the ancient city of Geneva, then on the
outskirts of the Swiss confederation. It was Calvin who organized the *Presbyterian Church* and formulated its beliefs. He
was born in northern France in 1509; he belonged, therefore,
to the second generation of Protestants. He was early influenced by the Lutheran teachings, which had already found
their way into France. A persecution of the Protestants under

Francis I drove him out of the country and he settled for a time in Basel.

Here he issued the first edition of his great work, *The Institute of the Christian Religion,* which has been more widely discussed than any other Protestant theological treatise. It was the first orderly exposition of the principles of Christianity from a Protestant standpoint, and formed a convenient manual for study and discussion. The *Institute* is based upon the infallibility of the Bible and rejects the infallibility of the Church and the pope. Calvin possessed a remarkably logical mind and a clear and admirable style. The French version of his great work is the first example of the successful use of that language in an argumentative treatise.

Calvin was called to Geneva about 1540 and intrusted with the task of reforming the town, which had secured its independence of the Duke of Savoy. He drew up a constitution and established an extraordinary government in which the Church and the civil government were as closely associated as they had ever been in any Catholic country. Calvin intrusted the management of church affairs to the ministers and the elders, or *presbyters;* hence the name "Presbyterian." The Protestantism which found its way into France was that of Calvin, not that of Luther, and the same may be said of Scotland.

How England Fell Away from the Papacy

When Erasmus came to England about the year 1500 he was delighted with the people he met there. Henry VII was still alive. It will be remembered that it was he that brought order into England after the Wars of the Roses. His son, who was to become the famous Henry VIII, impressed Erasmus as a very promising boy. We may assume that the intelligent men whom Erasmus met in England agreed with him in regard to the situation in the Church and the necessity of reform. He was a good friend of Sir Thomas More, who is best known for his little book called *Utopia,* which means "Nowhere." In it More pictures the happy conditions in an undiscovered land where the government was perfect and all the evils that he saw about him were done away with. It was at More's house that Erasmus wrote his *Praise of Folly* and dedicated it to him.

Henry VIII came to the English throne when he was eighteen years old. His chief adviser, Cardinal Wolsey, deserves great credit for having constantly striven to discourage his sovereign's ambition to take part in the wars on the Continent. The cardinal's argument that England could become great by peace better than by war was a momentous discovery. Peace he felt would be best secured by maintaining the *balance of power* on the Continent, so that no ruler should become dangerous by unduly extending his sway. For example, he thought it good policy to side with Charles V when Francis I was successful, and then with Francis after his terrible defeat at Pavia (1525) when he fell into the hands of Charles. This idea of the balance of power came to be recognized later by the European countries as a very important consideration in determining their policy. But Wolsey was not long to be permitted to put his enlightened ideas in practice. His fall and the progress of Protestantism in England are both closely associated with the notorious divorce case of Henry VIII.

It will be remembered that Henry had married Catherine of Aragon, the aunt of Charles V. Only one of their children, Mary, survived to grow up. As time went on Henry was very anxious to have a son and heir, for he was fearful lest a woman might not be permitted to succeed to the throne. Moreover, he had tired of Catherine, who was considerably older than he.

Catherine had first married Henry's older brother, who had died almost immediately after the marriage. Since it was a violation of the rule of the Church to marry a deceased brother's wife, Henry professed to fear that he was committing a sin by retaining Catherine as his wife and demanded to be divorced from her on the ground that his marriage had never been legal. His anxiety to rid himself of Catherine was greatly increased by the appearance at court of a black-eyed girl of sixteen, named Anne Boleyn, with whom the king fell in love.

[309]

Unfortunately for his case, his marriage with Catherine had been authorized by a dispensation from the pope, so that Clement VII, to whom the king appealed to annul the marriage, could not, even if he had been willing to run the risk of angering the queen's nephew, Charles V, have granted Henry's request.

Wolsey's failure to induce the pope to permit the divorce excited the king's anger, and with rank ingratitude for his minister's great services, Henry drove him from office (1529) and seized his property. From a life of wealth which was fairly regal, Wolsey was precipitated into extreme poverty. An imprudent but innocent act of his soon gave his enemies a pretext for charging him with treason; but the unhappy man died on his way to London and thus escaped being beheaded as a traitor.

Cardinal Wolsey had been the pope's representative in England. Henry VIII's next move was to declare the whole clergy of England guilty in obeying Wolsey, since an old law forbade any papal agent to appear in England without the king's consent.[1] The king refused to forgive them until they had solemnly acknowledged him supreme head of the English Church.[2] He then induced Parliament to cut off some of the pope's revenue from England; but, as this did not bring Clement VII to terms, Henry lost patience and secretly married Anne Boleyn, relying on getting a divorce from Catherine later.

His method was a simple one. He summoned an English church court which declared his marriage with Catherine null and void. He had persuaded Parliament to make a law providing that all lawsuits should be definitely decided within the realm and in this way cut off the possibility of the queen's appealing to the pope.

[1] Henry had, however, agreed that Wolsey should accept the office of papal legate.
[2] The clergy only recognized the king as "Head of the Church and Clergy so far as the law of Christ will allow." They did not abjure the headship of the pope over the whole Church.

Parliament, which did whatever Henry VIII asked, also declared Henry's marriage with Catherine unlawful and that with Anne Boleyn legal. Consequently it was decreed that Anne's daughter Elizabeth, born in 1533, was to succeed her father on the English throne instead of Mary, the daughter of Catherine.

In 1534 the English Parliament completed the revolt of the English Church from the pope by assigning to the king the right to appoint all the English prelates and to enjoy all the income which had formerly found its way to Rome. In the Act of Supremacy, Parliament declared the king to be "the only supreme head in earth of the Church of England," and that he should enjoy all the powers which the title naturally carried with it.

Two years later every officer in the kingdom was required to swear to renounce the authority of the bishop of Rome. Refusal to take this oath was to be adjudged high treason. Many were unwilling to deny the pope's headship merely because king and Parliament renounced it, and this legislation led to a persecution in the name of treason which was even more horrible than that which had been carried on in the supposed interest of religion.

It must be carefully observed that Henry VIII was not a Protestant in the usual sense of the word. He was led, it is true, by Clement VII's refusal to declare his first marriage illegal, to break the bond between the English and the Roman Church, and to induce the English clergy and Parliament to acknowledge the king as supreme head in the religious as well as in the worldly interests of the country. Important as this was, it did not lead Henry to accept the teachings of Protestant leaders, like Luther, Zwingli, and Calvin.

Henry was anxious to prove that he was orthodox, especially after he had seized the property of the monasteries and the gold and jewels which adorned the receptacles in which the relics of the saints were kept. He presided in person over the trial of one who accepted the opinions of Zwingli, and he quoted Scripture to prove the contrary. The prisoner was condemned and burned as a heretic. Henry also authorized a new translation of the Bible into English. A fine edition of this was printed (1539), and every parish was ordered to obtain a copy and place it in the parish church, where all the people could readily make use of it.

Henry VIII was heartless and despotic. With a barbarity not uncommon in those days, he allowed his old friend and adviser, Sir Thomas More, to be beheaded for refusing to pronounce the marriage with Catherine void. He caused numbers of monks to be executed for refusing to swear that his first marriage was illegal and for denying his title to supremacy in the Church. Others he permitted to die of starvation and disease in the filthy prisons of the time. Many Englishmen would doubtless have agreed with one of the friars who said humbly: "I profess that it is not out of obstinate malice or a mind of rebellion that I do disobey the king, but only for the fear of God, that I offend not the Supreme Majesty; because our Holy Mother, the Church, hath decreed and appointed otherwise than the king and Parliament hath ordained."

Henry wanted money; some of the English abbeys were rich, and the monks were quite unable to defend themselves against the charges which were brought against them. The king sent commissioners about to inquire into the state of the monasteries. A large number of scandalous tales were easily collected, some of which were undoubtedly true. The monks were doubtless often indolent and sometimes wicked. Nevertheless they were kind landlords, hospitable to the stranger, and good to the poor. The plundering of the smaller monasteries, with which the king began, led to a revolt, due to a rumor that the king would next proceed to despoil the parish churches as well.

This gave Henry an excuse for attacking the larger monasteries. The abbots and priors who had taken part in the revolt were hanged and their monasteries confiscated. Other abbots, panic-stricken, confessed that they and their monks had been committing the most loathsome sins and asked to be permitted to give up their monasteries to the king. The royal commis-

PL. XIV. HENRY VIII, BY HOLBEIN

PL. XV. QUEEN MARY OF ENGLAND, BY ANTONIO MORO

sioners then took possession, sold every article upon which they could lay hands, including the bells and even the lead on the roofs. The picturesque remains of some of the great abbey churches are still among the chief objects of interest to the sight-seer in England. The monastery lands were, of course, appropriated by the king. They were sold for the benefit of the government or given to nobles whose favor the king wished to secure.

Along with the destruction of the monasteries went an attack upon the shrines and images in the churches, which were adorned with gold and jewels. The shrine of St. Thomas of Canterbury was destroyed, and the bones of the saint were burned. An old wooden figure which was revered in Wales was used to make a fire to burn an unfortunate friar who maintained that in religious matters the pope rather than the king should be obeyed. These acts resembled the Protestant attacks on images which occurred in Germany, Switzerland, and the Netherlands. The main object of the king and his party was probably to get money, although the reason urged for the destruction was the superstitious veneration in which the relics and images were popularly held.

Henry's family troubles by no means came to an end with his marriage to Anne Boleyn. Of her, too, he soon tired, and three years after their marriage he had her executed on a series of monstrous charges. A few days later he married his third wife, Jane Seymour, who was the mother of his son and successor, Edward VI. Jane died a few days after her son's birth, and later Henry married in succession three other women, who are historically unimportant, since they left no children as claimants for the crown. Henry took care that his three children, all of whom were destined to reign, should be given their due place in the line of inheritance by act of Parliament.[1] His death in 1547 left the great problem of Protestantism and Catholicism to be settled by his son and daughters.

[1] Henry VIII, m. (1) Catherine, m. (2) Anne Boleyn, m. (3) Jane Seymour

| Mary (1553-1558) | Elizabeth (1558-1603) | Edward VI (1547-1553) |

It was arranged that the son was to succeed to the throne. In case he died without heirs, Mary and then Elizabeth were to follow.

England Becomes Protestant

While the revolt of England against the papacy was carried through by the government at a time when the greater part of the nation was still Catholic, there was undoubtedly, under Henry VIII, an ever-increasing number of aggressive and ardent Protestants who applauded the change. During the six years of the boy Edward's reign—he died in 1553 at the age of sixteen—those in charge of the government favored the

EDWARD VI, BY HOLBEIN

This interesting sketch was made before Edward became king, and he could have been scarcely six years old, as Holbein died in 1543

Protestant party and did what they could to change the faith of all the people by bringing Protestant teachers from the Continent.

A general demolition of all the sacred images was ordered; even the beautiful stained glass, the glory of the cathedrals, was destroyed, because it often represented saints and angels. The king was to appoint bishops without troubling to observe the old forms of election, and Protestants began to be put into the high offices of the Church. Parliament turned over to the king the funds which had been established for the purpose of having masses chanted for the dead, and decreed that thereafter the clergy should be free to marry.

A prayer book in English was prepared under the auspices of Parliament, not very unlike that used in the Church of England to-day. Moreover, forty-two articles of faith were drawn up by the government, which were to be the standard of belief for the country. These, in the time of Queen Elizabeth, were revised and reduced to the famous "Thirty-Nine Articles," which still constitute the official statement of the tenets of the Church of England.

The changes in the church services must have sadly shocked a great part of the English people, who had been accustomed to watch with awe and expectancy the various acts associated with the many church ceremonies and festivals. Earnest men who deplored the policy of those who conducted Edward's government in the name of Protestantism must have concluded that the reformers were chiefly intent upon advancing their own interests by plundering the Church. We get some idea of the desecrations of the time from the fact that Edward was forced to forbid "quarreling and shooting in churches" and "the bringing of horses and mules through the same, making God's house like a stable or common inn." Although many were heartily in favor of the recent changes, it is no wonder that after Edward's death there was a revulsion in favor of the old religion.

Edward VI was succeeded in 1553 by his half sister Mary, the daughter of Catherine, who had been brought up in the Catholic faith and held firmly to it. Her ardent hope of bringing her kingdom back once more to her religion did not seem altogether ill-founded, for the majority of the people were still Catholics at heart, and many who were not disapproved of the policy of Edward's ministers, who had removed abuses "in the devil's own way, by breaking in pieces."

The Catholic cause appeared, moreover, to be strengthened by Mary's marriage with the Spanish prince, Philip II, the son of the orthodox Charles V. But although Philip later distinguished himself, as we shall see, by the merciless way in which he strove to put down heresy within his realms, he never gained any great influence in England. By his marriage with Mary he acquired the title of king, but the English took care that he should have no hand in the government nor be permitted to succeed his wife on the English throne.

Mary succeeded in bringing about a nominal reconciliation between England and the Roman Church. In 1554 the papal legate restored to the communion of the Catholic Church the "Kneeling" Parliament, which theoretically, of course, represented the nation.

During the last four years of Mary's reign the most serious religious persecution in English history occurred. No less than two hundred and seventy-seven persons were put to death for denying the teachings of the Roman Church. The majority of the victims were humble artisans and husbandmen. The three most notable sufferers were the bishops Cranmer, Latimer, and Ridley, who were burned in Oxford.

It was Mary's hope and belief that the heretics sent to the stake would furnish a terrible warning to the Protestants and check the spread of the new teachings, but Catholicism was not promoted; on the contrary, doubters were only convinced of the earnestness of the Protestants who could die with such constancy.

The Catholics, it should be noted, later suffered serious persecution under Elizabeth and James I, the Protestant successors of Mary. Death was the penalty fixed in many cases for those who obstinately refused to recognize the monarch as the rightful head of the English Church, and heavy fines were imposed for the failure to attend Protestant worship. Two hundred Catholic priests are said to have been executed under Elizabeth, Mary's sister, who succeeded her on the throne; others were tortured or perished miserably in prison. These executions, in contrast with those under Mary, were political rather than religious in nature. The victims were accused of conspiracy and *treason* rather than *heresy*.

CHAPTER XIV

THE SO-CALLED WARS OF RELIGION

*The Council of Trent: The Jesuits. Philip II and the Revolt of the
Netherlands. The Huguenot Wars in France. England under
Queen Elizabeth. The Thirty Years' War. The Beginnings
of our Scientific Age*

The Council of Trent: the Jesuits

IN the preceding chapters we have seen how northern
Germany, England, and portions of Switzerland seceded
from the papacy and established independent Protestant
churches. A great part of western Europe, however, remained
faithful to the pope and to the old beliefs which had been
accepted for so many centuries. In order to consider the great
question of reforming the Catholic Church and to settle disputed questions of religious belief a great Church council was
summoned by the pope to meet in Trent, on the confines of
Germany and Italy, in the year 1545. Charles V hoped that
the Protestants would come to the council and that their ideas
might even yet be reconciled with those of the Catholics. But
the Protestants did not come, for they were too suspicious of an
assembly called by the pope to have any confidence in its
decisions.

The Council of Trent (1545-1563) was interrupted after a
few sessions and did not complete its work for nearly twenty
years after it first met. It naturally condemned the Protestant beliefs so far as they differed from the views held by the
Catholics, and it sanctioned those doctrines which the Catholic
Church still holds. It accepted the pope as the head of
the Church; it declared accursed any one who, like Luther,
believed that man would be saved by faith in God's promises
alone; for the Church held that man, with God's help, could
increase his hope of salvation by good works. It ratified all
the seven sacraments, several of which the Protestants had
rejected. The ancient Latin translation of the Bible—the Vul-
gate, as it is called—was proclaimed the standard of belief, and

[317]

no one was to publish any views about the Bible differing from those approved by the Church.

The Council suggested that the pope's officials should compile a list of dangerous books which faithful Catholics might not read for fear that their faith in the old Church would be disturbed. Accordingly, after the Council broke up, the pope issued the first "Index," or list of books which were not to be further printed or circulated on account of the false religious teachings they contained. Similar lists have since been printed from time to time. The establishment of this "Index of Prohibited Books" was one of the most famous of the Council's acts. It was hoped that in this way the spread of heretical and immoral ideas through the printing press could be checked.

Although the Council of Trent would make no compromises with the Protestants, it took measures to do away with certain abuses of which both Protestants and devout Catholics complained. All clergymen were to attend strictly to their duties, and no one was to be appointed who merely wanted the income from his office. The bishops were ordered to preach regularly and to see that only good men were ordained priests. A great improvement actually took place—better men were placed in office and many practices which had formerly irritated the people were permanently abolished.

Among those who, during the final sessions of the Council, sturdily opposed every attempt to reduce in any way the exalted power of the pope, was the head of a new religious society which was becoming the most powerful Catholic organization in Europe. The Jesuit order, or Society of Jesus, was founded by a Spaniard, Ignatius Loyola (1491-1556). He had been a soldier in his younger days, and while bravely fighting for his king, Charles V, had been wounded by a cannon ball (1521). Obliged to lie inactive for weeks, he occupied his time in reading the lives of the saints and became filled with a burning ambition to emulate their deeds. Upon recovering, he dedicated himself to the service of the Church, donned a beggar's gown, and started on a pilgrimage to Jerusalem. Once there he began to realize that he could do little without an education. So he returned to Spain and, although already thirty-three years old, took his place beside the boys who were learning the elements of Latin grammar. After two years he entered a Spanish university, and later went to Paris to carry on his theological studies.

In Paris he sought to influence his fellow students at the university, and finally, in 1534, seven of his companions agreed to follow him to Palestine or, if they were prevented from doing that, to devote themselves to the service of the pope. On arriving in Venice they found that war had broken out between that republic and the Turks. They accordingly gave up their plan for converting the infidels in the Orient and began to preach in the neighboring towns. When asked to what order they belonged, they replied, "To the Society of Jesus."

In 1538 Loyola summoned his followers to Rome, and there they worked out the principles of their order. When this had been done the pope gave his sanction to the new society. Loyola had been a soldier, and he laid great and constant stress upon absolute and unquestioning obedience. This he declared to be the mother of all virtue and happiness. Not only were all the members to obey the pope as Christ's representative on earth, and to undertake without hesitation any journey, no matter how distant or perilous, which he might command, but each was to obey his superiors in the order as if he were receiving directions from Christ in person. He must have no will or preference of his own, but must be as the staff which supports and aids its bearer in any way in which he sees fit to use it. This admirable organization and incomparable discipline were the great secret of the later influence of the Jesuits.

The object of the society was to cultivate piety and the love of God, especially through example. The members were to pledge themselves to lead a pure life of poverty and devotion. A great number of its members were priests, who went about preaching, hearing confession, and encouraging devotional exercises. But the Jesuits were teachers as well as preachers and confessors. They clearly perceived the advantage of bringing young people under their influence; they opened schools and seminaries and soon became the schoolmasters of Catholic Europe. So successful were their methods of instruction that even Protestants sometimes sent their children to them.

Before the death of Loyola over a thousand persons had joined the society. Under his successor the number was trebled, and it went on increasing for two centuries. The founder

PRINCIPAL JESUIT CHURCH IN VENICE

The Jesuits believed in erecting magnificent churches. This is a good example. The walls are inlaid with green marble in an elaborate pattern, and all the furnishings are very rich and gorgeous

of the order had been, as we have seen, attracted to missionary work from the first, and the Jesuits rapidly spread not only over Europe but throughout the whole world. Francis Xavier, one of Loyola's original little band, went to Hindustan, the Moluccas, and Japan. Brazil, Florida, Mexico, and Peru were soon fields of active missionary work at a time when Protestants as yet scarcely dreamed of carrying Christianity to the heathen. We owe to the Jesuits' reports much of our knowledge of the condition of America when white men first began to explore Canada and the Mississippi valley, for the followers of Loyola boldly penetrated into regions unknown to Europeans, and settled among the natives with the purpose of bringing the Gospel to them.

Dedicated as they were to the service of the pope, the Jesuits early directed their energies against Protestantism. They sent their members into Germany and the Netherlands, and even made strenuous efforts to reclaim England. Their success was most apparent in southern Germany and Austria, where they became the confessors and confidential advisers of the rulers. They not only succeeded in checking the progress of Protestantism, but were able to reconquer for the Catholic Church some districts in which the old faith had been abandoned.

Protestants soon realized that the new order was their most powerful and dangerous enemy. Their apprehensions produced a bitter hatred which blinded them to the high purposes of the founders of the order and led them to attribute an evil purpose to every act of the Jesuits. The Jesuits' air of humility the Protestants declared to be mere hypocrisy under which they carried on their intrigues. They were popularly supposed to justify the most deceitful and immoral measures on the ground that the result would be "for the greater glory of God." The very obedience on which the Jesuits laid such stress was viewed by the hostile Protestant as one of their worst offenses, for he believed that the members of the order were the blind tools of their superiors and that they would not hesitate even to commit a crime if so ordered.[1]

Philip II and the Revolt of the Netherlands

The chief ally of the pope and the Jesuits in their efforts to check Protestantism in the latter half of the sixteenth century

[1] As time went on the Jesuit order degenerated just as the earlier ones had done. In the eighteenth century it undertook great commercial enterprises, and for this and other reasons lost the confidence and respect of even the Catholics. The king of Portugal was the first to banish the Jesuits from his kingdom, and then France, where they had long been very unpopular with an influential party of Catholics, expelled them in 1764. Convinced that the order had outgrown its usefulness, the pope abolished it in 1773. It was, however, restored in 1814, and now again has thousands of members.

was the son of Charles V, Philip II. Like the Jesuits he enjoys a most unenviable reputation among Protestants. He was no thorough-going devil, however, and wrote charming letters to his children about the spring flowers. Certain it is, nevertheless, that Protestant heretics had no more terrible enemy among the rulers of the day than he. He eagerly forwarded every plan to attack England's Protestant queen, Elizabeth, and finally manned a mighty fleet with the purpose of overthrowing her (see below, p. 338). He resorted, moreover, to great cruelty in his attempts to bring back his possessions in the Netherlands to what he believed to be the true faith.

Charles V, crippled with the gout and old before his time, laid down the cares of government in 1555-1556. To his brother Ferdinand, who had acquired by marriage the kingdoms of Bohemia and Hungary, Charles had earlier transferred the German possessions of the Hapsburgs. To his son, Philip II (1556-1598), he gave Spain with its great American colonies, Milan, the kingdom of the Two Sicilies, and the Netherlands.[1]

Charles had constantly striven to maintain the old religion within his dominions. He had never hesitated to use the Inquisition in Spain and the Netherlands, and it was the great disappointment of his life that a part of his empire had become Protestant. He was, nevertheless, no fanatic. Like many of the princes of the time, he was forced to take sides on the religious question without, perhaps, himself having any deep religious sentiments. The maintenance of the Catholic faith

[1] Division of the Hapsburg possessions between the Spanish and the German branches:

Maximilian I (d. 1519), m. Mary of Burgundy (d. 1482)
|
Philip (d. 1506), m. Joanna the Insane (d. 1555)
|

Charles V (d. 1558)	Ferdinand (d. 1564), m. Anna, heiress to kingdoms
Emperor, 1519-1556	Emperor, 1556-1564	of Bohemia and Hungary
Philip II (d. 1598)	Maximilian II (d. 1576)
inherits Spain, the Netherlands,	Emperor, and inherits Bohemia,
and the Italian possessions of	Hungary, and the Austrian pos-
the Hapsburgs	sessions of the Hapsburgs

he believed to be necessary in order that he should keep his hold upon his scattered and diverse dominions.

On the other hand, the whole life and policy of his son Philip were guided by a fervent attachment to the old religion. He was willing to sacrifice both himself and his country in his long fight against the detested Protestants within and without his realms. And he had vast resources at his disposal, for Spain was a strong power, not only on account of her income from America, but also because her soldiers and their commanders were the best in Europe at this period.

The Netherlands, which were to cause Philip his first and greatest trouble, included seventeen provinces which Charles V had inherited from his grandmother, Mary of Burgundy. They occupied the position on the map where we now find the kingdoms of Holland and Belgium. Each of the provinces had its own government, but Charles V had grouped them together and arranged that the Holy Roman Empire should protect them. In the north the hardy Germanic population had been able, by means of dikes which kept out the sea, to reclaim large tracts of lowlands. Here considerable cities had grown up—Harlem, Leiden, Amsterdam, and Rotterdam. To the south were the flourishing towns of Ghent, Bruges, Brussels, and Antwerp, which had for hundreds of years been centers of manufacture and trade.

Charles V, in spite of some very harsh measures, had retained the loyalty of the people of the Netherlands, for he was himself one of them, and they felt a patriotic pride in his achievements. Toward Philip II their attitude was very different. His haughty manner made a disagreeable impression upon the people at Brussels when his father first introduced him to them as their future ruler. He was to them a Spaniard and a foreigner, and he ruled them as such after he returned to Spain.

Instead of attempting to win them by meeting their legitimate demands, he did everything to alienate all classes in his Burgundian realm and to increase their natural hatred and suspicion of the Spaniards. The people were forced to house Spanish soldiers whose insolence drove them nearly to desperation.

What was still worse, Philip proposed that the Inquisition should carry on its work far more actively than hitherto and put an end to the heresy which appeared to him to defile his fair realms. The Inquisition was no new thing to the provinces. Charles V had issued the most cruel edicts against the followers of Luther, Zwingli, and Calvin. According to a law of 1550, heretics who persistently refused to recant were to be burned alive. Even those who confessed their errors and abjured their heresy were, if men, to lose their heads; if women, to be buried alive. In either case their property was to be confiscated. The lowest estimate of those who were executed in the Netherlands during Charles's reign is fifty thousand. Although these terrible laws had not checked the growth of Protestantism, all of Charles's decrees were solemnly re-enacted by Philip in the first month of his reign.

For ten years the people suffered Philip's rule; nevertheless their king, instead of listening to the protests of their leaders, who were quite as earnest Catholics as himself, appeared to be bent on the destruction of the land. So in 1566 some five hundred of the nobles ventured to protest against Philip's policy Thereupon Philip took a step which led finally to the revolt of the Netherlands. He decided to dispatch to the low countries the remorseless Duke of Alva, whose conduct has made his name synonymous with blind and unmeasured cruelty.

The report that Alva was coming caused the flight of many of those who especially feared his approach. William of Orange, who was to be the leader in the approaching war against Spain, went to Germany. Thousands of Flemish weavers fled across the North Sea, and the products of their looms became before long an important article of export from England.

Alva brought with him (1567) a fine army of Spanish soldiers, ten thousand in number and superbly equipped. He appeared to think that the wisest and quickest way of pacifying the discontented provinces was to kill all those who ventured to criticize "the best of kings," of whom he had the honor to be the faithful servant. He accordingly established a special court for the speedy trial and condemnation of all those whose fidelity to Philip was suspected. This was popularly known as the Council of Blood, for its aim was not justice but butchery. Alva's administration from 1567 to 1573 was a veritable reign of terror.

The Netherlands found a leader in William, Prince of Orange and Count of Nassau (1533-1584). He is a national hero whose career bears a striking resemblance to that of Washington. Like the American patriot, he undertook the seemingly hopeless task of freeing his people from the oppressive rule of a distant king. To the Spaniards he appeared to be only an impoverished nobleman at the head of a handful of armed peasants and fishermen, contending against the sovereign of the richest realm in the world.

William had been a faithful subject of Charles V and would gladly have continued to serve his son after him had the oppression and injustice of the Spanish dominion not become intolerable. But Alva's policy convinced him that it was useless to send any more complaints to Philip. He accordingly collected a little army in 1568 and opened the long struggle with Spain.

William found his main support in the northern provinces, of which Holland was the chief. The Dutch, who had very generally accepted Protestant teachings, were German in blood, while the people of the southern provinces, who adhered (as they still do) to the Roman Catholic faith, were more akin to the population of northern France.

The Spanish soldiers found little trouble in defeating the troops which William collected. Like Washington, again, he seemed to lose almost every battle and yet was never conquered. The first successes of the Dutch were gained by the mariners who captured Spanish ships and sold them in Protestant England. Encouraged by this, many of the towns in the northern provinces of Holland and Zealand ventured to choose William as their governor (1572), although they did not throw off their allegiance to Philip. In this way these two provinces became the nucleus of the United Netherlands.

Alva recaptured a number of the revolted towns and treated their inhabitants with his customary cruelty; even women and children were slaughtered in cold blood. But instead of quenching the rebellion, he aroused the Catholic southern provinces to revolt.

After six years of this tyrannical and mistaken policy, Alva was recalled. His successor soon died and left matters worse than ever. The leaderless soldiers, trained in Alva's school, indulged in wild orgies of robbery and murder; they plundered and partially reduced to ashes the rich city of Antwerp. The "Spanish fury," as this outbreak was called, together with the hated taxes, created such general indignation that representatives from all of Philip's Burgundian provinces met in Ghent in 1576 with the purpose of combining to put an end to the Spanish tyranny.

This union was, however, only temporary. Wiser and more moderate governors were sent by Philip to the Netherlands, and they soon succeeded in again winning the confidence of the southern Catholic provinces. So the northern provinces went their own way. Guided by William the Silent, they refused to consider the idea of again recognizing Philip as their king. In 1579 seven provinces (Holland, Zealand, Utrecht, Gelderland, Overijssel, Groningen, and Friesland, all lying north of the mouths of the Rhine and the Scheldt) formed the new and firmer Union of Utrecht. The articles of this union served as a constitution for the United Provinces which, two years later, at last formally declared themselves independent of Spain.

Philip realized that William was the soul of the revolt and that without him it might not improbably have been put down. The king therefore offered a patent of nobility and a large sum of money to any one who should make way with the Dutch patriot. After several unsuccessful attempts, William, who had been chosen hereditary governor of the United Provinces, was shot in his house at Delft, 1584. He died praying the Lord to have pity upon his soul and "on this poor people."

The Dutch had long hoped for aid from Queen Elizabeth or from the French, but had heretofore been disappointed. At last the English queen decided to send troops to their assistance. While the English rendered but little actual help, Elizabeth's policy so enraged Philip that he at last decided to attempt the conquest of England. The destruction of the "Armada," the great fleet which he equipped for that purpose, interfered with further attempts to subjugate the United Provinces, which might otherwise have failed to maintain their liberty. Moreover, Spain's resources were being rapidly exhausted, and the State was on the verge of bankruptcy in spite of the wealth which it had been drawing from across the sea. But even though Spain had to surrender the hope of winning back the lost provinces, which now became a small but important European power, she refused formally to acknowledge their independence until 1648 (Peace of Westphalia).

The Huguenot Wars in France

The history of France during the latter part of the sixteenth century is little more than a chronicle of a long and bloody series of civil wars between the Catholics and Protestants.

Protestantism began in France in much the same way as in England. Those who had learned from the Italians to love the Greek language turned to the New Testament in the original and commenced to study it with new insight. Lefèvre (1450-1537), the most conspicuous of these Erasmus-like reformers, translated the Bible into French and began to preach justification by faith before he had ever heard of Luther, whose influence must not be overrated.

The Sorbonne, the famous theological school at Paris, soon began to arouse the suspicions of Francis I against the new ideas. He had no special interest in religious matters, but he was shocked by an act of desecration ascribed to the Protestants, and in consequence forbade the circulation of Protestant books. About 1535 several adherents of the new faith were burned, and Calvin was forced to flee to Basel, where he prepared a defense of his beliefs in his *Institute of the Christian Religion* (see above, p. 308). This is prefaced by a letter to Francis in which he pleads with him to protect the Protestants. Francis, before his death, became so intolerant that he ordered (1545) the massacre of three thousand defenseless peasants who dwelt on the slopes of the Alps, and whose only offense was adherence to the simple teachings of the Waldensians.[1]

Francis's son, Henry II (1547-1559), swore to extirpate the Protestants, and hundreds of them were burned. Nevertheless, Henry II's religious convictions did not prevent him from willingly aiding the German Protestants against his enemy Charles V, especially when they agreed to hand over to him three bishoprics which lay on the French boundary—Metz, Verdun, and Toul.

Henry II was accidentally killed in a tourney and left his kingdom to three weak sons, the last scions of the House of Valois, who succeeded in turn to the throne during a period of unprecedented civil war and public calamity. The eldest son, Francis II, a boy of sixteen, followed his father. His chief importance for France arose from his marriage with the daughter of King James V of Scotland, Mary Stuart, who became famous as Mary Queen of Scots. Her mother was the sister of two very ambitious French nobles, the Duke of Guise and the cardinal of Lorraine. Francis II was so young that Mary's uncles, the Guises, eagerly seized the opportunity to manage his affairs for him. The duke put himself at the head of the army, and the cardinal of the government. When the king died (1560), after reigning but a year, the Guises were naturally reluctant to surrender their power, and many of the woes of France for the next forty years were due to the machinations which they carried on in the name of the Holy Catholic religion.

The new king, Charles IX (1560-1574), was but ten years old, so that his mother, Catherine of Medici, of the famous

[1] See above, p. 159.

Florentine family, claimed the right to conduct the government for her son until he reached manhood.

By this time the Protestants in France had become a powerful party. They were known as *Huguenots* [1] and accepted the

FRANCIS II OF FRANCE

This is from a contemporaneous engraving. The boy king, the first husband of Mary Queen of Scots, died when he was only 17 years old

religious teachings of their fellow countryman, Calvin. Many of them, including their great leader Coligny, belonged to the nobility. They had a strong support in the king of the little realm of Navarre, on the southern boundary of France. He belonged to a side line of the French royal house, known as the Bourbons, who were later to occupy the French throne

[1] The origin of this name is uncertain.

[329]

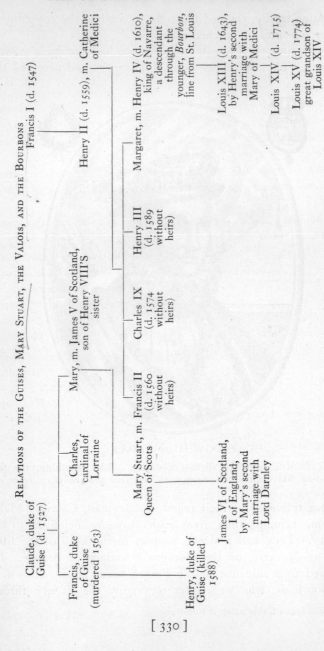

RELATIONS OF THE GUISES, MARY STUART, THE VALOIS, AND THE BOURBONS

Claude, duke of Guise (d. 1527)

Francis, duke of Guise (murdered 1563)

Charles, cardinal of Lorraine

Mary, m. James V of Scotland, son of Henry VIII's sister

Mary Stuart, m. Francis II (d. 1560 without heirs), Queen of Scots

Henry, duke of Guise (killed 1588)

James VI of Scotland, I of England, by Mary's second marriage with Lord Darnley

Francis I (d. 1547)

Henry II (d. 1559), m. Catherine of Medici

Francis II (d. 1560 without heirs)

Charles IX (d. 1574 without heirs)

Henry III (d. 1589 without heirs)

Margaret, m. Henry IV (d. 1610), king of Navarre, a descendant through the younger, *Bourbon*, line from St. Louis

Louis XIII (d. 1643), by Henry's second marriage with Mary of Medici

Louis XIV (d. 1715)

Louis XV (d. 1774) great grandson of Louis XIV

(see genealogical table). It was inevitable that the Huguenots should try to get control of the government, and they consequently formed a *political* as well as a *religious* party and were often fighting, in the main, for worldly ends.

Catherine tried at first to conciliate both Catholics and Huguenots, and granted a Decree of Toleration (1562) suspending the former edicts against the Protestants and permitting them to assemble for worship during the daytime and outside of the towns. Even this restricted toleration of the Protestants appeared an abomination to the more fanatical Catholics, and a savage act of the Duke of Guise precipitated civil war.

As he was passing through the town of Vassy on a Sunday he found a thousand Huguenots assembled in a barn for worship. The duke's followers rudely interrupted the service, and a tumult arose in which the troops killed a considerable number of the defenseless multitude. The news of this massacre aroused the Huguenots and was the beginning of a war which continued, broken only by short truces, until the last weak descendant of the House of Valois ceased to reign. As in the other religious wars of the time, both sides exhibited the most inhuman cruelty. France was filled for a generation with burnings, pillage, and every form of barbarity. The leaders of both the Catholic and Protestant parties, as well as two of the French kings themselves, fell by the hands of assassins, and France renewed in civil war all the horrors of the English invasion in the fourteenth and fifteenth centuries.

In 1570 a brief peace was concluded. The Huguenots were to be tolerated, and certain towns were assigned to them, where they might defend themselves in case of renewed attacks from the Catholics. For a time both Charles IX and his mother, Catherine of Medici, were on the friendliest terms with the Huguenot leader Coligny, who became a sort of prime minister. He was anxious that Catholics and Protestants should join in a great national war against France's old enemy, Spain. In this way the whole people of France might sink their religious differences in a patriotic effort to win Franche-Comté (see above, p. 268), which seemed naturally to belong to France rather than to Spain.

The strict Catholic party of the Guises frustrated this plan by a most fearful expedient. They easily induced Catherine of Medici to believe that she was being deceived by Coligny, and an assassin was engaged to put him out of the way; but the scoundrel missed his aim and only wounded his victim. Fearful lest the young king, who was faithful to Coligny, should discover her part in the attempted murder, Catherine invented a story of a great Huguenot conspiracy. The credulous king was deceived, and the Catholic leaders at Paris arranged that at a given signal not only Coligny, but all the Huguenots, who had gathered in great numbers in the city to witness the marriage of the king's sister to the Protestant Henry of Navarre, should be massacred on the eve of St. Bartholomew's Day (August 23, 1572).

The signal was duly given, and no less than two thousand persons were ruthlessly murdered in Paris before the end of the next day. The news of this attack spread into the provinces, and it is probable that, at the very least, ten thousand more Protestants were put to death outside of the capital. Civil war again broke out, and the Catholics formed the famous Holy League, under the leadership of Henry of Guise, for the advancement of their interests, the destruction of the Huguenots, and the extirpation of heresy.

Henry III (1574-1589), the last of the sons of Henry II, who succeeded Charles IX, had no heirs, and the great question of succession arose. The Huguenot Henry of Navarre was the nearest male relative, but the League could never consent to permit the throne of France to be sullied by heresy, especially as their leader, Henry of Guise, was himself anxious to become king.

Henry III was driven weakly from one party to the other, and it finally came to a war between the three Henrys— Henry III, Henry of Navarre, and Henry of Guise (1585-1589). It ended in a way characteristic of the times. Henry the king had Henry of Guise assassinated. The sympathizers of the League then assassinated Henry the king, which left the field to Henry of Navarre. He ascended the throne as Henry IV in 1589 and is an heroic figure in the line of French kings.

The new king had many enemies, and his kingdom was devastated and demoralized by years of war. He soon saw that he must accept the religion of the majority of his people if he wished to reign over them. He accordingly asked to be readmitted to the Catholic Church (1593), excusing himself—it is said but not known—on the ground that "Paris was worth a mass." He did not forget his old friends, however, and in 1598 he issued the Edict of Nantes.

By this edict of toleration the Calvinists were permitted to hold services in all the towns and villages where they had previously held them, but in Paris and a number of other towns all Protestant services were prohibited. The Protestants were to enjoy the same political rights as Catholics, and to be eligible to government offices. A number of fortified towns were to remain in the hands of the Huguenots, particularly La Rochelle, Montauban, and Nîmes. Henry's only mistake lay in granting the Huguenots the right to control fortified towns. In the next generation this privilege aroused the suspicion of the king's minister, Richelieu, who attacked the Huguenots, not so much on religious grounds as on account of their independent position in the state, which suggested that of the older feudal nobles.

Henry IV chose Sully, an upright and able Calvinist, for his chief minister. Sully set to work to reëstablish the kingly power, which had suffered greatly under the last three brothers of the House of Valois. He undertook to lighten the tremendous burden of debt which weighed upon the country. He laid out new roads and canals, and encouraged agriculture and commerce; he dismissed the useless noblemen and officers whom the government was supporting without any advantage to itself. Had his administration not been prematurely interrupted, it might have brought France unprecedented power and prosperity; but religious fanaticism put an end to his reforms.

In 1610 Henry IV, like William the Silent, was assassinated

just in the midst of his greatest usefulness to his country. Sully could not agree with the regent, Henry's widow, and so gave up his position and retired to private life.

Before many years Richelieu, perhaps the greatest minister France has ever had, rose to power, and from 1624 to his death in 1642 he governed France for Henry IV's son, Louis XIII (1610-1643). Something will be said of his policy in connection with the Thirty Years' War.

England under Queen Elizabeth

The long and disastrous civil war between Catholics and Protestants, which desolated France in the sixteenth century, had happily no counterpart in England. During her long reign Queen Elizabeth (1558-1603) succeeded not only in maintaining peace at home, but in frustrating the conspiracies and attacks of Philip II, which threatened her realm from without. Moreover, by her interference in the Netherlands, she did much to secure their independence of Spain.

Upon the death of Catholic Mary and the accession of her sister Elizabeth in 1558, the English government became once more Protestant. The new queen had a new revised edition issued of the Book of Common Prayer which had been prepared in the time of her brother, Edward VI. This contained the services which the government ordered to be performed in all the churches of England. All her subjects were required to accept the queen's views and to go to church, and ministers were to use nothing but the official prayer book. Elizabeth did not adopt the Presbyterian system advocated by Calvin but retained many features of the Catholic church, including the bishops and archbishops. So the Anglican church followed a middle path halfway between Lutherans and Calvinists on the one hand and Catholics on the other.

The Catholic churchmen who had held positions under Queen Mary were naturally dismissed and replaced by those who would obey Elizabeth and use her Book of Prayer. Her first Parliament gave the sovereign the *powers* of supreme head of the Church of England, although the *title,* which her father, Henry VIII, had assumed, was not revived.

The Church of England still exists in much the same form in which it was established in the first years of Elizabeth's reign and the prayer book is still used, although Englishmen are no longer required to attend church and may hold any religious views they please without being interfered with by the government.

While England adopted a middle course in religious matters Scotland became Presbyterian, and this led to much trouble for Elizabeth. There, shortly after her accession, the ancient Catholic Church was abolished, for the nobles were anxious to get the lands of the bishops into their own hands and enjoy the revenue from them. John Knox, a veritable second Calvin in his stern energy, secured the introduction of the Presbyterian form of faith and church government which still prevails in Scotland.

In 1561, the Scotch queen, Mary Stuart, whose French husband, Francis II, had just died, landed at Leith. She was but nineteen years old, of great beauty and charm, and, by reason of her Catholic faith and French training, almost a foreigner to her subjects. Her grandmother was a sister of Henry VIII, and Mary claimed to be the rightful heiress to the English throne should Elizabeth die childless. Consequently the beautiful Queen of Scots became the hope of all those who wished to bring back England and Scotland to the Roman Catholic faith. Chief among these were Philip II of Spain and Mary's relatives the Guises in France.

Mary quickly discredited herself with both Protestants and Catholics by her conduct. After marrying her second cousin, Lord Darnley, she discovered that he was a dissolute scapegrace and came to despise him. She then formed an attachment for a reckless nobleman named Bothwell. The house near Edinburgh in which Darnley was lying ill was blown up one night with gunpowder, and he was killed. The public suspected that both Bothwell and the queen were implicated. How far Mary was responsible for her husband's death no one can be sure. It is certain that she later married Bothwell and that her indignant subjects thereupon deposed her as a murderess. After fruitless attempts to regain her power, she abdicated in favor of her infant son, James VI, and then fled to England (1568) to appeal to Elizabeth. While the prudent Elizabeth denied the right of the Scotch to depose their queen, she took good care to keep her rival practically a prisoner.

As time went on it became increasingly difficult for Elizabeth to adhere to her policy of moderation in the treatment of the Catholics. A rising in the north of England (1569) showed that there were many who would gladly reëstablish the Catholic faith by freeing Mary and placing her on the English throne. This was followed by the excommunication of Elizabeth by the pope, who at the same time absolved her subjects from their allegiance to their heretical leader. Happily for Elizabeth the rebels could look for no help either from Philip II or the French king. The Spaniards had their hands full, for the war in the Netherlands had just begun; and Charles IX, who had accepted Coligny as his adviser, was at that moment in hearty accord with the Huguenots. The rising in the north was suppressed, but the English Catholics continued to look to Philip for help. They opened correspondence with Alva and invited him to come with six thousand Spanish troops to dethrone Elizabeth and make Mary Stuart queen of England in her stead. Alva hesitated, for he characteristically thought that it would be better to kill Elizabeth, or at least capture her. Meanwhile the plot was discovered and came to naught.

Although Philip found himself unable to harm England, the English mariners caused great loss to Spain. In spite of the fact that Spain and England were not openly at war, Elizabeth's seamen extended their operations as far as the West Indies, and seized Spanish treasure ships, with the firm conviction that in robbing Philip they were serving God. The daring Sir Francis Drake even ventured into the Pacific, where only the Spaniards had gone heretofore, and carried off much booty on his little vessel, the *Pelican*. At last he took "a great vessel with jewels in plenty, thirteen chests of silver coin,

PL. XVI. QUEEN ELIZABETH

PL. XVII. MARY QUEEN OF SCOTS AND DARNLEY

eighty pounds weight of gold, and twenty-six tons of silver." He then sailed around the world, and on his return presented his jewels to Elizabeth, who paid little attention to the expostulations of the king of Spain.

One hope of the Catholics has not yet been mentioned, namely, Ireland, whose relations with England from very early times down until a very recent date may safely be said to form one of the most cheerless pages in the history of Europe. The population was divided into numerous clans, and their chieftains fought constantly with one another as well as with the English, who were vainly endeavoring to subjugate the island. Under Henry II and later kings England had conquered a district in the eastern part of Ireland, and here the English managed to maintain a foothold in spite of the anarchy outside. Henry VIII had suppressed a revolt of the Irish and assumed the title of king of Ireland. Queen Mary of England had hoped to promote better relations by colonizing Kings County and Queens County with Englishmen. This led, however, to a long struggle which only ended when the colonists had killed all the natives in the district they occupied.

Elizabeth's interest in the perennial Irish question was stimulated by the probability that Ireland might become a base for Catholic operations, since Protestantism had made little progress among its people. Her fears were realized. Several attempts were made by Catholic leaders to land troops in Ireland with the purpose of making the island the base for an attack on England. Elizabeth's officers were able to frustrate these enterprises, but the resulting disturbances greatly increased the misery of the Irish. In 1582 no less than thirty thousand people are said to have perished, chiefly from starvation.

As Philip's troops began to get the better of the opposition in the southern Netherlands, the prospect of sending a Spanish army to England grew brighter. Two Jesuits were sent to England in 1580 to strengthen the adherents of their faith and urge them to assist the foreign force against their queen when it should come. Parliament now grew more intolerant and ordered fines and imprisonment to be inflicted on those who said or heard mass, or who refused to attend the English services. One of the Jesuit emissaries was cruelly tortured and executed for treason, the other escaped to the Continent.

In the spring of 1582 the first attempt by the Catholics to assassinate the heretical queen was made at Philip's instigation. It was proposed that, when Elizabeth was out of the way, the Duke of Guise should see that an army was sent to England in the interest of the Catholics. But Guise was kept busy at home by the War of the Three Henrys, and Philip was left to undertake the invasion of England by himself.

Mary Queen of Scots did not live to witness the attempt. She became implicated in another plot for the assassination of Elizabeth. Parliament now realized that as long as Mary lived Elizabeth's life was in constant danger; whereas, if Mary were no longer living, Philip II would have nothing to gain by the death of Elizabeth, since Mary's son, James VI of Scotland, who would succeed Elizabeth on the English throne, was also a Protestant. Elizabeth was therefore reluctantly persuaded by her advisers to sign a warrant for Mary's execution in 1587.

Philip II, however, by no means gave up his project of reclaiming Protestant England. In 1588 he brought together a great fleet, including his best and largest warships, which was proudly called by the Spaniards the "Invincible Armada" (that is, fleet). This was to sail through the English Channel to the Netherlands and bring over the Duke of Parma and his veterans, who, it was expected, would soon make an end of Elizabeth's raw militia. The English ships were inferior to those of Spain in size although not in number, but they had trained commanders, such as Francis Drake and Hawkins.

These famous captains had long "sailed the Spanish Main" and knew how to use their cannon without getting near enough to the Spaniards to suffer from their short-range weapons. When the Armada approached, it was permitted by the English fleet to pass up the Channel before a strong wind, which later became a storm. The English ships then followed, and both fleets were driven past the coast of Flanders. Of the hundred and twenty Spanish ships, only fifty-four returned home; the rest had been destroyed by English valor or by the gale to which Elizabeth herself ascribed the victory. The defeat of the Armada put an end to the danger from Spain.

As we look back over the period covered by the reign of Philip II, it is clear that it was a most notable one in the history of the religious history of western Europe. When he ascended the throne in 1556, Germany, as well as Switzerland and the Netherlands, had become largely Protestant. England, however, under his Catholic wife, Mary, seemed to be turning back to the old religion, while the French monarchs showed no inclination to tolerate the heretical Calvinists. Moreover, the new and enthusiastic order of the Jesuits promised to be a powerful agency in inducing the Protestants to accept once more the supremacy of the pope and the doctrines of the Catholic Church as formulated by the Council of Trent. The tremendous power and apparently boundless resources of Spain itself, which were viewed by the rest of Europe with terror, Philip was prepared to dedicate to the destruction of Protestantism throughout western Europe.

But when Philip II died in 1598, England was hopelessly Protestant; the "Invincible Armada" had been miserably wrecked and Philip's plan for bringing England once more within the fold of the Roman Catholic Church was forever frustrated. In France the terrible wars of religion were over, and a powerful king, lately a Protestant himself, was on the throne, who not only tolerated the Protestants but chose one of them for his chief minister and would brook no more meddling of Spain in French affairs. A new Protestant state, the United Netherlands, had actually appeared within the bounds of the realm bequeathed to Philip by his father. In spite of its small size this state was destined to play, from that time on, quite as important a part in European affairs as the harsh Spanish stepmother from whose control it had escaped. It proved, too, a refuge for "free thinkers" suspected alike by Protestants as well as Catholics.

Spain itself had suffered most of all from Philip's reign. His domestic policy and his expensive wars had sadly wrecked the country. The income from across the sea was bound to decrease as the mines were exhausted. The final expulsion of the industrious Moors, shortly after Philip's death (see above, p. 263), left the indolent Spaniards to till their own fields, which rapidly declined in fertility under their careless cultivation. Some one once ventured to tell a Spanish king that "not gold and silver but sweat is the most precious metal, a coin which is always current and never depreciates"; but it was a rare form of currency in the Spanish peninsula. After Philip II's death Spain sank to the rank of a secondary European power.

The Thirty Years' War

The last great conflict ostensibly caused by the differences between the Catholics and Protestants was fought out in Germany during the first half of the seventeenth century. It is generally known as the Thirty Years' War (1618-1648), but there was in reality a series of wars; and although the fighting was done upon German territory, Sweden, France, and Spain played quite as important a part in the struggle as the various German states.

Just before the abdication of Charles V, the Lutheran princes had forced the emperor to acknowledge their right to their own religion and to the church property which they had appropriated. The religious Peace of Augsburg had, however, as we have seen,[1] two great weaknesses. In the first place only those Protestants who held the Lutheran faith were to be tolerated. The Calvinists, who were increasing in numbers, were not included in the peace. In the second place the peace did not put a stop to the seizure of church property by the Protestant princes.

Protestantism, however, made rapid progress and invaded the Austrian possessions and, above all, Bohemia. So it looked for a time as if even the Catholic Hapsburgs were to see large portions of their territory falling away from the old Church.

---

[1] See above, p. 304 f.

But the Catholics had in the Jesuits a band of active and efficient missionaries. They not only preached and founded schools, but also succeeded in gaining the confidence of some of the German princes, whose chief advisers they became. Conditions were very favorable, at the opening of the seventeenth century, for a renewal of the religious struggle.

The long war began in Bohemia in 1618. This portion of the Austrian possessions was strongly "Protestant" and had been from the days of Huss. Its leaders decided that the best policy was to declare its independence of the Hapsburgs and set up a king of its own. It chose Frederick, the elector of the Palatinate, a Calvinist who would, it was hoped, enjoy the support of his father-in-law, King James I of England. So Frederick and his English wife moved from Heidelberg to Prague. But their stay there was brief, for the Hapsburg emperor (Ferdinand II) with the aid of the ruler of Bavaria put to flight the poor "winter king," as Frederick was called on account of his reign of a single season.

This was regarded as a serious defeat by the Protestants, and the Protestant king of Denmark decided to intervene. He remained in Germany for four years, but was so badly beaten by the emperor's able general, Wallenstein, that he retired from the conflict in 1629.

The emperor was encouraged by the successes of the Catholic armies in defeating the Bohemian and Danish Protestant armies to issue that same year an Edict of Restitution (1629). In this he ordered the Protestants throughout Germany to give back all the church possessions which they had seized since the religious Peace of Augsburg (1555). These included two archbishoprics (Magdeburg and Bremen), nine bishoprics, about one hundred and twenty monasteries, and other church foundations. Moreover, he decreed that only the Lutherans might hold religious meetings; the other "sects," including the Calvinists, were to be broken up. As Wallenstein was preparing to execute this decree in his usual merciless fashion, the war took a new turn.

The Catholic League, which had been formed some time before, had become jealous of a general who threatened to become too powerful, and it accordingly joined in the complaints, which came from every side, of the terrible extortions and incredible cruelty practiced by Wallenstein's troops. The emperor consented, therefore, to dismiss this most competent commander. Just as the Catholics were thus weakened, a new enemy arrived upon the scene who proved far more dangerous than any they had yet had to face, namely Gustavus Adolphus, king of Sweden.

We have had no occasion hitherto to speak of the Scandinavian kingdoms of Norway, Sweden, and Denmark, which the northern German peoples had established about Charlemagne's time; but from now on they begin to take part in the affairs of central Europe. The Union of Calmar (1397) had brought these three kingdoms, previously separate, under a single ruler. About the time that the Protestant revolt began in Germany the union was broken by the withdrawal of Sweden, which became an independent kingdom. Gustavus Vasa, a Swedish noble, led the movement and was subsequently chosen king of Sweden (1523). In the same year Protestantism was introduced. Vasa confiscated the church lands, got the better of the aristocracy,—who had formerly made the kings a great deal of trouble,—and started Sweden on its way toward national greatness.

Gustavus Adolphus (1594-1632) was induced to invade Germany for two reasons. In the first place, he was a sincere and enthusiastic Protestant and by far the most generous and attractive figure of his time. He was genuinely afflicted by the misfortunes of his Protestant brethren and anxious to devote himself to their welfare. Secondly, he undoubtedly hoped by his invasion not only to free his fellow Protestants from the oppression of the emperor and of the Catholic League, but to gain a strip of German territory for Sweden.

Gustavus was not received with much cordiality at first by the Protestant princes of the north, but they were brought to their senses by the awful destruction of Magdeburg by the troops of the Catholic League under General Tilly. Magdeburg was the most important town of northern Germany. When it finally succumbed after an obstinate and difficult siege, twenty thousand of its inhabitants were killed and the town burned to the ground (1631). Although Tilly's reputation for cruelty is quite equal to that of Wallenstein, he was probably not responsible for the fire. After Gustavus Adolphus had met Tilly near Leipzig and victoriously routed the army of the League, the Protestant princes began to look with more favor on the foreigner.

The next spring Gustavus entered Bavaria and once more defeated Tilly (who was mortally wounded in the battle) and forced Munich to surrender. There seemed now to be no reason why he should not continue his progress to Vienna. At this juncture the emperor recalled Wallenstein, who collected a new army over which he was given absolute command. After some delay Gustavus met Wallenstein on the field of Lützen, in November, 1632, where, after a fierce struggle, the Swedes gained the victory. But they lost their leader and Protestantism its hero, for the Swedish king ventured too far into the lines of the enemy and was surrounded and killed.

The Swedes did not, however, retire from Germany, but continued to participate in the war, which now degenerated into a series of raids by leaders whose soldiers depopulated the land by their unspeakable atrocities. Wallenstein, who had long been detested by even the Catholics, was deserted by his soldiers and murdered (in 1634), to the great relief of all parties.

Just at this moment Richelieu decided that it would be to the interest of France to renew the old struggle with the Hapsburgs by sending troops against the emperor. France was still shut in, as she had been since the time of Charles V, by the Hapsburg lands. Except on the side toward the ocean her boundaries were in the main artificial ones, and not those established by great rivers and mountains. She therefore longed to weaken her enemy and strengthen herself by winning Roussillon on the south, and so make the crest of the Pyrenees the line of demarcation between France and Spain. She dreamed, too, of extending her sway toward the Rhine by adding the county of Burgundy (that is, Franche-Comté) and a number of fortified towns which would afford protection against the Spanish Netherlands.

Richelieu declared war against Spain in May, 1635. He had already concluded an alliance with the chief enemies of the House of Austria. So the war was renewed, and French, Swedish, Spanish, and German soldiers ravaged an already exhausted country for a decade longer. The dearth of provisions was so great that the armies had to move quickly from place to place in order to avoid starvation. After a serious defeat by the Swedes, the emperor (Ferdinand III, 1637-1657) sent a Dominican monk to expostulate with Cardinal Richelieu for his crime in aiding the German and Swedish heretics against Catholic Austria.

The cardinal had, however, just died (December, 1642), well content with the results of his diplomacy. The French were in possession of Roussillon and of Lorraine and Alsace. The military exploits of the French generals, especially Turenne and Condé, during the opening years of the reign of Louis XIV (1643-1715), showed that a new period had begun in which the military and political supremacy of Spain was to give way to that of France.

The participants in the war were now so numerous and their objects so various and conflicting that it is not strange that it required some years to arrange the conditions of peace, even after every one was ready for it. It was agreed (1644) that France and the Empire should negotiate at Münster, and the emperor and the Swedes at Osnabrück—both of which towns lie in Westphalia. For four years the representatives of the several powers worked upon the difficult problem of satisfying every one, but at last the treaties of Westphalia were signed late in 1648.

The religious troubles in Germany were settled by extending the toleration of the Peace of Augsburg so as to include the Calvinists as well as the Lutherans. The Protestant princes were to retain the lands which they had in their possession in the year 1624, regardless of the Edict of Restitution, and each ruler was still to have the right to determine the religion of his state. The dissolution of the Holy Roman Empire was practically acknowledged by permitting the individual states to make treaties among themselves and with foreign powers; this was equivalent to recognizing the practical independence which they had, as a matter of fact, already long enjoyed. While portions of northern Germany were ceded to Sweden, this territory did not cease to form a part of the Empire, for Sweden was thereafter to have three votes in the German diet.

The emperor also ceded to France three important towns— Metz, Verdun, and Toul—and all his rights in Alsace, although the city of Strasbourg was to remain with the Empire. Lastly, the independence both of the United Netherlands and of Switzerland was acknowledged.

The accounts of the misery and depopulation of Germany caused by the Thirty Years' War are well-nigh incredible. Thousands of villages were wiped out altogether; in some regions the population was reduced by one-half, in others to a third, or even less, of what it had been at the opening of the conflict. The flourishing city of Augsburg was left with but sixteen thousand souls instead of eighty thousand. The people were fearfully barbarized by privation and suffering and by the atrocities of the soldiers of all the various nations. Until the end of the eighteenth century Germany remained too exhausted and impoverished to make any considerable contribution to the culture of Europe.

The Beginnings of Our Scientific Age

We have now reviewed the most conspicuous events and issues associated with the break-up of the Medieval Church and the appearance of Protestant churches. Each reader may be left to decide for himself how far "religion," in the particular sense in which he may be inclined to use that term, played its part in the wars, massacres, persecutions, dynastic rivalries, hatreds, and dissensions of the sixteenth and seventeenth centuries. All enterprises tended to assume a religious complexion and proffer religious sanctions and justifications. There were Henry VIII's divorce suit, the Schmalcaldic war in Germany, the massacre of Vassy and the terrible slaughter of St. Bartholomew, the murder of William the Silent, the Spanish Armada, the war of the Three Henrys, the Thirty Years' War,—all conducted under pious auspices and in God's name.

So far as the ordeal of Western civilization is concerned we may be permitted to narrow down the problem to the question of whether religion, its doctrines, organization, and practices, were to be regarded as public concerns under governmental control, or a matter of individual conviction, preference, and voluntary association. In 380 the Roman Emperor Theodosius I issued a decree declaring that all those who did not agree with the conceptions of "the blessed Trinity" held by the bishops of Rome and of Alexandria were to be regarded by the imperial government as "mad and demented"; such infamous persons were to suffer first "the wrath of God, then the punishment which in accordance with divine judgment we shall inflict." This responsibility of the civil government to enforce religious conformity persisted, as has been clearly shown, down to the Protestant secession. And it continued to persist, for the Protestant rulers assumed the headship of their established churches. The medieval struggles between Church and State, which continued in various European countries down into the nineteenth century, tended to merge into the question of religious toleration or the right of the individual to embrace any religious beliefs he chose and to put his convictions in practice so far as he could without violating the secular laws of the land. This religious freedom has finally become the rule of Western civilization. As we proceed we may note the various ways in which religious freedom has been achieved. In short, modern governments, in contrast with those of earlier times, usually explicitly repudiate any right to interfere with the religious beliefs and worship of their subjects. To many this still seems a sign of religious and moral degeneration, but there can be no doubt that the secularization of human affairs and the decline of a public reckoning with the supernatural is one of the most striking trends of modern times.

In effecting this momentous change of attitude much influence is to be ascribed to the growth of scientific knowledge and the steady discrediting of ancient beliefs about the heavens and earth.

The battles of the Thirty Years' War are now well-nigh forgot, and few people are interested in Tilly, Wallenstein, and Gustavus Adolphus. It seems as if the war did little but destroy men's lives and property, and that no great ends were accomplished by all the suffering it involved. But during the years that it raged certain men were quietly devoting themselves to scientific research which was to change the world more than all the battles that have ever been fought. These men adopted a new method. They perceived that the books of ancient writers, especially Aristotle, which were used as textbooks in the universities, were full of statements that could not be proved. They maintained that the only way to advance science was to set to work and try experiments, and by careful thought and investigation to determine the laws of nature without regard to what previous generations had thought.

The Polish astronomer Copernicus published a work in 1543 in which he refuted the old idea that the sun and all the stars revolved around the earth as a center, as was then taught in all the universities. He showed that, on the contrary, the sun was the center about which the earth and the rest of the planets revolved, and that the reason that the stars seem to go around the earth each day is because our globe revolves on its axis. Although Copernicus had been encouraged to write his book by a cardinal and had dedicated it to the pope, the Catholic as well as the Protestant theologians declared that the new theory did not correspond with the teachings of the Bible, and they therefore rejected it. But we know now that Copernicus was right and the theologians and universities wrong. The earth is a mere speck in the universe, and even the sun is a relatively small body compared with many of the stars, and so far as we know the universe as a whole has no center.

The Italian scientist Galileo (1564-1642), by the use of a little telescope he contrived, was able in 1610 to see the spots on the sun; these indicated that the sun was not, as Aristotle had taught, a perfect, unchanging body, and showed also that it revolved on its axis, as Copernicus had guessed that the earth did. Galileo made careful experiments by dropping objects from the leaning tower of Pisa, which proved that Aristotle was wrong in assuming that a body weighing a hundred pounds fell a hundred times as fast as a body weighing but one. To Galileo we owe, besides, many new ideas in the science of mechanics. He wrote in Italian as well as Latin, and this, too, gave offense to those who pinned their faith to Aristotle. They would have forgiven Galileo if he had confined his discussions to the learned who could read Latin, but they thought it highly dangerous to have the new ideas set forth in such a way that the people at large might find out about them and so come to doubt what the theologians and universities were teaching. Galileo was finally summoned before the Inquisition and some of his theories condemned by the church authorities.

Just as the Thirty Years' War was beginning, a young Frenchman by the name of Descartes had finished his education at a Jesuit college and decided to get some knowledge of the world by going into the war for a short time. He did much more thinking than fighting, however. Sitting by the stove during the winter lull in hostilities, deep in meditation, it occurred to him one day that he had no reason for believing anything. He saw that everything that he accepted had come to him on the authority of some one else, and he failed to see any reason why the old authorities should be right. So he boldly set to work to think out a wholly new philosophy that should be entirely the result of his own reasoning. He decided, in the first place, that one thing at least was true. He was *thinking*, and therefore he must exist. This he expressed in Latin in the famous phrase *Cogito, ergo sum,* "I think, therefore I am." He also decided that God must exist and that He had given men such good minds that, if they only used them *carefully*, they would not be deceived in the conclusions they

PL. XVIII. GALILEO

Pl. xix. Francis Bacon

reached. In short, Descartes held that *clear* thoughts must be *true* thoughts.

Descartes not only founded modern philosophy, he was also greatly interested in science and mathematics. He was impressed by the wonderful discovery of Harvey in regard to the circulation of the blood, which he thought well illustrated what scientific investigation might accomplish. His most famous book, called *An Essay on Method,* was written in French and addressed to intelligent men who did not know Latin. He says that those who use their own heads are much more likely to reach the truth than those who read old Latin books. Descartes wrote clear textbooks on algebra and that branch of mathematics known as analytical geometry, of which he was the discoverer.

Francis Bacon, an English lawyer and government official, spent his spare hours explaining how men could increase their knowledge. He too wrote in his native tongue as well as in Latin.[1] He was the most eloquent representative of the new science which renounced *authority* and relied upon *experiment.* "We are the ancients," he declared, not those who lived long ago when the world was young and men ignorant. Late in life he wrote a little book, which he never finished, called the *New Atlantis.* It describes an imaginary state which some Europeans were supposed to have come upon in the Pacific Ocean. The chief institution was a "House of Solomon," a great laboratory for carrying on scientific investigation in the hope of discovering new facts and using them for bettering the condition of the inhabitants. This House of Solomon became a sort of model for the Royal Society, which was established in London some fifty years after Bacon's death. It still exists and still publishes its proceedings regularly.

The earliest societies for scientific research grew up in Italy. Later the English Royal Society and the French Institute were established, as well as similar associations in Germany. These were the first things of the kind in the history of the world.

[1] *The Advancement of Learning* is a book easy to get and astonishing to read.

Their object was not, like that of the old Greek schools of philosophy and the medieval universities, merely to hand down the knowledge derived from the past, but to find out what had never been known before.

We have seen how in the thirteenth and fourteenth centuries new inventions were made, such as the compass, paper, spectacles, gunpowder, and, in the fifteenth century, the printing press. But in the seventeenth century progress began to be much more rapid, and an era of invention opened, in the midst of which we still live. The microscope and telescope made it possible to discover innumerable scientific truths that were hidden to the Greeks and Romans. In time this scientific advance produced a *spirit of reform,* also new in the world (see below, Chapter XX).

CHAPTER XV

DISCOVERY OF CONSTITUTIONAL GOVERNMENT IN ENGLAND

James I and the Divine Right of Kings. How Charles I Got Along Without Parliament. How Charles I Lost His Head. Oliver Cromwell: England a Republic. The Restoration. The Revolution of 1688

James I and the Divine Right of Kings

IN the development of our Western civilization during the seventeenth century England played the most conspicuous part. Her experiments in government and the final discrediting of the sacredness of monarchy set an example to be later followed by most of the world. Her thinkers, of whom, unhappily, little can be told here, began questioning a great part of the old ideas of things heavenly and earthly. They wrote in a vigorous style, and exercised a great influence upon other countries, notably France.

On the death of Elizabeth in 1603, James I, the first of the Scotch family of Stuart, ascended the throne. It will be remembered that he was the son of Mary Stuart, Queen of Scots, and through her a descendant of Henry VII (see table, p. 330). In Scotland he reigned as James VI; consequently the two kingdoms were now brought together under the same ruler. This did not, however, make the relations between the two countries much more cordial than they had been in the past.

The chief interest of the period of the Stuarts, which began with the accession of James I in 1603 and ended with the flight from England of his grandson, James II, eighty-five years later, is the long and bitter struggle between the kings and Parliament. The vital question was, Should the Stuart kings, who claimed to be God's representatives on earth, do as they thought fit, or should Parliament control them and the government of the country?

We have seen how the English Parliament originated in the time of Edward I and how his successors were forced to pay attention to its wishes (see above, pp. 243 ff.). Under the

Tudors—that is, from the time of Henry VII to Elizabeth—the monarchs had been able to manage Parliament so that it did, in general, just what they wished. Henry VIII was a heartless tyrant, and his daughter Elizabeth, like her father, had ruled the nation in a high-handed manner, but neither of them had been accustomed to say much of their rights.

James I, on the other hand, had a very irritating way of discussing his claim to be the sole and supreme ruler of England. "It is atheism and blasphemy," he declared, "to dispute what God can do; . . . so it is presumption and high contempt in a subject to dispute what a king can do, or say that a king cannot do this or that." James was a learned man and fond of writing books. He denounced the smoking of tobacco and stoutly defended the belief in witches against manly repudiation of this superstition by Reginald Scott, who had written in Elizabeth's time. He also published a work on monarchs, in which he claimed that the king could make any law he pleased without consulting Parliament; that he was the master of every one of his subjects, high and low, and might put to death whom he pleased. A good king would act according to law, but is not bound to do so and has the power to change the law at any time to suit himself. This was the doctrine of Elizabeth's ecclesiastical supporters who had composed a collection of sermons to be read in the churches. Neither James I nor Louis XIV could outrun the *Homilies* in the matter of divine right.

These theories seem strange and very unreasonable to us, but James was only trying to justify the powers which the Tudor monarchs had actually exercised and which the kings of France enjoyed down to the French Revolution of 1789. According to the theory of "the divine right of kings" it had pleased God to appoint the monarch the father of his people. His subjects must obey him as they would God and ask no questions. The king was responsible to God alone, to whom he owed his powers, not to Parliament or the nation (see below, p. 371).

It is unnecessary to follow the troubles between James I and Parliament, for his reign only forms the preliminary to the fatal experiences of his son Charles I, who came to the throne in 1625.

The writers of James's reign constituted its chief glory. They outshone those of any other European country. Shakespeare is generally admitted to be the greatest dramatist that the world has produced. While he wrote many of his plays before the death of Elizabeth, some of his finest—*Othello, King Lear,* and *The Tempest,* for example—belong to the time of James I. During the same period Francis Bacon was writing his *Advancement of Learning,* which he dedicated to James I in 1605 and in which he urged that men should cease to rely upon the old textbooks, like Aristotle, and turn to a careful examination of animals, plants, and chemicals, with a view of learning about them and using the knowledge thus gained to improve the condition of mankind. Bacon's ability to write English is equal to that of Shakespeare, but he chose to write prose, not verse. It was in James's reign that the authorized English translation of the Bible was made which is still used in all countries where English is spoken.

An English physician of this period, William Harvey, examined the workings of the human body more carefully than any previous investigator and made the great discovery of the manner in which the blood circulates from the heart through the arteries and capillaries and back through the veins—a matter which had previously been entirely misunderstood.

How Charles I Got Along Without Parliament

Charles I (1625-1649), James I's son and successor, was somewhat more dignified than his father, but he was quite as obstinately set upon having his own way and showed no more skill in winning the confidence of his subjects. He did nothing to remove the disagreeable impressions of his father's reign and began immediately to quarrel with Parliament. When that body refused to grant him any money, mainly because they thought that it was likely to be wasted by his favorite, the Duke of Buckingham, Charles formed the plan of winning their favor by a great military victory.

He hoped to gain popularity by prosecuting a war against Spain, whose king was energetically supporting the Catholic League in the Thirty Years' War. Accordingly, in spite of Parliament's refusal to grant him the necessary funds, he embarked in war. With only the money which he could raise by irregular means, Charles arranged an expedition to capture the Spanish treasure ships which arrived in Cadiz once a year from America, laden with gold and silver; but this expedition failed.

In his attempts to raise money without a regular grant from Parliament, Charles resorted to vexatious exactions. The law prohibited him from asking for *gifts* from his people, but it did not forbid his asking them to *lend* him money, however little prospect there might be of his ever repaying it. Five gentlemen who refused to pay such a forced loan were imprisoned by the mere order of the king. This raised the question of whether the king had the right to send to prison those whom he wished without any legal reasons for their arrest.

This and other attacks upon the rights of his subjects aroused Parliament. In 1628 that body drew up the celebrated *Petition of Right*, which is one of the most important documents in the history of the English Constitution. In it Parliament called the king's attention to his unlawful exactions, and to the acts of his agents who had in sundry ways molested and disquieted the people of the realm. Parliament therefore "humbly prayed" the king that no man need thereafter "make or yield any gift, loan, benevolence, tax, or such like charge" without consent of Parliament; that no free man should be imprisoned or suffer any punishment except according to the laws and statutes of the realm as presented in the Great Charter; and that soldiers should not be quartered upon the people on any pretext whatever. Very reluctantly Charles consented to this restatement of the limitations which the English had always, in theory at least, placed upon the arbitrary power of their king.

The disagreement between Charles and Parliament was rendered much more serious by religious differences. The king had married a French Catholic princess, and the Catholic cause

PL. XX. CHARLES I, BY VAN DYCK

PL. XXI. CHILDREN OF CHARLES I, BY VAN DYCK

seemed to be gaining on the Continent. The king of Denmark had just been defeated by Wallenstein and Tilly, and Richelieu had succeeded in depriving the Huguenots of their cities of refuge. Both James I and Charles I had shown their readiness to enter into agreements with France and Spain to protect Catholics in England, and there was evidently a growing inclination in England to revert to the older ceremonies of the Church, which shocked the more strongly Protestant members of the House of Commons. The communion table was again placed by many clergymen at the eastern end of the church and became fixed there as an altar, and portions of the service were once more chanted.

These "popish practices," as the Protestants called them, with which Charles was supposed to sympathize, served to widen the breach between him and the Commons, which had been caused by the king's attempt to raise taxes on his own account. The Parliament of 1629, after a stormy session, was dissolved by the king, who determined to rule thereafter by himself. For eleven years no new Parliament was summoned.

Charles was not well fitted by nature to run the government of England by himself. He had not the necessary tireless energy. Moreover, the methods resorted to by his ministers to raise money without recourse to Parliament rendered the king more and more unpopular and prepared the way for the triumphant return of Parliament. For example, Charles applied to his subjects for "ship money." He was anxious to equip a fleet, but instead of requiring the various ports to furnish ships, as was the ancient custom, he permitted them to buy themselves off by contributing money to the fitting out of large ships owned by himself. Even those living inland were asked for ship money. The king maintained that this was not a tax but simply a payment by which his subjects freed themselves from the duty of defending their country.

John Hampden, a squire of Buckinghamshire, made a bold stand against this illegal demand by refusing to pay twenty shillings of ship money which was levied upon him. The case was tried before the king's judges, and he was convicted, but by a bare majority. The trial made it tolerably clear that the country would not put up long with the king's despotic policy.

In 1633 Charles made William Laud Archbishop of Canterbury. Laud believed that the English Church would strengthen both itself and the government by following a middle course which should lie between that of the Church of Rome and that of Calvinistic Geneva. He declared that it was the part of good citizenship to conform outwardly to the services of the state church, but that the State should not undertake to oppress the individual conscience, and that every one should be at liberty to make up his own mind in regard to the interpretation to be given to the Bible and to the church fathers. As soon as he became archbishop he began a series of visitations through his province. Every clergyman who refused to conform to the prayer book, or opposed the placing of the communion table at the east end of the church, or declined to bow at the name of Jesus, was, if obstinate, to be brought before the king's special Court of High Commission to be tried and, if convicted, to be deprived of his position.

Laud's conduct was no doubt gratifying to the High Church party among the Protestants, that is, those who still clung to some of the ancient practices of the Roman Church, although they rejected the doctrine of the Mass and refused to regard the pope as their head. The Low Church party, or *Puritans,* on the contrary, regarded Laud and his policy with aversion. While, unlike the Presbyterians, they did not urge the abolition of the bishops, they disliked all "superstitious usages," as they called the wearing of the surplice by the clergy, the use of the sign of the cross at baptism, the kneeling posture in partaking of the communion, and so forth. The Presbyterians, who are often confused with the Puritans, agreed with them in many respects, but went farther and demanded the introduction of Calvin's system of church government.

Lastly, there was an ever-increasing number of Separatists, or Independents. These rejected both the organization of the Church of England and that of the Presbyterians, and desired that each religious community should organize itself independently. The government had forbidden these Separatists to hold their little meetings, which they called *conventicles,* and about 1600 some of them fled to Holland. The community of them which established itself at Leiden dispatched the *Mayflower,* in 1620, with colonists—since known as the Pilgrim Fathers—to the New World across the sea.[1] The form of worship which they established in their new home is still known as Congregational.

How Charles I Lost His Head

In 1640 Charles found himself forced to summon Parliament, for he was involved in a war with Scotland which he could not carry on without money. There the Presbyterian system had been pretty generally introduced by John Knox in Elizabeth's time. An attempt on the part of Charles to force the Scots to accept a modified form of the English prayer book led to the signing of the National Covenant in 1638. This pledged those who attached their names to it to reëstablish the purity and liberty of the Gospel, which, to most of the Covenanters, meant Presbyterianism.

Charles thereupon undertook to coerce the Scots. Having no money, he bought on credit a large cargo of pepper, which had just arrived in the ships of the East India Company, and sold it cheap for ready cash. The soldiers, however, whom he got together showed little inclination to fight the Scots, with whom they were in tolerable agreement on religious matters. Charles was therefore at last obliged to summon a Parliament (1640), which, owing to the length of time it remained in session, is known as the Long Parliament.

The Long Parliament began by imprisoning Archbishop Laud in the Tower of London. They declared him guilty of treason, and he was executed in 1645, in spite of Charles's efforts to save him. Parliament also tried to strengthen its

[1] The name "Puritan," it should be noted, was applied loosely to the English Protestants, whether Low Churchmen, Presbyterians, or Independents, who aroused the antagonism of their neighbors by their offensive piety and their opposition to popular pastimes, especially on Sunday.

position by passing the Triennial Bill, which provided that it should meet at least once in three years, even if not summoned by the king. In fact, Charles's whole system of government was abrogated. Parliament drew up a "Grand Remonstrance" in which all of Charles's errors were enumerated and a demand was made that the king's ministers should thereafter be responsible to Parliament. This document Parliament ordered to be printed and circulated throughout the country.

Exasperated at the conduct of the Commons, Charles attempted to intimidate the opposition by undertaking to arrest five of its most active leaders, whom he declared to be traitors. But when he entered the House of Commons and looked around for his enemies, he found that they had taken shelter in London, whose citizens later brought them back in triumph to Westminster, where Parliament held its meetings.

Both Charles and Parliament now began to gather troops for the inevitable conflict, and England was plunged into civil war. Those who supported Charles were called *Cavaliers*. They included not only most of the aristocracy and the Catholic party, but also a number of members of the House of Commons who were fearful lest Presbyterianism should succeed in doing away with the English Church. The parliamentary party was popularly known as the *Roundheads*, since some of them cropped their hair close because of their dislike for the long locks of their more aristocratic and worldly opponents.

The Roundheads soon found a distinguished leader in Oliver Cromwell (b. 1599), a country gentleman and member of Parliament, who was later to become the most powerful ruler of his time. Cromwell organized a compact army of God-fearing men, who were not permitted to indulge in profane words or light talk, as is the wont of soldiers, but advanced upon their enemies singing psalms. The king enjoyed the support of northern England, and also looked for help from Ireland, where the royal and Catholic causes were popular.

The war continued for several years, and a number of battles were fought which, after the first year, went in general against

[358]

the Cavaliers. The most important of these were the battle of Marston Moor in 1644, and that of Naseby the next year, in which the king was disastrously defeated. The enemy came into possession of his correspondence, which showed them how their king had been endeavoring to bring armies from France and Ireland into England. This encouraged Parliament to prosecute the war with more energy than ever. The king, defeated on every hand, put himself in the hands of the Scotch army which had come to the aid of Parliament (1646), and the Scotch soon turned him over to Parliament. During the next two years Charles was held in captivity.

There were, however, many in the House of Commons who still sided with the king, and in December, 1648, that body declared for a reconciliation with the monarch, whom they had safely imprisoned in the Isle of Wight. The next day Colonel Pride, representing the army,—which constituted a party in itself and was opposed to all negotiations between the king and the Commons,—stood at the door of the House with a body of soldiers and excluded all the members who took the side of the king. This outrageous act is known in history as "Pride's Purge."

In this way the House of Commons was brought completely under the control of those most bitterly hostile to the king, whom they immediately proposed to bring to trial. They declared that the House of Commons, since it was chosen by the people, was supreme in England and the source of all just power, and that consequently neither king nor House of Lords was necessary. The mutilated House of Commons appointed a special High Court of Justice made up of Charles's sternest opponents, who alone would consent to sit in judgment on him. They passed sentence upon him, and on January 30, 1649, Charles was beheaded in front of his palace of Whitehall, London. It must be clear from the above account that it was not the nation at large which demanded Charles's death, but a very small group of extremists who claimed to be the representatives of the nation.

Oliver Cromwell: England a Republic

The "Rump Parliament," as the remnant of the House of Commons was contemptuously called, proclaimed England to be thereafter a "commonwealth," that is, a republic, without a king or House of Lords. But Cromwell, the head of the army, was nevertheless the real ruler of England. He derived his main support from the Independents; and it is very surprising that he was able to maintain himself so long, considering what a small portion of the English people was in sympathy with the religious ideas of that sect and with the abolition of kingship. Even the Presbyterians were on the side of Charles I's son, Charles II, the legal heir to the throne. Cromwell was a vigorous and skillful administrator and had a well-organized army of fifty thousand men at his command, otherwise the republic could scarcely have lasted more than a few months.

Cromwell found himself confronted by every variety of difficulty. The three kingdoms had fallen apart. The nobles and Catholics in Ireland proclaimed Charles II as king, and Ormond, a Protestant leader, formed an army of Irish Catholics and English royalist Protestants with a view of overthrowing the Commonwealth. Cromwell accordingly set out for Ireland, where, after taking Drogheda, he mercilessly slaughtered two thousand of the "barbarous wretches," as he called them. Town after town surrendered to Cromwell's army, and in 1652, after much cruelty, the island was once more conquered. A large part of it was confiscated for the benefit of the English, and the Catholic landowners were driven into the mountains. In the meantime (1650) Charles II, who had taken refuge in France, had landed in Scotland, and upon his agreeing to be a Presbyterian king, the whole Scotch nation was ready to support him. But Scotland was subdued by Cromwell even more promptly than Ireland had been. So completely was the Scottish army destroyed that Cromwell found no need to draw the sword again in the British Isles.

Although it would seem that Cromwell had enough to keep him busy at home, he had already engaged in a victorious foreign war against the Dutch, who had become dangerous commercial rivals of England. The ships which went out from

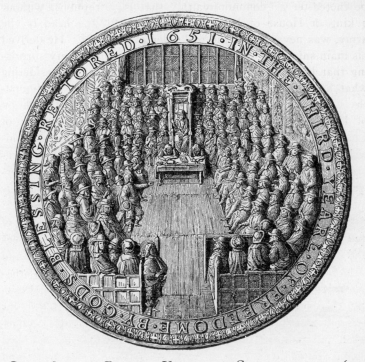

GREAT SEAL OF ENGLAND UNDER THE COMMONWEALTH, 1651

This seal is reduced considerably in the reproduction. It gives us an idea of the appearance of a session of the House of Commons when England was for a short period a republic. It is still to-day the custom for members to sit with their hats on, except when making a speech

Amsterdam and Rotterdam were the best merchant vessels in the world and had got control of the carrying trade between Europe and the colonies. In order to put an end to this, the English Parliament passed the Navigation Act (1651), which permitted only English vessels to bring goods to England, unless the goods came in vessels belonging to the country which had produced them. This led to a commercial war between Holland and England, and a series of battles was fought between the English and Dutch fleets, in which sometimes one and sometimes the other gained the upper hand. This war is notable as an early example of the commercial

DUTCH WAR VESSEL IN CROMWELL'S TIME

This should be compared with the next illustration to realize the change that had taken place in navigation since the palmy days of the Hanseatic League. (See above, pp. 176 f.).

struggles which were thereafter to take the place of the religious conflicts of the preceding period.

Cromwell failed to get along with Parliament any better than Charles I had done. The Rump Parliament had become very unpopular, for its members, in spite of their boasted piety, accepted bribes and were zealous in the promotion of their relatives in the public service. At last Cromwell upbraided them angrily for their injustice and self-interest, which were injuring the public cause. On being interrupted by a member, he cried out, "Come, come, we have had enough of this! I'll put an end to this. It's not fit that you should sit here any longer," and calling in his soldiers he turned the members out of the House and sent them home. Having thus made an end of the Long Parliament (April, 1653), he summoned a Parliament of his own, made up of "God-fearing" men whom he and the officers of his army chose. This extraordinary body is known as Barebone's Parliament, from a distinguished member, a London merchant, with the characteristically Puritan name of Praisegod Barebone. Many of these godly men were unpractical and hard to deal with. A minority of the more sensible ones got up early one winter morning (December, 1653) and, before their opponents had a chance to protest, declared Parliament dissolved and placed the supreme authority in the hands of Cromwell.

A SHIP OF THE HANSEATIC LEAGUE

This is taken from a picture at Cologne, painted in 1409. It, as well as other pictures of the time, makes it clear that the Hanseatic ships were tiny compared with those used two hundred and fifty years later, when Cromwell fought the Dutch

For nearly five years Cromwell was, as Lord Protector,—a title equivalent to that of Regent,—practically king of England, although he refused actually to accept the royal insignia. He did not succeed in permanently organizing the government at home but showed remarkable ability in his foreign negotiations. He formed an alliance with France, and English troops aided the French in winning a great victory over Spain. England gained thereby Dunkirk, and the West Indian island of Jamaica. The French king, Louis XIV, at first hesitated to address Cromwell, in the usual courteous way of monarchs, as "my cousin," but soon admitted that he should have even to call Cromwell "father" should he wish it, as the Protector was undoubtedly the most powerful person in Europe. Indeed, he found himself forced to play the part of a monarch, and it seemed to many persons that he was quite as despotic as James I and Charles I.

In May, 1658, Cromwell fell ill, and as a great storm passed over England at that time, the Cavaliers asserted that the devil had come to fetch home the soul of the usurper. Cromwell was dying, it is true, but he was no instrument of the devil. He closed a life of honest effort for his fellow beings with a last touching prayer to God, whom he had consistently sought to serve: "Thou hast made me, though very unworthy, a mean instrument to do Thy people some good and Thee service: and many of them have set too high a value upon me, though others wish and would be glad of my death. Pardon such as desire to trample upon the dust of a poor worm, for they are Thy people too; and pardon the folly of this short prayer, even for Jesus Christ's sake, and give us a good night, if it be Thy pleasure. Amen."

The Restoration

After Cromwell's death, his son Richard, who succeeded him, found himself unable to carry on the government. He soon abdicated, and the remnants of the Long Parliament met once more. But the power was really in the hands of the soldiers. In 1660 George Monk, who was in command of the forces in Scotland, came to London with a view of putting an end to the anarchy. He soon concluded that no one cared to support the Rump, and that body peacefully disbanded of its own accord. Resistance would have been vain in any case with the army against it. The nation was glad to acknowledge Charles II, whom every one preferred to a government by soldiers. A new Parliament, composed of both houses, was assembled, which welcomed a messenger from the king and solemnly resolved that, "according to the ancient and fundamental laws of this kingdom, the government is, and ought to be, by king, lords, and commons." Thus the Puritan revolution and the short-lived republic was followed by the *Restoration* of the Stuarts.

Charles II was quite as fond as his father of having his own way, but he was a man of more ability. He disliked to be ruled by Parliament, but, unlike his father, he was too wise to arouse the nation against him. He did not propose to let anything happen which would send him on his travels again. He and his courtiers were fond of pleasure of a light-minded kind. The immoral dramas of the Restoration seem to indicate that those who had been forced by the Puritans to give up their legitimate pleasures now welcomed the opportunity to indulge in reckless gayety without regard to the bounds imposed by custom and decency.

Charles's first Parliament was a moderate body, but his second was made up almost wholly of Cavaliers, and it got along, on the whole, so well with the king that he did not dissolve it for eighteen years. It did not take up the old question, which was still unsettled, as to whether Parliament or the king was really supreme. It showed its hostility, however, to the Puritans by a series of intolerant acts, which are very important in English history. It ordered that no one should hold a town office who had not received the communion according to the rites of the Church of England. This was aimed at both the Presbyterians and the Independents. By the Act of Uniformity (1662) every clergyman who refused to accept everything contained in the Book of Common Prayer was to be excluded from holding his benefice. Two thousand clergymen thereupon resigned their positions for conscience's sake.

These laws tended to throw all those Protestants who refused to conform to the Church of England into a single class, still known to-day as *Dissenters*. It included the Independents, the Presbyterians, the Baptists and the more recent Society of

Friends, commonly known as Quakers. These sects abandoned any idea of controlling the religion or politics of the country, and asked only that they might be permitted to worship in their own way outside of the English Church.

Toleration found an unexpected ally in the king, who, in spite of his dissolute habits, had interest enough in religion to have secret leanings toward Catholicism. He asked Parliament to permit him to moderate the rigor of the Act of Uniformity by making some exceptions. He even issued a declaration in the interest of toleration, with a view of bettering the position of the Catholics and Dissenters. Suspicion was, however, aroused lest this toleration might lead to the restoration of "popery,"—as the Protestants called the Catholic beliefs,—and Parliament passed the harsh Conventicle Act (1664).

Any adult attending a conventicle—that is to say, any religious meeting not held in accordance with the practice of the English Church—was liable to penalties which might culminate in transportation to some distant colony. Samuel Pepys, who saw some of the victims of this law upon their way to a terrible exile, notes in his famous diary: "They go like lambs without any resistance. I would to God that they would conform, or be more wise and not be catched." A few years later Charles II issued a declaration giving complete religious liberty to Roman Catholics as well as to Dissenters. Parliament not only forced him to withdraw this enlightened measure but passed the Test Act, which excluded every one from public office who did not accept the views of the English Church.

The old war with Holland, begun by Cromwell, was renewed under Charles II, who was earnestly desirous to increase English commerce and to found new colonies. The two nations were very evenly matched on the sea, but in 1664 the English seized some of the West Indian Islands from the Dutch and also their colony on Manhattan Island, which was renamed New York in honor of the king's brother, the Duke of York. In 1667 a treaty was signed by England and Holland which confirmed these conquests.

The Revolution of 1688

Upon Charles II's death he was succeeded by his brother, James II (1685-1688), who was an avowed Catholic and had married, as his second wife, Mary of Modena, who was also a Catholic. He was ready to reëstablish Catholicism in England regardless of what it might cost him. Mary, James's daughter by his first wife, had married her cousin, William III, Prince of Orange, the head of the United Netherlands. The nation might have tolerated James so long as they could look forward to the accession of his Protestant daughter. But when a son was born to his Catholic second wife, and James showed unmistakably his purpose of favoring the Catholics, messengers were dispatched by a group of Protestants to William of Orange, asking him to come and rule over them.

William landed in November, 1688, and marched upon London, where he received general support from all the English Protestants, regardless of party. James II started to oppose William, but his army refused to fight and his courtiers deserted him. William was glad to forward James's flight to France, as he would hardly have known what to do with him had James insisted on remaining in the country. A new Parliament declared the throne vacant, on the ground that King James II, "by the advice of the Jesuits and other wicked persons, having violated the fundamental laws and withdrawn himself out of the kingdom, had abdicated the government."

```
              Charles I, m. Henrietta Maria of France
              (1625-1649)

Charles II   Mary, m. William II,   Anne Hyde, m. James II, m. Mary of Modena
(1660-1685)         Prince of                   (1685-1688)
                    Orange

       William III, m. Mary   Anne        James Francis Edward,
       (1688-1702)        (1702-1714)        the Old Pretender
```

The new sovereigns accepted those conditions (later formally rehearsed in the famous Bill of Rights) which the irregular Parliament imposed upon them, and William and Mary were proclaimed king and queen in February, 1689. This "Glorious Revolution" of 1688 made it clear that the English Parliament and not the monarch was really supreme. Professor Cheyney points out that the revolution accomplished rather less than is ordinarily claimed. "No new classes were given the right to vote and there was no effort to represent the people more completely in Parliament. It brought few if any advantages to the common people. It was a very successful revolution, but not one that extended very deeply or affected very many interests of the people."

The Bill of Rights enumerated the ways in which the late James II "by the assistance of divers evil counsellors, judges and ministers employed by him, did endeavor to subvert and extirpate the Protestant religion, and the laws and liberties of this kingdom," by suspending the laws, establishing a special court, levying money without the consent of Parliament, exacting excessive bail, and imposing illegal and cruel punishments. All these things, "utterly and directly contrary to the known laws and statutes and freedom of this realm," were recognized as such by the new rulers. They agreed, too, that there should be complete freedom of speech in Parliament.

This Bill of Rights became a sort of model for the American Declaration of Independence and for the bills of rights in many of the state constitutions, as well as for the one appended to the United States Constitution in the form of the first ten amendments.

A Toleration Act was passed, granting the right of public worship to Dissenters. Roman Catholics and Unitarians—those who deny the Trinity—were not included. Later the liberty of the press was established by revoking all the former laws for government censorship and the licensing of books—measures which John Milton had denounced in his eloquent *Areopagitica*, written while the Long Parliament was in session. But a writer could still be adjudged guilty of sedition, blasphemy, and libel—to wit, needless abuse of the government, God, or his fellow man. Latterly governments have become less sensitive in regard to God's honor, but it was discovered during the World War that even the United States government could surprise disrespect of itself in the most unexpected quarters. Nonetheless the action of the English Parliament was a significant innovation in frankly giving up all efforts to have books examined in manuscript by government agents and approved before they could be legally printed.

CHAPTER XVI

THE AGE OF LOUIS XIV

The French Monarchy at Its Height. Louis XIV Attacks His Neighbors. Renewed Religious Persecution. War of the Spanish Succession.

The French Monarchy at Its Height

UNDER the despotic rule of Louis XIV (1643-1715) France enjoyed a commanding influence in European affairs. After the wars of religion were over, the royal authority had been reëstablished by the wise conduct of Henry IV. Later, Richelieu had solidified the monarchy by depriving the Huguenots of the exceptional privileges granted to them for their protection by Henry IV; he had also destroyed the fortified castles of the nobles, whose power had greatly increased during the turmoil of the Huguenot wars. His successor, Cardinal Mazarin, who conducted the government during Louis XIV's boyhood, was able to put down a last rising of the discontented nobility.

When Mazarin died, in 1661, he left the young monarch with a solidified kingdom such as no previous French king had enjoyed. The nobles, who for centuries had disputed the power of the king, were no longer feudal lords but only courtiers. The Huguenots, whose claim to a place in the State beside the Catholics had led to the terrible civil wars of the sixteenth century, were reduced in numbers and no longer held fortified towns from which they could defy the king's officers. Richelieu and Mazarin had successfully taken a hand in the Thirty Years' War, and France had come out of it with enlarged territory and increased importance in European affairs.

Louis XIV carried the work of these great ministers still farther. During his reign the French monarchy assumed the character which it retained until the French Revolution. He made himself the very mirror of kingship. His marvelous court at Versailles became the model and the despair of other less opulent and powerful princes, who accepted his theory of the absolute power of kings but could not afford to imitate his luxury. By his incessant wars he kept Europe in turmoil for over half a century. The distinguished generals who led his newly organized troops, and the wily diplomats who arranged his alliances and negotiated his treaties, made France feared and respected by even the most powerful of the other European states.

Louis XIV had the same idea of kingship that James I had tried in vain to induce the English people to accept. God had given kings to men, and it was His will that monarchs should be regarded as His lieutenants and that all those subject to them should obey them absolutely, without asking any questions or making any criticisms; for in submitting to their prince they were really submitting to God Himself. If the king were good and wise, his subjects should thank the Lord; if he proved foolish, cruel, or perverse, they must accept their evil ruler as a punishment which God had sent them for their sins. But in no case might they limit his power or rise against him. All this was set forth by the elegant bishop Bossuet in his treatise on *Government as Based on the Very Words of Scripture*.[1]

Louis XIV had two great advantages over James I. In the first place, the English nation has always shown itself more reluctant than France to place absolute power in the hands of its rulers. By its Parliament, its courts, and its various declarations of the nation's rights, it had built up traditions which made it impossible for the Stuarts permanently to establish their claim to be absolute rulers. In France, on the other hand, there was no Great Charter or Bill of Rights; the Estates General did not hold the purse strings, and the king was permitted to raise money without asking their permission or previously redressing the grievances which they chose to point out. They were therefore only summoned at irregular intervals. When Louis XIV took charge of the government, forty-seven years had passed without a meeting of the Estates General, and a century and a quarter was still to elapse before another call to the representatives of the nation was issued in 1789.

[1] Louis XIV does not appear to have himself used the famous expression "*I* am the *State*," usually attributed to him, but it exactly corresponds to his idea of the relation of the king and the State.

Moreover, the French people placed far more reliance upon a powerful king than the English, perhaps because they were not protected by the sea from their neighbors, as England was. On every side France had enemies ready to take advantage of any weakness or hesitation which might arise from dissension between a parliament and the king. So the French felt it best, on the whole, to leave all in the king's hands, even if they suffered at times from his tyranny.

Louis had another great advantage over James. He was a handsome man, of elegant and courtly mien, and possessed the most exquisite perfection of manner and a fine reticence. Even when playing billiards he is said to have retained an air of world mastery. The first of the Stuarts, on the contrary, was a very awkward man, whose slouching gait, intolerable manners, and pedantic conversation were utterly at variance with his lofty pretensions. Louis added, moreover, to his graceful exterior a sound judgment and quick apprehension. He said neither too much nor too little. He was, for a king, a hard worker and spent several hours a day attending to the business of government.

It requires, in fact, a great deal of energy and application to be a real despot. In order thoroughly to understand and to solve the problems which constantly face the ruler of a great state, a monarch must, like Frederick the Great or Napoleon, rise early and toil late. Louis XIV was greatly aided by the able ministers who sat in his council, but he always retained for himself the place of first minister. He would never have consented to be dominated by an adviser, as his father had been by Richelieu. "The profession of the king," he declared, "is great, noble, and delightful if one but feels equal to performing the duties which it involves,"—and he never harbored a doubt that he himself was born for the business.

Louis XIV was careful that his surroundings should suit the grandeur of his office. His court was magnificent beyond anything that had been dreamed of in the West. He had an enormous palace constructed at Versailles, just outside of Paris, with interminable halls and apartments and a vast garden stretching away behind it. About this a town was laid out, where those who were privileged to be near his majesty or supply the wants of the royal court lived. This palace and its outlying buildings, including two or three less gorgeous residences for the king when he occasionally tired of the ceremony of Versailles, probably cost the nation about a hundred million dollars, in spite of the fact that thousands of peasants and soldiers were forced to turn to and work without pay. The furnishings and decorations were as rich and costly as the

ONE OF THE HALLS OF VERSAILLES

palace was splendid and still fill the visitor with wonder. For over a century Versailles continued to be the home of the French kings and the seat of their government.

This splendor and luxury helped to attract the nobility, who no longer lived on their estates in well-fortified castles, planning how they might escape the royal control. They now dwelt in the effulgence of the king's countenance. They saw him to bed at night and in stately procession they greeted him in the morning. It was deemed a high honor to hand him his shirt as he was being dressed or, at dinner, to provide him with a fresh napkin. Only by living close to the king could the courtiers hope to gain favors, pensions, and lucrative offices for themselves and their friends, and perhaps occasionally to exercise some little influence upon the policy of the government. For they were now entirely dependent upon the good will of their monarch.

The reforms which Louis XIV carried out in the earlier part of his reign were largely the work of the great financier Colbert, to whom France still looks back with gratitude. He early discovered that the king's officials were stealing and wasting huge sums. The offenders were arrested and forced to disgorge, and a new system of bookkeeping was introduced, similar to that employed by business men. He then turned his attention to increasing the manufactures of France by establishing new industries and seeing that the older ones kept to a high standard, which would make French goods sell readily in foreign markets. He argued justly that if foreigners could be induced to buy French goods, these sales would bring gold and silver into the country and so enrich it. He made rigid rules as to the width and quality of cloths which the manufacturers might produce and the dyes which they might use. He even reorganized the old medieval guilds; for through them the government could keep its eye on all the manufacturing that was done; this would have been far more difficult if every one had been free to carry on any trade which he might choose.

It was, however, as a patron of art and literature that Louis XIV gained much of his celebrity. Molière, who was at once a playwright and an actor, delighted the court with comedies in which he delicately satirized the foibles of his time. Corneille, who had gained renown by the great tragedy of *The Cid* in Richelieu's time, found a worthy successor in Racine, the most distinguished, perhaps, of French tragic poets. The charming letters of Madame de Sévigné are models of prose style and serve at the same time to give us a glimpse into the more refined life of the court circle. In the famous memoirs of Saint-Simon, the weaknesses of the king, as well as the numberless intrigues of the courtiers, are freely exposed with inimitable skill and wit.

Men of letters were generously aided by the king with pensions. Colbert encouraged the French Academy, which had been created by Richelieu. This body gave special attention to making the French tongue more eloquent and expressive by determining what words should be used. It is now the greatest honor that a Frenchman can obtain to be made one of the forty members of this association. A magazine which still exists, the *Journal des Savants,* was founded for the promotion of science at this time. Colbert had an astronomical observatory built at Paris; and the Royal Library, which possessed only about sixteen thousand volumes, began to grow into that great collection of two and a half million volumes—the largest in existence—which to-day attracts scholars to Paris from all parts of the world. In short, Louis XIV and his ministers believed one of the chief objects of any government to be the promotion of art, literature, and science, and the example they set has been followed by almost every modern state.

Louis XIV Attacks His Neighbors

Unfortunately for France, the king's ambitions were by no means exclusively peaceful. Indeed, he regarded his wars as his chief glory. He employed a carefully reorganized army and the skill of his generals in a series of inexcusable attacks on his neighbors, in which he finally squandered all that Colbert's economies had accumulated and led France to the edge of financial ruin.

Louis XIV's predecessors had had, on the whole, little time to think of conquest. They had first to consolidate their realms and gain the mastery of their feudal dependents, who shared the power with them; then the claims of the English Edwards and Henrys had to be met, and the French provinces freed from their clutches; lastly, the great religious dispute was only settled after many years of disintegrating civil war. But Louis XIV was now at liberty to look about him and consider how he might best realize the dream of his ancestors and perhaps reëstablish the ancient boundaries which Cæsar reported that the Gauls had occupied. The "natural limits" of France appeared to be the Rhine on the north and east, the Jura Mountains and the Alps on the southeast, and to the south the Mediterranean and the Pyrenees. Richelieu had believed that it was the chief end of his ministry to restore to France the boundaries determined for it by nature. Mazarin had labored hard to win Savoy and Nice and to reach the Rhine on the north. Before his death France at least gained Alsace and reached the Pyrenees, "which," as the treaty with Spain says (1659), "formerly divided the Gauls from Spain."

Louis XIV first turned his attention to the conquest of the Spanish Netherlands, to which he laid claim through his wife, the elder sister of the Spanish king, Charles II (1665-1700). In 1667 he surprised Europe by publishing a little treatise in which he set forth his claims not only to the Spanish Netherlands, but even to the whole Spanish monarchy. By confounding the kingdom of France with the old empire of the Franks he could maintain that the people of the Netherlands were his subjects.

In 1667 Louis placed himself at the head of the army which he had re-formed and reorganized, and announced that he was to undertake a "journey," as if his invasion was only an expedition into another part of his undisputed realms. He easily took a number of towns on the border of the Netherlands and then turned south and completely conquered Franche-Comté. This was an outlying province of Spain, isolated from her other lands, and a most tempting morsel for the hungry king of France.[1]

These conquests alarmed Europe, and especially Holland, which could not afford to have the barrier between it and France removed, for Louis XIV would be an uncomfortable neighbor. A Triple Alliance, composed of Holland, England, and Sweden, was accordingly organized to induce France to make peace with Spain. Louis contented himself for the moment with the dozen border towns that he had taken and

---

[1] See above, pp. 268 and 332. The long struggle over Franche-Comté is a bore to the historical student. It keeps coming into the narrative in spite of its general irrelevance to our interests to-day.

which Spain ceded to him on condition that he would return Franche-Comté.

The success with which Holland had held her own against the navy of England and brought the proud king of France to a halt produced an elation on the part of that tiny country which was very aggravating to Louis XIV. He was thoroughly vexed that he should have been blocked by so trifling an obstacle as Dutch intervention. He consequently conceived a strong dislike for the United Provinces, which was increased by the protection that they afforded to writers who annoyed him with their attacks. He broke up the Triple Alliance by inducing Charles II of England to conclude a treaty which pledged England to help France in a new war against the Dutch.

Louis XIV then startled Europe again by seizing the duchy of Lorraine, which brought him to the border of Holland. At the head of a hundred thousand men he crossed the Rhine (1672) and easily conquered southern Holland. For the moment the Dutch cause appeared to be lost. But William of Orange showed the spirit of his great ancestor William the Silent; the sluices in the dikes were opened and the country flooded, so the French army was checked before it could take Amsterdam and advance into the north. The emperor sent an army against Louis, and England deserted him and made peace with Holland.

When a general peace was concluded at the end of six years (at Nimwegen, 1678), the chief provisions were that Holland should be left intact, and that France should this time retain Franche-Comté, which had been conquered by Louis XIV in person. This bit of the Burgundian heritage thus became at last a part of France, after France and Spain had quarreled over it for a century and a half. For the ten years following there was no open war, but Louis seized the important free city of Strasbourg and made many other less conspicuous but equally unwarranted additions to his territory. The emperor was unable to do more than protest against these outrageous encroachments, for he was fully occupied with the Turks, who had just laid siege to Vienna.

Renewed Religious Persecution

Louis XIV exhibited as woeful a want of statesmanship in the treatment of his Protestant subjects as in the prosecution of disastrous wars. The Huguenots, deprived of their former military and political power, had turned to manufacture, trade, and banking; "as rich as a Huguenot" had become a proverb in France. There were perhaps a million of them among fifteen million Frenchmen, and they undoubtedly formed by far the most thrifty and enterprising part of the nation. The Catholic clergy, however, did not cease to urge the complete suppression of heresy.

Louis XIV had scarcely taken the reins of government into his own hands before the perpetual nagging and injustice to which the Protestants had been subjected at all times took a more serious form. Upon one pretense or another their churches were demolished. Children were authorized to renounce Protestantism when they reached the age of seven. Rough dragoons were quartered upon the Huguenots with the hope that the insulting behavior of the soldiers might frighten the heretics into accepting the religion of the king.

At last Louis XIV was led by his officials to believe that practically all the Huguenots had been converted by these harsh measures. In 1685, therefore, he revoked the Edict of Nantes, and the Protestants thereby became outlaws and their ministers subject to the death penalty. Even liberal-minded Catholics, like the kindly writer of fables, La Fontaine, and the charming letter writer, Madame de Sévigné, hailed this reëstablishment of "religious unity" with delight. They believed that only an insignificant and seditious remnant still clung to the beliefs of Calvin. But there could have been no more serious mistake. Thousands of the Huguenots succeeded in eluding the vigilance of the royal officials and fled, some to England, some to Prussia, some to America, carrying with them their skill and industry to strengthen France's rivals. This was the last great and terrible example in western Europe of that fierce religious intolerance which had produced the Albigensian

Crusade, the Spanish Inquisition, and the Massacre of St. Bartholomew.

Louis XIV now set his heart upon conquering the Palatinate, a Protestant land, to which he easily discovered that he had a claim. The rumor of his intention and the indignation occasioned in Protestant countries by the revocation of the Edict of Nantes resulted in an alliance against the French king headed by William of Orange. Louis speedily justified the suspicions of Europe by a frightful devastation of the Palatinate, burning whole towns and destroying many castles, including the exceptionally beautiful one of the elector at Heidelberg. Ten years later, however, Louis agreed to a peace in which he surrendered the districts which the French had occupied. He was preparing for the final and most ambitious undertaking of his life, which precipitated the longest and bloodiest war of all his warlike reign.

War of the Spanish Succession

The king of Spain, Charles II, was childless and brotherless, and Europe had long been discussing what would become of his vast realms when his sickly existence should come to an end. Louis XIV had married one of his sisters, and the emperor, Leopold I, another, and these two ambitious rulers had been considering for some time how they might divide the Spanish possessions between the Bourbons and the Hapsburgs. But when Charles II died, in 1700, it was discovered that he had left a will in which he made Louis's younger grandson, Philip, the heir to his twenty-two crowns, but on the condition that France and Spain should never be united.

It was a weighty question whether Louis XIV should permit his grandson to accept this hazardous honor. Should Philip become king of Spain, Louis and his family would control all of southwestern Europe from Holland to Sicily, as well as a great part of North and South America. This would mean the establishment of an empire more powerful than that of Charles V. It was clear that the disinherited emperor and the ever watchful William of Orange, now king of England, would never permit this unprecedented extension of French influence. They had already shown themselves ready to make great sacrifices in order to check far less serious aggressions on the part of the French king. Nevertheless, family pride and personal ambition led Louis criminally to risk the welfare of his country. He accepted the will and informed the Spanish ambassador at the French court that he might salute Philip V as his new king. The leading French newspaper of the time boldly proclaimed that the Pyrenees were no more.

King William soon succeeded in forming a new Grand Alliance (1701) in which Louis's old enemies, England, Holland, and the emperor, were the most important members. William himself died just as hostilities were beginning, but the long War of the Spanish Succession was carried on vigorously by the great English general, the Duke of Marlborough, and the Austrian commander, Eugene of Savoy. The conflict was more general than the Thirty Years' War; even in America there was fighting between French and English colonists, which passes in American histories under the name of Queen Anne's War. All the more important battles went against the French, and after ten years of war, which was rapidly ruining the country by the destruction of its people and its wealth, Louis XIV was willing to consider some compromise, and after long discussion a peace was arranged in 1713.

The Treaty of Utrecht changed the map of Europe as no previous treaty had done, not even that of Westphalia. Each of the chief combatants got his share of the Spanish booty over which they had been fighting. The Bourbon Philip V was permitted to retain Spain and its colonies on condition that the Spanish and French crowns should never rest on the same head. To Austria fell the Spanish Netherlands, hereafter called the Austrian Netherlands, which continued to form a barrier between Holland and France. Holland received certain fortresses to make its position still more secure. The Spanish possessions in Italy, that is, Naples and Milan, were also given to Austria, and in this way Austria got the hold on Italy which it retained until 1866. From France, England acquired Nova

Chicago Public Library
Sulzer Regional
2/10/2009 4:18:47 PM

- PATRON RECEIPT -
- RENEWALS -

1: Item Number: R0026560735
 Title: The ordeal of civili
 Renewed Until: 3/3/2009

------- Please Keep this Slip -------

War of Sp. Succ.

Louis XIV

{
Eng
Holland -
Emperor Leopold
}

Duke of Marlborough &
Eugene of Savoy

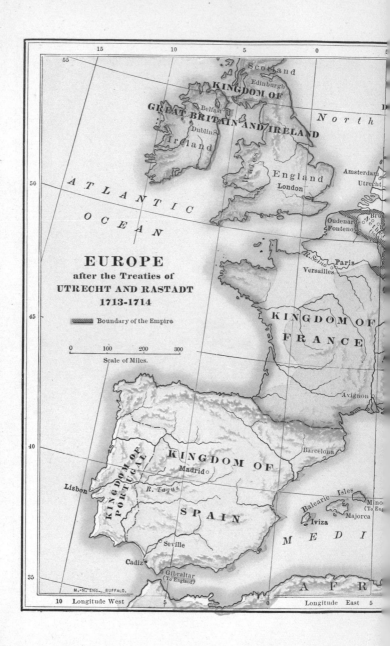

EUROPE
after the Treaties of
UTRECHT AND RASTADT
1713-1714

▨▨▨ Boundary of the Empire

0   100   200   300
Scale of Miles.

15   10   5   0

55

50

ATLANTIC

OCEAN

45

40

35

Scotland

Edinburgh

KINGDOM OF

Belfast

GREAT BRITAIN AND IRELAND

Dublin

Ireland

England

London

North

Amsterdam

Utrecht

Oudenar

Fontenoy

Bru

Ne che

R. Seine

Paris

Versailles

KINGDOM OF

FRANCE

Avignon

Barcelona

KINGDOM OF

Madrid

R. Tagus

Lisbon

KINGDOM OF PORTUGAL

SPAIN

Balearic Isles

Mino
(To Eng

Majorca

Iviza

Seville

M E D I

Cadiz

Gibraltar
(To England)

A F R

M. N. ENG. BUFFALO.

10   Longitude West   5   0   Longitude East   5

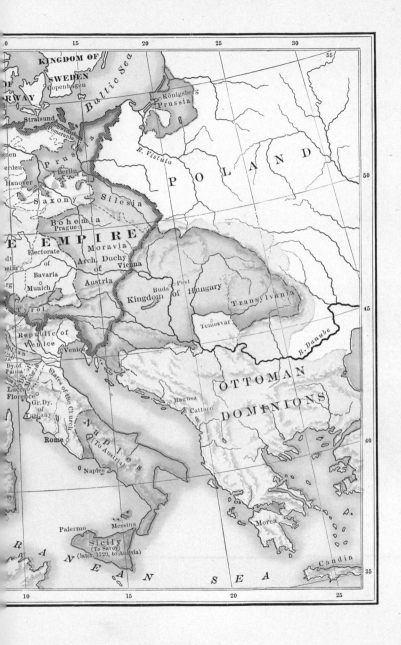

Scotia, Newfoundland, and the Hudson Bay region, and so began the expulsion of the French from North America. Besides these American provinces she received the rock and fortress of Gibraltar, which still gives her command of the narrow entrance to the Mediterranean.

Louis XIV outlived his son and his grandson and left a sadly demoralized kingdom to his five-year-old great-grandson, Louis XV (1715-1774). The national treasury was depleted, the people were reduced in numbers and were in a miserable state, and the army, once the finest in Europe, was in no condition to gain further victories.

It seems as if the historian found himself almost inevitably taxing his readers' attention by accounts of wars. Most of them seem scandalous in their origin, wicked in their prosecution, and futile and destructive in their consequences. The eighteenth century was, as we shall see, not behind the seventh or the sixteenth in illustrating the fact that the State has hitherto been a predatory institution which even in western Europe has usually devoted a great part of its resources to fighting. The nineteenth and the twentieth centuries opened with widespread and tremendous armed conflicts. Grotesque as war may seem in its growing inappropriateness, it has been so universal, and sometimes so important in its effects on the growth of states, that it must be assigned a conspicuous place in the story of Western civilization.

Then if wars are to be prevented some means will have to be discovered for obviating the conditions which produce them. No one can take an intelligent part in the modern efforts to secure and maintain peace unless he is familiar with the ancient and inveterate warlike habits of Western governments. Peace is one of the most important issues of our day and some study of wars, their ostensible causes and results, is an essential to a wise participation in the movement.

The denunciation of war and projects for peace among nations can be traced back to the days of Philip the Fair of France, when an ingenious lawyer of the time, Pierre Dubois, submitted to the king about the year 1300 a short treatise explaining how wars might be prevented by international arbitration and the boycotting of aggressors. A quarter of a century later Marsiglio of Padua published his *Defender of the Peace* in which he pronounced the Church and Pope, with their property and governmental rights, the chief disturbers of the peace. He proposed to deprive them of their property and secular powers. Both Erasmus and Sir Thomas More wrote ardently against war and the kingly governments of their day.

With Grotius, who published his *War and Peace* in 1625, the history of *International Law* begins. Grotius was followed, a half a century later, by Pufendorf with his *Law of Nature and of Nations*. These onlookers perceived that the incessant wars and great alliances of their day made necessary clearer rules in the international relations of the powers. For example, what protection were ambassadors to enjoy? What was to be the status of neutral vessels? What should be considered fair and permissible in actual war and in the treatment of prisoners? International law has so far been a high aspiration—or at least a sort of *diplomatique* etiquette—rather than an effective barrier to aggression and military horrors. But the League of Nations has proposed a committee of experts to codify international law in a far more impressive way than it has heretofore been presented by more or less academic writers. Hitherto it has been a grave question whether international law was "law" at all in the usual juridical sense of the term.

Peter the Great

Louis XIV

Pl. XXII

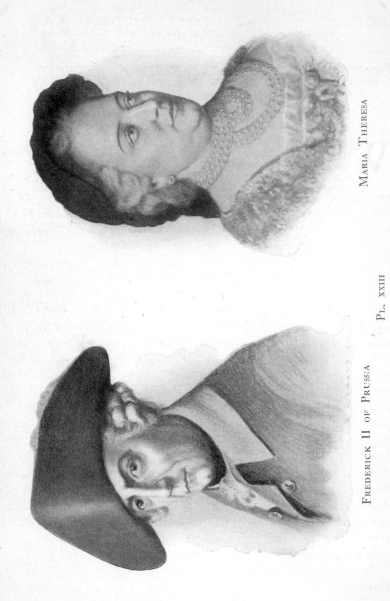

FREDERICK II OF PRUSSIA   MARIA THERESA

PL. XXIII

CHAPTER XVII

EIGHTEENTH-CENTURY RULERS: THEIR WARS AND REFORMS

Beginnings of Russia. Peter the Great. How Prussia Became a Great Power. The Wars of Frederick the Great. The Partition of Poland. The Austrian Realms: Maria Theresa and Joseph II

Beginnings of Russia

WE have had little occasion hitherto, in dealing with the history of western Europe, to speak of the Slavic peoples, to whom the Russians, Poles, Bohemians, and two important Balkan nations belong. Together they form the most numerous linguistic group in Europe. In the eighteenth century Russia began to take an increasingly important part in European affairs, and it is now a great problem in the affairs of the world. The realms of the Tsar in Europe before the World War exceeded in extent those of all the other rulers of the Continent put together, and yet they were scarcely more than a quarter of his whole dominion, which embraced northern and central Asia, and formed together an empire occupying nearly three times the area of the United States.

The Slavs were settled along the Dneiper, Don, and Vistula rivers long before the Christian era. After the East Goths had penetrated into the Roman Empire the Slavs followed their example and invaded, ravaged, and conquered the Balkan peninsula, where the medieval kingdoms of Bulgaria and Serbia grew up. When the German Lombards went south into Italy, about 569, the Slavs pressed behind them into the eastern Alps, where they later continued to live until recently within the bounds of the Austrian empire. Other Slavic hordes had driven the Germans across the Oder and the upper Elbe. The German emperors, beginning with Charlemagne, began to push them back, but the Bohemians and Moravians, who are Slavs, still hold an advanced position on the borders of Germany.

In the ninth century some of the Northmen invaded the districts to the east of the Baltic, while their relatives were causing grievous trouble in France and England. It is generally supposed that one of their leaders, Rurik, was the first to consolidate the Slavic tribes about Novgorod into a sort of state, in 862. Rurik's successor extended the bounds of the new empire to the south as far as the Dnieper River. The word "Russia" is probably derived from *Rous*, the name given by the neighboring Finns to the Norman adventurers. Before the end of the tenth century the Greek form of Christianity was introduced and the Russian ruler was baptized. The frequent intercourse with Constantinople might have led to rapid advance in civilization had it not been for a great disaster which put Russia back for centuries.

Russia is geographically nothing more than an extension of the vast plain of northern Asia, which the Russians were destined finally to conquer. It was therefore exposed to the great invasion of the Tartars, or Mongols, who swept in from the east in the thirteenth century. The powerful Tartar ruler, Genghis Khan (1162-1227), conquered northern China and central Asia, and the mounted hordes of his successors crossed into Europe and overran Russia, which had fallen apart into numerous principalities. The Russian princes became the dependents of the Great Khan, and had frequently to seek his far-distant court, some three thousand miles away, where he freely disposed of both their crowns and their heads. The Tartars exacted tribute of the Russians but left them undisturbed in their laws and religion.

The original center of Russian power was Kiev, but, later, the princes of Moscow so increased their power and the extent of their realms that they were able to make terms with the various Mongolian khans who continued to rule southern Russia after the break-up of the vast empire of Genghis. In due time the khanates were conquered by the princes of Moscow and added to Russia. In 1547 Ivan the Terrible assumed the title of "Tsar" which was the Slavic equivalent for "king" or "emperor." [1] Russian civilization was deeply affected by that

---

[1] The word "Tsar," or "Czar," is derived from "Cæsar" (German, *Kaiser*), but was used in Slavic books for the title of the kings of antiquity as well as for the Roman emperors. Peter the Great called himself "Impera-

of Constantinople, with which its rulers had from the begin-ning been in contact. The pomp of the Russian princes, the Russian religion, and the Russian alphabet derive from the Eastern Empire. So it is probable that the "Oriental" characteristics of Russia were due not so much to the invading Mongols, as has sometimes been supposed, but rather to Byzantine example. It was the life work of Peter the Great to introduce Western civilization into Russia. In this way there was a tendency of eastern Europe to enter into constantly more intimate relations with the west.

Peter the Great

At the time of Peter's accession, in 1672, Russia, which had grown greatly under Ivan the Terrible and other enterprising rulers, still had no outlet to the sea. In manners and customs the kingdom was Oriental, and its government was a good deal like that of a Tartar prince. Peter had no objection to the despotic power which fell to him, but he knew that Russia was very much behind the rest of Europe and that his crudely equipped soldiers could never make headway against the well-armed and well-disciplined troops of the West. He had no seaport and no ships, and without these Russia could never hope to take part in the world's affairs. His three great tasks were therefore to improve the Russian government, to introduce Western habits, and to "make a window," as he expressed it, through which Russia might look abroad.

In 1697-1698 Peter himself visited Germany, Holland, and England with a view to investigating every art and science of the West, as well as the most-approved methods of manufacture, from the making of a man-of-war to the etching of an engraving. Nothing escaped the keen eyes of this rude, half-savage northern giant. For a week he put on the wide breeches of a Dutch laborer and worked in the shipyard at Zaandam near Amsterdam. In England, Holland, and Germany he engaged artisans, scientific men, architects, ship captains, and

---

tor," that is, "emperor." The Tsar was also known as "Autocrat of all the Russias."

those versed in artillery and in the training of troops—all of whom he took back with him to aid in the reform and development of Russia.

He was called home by the revolt of Russian nobles and churchmen who were horrified at Peter's desertion of the habits and customs of his forefathers. They hated what they called "German ideas," such as short coats, tobacco smoking, and beardless faces. Peter took a fearful revenge upon the rebels and is said to have himself cut off the heads of many of them. Like the barbarian that he was at heart, he left their heads and bodies lying about all winter, unburied, in order to make the terrible results of revolt against his power quite plain to all.

Peter's reforms extended through his whole reign. He made his people give up their cherished Oriental beards and long flowing garments. He forced the women of the richer classes, who had been kept in a sort of Oriental harem, to come out and meet the men in social assemblies, such as were common in the West. He invited foreigners to settle in Russia, and sent young Russians abroad to study. He reorganized the government officials on the model of a Western kingdom, and made over his army in the same way. He reconstructed the monetary system, and encouraged the printing of Russian books.

Finding that the old capital, Moscow, clung persistently to its ancient habits, he prepared to found a new capital for his new Russia. He selected for this purpose a bit of territory on the Baltic which he had conquered from Sweden—very marshy, it is true, but where he might hope to construct Russia's first real port. Here he built St. Petersburg [1] at enormous expense and colonized it with Russians and foreigners. Russia was at last becoming a European power.

The next problem was to get control of the provinces lying between the Russian boundary and the Baltic Sea. These

---

[1] Changed to *Petrograd* during the war with Germany in 1914, so that the Russian capital should no longer be called by a German name. Then the Bolsheviki later renamed the city after their hero, Leningrad.

belonged to Sweden, which happened to have at that time a very warlike young monarch, Charles XII. He filled Europe with astonishment for a time by engaging in war with Denmark, Saxony, and Russia and gaining many surprising victories. But his attempt to penetrate into Russia proved as fatal to him as a similar attempt did to Napoleon a century later. His prowess only served to set back Russia's plans for the moment. Three years after his death, which occurred in 1718, Peter forced Sweden to cede to him Livonia, Esthonia, and other Swedish territory which had previously cut Russia off from the sea.

Peter looked with longing eyes on the possessions of the Turks to the south of him, and he made vain attempts to extend the Russian control as far as the Black Sea. He did not succeed in this, but it had become evident that if the Turks were to be driven from Europe, Russia would prove a mighty rival of the other European powers in the divisions of the spoils.

For a generation after the death of Peter the Great, Russia fell into the hands of incompetent rulers. It only appears again as a European state when the great Catherine II came to the throne, in 1762. From that time on, the Western powers had always to consider the vast Slavic empire in all their great struggles. They had also to consider a new kingdom in northern Germany, which was just growing into a great power that was to prove a potent factor in world affairs. This was Prussia, whose beginnings we must now consider.

How Prussia Became a Great Power

The electorate of Brandenburg had figured on the German map for centuries, but there was no particular reason to suppose that it was to become one day the dominant state in Germany. Early in the fifteenth century the old line of electors had died out, and Emperor Sigismund, in the days of the Council of Constance, had sold Brandenburg to a hitherto unimportant house, the Hohenzollerns, which is known to us now through such names as those of Frederick the Great, of William I, the first German emperor, and of his grandson, William II, the "Kaiser." Beginning with a strip of territory extending some ninety or a hundred miles to the east and to the west of the little town of Berlin, the successive representatives of the line gradually extended their boundaries until the kingdom of Prussia embraced nearly two-thirds of Germany. Of the earlier little annexations nothing need be said. While it has always been the boast of the Hohenzollern family that almost every one of its reigning members has added something to what his ancestors handed down to him, no great

VIEW OF BERLIN IN 1717

Berlin was only a small town until the days of the Great Elector. It increased from about 8,000 inhabitants in 1650 to about 20,000 in 1688. It is therefore not really an ancient city like Paris. Most of its great growth has taken place in the nineteenth and twentieth centuries

extension took place until just before the Thirty Years' War. About that time the elector of Brandenburg inherited Cleves and Mark, and thus got his first hold on the Rhine district (see map, p. 394).

What was quite as important, he won, far to the east, the duchy of Prussia, which was separated from Brandenburg by Polish territory. Prussia was originally the name of a region on the Baltic inhabited by heathen Borussians. These had been conquered in the thirteenth century by one of the orders of crusading knights (the Teutonic order), who, when the conquest of the Holy Land was abandoned, looked about for other occupation.

After the German knights had conquered Prussia it began to fill up with German colonists. In Luther's day (1525) the knights were converted to Protestantism and dissolved their order. They then formed their lands into the duchy of Prussia, and their Grand Master, who was a relative of the elector of Brandenburg, became their first duke. About a hundred years later (1618) this branch of the Hohenzollerns died out, and the duchy then fell to the elector of Brandenburg.

Notwithstanding this substantial territorial gain, there was little promise that the hitherto obscure electorate would ever become a formidable power when, in 1640, Frederick William, known as the Great Elector, came to the throne of Brandenburg. His territories were scattered from the Rhine to the Vistula, his army was of small account, and his authority disputed by powerful nobles. The center of his domain was Brandenburg. Far to the west was Mark, bordering on the Rhine valley, and Cleves, lying on both banks of that river. Far to the east, beyond the Vistula, was the duchy of Prussia.

The Great Elector was, however, well fitted for the task of welding these domains into a powerful state. He was heartless in destroying opponents, treacherous in diplomatic negotiations, and entirely devoid of the refinement which distinguished Louis XIV and his court. He unscrupulously set to work to increase his territories and his power.

By shrewd tactics during the closing days of the Thirty Years' War he managed to secure, by the Treaty of Westphalia, the bishoprics of Minden and Halberstadt and the duchy of Farther Pomerania, which gave him a good shore line on the Baltic.

Knowing that the interests of his house depended on military strength, he organized, in spite of the protests of the taxpayers, an army out of all proportion to the size and wealth of his dominions, and this was the beginning of that great Prussian war machine which showed its terrible efficiency in the conflict of 1914. He succeeded in creating an absolute monarchy on the model furnished by his contemporary, Louis XIV. He joined with England and Holland in their alliances against Louis, and the army of Brandenburg began to be known and feared.

Though a good Protestant, the Great Elector permitted religious freedom to a remarkable degree. He made Catholics

MILITARY PUNISHMENT

The armies of the old régime were mostly made up of hired soldiers or serfs, and the officers maintained discipline by cruel punishments. In this picture of a Prussian regiment one soldier is being flogged while half suspended by his wrists; another is forced to walk between two files of soldiers who must beat his bared back with heavy rods. It has been said that Prussian soldiers found war a relief from the terrors of peace, since in war time the punishments were lessened

eligible to office and, on the other hand, gave asylum to the persecuted Huguenots of France, even offering them special inducements to settle in his realms.

It was accordingly an enriched legacy which the Great Elector left in 1688 to his son, Frederick, and although the career of the latter was by no means so brilliant as that of his father, he induced the emperor to permit him to change his title from "elector" to "king" and so to transform his *electorate* into a *kingdom*.[1]

The title "King in Prussia" was deemed preferable to the more natural "King of Brandenburg" because Prussia lay wholly without the bounds of the empire, and consequently its ruler was not in any sense subject to the emperor but was entirely independent.[2]

The second ruler of the new kingdom, Frederick William I (1713-1740), the father of Frederick the Great, was a rough and boorish king who devoted himself entirely to governing his realm, collecting tall soldiers, drilling his battalions, hunting wild game, and smoking strong tobacco. He was passionately fond of military life from his childhood. He took special pride in stalwart soldiers and collected them at great expense from all parts of Europe. He raised the Prussian army, which numbered twenty-seven thousand in the days of the Great Elector, to eighty-four thousand, making it almost equal to that maintained by France or Austria. He was constantly drilling and reviewing his men, of whose military appearance he was inordinately proud.

Moreover, by strict management, miserly thrift, and entire indifference to luxury, Frederick William treasured up a huge sum of money. He discharged a large number of court servants, sold at auction many of the royal jewels, and had a great portion of the family table silver coined into money. Consequently he was able to leave to his son, Frederick II, not only a strengthened army but an ample supply of gold. Indeed, it was his toil and economy that made possible the warlike achievements of his far better-known son.

The Wars of Frederick the Great

In his early years Frederick II grieved and disgusted his boorish old father by his dislike for military life and his interest in books and music. He was a particular admirer of the

[1] As king of Prussia his title was Frederick I.

[2] He was not king of all of Prussia. Frederick the Great changed his title to "King of Prussia" after the incorporation of the rest, in the partition of Poland.

French and wrote all his works in their tongue. No sooner had he become king, however, than he suddenly developed marvelous energy and ruthlessness in warlike enterprises. Chance favored his designs. The emperor Charles VI, the last representative of the direct male line of the Hapsburgs, died in 1740, just a few months before Frederick ascended the throne, leaving only a daughter, Maria Theresa, to inherit his vast and miscellaneous dominions. He had induced the other European powers to promise to accept the "pragmatic sanction," or solemn will, in which he left everything to the young Maria Theresa; but she had no sooner begun to reign than her greedy neighbors prepared to seize her lands. Her greatest enemy was the newly crowned king of Prussia, who at first pretended friendship for her. Frederick determined to seize Silesia, a strip of Hapsburg territory lying to the southeast of Brandenburg. He marched his army into the coveted district and occupied the important city of Breslau without declaring war or offering any excuse except a vague claim to part of the land.[1]

Within a short time France had joined with Bavaria in the attack upon Maria Theresa. It seemed for a time as if her struggle to keep her realm intact would be vain, but the loyalty of all the various peoples under her scepter was roused by her extraordinary courage and energy. The French were driven back, but Maria Theresa was forced to grant Silesia to Frederick in order to induce him to retire from the war. Finally, England and Holland joined in an alliance for maintaining the balance of power, for they had no desire to see France annex the Austrian Netherlands. A few years later (1748) all the powers, tired of the war,—which is known as the War of the Austrian Succession,—laid down their arms and

---

[1] As no woman had ever been elected empress, the Duke of Bavaria managed to secure the Holy Roman Empire, as Emperor Charles VII. Upon his death, however, in 1745, Maria Theresa's husband, Francis, duke of Lorraine, was chosen emperor. Their son, Joseph II, succeeded his father in 1765, and upon his death, in 1790, his brother Leopold II was elected. When he died, in 1792, the empire fell to his son Francis II, who was the last of the "Roman" emperors but assumed the new title "Emperor of Austria." See below, p. 510.

agreed to what is called in diplomacy the *status quo ante bellum*, which simply means that things were to be restored to the condition in which they had been before the opening of hostilities, regardless of the sacrifice of blood and treasure.

Frederick, however, retained possession of Silesia, which increased his dominions by about one-third of their former extent. He now turned his attention to making his subjects more prosperous, by draining the swamps, promoting industry, and drawing up a new code of laws. He found time, also, to gratify his interest in men of letters, and invited Voltaire [1] to make his home at Berlin. It will not seem strange to any one who knows anything of the character of these two men, that they quarreled after two or three years, and that Voltaire left the Prussian king with very bitter feelings.

Maria Theresa was by no means reconciled to the loss of Silesia, and she began to lay her plans for expelling the perfidious Frederick and regaining her lost territory. This led to one of the most important wars in modern history, in which not only almost every European power joined but which involved the whole world, from the Indian rajahs of Hindustan to the colonists of Virginia and New England. This Seven Years' War (1756-1763) will be considered in its broader aspects in the next chapter. We note here only the part played in it by the king of Prussia.

Maria Theresa's ambassador at Paris was so skillful in his negotiations with the French court that in 1756 he induced it, in spite of its two hundred years of hostility to the House of Hapsburg, to enter into an alliance with Austria against Prussia. Russia, Sweden, and Saxony also agreed to join in a concerted attack on Prussia. Their armies, coming as they did from every point of the compass, threatened the complete annihilation of Austria's rival. It seemed as if the new kingdom of Prussia might disappear altogether from the map of Europe.

However, it was in this war that Frederick earned his title of "the Great," and because of his successes he has often been

[1] See below, pp. 440 ff.

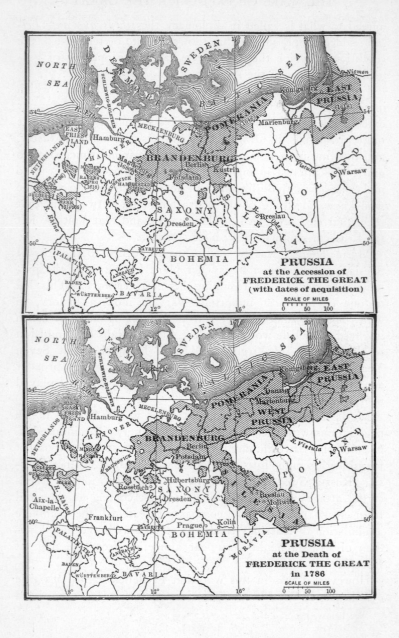

PRUSSIA
at the Accession of
FREDERICK THE GREAT
(with dates of acquisition)

SCALE OF MILES
0   50   100

PRUSSIA
at the Death of
FREDERICK THE GREAT
in 1786

SCALE OF MILES
0   50   100

classed with the ablest generals the world has seen. Learning the object of the allies, he did not wait for them to declare war against him, but occupied Saxony at once and then moved on into Bohemia, where he nearly succeeded in taking the capital, Prague. Here he was forced to retire, but in 1757 he defeated the French and his German enemies in the most famous, perhaps, of his battles, at Rossbach. A month later he routed the Austrians brilliantly at Leuthen, not far from Breslau. Thereupon the Swedes and the Russians retired from the field and left Frederick for the moment master of the situation.

Great Britain now engaged the French and left Frederick at liberty to deal with his other enemies. While he exhibited great military skill, he was by no means able to gain all the battles in which he engaged. Money paid him by the English government helped him to stay in the field, but for a time it looked as if he might, after all, be vanquished. But the accession of a new Tsar, who was an ardent admirer of Frederick, led Russia to conclude peace with Prussia, whereupon Maria Theresa reluctantly agreed to give up once more her struggle with her inveterate enemy. Shortly afterwards England and France came to terms, and a general settlement was made at Paris in 1763.

The Partition of Poland

Frederick's success in seizing and holding one of Austria's finest provinces did not satisfy him. The central portions of his kingdom—Brandenburg, Silesia, and Pomerania—were completely cut off from East Prussia by a considerable tract known as West Prussia, which belonged to the kingdom of Poland. The map will show how great must have been Frederick's temptation to fill this gap, especially as Poland was in no condition to defend its possessions.

With the exception of Russia, Poland was the largest kingdom in Europe. It covered an immense plain with no natural boundaries, and the population, which was very thinly scattered, belonged to several races. Besides the Poles themselves, there were Germans in the cities of West Prussia and Russians in Lithuania. The Jews were very numerous everywhere, forming half of the population in some of the towns. The Poles were usually Catholics, while the Germans were Protestants and the Russians adhered to the Greek Church. These differences in religion, added to those of race, created endless difficulties and dissensions.

The government of Poland was the worst imaginable. Instead of having developed a strong monarchy, as her neighbors—Prussia, Russia, and Austria—had done, she remained in a state of feudal anarchy, which the nobles had taken the greatest pains to perpetuate by binding their kings in such a way that they had no power either to maintain order or to defend the country from attack. The king could not declare war, make peace, impose taxes, or pass any law, without the consent of the diet. As the diet was composed of representatives of the nobility, any one of whom could freely veto any measure,—for no measure could pass that had even one vote against it,—most of the diets broke up without accomplishing anything.

The kingship was not hereditary in Poland, but whenever the ruler died, the nobles assembled and chose a new one, commonly a foreigner. These elections were tumultuous, and the various European powers regularly interfered, by force or bribery, to secure the election of a candidate who they believed would favor their interests.

The nobles in Poland were numerous. There were perhaps a million and a half of them, mostly very poor, owning only a trifling bit of land. There was a saying that the poor noble's dog, even if he sat in the middle of the estate, was sure to have his tail upon a neighbor's land. There was no middle class except in the few German towns. The peasants were miserable indeed. They had sunk from serfs to slaves over whom their lords had the right of life and death.

It required no great insight to foresee that Poland was in danger of falling a prey to her greedy and powerful neighbors, Russia, Prussia, and Austria, who clamped in the unfortunate kingdom on all sides. They had long shamelessly interfered in its affairs and had actually taken active measures to oppose all reforms of the constitution in order that they might profit by the chronic anarchy.

The ruler of Russia was the famous Catherine II, who arranged with Frederick the Great to prevent any improvement in Poland and to keep up and encourage the disorder. Finally, Poland's kind neighbors, including Austria, agreed, in 1772, each to take a slice of the unhappy kingdom.

A CARTOON OF THE PARTITION OF POLAND

Catherine II, Joseph II of Austria, and Frederick the Great are pointing out the part of the map of Poland they each propose to take. The king of Poland is trying to hold his crown from falling off his head. Poland is pushed out into the Baltic

Austria was assigned a strip inhabited by almost three million Poles and Russians, and thus added two new kinds of people and two new languages to her already varied collection of races and tongues. Prussia was given a smaller piece, but it was the coveted West Prussia, which she needed to fill out her boundaries, and its inhabitants were to a considerable extent Germans and Protestants. Russia's strip, on the east, was inhabited entirely by Russians. The Polish diet was forced, by the advance of Russian troops to Warsaw, to approve the partition.

Poland seemed at first, however, to have learned a great lesson from the disaster. During the twenty years following its first dismemberment there was an extraordinary revival in education, art, and literature. Historians and poets sprang up to give distinction to the last days of Polish independence. The constitution which had made Poland the laughingstock and the victim of its neighbors was abolished, and an entirely new one worked out (1791). It did away with the free veto of the nobles, made the crown hereditary, and established a parliament somewhat like that of England.

Russia had no desire that Poland should become a strong monarchy, and it sent soldiers to help the enemies of the new constitution on the ground that Russia could not bear to see any changes in the government "under which the Polish commonwealth had flourished for so many centuries." Russia and Prussia, having secured the continuance of disorder in Poland, declared that they could not put up with such a dangerous neighbor and proceeded to a second partition in 1793. Prussia cut deep into Poland, added a million and a half of Poles to her subjects, and acquired the towns of Thorn, Danzig, and Posen. Russia's gains were three millions of people, who at least belonged to her own race. On this occasion Austria was put off with the promises of her confederates, Russia and Prussia, that they would use their good offices to secure Bavaria for her in exchange for the Austrian Netherlands.

At this juncture the Poles found a national leader in the brave Kosciusko, who had fought under Washington for American liberty. With the utmost care and secrecy he organized an insurrection in the spring of 1794 and summoned the Polish people to join his standard of national independence. The Poles who had been incorporated into the Prussian monarchy thereupon rose and forced Prussia to withdraw its forces.

Russia was ready, however, to crush the patriots. Kosciusko was wounded and captured in battle, and by the end of the year Russia was in control of Warsaw. The Polish king was compelled to abdicate, and the remnants of the dismembered kingdom were divided (1795), after much bitter contention, among Austria, Russia, and Prussia. In the three partitions which blotted out the kingdom of Poland from the map of Europe, Russia received nearly twice the combined shares of Austria and Prussia.

The Austrian Realms: Maria Theresa and Joseph II

While the Hohenzollerns of Prussia from their capital at Berlin had been extending their power over northern Germany, the ancient house of Hapsburg, established in the southeastern corner of Germany, with its capital at Vienna, had been grouping together, by conquest or inheritance, the vast realm over much of which they ruled down to the end of the World War. It will be remembered that Charles V, shortly after his accession, ceded to his brother, Ferdinand I, the German or Austrian possessions of the house of Hapsburg,[1] while he himself retained the Spanish, Burgundian, and Italian dominions. Ferdinand, by a fortunate marriage with the heiress of the kingdoms of Bohemia and Hungary, greatly augmented his territory. Hungary was, however, almost completely under the Turks at that time, and till the end of the seventeenth century the energies of the Austrian rulers were largely absorbed in a long struggle against the Mohammedans.

A Turkish tribe from western Asia had, at the opening of the thirteenth century, established themselves in western Asia Minor under their leader Othman (d. 1326). It was from him that they derived their name of Ottoman Turks, to distinguish them from the Seljuk Turks, with whom the crusaders had come into contact. The leaders of the Ottoman Turks showed great energy. They not only extended their Asiatic territory far toward the east, and later into Africa, but they gained a footing in Europe as early as 1353. They gradually conquered the Slavic peoples of the Balkan peninsula and occupied the territory about Constantinople, although it was a hundred

[1] For the origin of the Austrian dominions, see above, pp. 259 ff.

years before they succeeded in capturing the ancient capital of the Eastern Empire.

This advance of the Turks naturally aroused grave fears in the states of western Europe lest they too might be deprived of their independence. The brunt of the defense against the common foe devolved upon Venice and the German Hapsburgs, who carried on an almost continuous war with the Turks for nearly two centuries. As late as 1683 the Mohammedans collected a large force and besieged Vienna, which might very well have fallen into their hands had it not been for the timely assistance which the city received from the king of Poland. From this time on, the power of the Turks in Europe rapidly decreased, and the Hapsburgs were able to regain the whole territory of Hungary and Transylvania, their possession of which was formally recognized by the Sultan in 1699.

The conquest of Silesia by Frederick the Great was more than a severe blow to the pride of Maria Theresa; for, since it was inhabited by Germans, its loss lessened the Hapsburg power inside the empire. In extent of territory the Hapsburgs more than made up for it by the partitions of Poland, but since the Poles were an alien race, they added one more difficulty to the very serious problem of ruling so many different peoples, each of whom had a different language and different customs and institutions. The Hapsburg possessions were inhabited by Germans in Austria proper, a Slav people (the Czechs) mixed with Germans in Bohemia and Moravia, Poles in Galicia, Hungarians or Magyars along with Rumanians and smaller groups of other peoples in Hungary; Croats and Slovenes (both Slavs) in the south, Italians in Milan and Tuscany, and Flemish and Walloons in the Netherlands.

Maria Theresa ruled these races with energy and skill. She patiently attended to all the tiresome matters of state, read long documents and reports, and conferred with the ambassadors of foreign powers. After her long reign of forty years her son Joseph, who had already been elected emperor as Joseph II, tried in the ten years of his rule (1780-1790) to modernize these backward states of southeastern Europe by a series of sweeping reforms. He was a very enlightened man and with something of the impetuous zeal of Peter the Great tried to sweep away at once the old abuses of feudalism, to introduce more general education, and to lessen the power of the clergy. He even abolished six hundred monasteries. Besides this he attempted to govern more and more from one center where he could oversee matters himself, a scheme which also seemed to promise greater unity to his realms. But his peoples did not understand his ideas or feared the growth of his power, and he was opposed on every hand. He died just as the Revolution in France was beginning to show that a nation could do for itself in a few months what a king could not do in a lifetime.

It must be admitted, however, that the problems which confronted Maria Theresa and Joseph II were much more difficult than those of France or England. Poles, Italians, Magyars, and Germans could never be united into one state by such common interests as Englishmen or Frenchmen have felt so keenly in the last two centuries. Instead of fusing together to form a nation, the peoples ruled over by the Hapsburgs were on such bad terms with each other that it often seemed as if they would split apart, forming separate nations. Moreover, since some of these peoples, especially the Slavs, Poles, and Rumanians, lived in neighboring states as well, the Hapsburg monarchy was always much concerned in what happened outside its borders. The immediate cause of the terrible war of 1914-1918 was trouble between Austria and her neighbor Serbia. So if one hopes to understand the great questions of our own time, he must follow carefully the complicated history of Austria and her ever-changing realms.

This review of the wars and reforms of the eighteenth-century rulers is incomplete. There were more wars than have been mentioned and more reforms than have been enumerated. Frederick the Great, Catherine of Russia, Charles III of Spain, as well as some minor rulers, are usually classified as the "enlightened" or "benevolent" despots of the eighteenth century. They, like Joseph II, tried to eliminate the ancient complications and eradicate or reduce the persistent medieval traditions of feudalism, the manor, monasticism, and the traditional claims of the clergy and pope. They had, however, their own power in mind rather than any theory of democracy.

Although the attempted reforms of the benevolent despots and their attacks on old institutions and anachronisms had rather little immediate effect, they cast a great deal of light on the sweeping reforms of the French Revolution, which we shall soon reach. It does not seem to come out of a clear sky when we realize that many of its innovations had already been contemplated by the very "despots" against which the revolutionary leaders directed the shafts of their scorn.

CHAPTER XVIII

FOUNDATION OF BRITAIN'S RULE OVERSEAS

England after the Revolution of 1688. How Europe Began to Extend Its Commerce over the Whole World. The Contest between France and England in India and North America. Revolt of the American Colonies from England

England after the Revolution of 1688

IN the last chapter we reviewed the progress of affairs in eastern Europe and noted the development of two new European powers, Prussia and Russia, which have for the past two centuries played a great part in the affairs of the world. In the west, Great Britain was rapidly becoming the most important state. While she did not greatly influence the course of the wars on the Continent, she was already beginning to make herself mistress of the seas—a position which she was able to maintain owing to her colonies and her unrivaled fleet.

At the close of the War of the Spanish Succession her navy was superior to that of any other power, for both France and Spain had been greatly weakened by the long conflict. Fifty years after the Treaty of Utrecht, England had succeeded in driving out the French both from North America and from India and in planting her vast empire beyond the seas, which still gives her the commercial supremacy of the world.

With the accession of William and Mary in 1688 [1] England may be said to have settled the two great questions that had produced such serious dissensions during the previous fifty years. In the first place, the nation had clearly shown that it proposed to remain Protestant in spite of the Catholic sympathies of her Stuart kings; and the relations between the Church of England and the Dissenters were gradually being satisfactorily adjusted. In the second place, the powers of the king had been carefully defined, and from the opening of the

---

[1] See above, pp. 367 ff.

eighteenth century to the present time no English monarch has ventured to veto an act of Parliament.[1]

William III was succeeded in 1702 by his sister-in-law, Anne, a younger daughter of James II. Far more important than the war which her generals carried on against Spain was the final union of England and Scotland. As we have seen, the difficulties between the two countries had led to much bloodshed and suffering ever since Edward I's futile attempt to conquer Scotland.[2] The two countries had, it is true, been under the same ruler since the accession of James I, but each had

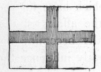

England (St. George)   Scotland (St. Andrew)   Ireland (St. Patrick)

Great Britain   Great Britain and Ireland

THE UNION JACK[3]

maintained its own independent parliament and system of government. Finally, in 1707, both nations agreed to unite their governments into one. Forty-five members of the British House of Commons were to be chosen thereafter in Scotland, and sixteen Scotch lords were to be added to the British House of Lords. In this way the whole island of Great Britain was placed under a single government, and the occasions for strife were thereby greatly reduced.

[1] The last instance in which an English ruler vetoed a measure passed by Parliament was in 1707.

[2] See above, pp. 246 ff.

[3] The flag of Great Britain, combining the crosses of St. George and St. Andrew, was called the Union Jack from *Jacques*, the French form of James I, the first king of Great Britain. The cross of Ireland was added upon its union with Great Britain in 1801. Upright lines indicate red; horizontal lines, blue.

[Hereafter, if a common inaccuracy is to be avoided, England, as a European power, should be referred to as *Great Britain*.] With the union of England and Scotland the whole island of "Greater" Britannia (originally distinguished in this way from "Lesser" Britannia or Bretagne, across the Channel), including Wales, came under one government. With the addition of Ireland in 1801 the British state was officially known as The United Kingdom of Great Britain and Ireland. This had to be slightly altered with the establishment of the Irish Free State. In spite of these facts the familiar "England" and "English" will continue to occur throughout this narrative. Let no one take offense!

Since none of Anne's seventeen children survived her, she was succeeded, according to an arrangement made before her accession, by the nearest Protestant heir. This was the son of James I's granddaughter Sophia. She had married the elector of Hanover; [1] consequently the new king of England, George I

[1] Originally there had been seven electors (see above, p. 270), but the Duke of Bavaria had been made an elector during the Thirty Years' War, and in 1692 the father of George I had been permitted to assume the title of "Elector of Hanover."

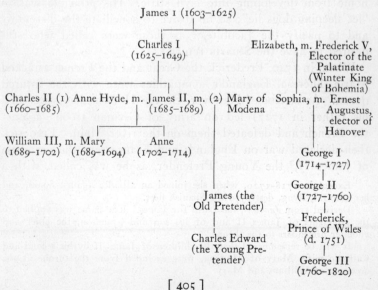

James I (1603–1625)

Charles I (1625–1649)   Elizabeth, m. Frederick V, Elector of the Palatinate (Winter King of Bohemia)

Charles II (1) Anne Hyde, m. James II, m. (2) Mary of Modena   Sophia, m. Ernest Augustus, elector of Hanover
(1660–1685)

William III, m. Mary   Anne
(1689–1702) (1689–1694) (1702–1714)

James (the Old Pretender)

Charles Edward (the Young Pretender)

George I (1714–1727)

George II (1727–1760)

Frederick, Prince of Wales (d. 1751)

George III (1760–1820)

(1714-1727), was also elector of Hanover and a member of the Holy Roman Empire.

William of Orange had been a continental statesman before he became king of England, and his chief aim had always been to prevent France from becoming overpowerful. He had joined in the War of the Spanish Succession in order to maintain the "balance of power" between the various European countries. During the eighteenth century England continued, for the same reason, to engage in the struggles between the continental powers, although she had no expectation of attempting to extend her sway across the Channel. The wars which she waged in order to increase her own power and territory were carried on in distant parts of the world, and more often on sea than on land.

For a quarter of a century after the Treaty of Utrecht, England enjoyed peace.[1] Under the influence of Walpole, who for twenty-one years directed the government and who was the first to be called prime minister, peace was maintained within and without. Not only did Walpole avoid going to war with other countries, but he was careful to prevent the ill feeling at home from developing into civil strife. His principle was to "let sleeping dogs lie"; so he strove to conciliate the dissenters and to pacify the Jacobites,[2] as those were called who still desired to have the Stuarts return.

When, in 1740, Frederick the Great and the French attacked Maria Theresa, England's sympathies were with the injured queen. As elector of Hanover, George II (who had succeeded his father in 1727) led an army of German troops against the French and defeated them on the river Main. Frederick then declared war on England; and France sent the grandson of James II,[3] the Young Pretender, as he was called, with a

[1] Except in 1718-1720, when she joined an alliance against Spain, and her admiral, Byng, destroyed the Spanish fleet.

[2] Derived from *Jacobus*, the Latin for James. The name was applied to the adherents of James II and of his son and grandson, the elder and younger pretenders to the throne.

[3] It will be remembered that the children of James II by his second and Catholic wife, Mary of Modena, were excluded from the throne at the accession of William and Mary.

fleet to invade England. The attempt failed, for the fleet was dispersed by a storm. In 1745 the French defeated the English and Dutch forces in the Netherlands; this encouraged the Young Pretender to make another attempt to gain the English crown. He landed in Scotland, where he found support among the Highland chiefs, and even Edinburgh welcomed "Prince Charlie." He was able to collect an army of six thousand men, with which he marched into England. He was quickly forced back into Scotland, however, and after a disastrous defeat on Culloden Moor (1746) and many romantic adventures, he was glad to reach France once more in safety.

Soon after the close of the War of the Austrian Succession in 1748, England entered upon a series of wars which were destined profoundly to affect not only her position, but also the fate of distant portions of the globe. In order to follow these changes intelligently we must briefly review the steps by which the various European states had extended their sway over regions separated from them by the ocean.

How Europe Began to Extend Its Commerce over the Whole World

The long and disastrous wars of the eighteenth century were much more than merely quarrels of monarchs. They were also caused by commercial and colonial rivalries, and they extended to the most distant parts of the world. In the War of the Spanish Succession, the trade of Spain was at stake as well as the throne. From the seventeenth century on, the internal affairs of each country have been constantly influenced by the demands of its merchants and the achievements of its sailors and soldiers, fighting rival nations or alien peoples thousands of miles from London, Paris, or Vienna. The great manufacturing towns of England—Leeds, Manchester, and Birmingham—owe their prosperity to India, China, and Australia. Liverpool, Amsterdam, and Hamburg, with their long lines of docks and warehouses and their fleets of merchant vessels, would dwindle away if their trade were confined to the demands of their European neighbors.

[407]

Europe includes scarcely a twelfth of the land upon the globe and yet over three-fifths of the world is to-day either occupied by peoples of European origin or ruled by European states. The possessions of France in Asia and Africa exceed the entire area of Europe; even the little kingdom of the Netherlands

A NAVAL BATTLE BETWEEN SAILING SHIPS

This is the way the rival navies of Holland, France, and England fought in the seventeenth and eighteenth centuries. Note how the ships sail right up to the foe and fire broadsides at close range. The large ship in front has rammed an enemy ship; this was often done, not with the idea of sinking it, since the heavily timbered wooden ships did not sink so easily as ironclads will, but in order that a boarding party could clamber over onto its decks. Thus naval warfare still resembled somewhat the method of fighting of the Greeks and Romans

administers a colonial dominion three times the size of the German empire. The British empire, of which the island of Great Britain constitutes but a hundredth part, includes one-fifth of the world's dry land. Moreover, European peoples have populated the United States (which is nearly as large as all of Europe), Mexico, and South America.

HOW EUROPE BEGAN TO EXTEND ITS COMMERCE

The widening of the field of European history is one of the most striking features of modern times. Though the Greeks and Romans carried on a large trade in silks, spices, and precious stones with India and China, they really knew little of the world beyond southern Europe, northern Africa, and western Asia, and much that they knew was forgotten during the Middle Ages. Slowly, however, the interest in the East revived, and travelers began to add to the scanty knowledge handed down from antiquity.

The voyages which had brought America and India within the ken of Europe during the fifteenth and early sixteenth centuries were, as we know, mainly undertaken by the Portuguese and the Spaniards. Portugal was the first to realize the advantage of extending her commerce by establishing stations in India after Vasco da Gama rounded the Cape of Good Hope in 1498; [1] and later by founding posts on the Brazilian coast of South America; then Spain laid claim to Mexico, the West Indies, and a great part of South America. These two powers later found a formidable rival in the Dutch, who succeeded in expelling the Portuguese from a number of their settlements in India and the Spice Islands, and brought Java, Sumatra, and other tropical regions under Dutch control.

In North America the chief rivals were England and France, both of which succeeded in establishing colonies in the early part of the seventeenth century. Englishmen settled at Jamestown in Virginia (1607), then in New England, Maryland, Pennsylvania, and elsewhere. The colonies owed their growth in part to the influx of refugees,—Puritans, Catholics, and Quakers,—who exiled themselves in the hope of gaining the right freely to enjoy their particular forms of religion. On the other hand, many came in order to better their fortunes in the New World, and thousands of bond servants and slaves were brought over as laborers.

Just as Jamestown was being founded by the English the French were making their first successful settlement in Nova Scotia and at Quebec. Although England made no attempt to

[1] See above, pp. 224 ff.

[409]

oppose it, the French occupation of Canada progressed very slowly. In 1673 Marquette, a Jesuit missionary, and Joliet, a merchant, explored a part of the Mississippi River. La Salle sailed down the great stream and named the new country which he entered, Louisiana, after his king. The city of New Orleans was founded, near the mouth of the river, in 1718, and the French established a chain of forts between it and Montreal.

The Contest between France and England in India and North America

The contest between England and France for the supremacy in North America was responsible for almost continuous border war, which burst out more fiercely with each war in the Old World. Finally, England was able, by the Treaty of Utrecht, to establish herself in the northern regions, for France thereby ceded to her Newfoundland, Nova Scotia, and the borders of Hudson Bay. While the English in North America at the beginning of the Seven Years' War numbered over a million, the French did not reach a hundred thousand.

The rivalry of England and France was not confined to the wildernesses of North America, occupied by half a million of savage red men. At the opening of the eighteenth century both countries had gained a firm foothold on the borders of the vast Indian empire, inhabited by two hundred millions of people and the seat of an ancient and highly developed civilization. One may gain some idea of the extent of India by laying the map of Hindustan upon that of the United States. If the southernmost point, Cape Comorin, be placed over New Orleans, Calcutta will lie nearly over New York City, and Bombay in the neighborhood of Des Moines, Iowa.

A generation after Vasco da Gama rounded the Cape, a Mongolian conqueror, Baber, had established his empire in India. The dynasty of Mongolian rulers which he founded was able to keep the whole country under its control for nearly two centuries; then after the death of the Great Mogul Aurungzeb, in 1707, their empire began to fall apart in much the same way as that of Charlemagne had done. Like the counts and dukes of the Carolingian period, the emperor's officials, the

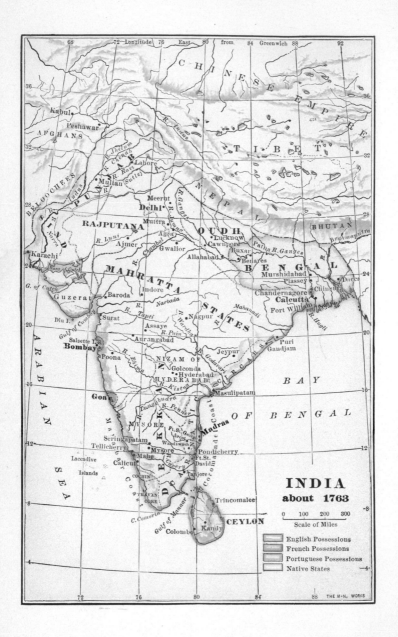

INDIA
about 1763

0   100   200   300
Scale of Miles

English Possessions
French Possessions
Portuguese Possessions
Native States

THE M·N· WORKS

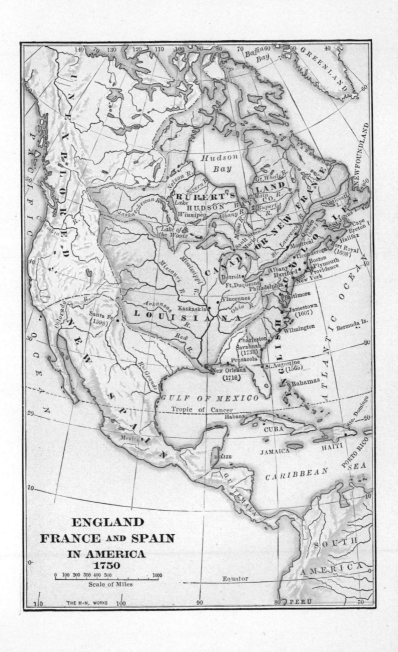

ENGLAND
FRANCE AND SPAIN
IN AMERICA
1750

0 100 200 300 400 500   1000
Scale of Miles

THE M-N. WORKS

subahdars and nawabs (nabobs) and the rajahs (Hindu princes who had been subjugated by the Mongols) had gradually got the power in their respective districts into their own hands. Although the emperor, or Great Mogul, as the English called him, continued to maintain himself in his capital of Delhi, he could no longer be said to rule the country at the opening

THE TAJ MAHAL

This mausoleum of a princess was built at Agra, India, in 1632. It has been described as "the most splendidly poetic building in the world . . . a dream in marble, which justifies the saying that the Moguls designed like Titans but finished like jewelers." The entire building is of white marble, inlaid with precious stones. Although this is regarded as the most perfect monument, India has many others of great magnificence, witnesses of the power and wealth of her princes

of the eighteenth century when the French and English were beginning to turn their attention seriously to his coasts.

In the time of Charles I (1639) a village had been purchased by the English East India Company on the southeastern coast of Hindustan, which grew into the important English station of Madras. About the same time posts were established in the district of Bengal, and later Calcutta was fortified. Bombay was already an English station. The Mongolian emperor of India at first scarcely deigned to notice the presence of a few foreigners on the fringe of his vast realms, but before the end of the seventeenth century hostilities began between the English East India Company and the native rulers, which made it plain that the foreigners would be forced to defend themselves.

The English had to face not only the opposition of the natives, but that of a European power as well. France also had an East India Company, and at the opening of the eighteenth century Pondicherry was its chief center, with a population of sixty thousand, of which two hundred only were Europeans. It soon became apparent that there was little danger from the Great Mogul; moreover the Portuguese and Dutch were out of the race, so the native princes and the French and English were left to fight among themselves for the supremacy.

Just before the clash of European rulers, known as the Seven Years' War, came, in 1756, the French and English had begun their struggle in both America and India. In America the so-called French and Indian War began in 1754 between the English and French colonists. General Braddock was sent from England to capture Fort Duquesne, which the French had established to keep their rivals out of the Ohio valley. Braddock knew nothing of border warfare, and he was killed and his troops routed. Fortunately for England, France, as the ally of Austria, was soon engaged in a war with Prussia that prevented her from giving proper attention to her American possessions. A famous statesman, the elder Pitt,[1] was now at the head of the English ministry. He was able not only to succor the hard-pressed king of Prussia with money and men, but also to support the militia of the thirteen American colonies in their attacks upon the French. The French forts at Ticonderoga and Niagara were taken; Quebec was won in Wolfe's heroic attack, 1759; and the next year all Canada submitted to the English. England's supremacy on the sea was demonstrated by three admirals, each of whom destroyed a French fleet.

[1] So called to distinguish him from his son, prime minister later.

THE CONTEST BETWEEN FRANCE AND ENGLAND

In India conflicts between the French and the English had occurred during the War of the Austrian Succession. The governor of the French station of Pondicherry was Dupleix, a soldier of great energy, who proposed to drive out the English and firmly establish the power of France over Hindustan. His chances of success were greatly increased by the quarrels among the native rulers, some of whom belonged to the earlier Hindu inhabitants and some to the Mohammedan Mongolians who had conquered India in 1526. Dupleix had very few French soldiers, but he began the enlistment of the natives, a custom eagerly adopted by the English. These native soldiers, whom the English called Sepoys, were taught to fight in the manner of Europeans.

But the English colonists, in spite of the fact that they were mainly traders, discovered among the clerks in Madras a leader equal in military skill and energy to Dupleix himself. Robert Clive, who was but twenty-five years old at this time, organized a large force of Sepoys and gained a remarkable ascendency over them by his astonishing bravery.

At the moment that the Seven Years' War was beginning, bad news reached Clive from the English settlement of Calcutta, about a thousand miles to the northeast of Madras. The nawab of Bengal had seized the property of some English merchants and imprisoned one hundred and forty-five Englishmen in a little room,—the "black hole" of Calcutta,—where most of them died of suffocation before morning. Clive hastened to Bengal, and with a little army of nine hundred Europeans and fifteen hundred Sepoys he gained a great victory at Plassey, in 1757, over the nawab's army of fifty thousand men. Clive then replaced the nawab of Bengal by a man whom he believed to be friendly to the English. Before the Seven Years' War was over, the English had won Pondicherry and deprived the French of all their former influence in the region of Madras, and had begun to extend their control over the great plains of northern India.

When the Seven Years' War was brought to an end, in 1763, by the Treaty of Paris, it was clear that England had

[413]

gained far more than any other power. She was to retain her two forts commanding the Mediterranean—Gibraltar, and Port Mahon on the island of Minorca; in America, France ceded to her the vast region of Canada and Nova Scotia, as well as several of the islands in the West Indies. The region beyond the Mississippi was ceded to Spain by France, who thus gave up all her claims to North America. In India, France, it is true, received back the towns which the English had taken from her, but she had permanently lost her influence over the native rulers, for Clive had made the English name greatly feared among them.

Revolt of the American Colonies from England

England had, however, no sooner added Canada to her possessions and driven the French from the broad region which lay between her dominions and the Mississippi than she lost the better part of her American empire by the revolt of the irritated colonists, who refused to submit to her interference in their government and commerce.

The English settlers had been left alone, for the most part, by the home government and had enjoyed far greater freedom in the management of their affairs than had the colonies of France and Spain. Virginia established its own assembly in 1619, and Massachusetts became almost an independent commonwealth. England had been busied during the seventeenth century with a great struggle at home and with the wars stirred up by Louis XIV. After the Peace of Utrecht, Walpole for twenty years prudently refused to interfere with the colonies. The result was that by the end of the Seven Years' War the colonists numbered over two millions. Their rapidly increasing wealth and strength, their free life in a new land, and the confidence they had gained in their successful conflict with the French—all combined to render the renewed interference of the home government intolerable to them.

During the war with the French, England began to realize for the first time that the colonies had money, and so Parliament decided that they should be required to pay part of the expenses of the recent conflict and support a small standing army of English soldiers. The Stamp Act was therefore passed (1765), which taxed the colonists by requiring them to pay the English government for stamps which had to be used upon leases, deeds, and other legal documents in order to make them binding. The colonists were indignant, for, while they were not unwilling to contribute to the mother country, they declared that according to the principles of the English constitution, a Parliament in which they were not represented had no right to tax them. Representatives of the colonies met in New York in 1765 and denounced the Stamp Act as indicating "a manifest tendency to subvert the rights and liberties of the colonies."

More irritating than the attempts of Great Britain to tax the colonists were the vexatious navigation and trade laws by which, like the other nations of the time, she tried to keep all the benefits of colonial trade and industry to herself. The early navigation laws passed under Cromwell and Charles II were specially directed against the enterprising Dutch traders. They provided that all products grown or manufactured in Asia, Africa, or America should be imported into England or her colonies only in English ships. But if the laws were directed against the Dutch, they worked hardships to the colonists as well. Thus if a Dutch merchant vessel laden with cloves, cinnamon, teas, and silks from the Far East anchored in the harbor of New York, the inhabitants could not lawfully buy of the ship's master, no matter how much lower his prices were than those offered by English shippers. Furthermore, another act provided that no commodity of European production or manufacture should be imported into any of the colonies without being shipped through England and carried in ships built in England or the colonies. So if a colonial merchant wished to buy French wines or Dutch watches, he would have to order through English merchants. Again, if a colonist desired to sell to a European merchant such products as the law permitted him to sell to foreigners, he had to export them in English ships and even send them by way of England.

What was still worse for the colonists, certain articles in which they were most interested, such as sugar, tobacco, cotton, and indigo, could be sold only in England. Certain other things they were forbidden to export at all or even to produce. For instance, though they possessed furs in abundance, they could not export any caps or hats to England or to any foreign country. They had iron ore in inexhaustible quantities at their disposal, but by a law of 1750 they were forbidden to erect any rolling mill or furnace for making steel, in order that English steel manufacturers might enjoy a monopoly of that trade.

The colonists naturally evaded these laws as far as possible; they carried on a prosperous smuggling trade and built up industries in spite of them. Tobacco, sugar, hemp, flax, and cotton were grown, and cloth was manufactured. Furnaces, foundries, nail mills and wire mills supplied pig iron and bar iron, chains, anchors, and other hardware. It is clear that where so many people were interested both in manufacturing and in commerce a loud protest was sure to be raised against the continued attempts of England to restrict the business of the colonists in favor of her own merchants.

Parliament withdrew the unpopular stamp tax, but declared that it had a perfect right to tax the colonies as well as to make laws for them. Soon new duties on glass, paper, and tea were imposed, and a government board was established to secure a firm observance of the navigation laws and other restrictions. But the protests of the colonists finally induced Parliament to remove all the duties except that on tea, which was retained to prove England's right to tax the colonists and was later used to benefit the English East India Company.

The effort to make the Americans pay a very moderate import duty on tea and to force upon Boston markets the company's tea at a low price produced trouble in 1773. The young men of Boston seditiously boarded a tea ship in the harbor and threw the cargo into the water. Burke, perhaps the most able member of the House of Commons, urged the ministry to allow the Americans to tax themselves, but George III, and Parliament as a whole, could not forgive the colonists for their opposition. They believed that the trouble was largely confined to New England and could easily be overcome. In 1774 acts were passed prohibiting the landing and shipping of goods at Boston; and the colony of Massachusetts was deprived of its former right to choose its judges and the members of the upper house of its legislature, who were thereafter to be selected by the king.

These measures, instead of bringing Massachusetts to terms, so roused the apprehension of the rest of the colonists that a congress of all the colonists was held at Philadelphia in 1774. This congress decided that all trade with Great Britain should cease until the grievances of the colonies had been redressed. The following year the Americans attacked the British troops at Lexington and made a brave stand against them in the battle of Bunker Hill. The second congress decided to prepare for war, and raised an army which was put under the command of George Washington, a Virginia planter who had gained some distinction in the late French and Indian War. Up to this time the colonies had not intended to secede from the mother country, but the proposed compromises came to nothing, and in July, 1776, Congress declared that "these United States are, and of right ought to be, free and independent."

This occurrence naturally excited great interest in France. The outcome of the Seven Years' War had been most lamentable for that country, and any trouble which came to her old enemy, England, could not but be a source of congratulation to the French. The United States therefore regarded France as their natural ally and immediately sent Benjamin Franklin to Versailles in the hope of obtaining the aid of the new French king, Louis XVI. The king's ministers were uncertain whether the colonies could long maintain their resistance against the overwhelming strength of the mother country. It was only after the Americans had defeated Burgoyne at Saratoga that France, in 1778, concluded a treaty with the United States in which the independence of the new republic was recognized. This was tantamount to declaring war upon England. The enthusiasm for the Americans was so great in France that a number of the younger nobles, the most conspicuous of whom was the Marquis de Lafayette, crossed the Atlantic to fight in the American army.

In spite of the skill and heroic self-sacrifice of Washington the Americans lost more battles than they gained. It is extremely doubtful whether they would have succeeded in bringing the war to a favorable close, by forcing the English general, Cornwallis, to capitulate at Yorktown (1781), had it not been for the aid of the French fleet. The chief result of the war was the recognition by England of the independence of the United States, whose territory was to extend to the Mississippi River. To the west of the Mississippi the vast territory of Louisiana still remained in the hands of Spain, and Spain also held Florida, which England had held since 1763 but now gave back.

Spain and Portugal were able to hold their American possessions a generation longer than were the English, but in the end nearly all of the western hemisphere, with the exception of Canada, completely freed itself from the domination of the European powers. Cuba, one of the last vestiges of Spanish rule in the West, gained its independence with the aid of the United States, in 1898.

CHAPTER XIX

MEDIEVAL SURVIVALS IN THE EIGHTEENTH CENTURY

Country Life: Serfdom. The Towns. The Nobility and the Monarch. The Catholic Church. The English Church and the Dissenters

Country Life: Serfdom

IF a peasant who had lived on a manor in the time of the Crusades had been permitted to return to earth and travel about Europe at the opening of the eighteenth century, he would have found much to remind him of the conditions under which, seven centuries earlier, he had extracted a scanty living from the soil. It is true that the gradual extinction of serfdom in western Europe appears to have begun as early as the twelfth century, but it proceeded at very different rates in different countries. In France the old type of serf had largely disappeared by the fourteenth century, and in England a hundred years later. In Prussia, Austria, Poland, Russia, Italy, and Spain, on the contrary, the great mass of the country people were still bound to the soil in the eighteenth century.

Even in France there were still many annoying traces of the old system. The peasant was, it is true, no longer bound to a particular manor; he could buy or sell his land at will, could marry without consulting the lord, and could go and come as he pleased. Many bought their land outright, while others disposed of their holdings and settled in town. But the lord might still require all those on his manor to grind their grain at his mill, bake their bread in his oven, and press their grapes in his wine press. The peasant might have to pay a toll to cross a bridge or ferry which was under the lord's control, or a certain sum for driving his flock past the lord's mansion. Many of the old arrangements still forced the peasant occupying a particular plot of land to turn over to the lord a certain portion of his crops, and, if he sold his land, to pay the lord a part of the money he received for it.

In England in the eighteenth century the prominent features of serfdom had disappeared much more completely than in

[419]

France. The services in labor due to the lord had long been commuted into money payments, and the peasant was thus transformed into a renter or owner of his holding.

In central, southern, and eastern Europe the medieval system still prevailed; the peasant lived and died upon the same manor, and worked for his lord in the same way that his ancestors had worked a thousand years before. Everywhere the same crude

THE OVEN OF THE MANOR

The oven at which those on the manor had to bake their bread was sometimes a large stone structure in the open air. The one in the picture has fallen into ruins since now the country people bake at home and so avoid paying the owner of the oven a part of the flour or bread for its use

agricultural instruments were still used, and most of the implements and tools were roughly made in the village itself. The wooden plows commonly found even on English farms were constructed on the model of the old Roman plow; wheat was cut with a sickle, grass with an unwieldy scythe, and the rickety cart wheels were supplied with only wooden rims.

The houses occupied by the country people differed greatly from Sicily to Pomerania, and from Ireland to Poland; but, in general, they were small, with little light or ventilation, and often they were nothing but wretched hovels with dirt floors and neglected thatch roofs. The pigs and the cows were frequently as well housed as the people, with whom they associated upon very familiar terms, since the barn and the house were commonly in the same building. The drinking water was bad, and there was no attempt to secure proper drainage. Fortunately every one was out of doors a great deal of the time,

INTERIOR OF PEASANT'S HUT

The house consists of one room. Milk jugs, kettles, and pails stand around the fireplace, where the cooking is done. In the corner stands the bed, curtained off from the room to secure privacy. Often the bed occupied a recess in the wall

for the women as well as the men usually worked in the fields, cultivating the soil and helping to gather in the crops.

Country life in the eighteenth century was obviously very arduous and unattractive for the most part. The peasant had no newspapers to tell him of the world outside his manor, nor could he have read them if he had had them. Even in England not one peasant in five thousand, it is said, could read at all; and in France the local tax collectors were too uneducated to make out their own reports. Farther east conditions must have been still more cheerless, for a Hungarian peasant complains that he owed four days of his labor to his lord, spent the fifth and sixth hunting and fishing for him, while the seventh belonged to God.

The Towns

Even in the towns there was much to remind one of the Middle Ages. The narrow, crooked streets, darkened by the overhanging buildings and scarcely lighted at all by night, the rough cobblestones, the disgusting odors even in the best quarters—all offered a marked contrast to the European cities of to-day, which have grown tremendously in the last hundred years in size, beauty, and comfort.

In 1760 London had half a million inhabitants, or less than a tenth of its present population. There were of course no street cars or omnibuses, to say nothing of the thousands of automobiles which now thread their way in and out through the press of traffic. A few hundred hackney coaches and sedan chairs served to carry those who had not private conveyances and could not, or would not, walk. The ill-lighted streets were guarded at night by watchmen who went about with lanterns, but afforded so little protection against the roughs and robbers that gentlemen were compelled to carry arms when passing through the streets after nightfall.

Paris was somewhat larger than London and had outgrown its medieval walls. The police were more efficient there, and the highway robberies which disgraced London and its suburbs were almost unknown. The great park, the *Champs Élysées,* and many of the boulevards which now form so distinguished a feature of Paris were already laid out; but, in general, the streets were still narrow, and there were none of the fine broad avenues which now radiate from a hundred centers. There were few sewers to carry off the water which, when it rained, flowed through the middle of the streets. The filth and the bad smells of former times still remained, and the people relied upon easily polluted wells or the dirty River Seine for their water supply.

In Germany very few of the towns had spread beyond their medieval walls. They had, for the most part, lost their former prosperity, which was still attested by the fine old houses of the merchants and of the once flourishing guilds. Berlin had a population of only about two hundred thousand. Vienna, the largest city in Austria, was slightly larger. This city then employed from thirty to a hundred street cleaners and boasted that the street lamps were lighted every night, while many towns contented themselves with dirty streets and with light during the winter months, and then only when the moon was not scheduled to shine.

Even the famous cities of Italy,—Milan, Genoa, Florence, Rome,—notwithstanding their beautiful palaces and public buildings, were, with the exception of water-bound Venice, crowded into the narrow compass of the town wall, and their streets were narrow and crooked.

Another contrast between the towns of the eighteenth century and those of to-day lay in the absence of the great wholesale warehouses, the vast factories with their tall chimneys, and the vast department stores which may now be found in every city from Dublin to Budapest. Commerce and industry were in general conducted upon a very small scale, except at the great ports like London, Antwerp, or Amsterdam, where goods coming from and going to the colonies were brought together.

The growth of industry under the influence of the various machines which were being invented during the latter part of the eighteenth century will form the subject of a later chapter. It is clear, however, that before the introduction of railroads, steamships, and machine-equipped factories, all business operations must have been carried on in what would seem to us a slow and primitive fashion.

A great part of the manufacturing still took place in little shops where the articles when completed were offered for sale. Generally all those who owned the several shops carrying on a particular trade, such as tailoring, shoemaking, baking, tanning, bookbinding, hair cutting, or the making of candles,

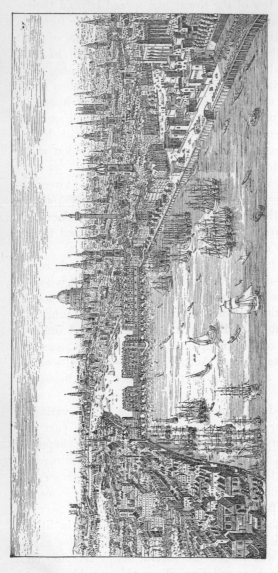

LONDON IN THE EIGHTEENTH CENTURY

London was almost destroyed by a great fire in 1666. The old city had been a picturesque mass of timbered houses; the new one was built of brick and stone. In the center rose the new St. Paul's Cathedral, whose dome, 370 feet high, is still higher than any other building in the city. Its architect, Sir Christopher Wren, also built most of the churches whose spires are visible here, the eighteenth-century artist having drawn them, indeed, somewhat out of proportion in order to attract attention to them. The column with a gallery around it is "The Monument," erected to commemorate the great fire. At the lower right-hand side is the Tower. Note the houses on London Bridge. The two towers farthest up the river are those of Westminster Abbey, and the roof of the old Parliament buildings can be just made out below them, beside the bridge knives, hats, artificial flowers, swords, or wigs, were organized into a guild, as they had been in the Middle Ages. The main object of the guild was to prevent all other citizens from making or selling the articles in which its members dealt. The number of master workmen who might open a shop of their own was often limited by the guild, as well as the number of apprentices each master could train. The period of apprenticeship was long, sometimes seven or even nine years, on the ground that it took years to learn the trade properly, but really because the guild wished to maintain its monopoly by keeping down the number who could become masters. When the apprenticeship was over, the workman became a "journeyman" and might never perhaps become a master workman and open a shop of his own.

PUBLIC LETTER WRITER

Since most common people could not read or write, they had to employ letter writers, who often had stalls like this along the street

Everywhere a workman had to stick to his trade; if a cobbler should venture to make a pair of new boots, or a baker should roast a piece of meat in his oven, he might be expelled from the guild unless he made amends. In Paris a hatter, who had greatly increased his trade by making hats of wool mixed with silk, had his stock destroyed by the guild authorities on the ground that the rules permitted hats to be made only of wool and said nothing of silk.

The guilds differed from the modern trade unions in several important respects. In the first place, only the master workmen, who owned the shops, tools, or machines, belonged to them. The apprentices and journeymen, that is, the ordinary workmen, were excluded and had no influence whatever upon the policy of the organization. In the second place, the government enforced the decisions of the guilds. Lastly, the guilds were confined to the old-established industries which were still carried on, as they had been during the Middle Ages, on a small scale in the master's house.

In spite, however, of the seeming strength of the guilds, they were really giving way before the entirely new conditions which had arisen. Thoughtful persons disapproved of them on the ground that they hampered industry and prevented progress by their outworn restrictions. In many towns the regulations were evaded or had broken down altogether, so that enterprising workmen and dealers carried on their business as they pleased. Then, as we have said, it was only the old industries that were included in the guild system.

The Nobility and the Monarch

Not only had the medieval manor and the medieval guilds maintained themselves down into the eighteenth century, but the successors of the feudal lords continued to exist as a conspicuous and powerful class. They enjoyed various privileges and distinctions denied to the ordinary citizen, although they were, of course, shorn of the great power that the more important dukes and counts had enjoyed in the Middle Ages, when they ruled over vast tracts, could summon their vassals to assist them in their constant wars with their neighbors, and dared defy even the authority of the king himself.

The English, French, and Spanish kings had gradually subjugated the turbulent barons and brought the great fiefs directly under royal control. The monarchs met with such success that in the eighteenth century the nobles no longer held aloof but eagerly sought the king's court. Those whose predecessors had once been veritable sovereigns within their own domains, had declared war even against the king, coined money, made laws for their subjects, and meted out justice in their castle halls, had, by the eighteenth century, deserted their war

A NOBLE FAMILY OF THE OLD RÉGIME

Extravagance in dress, of which the men were as guilty as the women, was largely due to the influence of court life, where so many nobles were rivaling each other in display. This brought hardship to the people on their estates in the country, since they had to support their master's expenses

horses and laid aside their long swords; in their velvet coats and high-heeled shoes they were contented with the privilege of helping the king to dress in the morning and attending him at dinner. The battlemented castle, once the stronghold of independent chieftains, was transformed into a tasteful country residence where, if the king honored the owner with a visit, the host was no longer tempted, as his ancestors had been, to shower arrows and stones upon the royal intruder.

The French noble, unlike the English, was not fond of the country but lived with the court at Versailles whenever he could afford to do so, and often when he could not. He liked the excitement of the court, and it was there that he could best advance his own and his friends' interests by obtaining lucrative offices in the army or Church or in the king's palace. By their prolonged absence from their estates the nobles lost the esteem of their tenants, while their stewards roused the hatred of the peasants by strictly collecting all the ancient manorial dues in order that the lord might enjoy the gayeties at Versailles.

The unpopularity of the French nobility was further increased by their exemptions from some of the heavy taxes, on the ground that they were still supposed to shed their blood in fighting for their king instead of paying him money like the unsoldierly burghers and peasants. They enjoyed, moreover, the preference when the king had desirable positions to grant. They also claimed a certain social superiority, since they were excluded by their traditions of birth from engaging in any ordinary trade or industry, although they might enter some professions, such as medicine, law, the Church, or the army, or even participate in maritime trade without derogating from their rank. In short, the French nobility, including some one hundred and thirty thousand or one hundred and forty thousand persons, constituted a *privileged* class, although they no longer performed any of the high functions which had been exercised by their predecessors.

To make matters worse, very few of the nobles really belonged to old feudal families. For the most part they had been ennobled by the king for some supposed service, or had bought an office, or a judgeship in the higher courts, to which noble rank was attached. Naturally this circumstance served to rob them of much of the respect that their hereditary dignity and titles might otherwise have gained for them.

In England the feudal castles had disappeared earlier even than in France, and the English law did not grant to any one, however long and distinguished his lineage, special rights or privileges not enjoyed by every freeman. Nevertheless, there was a distinct noble class in England. The monarch had formerly been accustomed to summon his earls and some of his barons to take council with him, and in this way the *peerage* developed; this included those whose title permitted them to sit in the House of Lords and to transmit this honorable prerogative to their eldest sons. But the peers paid the same taxes as every other subject and were punished in the same manner if they were convicted of an offense. Moreover, only the eldest surviving son of a noble father inherited his rank, while on the Continent all the children became nobles. In this way the number of the English nobility was greatly restricted, and their social distinction roused little antagonism.

In Germany, however, the nobles continued to occupy very much the same position which their ancestors held in the Middle Ages. There had been no king to do for Germany what the French kings had done for France; no mighty man had risen strong enough to batter down castle walls and bend all barons, great and small, to his will. The result was that there were in Germany in the eighteenth century hundreds of nobles dwelling in strong old castles and ruling with a high hand domains which were sometimes no larger than a big American farm. They levied taxes, held courts, coined money, and maintained standing armies of perhaps only a handful of soldiers.

In all the countries of Europe the chief noble was of course the monarch himself, to whose favor almost all the lesser nobles owed their titles and rank. He was, except in a few cases, always despotic, permitting the people no share in the management of the government and often rendering them miserable by needless wars and ill-advised and oppressive taxes. He commonly maintained a very expensive court and gave away to unworthy courtiers much of the money which he had wrung from his people. He was permitted to imprison his subjects upon the slightest grounds and in the most unjust manner; nevertheless he usually enjoyed their loyalty and respect, since they were generally ready to attribute his bad acts to evil councilors.

[429]

On the whole, the king merited the respect paid him. He it was who had destroyed the power of innumerable lesser despots and created something like a nation. He had put a stop to the private warfare and feudal brigandage which had disgraced the Middle Ages. His officers maintained order throughout the country so that merchants and travelers could go to and fro with little danger. He opened highroads for them and established a general system of coinage, which greatly facilitated business operations. He interested himself more and more in commerce and industry and often encouraged learning. Finally, by consolidating his realms and establishing a regular system of government, he prepared the way for the European State of to-day in which the people are either given more or less control over lawmaking and the disposition of the public revenue, or, as in the case of France, the monarch has been discarded altogether as no longer needful. Democracy and political equality would, in fact, have been impossible if monarchs had not leveled the proud and mighty nobles who aspired to be petty kings in their domains.

The Catholic Church

The eighteenth century had inherited from the Middle Ages the nobility with their peculiar privileges. At the same time, the clergy, especially in Catholic countries, still possessed prerogatives which set them off from the nation at large. They were far more powerful and better organized than the nobility and exercised a great influence in the State.

The Catholic Church did not rely for its entire support upon the voluntary contributions of its members, but still enjoyed the revenue from vast domains which kings, nobles, and other landholders had from time to time (especially during the Middle Ages) given to the churches and monasteries. In addition to the income from its lands, the Church had the right, like the State, to impose a regular tax which was called the tithe. All who were subject to this were forced to pay it, whether they cared anything about religion or not, just as we are all compelled to pay taxes imposed by the government under which we live.

In spite of the changes which had overtaken the Church since the Middle Ages, it still retained its ancient external appearance in the eighteenth century—its gorgeous ceremonial, its wealth, its influence over the lives of men, its intolerance of those who ventured to differ from the conceptions of Christianity which it held. The Church could fine and imprison those whom it convicted of blasphemy, contempt of religion, or heresy. The clergy managed the schools in which, of course, the children were brought up in the orthodox faith. Hospitals and other charitable institutions were under their control. They registered all births and deaths, and only the marriages which they sanctified were regarded by the State as legal. The monasteries still existed in great numbers and owned vast tracts of land. A map of Paris made in 1789 shows no less than sixty-eight monasteries and seventy-three nunneries within the walls.

Both the Catholic and the Protestant churches were still intolerant, and in this were usually supported by the government, which was ready to punish or persecute those who refused to conform to the State religion, whatever it might be, or ventured to speak or write against its doctrines. There was none of that freedom which is so general now, and which permits a man to worship or not as he pleases, and even to criticize religion in any or all its forms without danger of imprisonment, loss of citizenship, or death.

In France, after the revocation of the Edict of Nantes in 1685, Protestants had lost all civil rights. According to a decree of 1724, those who assembled for any form of worship other than the Roman Catholic were condemned to lose their property; the men were to be sent to the galleys and the women imprisoned for life.

Books and pamphlets were carefully examined in order to see whether they contained any attacks upon the orthodox Catholic beliefs or might in any way serve to undermine the authority of the Church or of the king. The king of France, as late as 1757, issued a declaration establishing the *death* penalty for those who wrote, printed, or distributed any work which appeared to be an attack upon religion. A considerable number of the books issued in France in the eighteenth century, which ventured to criticize the government or the Church, were condemned by either the clergy or the king's courts, and were burned by the common hangman or suppressed. Not infrequently, the authors, if they could be discovered, were imprisoned.

Nevertheless, books attacking the old ideas and suggesting reforms in Church and State constantly appeared and were freely circulated.[1] The writers took care not to place their names or those of the publishers upon the title-pages, and many such books were printed at Geneva or in Holland, where great freedom prevailed.

In Spain, Austria, and Italy, however, and especially in the Papal States, the clergy, particularly the Jesuits, were more powerful and enjoyed more privileges than in France. In Spain the censorship of the press and the Inquisition constituted a double bulwark against change until the latter half of the eighteenth century.

In Germany the position of the Church varied greatly. The southern states were Catholic, while Prussia and the northern rulers had embraced Protestantism. Many of the archbishops, bishops, and abbots ruled as princes over their own lands.

The English Church and the Dissenters

In England Henry VIII had thrown off his allegiance to the pope and declared himself the head of the English Church. Under his daughter, Queen Elizabeth, Parliament had established the Church of England. It abolished the Mass and sanctioned the Book of Common Prayer, which has since remained the official guide to the services in the Anglican Church. The beliefs of the Church were brought together in the Thirty-Nine Articles, from which no one was to vary or depart in the least degree. The system of government of the Roman Catholic Church, with its archbishops, bishops, and priests, was retained,

[1] See following chapter.

but the general charge of religious matters and the appointment of bishops were put in the hands of the monarch or his ministers. All clergymen were required to subscribe solemnly to the Thirty-Nine Articles. All public religious services were to be conducted according to the Prayer Book, and those who failed to attend services on Sunday and holydays were to be fined.

But there were many Protestants, as we have seen, who did not approve of the Anglican Church as established by law. These "Dissenters" developed gradually into several sects with differing views. By far the most numerous of the Dissenters were the Baptists. They spread to America, and were the first Protestant sect to undertake foreign missions on a large scale, having founded a society for that purpose as early as 1792.

Another English sect which was destined also to be conspicuous in America was the Society of Friends, or Quakers, as they are commonly called. This group owes its origin to George Fox, who began his preaching in 1647. The Friends were distinguished by their simplicity of life and dress, and their rejection of all ceremonial and sacraments, including even the Lord's Supper. The chief stronghold of the Quakers in America has always been in Pennsylvania, more particularly Philadelphia and its neighborhood, where they settled under the leadership of William Penn.

The Quakers were the first religious sect to denounce war ever and always, and they should have the credit of beginning the movement against war which has gained much headway as a result of the World War.

The last of the great Protestant sects to appear was that of the Methodists. Their founder, John Wesley (d. 1791), when at Oxford had established a religious society among his fellow students. Their piety and the regularity of their habits gained for them the nickname of "Methodists."

Only gradually did the Methodists separate themselves from the Church of England, of which they at first considered themselves members. In 1784 the numerous American Methodists were formally organized into the Methodist Episcopal

Church, and early in the nineteenth century the English Methodists became an independent organization. At the time of Wesley's death his followers numbered over fifty thousand, and there are now in the United States over six millions, including the various branches of the Church.

Parliament under Charles II showed itself very intolerant toward all Dissenters alike—Presbyterians, Independents, Baptists, Quakers, Unitarians. Upon the accession of William and Mary, however, the Act of Toleration was passed in 1689, which permitted Dissenters to hold meetings; but "Papists and such as deny the Trinity" (namely, Unitarians) were explicitly excluded, so England still continued to maintain a somewhat intolerant system in the eighteenth century. It had a State Church (which still exists) with a particular form of belief and of services established by the government in Elizabeth's time. Even if the Dissenters were permitted to hold services in their own way, they were excluded from government offices, nor could they obtain a degree at the universities. Only the members of the Anglican Church could hold a Church benefice. Its bishops had seats in the House of Lords and its priests enjoyed a social preëminence denied to the dissenting ministers.

Roman Catholics were forbidden to enter England.[1] The celebration of the Mass was strictly prohibited. All public offices were closed to Catholics and of course they could not sit in Parliament. Indeed, legally, they had no right whatever to be in England at all.

Nevertheless, in spite of the old intolerant laws and the special privileges of the Anglican Church, men were very free in the eighteenth century in England to believe what they wished and say what they wished. One desiring to publish a book or pamphlet did not have to obtain the permission of

[1] It may be noted here that the Catholics as well as dissenting Protestant sects found a refuge in America from their persecutors, as did the Huguenots who fled from the oppression of the Catholic government in France. The colony of Maryland was founded by Lord Baltimore in 1634 and named after the French wife of Charles I. In the nineteenth century the number of Catholics in the United States was vastly increased by immigration from Ireland, Italy, and other countries, so that there are over sixteen millions to-day who have been baptized into the Roman Catholic Church,

the government, as was required in France. The result was that there was a vast amount of discussion of religious, scientific, and political matters beyond anything that went on in any other European country. The books of the English reformers had a great influence upon the French, as will become apparent in the following chapter.

England was celebrated throughout Europe for its parliamentary government. The English sovereign did not enjoy the despotic powers of the French, Prussian, or Russian monarch but was controlled by the House of Lords and the House of Commons. He left the management of affairs largely in the hands of the *cabinet*, which was really a committee of the House of Commons. This important matter of England's government will be taken up later.

CHAPTER XX

MODERN SCIENCE AND THE IDEA OF PROGRESS

The Advance of Modern Science. How the Scientific Discoveries Produced a Spirit of Reform: Voltaire. The Encyclopædia: Rousseau

The Advance of Modern Science

A THOUGHTFUL observer in the eighteenth century would, as we have seen, have discovered many medieval institutions which had persisted in spite of the considerable changes which had taken place in conditions and ideas during the previous five hundred years. Serfdom, the guilds, the feudal dues, the nobility and clergy with their peculiar privileges, the declining monastic orders, the confused and cruel laws—these were a part of the heritage which Europe had received from what was coming to be regarded as a dark and barbarous period. People began to be keenly alive to the deficiencies of the past, and to look to the future for better things, even to dream of progress beyond the happiest times of which they had any record. They came to feel that the chief obstacles to progress were the outworn institutions, the ignorance and prejudices of their forefathers, and that if they could only be freed from this burden, they would find it easy to create new and enlightened laws and institutions to suit their needs.

This attitude of mind seems natural enough in our progressive age, but two centuries ago it was distinctly new. Mankind has in general shown an inordinate respect and veneration for the past. Until the opening of the eighteenth century the former times were commonly held to have been better than the present; for the evils of the past were little known, while those of the present were, as always, only too apparent. Men looked backward rather than forward. They aspired to fight as well, or be as saintly, or write as good books, or paint as beautiful pictures, as the great men of old. That they might excel the achievements of their predecessors did not occur to them. Knowledge was sought not by studying the world about them but in some ancient authority. In Aristotle's vast range of works on various branches of science, the universities of the Middle Ages felt that they had a mass of authentic information which it should be their main business to explain and impart rather than to increase or correct by new investigations. Men's ideals centered in the past, and improvement seemed to them to consist in reviving, so far as possible, the "good old days."

It was mainly to the patient men of science that the western world owed its first hopes of future improvement. It is they who have shown that the ancient writers were mistaken about many serious matters and that they had at best a very crude and imperfect notion of the world. They have gradually robbed men of their old blind respect for the past, and by their discoveries have pointed the way to indefinite advance, so that now we expect constant change and improvement and are scarcely astonished at the most marvelous inventions.

In the Middle Ages the scholars and learned men had been but little interested in the world about them. They devoted far more attention to philosophy and theology than to what we should call the natural sciences. They were satisfied in the main to get their knowledge of nature from reading the works of the ancients above all, those of Aristotle.

We have seen how early in the seventeenth century men like Lord Bacon, Galileo, and Descartes advocated a new kind of science. They were tired of all the talk about things of which people knew very little and proposed that natural objects and changes should be examined with great care so as to discover exactly what happened in any given case. But the new scientists were not contented with the mere observation of what they saw around them, they began to perform experiments and so made things happen in ways that they could conveniently watch and study. Nowadays *experimentation* is, of course, constantly used by scientific investigators who establish specially equipped laboratories for the purpose. In this way they learn many things that the most careful observation of what takes place naturally in the world would not reveal.

Lastly, in order to carry on experiments and make careful observations and measurements, *apparatus* had to be devised, such as microscopes, telescopes, thermometers, barometers, accurate clocks and balances. The Greeks and Romans and the professors in the medieval universities had none of these things. They were all either invented or used for the first time on a large scale in the seventeenth century.

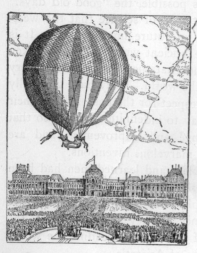

BALLOON ASCENSION, 1783

The crowds along paths of the garden of the Tuileries palace in Paris, on December 1, 1783, saw for the first time two men ascend 2,000 feet in a balloon

This new way of studying the world led to the most wonderful discoveries, so that now we can do things that even magicians never claimed to do in the Middle Ages. Our modern machinery has changed the world more than all the battles that ever happened. Our locomotives and steamships take us swiftly to all parts of the globe; our telegraphs and telephones enable us to communicate with people at great distances; our cameras and phonographs reproduce the faces and voices of the dead or absent. And these are but very few of the marvels of modern scientific invention which were wholly unknown to people in the eighteenth century.

The path of the scientific investigator has not always been without its thorns. Mankind has changed its notions with reluctance. The churchmen and the professors in the universities were wedded to the conceptions of the world which the medieval theologians and philosophers had worked out, mainly from the Bible and Aristotle. They clung to the textbooks which they and their predecessors had long used in teaching, and had no desire to work in laboratories or to keep up with the ideas of the scientists.

Many theologians looked with grave suspicion on the scientific discoveries of the day, on the ground that they did not harmonize with the teachings of the Bible as commonly accepted. It was naturally a great shock to them, and also to the public at large, to have it suggested that man's dwelling place, instead of being God's greatest work, to which he had subordinated everything and around which the whole starry firmament revolved, was after all but a tiny speck in comparison with the whole universe, and its sun but one of an innumerable host of similar glowing bodies of stupendous size, each of which might have its particular family of planets revolving about it.

The bolder thinkers were consequently sometimes made to suffer for their ideas, and their books prohibited or burned.

How the Scientific Discoveries Produced a Spirit of Reform: Voltaire

Those who accepted the old views of the world and of religion, and opposed change, were quite justified in suspecting that scientific investigation would sooner or later make them trouble. It taught men to distrust, and even to scorn, the past which furnished so many instances of ignorance and superstition. Instead of accepting the teachings of the theologians, both Catholic and Protestant, that mankind through Adam's fall was rendered utterly vile, and incapable (except through God's special grace) of good thoughts or deeds, certain thinkers began to urge that man was by nature good; that he should freely use his own God-given reason; that he was capable of becoming increasingly wise by a study of nature's laws, and that he could indefinitely better his own condition and that of his fellows if he would but free himself from the shackles of error and superstition. Those who had broadened their views of mankind and of the universe came to believe that God had revealed himself not only to the Jewish people but also, in greater or less degree, to all his creatures in all ages and in all parts of a boundless universe where everything was controlled

[439]

by his immutable laws. This is illustrated in the famous "Universal Prayer" of Alexander Pope, written about 1737:

> Father of all! in ev'ry age,
>   In ev'ry clime adored,
> By saint, by savage, and by sage,
>   Jehovah, Jove, or Lord!
>
> . . . .
>
> Yet not to earth's contracted span
>   Thy goodness let me bound,
> Or think Thee Lord alone of man,
>   When thousand worlds are 'round.

Such ideas of God's providence had in them nothing essentially unchristian, for they are to be found in writings of early Church fathers. But those who advanced them now were often "free thinkers," who attacked the Christian religion in no doubtful terms, and whose books were eagerly read and discussed. These "deists" maintained that their conception of God was far worthier than that of the Christian believer, who, they declared, accused the deity of violating his own laws by miracles and of condemning a great part of his children to eternal torment.[1]

In the year 1726 there landed in England a young and gifted Frenchman, who was to become the great prophet of this new view. Voltaire, who was then thirty-two years old, had already deserted the older religious beliefs and was consequently ready to follow enthusiastically the more radical of the English thinkers, who discussed matters with an openness which filled him with astonishment. He became an ardent

---

[1] Locke rejected the notion that man was born with certain divinely implanted ideas, and maintained that we owe all that we know to the sensations and impressions which come to us from without. Locke was a man of extraordinary modesty, good sense, and caution, and he and his gifted successor, Bishop Berkeley, did much to forward modern psychology. Berkeley's *New Theory of Vision* is a clear account of the gradual way in which we learn to see. He shows that a blind man, if suddenly restored to sight, would make little or nothing of the confused colors and shapes which would first strike his eye. He would learn only from prolonged experience that one set of colors and contours meant a man and another a horse or a table, no matter how readily he might recognize the several objects by touch.

admirer of the teachings of Newton, whose stately funeral he attended shortly after his arrival. He regarded the discoverer of universal gravitation as greater than an Alexander the Great or a Cæsar, and did all he could to popularize Newton's work in France. "It is to him who masters our minds by the force of truth, not to those who enslave men by violence; it is to him who understands the universe, not to those who disfigure it, that we owe our reverence."

Voltaire was deeply impressed by the Quakers—their simple life and their hatred of war. He admired the English liberty of speech and writing; he respected the general esteem for the merchant class. In France, he said, "the merchant so constantly hears his business spoken of with disdain that he is fool enough to blush for it; yet I am not sure that the merchant who enriches his country, gives orders from his countinghouse at Surat or Cairo, and contributes to the happiness of the globe is not more useful to a state than the thickly bepowdered lord who knows exactly what time the king rises and what time he goes to bed, and gives himself mighty airs of greatness while he plays the part of a slave in the minister's anteroom."

Voltaire proceeded to enlighten his countrymen by a volume of essays in which he sets forth his impressions of England; but the high court of justice (the *parlement*) of Paris condemned these *Letters on the English* to be publicly burned, as scandalous and lacking in the respect due to the kings and governments. Voltaire was not discouraged and remained, during the rest of a long life, the chief advocate throughout Europe of reliance upon reason and of confidence in progress. He was interested in almost everything; he wrote histories, dramas, philosophic treatises, romances, and innumerable letters to his innumerable admirers. The vast range of his writings enabled him to bring his views to the attention of all sorts and conditions of men—not only to the general reader but even to the careless playgoer.

While Voltaire was successfully encouraging free criticism in general, he led a relentless attack upon the most venerable, probably the most powerful, institution in Europe, the Roman

Catholic Church. The absolute power of the king did not trouble him, but the Church appeared to him to be opposed to a free exercise of reason and hostile to reform, and he declared that it interfered with human progress. The Church, as it fully realized, had never encountered a more deadly enemy.

Were there space at command, a great many good things, as well as plenty of bad ones, might be told of this extraordinary man. He was often superficial in his judgments, and sometimes jumped to unwarranted conclusions. He saw only evil in the Church and seemed incapable of understanding all that it had done for mankind during the bygone ages. He attributed to evil motives teachings which were accepted by honest and good men. He bitterly ridiculed cherished religious ideas, along with the censorship of the press and the quarrels of the theologians.

He could, and did, however, fight against wrong and oppression. The abuses which he attacked were in large part abolished by the French Revolution. It is unfair to notice only Voltaire's mistakes and exaggerations, as many writers, both Catholic and Protestant, have done; for he certainly did much to prepare the way for great and permanent reforms which every one would now approve.[1]

The Encyclopædia: Rousseau

Voltaire had many admirers and powerful allies. Among these none were more important than Denis Diderot and the scholars whom Diderot induced to coöperate with him in preparing articles for a new *Encyclopædia,* which was designed to spread among a wide range of intelligent readers a knowledge of scientific advance and rouse enthusiasm for reform and progress. An encyclopædia was by no means a new thing. Diderot's plan had been suggested by a proposal to publish a

[1] Voltaire repudiated the beliefs of the Protestant churches as well as of the Catholic Church. He was, however, no atheist, as his enemies—and they have been many and bitter—have so often asserted. He believed in God, and at his country home, near Geneva, he dedicated a temple to him. Like many of his contemporaries, he was a deist, and held that God had revealed himself in nature and in our own hearts, not in Bible or Church.

French translation of Chambers's *Cyclopædia*. Before his first volume appeared, a vast *Universal Dictionary* had been completed in Germany in sixty-four volumes. But few people outside of that country could read German in those days, whereas the well-written and popular articles of Diderot and his helpers, ranging from "abacus," "abbey," and "abdication" to "Zoroaster," "Zurich," and "zymology," were in a language that many people all over Europe could understand.

Diderot and his fellow editors endeavored to rouse as little opposition as possible. They respected current prejudices and gave space to ideas and opinions with which they were not personally in sympathy. They furnished material, however, for refuting what they believed to be mistaken notions, and Diderot declared that "time will enable people to distinguish what we have thought from what we have said." But no sooner did the first two volumes appear in 1752 than the king's ministers, to please the officials of the Church, suppressed them, as containing principles hostile to royal authority and religion, although they did not forbid the continuation of the work.

As volume after volume appeared, the subscribers increased; but so did the opposition. The Encyclopædists were declared to be a band bent upon the destruction of religion and the undermining of society; the government again interfered, withdrew the license to publish the work, and prohibited the sale of the seven volumes that were already out. Nevertheless seven years later Diderot was able to deliver the remaining ten volumes to the subscribers in spite of the government's prohibition.

The *Encyclopædia* criticized temperately, but effectively, religious intolerance, the bad taxes, the slave trade, and the atrocities of the criminal law; it encouraged men to turn their minds to natural science with all its possibilities. The article "Legislator," written by Diderot, says: "All the men of all lands have become necessary to one another for the exchange of the fruits of industry and the products of the soil. Commerce is a new bond among men. In these days every nation has an interest in the preservation by every other nation of its wealth, its industry, its banks, its luxury, its agriculture. The ruin of Leipzig, of Lisbon, of Lima, has led to bankruptcies on all the exchanges of Europe and has affected the fortunes of many millions of persons." The English statesman, John Morley, has given us an enthusiastic account of Diderot and his companions, declaring that "it was this band of writers, organized by a harassed man of letters, and not the nobles swarming around Louis XV, nor the churchmen singing masses, who first grasped the great principle of modern society, the honour that is owed to productive industry. They were vehement for the glories of peace and passionate against the brazen glories of war."

Next to Voltaire, the writer who did most to cultivate discontent with existing conditions was Jean Jacques Rousseau (1712-1778). Unlike Voltaire and Diderot, Rousseau believed that people thought too much, not too little; that we should trust to our hearts rather than to our heads, and may safely rely upon our natural feelings and sentiments to guide us. He declared that Europe was overcivilized, and summoned men to return to nature and simplicity. His first work was a prize essay written in 1750, in which he sought to prove that the development of the arts and sciences had demoralized mankind, inasmuch as they had produced luxury, insincerity, and arrogance. He extolled the rude vigor of Sparta and denounced the refined and degenerate life of the Athenians.

Rousseau's plea for the simple life went to the heart of many a person who was weary of artificiality. Others were attracted by his firm belief in the natural equality of mankind and the right of every man to have a voice in the government. In his celebrated little treatise, *The Social Contract,* he takes up the question, By what right does one man rule over others? The book opens with the words: "Man is born free and yet is now everywhere in chains. One man believes himself the master of others and yet is after all more of a slave than they. How did this change come about? I do not know. What can render it legitimate? I believe that I can answer that question." It is, Rousseau declares, the will of the people that renders govern-

Turgot

Jean Jacques Rousseau

Joseph II

Pl. xxiv

NEWTON

DIDEROT

VOLTAIRE

Pl. xxv. Leaders of the Revolution of Thought

ment legitimate. The real sovereign is the people. Although they may appoint a single person, such as a king, to manage the government for them, they should make the laws, since it is they who must obey them. We shall find that the first French constitution accepted Rousseau's doctrine and defined law as "the expression of the general will"—not the will of a king reigning by the grace of God.

About the middle of the eighteenth century a new social science was born, namely, political economy. Scholars began to investigate the sources of a nation's wealth, the manner in which commodities were produced and distributed, the forces determining demand and supply, the function of money and credit, and their influence upon industry and commerce. Previous to the eighteenth century these matters had seemed to most people unworthy of scientific discussion.

The first great systematic work upon political economy was published by a Scotch philosopher, Adam Smith, in 1776. His *Inquiry into the Nature and Causes of the Wealth of Nations* became the basis of all further progress in the science.

While the economists in France and England by no means agreed in details, they brought the light of reason to bear, for example, upon the various bungling and iniquitous old methods of taxation then in vogue, and many of them advocated a single tax which should fall directly upon the landowner. They wrote treatises on practical questions, scattered pamphlets broadcast, and even conducted a magazine or two in the hope of bringing home to the people at large the existing economic evils.

It is clear from what has been said that the eighteenth century was a period of unexampled advance in general enlightenment. New knowledge spread abroad by the Encyclopædists, the economists, and writers on government led people to see the vices of the existing system and gave them at the same time new hope of bettering themselves by abandoning the mistaken beliefs and imperfect methods of their predecessors. The spirit of reform penetrated even into kings' palaces, and we must now turn to the events which led up to the French Revolution, which deeply affected the course of Western civilization.

CHAPTER XXI

THE FRENCH REVOLUTION

The Old Régime in France. Louis XVI as Benevolent Despot. Meeting of the Estates General in 1789. First Reforms of the National Assembly. The National Assembly in Paris. Revolutionary France and the European Powers. The First French Republic. The Reign of Terror

The Old·Régime in France

IT was France that first carried out the great reforms that did away with most of the old institutions and confusion that had come down from the Middle Ages. It is true that some of the monarchs of the time ("benevolent despots," as they are called), especially Frederick the Great, and Catherine II of Russia, and the Emperor Joseph II, introduced some reforms, largely in their own interests, but even in England little was done in the eighteenth century to remedy the great abuses of which the reformers complained. But in 1789 the king of France asked his people to submit their grievances to him and to send representatives to Versailles to confer with him upon the state of the realm and the ways in which the government might be improved so as to increase the general happiness and the prosperity of the kingdom. And then the miracle happened! The French National Assembly swept away the old abuses with an ease and thoroughness which put the petty reforms of the benevolent despots to shame. It accomplished more in a few months than the reforming kings had done in a century; for the kings had not been in the habit of calling in the representatives of the people to aid them. Instead of availing themselves of the great forces of the nation, they had tried to do everything alone by royal decrees, and so had failed.

The unique greatness of the reformation accomplished by the French Assembly is, however, often obscured by the disorder which accompanied it. When one meets the words "French Revolution," he is pretty sure to call up before his mind's eye the guillotine and its hundreds of victims, and the Paris mob shouting the hymn of the Marseillaise as they paraded the streets with the heads of unfortunate "aristocrats" on their pikes. Every one has heard of this terrible episode in French history even if he knows practically nothing of the permanent good which was accomplished at the time. Indeed, it has made so deep an impression on posterity that the Reign of Terror is often mistaken for the real Revolution. It was, however, only a sequel to it, an unhappy accident which seems less and less important as the years go on, while the achievements of the Revolution itself loom larger and larger. The Reign of Terror will be explained in good time, but it is a matter of far greater importance to understand clearly how the fundamental and permanent reforms were wrought out, and how France won the proud distinction of being the first nation to do away with the absurd and vexatious institutions which weighed upon Europe in the eighteenth century.

We have already examined these institutions which were common to most of the European countries,—despotic kings, arbitrary imprisonment, unfair taxation, censorship of the press, serfdom, feudal dues, friction between Church and State,—all of which the reformers had been busy denouncing as contrary to reason and humanity, and some of which the benevolent despots and their ministers had, in a half-hearted way, attempted to remedy. The various relics of bygone times and of outlived conditions which the Revolution abolished forever are commonly called in France the old régime.[1] In order to see why France took the lead of other European countries in modernizing itself, it is necessary to examine somewhat carefully the particular causes of discontent there. We shall then see how almost every one, from the king to the peasant, came to realize that the old system was bad and consequently resolved to do away with it and substitute a more rational plan of government for the long-standing disorder.

Of the evils which the Revolution abolished, none was more important than the confusion in France due to the fact that it was not in the eighteenth century a well-organized, homogeneous state whose citizens all enjoyed the same rights and privi-

[1] From the French *ancien régime*, the old or former system.

leges. A long line of kings had patched it together, adding bit by bit as they could. By conquest and bargain, by marrying heiresses, and through the extinction of the feudal dynasties, the original restricted domains of Hugh Capet about Paris and Orléans had been gradually increased by his descendants. We have seen how Louis XIV gained Alsace and Strasbourg and some towns on the borders of the Spanish Netherlands.

THE PROVINCES OF FRANCE IN THE EIGHTEENTH CENTURY,
SHOWING INTERIOR CUSTOMS LINES

Louis XV added Lorraine in 1766. Two years later the island of Corsica was ceded to France by Genoa. So when Louis XVI came to the throne in 1774 he found himself ruler of practically the whole territory which makes up France to-day. But these different parts had different institutions.

Some of the districts which the kings of France brought under their sway, like Languedoc, Provence, Brittany, and

Dauphiny, were considerable states in themselves, each with its own laws, customs, and system of government. When these provinces had come, at different times, into the possession of the king of France, he had not changed their laws so as to make them correspond with those of his other domains. He was satisfied if a new province paid its due share of the taxes and treated his officials with respect. In some cases the provinces retained their local assemblies, and controlled, to a certain extent, their own affairs. The provinces into which France was divided before the Revolution were not, therefore, merely artificial divisions created for the purposes of convenience, like the modern French *departments*,[1] but represented real historical differences.

THE SALT TAX

Showing the different amounts paid in the various parts of France in the eighteenth century for a given amount of salt

While in a considerable portion of southern France the Roman law still prevailed, in the central parts and in the west and north there were no less than two hundred and eighty-five different local codes of law in force; so that one who moved from his own to a neighboring town might find a wholly unfamiliar legal system.

One of the heaviest taxes was that on salt. This varied greatly, so greatly in different parts of France that the government had to go to great expense to guard the boundary lines between the various districts, for there was every inducement to smugglers to carry salt from those parts of the country

[1] See below, p. 471.

where it was cheap into the regions where it sold for a high price on account of the tax.

Besides these unfortunate local differences, there were the old class differences which caused great discontent. All Frenchmen did not enjoy the same rights as citizens. Two small but very important classes, the nobility and the clergy, were treated differently by the State from the rest of the people. They did not have to pay one of the heaviest of the taxes, the notorious *taille;* and on one ground or another they escaped other burdens which the rest of the citizens bore. For instance, they were not required to serve in the militia or help build the roads.

We have seen how great and powerful the Medieval Church was. In France, as in other Catholic countries of Europe, it still retained in the eighteenth century a considerable part of the power that it had possessed in the thirteenth, and it still performed important public functions. It took charge of education and of the relief of the sick and the poor. It was very wealthy and is supposed to have owned one-fifth of all the land in France. The clergy claimed that their property, being dedicated to God, was not subject to taxation. They consented, however, to help the king from time to time by a "free gift," as they called it. The Church still collected the tithes from the people, and its vast possessions made it very independent.

A great part of the enormous income of the Church went to the higher clergy—the bishops, archbishops, and abbots. Since they were appointed by the king, often from among his courtiers, they tended to neglect their duties as officers of the Church and to become little more than "great lords with a hundred thousand francs income." But while they were spending their time at Versailles the real work was performed—and well performed—by the lower clergy, who often received scarcely enough to keep soul and body together. This explains why, when the Revolution began, the parish priests sided with the people instead of with their ecclesiastical superiors.

The privileges of the nobles, like those of the clergy, had originated in the medieval conditions described in an earlier chapter. A detailed study of their rights would reveal many survivals of the institutions which prevailed in the eleventh and twelfth centuries, when the great majority of the people were serfs living upon the manors. While serfdom had largely disappeared in France long before the eighteenth century, and the peasants were generally free men who owned or rented their land, it was still the theory of the French law that there was "no land without its lord." Consequently the lords still enjoyed the right to collect a variety of time-honored dues from the inhabitants living within the limits of the former manors.

The privileges and dues enjoyed by the nobles varied greatly in different parts of France. It was quite common for the noble landowner to have a right to a certain portion of the peasant's crops; occasionally he could still collect a toll on sheep and cattle driven past his house. In some cases the lord maintained, as he had done in the Middle Ages, the only mill, wine press, or oven within a certain district, and could require every one to make use of these and pay him a share of the product. Even when a peasant owned his land, the neighboring lord usually had the right to exact one-fifth of its value every time it was sold.

The nobles, too, enjoyed the exclusive privilege of hunting, which was deemed an aristocratic pastime. The game which they preserved for their amusement often did great damage to the crops of the peasants, who were forbidden to interfere with hares and deer. Many of the manors had great pigeon houses, built in the form of a tower, in which there were one or two thousand nests. No wonder the peasants detested these, for they were not permitted to protect themselves against the innumerable pigeons and their progeny, which spread over the fields, devouring newly sown seed. These dovecotes constituted, in fact, one of the chief grievances of the peasants.

The higher offices in the army were reserved for the nobles, as well as the easiest and most lucrative places in the Church and about the king's person. All these privileges were vestiges of the powers which the nobles had enjoyed when they ruled their estates as feudal lords. Louis XIV had, as we know, induced them to leave their domains and gather round him at Versailles, where all who could afford it lived for at least a part of the year.

Only a small part of the nobility in the eighteenth century were, however, descendants of the ancient and illustrious feudal families of France. The greater part of them had been ennobled in recent times by the king, or had purchased or inherited a government office or judgeship which carried the privileges of nobility with it. This fact rendered the rights and exemptions claimed by the nobility even more odious to the people at large than they would otherwise have been.

A CHÂTEAU AND PIGEON HOUSE

The round tower at the right hand in front is a pigeon house. The wall inside is honeycombed with nests, and the pigeons fly in and out at the side of the roof

Everybody who did not belong to either the clergy or the nobility was regarded as being of the third estate. The third estate was therefore really the nation at large, which was made up in 1789 of about twenty-five million souls. The privileged classes can scarcely have counted altogether more than two hundred or two hundred and fifty thousand individuals. A great part of the third estate lived in the country and tilled the soil. Most historians have been inclined to make out their condition as very wretched. They were certainly oppressed by an abominable system of taxation and were irritated by the dues which they had to pay to the lords. They also suffered frequently from local famines. Yet there is no doubt that the evils of their situation have been greatly exaggerated. When Thomas Jefferson traveled through France in 1787 he

COURT SCENE AT VERSAILLES

The king is surrounded by princes of the royal family and the greatest nobles of France while he dresses and shaves upon rising in the morning (the *levée*). Similar ceremonies were performed when the king went to bed at night (the *couchée*). The bed, hung with rich tapestries, is behind the railing. The door at the left leads into a small room—called the Bull's Eye Room (*Salon de l'Œil de Bœuf*) from the round window above the door—where the ambassadors and other dignitaries waited to be admitted, and while waiting often planned and plotted how to win the king's favor. Louis XIV's bedroom at Versailles is still preserved, in much of its old-time splendor; for the palace is now a museum

reported that the country people appeared to be comfortable and that they had plenty to eat. Arthur Young, a famous English traveler who has left us an admirable account of his journeys in France during the years 1787 and 1789, found much prosperity and contentment, although he gives, too, some forlorn pictures of destitution.

The latter have often been unduly emphasized by historical writers; for it has commonly been thought that the Revolution was to be explained by the misery and despair of the people, who could bear their burdens no longer. If, however, instead of comparing the situation of the French peasant under the old régime with that of an English or American farmer to-day, we contrast his position with that of his fellow peasant in Prussia, Russia, Austria, Italy, or Spain, in the eighteenth century, it will be clear that in France the agricultural classes were really much better off than elsewhere on the Continent. In almost all the other European countries, except England, the peasants were still serfs: they had to work certain days in each week for their lord; they could not marry or dispose of their land without his permission. Moreover, the fact that the population of France had steadily increased from seventeen millions after the close of the wars of Louis XIV to about twenty-five millions at the opening of the Revolution indicates that the general condition of the people was improving rather than growing worse.

The real reason why France was the first among the European countries to carry out a great reform and do away with the irritating survivals of feudalism was not that the nation was miserable and oppressed above all others, but that it was sufficiently free and enlightened to realize the evils and absurdities of the old régime. Mere oppression and misery do not account for a revolution; there must also be *active discontent;* and of that there was a great abundance in France, as we shall see. The French peasant no longer looked up to his lord as his ruler and protector, but viewed him as a sort of legalized robber who demanded a share of his precious harvest, whose officers awaited the farmer at the crossing of the river to claim a toll, who would not let him sell his produce when he wished, or permit him to protect his fields from the ravages of the pigeons which it pleased his lord to keep.

In the eighteenth century France was still the despotism that Louis XIV had made it. Louis XVI once described it very well in the following words: "The sovereign authority resides exclusively in my person. To me solely belongs the power of making the laws, and without dependence or coöperation. The entire public order emanates from me, and I am its supreme protector. My people are one with me. The rights and interests of the nation are necessarily identical with mine and rest solely in my hands." In short, the king still ruled "by the grace of God," as Louis XIV had done. He needed to render account to no man for his governmental acts; he was responsible to God alone. The following illustrations will make clear the dangerous extent of the king's power.

In the first place, it was he who levied each year the heaviest of the taxes, the hated *taille,* from which the privileged classes were exempted. This tax brought in about one-sixth of the whole revenue of the State. The amount collected was kept secret, and no report was made to the nation of what was done with it or, for that matter, with any other part of the king's income. Indeed, no distinction was made between the king's private funds and the State treasury, whereas in England the monarch was given a stated allowance. The king of France could issue as many drafts payable to bearer as he wished; the royal officials must pay all such orders and ask no questions. Louis XV is said to have spent no less than seventy million dollars in this irresponsible fashion in a single year.

But the king not only controlled his subjects' purses; he had a terrible authority over their persons as well. He could issue orders for the arrest and arbitrary imprisonment of any one he pleased. Without trial or formality of any sort a person might be cast into a dungeon for an indefinite period, until the king happened to remember him again or was reminded of him by the poor man's friends. These notorious orders of arrest were called *lettres de cachet,* that is, sealed letters. They were not difficult to obtain for any one who had influence with the king or his favorites, and they furnished a particularly easy and efficacious way of disposing of an enemy. These arbitrary orders lead one to appreciate the importance of the provision of Magna Charta, which runs: "No freeman shall be taken or imprisoned except by the lawful judgment of his peers and in accordance with the law of the land." Some of the most eminent men of the time were shut up by the king's order, often on account of books or pamphlets written by them which displeased the king or those about him. The distinguished statesman, Mirabeau, when a young man, was imprisoned several times through *lettres de cachet* obtained by his father as a means of checking his reckless dissipation.

A ROYAL SESSION OF PARLEMENT, AT VERSAILLES, 1776

The name *lit de justice* (couch of justice) is supposed to come from the fact that the king once reclined on a couch, but here he is seated on a throne. The members of the *parlement*, with long gowns and caps, can be distinguished from the nobles and princes in their richer court dress. Each person had his exact place assigned him, in order of rank

Yet, notwithstanding the seemingly unlimited powers of the French king, and in spite of the fact that France had no written constitution and no legislative body to which the nation sent representatives, the monarch was by no means absolutely free to do just as he pleased. In the first place, the high courts of law, the so-called *Parlements*, could often hamper the king.

These resembled the English Parliament in almost nothing but name. The French *parlements*—of which the most important one was at Paris and a dozen more were scattered about the provinces—did not, however, confine themselves solely to the business of trying lawsuits. They claimed, and quite properly, that when the king decided to make a new law he must send it to them to be registered, for how, otherwise, could they adjust their decisions to it? Now although they acknowledged that the right to make the laws belonged to the monarch, they nevertheless often sent a "protest" to the king instead of registering an edict which they disapproved. They would urge that the ministers had abused his Majesty's confidence. They would also take pains to have their protest printed and sold on the streets at a penny or two a copy, so that people should get the idea that the *parlement* was defending the nation against the oppressive measures of the king's ministers.

When the king received one of these protests two alternatives were open to him. He might recall the distasteful decree altogether, or modify it so as to suit the court; or he could summon the *parlement* before him and in a solemn session (called a *lit de justice*) command it with his own mouth to register the law in its records. The *parlement* would then reluctantly obey; but as the Revolution approached it began to claim that a decree registered against its will was not valid.

Struggles between the *parlements* and the king's ministers were very frequent in the eighteenth century. They prepared the way for the Revolution, first, by bringing important questions to the attention of the people; for there were no newspapers, and no parliamentary or congressional debates, to enable the public to understand the policy of the government. Secondly, the *parlements* not only frankly criticized the proposed measures of the king and his ministers, but they familiarized the nation with the idea that the king was not really at liberty to alter what they called "the fundamental laws" of the State. By this they meant that there was an unwritten constitution, which limited the king's power and of which they were the guardians. In this way they promoted the growing discontent with a government which was carried on in secret and which left the nation at the mercy of the men in whom the king might for the moment repose confidence.

In addition to the *parlements* public opinion often exercised a powerful check upon the king, even under the autocratic old régime. It was, Necker declared, "an invisible power which, without treasury, guards, or an army, ruled Paris and the court, —yes, the very palace of the king." The latter half of the eighteenth century was a period of outspoken and acrid criticism of the whole existing social and governmental system. Reformers, among whom many of the king's ministers were counted, loudly and eloquently discussed the numerous abuses and the vicious character of the government, which gradually came to seem just as bad to the intelligent people of that day as it does to us now.

Although there were no daily newspapers to discuss public questions, large numbers of pamphlets were written and circulated by individuals whenever there was an important crisis, and they answered much the same purpose as the editorials in a modern newspaper. We have already seen how French philosophers and reformers, like Voltaire and Diderot, had been encouraged by the freedom of speech which prevailed in England, and how industriously they had sown the seeds of discontent in their own country. We have seen how in popular works, in poems and stories and plays, and above all in the *Encyclopædia*, they explained the new scientific discoveries, attacked the old beliefs and misapprehensions, and encouraged progress.

Louis XVI as Benevolent Despot

In 1774 Louis XV [1] died, after a disgraceful reign of which it has not seemed necessary to say much. His unsuccessful wars, which had ended with the loss of all his American possessions and the victory of his enemies in India, had brought France to the verge of bankruptcy; indeed in his last years his ministers repudiated a portion of the government's obligations. The taxes were already so oppressive as to arouse universal discontent, and yet the government was running behind seventy millions of dollars a year—a great sum for those days.

---

[1] He came to the throne in 1715 as a boy of five, on the death of Louis XIV, his great-grandfather.

LOUIS XVI AS BENEVOLENT DESPOT

The king's personal conduct was scandalous, and he allowed his mistresses and courtiers to meddle in public affairs and plunder the royal treasury for themselves and their favorites. When at last he was carried off by smallpox every one hailed, with hopes of better times, the accession of his grandson and successor, Louis XVI.

The new king was but twenty years old, ill educated, indolent, unsociable, and very fond of hunting and of pottering about in a workshop, where he spent his happiest hours. He was a well-meaning young man, with none of his grandfather's vices, who tried now and then to attend to the disagreeable business of government, and would gladly have made his people happy if that had not required more energy than he possessed. He had none of the restless interest in public affairs that we found in Frederick the Great, Catherine II, or his brother-in-law, Joseph II; he was never tempted to rise at five o'clock in the morning in order to read State papers.

His wife was the beautiful Marie Antoinette, daughter of Maria Theresa. The marriage had been arranged in 1770 with a view of maintaining the alliance which had been concluded between France and Austria in 1756.[1] The queen was only nineteen years old when she came to the throne, light-hearted and on pleasure bent. She disliked the formal etiquette of the court at Versailles and shocked people by her thoughtless pranks. She rather despised her heavy husband, who did not care to share in the amusements which pleased her best. She did not hesitate to interfere in the government when she wished to help one of her favorites or to make trouble for some one she disliked.

At first Louis XVI took his duties very seriously. It seemed for a time that he might find a place among the benevolent despots who were then ruling in Europe. He almost immediately placed the ablest of all the French economists, Turgot, in the most important of the government offices, that of controller general. Turgot was an experienced government official as well as a scholar.

[1] See above, p. 393.

The first and most natural measure was economy, for only in that way could the government be saved from bankruptcy and the burden of taxation be lightened. Turgot felt that the

A LETTER OF MARIE ANTOINETTE

A page of a letter written July 12, 1770, to her mother, Maria Theresa. The handwriting, mistakes in spelling, and general carelessness show what an undeveloped girl she was when she came to the gay court of Versailles. She says in the letter that she has no other time to write than while she is dressing and cannot reply exactly to the last letter because she has burned it. Now she must stop in order to dress and go to mass in the king's chapel. She adds in postscript that she is sending a list of the wedding presents, thinking that that will entertain (*amuser*) her mother

vast amount spent in maintaining the luxury of the royal court at Versailles should be reduced. The establishments of the king, the queen, and the princes of the blood royal cost the State annually about twelve million dollars. Then the French king had long been accustomed to grant "pensions" in a reckless manner to his favorites, and this required nearly twelve million dollars more.

Any attempt, however, to reduce this amount would arouse the immediate opposition of the courtiers, and it was the courtiers who really governed France. They had every opportunity to influence the king's mind against a man whose economies they disliked. They were constantly about the monarch from the moment when he awoke in the morning until he went to bed at night; therefore they had an obvious advantage over Turgot, who saw him only in business hours.

An Italian economist, when he heard of Turgot's appointment, wrote to a friend in France as follows: "So Turgot is controller general! He will not remain in office long enough to carry out his plans. He will punish some scoundrels; he will bluster about and lose his temper; he will be anxious to do good, but will run against obstacles and rogues at every turn. Public credit will fall; he will be detested; it will be said that he is not fitted for his task. Enthusiasm will cool; he will retire or be sent off, and we shall have a new proof of the mistake of filling a position like his in a monarchy like yours with an upright man and a philosopher."

The Italian could not have made a more accurate statement of the case had he waited until after the dismissal of Turgot, which took place in May, 1776, much to the satisfaction of the court. Although the privileged classes so stoutly opposed Turgot's reforms that he did not succeed in abolishing the abuses himself,[1] he did a great deal to forward their destruction not many years after his retirement.

Necker, who after a brief interval succeeded Turgot, contributed to the progress of the coming revolution in two ways. He borrowed vast sums of money in order to carry on the war which France, as the ally of the United States, had undertaken against England. This greatly embarrassed the treasury later and helped to produce the financial crisis which was the imme-

---

[1] Turgot succeeeded in inducing the king to abolish the guilds and the forced labor on the roads, but the decrees were revoked after Turgot's dismissal.

diate cause of the Revolution. Secondly, he gave the nation its first opportunity of learning what was done with the public funds, by presenting to the king (February, 1781) a *report* on the financial condition of the kingdom; this was publicly printed and eagerly read. There the people could see for the first time how much the *taille* and the salt tax actually took from them, and how much the king spent on himself and his favorites.

Necker was soon followed by Calonne, who may be said to have precipitated the French Revolution. He was very popular at first with king and courtiers, for he spent the public funds far more recklessly than his predecessors. But, naturally, he soon found himself in a position where he could obtain no more money. The *parlements* would consent to no more loans in a period of peace, and the taxes were as high as it was deemed possible to make them. At last Calonne, finding himself desperately put to it, informed the astonished king (August, 1786) that the State was on the verge of bankruptcy and that in order to save it a radical reformation of the whole public order was necessary. This report of Calonne's may be taken as the beginning of the French Revolution, for it was the first of the series of events that led to the calling of a representative assembly which abolished the old régime and gave France a written constitution.

Meeting of the Estates General in 1789

It was necessary, in order to avoid ruin, Calonne claimed, "to reform everything vicious in the State." He proposed, therefore, to reduce the *taille*, reform the salt tax, do away with the interior customs lines, correct the abuses of the guilds, etc. But the chief reform, and by far the most difficult one, was to force the privileged classes to surrender their important exemptions from taxation. He hoped, however, that if certain concessions were made to them they might be brought to consent to a land tax to be paid by all alike. So he proposed to the king that he should summon an assembly of persons prominent in Church and State, called *Notables,* to ratify certain changes which would increase the prosperity of the country and give the treasury money enough to meet the necessary expenses.

The summoning of the Notables in 1786 was really a revolution in itself. It was a confession on the part of the king that he found himself in a predicament from which he could not escape without the aid of his people. The Notables whom he selected—bishops, archbishops, dukes, judges, high government officials—were practically all members of the privileged classes; but they still represented the nation, after a fashion, as distinguished from the king's immediate circle of courtiers. At any rate it proved an easy step from calling the Notables to summoning the ancient Estates General, and that, in its turn, speedily became a modern representative body.

In his opening address Calonne gave the Notables an idea of the sad financial condition of the country. The government was running behind some forty million dollars a year. He could not continue to borrow, and economy, however strict, would not suffice to cover the deficit. "What, then," he asked, "remains to fill this frightful void and enable us to raise the revenue to the desired level? *The Abuses!* Yes, gentlemen, the abuses offer a source of wealth which the State should appropriate, and which should serve to reëstablish order in the finances. . . . The abuses which must now be destroyed for the welfare of the people are the most important and the best guarded of all, the very ones which have the deepest roots and the most spreading branches. For example, those which weigh on the laboring classes, the privileges, exceptions to the law which should be common to all, and many an unjust exemption which can only relieve certain taxpayers by embittering the condition of others; the general want of uniformity in the assessment of the taxes and the enormous difference which exists between the contributions of different provinces and of the subjects of the same sovereign";—all these evils, which public-spirited citizens had long deprecated, Calonne proposed to do away with forthwith.

The Notables, however, had no confidence in Calonne, and refused to ratify his program of reform. The king then dismissed him and soon sent them home, too (May, 1787). Louis XVI then attempted to carry through some of the more pressing financial reforms in the usual way by sending them to the *parlements* to be registered.

The *parlement* of Paris resolved, as usual, to make the king's ministry trouble and gain popularity for itself. This time it resorted to a truly extraordinary measure. It not only refused to register two new taxes which the king desired but asserted that *"Only the nation assembled in the Estates General can give the consent necessary to the establishment of a permanent tax."* "Only the nation," the *parlement* continued, "after it has learned the true state of the finances can destroy the great abuses and open up important resources." This declaration was followed in a few days by the humble request that the king assemble the Estates General of his kingdom. The *parlements* not only refused to register taxes but continued during the following months to do everything that they could to embarrass the king's ministers. There seemed no other resort except to call the representatives of the people together. The Estates General were accordingly summoned to meet on May 1, 1789.

It was now discovered that no one knew much about this body of which every one was talking, for it had not met since 1614. The king accordingly issued a general invitation to scholars to find out all they could about the customs observed in the former meetings of the Estates. The public naturally became very much interested in a matter which touched them so closely, and there were plenty of readers for the pamphlets which now began to appear in great numbers. The old Estates General had been organized in a way appropriate enough to the feudal conditions under which they originated.[1] All three of the estates of the realm—clergy, nobility, and third estate— were accustomed to send an *equal* number of representatives, who were expected to consider not the interests of the nation but the special interests of the particular social class to which they respectively belonged. Accordingly, the deputies of the

[1] See above, p. 250.

three estates did not sit together, or vote as a single body. The members of each group first came to an agreement among themselves, and then a single vote was cast for the whole order.

Conditions had so changed that this system seemed preposterous to the thoughtful Frenchman in 1788. If the Estates should be convoked according to the ancient forms, the two privileged classes would be entitled to twice the number of representatives allotted to the nation at large. What was much worse, it seemed impossible that any important reforms could be adopted in an assembly where those who had every selfish reason for opposing the most necessary changes were given two votes out of three. Necker, whom the king had recalled in the hope that he might succeed in adjusting the finances, agreed that the third estate might have as many deputies as both the other orders put together, namely six hundred, but he would not consent to having the three orders sit and vote together like a modern representative body.

Besides the great question as to whether the deputies should vote *by head* or *by order,* the pamphlets discussed what reforms the Estates should undertake. We have, however, a still more interesting and important expression of public opinion in France at this time, in the *cahiers,* or lists of grievances and suggestions for reform which, in pursuance of an old custom, the king asked the nation to prepare. Each village and town throughout France had an opportunity to tell quite frankly exactly what it suffered from the existing system, and what reforms it wished that the Estates General might bring about. These *cahiers* were the "last will and testament" of the old régime, and they constitute a unique historical document, of unparalleled completeness and authenticity. No one can read the *cahiers* without seeing that the whole nation was ready for the great transformation which within a year was to destroy a great part of the social and political system under which the French had lived for centuries.

Almost all the *cahiers* agreed that the prevailing disorder and the vast and ill-defined powers of the king and his ministers were perhaps the fundamental evils. One of the *cahiers* says: "Since arbitrary power has been the source of all the evils which afflict the state, our first desire is the establishment of a really national constitution, which shall define the rights of all and provide the laws to maintain them." No one dreamed at this time of displacing the king or of taking the government out of his hands. The people only wished to change an absolute monarchy into a limited, or constitutional, one. All that was necessary was that the things which the government might *not* do should be solemnly and irrevocably determined and put upon record, and that the Estates General should meet periodically to grant the taxes, give the king advice in national crises, and expostulate, if necessary, against any violations of the proposed charter of liberties.

With these ideas in mind, the Estates assembled in Versailles and held their first session on May 5, 1789. The king had ordered the deputies to wear the same costumes that had been worn at the last meeting of the Estates in 1614; but no royal edict could call back the spirit of earlier centuries. In spite of the king's commands the representatives of the third estate refused to organize themselves in the old way as a separate order. They sent invitation after invitation to the deputies of the clergy and nobility, requesting them to join the people's representatives and deliberate in common on the great interests of the nation. Some of the more liberal of the nobles— Lafayette, for example—and a large minority of the clergy wished to meet with the deputies of the third estate. But they were outvoted, and the deputies of the third estate, losing patience, finally declared themselves, on June 17, a "National Assembly." They argued that, since they represented at least ninety-six per cent of the nation, the deputies of the privileged orders might be neglected altogether. This usurpation of power on the part of the third estate transformed the old feudal Estates, voting by orders, into the first modern national representative assembly on the continent of Europe.

Under the influence of his courtiers the king tried to restore the old system by arranging a solemn joint session of the three orders, at which he presided in person. He presented a long

THE TENNIS COURT OATH

This picture, from a painting by a famous artist of the Revolutionary period, shows the excited crowd of deputies in the barnlike court, in the act of swearing that they will not separate until they shall have prepared a constitution for France. Notice the members of the clergy fraternizing with the representatives of the third estate program of excellent reforms, and then bade the Estates sit apart, according to the old custom. But it was like bidding water to run up hill. Three days before, when the commons had found themselves excluded from their regular place of meeting on account of the preparations for the royal session, they had betaken themselves to a neighboring building called the "Tennis Court." Here, on June 20, they took the famous "Tennis Court" oath, "to come together wherever circumstances may dictate, until the constitution of the kingdom shall be established."

Consequently, when the king finished his address and commanded the three orders to disperse immediately in order to resume their separate sessions, most of the bishops, some of the parish priests, and a great part of the nobility obeyed; the rest sat still, uncertain what they should do. When the master of ceremonies ordered them to comply with the king's commands, Mirabeau, the most distinguished statesman among the deputies, told him bluntly that they would not leave their places except at the point of the bayonet. The weak king almost immediately gave in and a few days later ordered all the deputies of the privileged orders who had not already done so to join the commons.

First Reforms of the National Assembly

The National Assembly now began in earnest the great task of preparing a constitution and regenerating France. It was soon interrupted, however, by events at Paris. The king had been advised by those about him to gather together the Swiss and German troops who formed the royal guard, so that if he decided to send the insolent deputies home he would be able to put down any disorder which might result. He was also induced to dismiss Necker, who enjoyed a popularity that he had done little to merit. When the people of Paris saw the troops gathering and when they heard of the dismissal of Necker, there was general excitement and some disorder.

On July 14 crowds of people assembled, determined to procure arms to protect themselves and mayhap to perform some daring "deed of patriotism." One of the mobs, led by the old Parisian guards, turned to the ancient fortress of the Bastille, on the parapets of which guns had been mounted which made the inhabitants of that part of the city very nervous. The castle had long had a bad reputation as a place of confinement for prisoners of State and for those imprisoned by *lettres de cachet*. When the mob demanded admission, it was naturally denied them, and they were fired upon and nearly a hundred were killed. After a brief attack the place was surrendered. The mob rushed into the gloomy pile, slew the garrison and paraded the commander's head about the streets. They found only seven prisoners, but one poor fellow had lost his wits and another had no idea why he had been kept there for years. The captives were freed amidst great enthusiasm, and the people soon set to work to demolish the walls.

The capture of the Bastille was an example of the cruelty of the Paris mob, very ugly in its details; but it was immediately exalted into a deed of brave patriotism. Its anniversary is still celebrated as the great national holiday of France. The rising of "the people" to protect themselves against the machinations of the king's associates who wished to block reform, and the successful attack on a monument of ancient tyranny appeared to be the opening of a new era of freedom. The disorders of these July days led to the formation of the "National Guard." This was made up of volunteers from among the more prosperous citizens, who organized themselves to maintain order and so took from the king every excuse for calling in the regular troops for that purpose. Lafayette was put in command of this body.

The government of Paris was organized, and a mayor, chosen from among the members of the National Assembly, was put at the head of the new *Commune*, as the municipal government was called. The other cities of France also began with one accord, after the dismissal of Necker and the fall of the Bastille, to promote the Revolution by displacing or supplementing their old royal or aristocratic governments by committees of their citizens. These improvised communes, or city governments, established national guards, as Paris had done, and thus maintained order. The Commune of Paris later played a very important rôle in the Reign of Terror and in 1871.

About the first of August news began to reach the National Assembly of the serious disorders in the provinces. In some cases the peasants burned the country houses of the nobles

THE TAKING OF THE BASTILLE

This picture of the capture of the Bastille, by a contemporary artist, shows the mob assisting the attacking party, who have passed the outer works by the drawbridge on the right and are already crowding into the stronghold itself by the inner drawbridge

so as to destroy the registers enumerating the feudal dues. This led to the first important reforms of the Assembly. A momentous resolution abolishing the survivals of serfdom and other institutions of feudalism was passed in a night session (August 4-5) amid great excitement, the representatives of the privileged orders vying with each other in surrendering the ancient privileges they could no longer keep. The exclusive right of the nobility to hunt and to maintain pigeon houses was abolished, and the peasant was permitted to kill game which he found on his land. The tithes of the Church were done away with. Exemptions from the payment of taxes were abolished forever. It was decreed that "taxes shall be collected from all citizens and from all property in the same manner and in the same form," and that "all citizens, without distinction of birth, are eligible to any office or dignity." Moreover, "all the peculiar privileges, pecuniary or otherwise, of the provinces, principalities, districts, cantons, cities and communes, are once for all abolished and are absorbed into the law common to all Frenchmen."

This decree established the equality and uniformity for which the French people had sighed so long. The injustice of the former system of taxation could never be reintroduced. All France was to have the same laws, and its citizens were henceforth to be treated in the same way by the State, whether they lived in Brittany or Dauphiny. The Assembly soon went a step farther in consolidating and unifying France. It wiped out the old provinces altogether, by dividing the whole country into districts of convenient size, called *departments*. These were much more numerous than the ancient divisions, and were named after rivers and mountains. This obliterated from the map all reminiscences of the feudal disunion.

Many of the *cahiers* had suggested that the Estates should draw up a clear statement of the rights of the individual citizen. The National Assembly consequently determined to prepare such a declaration in order to reassure the people and to form a basis for the new constitution.

This Declaration (completed August 26) is one of the most notable documents in the history of Europe. It not only aroused general enthusiasm when it was first published, but it appeared over and over again, in a modified form, in the succeeding French constitutions down to 1848, and has been the model for similar declarations in many of the other continental states. It was a dignified repudiation of the abuses described in the preceding chapter. Behind each article there was some crying evil of long standing against which the people wished to be forever protected.

The Declaration sets forth that "Men are born and remain equal in rights. Social distinctions can only be founded upon the general good." "Law is the expression of the general will. Every citizen has a right to participate, personally or through his representative, in its formation. It must be the same for all." "No person shall be accused, arrested, or imprisoned except in the cases and according to the forms prescribed by law." "No one shall be disquieted on account of his opinions, including his religious views, provided that their manifestation does not disturb the public order established by law." "The free communication of ideas and opinions is one of the most precious of the rights of man. Every citizen may, accordingly, speak, write, and print with freedom, being responsible, however, for such abuses of this freedom as shall be defined by law." "All citizens have a right to decide, either personally or by their representative, as to the necessity of the public contribution, to grant this freely, to know to what uses it is put, and to fix the proportion, the mode of assessment and of collection, and the duration of the taxes." "Society has the right to require of every public agent an account of his administration." Well might the Assembly claim, in its address to the people, that "the rights of man had been misconceived and insulted for centuries," and boast that they were "reëstablished for all humanity in this declaration, which shall serve as an everlasting war cry against oppressors."

The National Assembly in Paris

The king hesitated to ratify the Declaration of the Rights of Man, and about the first of October rumors became current that, under the influence of the courtiers, he was calling together troops and preparing for another attempt to put an end to the Revolution, similar to that which the attack on the Bastille had frustrated. It was said that the new national colors—red, white, and blue—had been trampled under foot at a banquet at Versailles. These things, along with the scarcity of food due to the poor crops of the year, aroused the excitable Paris populace.

On October 5 several thousand women and a number of armed men marched out to Versailles to ask bread of the king, in whom they had great confidence personally, however suspicious they might be of his friends and advisers. Lafayette marched after the mob with the National Guard to keep order, but did not prevent some of the rabble from invading the king's palace the next morning and nearly murdering the queen, who had become very unpopular. She was believed to be still an Austrian at heart and to be in league with the counter-revolutionary party.

The mob declared that the king must accompany them to Paris, and he was obliged to consent. Far from being disloyal,

MARCH OF THE WOMEN TO VERSAILLES

they assumed that the presence of the royal family would insure plenty and prosperity. So they gayly escorted the "baker and the baker's wife and the baker's boy," as they jocularly termed the king and queen and the little dauphin, to the Palace of the Tuileries, where the king took up his residence, practically a prisoner, as it proved. The National Assembly soon followed him and resumed its sittings in a riding school near the Tuileries.

This transfer of the king and the Assembly to the capital was the first great misfortune of the Revolution. At a serious crisis the government was placed at the mercy of the leaders of the disorderly elements of Paris. We shall see how the municipal council of Paris finally usurped the powers of the national government.

As we have seen, the Church in France was very rich and retained many of its medieval prerogatives and privileges. Its higher officials, the bishops and abbots, received very large revenues and often a single prelate held a number of rich benefices, the duties of which he utterly neglected. The parish priests, on the other hand, who really performed the manifold and important functions of the Church, were scarcely able to live on their incomes. This unjust apportionment of the vast revenue of the Church naturally suggested the idea that, if the State confiscated the ecclesiastical possessions, it could see that those who did the work were properly paid for it, and might, at the same time, secure a handsome sum which would help the government out of its financial troubles. Those who sympathized with Voltaire's views were naturally delighted to see their old enemy deprived of its independence and made subservient to the State, and even many good Catholics could not but hope that the new system would be an improvement upon the old.

The tithes had been abolished in August along with the feudal dues. That deprived the Church of perhaps thirty million dollars a year. On November 2, 1789, a decree was passed providing that "All the ecclesiastical possessions are at the disposal of the nation on condition that it provides properly for the expenses of maintaining religious services, for the support of those who conduct them and for the succor of the poor." [1] This decree deprived the bishops and priests of their benefices and made them dependent on salaries paid by the State. The monks, monasteries, and convents, too, lost their property.

The National Assembly resolved to issue a paper currency for which the newly acquired lands should serve as security. Of these *assignats,* as this paper money was called, about forty billions of francs were issued in the next seven years. But

[1] This property never reverted to the Church again. Consequently even cathedrals and churches remained national property.

since so much land was thrown on the market, they were worth less and less as time went on, and ultimately a great part of them was repudiated.

The Assembly set to work completely to reorganize the Church. The anxiety for complete uniformity shows itself in the reckless way that it dealt with this most venerable institution of France, the customs of which were hallowed by age and religious veneration. The one hundred and thirty-four ancient bishoprics, some of which dated back to the

ASSIGNAT

This piece of paper money, which resembled the bank note of to-day, was of the face value of 10 *livres;* but before the Revolution was over it was almost worthless. So many were printed, however, that one can still find examples in old curiosity shops

Roman Empire, were replaced by the eighty-three new departments into which France had already been divided.[1] Each of these became the diocese of a bishop, who was looked upon as an officer of the State and was to be elected by the people. The priests, too, were to be chosen by the people, and their salaries were much increased, so that even in the smallest villages they received over twice the minimum amount paid under the old régime.

This Civil Constitution of the Clergy was the first serious mistake on the part of the National Assembly. While the

[1] See above, p. 471.

half-feudalized Church had sadly needed reform, the worst abuses might have been remedied without shocking and alienating thousands of those who had hitherto enthusiastically applauded the great reforms which the Assembly had effected. Louis XVI gave his assent to the changes, but with the feeling that he might be losing his soul by so doing. From that time on, he became at heart an enemy of the Revolution.

The discontent with the new system on the part of the clergy led to another serious error on the part of the Assembly. It required the clergy to take an oath to be faithful to the law and "to maintain with all their might the constitution decreed by the Assembly." Only six of the bishops consented to this and but a third of the lower clergy, although they were much better off under the new system. Forty-six thousand parish priests refused to sacrifice their religious scruples, and before long the pope forbade them to take the required oath to the constitution. As time went on, the "nonjuring" clergy were dealt with more and more harshly by the government, and the way was prepared for the horrors of the Reign of Terror.

Revolutionary France and the European Powers

We have now studied the progress and nature of the revolution which destroyed the old régime and created modern France. Through it the unjust privileges, the perplexing irregularities, and the local differences were abolished, and the people admitted to a share in the government. This vast reform had been accomplished without serious disturbance and, with the exception of some of the changes in the Church, it had been welcomed with enthusiasm by the French nation.

This permanent, peaceful revolution, or reformation, was followed by a second revolution of unprecedented violence, which for a time destroyed the French monarchy. It also introduced a series of further changes, many of which were absurd and unnecessary and could not endure since they were approved by only a few fanatical leaders. France, moreover, became involved in a war with most of the powers of western

Pl. xxvi. The Opening of the Estates General.

DANTON

LOUIS XVI

MAXIMILIEN ROBESPIERRE

PL. XXVII

Europe. The weakness of her government which permitted the forces of disorder and fanaticism to prevail, combined with the imminent danger of an invasion by the united powers of Europe, produced the Reign of Terror.

While practically the whole of the nation heartily rejoiced in the earlier reforms introduced by the National Assembly and celebrated the general satisfaction and harmony by a great national festival held at Paris on the first anniversary of the fall of the Bastille, some of the higher nobility refused to remain in France. The king's youngest brother, the count of Artois, set the example by leaving the country. He was followed by others who were terrified or disgusted by the burning of their country houses, the loss of their privileges, and the unwise abolition of hereditary nobility by the National Assembly in June, 1790. Before long these *emigrant nobles* (*émigrés*), among whom were many military officers, organized a little army across the Rhine, and the count of Artois began to plan an invasion of France. He was ready to ally himself with Austria, Prussia, or any other foreign government which he could induce to help undo the Revolution and give back to the French king his former absolute power and to the nobles their old privileges.

The threats and insolence of the emigrant nobles and their shameful negotiations with foreign powers discredited the members of their class who still remained in France. The people suspected that the plans of the runaways met with the secret approval of the king, and more especially of the queen, whose brother was now emperor and ruler of the Austrian dominions. This, added to the opposition of the nonjuring clergy, produced a bitter hostility between the so-called "patriots" and those who, on the other hand, were supposed to be secretly hoping for a counter revolution which would reëstablish the old régime.

The worst fears of the people appeared to be justified by the secret flight of the royal family from Paris, in June, 1791. Ever since the king had reluctantly signed the Civil Constitution of the Clergy, flight had seemed to him his only resource.

[477]

There was a body of French troops on the northeastern boundary; if he could escape from Paris and join them he hoped that, aided by a demonstration on the part of the queen's brother, Emperor Leopold II, he might march back and check the further progress of the revolutionary movement with which he could no longer sympathize. He and the queen were, however, arrested on the way, at Varennes, and speedily brought back to Paris.

The desertion of the king appears to have terrified rather than angered the nation. The grief of the people at the thought of losing, and their joy at regaining, a poor weak ruler like Louis XVI clearly shows that France was still profoundly royalist in its sympathies. The National Assembly pretended that the king had not fled, but that he had been carried off. This gratified France at large; still in Paris there were some who advocated the deposition of the king, and for the first time a *republican* party appeared, though it was still small.

CARICATURE: LOUIS XVI
AS CONSTITUTIONAL
MONARCH [1]

The National Assembly at last put the finishing touches to the new constitution upon which it had been working for two years, and the king readily swore to observe it faithfully. All the discord and suspicion of the past months were to be forgotten. The National Assembly had completed its appointed task, perhaps the greatest that a single body of men ever undertook. It had made France over and had given her an elaborate constitution. It was now ready to give way to the regular Legislative Assembly provided for in the constitution. This held its first session October 1, 1791.

[1] The formerly despotic king is represented as safely caged by the National Assembly. When asked by Marie Antoinette's brother, the Emperor Leopold, what he is doing, Louis XVI replies, "I am signing my name."

In spite of the great achievement of the National Assembly it left France in a critical situation. Besides the emigrant nobles abroad, there were the nonjuring clergy at home and a king who was secretly corresponding with foreign powers with the hope of securing their aid. When the news of the arrest of the king and queen at Varennes reached the ears of Marie Antoinette's brother Leopold, he declared that the violent arrest of the king sealed with unlawfulness all that had been done in France and "compromised directly the honor of all the sovereigns and the security of every government." He therefore proposed to the rulers of Russia, England, Prussia, Spain, Naples, and Sardinia that they should come to some understanding among themselves as to how they might "reëstablish the liberty and honor of the most Christian king and his family, and place a check upon the dangerous excesses of the French Revolution, the fatal example of which it behooves every government to repress."

On August 27 Leopold had issued, in conjunction with the king of Prussia, the famous Declaration of Pillnitz. In this the two sovereigns state that, in accordance with the wishes of the king's brothers (the leaders of the emigrant nobles), they are ready to join the other European rulers in an attempt to place the king of France in a position to establish a form of government "that shall be once more in harmony with the rights of sovereigns and shall promote the welfare of the French nation." In the meantime they promised to prepare their troops for active service.

The Declaration was little more than an empty threat; but it seemed to the French people a sufficient proof that the monarchs were ready to help the seditious French nobles to reëstablish the old régime against the wishes of the nation and at a cost of infinite bloodshed. The idea of foreign rulers intermeddling with their internal affairs would in itself have been intolerable to a proud people like the French, even if the permanence of the new reforms had not been endangered. Had it been the object of the allied monarchs to hasten instead of to prevent the deposition of Louis XVI, they could hardly have chosen a more efficient means than the Declaration of Pillnitz.

The political excitement and the enthusiasm for the Revolution were kept up by the newspapers which had been established, especially in Paris, since the meeting of the Estates General. The people did not need longer to rely upon an occasional pamphlet, as was the case before 1789. Many journals of the most divergent kinds and representing the most diverse opinions were published. Some were no more than a periodical editorial written by one man; for example, the notorious *L'ami du Peuple,* by the insane Marat. Others, like the famous *Moniteur,* were much like our papers of to-day and contained news, reports of the debates in the Assembly and announcements of theaters. Some of the papers were illustrated, and the representations of contemporaneous events, especially the numerous caricatures, are highly diverting.

Of the various political clubs, by far the most famous was that of the "Jacobins." When the Assembly moved into Paris, some of the representatives of the third estate rented a large room in the monastery of the Jacobin monks, not far from the building where the National Assembly itself met. The aim of this society was to discuss questions which were about to come before the National Assembly. The club decided beforehand what should be the policy of its members and how they should vote; and in this way they successfully combined to counteract the schemes of the aristocratic party in the Assembly. The club rapidly grew and soon admitted some who were not deputies to its sessions. In October, 1791, it decided to permit the public to attend its discussions.

Gradually similar societies were formed in the provinces.[1] These affiliated themselves with the "mother" society at Paris and kept in constant communication with it. In this way the Jacobins of Paris stimulated and controlled public opinion throughout France, and kept the opponents of the old régime alert. When the Legislative Assembly met, the Jacobins had

[1] By June, 1791, there were four hundred and six of these affiliated clubs.

not as yet become republicans, but they believed that the king should have hardly more power than the president of a republic.

The growing discord in the nation was increased by the severe edicts that the Legislative Assembly directed against the emigrant nobles and the nonjuring clergy. "The Frenchmen assembled on the frontier" were declared under suspicion of conspiring against their country. If they did not return to France by January 1, 1792, they were to be regarded as convicted traitors, to be punished, if caught, with death; their property was to be confiscated.

The harsh treatment of the emigrant nobles was perhaps justified by their desertion and treasonable intrigues; but the conduct of the Assembly toward the clergy was both unstatesmanlike and iniquitous. Those who had refused to take the oath to support the Civil Constitution of the Clergy were commanded to do so within a week on penalty of losing their income from the State and being watched as suspects. As this failed to bring the clergy to terms, the Assembly later (May, 1792) ordered the deportation from the country of those who steadily persisted in their refusal. In this way the Assembly aroused the active hostility of a great part of the most conscientious among the lower clergy, who had loyally supported the commons in their fight against the privileged orders. It also lost the confidence of the great mass of faithful Catholics,—merchants, artisans, and peasants,—who had gladly accepted the abolition of the old abuses, but who would not consent to desert religious leaders.

By far the most important act of the Legislative Assembly during the one year of its existence was its starting a war between France and Austria. It little dreamed that this was the beginning of wars between revolutionary France and the rest of western Europe which were to last, with slight interruptions, for over twenty years.

To many of the leaders in the Assembly it seemed that the existing conditions were intolerable. The emigrant nobles were forming little armies on the boundaries of France and had, as we have seen, induced Austria and Prussia to consider interfering in French affairs. The Assembly suspected that Louis was negotiating with foreign rulers and would be glad to have them intervene and reëstablish him in his old despotic power. The deputies argued, therefore, that a war against the hated Austria would unite the sympathies of the nation and force the king to show his true character; for he would be obliged either to become the nation's leader or show himself the traitor they suspected him to be.

The First French Republic

It was with a heavy heart that the king, urged on by the clamors of the Assembly, declared war upon Austria in April, 1792. The unpopularity of the king only increased, however. He refused to ratify certain popular measures of the Assembly and dismissed the ministers who had been forced upon him by the Assembly. In June a mob of Parisians invaded the Palace of the Tuileries, and the king might have been killed had he not consented to don the "cap of liberty," the badge of the "citizen patriots."

When France declared war, Prussia immediately allied itself with Austria. Both powers collected their forces and, to the great joy of the emigrant nobles, who joined them, prepared to march upon France. The early attempts of the French to get a footing in the Austrian Netherlands were not successful, and the troops and people accused the nobles, who were in command of the French troops, of treason. As the allies approached the boundaries it became clearer and clearer that the king was utterly incapable of defending France, and the Assembly began to consider the question of deposing him. The Duke of Brunswick, who was at the head of the Prussian forces, took the very worst means of helping the king, by issuing a manifesto in which he threatened utterly to destroy Paris should the king suffer any harm.

Angered by this declaration and aroused by the danger, the populace of Paris again invaded the Tuileries, August 10, 1792, and the king was obliged to take refuge in the building in which the Assembly was in session. Those who instigated the attack were men who had set their heart upon doing away with the king altogether and establishing a republic. A group of them had taken possession of the city hall, pushed the old members of the municipal council off their seats, and taken the government in their own hands. In this way the members of the Paris Commune became the leaders in the new revolution which established the first French republic.

The Assembly agreed with the Commune in desiring a republic. If, as was proposed, France was henceforth to do without a king, it was obviously necessary that the monarchical constitution so recently completed should be replaced by a republican one. Consequently, the Assembly arranged that the people should elect delegates to a constitutional *Convention,* which should draw up a new system of government. The Convention met on September 21, and its first act was to abolish the ancient monarchy and proclaim France a republic. It seemed to the enthusiasts of the time that a new era of liberty had dawned, now that the long oppression by "despots" was ended forever. The twenty-second day of September, 1792, was reckoned as the first day of the Year One of French liberty.[1]

Meanwhile the usurping Paris Commune had taken matters into its own hands and had brought discredit upon the cause of liberty by one of the most atrocious acts in history. On the pretext that Paris was full of traitors, who sympathized with the Austrians and the emigrant nobles, they had filled the prisons with some three thousand citizens. On September 2 and 3 hundreds of these were executed with scarcely a pretense of a trial. The members of the Commune who perpetrated this deed probably hoped to terrify those who might still dream of returning to the old system of government.

[1] A committee of the Convention was appointed to draw up a new republican calendar. The year was divided into twelve months of thirty days each. The five days preceding September 22, at the end of the year, were holidays. Each month was divided into three *decades,* and each "tenth day" (*décadi*) was a holiday. The days were no longer dedicated to saints, but to agricultural implements, vegetables, domestic animals, etc.

Late in August the Prussians crossed the French boundary and on September 2 took the fortress of Verdun. It now seemed as if there was nothing to prevent their marching upon Paris. The French general, Dumouriez, blocked their advance, however, and without a pitched battle caused the enemy to retreat.

LOUIS XVI ON THE ROOF
OF HIS PRISON

The prison to which the royal family was taken on August 13 was known as the Temple, because it had been part of the building of the Knights Templar in Paris. It was a gloomy tower with massive walls.

It was torn down in 1811

Notwithstanding the fears of the French, the king of Prussia had but little interest in the war; the Austrian troops were lagging far behind, and both powers were far more absorbed in a second partition of Poland,[1] which was imminent, than in the fate of the French king. The French now invaded Germany and took several important towns on the Rhine, including Mainz, which gladly opened its gates to them. They also occupied the Austrian Netherlands and Savoy.

Meanwhile the new Convention was puzzled to determine what would best be done with the king. A considerable party felt that he was guilty of treason in secretly encouraging the foreign powers to come to his aid. He was therefore brought to trial, and when it came to a final vote, he was, by a small majority, condemned to death. He mounted the scaffold on January 21, 1793, with the fortitude of a martyr. Nevertheless, one cannot but feel that through his earlier weakness and indecision he brought untold misery upon

[1] See above, p. 398.

his own kingdom and upon Europe at large. The French people had not dreamed of a republic until his absolute incompetence forced them, in self-defense, to abolish the monarchy in the hope of securing a more efficient government.

The exultation of the Convention over the conquests which their armies were making encouraged them to offer the assistance of the new republic to any country that wished to establish its freedom by throwing off the yoke of monarchy. They even proposed a republic to the English people. One of the French ministers declared, "We will hurl thither fifty thousand caps of liberty, we will plant there the sacred tree of liberty." February 1, 1793, France greatly added to her embarrassments by declaring war on Great Britain, a power which proved her most persistent and inveterate enemy.

The war now began to go against the French. The allies had hitherto been suspicious of one another and fearful lest Russia should take advantage of their preoccupation with France to seize more than her share of Poland. They now came to an agreement.

The adjustment of the differences between the allies gave a wholly new aspect to the war with France. When in March, 1793, Spain and the Holy Roman Empire joined the coalition, France was at war with all her neighbors. The Austrians defeated Dumouriez at Neerwinden and drove the French out of the Netherlands. Thereupon Dumouriez, disgusted by the failure of the Convention to support him and by their execution of the king, deserted to the enemy with a few hundred soldiers who consented to follow him.

The Reign of Terror

The loss of the Netherlands and the treason of their best general made a deep impression upon the members of the Convention. If the new French republic was to defend itself against the "tyrants" without and its many enemies within, it could not wait for the Convention to draw up an elaborate, permanent constitution. An efficient, if temporary, government must be devised immediately to maintain the loyalty of the nation to the republic and to raise and equip armies and direct their commanders. The Convention accordingly (April, 1793), put the government into the hands of a small committee, consisting originally of nine, later of twelve, of its members. This famous Committee of Public Safety was given practically unlimited powers. "We must," one of the leaders exclaimed, "establish the despotism of liberty in order to crush the despotism of kings."

Within the Convention itself there were two groups of active men who came into bitter conflict over the policy to be pursued. There was, first, the party of the Girondists, so called because their leaders came from the department of Gironde, in which the great city of Bordeaux lay. They were moderate republicans and counted among their numbers some speakers of remarkable eloquence. The Girondists had enjoyed the control of the Legislative Assembly in 1792 and had been active in bringing on the war with Austria and Prussia. They hoped in that way to complete the Revolution by exposing the bad faith of the king and his sympathy with the emigrant nobles. They were not, however, men of sufficient decision to direct affairs in the terrible difficulties in which France found herself after the execution of the king. They consequently lost their influence, and a new party, called the Mountain from the high seats that they occupied in the Convention, gained the ascendency.

This was composed of the most vigorous and uncompromising republicans. They believed that the French people had been depraved by the slavery to which their kings had subjected them. Everything, they argued, which suggested the former rule of kings must be wiped out. A new France should be created, in which liberty, equality, and fraternity should take the place of the tyranny of princes, the insolence of nobles, and the exactions of the priests. The leaders of the Mountain held that the mass of the people were by nature good and upright, but that there were a number of adherents of the old system who would, if they could, undo the great work of the Revolution and lead the people back to slavery, under the king. All who were suspected by the Mountain of having the least sympathy with the nobles or persecuted priests were branded as counter-revolutionary. The Mountain was willing to resort to any measures, however shocking, to rid the nation of those suspected of counter-revolutionary tendencies, and its leaders relied upon the populace of Paris, which had been disappointed that "liberty" had not bettered the hard conditions of life as it had hoped, to aid them in reaching their ends.

The Girondists, on the other hand, abhorred the furious Paris mob and the cruel fanatics who composed the Commune of the capital. They argued that Paris was not France, and that it had no right to assume a despotic rule over the nation. They proposed that the Commune should be dissolved and that the Convention should remove to another town where they would not be subject to the intimidation of the Paris mob. The Mountain thereupon accused the Girondists of an attempt to break up the republic, "one and indivisible," by questioning the supremacy of Paris and the duty of the provinces to follow the lead of the capital. The mob, thus encouraged, rose against the Girondists. On June 2, 1793, it surrounded the meeting place of the Convention, and deputies of the Commune demanded the expulsion from the Convention of the Girondist leaders, who were placed under arrest.

The conduct of the Mountain and its ally, the Paris Commune, now began to arouse opposition in various parts of France, and the country was threatened with civil war at a time when it was absolutely necessary that all Frenchmen should combine in the loyal defense of their country against the invaders who were again approaching its boundaries. The first and most serious opposition came from the peasants of Brittany, especially in the department of La Vendée. There the people still loved the monarchy and their priests and even the nobles; they refused to send their sons to fight for a republic which had killed their king and was persecuting the clergymen who declined to take an oath which their consciences forbade. The Vendean royalists defeated several corps of the

National Guard which the Convention sent against them, and it was not until autumn that the distinguished general Kléber was able to put down the insurrection.

The great cities of Marseille and Bordeaux were indignant at the treatment to which the Girondist deputies were subjected in Paris, and organized a revolt against the Convention. In the manufacturing city of Lyon the merchants hated the Jacobins and their republic, since the demand for silk and other luxuries produced at Lyon had come from the nobility

THE PALACE OF JUSTICE (LAW COURTS) IN PARIS [1]

and clergy, who were now no longer in a position to buy. The prosperous classes were therefore exasperated when the commissioners of the Convention demanded money and troops. The citizens gathered an army of ten thousand men and placed it under a royalist leader. The Convention, however, called

[1] In the thirteenth century part of the royal palace on the island in the Seine was made over to the lawyers of the court, and it has remained ever since the seat of the chief law courts of France. The square clock tower at the corner, the round towers and the chapel (Sainte-Chapelle, just visible at the left), all date from the old palace—also the lower floor and cellar facing the river, made over into the prison of the Conciergerie. In it Marie Antoinette and many other illustrious prisoners were kept when tried by the Revolutionary Tribunal.

in troops from the armies on the frontier, bombarded and captured the city, and wreaked a terrible vengeance upon those
who had dared to revolt against the Mountain. Frightened
by the experience of Lyon, Bordeaux and Marseille decided
that resistance was futile and admitted the troops of the
Convention. The Convention's Committee of Public Safety
showed itself far more efficient than the scattered and dis-
united opponents who questioned its right to govern France.

[While the Committee of Public Safety had been suppressing
the revolts within the country, it had taken active measures to
meet its foreign enemies.] The distinguished military organizer,
Carnot, had become a member of the committee in August and
immediately called for a general levy of troops. He soon had
seven hundred and fifty thousand men; these he divided into
thirteen armies and dispatched them against the allies. The
English and Hanoverians, who were besieging Dunkirk, were
driven off and the Austrians were defeated, so that by the
close of the year 1793 all danger from invasion was past, for
the time being at least.

[In spite of the marvelous success with which the Committee
of Public Safety had crushed its opponents at home and repelled the forces of the coalition, it continued its policy of
stifling all opposition by terror.] Even before the fall of the
Girondists a special court had been established in Paris, known
as the Revolutionary Tribunal. Its duty was to try all those
who were suspected of treasonable acts. At first the cases were
very carefully considered, and few persons were condemned.

In September, after the revolt of the cities, two new men,
who had been implicated in the September massacres, were
added to the Committee of Public Safety. They were selected
with the particular purpose of intimidating the counter-
revolutionary party by bringing all the disaffected to the
guillotine.[1] A terrible law was passed, declaring all those to

---

[1] In former times it had been customary to inflict capital punishment by
decapitating the victim with the sword. At the opening of the Revolution
a certain Dr. Guillotin recommended a new device, which consisted of a
heavy knife sliding downward between two uprights. This instrument,
called, after him, the guillotine, which is still used in France, was more

be suspects who by their conduct or remarks had shown themselves enemies of liberty. The former nobles, including the wives, fathers, mothers, and children of the "emigrants," unless they had constantly manifested their attachment to the Revolution, were ordered to be imprisoned.

In October, 1793, the queen, Marie Antoinette, after a trial in which false and atrocious charges were brought against her,[1] was executed in Paris, and a number of high-minded and distinguished persons suffered a like fate. But the most horrible acts of the Reign of Terror were perpetrated in the provinces where deputies of the Committee of Public Safety were sent with almost absolute military power to crush rebellions. A representative of the Convention had thousands of the people of Nantes shot down or drowned. The Convention proposed to destroy the great city of Lyon altogether, and, though this decree was only partially carried out, thousands of its citizens were executed.[2]

Soon the radical party which was conducting the government began to disagree among themselves. Danton, a man of fiery zeal for the republic, who had hitherto enjoyed great popularity with the Jacobins, became tired of bloodshed and believed that the system of terror was no longer necessary. On the other hand, Hébert, the leader of the Commune, felt that the revolution was not yet complete. He proposed, for example, that the worship of Reason should be substituted for the worship of God, and arranged a service in the great church of Notre Dame, where Reason, in the person of a handsome actress, took her place on the altar. The most powerful member of the

---

speedy and certain in its action than the sword in the hands of the executioner.

[1] She had, like the king, been guilty of encouraging the enemies of France to intervene.

[2] It should not be forgotten that very few of the people at Paris stood in any fear of the guillotine. The city during the Reign of Terror was not the gloomy place that we might imagine. Never did the inhabitants appear happier, never were the theaters and restaurants more crowded. The guillotine was making away with the enemies of liberty, so the women wore tiny guillotines as ornaments, and the children were given toy guillotines and amused themselves decapitating the figures of "aristocrats."

Committee of Public Safety was Robespierre, who, although he was insignificant in person and a tiresome speaker, enjoyed a great reputation for republican virtue. He disapproved alike of Danton's moderation and of the worship of Reason advocated by the Commune. Through his influence the leaders of both the moderate and the extreme party were arrested and executed (March and April, 1794).

It was, of course, impossible for Robespierre to maintain his dictatorship for long. When he had the Revolutionary Tribunal divided into sections and greatly increased the rapidity of the executions with a view of destroying all his enemies, his colleagues in the Convention began to fear that he would demand their heads next. A coalition was formed against him, and the Convention ordered his arrest, July 27, 1794.[1] He called upon the Commune to defend him, but the Convention roused Paris against the Commune, which was no longer powerful enough to intimidate the whole city, and he and his supporters were sent to the guillotine.

In successfully overthrowing Robespierre, the Convention and Committee of Public Safety had rid the country of the only man who, owing to his popularity and his reputation for uprightness, could have prolonged the Reign of Terror. There was an immediate reaction after his death, for the country was weary of executions. The Revolutionary Tribunal henceforth convicted very few indeed of those who were brought before it. Indeed, it turned upon those who had themselves been the leaders in the worst atrocities, for example, as the public prosecutor, who had brought hundreds of victims to the guillotine in Paris, and the brutes who had ordered the massacres at Nantes and Lyon. Within a few months the Jacobin Club at Paris was closed by the Convention, and the Commune abolished.

The Convention now at last turned its attention to the great work for which it had originally been summoned, and drew up a constitution for the republic. This provided that the law-

[1] The date of Robespierre's fall is generally known as the Ninth of Thermidor, the day and month of the republican calendar.

making power should be vested in a legislative assembly consisting of two houses. The lower house was called the Council of the Five Hundred, and the upper chamber the Council of the Elders. Members of the latter were required to be at least forty years of age. The executive powers were put in the hands of a *Directory* of five persons, to be chosen by the two chambers.

In October, 1795, the Convention finally dissolved itself, having governed the country during three years of unprecedented excitement, danger, and disorder. While it was responsible for the horrors of the Reign of Terror, its committees had carried France through the terrible crisis of 1793. The civil war had been brought to a speedy end, and the coalition of foreign powers had been defeated. Meanwhile other committees appointed by the Convention had been quietly working upon the problem of bettering the system of education, which had been taken by the State out of the hands of the clergy. Progress had also been made toward establishing a single system of law for the whole country to replace the old confusion. The new republican calendar was not destined to survive many years, but the metric system of weights and measures introduced by the Convention has now been adopted by most European countries, and is used by men of science in England and America.

On the other hand, the Reign of Terror, the depreciated paper currency,[1] and many hasty and unwise laws passed by the Convention had produced all sorts of disorder and uncertainty. The Directory did little to better conditions, and it was not until Napoleon's strong hand grasped the helm of government in the year of 1800 that order was really restored.

[1] See above, pp. 474 f. There were about forty billions of francs in assignats in circulation at the opening of 1796. At that time it required nearly three hundred francs in paper money to procure one in specie.

CHAPTER XXII

EUROPE AND NAPOLEON

General Bonaparte. Bonaparte Master of France. Peace of 1801: The Consolidation of Germany. Bonaparte Restores Order and Prosperity. Disappearance of the Holy Roman Empire. Defeat of Prussia: The Continental Blockade. Napoleon at His Zenith. The Fall of Napoleon

General Bonaparte

THE aristocratic military leaders of old France had either run away or been discredited along with the noble class to which they belonged. Among the commanders who, through exceptional ability, arose in their stead, one was soon to dominate the history of Europe as no man before him had ever done. For fifteen years his biography and the political history of Europe are so nearly synonymous that the period that we are now entering upon may properly be called after him, the Napoleonic Period.

Napoleon Bonaparte was hardly a Frenchman in origin. It is true that the island of Corsica, where he was born August 15, 1769, had at that time belonged to France for a year. But Napoleon's native language was Italian, he was descended from Italian ancestors who had come to the island in the sixteenth century, and his career revives, on a magnificent scale, the ambitions and the policy of a *condottiere* despot of the fifteenth century.[1]

When he was ten years old he was taken to France by his father. After learning a little of the French language, which he is said never to have mastered perfectly, he was put into a military school, where he remained for six years. He soon came to hate the young French aristocrats with whom he was associated. He wrote to his father, "I am tired of exposing my poverty and seeing these shameless boys laughing over it, who are superior to me only in their wealth, but infinitely beneath me in noble sentiments." Gradually the ambition to

[1] See above, pp. 188 ff.

[493]

free his little island country from French control developed in him.

On completing his course in the military school he was made second lieutenant. Poor and without influence, he had little hope of any considerable advance in the French army, and he was drawn to his own country by a desire both to play a political rôle there and to help his family, which had been left in straitened circumstances by his father's death. He therefore absented himself from his command as often and as long as he could, and engaged in a series of intrigues in Corsica with a hope of getting control of the forces of the island. He fell out, however, with the authorities, and he and his family were banished in 1793 and fled to France.

The following three years were for Bonaparte a period of great uncertainty. He had lost his love for Corsica and as yet he had no foothold in France. He managed, however, to demonstrate his military skill and decision on two occasions and gained thereby the friendship of the Directory. In the spring of 1796 he was made the Directory commander-in-chief of the army of Italy. This important appointment at the age of twenty-seven forms the opening of a military career which in extent and military glory hardly finds a parallel in history, except that of Alexander the Great. And of all Bonaparte's campaigns, none is more interesting perhaps than his first, that in Italy in 1796-1797.

After the armies raised by the Committee of Public Safety had driven back their enemies in the autumn of 1793, the French occupied the Austrian Netherlands, Holland, and that portion of Germany which lies on the left, or west, bank of the Rhine. Austria and Prussia were again busy with a new, and this time final, partition of Poland. As Prussia had little real interest in the war with France, she soon concluded peace with the new republic, April, 1795. Spain followed her example and left Austria, England, and the kingdom of Sardinia to carry on the war. General Bonaparte had to face the combined armies of Austria and of the king of Sardinia. By marching north from Savona he skillfully separated his two enemies, forced the

Sardinian troops back toward their capital, Turin, and compelled the king of Sardinia to conclude a truce with France.[1]

This left him free to advance against the Austrians. These he outflanked and forced to retreat. On May 15, 1796, he entered Milan. The Austrian commander then shut himself up in the well-nigh impregnable fortress of Mantua, where Bonaparte promptly besieged him. There is no more exciting chapter in the history of warfare than the story of the audacious maneuvers by which Bonaparte successfully repulsed four attempts on the part of the Austrians to relieve Mantua, which was finally forced to capitulate at the beginning of February of the following year. As soon as he had removed all danger of an attack in the rear, the young French general led his army to within a hundred miles of Vienna, and by April, 1797, the Austrian court was glad to sign a preliminary peace.

The provisions of the definitive peace, which was concluded at Campo-Formio October, 1797, illustrate the unscrupulous manner in which Austria and the French republic disposed of the helpless lesser states. It inaugurated the bewilderingly rapid territorial redistribution of Europe, which was so characteristic of the Napoleonic Period. Austria ceded to France the Austrian Netherlands and secretly agreed to use its good offices to secure for France a great part of the left bank of the Rhine. Austria also recognized the Cisalpine republic which Bonaparte had created out of the smaller states of northern Italy, and which was under the "protection" of France. This new state included Milan, Modena, some of the papal dominions, and, lastly, a part of the possessions of the venerable and renowned but now defenseless republic of Venice, which Napolean had iniquitously destroyed. Austria received as a partial indemnity the rest of the possessions of the Venetian republic, including Venice itself.

While the negotiations were going on at Campo-Formio, the young general had established a brilliant court. "His salons,"

[1] The island of Sardinia had in 1720 been given to the Duke of Savoy, who was also ruler of Piedmont. The duke thereupon assumed the title King of Sardinia, but Piedmont with its capital remained the most important part of the kingdom of Sardinia.

an observer informs us, "were filled with a throng of generals, officials, and purveyors, as well as the highest nobility and the most distinguished men of Italy, who came to solicit the favor of a glance or a moment's conversation." He appears already to have conceived the rôle that he was to play later. We have

CENTRAL EUROPE, TO ILLUSTRATE NAPOLEON'S CAMPAIGNS, 1796-1801

a report of a most extraordinary conversation which occurred at this time.

"What I have done so far," he declared, "is nothing. I am but at the opening of the career that I am to run. Do you suppose that I have gained my victories in Italy in order to advance the lawyers of the Directory? . . . Do you think either that my object is to establish a republic? What a notion! . . . What the French want is glory and the satisfaction of

PL. XXVIII.   NAPOLEON I

their vanity; . . . Let the Directory attempt to deprive me of my command and they will see who is the master. The nation must have a head, a head who is rendered illustrious by glory and not by theories of government, fine phrases, or the talk of idealists." There is no doubt whom General Bonaparte had in mind when he spoke of the needed head of the French nation who should be "rendered illustrious by glory." This son of a poor Corsican lawyer, but yesterday a mere unlucky adventurer, had arranged his program; two years and a half later, at the age of thirty, he was the master of the French republic.

Bonaparte was a short man, at this time extremely thin, but his striking features, quick, searching eye, abrupt, animated gestures and rapid speech, incorrect as it was, made a deep impression upon those who came in contact with him. He possessed in a supreme degree two qualities that are ordinarily incompatible. He was a dreamer, and at the same time a man whose practical skill and mastery of detail amounted to genius. He once told a friend that he was wont, when a poor lieutenant, to allow his imagination full play and fancy things just as he would have them. Then he would coolly consider the exact steps to be taken if he were to try to make his dream come true. At the age of twenty-eight he had become the chief general of France; at that of thirty he was to become master of the country.

In order to explain Bonaparte's success it must be remembered that he was not hampered or held back by the fear of doing wrong. He was utterly unscrupulous, whether dealing with an individual or a nation, and appears to have been absolutely without any sense of moral responsibility. Affection for his friends and relatives never stood in the way of his personal aggrandizement. To these traits must be added unrivaled military genius and the power of intense and almost uninterrupted work.

But even Bonaparte, unexampled as were his abilities, could never have extended his power over all of western Europe, had it not been for the peculiar political weakness of most of the states with which he had to deal. There was no strong German empire in his day, no mighty Prussian army; Austria was already humbled, and its defeat had opened Italy to the French. In short, the French republic was surrounded by small states almost defenseless against an unscrupulous invader.

Bonaparte Master of France

After arranging the Peace of Campo-Formio, General Bonaparte returned to Paris. He at once perceived that France, in spite of her enthusiasm for him, was not yet ready to accept him as her ruler. He saw, too, that he would soon sacrifice his prestige if he lived quietly in Paris like an ordinary person. His active mind soon conceived a plan which would forward his interests. France was still at war with England, its most persevering enemy during this period. Bonaparte convinced the Directory that England could best be ruined in the long run by seizing Egypt and threatening her commerce through the Mediterranean, and perhaps ultimately her dominion in India.[1] Bonaparte, fascinated by the career of Alexander the Great, pictured himself riding to India on the back of an elephant and dispossessing England of her most precious colonial dependencies. He had, however, still another, and a characteristic, reason for undertaking the expedition. France was on the eve of a new war with the European powers. Bonaparte foresaw that, if he could withdraw with him some of France's best officers, the Directory might soon find itself so embarrassed that he could return as a national savior. And even so it fell out.

The French fleet left Toulon May 19, 1798. It was so fortunate as to escape the English squadron under Nelson, which sailed by it in the night. Bonaparte arrived at Alex-

---

[1] The expedition to Egypt did not establish a new empire, but it led to the opening up of thousands of years of ancient history. A band of French scholars accompanied the army and started collecting the remains of monuments and tombs.

The tombs were covered with hieroglyphs which no one could read; but in the spoil collected—and captured by Nelson so that it is now in the British Museum—was a stone with both Greek text and hieroglyphs, which a French scholar used, a few years later, as a key to unlock the literature of ancient Egypt. See Breasted, *Conquest of Civilization*, p. 456.

andria July 1, and easily defeated the Turkish troops in the famous battle of the Pyramids, near Cairo. Meanwhile Nelson, who did not know the destination of the enemy's fleet, had returned from the Syrian coast, where he looked for the French in vain. He discovered Bonaparte's ships in the harbor of Alexandria and annihilated them in the first battle of the Nile (August 1, 1798). The French troops were now completely cut off from Europe.

The Porte (that is, the Turkish government) declared war against France, and Bonaparte resolved to attack Turkey by land. He accordingly marched into Syria in the spring of 1799, but was repulsed at Acre, where the Turkish forces were aided by the English fleet. Pursued by pestilence, the army regained Cairo in

EGYPTIAN CAMPAIGN

June, after terrible suffering and loss. It was still strong enough to annihilate a Turkish army that landed at Alexandria; but news now reached Bonaparte from Europe which convinced him that the time had come for him to hasten back. Northern Italy, which he had won, was lost; the allies were in arms again and were about to invade France, and the Directory was completely demoralized. Bonaparte accordingly secretly deserted his army and managed, by a series of happy accidents, to reach France with a few of his best officers by October 9, 1799.

The Directory, one of the most corrupt and inefficient governmental bodies that the world has ever seen, had completely disgraced itself. Bonaparte readily found others to join with him in a conspiracy to overthrow it. A plan was formed for abruptly destroying the old government and replacing it by a new one. This is a procedure so familiar in France during the past century that it is known even in English as a *coup d'état*. Bonaparte's "stroke of state" is known as the *coup d'état* of the 18th Brumaire—November 9, 1799. The conspirators had a good many friends in the two assemblies, especially the "Elders." Nevertheless, Bonaparte had to order his soldiers to invade the hall in which the Assembly of the Five Hundred was in session and scatter his opponents before he could accomplish his purpose. A chosen few were then reassembled under the presidency of Lucien Bonaparte, one of Napoleon's brothers, who was a member of the assembly. They voted to put the government in the hands of General Bonaparte and two others, to be called *Consuls*. These were to proceed, with the aid of a commission and of the "Elders," to draw up a new constitution.

The new constitution (that of the year eight of French liberty) was a very cumbrous and elaborate one. It provided for no less than four assemblies, one to propose the laws, one to consider them, one to vote upon them, and one to decide on their constitutionality. But Bonaparte saw to it that as First Consul he himself had practically all the power in his own hands.

In each department he put an officer called a *prefect*, in each subdivision of the department a *subprefect*. These, together with the mayors and police commissioners of the towns, were all appointed by the First Consul. The prefects, "little First Consuls," as Bonaparte called them, resembled the intendants —the king's officers under the old régime. Indeed, the new government suggested in several important respects that of Louis XIV.

The new ruler objected as decidedly as Louis XIV had done to the idea of being controlled by the people, who, he believed, knew nothing of public affairs. It was enough, he thought, if they were allowed to say whether they wished a certain form of government or not. He therefore introduced what he called

PL. XXX. PIUS VII AND HIS LEGATE TO FRANCE, BY DAVID

PL. XXXI. A LADY OF THE TIME OF THE DIRECTORY, BY DAVID

a *plébiscite*. The new constitution when completed was submitted to the nation at large, and all were allowed to vote "yes" or "no" on the expediency of its adoption. Over three million voted in favor of it and only fifteen hundred and sixty-two against it. This did not necessarily mean, however, that practically the whole nation wished to have General Bonaparte as its ruler. A great many may have preferred what seemed to them an objectionable form of government to the risk of rejecting it. Herein lies the injustice of the plébiscite. There are so many questions that cannot be answered by a simple "yes" or "no!"

Yet the accession of the popular young general to power was undoubtedly grateful to the majority of citizens, who longed above all for a stable government. The Swedish envoy wrote just after the *coup d'état:* "A legitimate monarch has perhaps never found a people more ready to do his bidding than Bonaparte, and it would be inexcusable if this talented general did not take advantage of this to introduce a better form of government upon a firmer basis. It is literally true that France will perform impossibilities in order to aid him in this. The people (with the exception of a despicable horde of anarchists) are so sick and weary of revolutionary horrors and folly that they believe that any change cannot fail to be for the better. . . . Even the royalists, whatever their views may be, are sincerely devoted to Bonaparte, for they attribute to him the intention of gradually restoring the old order of things. The indifferent element regard him as the one most likely to give France peace. The enlightened republicans, although they tremble for their form of government, prefer to see a single man of talent possess himself of the power than a club of intriguers."

Upon becoming First Consul, General Bonaparte found France at war with England, Russia, Austria, Turkey, and Naples. These powers had formed a coalition in December, 1798, had defeated the armies that the Directory sent against them, and undone Bonaparte's work in Italy. It now devolved upon him to reëstablish the prestige of France abroad, as well as to restore order and prosperity at home. Besides, he must

keep himself before the people as a military hero if he wished
to maintain his supremacy.

Peace of 1801: The Consolidation of Germany

Early in the year 1800 Bonaparte began secretly to collect
an army near Dijon. This he proposed to direct against an
Austrian army which was besieging the French in Genoa.
Instead of marching straight into Italy, as would have been
most natural, the First Consul resolved to take the Austrian
forces in the rear. Emulating Hannibal, he led his troops over
the famous Alpine pass of the Great St. Bernard, dragging his
cannon over in the trunks of trees which had been hollowed
out for the purpose. He arrived safely in Milan on the second
of June, to the utter astonishment of the Austrians, who were
taken completely by surprise.

Bonaparte now moved westward and defeated the Austrians
in the famous battle of Marengo (June 14), and added one
more to the list of his great military successes. A truce was
signed next day, and the Austrians retreated behind the Min-
cio River, leaving Bonaparte to restore French influence in
Lombardy. The districts that he had "freed" had to support
his army, and the reëstablished Cisalpine republic was forced
to pay a monthly tax of two million francs.

A second victory gained by the French in December of the
same year brought Austria to terms, and she agreed to conclude a separate peace with the French republic. This was
the beginning of a general pacification. During the year 1801
treaties were signed with all the powers with which France
had been at war, even with England, who had not laid down
her arms since war was first declared in 1793.

Among many merely transitory results of these treaties there
were two provisions of momentous import. The first of these,
Spain's cession of Louisiana to France in exchange for certain
advantages in Italy, does not concern us here directly. When
war again broke out, Bonaparte sold the district to the United
States, and among the many transfers of territory that he made
during his reign, none was more important than this. We must,

however, treat with some patience the second of the great changes, for it led to the complete reorganization of Germany and ultimately rendered possible the establishment of the German empire of the nineteenth century.

In the treaty signed by Austria at Lunéville in February, 1801, the emperor agreed, on his own part and on the part of the Holy Roman Empire, that the French republic should thereafter possess in full sovereignty the territories lying on the left bank of the Rhine which belonged to the Holy Roman Empire, and that thereafter the Rhine should form the boundary of France from the point where it left Switzerland to where it flowed into Dutch territory. As a natural consequence of this cession, various princes and states of the empire found themselves dispossessed, either wholly or in part, of their lands. The empire bound itself to furnish the *hereditary* princes who had lost possessions on the left bank of the Rhine with "an indemnity within the empire."

This provision implied a veritable transformation of the old Holy Roman Empire, which, except for the development of Prussia, was still in pretty much the same condition as in Luther's time.[1] There was no unoccupied land to give the dispossessed princes; but there were two classes of states in the empire that did not belong to *hereditary* princes; namely, the ecclesiastical states and the free towns. As the churchmen,—archbishops, bishops, and abbots,—who ruled over the ecclesiastical states, were forbidden by the rules of the Church to marry,[2] they could of course have no lawful heirs. Should an ecclesiastical ruler be deprived of his realms, it was possible, therefore, to indemnify him by a pension for life, with no fear of any injustice to heirs, since there could be none. The transfer of the lands of an ecclesiastical prince to a lay, that is, hereditary, prince was called *secularization*. As for the "free" towns, once so powerful and important, they had lost their former influence and seemed as much of an anomaly in the German Confederation as the ecclesiastical states.

[1] See above, pp. 270 ff.
[2] This carries us back to the chapter on "Popes and Emperors." Such is history!

' *Reichdeputationshauptschluss*—one of the most important decisions of modern history—was the high-sounding German name of the great decree issued by the imperial diet in 1803, redistributing the territory so as to indemnify the hereditary princes dispossessed by the cession of the left bank of the Rhine to France. All the ecclesiastical states, except the electorate of Mainz, were turned over to lay rulers. Of the forty-eight imperial cities, only six were left. Three of these still exist as republican members of the present German federation; namely, the Hanseatic towns—Hamburg, Bremen, and Lübeck. Bavaria received the bishoprics of Würzburg, Bamberg, Augsburg, Freising, and a number of the imperial cities. Baden received the bishoprics of Constance, Basel, Speyer, etc. The knights—now a feeble folk—who had lost their possessions on the left bank were not indemnified, and those on the right bank were deprived of their political rights within the next two or three years, by the several states within whose boundaries they lay.

The final distribution was preceded by a bitter and undignified scramble among the princes for additional bits of territory. All turned to Paris for favors, since the First Consul, and not the German diet, was really the arbiter in the matter. Germany never sank to a lower degree of national degradation than at this period. But this amalgamation was, nevertheless, the beginning of her political regeneration; for without the consolidation of the hundreds of practically independent little states into a few well-organized monarchies, such a union as the later German empire would have been impossible, and the country must have remained indefinitely in its traditional impotency. *Thus Germany owes to a French ruler, not to any of its emperors or to Prussia, the first measures which resulted in the German empire!*

The treaties of 1801 left France in possession of the Austrian Netherlands and the left bank of the Rhine, to which increase of territory Piedmont was soon added. Bonaparte found a further resource in the dependencies, which it was his consistent policy to create. Holland became the Batavian republic, and, with the Italian (originally the Cisalpine) republic, came under French control and contributed money and troops for the forwarding of French interests. The constitution of Switzerland was improved in the interests of the First Consul and, incidentally, to the great advantage of the country itself.

Bonaparte Restores Order and Prosperity

The activity of the extraordinary man who had placed himself at the head of the French republic was by no means confined to the important alterations of the map of Europe described in the previous chapter. He was indefatigable in carrying out a series of internal reforms, second only in importance to those of the great Revolution of 1789. The Reign of Terror and the incompetence of the Directory's government had left France in a very bad plight.[1] Bonaparte's reorganization of the government has already been noticed. The finances were in a terrible condition. These the First Consul adjusted with great skill, quickly restored the national credit, and established the Bank of France.

He then set about settling the great problem of the nonjuring clergy, who were still under suspicion for refusing to sanction the Civil Constitution of the Clergy.[2] Under the slack rule of the Directory persecution had ceased and priests were again officiating in thousands of parishes. Their churches were now formally given back to them. All imprisoned priests were now freed, on promising not to oppose the constitution. Their churches were given back to them, and the distinction between "nonjuring" and "constitutional" clergymen was obliterated. Sunday, which had been abolished by the republican calendar, was once more observed, and all the revolutionary holidays, except July 14—the anniversary of the fall of the Bastille—and the first day of the republican year, were done

---

[1] The roads were dilapidated and the harbors filled with sand; taxes were unpaid, robbery prevailed, and business had greatly fallen off. A manufacturer in Paris who had employed from sixty to eighty workmen now had but ten. The lace, paper, and linen industries were as good as destroyed.

[2] See above, p. 475.

away with. A formal treaty with the pope, the Concordat of 1801, was concluded, which revoked some of the provisions of the Civil Constitution, especially the election of the priests and bishops by the people, and recognized the pope as the head of the Church. It is noteworthy, however, that Bonaparte did not restore to the Church its ancient possessions and that he reserved to himself the right to appoint the bishops, as the former kings had done.

As for the emigrant nobles, Bonaparte decreed that no more names should be added to the lists. The striking of names from the list and the return of confiscated lands that had not already been sold, he made favors to be granted by himself. Parents and relatives of emigrants were no longer to be regarded as incapable of holding public offices. In April, 1802, a general amnesty was issued, and no less than forty thousand families returned to France.

There was a gradual reaction from the innovations of the Reign of Terror. The old titles of address, "Monsieur" and "Madame," were again used instead of the revolutionary "Citizen." Streets which had been rebaptized with republican names resumed their former ones. Old titles of nobility were revived, and something very like a royal court began to develop at the Palace of the Tuileries; for, except in name, Bonaparte was already a king, and his wife, Josephine, a queen. It had been clear for some years that the nation was weary of political agitation. How great a blessing after the anarchy of the past to put all responsibility upon one who showed himself capable of concluding a long war with unprecedented glory for France and of reëstablishing order and the security of person and property, the necessary conditions for renewed prosperity! How natural that the French should welcome a despotism to which they had been accustomed for centuries, after suffering as they had under nominally republican institutions!

One of the greatest and most permanent of Bonaparte's achievements still remains to be noted. The heterogeneous laws of the old régime had been much modified by the legislation of the successive assemblies. All this needed a final revision, and Bonaparte appointed a commission to undertake this great task. Their draft of the new code was discussed in the Council of State, and the First Consul had many suggestions to make. The resulting codification of the civil law—the *Code Napoléon*—is still used to-day, not only in France but also, with some modifications, in Rhenish Prussia, Bavaria, Baden, Holland, Belgium, Italy, and even in the state of Louisiana. The criminal and commercial law also was codified. These codes carried with them into foreign lands the principles of equality upon which they were based, and thus diffused the benefits of the Revolution beyond the borders of France.

Bonaparte was able gradually to modify the constitution so that his power became more and more absolute. In 1802 he was appointed consul for life and given the right to name his successor. Even this did not satisfy his insatiable ambition, which demanded that his actual power should be clothed with all the attributes and surroundings appropriate to an hereditary ruler. In May, 1804, he was accordingly given the title of "Emperor," and (in December) crowned, as the successor of Charlemagne, with great pomp in the cathedral of Notre Dame. He at once proceeded to establish a new nobility to take the place of that abolished by the first National Assembly in 1790.

From this time on he became increasingly tyrannical and hostile to criticism. At the very beginning of his administration he had suppressed a great part of the numerous political newspapers and forbidden the establishment of new ones. As emperor he showed himself still more exacting. His police furnished the news to the papers and carefully omitted all that might offend their suspicious master. He ordered the journals to "put in quarantine all news that might be disadvantageous or disagreeable to France." His ideal was to suppress all newspapers but one, which should be used for official purposes.

Disappearance of the Holy Roman Empire

A great majority of the French undoubtedly longed for peace, but Napoleon's position made war a personal necessity for him. No one saw this more clearly than he. "If," he said to his Council of State in the summer of 1802, "the European states intend ever to renew the war, the sooner it comes the better. Every day the remembrance of their defeats grows dimmer and at the same time the prestige of our victories pales. . . . France needs glorious deeds, and hence war. She must be the first among the states, or she is lost. I shall put up with peace as long as our neighbors can maintain it, but I shall regard it as an advantage if they force me to take up my arms again before they are rusted. . . . In our position I shall look on each conclusion of peace as simply a short armistice, and I regard myself as destined during my term of office to fight almost without intermission."

On another occasion, in 1804, Napoleon said, "There will be no rest in Europe until it is under a single chief—an emperor who shall have kings for officers, who shall distribute kingdoms to his lieutenants, and shall make this one king of Italy, that one of Bavaria; this one ruler of Switzerland, that one governor of Holland, each having an office of honor in the imperial household." This was the ideal that he now found himself in a situation to carry out with marvelous exactness.

There were many reasons why the peace with Great Britain (concluded at Amiens in March, 1802) should be speedily broken, especially as the First Consul was not averse to a renewal of the war. The obvious intention of Napoleon to bring as much of Europe under his control as he could, and the imposition of high duties on English goods in those territories that he already controlled, filled commercial and industrial England with apprehension. The English people longed for peace, but peace appeared only to offer an opportunity to the Corsican usurper to ruin England by a continuous war upon her commerce. This was the secret of England's pertinacity. All the other European powers concluded peace with Napoleon at some time during his reign. Great Britain alone did not lay down her arms a second time until the emperor of the French was a prisoner.

War was renewed between Great Britain and France in 1803. Bonaparte promptly occupied Hanover, of which it will be remembered that the English king was elector,[1] and declared the coast blockaded from Hanover to Otranto. Holland, Spain, Portugal, and the Ligurian republic—formerly the republic of Genoa—were, by hook or by crook, induced to agree to furnish each their contingent of men or money to the French army and to exclude English ships from their ports.

To cap the climax, England was alarmed by the appearance of a French army at Boulogne, just across the Channel. A great .number of flatboats were collected, and troops trained to embark and disembark. Apparently Napoleon harbored the firm purpose of invading the British Isles. Yet the transportation of a large body of troops across the English Channel, trifling as is the distance, would have been very hazardous, and by many it was deemed downright impossible. No one knows whether Napoleon really seriously expected to make the trial. It is quite possible that his main purpose in collecting an army at Boulogne was to have it in readiness for the continental war which he saw immediately ahead of him. He succeeded, at any rate, in terrifying England, who prepared to defend herself.

The Tsar, Alexander I, had submitted a plan for the reconciliation of France and England in August, 1803. The rejection of this and the evident intention of Napoleon to include the eastern coast of the Adriatic in his sphere of influence led Russia to join a new coalition which, by July, 1805, included Austria, Sweden, and, of course, Great Britain. Austria was especially affected by the increase of Napoleon's power in Italy. He had been crowned king of Italy in May, 1805, had created a little duchy in northern Italy for his sister, and had annexed the Ligurian republic to France. There were rumors, too, that he was planning to seize the Venetian territories which had been given to Austria.

War was declared against Austria, August 23, 1805, and four days later the army at Boulogne was ordered eastward. One

[1] See above, p. 405.

of the Austrian commanders exhibited the most startling incapacity in allowing himself to be shut up in Ulm, where he was forced to capitulate with all his troops (October 20). Napoleon then marched down the Danube with little opposition, and before the middle of November Vienna was in the possession of French troops. Napoleon thereupon led his forces north to meet the allied armies of Austria and Russia; these he defeated on December 2, 1805, in the terrible winter battle of Austerlitz. Russia then withdrew for a time and signed an armistice; and Austria was obliged to submit to a humiliating peace, the Treaty of Pressburg.

By this treaty Austria recognized all Napoleon's changes in Italy, and ceded to his kingdom of Italy that portion of the Venetian territory that she had received at Campo-Formio. Moreover, she ceded Tyrol to Bavaria, which was friendly to Napoleon, and other of her possessions to Württemberg and Baden, also friends of the French emperor. She further agreed to ratify the assumption on the part of the rulers of Bavaria and Württemberg of the titles of "King." Napoleon was now in a position still further to reorganize western Europe, with a view to establishing a great international federation of which he should be the head.

Napoleon had no desire to unify Germany completely; he merely wished to maintain a certain number of independent states, or groups of states, which he could conveniently control. He had provided, in the Treaty of Pressburg, that the newly created sovereigns should enjoy the "plenitude of sovereignty" and all the rights derived therefrom, precisely as did the rulers of Austria and Prussia.

This treaty, by explicitly declaring several of the most important of the German states altogether independent of the emperor, rendered the further existence of the Holy Roman Empire impossible. The emperor, Francis II, took the hint and abdicated, August 6, 1806. Thus the most imposing and enduring political office known to history was formally abolished.

Francis II did not, however, lose his title of "Emperor." Shortly after the First Consul had received that title, Francis adopted the formula "Emperor of Austria," to designate him as the ruler of all the possessions of his house.[1] Hitherto he had been officially known as King of Hungary, Bohemia, Dalmatia, Croatia, Galicia, and Laodomeria, Duke of Lorraine, Venice, Salzburg, etc., Grand Duke of Transylvania, Margrave of Moravia, etc.

Meanwhile Napoleon had organized a union of the southern German states, called the Confederation of the Rhine, and had assumed its headship as "Protector." This he had done, he assured Europe, "in the dearest interests of his people and of his neighbors," adding the pious hope that the French armies had crossed the Rhine for the last time, and that the people of Germany would witness no longer, "except in the annals of the past, the horrible pictures of disorder, devastation, and slaughter that war invariably brings with it." In reality, however, Napoleon was enlarging his empire by erecting dependent states east of the Rhine.

Immediately after the battle of Austerlitz, Napoleon proclaimed that the king of Naples, who had allied himself with the English, had ceased to reign, and French generals were ordered to occupy Naples. In March, 1806, he made his brother Joseph king of Naples and Sicily, his brother Louis king of Holland, and his brother-in-law, Murat, duke of Cleves and Berg. These states and those of his German allies constituted what he called "the real French Empire."

Defeat of Prussia: The Continental Blockade

One of the most important of the continental states, it will have been noticed, had taken no part as yet in the opposition to the extension of Napoleon's power. Prussia, the first power to conclude peace with the new French Republic in 1795, had since that time maintained a strict neutrality. Had it yielded to Tsar Alexander's persuasions and joined the coalition in 1805,

[1] Thus Francis II of the Holy Roman Empire became Francis I of Austria.

it might have turned the tide at Austerlitz, or at any rate have encouraged further resistance to the conqueror. The hesitation of Frederick William III cost him dear, for Napoleon now forced him into war at a time when he could look for no efficient assistance from Russia or the other powers. The immediate cause of the declaration of war was the disposal of Hanover. This electorate Frederick William had consented to hold provisionally, pending its possible transfer to him should the English king give his assent. Prussia was anxious to get possession of Hanover because it lay just between her older possessions and the territory which she had gained in the redistribution of 1803.

NELSON'S COLUMN, TRAFALGAR SQUARE, LONDON

The English regard Nelson as the man who safeguarded their liberty by the victories of the fleet. Nelson was killed at Trafalgar and buried with great ceremony in the crypt of St. Paul's, under the very center of the dome. Some years later, "Trafalgar Square" was laid out at the point where the street leading to the Parliament buildings joins a chief business street—the Strand—and a gigantic column to Nelson erected, surmounted by a statue of the admiral

Napoleon, as usual, did not fail either to see or to use his advantage. His conduct toward Prussia was most insolent. After setting her at enmity with England and promising that she should have Hanover, he unblushingly offered to restore the electorate to George III. His insults now began to arouse the national spirit in Prussia, and the reluctant Frederick William III was forced by the party in favor of war, which included his beautiful queen Louise and the great statesman Stein, to break with Napoleon.

Her army was, however, as has been well said, "only that of Frederick the Great grown twenty years older"; one of Frederick's generals, the aged duke of Brunswick, who had issued the famous manifesto against the French Revolution in 1792, was its leader. A single defeat, near Jena (October 14, 1806), put Prussia completely in the hands of her enemy. This one disaster produced complete demoralization throughout the country. Fortresses were surrendered without resistance, and the king fled to the uttermost parts of his realm on the Russian boundary.

Napoleon now led his army into Poland, where he spent the winter in operations against Russia and her feeble Prussian ally. He closed an arduous campaign by a signal victory at Friedland (June 14, 1807), which was followed by the treaties of Tilsit with Russia and Prussia (July 7 and 9). Prussia was thoroughly defeated. Frederick William III lost all his possessions to the west of the Elbe and all that Prussia had gained in the second and third partitions of Poland. The Polish territory Napoleon made into a new subject kingdom called the grand duchy of Warsaw, and chose his friend, the king of Saxony, as its ruler. Out of the western lands of Prussia, which he later united with Hanover, he created the kingdom of Westphalia for his brother Jerome. Russia, on the other hand, was treated with marked consideration. The Tsar (Alexander I) finally consented to recognize all the sweeping territorial changes that Napoleon had made, and secretly agreed to enforce the blockade against England should that country refuse to make peace.

Napoleon's most persevering enemy, England, still remained unconquered and inaccessible. Just as Napoleon was undertaking his successful campaign against Austria in 1805, Nelson had annihilated a second French fleet in the renowned naval engagement at Trafalgar, off the coast of Spain. It seemed more than ever necessary, therefore, to ruin England commercially and industrially, since there was obviously no likelihood of subduing it by arms.

In May, 1806, the British government had declared the coast from the Elbe to Brest to be blockaded. Napoleon replied to this with the Berlin decree (November 21, 1806), in which he proclaimed it a monstrous abuse of the right for England to declare great stretches of coast in a state of blockade which her whole fleet would be unable to enforce. He retaliated with a "paper" [1] blockade of the British Isles, which forbade all commerce with them. Letters or packages directed to England or to an Englishman or written in the English language were not to be permitted to pass through the mails in the countries he controlled. Every English subject in countries occupied by French troops or in the territory of Napoleon's allies was to be regarded as a prisoner of war and his property as a lawful prize. All trade in English goods was forbidden.

A year later Great Britain established a similar paper blockade of the ports of the French Empire and its allies, but permitted the ships of neutral powers to proceed, provided that they touched at an English port, secured a license from the British government, and paid a heavy export duty. Napoleon promptly declared all ships that submitted to these humiliating regulations to be lawful prizes of French privateers. The ships of the United States were at this time the most numerous and important of the neutral carriers. The disastrous results of these restrictions led to the various embargo acts (the first of which was passed by Congress in December, 1807), and ultimately to the temporary destruction of the flourishing carrying trade of the United States.

Napoleon tried to render Europe permanently independent of the colonial productions brought from English colonies and by English ships. He encouraged the substitution of chicory for coffee, the cultivation of the sugar beet, and the discovery of new dyes to replace those coming from the tropics. But the distress caused by the disturbance in trade produced great dis-

---

[1] That is, a blockade obviously too extensive to be really carried out by the ships at the disposal of the power proclaiming it.

content, especially in Russia; it rendered the domination of Napoleon more and more distasteful, and finally contributed to his downfall.

Napoleon at His Zenith

France owed much to Napoleon, for he had restored order and guaranteed many of the beneficent achievements of the Revolution of 1789. His boundless ambition was, it is true, sapping her strength by forcing younger and younger men into his armies in order to build up the vast international federation of which he dreamed. But his victories and the commanding position to which he had raised France could not but fill the nation with pride.

He sought to gain popular approval by great public improvements. He built marvelous roads across the Alps and along the Rhine, which still fill the traveler with admiration. He beautified Paris by opening up wide streets and quays and building magnificent bridges and triumphal arches that kept fresh in the people's minds the recollection of his victories. By these means he gradually converted a medieval town into the most beautiful of modern capitals.

The whole educational system was reorganized and made as highly centralized and as subservient to the aims of the emperor as any department of government. Napoleon argued that one of the chief aims of education should be the formation of loyal subjects who would be faithful to the emperor and his successors. An imperial catechism was prepared, which not only inculcated loyalty to Napoleon but actually threatened with eternal perdition those who should fail in their obligations to him, including military service.

Napoleon created a new nobility, and he endeavored to assure the support of distinguished individuals by making them

---

[1] *En passant*—Those who complacently think that the United States can in some magical way maintain a noble isolation may well recall the difficulties of preserving the freedom of the seas in war time. The blockades of Napoleon's time have a singular resemblance to those of Germany and Great Britain during the World War, which ended in taking so many young men from the United States to fight overseas.

members of the Legion of Honor which he founded. The "Princes" whom he nominated received an annual income of two hundred thousand francs. The ministers of state, senators, members of his Council of State, and the archbishops received the title of "Count" and a revenue of thirty thousand francs, and so on. The army was not forgotten, for Napoleon felt that to be his chief support. The incomes of his marshals were enormous, and brave actions among the soldiers were rewarded with the decoration of the Legion of Honor.

As time went on Napoleon's despotism grew more and more oppressive. No less than thirty-five hundred prisoners of state were arrested at his command, one because he hated Napoleon, another because in his letters he expressed sentiments adverse to the government, and so on. No grievance was too petty to attract the attention of the emperor's jealous eye. He ordered the title of a *History of Bonaparte* to be changed to the *History of the Campaigns of Napoleon the Great.* He forbade the performance of certain of Schiller's and Goethe's plays in German towns, as tending to arouse the patriotic discontent of the people with his rule.

TRIUMPHAL ARCH OF PARIS

Begun by Napoleon in 1806, this largest arch of triumph in the world was not completed until 1836. It is 160 feet high and stands on a slight hill, with streets radiating from all sides, so that it is known as the Arch of Triumph of the Star. It is therefore visible from all over the western part of the city. The monument recalls the days of the Roman Empire, which inspired so many of the institutions and ideas of Republican and Napoleonic France

Napoleon was never content with his achievements or his glory. On the day of his coronation, December, 1806, he complained to his minister Decrès that he had been born too late, that there was nothing great to be done any more. On his minister's remonstrating he added: "I admit that my career has been brilliant and that I have made a good record. But what a difference there is if we compare ours with ancient times. Take Alexander the Great, for example. After announcing himself the son of Jupiter, the whole East, except his mother, Aristotle, and a few Athenian pedants, believed this to be true. But now, should I nowadays declare myself the son of the Eternal Father, there isn't a fishwife who would not hiss me. No, the nations are too sophisticated, there is nothing great any longer possible."

Up to this time Napoleon had had only the opposition of the several European rulers to overcome in the extension of his power. The people of the various states which he had conquered showed an extraordinary indifference toward the political changes. It was clear, however, that as soon as the national spirit was once awakened, the highly artificial system created by the French emperor would collapse. His first serious reverse came from the people and from an unexpected quarter.

Napoleon decided, after Tilsit, that the Spanish peninsula must be brought more completely under his control. Portugal was too friendly to the English, and Spain, owing to serious dissensions in the royal family, seemed an easy prey. In the spring of 1808 Napoleon induced both the king and the crown prince of Spain to meet him at Bayonne. Here he was able to persuade or force both of them to surrender their rights to the throne; on June 6 he appointed his brother Joseph king of Spain, making Murat king of Naples in his stead.

Joseph entered Madrid in July, armed with excellent intentions and a liberal constitution. The general rebellion in favor of the crown prince which immediately broke out had an element of religious enthusiasm in it, for the monks stirred up the people against Napoleon, on the ground that he was oppressing the pope and depriving him of his dominions. One French army was captured at Baylen, and another capitulated to the English forces which had landed in Portugal. Before the end of July, Joseph and the French troops had been compelled to retreat behind the Ebro River.

In November, 1808, the French emperor himself led a magnificent army into Spain, two hundred thousand strong, in the best of condition and commanded by his ablest marshals. The Spanish troops, perhaps one hundred thousand in number, were ill clad and inadequately equipped; what was worse, they were overconfident in view of their late victory. They were of course defeated, and Madrid surrendered December 4. Napoleon immediately abolished the Inquisition, the feudal dues, the internal customs lines, and two-thirds of the cloisters. This is typical of the way in which the French Revolution went forth in arms to spread its principles throughout western Europe.

The next month Napoleon was back in Paris, as he saw that he had another war with Austria on his hands. He left Joseph on his insecure throne, after assuring the Spanish that God was behind him. "It depends upon you alone," he said to the Spanish in his proclamation of December 7, "whether this moderate constitution that I offer you shall henceforth be your law. Should all my efforts prove vain, and should you refuse to justify my confidence, then nothing remains for me but to treat you as a conquered province and find a new throne for my brother. In that case I shall myself assume the crown of Spain and teach the ill-disposed to respect that crown, for God has given me power and will to overcome all obstacles." He was soon to discover, however, that these very Spaniards could maintain a guerrilla warfare against which his best troops and most distinguished generals were powerless. The English army under the Duke of Wellington slowly but surely drove the French back over the Pyrenees. His ultimate downfall was in no small measure due to this Peninsular War.

In April, 1809, Austria ventured to declare war once more on the "enemy of Europe," but this time she found no one to aid her. The great battle of Wagram, near Vienna (July 5-6), was not perhaps so unconditional a victory for the French as

that of Austerlitz, but it forced Austria into just as humiliating a peace as that of Pressburg. Austria's object had been
to destroy Napoleon's system of dependencies and "to restore
to their rightful possessors all those lands belonging to them
respectively before the Napoleonic usurpations." Instead of
accomplishing this end, Austria was obliged to cede more territory to Napoleon and his allies, and he went on adding to his
dependencies. After incorporating into France the kingdom
of Etruria and the papal dominions (1808-1809), Napoleon
was encouraged by his victory over Austria to annex Holland [1]
and the German districts to the north, including the Hanseatic
towns. Consequently, in 1810 France stretched from the confines of Naples to the Baltic. One might travel from Lübeck
to Rome without leaving Napoleon's realms.

Napoleon was anxious to have an heir to whom he could
transmit his vast dominions. As Josephine bore him no children, he decided to divorce her, and, after considering a Russian princess, he married the Archduchess Maria Louisa, the
daughter of the Austrian emperor and a grandniece of Marie
Antoinette. In this way the former Corsican adventurer
gained admission to one of the oldest and proudest of reigning families, the Hapsburgs. His new wife soon bore him a
son, who was styled King of Rome.

The Fall of Napoleon

Among the continental states Russia alone was entirely out
of Napoleon's control. There were plenty of causes for misunderstanding between the ardent young Tsar Alexander I
and Napoleon. Up to this time the agreement of Tilsit had
been maintained. Napoleon was, however, secretly opposing
Alexander's plans for adding the Danubian provinces and Finland to his possessions. Then the possibility of Napoleon's
reëstablishing Poland as a national kingdom which might
threaten Russia's interests was a constant source of apprehen-

---

[1] Louis Bonaparte, the father of Napoleon III, and the most conscientious
of the Bonaparte family, had been so harassed by his imperial brother that
he had abdicated as king of Holland.

sion to Alexander. By 1812 Napoleon believed himself to be in a condition to subdue this doubtful friend, who might at any moment become a dangerous enemy. Against the advice of his more far-sighted counselors, the emperor collected on the Russian frontier a vast army of four hundred thousand men, composed to a great extent of young conscripts and the contingents furnished by his allies.

MUSIC ROOM IN THE PALACE OF COMPIÈGNE

Napoleon used the various palaces erected by the previous rulers of France. That at Compiègne, 50 miles from Paris, was built by Louis XV. The smaller harp, to be seen in the picture, was made, it is said, for Napoleon's heir, "The King of Rome," as his father called him. The boy was but three years old, however, when Napoleon abdicated in 1814, and was carried off to Austria by his Austrian mother, Maria Louise. He was known by the Bonapartists as Napoleon II, but never ruled over France. His memory has been revived in recent times by Rostand's *L'Aiglon* and Sara Bernhardt

The story of the fearful Russian campaign which followed cannot be told here in detail. Napoleon had planned to take three years to conquer Russia, but he was forced on by the necessity of gaining at least one signal victory before he closed the season's campaign. The Russians simply retreated and led him far within a hostile and devastated country before they made a stand at Borodino (September 7). Napoleon won the battle, but his army was reduced to something over one hundred thousand men when he entered Moscow a week later. The town had been set on fire by the Russians before his arrival; he found his position untenable and had to retreat as winter came on. The cold, the want of food, and the harassing attacks of the people along the route made that retreat the most signal military tragedy on record. Napoleon regained Poland early in December with scarcely twenty thousand of the four hundred thousand with which he had started less than six months before.

Napoleon hastened back to Paris, where he freely misrepresented the true state of affairs—as was his wont—even declaring that the army was in a good condition up to the time that he turned it over to Murat in December. While the loss of men in the Russian campaign was enormous, just those few had naturally survived who would be most essential in the formation of a new army; namely, the officers. With their help, Napoleon soon had a force of no less than six hundred thousand men with which to return to the attack. This contained one hundred and fifty thousand conscripts who should not have been called into service until 1814, besides older men who had been hitherto exempted.

By the end of February, 1813, the timid Frederick William had been induced by public sentiment in Prussia to break with his oppressor and join Russia. On March 17, he issued a famous address "To my people," in which he called upon them to assist him in the recovery of Prussian independence. Up to the defeat of Jena, Prussia was far more backward in its social organization than France had been before 1789. The agricultural classes were serfs, who were bound to the land and compelled to work a certain part of each week for the lord without remuneration. The population was divided into strict social castes. Moreover, no noble could buy citizen or peasant land; no citizen, noble or peasant land; no peasant, noble or citizen land.

The overwhelming defeat of the Prussian army at Jena and the provisions of the Treaty of Tilsit, which reduced Prussia to territorial insignificance, forced the leaders of that old-fashioned country to consider whether its weakness was not partly due to its medieval institutions. Neither the king nor his usual advisers were ready for thoroughgoing reform, but there were some more progressive spirits, among whom Baron vom Stein and Prince Hardenberg were conspicuous, who induced the government to alter the old system.

The first step was taken in October, 1807, when a royal decree was issued which declared its purpose to be nothing less than "to remove every obstacle that has hitherto prevented the individual from attaining such a degree of prosperity as he is capable of reaching." Serfdom was formally abolished, and the old class system done away with, so that any one, regardless of social rank, was legally free to purchase and hold landed property, no matter to whom it had formerly belonged.

It is important to note that while serfs had practically disappeared in England and France hundreds of years earlier, it was not until the opening of the nineteenth century, and then under the stress of dire calamity, that Prussia sufficiently modernized herself to abolish the medieval manor and free the peasants until then bound to the soil and sold with it. Moreover, it took several decades to get over the ancient habits, and the former manorial lords, the so-called *Junkers,* remained rich and influential, and continued, with their ancient notions of kingship by the grace of God and military prowess, to exercise a fatal influence on the Prussian government. Furthermore, the mass of the Prussian people seemed to retain—down at least to the World War—something of their old servile attitude toward their masters.

The old army of Frederick the Great had been completely discredited, and a few days after the signing of the Treaty of Tilsit a commission for military reorganization was appointed. The object of the reformers was to introduce a novelty—universal military service. Napoleon permitted Prussia to maintain only a small force of not more than forty-two thousand men, but the Prussian patriots ingeniously arranged that this army should be continually recruited by new men, while those who had had some training should retire and form a reserve. In this way, in spite of Napoleon's restrictions on the size of the regular Prussian army, there were before long as many as a hundred and fifty thousand men sufficiently trained to fight when the opportunity should come. This system was later adopted by other European states and was the basis of the great armies of the Continent at the outbreak of the Great War in 1914.

While serfdom and the old system of social classes were being abolished in Prussia, attempts were being made to rouse the national spirit of the Germans and prepare them to fight against their French conquerors. A leader in this movement was the well-known philosopher Fichte. He arranged a course of public addresses in Berlin, just after the defeat at Jena, in which he laid the foundation for the modern German sense of superiority from which the world has suffered so much. He told his auditors, with impressive warmth and eloquence, that the Germans were the one really superior people in the whole world. All other nations were decadent and had, he was confident, seen their best days; but the future belonged to the Germans, who would in due time, owing to their supreme natural gifts, come into their own and be recognized as the leaders of the world. The German language was, he claimed, an "original" language—*Ursprache*—infinitely stronger than the feeble speech of the French and Italians, borrowed from ancient Latin. Unhappily, later German writers followed Fichte's lead in exaggerating the Germans' self-esteem and their contempt for every other race.

Napoleon had to face now not only the kings and the cabinets of Europe and the regular armies that they directed, but a people who were being organized to defend their country. The campaign which followed is known in Prussia as the "War of Liberation." Napoleon's soldiers were, however, still triumphant for a time. He met with no successful opposition, and on May 14, 1813, he occupied Dresden in the territory of his faithful ally, the king of Saxony. This he held during the summer, and inflicted several defeats upon the allies, who had been joined by Austria in August. He gained his last great victory, the battle of Dresden, August 26-27, 1813. Finding that the allied armies of the Russians, Prussians, and Austrians, which had at last learned the necessity of coöperating against their powerful common enemy, were preparing to cut him off from France, he retreated early in October and was totally defeated in the tremendous "Battle of the Nations," as it has since been called, in the environs of Leipzig (October 16-19).

As the defeated emperor crossed the Rhine with the remnants of his army, the whole fabric of his political edifice in

THE ABDICATION OF NAPOLEON—THE DOCUMENT IN HIS OWN HANDWRITING [1]

Germany and Holland collapsed. The members of the Confederation of the Rhine joined the allies. Jerome Bonaparte fled from his kingdom of Westphalia, and the Dutch drove the French officials from Holland. During the year 1813 the

[1] The document reads as follows: "Les puissances alliées ayant proclamé que l'Empereur Napoléon était le seul obstacle au rétablissement de la paix en Europe, l'Empereur, fidèle a son serment, déclare qu'il renonce, pour lui et pour ses successeurs, aux trônes de France et d'Italie, et qu'il, fidèle a son serment, n'est aucun sacrifice personnel, même celui de la vie, qu'il ne soit prêt a faire aux intérêts de la France."

"The allied powers having proclaimed that the Emperor Napoleon was the sole obstacle to the reëstablishment of peace in Europe, the Emperor, faithful to his oath, proclaims that he renounces, for himself and his successors, the thrones of France and of Italy, and that, faithful to his oath, there is no personal sacrifice, even that of life, that he is not ready to make for the interests of France."

Spanish, with the aid of the English under Wellington, had practically cleared their country of the French intruders.

In spite of these disasters, Napoleon refused the propositions of peace made on condition that he would content himself henceforth with his dominion over France. The allies consequently marched into France, and the almost superhuman

THE RETURN OF NAPOLEON FROM ELBA

Napoleon landed almost alone in France, but had a triumphal march to Paris. The old soldiers of the armies of the empire responded to his call, and even those sent against him yielded to the spell of his personality and joined his small but growing army. Louis XVIII fled from Paris and took refuge with the allies, until Waterloo ended this last great adventure of Napoleon, one hundred days later. The period is often known as "The Hundred Days"

activity of the hard-pressed emperor could not prevent their occupation of Paris (March 31, 1814). Napoleon was forced to abdicate, and the allies, in seeming derision, granted him full sovereignty over the tiny island of Elba and permitted him to retain his imperial title. In reality he was a prisoner on his island kingdom, and the Bourbons reigned again in France.

Within a year, encouraged by the dissensions of the allies and the unpopularity of the Bourbons, he made his escape, landed in France (March 1, 1815), and was received with enthusiasm by a portion of the army. Yet France as a whole was indifferent, if not hostile, to his attempt to reëstablish his power. Certainly no one could place confidence in his talk of peace and liberty. Moreover, whatever disagreement there might be among the allies on other matters, there was perfect unanimity in their attitude toward "the enemy and destroyer of the world's peace." They solemnly proclaimed him an outlaw and devoted him to public vengeance.

Upon learning that English troops under Wellington, the hero of the Peninsular War, and a Prussian army under Blücher, a hero of the War of Liberation, had arrived in the Netherlands, Napoleon decided to attack them with such troops as he could collect. In the first engagements he defeated and drove back the Prussians. Wellington then

TOMB OF NAPOLEON IN PARIS

Napoleon died at St. Helena in 1821. He wished that his ashes should rest amidst the people he had "so dearly loved." The body was brought to Paris in 1840 and placed with great military splendor in this sarcophagus of reddish-brown granite, which was hewn in Finland as a solid block, weighing 67 tons. Around it in the pavement are inscribed the names of Napoleon's greatest victories, while some 60 captured banners stand beside colossal statues of victory. The whole tomb is under the gilded dome of the church of the old soldiers' hospital, known as the Invalides, which rises 161 feet above it [1]

[1] The interior of General Grant's tomb in New York was obviously suggested by that of Napoleon.

took his station south of Brussels, at Waterloo. Napoleon advanced against him (June 18, 1815) but was unable to defeat the English and was finally routed when Blücher's Prussians arrived to aid Wellington. Thus Napoleon lost one of the most memorable of modern battles. Yet, even if he had not been defeated at Waterloo, he could not long have opposed the vast armies which were being concentrated to overthrow him. This time he was banished to the remote island of Saint Helena, where he could only brood over the past and prepare his *Memoirs*, in which he carefully strove to justify his career of ambition. He elaborated "The Napoleonic legend" which was destined to aid one of his relatives in reëstablishing later a second Napoleonic empire.

CHAPTER XXIII

EUROPE AFTER THE CONGRESS OF VIENNA

Marvels of the Past Century. Work of the Congress of Vienna. Influence of Metternich. The German Confederation of 1815. Independence of Latin America. Preliminary Revolutions in Italy. France from Napoleon I to Napoleon III

Marvels of the Past Century

WITH the passing of the spectacular figure of Napoleon from the European stage and the collapse of the vast French empire which he had so skillfully built up with the realms of his neighbors we enter a new phase of European history. We shall see that during the hundred years which separate the Napoleonic upheaval from the great disaster of our own generation, the map of Europe suffered many changes. In the nineteenth century the modern national states —great and small—developed strong sentiments of unity and self-importance. It was this nationalistic rivalry that finally precipitated the great war of 1914,—a catastrophe which, however, affected not only Europe but nearly every part of the globe. In order to discover how the conflicting ambitions of European states came to involve so large a portion of humanity we shall have to broaden our conception of the history of western Europe and take note of the way in which European nations had reached out with their colonies, their trade, and their business enterprise and *Europeanized* a large part of the earth.

This extension of European civilization and control throughout the world is one of the most striking phenomena of the nineteenth century. It was made possible by a series of astonishing inventions which substituted machinery for hand labor in manufacture, thereby multiplying indefinitely the possibility of the world's output of goods. The steam engine and steamboat revolutionized the means of transporting men, food, and goods back and forth across land and sea, and opened up ready access to far-distant countries. Later the telegraph, telephone, and radio established almost instantaneous communication between all parts of the earth. During the brief period which has elapsed since Napoleon's time the momentous changes which have taken place in the conditions of living, in business and commerce and science, have produced a world situation in which all the nations are as intimately involved in one another's affairs as the European powers were in 1815.

In such a changing world the peoples came gradually to change their ideas too. They began to think differently about kings and diplomats and the special privileges enjoyed for so long by a small group only. They began to see that they too might play some part in affairs, and so they questioned their relation to the government, to their own work, and to their chance of betterment in life.[1] So it came about that the arrangements made by the old-fashioned statesmen in 1815 to insure permanent peace by reëstablishing the old order proved but a temporary settlement, and the very tendencies which they took such careful measures to circumvent began, almost immediately, to show their strength.

Work of the Congress of Vienna

Immediately after Napoleon's abdication the allies reinstated the Bourbon dynasty on the throne of France in the person of Louis XVI's younger brother, the count of Provence, who became Louis XVIII.[2] They first restricted France to the boundaries that she had had at the beginning of 1792, but later deprived her of Savoy as a punishment for yielding to the domination of Napoleon after his return from Elba. A great congress of the European powers was summoned to meet at Vienna, where the allies proposed to settle all those difficult problems that faced them. They had no idea of reëstablishing things just as they were before the Napoleonic period, for

[1] During the English Revolution in Cromwell's time and the French Revolution of 1789 many new ideas in regard to government and human relations made their appearance, but it took the social, economic, and scientific revolutions of the nineteenth century to substantiate them and to spread them throughout the world.

[2] The son of Louis XVI had been imprisoned and maltreated by the terrorists. He died while still a boy in 1795, but nevertheless takes his place in the line of French kings as Louis XVII.

the simple reason that Austria, Russia, and Prussia all had schemes for their own advantage that precluded so simple an arrangement.

The Congress of Vienna began its sessions November 1, 1814. The allies quickly agreed that Holland should become a hereditary kingdom under the house of Orange, which had long played so conspicuous a rôle in the nominal republic. In order that Holland might be the better able to check any new encroachments on the part of France, the former Austrian Netherlands were given to her. Switzerland was declared independent, as were all the small Italian states which had existed prior to the innovations of Napoleon, except the ancient republics of Venice and Genoa, neither of which was restored. Genoa was given to the king of Sardinia; Venetia to Austria, as an indemnity for her losses in the Netherlands. Austria also received back her former territory of Milan, and became, by reason of her control of northern Italy, a powerful factor in determining the fate of the whole Italian peninsula. As to Germany, no one desired to undo the great work of 1803 and restore the old monarchy. The former members of the Rhine Confederation were bent upon maintaining the "sovereignty" which Napoleon had secured for them; consequently the allies determined that the several states of Germany should be independent, but "united in a federal union."

So far all was tolerably harmonious. Nevertheless, serious differences of opinion developed at the congress, which nearly brought on war among the allies themselves, and encouraged Napoleon's return from Elba. These concerned the disposition of the Polish territory that Napoleon had converted into the grand duchy of Warsaw. The Tsar was bent on restoring the kingdom of Poland as a separate state over which he was to rule as king, thus uniting Poland in a "personal union" with Russia. The king of Prussia was reluctantly persuaded to support the Tsar in this scheme on condition that Prussia should be indemnified for her losses in the East by annexing the lands of the king of Saxony. The Saxon king, they argued, merited this retribution for remaining faithful to Napoleon after the other members of the Confederation of the Rhine had repudiated him. Austria and England, on the other hand, were bitterly opposed to this arrangement. They did not favor dispossessing the king of Saxony and they were hotly against seeing Russian influence extended westward by giving Poland to the Tsar.

The great diplomatist, Talleyrand, who represented Louis XVIII at the congress, now saw his chance. The allies had resolved to treat France as a black sheep, and permit the other four great powers to arrange matters to suit themselves. But they were now hopelessly at odds. Talleyrand dexterously took advantage of this dissension to restore France to a place of importance. He offered to support Austria with arms, if necessary, against the schemes of the Tsar. In this way France became aligned with Austria and England against Russia and Prussia, and the disturber of the peace of Europe for the last quarter of a century was received back into the family of nations.

A compromise was finally reached, however. The Tsar was allowed to create a kingdom of Poland out of the grand duchy of Warsaw, but only half of the possessions of the king of Saxony were ceded to Prussia. As a further indemnity Frederick William III was given certain districts on the left bank of the Rhine which had belonged to ecclesiastical and petty lay princes before the Treaty of Lunéville. This seemingly innocent adjustment proved one of the most tremendous in its consequences of all the decisions of the Congress of Vienna. In ratifying it England and France had no suspicion that they were furnishing material for a far more terrible conflict than that from which they were emerging. Before Napoleon's time Prussia held only two or three bits of territory on the Rhine, north of Cologne. As the allies contemplated the feeble Frederick William III they could hardly have suspected that a future Prussian king would become the aggressive head of a united Germany and would take advantage of the fact that his boundaries were contiguous to those of Belgium, Luxemburg, and France. Furthermore, if one hundred years later

Castlereagh, Talleyrand, and the other diplomats at Vienna could have revisited the sleepy little towns of the Ruhr valley which they so negligently handed over to Prussia, they would have seen them transformed into busy centers for the production of the great modern machinery of commerce and war. For in Essen, Barmen, Düsseldorf, and Elberfeld they would have found hundreds of thousands of workers devoting their energy to the creation of Germany's national wealth and military preëminence.

Influence of Metternich

The representatives of the allies at Vienna were not only intent on arranging peace but were determined as well to keep such additional territory as they had gained during the Napoleonic wars. Austria had emerged from the disorder the dominant power in Europe, and, under the leadership of her astute statesman Count Metternich, for thirty years she held the foremost place in European affairs and dictated the policy of the Central European powers. The allies, however, restored in the smaller countries the monarchs who had been displaced by Napoleon and whom they regarded as "legitimately" entitled to rule. In Spain, Holland, northern Germany, and Naples the former ruling families were given back their thrones.

Having arranged the map of Europe as they desired, the statesmen of the four great powers determined to provide against any future revolutionary uprising which might undo their work. On the same day that the final treaty was signed embodying the decisions of the Congress of Vienna (November 20, 1815) Austria, Russia, Prussia, and England entered a secret alliance agreeing to hold meetings from time to time and to take such measures as might seem to them necessary to preserve order in Europe.[1]

[1] This Quadruple Alliance, as it is called, has often been confused with the Holy Alliance published in September, 1815. This was a pious document, promoted by the Tsar, in which the members viewed themselves as "delegates of Providence" ruling over various branches of the same family, and promised to base their policy on "the sublime truths which are taught by the eternal religion of God our Saviour." The Tsar and the king of Prussia were the only monarchs who took this alliance seriously. Owing

In attempting to restore the old aristocratic régime with its inequalities and unfairnesses Metternich and his associates made use of all the old machinery of intimidation and force. They seemed to have learned but little from the English or the French revolutions and to have believed that a small group of aristocrats could fasten permanently on the "underlying population" of Europe a system devised for its subjugation. They did not remember, or would not recognize, that in France at least men had experienced what it was to be free from the old feudal burdens, and that the idea of a constitution which explicitly stated what the king might do and might not do and what the rights of the common people were had fired the imagination of progressive men throughout Europe.

They also failed to appreciate the fundamental and persistent character of the tendency of those who speak the same language and feel bound by ties of kinship to unite in a common cause and form a government of their own. For all their shrewd diplomacy in dealing with one another, the statesmen at Vienna showed a singular obtuseness in dealing with their enemies. They built their hopes of tranquillity on secret treaties, alliances, espionage, censorship of speech and writing, imprisonment, and war. Although from 1815 to 1848 they were able to put down all revolutionary uprisings, not long after that the supporters of the system of Metternich found themselves outnumbered by the champions of constitutional government and national unity.

The German Confederation of 1815

One of the most important questions which the Congress of Vienna failed to settle satisfactorily was the problem of the federation of Germany. The formation of a strong union of German peoples as a protection against invasion by a foreign power had been the aspiration of German patriots ever since their disastrous defeat at Jena. The chief effects of the Napoleonic occupation of Germany were three in number:

---

probably to its picturesque title and conception, it has borne the responsibility for many of the deeds which were really the acts of the Quadruple Alliance.

First, the consolidation of territory that followed the cession of the left bank of the Rhine to France had, as has been explained, done away with the anomalous ecclesiastical states, the territories of the knights, and most of the free towns. Only thirty-eight German states, including four towns, were left when the Congress of Vienna took up the question of finding something to replace the defunct Holy Roman Empire.

Second, the external and internal conditions of Prussia had been so changed as to open the way for it eventually to supplant Austria as the controlling power in Germany. A great part of the Slavic possessions gained in the last two partitions of Poland had been lost, but as an indemnity Prussia had received half of the kingdom of Saxony, in the very center of Germany, and also the Rhine provinces, which later proved to be so important. Prussia, moreover, was comparatively free from the presence of non-German races, and in this respect offered a marked contrast to the heterogeneous population of its great rival Austria.

The internal changes were no less remarkable. The reforms carried out after Jena by the distinguished minister Stein and his successor, Hardenberg, had done for Prussia somewhat the same that the first National Assembly had done for France. The abolition of serfdom, which in reality required several decades to carry out, and the removal of the feudal restrictions on the buying and selling of land made the economic development of the country possible.[1] The reorganization of the whole military system prepared the way for Prussia's great victories in 1866 and 1870, which led to the formation of a new German empire under her headship.

Third, the agitations of the Napoleonic period had aroused the national spirit. The appeal to the people to aid in the freeing of their country from foreign oppression, and the idea of their participation in a government based upon a written constitution, had produced widespread discontent with the old absolute monarchy and a general demand that the rulers should grant constitutions to their subjects.

[1] See above, p. 522.

Pl. xxxii. The Congress of Vienna

ALEXANDER I

TALLEYRAND

METTERNICH

Pl. xxxiii. Important Members of the Congress of Vienna

When the form of union for the German states came up for discussion at the Congress of Vienna, two different plans were advocated. Prussia's representatives submitted a scheme for a firm union like that of the United States, in which the central government should control the individual states in all matters of general interest. This idea was opposed by Austria, who was supported by the other German rulers. Austria realized that her possessions, as a whole, could never be included in any real German union, for in the western portion of her territory there were many Slavs, while in Hungary and the southern provinces there were practically no Germans at all. She hoped, however, that she might be the leader in a very loose union in which all the members should be left practically independent. Her proposal of an international union of sovereign princes under her own headship was almost completely realized in the constitution which was adopted.

The confederation was not a union of the various *countries* involved, but of "The Sovereign Princes and Free Towns of Germany," including the emperor of Austria and the king of Prussia for such of their possessions as were formerly included in the Holy Roman Empire; the king of Denmark for Holstein; and the king of the Netherlands for the grand duchy of Luxemburg. The union thus included two sovereigns who were out-and-out foreigners, and did not include all the possessions of its most important two members.

The diet, which held its meetings at Frankfurt, was composed (as was perfectly logical), not of representatives of the people, but of plenipotentiaries of the rulers who were members of the confederation. The several states reserved to themselves the right of forming alliances of all kinds, but pledged themselves to make no agreement prejudicial to the safety of the union or of any of its members, or to make war upon any member of the confederation on any pretense whatsoever. The constitution could not be amended without the approval of *all* the states of the union. In spite of its obvious weaknesses, the confederation of 1815 lasted for a half a century, until Prussia

[535]

finally expelled Austria from the union by arms, and incorporated the rest of Germany in the German Empire.

The liberal and progressive party in Germany was sadly disappointed by the failure of the Congress of Vienna to weld Germany into a really national state. They were troubled, too, by the delay of the king of Prussia in granting the constitution that he had promised to his subjects. But Frederick William III was a timid monarch and had lived through such a

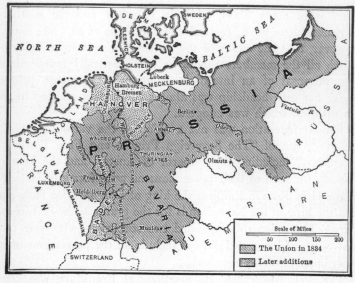

THE ZOLLVEREIN

period of revolutionary disorder that he was easily influenced by Metternich, who was devoting his energy to the suppression of every tendency toward democratic reform. When, therefore, German students began to form political societies and to join with other liberals in violent protests against a reactionary government, Metternich seized the opportunity to point out the terrible results which followed the freedom of speech and writing. He called a meeting at Carlsbad of the representatives of the larger German states and persuaded the diet to adopt drastic resolutions providing that the teaching of the professors in the universities should be supervised and those who taught dangerous doctrines dismissed. The general students' union, which was regarded as too revolutionary, was to be suppressed. Moreover, no newspaper, magazine, or pamphlet was to go to press without the previous approval of government officials, who were to determine whether it contained anything tending to foster discontent with the government.

This attack upon the freedom of the press, and especially the interference with the liberty of teaching in the great institutions of learning, which were already becoming the home of the highest scholarship, scandalized all the progressive spirits in Germany. Yet no successful protest was raised, and Germany as a whole acquiesced for a generation in Metternich's system of discouraging reform of all kinds.

Nevertheless, important progress was made in southern Germany. As early as 1818 the king of Bavaria granted his people a constitution in which he stated their rights and admitted them to a share in the government by establishing a parliament. His example was followed within two years by the rulers of Baden, Württemberg, and Hesse. These smaller German states had come to resent the interference of Austria in German affairs and were less afraid now that their "sovereign" rights would suffer from constitutional reform than from the dictation of Austria and Prussia.

Another change for the better was the gradual formation of a customs union—*Zollverein*—which permitted goods to be sent freely from one German state to another without the payment of duties at each boundary line. This yielded some of the advantages of a political union. This economic union, of which Prussia was the head, and from which Austria was excluded, created a sense of business unity among its members and was a harbinger of the future German empire.

Independence of Latin America

Napoleon had been as thoroughly despotic in his government as any of the monarchs who regained their thrones after his downfall, but he was a son of the Revolution and had no sympathy with the ancient abuses that it had done away with. In spite of his despotism, the spirit and reforms of the French Revolution had exercised a good deal of influence on the countries that had come under his influence. Nevertheless, the restored monarchs in many of the smaller European states proceeded to reëstablish the ancient feudal customs and to treat their subjects as if there had been no French Revolution and no such man as Napoleon. In Hesse-Cassel, which had formed a part of the kingdom of Westphalia, all the reforms introduced by Napoleon and his brother were abolished. The privileges of the nobility, and also the feudal burdens of the peasantry, were restored. The soldiers were even required to assume the discarded pigtails and powdered wigs of the eighteenth century. In Sardinia and Naples the returning monarchs pursued the same policy of reaction.

In Spain the reaction following the restoration of Ferdinand VII was especially striking. The constitution which enlightened liberals had succeeded in getting adopted in 1812 was annulled, all the decrees of the Cortes were declared void, and an absolute monarchy was reëstablished. The renewed power of the nobles and clergy was immediately evident in the revival of the old feudal privileges, the exemption of the clergy from taxation, and the restoration of the monasteries. At the urgent request of the clergy the Inquisition was reëstablished. The great mass of the peasants were under the influence of the clergy and saw in the return of the king only freedom from foreign rule and the triumph of the mother Church. They understood nothing of the character of the government, but had a slavish reverence for authority. On the other hand, the educated townspeople and liberals found themselves in a desperate plight. The leaders of the Cortes were imprisoned and, by an arbitrary decree of the king, sentenced to long terms of confinement, although they had been proved innocent of the charge of treason. The country was filled with brigands who preyed on the people. The mismanagement of the king's favorites had reduced the State to bankruptcy. Commerce and agriculture had fallen to ruin. Freedom of speech was denied, and books and newspapers were censored. Many liberals were seized and put in prison and in some cases executed. As time went on things grew worse rather than better.

Far more important, however, than the discontent at home was the revolt of the Spanish colonies in North and South America from the mother country. Spain had always treated her colonies harshly, monopolized their trade, and used them chiefly as a source of profit to her own grandees and merchants. As early as 1810 Mexico, New Granada (now Colombia), Venezuela, Peru, Argentina, and Chile, while they still professed to be loyal to the Spanish monarch, took their government into their own hands and drove out the Spanish officials. At first these revolts were put down with great cruelty; but in 1817, under the leadership of Bolivar, Venezuela won its entire independence. During the following five years the Spaniards also lost New Granada, Peru, Ecuador, Chile, Mexico, and lastly (1825) Upper Peru, which was named Bolivia after its liberator.

The revolt against Ferdinand's unyielding despotism that was growing throughout Spain finally spread to the army. Many of the soldiers had not received their pay for years, while sometimes even food was lacking. Moreover, thousands were sent to death in putting down the revolt in the South American colonies. At last in January, 1820, the army waiting at Cadiz to be dispatched overseas revolted. The revolution soon spread to Madrid, where a mob surrounded the palace and forced the king to take an oath to restore the constitution of 1812. Frederick called upon the great powers for aid, and in 1822 the members of the Quadruple Alliance met at Verona to consider what should be done. Great Britain, the only one of the powers with a fleet large enough to be of assistance, refused to aid Ferdinand in trying to regain the South American colonies. But Louis XVIII was induced to send an army across the Pyrenees. The French easily defeated the revolutionists and put Ferdinand in a position to take vengeance on his enemies.

The French government soon sickened of its part in the proceeding when it saw the bloodthirsty manner in which Ferdinand dealt with his foes.

The Spanish were so occupied with their difficulties at home that they had neither money nor ships to subdue the colonies. However, the threats of Metternich and his friends to help Spain force the colonies into submission led President Monroe to call the attention of the Congress of the United States to the danger of European interference and to state clearly what has since become famous as the Monroe Doctrine; namely, that the United States would consider any attempt on the part of the European powers to extend their system to any portion of this hemisphere as dangerous to the peace and safety of the United States, and as an unfriendly act.

Preliminary Revolutions in Italy

Italy was at this time what Metternich called only "a geographical expression"; it had no political unity whatever. Lombardy and Venetia, in the northern part, were in the hands of Austria; and Parma, Modena, and Tuscany belonged to members of the Austrian family. In the south, the considerable kingdom of the Two Sicilies was ruled over by a branch of the Spanish Bourbons. In the center, cutting the peninsula in twain, were the ancient Papal States, which extended north to the Po. The presence of Austria, and the apparent impossibility of inducing the pope to submit to any government but his own, seemed to preclude all hope of making Italy into a true nation. Yet fifty years later the kingdom of Italy, as it now appears on the map of Europe, came into existence through the final exclusion of Austria from the peninsula and the extinction of the political power of the pope.

Although Napoleon had governed Italy despotically he had introduced a great many important reforms. He had established political equality and an orderly administration, and had forwarded public improvements; the vestiges of the feudal régime had vanished at his approach. Moreover, he had held out the hope of a united Italy, from which the foreign powers who had plagued and distracted her for centuries should be banished. But his unscrupulous use of Italy to advance his personal ambitions disappointed those who at first had placed their hopes in him, and they came to desire his downfall as eagerly as did the nobility and the dispossessed clergy, whose hopes were centered in Austria. It became clear to the more thoughtful Italians that Italy must look to herself and her own resources if she were ever to become an independent European state.

The overthrow of Napoleon left Italy seemingly in a worse state than that in which he had found it. The hold of Austria was strengthened by her acquisition of Venice. The petty despots of Parma, Modena, and Tuscany, reseated on their thrones by the Congress of Vienna, hastened to sweep away the reforms of the Corsican and to reëstablish all the abuses of the old régime, now doubly conspicuous and obnoxious by reason of their temporary abolition. The lesser Italian princes, moreover, showed themselves to be heartily in sympathy with the hated Austria. Active discontent spread throughout the peninsula and led to the formation of numerous secret societies, which assumed strange names, practiced mysterious rites, and plotted darkly in the name of Italian liberty and independence. By far the most noted of these associations was that of the *Carbonari*, i.e., charcoal burners. Its objects were individual liberty, constitutional government, and national independence and unity; these it undertook to promote by agitation, conspiracy, and, if necessary, by revolution.

The Italian agitators had a superstitious respect for a constitution; they appear to have regarded it not so much as a form of government to be carefully adapted to the needs of a particular country and time, as a species of talisman which would insure liberty and prosperity to its happy possessor. So when the Neapolitans heard that the king of Spain had been forced by an insurrection to grant a constitution, they made the first attempt on the part of the Italian people to gain constitutional liberty by compelling their king to agree to accept the Spanish constitution (July, 1820). However, at the same time that the monarch was invoking the vengeance of God upon his own head should he violate his oath of fidelity to the constitution, he was casting about for foreign assistance to suppress the revolution and enable him to return to his old ways.

He had not long to wait. The alert Metternich invited Russia, Prussia, France, and England to unite in order to check the development of "revolt and crime." He declared that the liberal movements, if unrestrained, would prove "not less tyrannical and fearful" in their results than that against which the allies had combined in the person of Napoleon. "Revolution" appeared to him and his conservative sympathizers as heresy appeared to Philip II,—it was a fearful disease that not only destroyed those whom it attacked directly, but spread contagion wherever it appeared and justified prompt and sharp measures of quarantine and even violent intervention with a view of stamping out the devastating plague.

To the great joy of the king of Naples, Austria marched its troops into his territory (March, 1821) and, meeting but an ill-organized opposition, freed him from the limitations which his subjects had for the moment imposed upon him. An attempt on the part of the subjects of the king of Sardinia to win a constitution was also repressed by Austrian troops.

The weakness of the liberal movement in both southern and northern Italy appeared to be conclusively demonstrated. A new attempt ten years later, in Piedmont, Modena, and the Papal States, to get rid of the existing despotism was quite as futile as the revolution of 1820-1821. Yet there were two hopeful signs. Great Britain protested as early as 1820 against Metternich's theory of interfering in the domestic affairs of other independent states in order to prevent reforms of which he disapproved, and France emphatically repudiated the doctrine of intervention on the accession of Louis Philippe in 1830. A second and far more important indication of progress was the increasing conviction on the part of the Italians themselves that their country ought to be a single nation and not, as hitherto, a group of small independent states under foreign influence.

Bourbon line of monarchs in France. From this time on Louis ceased to oppose the actions of the ultra-royalists and permitted the parliament to pass various oppressive measures. He was even persuaded to coöperate with the allies in attempting to quell the revolution in Spain.

In 1824 the aged king died, and the count of Artois at last came to the throne as Charles X. The new king had a very different temperament from that of his predecessor. For thirty years he had been fretting to restore the lost authority of the Bourbons and he now determined to rule with the power if not the glory of Louis XIV. Regardless of the warnings of the past he proceeded to rouse antagonism on all sides by his tactless methods and offensive measures. He soon showed his contempt for the Charter and made it plain that he intended to govern as he saw fit. He reëstablished the power of the Catholic Church and put education once more in the hands of the priests. He greatly increased the number of his enemies by enacting a law which provided for the indemnifying of the *émigrés* for their losses in the Revolution. The sum of a billion francs was to be raised for this purpose by reducing the payment of interest on the 5-per-cent government bonds to 3 per cent and handing over the balance to the nobles. This measure greatly antagonized the merchants, business men, and bankers, who did not wish to see their income going into the pockets of the *émigrés*.

The royalists who had controlled the House of Deputies finally lost their influence, and republicans were elected in their places. When the king found that he was no longer in command of the Chamber, he dissolved it and boldly issued a series of decrees forbidding the publication of any journal without royal permission, limiting the vote to wealthy landholders, and providing that in future the king alone could make new laws. These ordinances took away from the French people practically all the rights granted in the Charter and placed them once more at the mercy of the king.

The following day (July 26, 1830), the newspapers published a protest and stated their intention to disregard the ordinances.

Encouraged by the stand which the journalists had taken, the republicans, who had never given up their dreams of 1792 and had maintained their secret societies all along, proceeded to organize an armed revolt. They were joined by workmen from the printing presses and from other establishments, and the revolt grew until Paris was in the hands of the insurgents. The king, who was at his palace at St. Cloud, refused to take the insurrection seriously, regarding it as a mere street fight.

When he finally realized the situation, he promised to repeal the offensive measures, but it was too late. A group of business men and bankers had already made plans to place on the throne Louis Philippe, a descendant of Henry IV through the Orleans branch of the Bourbon family.[1] Louis Philippe had associated with the Jacobins and fought in the army of the republic. Later he was exiled, but after the restoration he had become reconciled to Louis XVIII. He did not join the royalist party, however, but sought popular favor by professing democratic opinions and living the life of a plain citizen.

[1] THE BOURBON KINGS
Henry IV (the first of the Bourbon line; d. 1610)

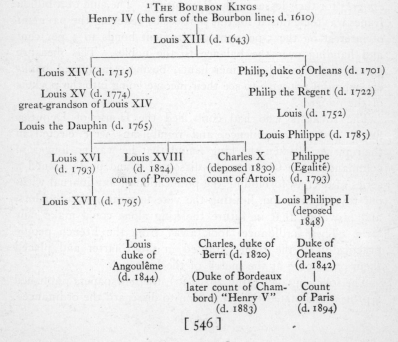

Louis XIII (d. 1643)

Louis XIV (d. 1715)   Philip, duke of Orleans (d. 1701)

Louis XV (d. 1774)   Philip the Regent (d. 1722)
great-grandson of Louis XIV
                                       Louis (d. 1752)
Louis the Dauphin (d. 1765)
                                       Louis Philippe (d. 1785)

Louis XVI   Louis XVIII   Charles X   Philippe
(d. 1793)   (d. 1824)   (deposed 1830)   (Egalité)
               count of Provence count of Artois (d. 1793)

Louis XVII (d. 1795)   Louis Philippe I
                                               (deposed
                                               1848)

        Louis   Charles, duke of   Duke of
        duke of   Berri (d. 1820)   Orleans
        Angoulême   (d. 1842)
        (d. 1844)   (Duke of Bordeaux
                       later count of Cham- Count
                       bord) "Henry V"   of Paris
                       (d. 1883)   (d. 1894)

He made friends with the bankers and business men of Paris and sent his children to the public schools. He was therefore the natural candidate for those who wished to retain a monarchy but to establish the middle class in control in place of the nobles and clergy. When Charles was convinced that he could no longer keep the crown, he abdicated, and Louis Philippe was made king of France. The republicans who had carried through the revolt were sadly disappointed, for they found that their party was not yet strong enough to prevent another monarch from gaining the French throne. Both the aristocrats and republicans had been forced to give way before the rising middle class of business men—the bourgeoisie.

The July revolution of 1830 had in reality brought few changes. The new king professed more liberal views, but the government was hardly more democratic than before. Parliament made the necessary changes in the Charter: freedom of the press was reaffirmed, and the provision which established the Roman Catholic religion as the religion of the State was stricken out; the tri-colored flag of the Revolution replaced the white banner of the Bourbons; but France was still a monarchy, and these changes seemed slight to the ardent republicans and to the new socialists (who wished to see the middle class divested of their wealth as the nobles and clergy formerly had been). They maintained that the king had too much power and could influence the parliament to make laws contrary to the wishes of the people. They also protested against the laws which excluded the poorer classes from voting (only two hundred thousand among a population of thirty million enjoyed that right), and demanded that every Frenchman should have the right to vote as soon as he reached maturity. As Louis Philippe grew older he became more and more suspicious of the liberal parties which had helped him to his throne. He not only opposed reforms himself, but also did all he could to keep the parliament and the newspapers from advocating any changes which the progressive parties demanded. Nevertheless, the strength of the republicans gradually increased. They found strong allies in the new group of socialistic writers who desired a fundamental reorganization of the state.[1]

On February 24, 1848, a mob attacked the Tuileries. The king abdicated in favor of his grandson, but it was too late; he and his whole family were forced to leave the country. The mob invaded the assembly, as in the time of the Reign of Terror, crying, "Down with the Bourbons, old and new! Long live the Republic!" A provisional government was established which included the writer Lamartine, Louis Blanc, a prominent socialist, two or three editors, and several politicians. The first decree of this body, ratifying the establishment of the republic, was solemnly proclaimed on the former site of the Bastille, February 27.

The provisional government was scarcely in session before it was threatened by the "red republic," whose representatives, the social democrats, desired to put the laboring classes in control of the government, and let them conduct it in their own interests. Some advocated community of property, and wished to substitute the red flag for the national colors.[2] The government went so far as to concede the so-called "right to labor," and agreed to establish national workshops, in which all the unemployed were to be given an opportunity to work.

A National Assembly had been convoked whose members were elected by the ballots of all Frenchmen above the age of twenty-one. The result of the election was an overwhelming defeat for the social democrats. Their leaders then attempted to overthrow the new assembly on the pretext that it did not represent the people; but the national guard frustrated the attempt. The number of men now enrolled in the merely promised "national workshops" had reached one hundred and seventeen thousand, each of whom received two francs a day in return for either useless labor or mere idleness. The abolition of this nuisance led to a serious revolt. Battle raged

[1] See close of following chapter.

[2] The red flag of the socialists typifies the essential blood that courses in the veins of rich and poor alike. To their enemies it is a symbol of bloody revolt. "Like a red rag to a bull," is the natural reflection of one who tries to be on his guard against the insidious workings of symbols.

in the streets of Paris for three days, and over ten thousand persons were killed, June, 1848.

This wild outbreak of the forces of revolution resulted in a general conviction that a strong hand was essential to the maintenance of peace. The new constitution decreed that the president of the republic should be chosen by the people at large. Their choice fell upon the nephew of Napoleon Bonaparte, Louis Napoleon, who had already made two futile attempts to make himself the ruler of France. Before the expiration of his four years' term he succeeded, by a *coup d'état* on the anniversary of the coronation of his uncle (December 2, 1851), in setting up a new government. He next obtained, by means of a plebiscite, the consent of the people to his remaining president for ten years. A year later (1852) the second empire was established, and Napoleon III became "Emperor of the French by the grace of God and the will of the people."

Two events, at least, during the period of Metternich's influence served to encourage the liberals of Europe. In 1821 the inhabitants of Greece had revolted against the oppressive government of the Turks, and succeeded in forcing the Sultan to acknowledge their independence in 1829.[1]

Another little kingdom—Belgium—was added to the European states by the revolt of the former Austrian Netherlands from the king of Holland, to whom they had been assigned by the Congress of Vienna. The southern Netherlands were still as different from the northern as they had been in the time of William the Silent. Holland was Protestant and German, while the southern provinces, to whom the union had always been distasteful, were Catholic and akin to the French in their sympathies. Encouraged by the revolution at Paris in 1830, the people of Brussels rose in revolt against their Dutch king, and forced his troops to leave the city. Through the influence of England and France the European powers agreed to recognize the independence of the Belgians, who established a kingdom and introduced an excellent constitution providing for a limited monarchy modeled upon that of England.

[1] See below, p. 651.

CHAPTER XXIV

THE DAWN OF OUR AGE OF MACHINES

*Machines for Spinning and Weaving. The Steam Engine. Effects of
the Factory System. Origin of Socialism*

Machines for Spinning and Weaving

IN the preceding chapters we have reviewed the startling
changes and reforms introduced by the leaders of the
French Revolution and by Napoleon Bonaparte, and the
reconstruction of Europe at the Congress of Vienna. These
were mainly the work of statesmen, warriors, and diplomats—
who have certainly done their part in making Europe what it
is to-day. But a still more fundamental revolution than that
which has been described had begun in England before the
meeting of the Estates General, in 1789.

The chief actors in this never stirred an assembly by their
fiery denunciation of abuses, or led an army to victory, or conducted a clever diplomatic negotiation. On the contrary, their
attention was concentrated upon the homely operations of
every-day life—the housewife drawing out her thread with
distaff or spinning wheel, the slow work of the weaver at his
primitive loom, the miner struggling against the water which
threatened to flood his mine. They busied themselves per-
severingly with wheels, cylinders, bands, and rollers, patiently
combining and recombining them, until, after many discourage-
ments, they made discoveries destined to alter the habits, ideas,
and prospects of the great mass of the people far more profoundly than all the edicts of the National Assembly and all
the conquests of Napoleon taken together.

The Greeks and Romans, notwithstanding their refined civilization, had, as has been pointed out, shown slight aptitude for
mechanical invention, and only a few important contrivances
had been added to their stock of human resources before the
middle of the eighteenth century. Up to that time the people of
western Europe for the most part continued to till their fields,
weave their cloth, and saw and plane their boards by hand,
much as the ancient Egyptians had done. Merchandise was

[550]

still transported in slow, lumbering carts, and letters were as long in passing from London to Rome as in the reign of Constantine. Could a peasant, a smith, or a weaver of the age of Cæsar Augustus have visited France or England eighteen hundred years later, he would have recognized the familiar flail, forge, distaff, and hand loom of his own day.

Suddenly, however, a series of ingenious devices were invented, which in a few generations eclipsed the achievements of ages and revolutionized every branch of business. This *Industrial Revolution* serves to explain the world in which we live, with its busy cities, its gigantic factories filled with complicated machinery, its commerce and vast fortunes, its trade-unions and labor parties, its bewildering variety of plans for bettering the lot of the great mass of the people. This story of mechanical invention has proved more revolutionary than the more familiar history of kings, parliaments, wars, treaties, and constitutions.

DISTAFF AND SPINDLE

The revolution in manufacture which has taken place in the last hundred and fifty years can be illustrated by the improvement in making cloth, which is so necessary to our comfort and welfare. In order to produce cloth one must first *spin* (that is, twist) the wool, cotton, or flax into thread; then by means of a loom the thread can be *woven* into a fabric. A simple way of spinning thread was discovered thousands of years ago but it was possible by the old methods for a person to make only a single thread at a time.[1] By 1767

---

[1] The hand spinner had bunches of wool, which had been combed into loose curls, on the end of a stick, or distaff, and then pulled and twisted these with her fingers into a yarn, which she wound on the spindle. By whirling the spindle around she could help twist. The spinning wheel was

James Hargreaves, an English spinner, invented what was called a spinning jenny, which enabled a single workman, by turning a wheel, to spin eight or ten threads at once, and thus do the work of eight or ten spinners. A year later a barber, Richard Arkwright, patented a device for drawing out thread by means of rollers, and made a large fortune—for his time —by establishing a great factory filled with power-driven machines. In 1779 Samuel Crompton made a happy combination of Hargreaves's spinning jenny and Arkwright's roller machine, which was called the mule. Before the end of the eighteenth century, machines spinning two hundred threads simultaneously had been invented, and as they were driven by power and required only one or two watchers, the hand workers could by no means compete with them. Such inventions as these produced the factory system of manufacture.

THE FIRST SPINNING JENNY

The enormous output of thread and yarn on these new machines made the weavers dissatisfied with the clumsy old hand loom, which had been little changed for many centuries until the eighteenth century. At length, in 1784, Dr. Cartwright, a clergyman of Kent, patented a new loom, which automatically threw the shuttle and shifted the weft. This machine was steadily improved during the nineteenth century until now a single machine watched by one workman can do as much weaving in a day as two hundred weavers could do with old-

invented to give a better twist to the spindle. It was used by our great-grandmothers, and became common in the sixteenth and seventeenth centuries. By means of the spinning wheel it was possible in some cases for one person to make two threads, one in one hand and the other in the other.

fashioned hand looms. Other inventions followed. The time required for bleaching was reduced from several months to a few days by the use of acids, instead of relying principally upon the sunlight. In 1792 Eli Whitney, in the United States, invented a power "gin," which, as it was improved, enabled one man to take the seeds out of over a thousand pounds of cotton a day instead of five or six pounds, which had been the limit for the hand worker.

MODERN SPINNING MULE

The effect of these inventions in increasing the amount of cloth manufactured was astonishing. In 1764 England imported only about four million pounds of raw cotton, but by 1841 she was using nearly five hundred million pounds annually. At the close of the Napoleonic wars Robert Owen, a distinguished manufacturer and reformer, declared that his two thousand workmen at New Lanark could do as much work with the new machinery which had been invented during the past forty years as all the operators of Scotland could do without it.

The Steam Engine

In order that inventions could further develop and become widely useful, two things were necessary. In the first place, there had to be available a sufficiently strong material out of which to construct the machinery, and for this purpose iron and steel have, with few exceptions, proved the most satisfactory. In the second place, some adequate power had to be found to propel the machinery, which is ordinarily too heavy to be run by hand or foot. Of course windmills were common, and waterfalls and running streams had long been used to turn water wheels, but these forces were too restricted and uncertain to suffice for the rapid development of machinery, which resulted from the beginnings we have described. Consequently while Arkwright, Hargreaves, and Crompton were successfully solving the problem of new methods of spinning and weaving, other inventors were improving the ways of melting and forging iron for the machines and of using steam to run them.

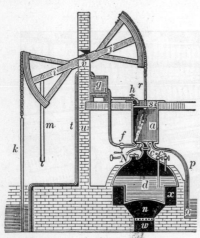

NEWCOMEN'S STEAM ENGINE

Newcomen's steam engines were run by condensing the steam in the cylinder (*a*) by cold water (*g*), so that the air on the piston (*s*) pressed it down on the vacuum. Watt covered both ends of the cylinder and used steam instead of air to push the piston

Although iron had been used for tools, weapons, and armor for hundreds of years, the processes of reducing the iron from the ore and of working it up were very crude. It was not until 1750 that coal began to be used instead of charcoal for melting, or softening, the metal. The old-fashioned bellows gave way to new ways of producing the blast necessary for melting iron, and steam hammers were invented to pound out the iron instead of doing it by hand.

Contrary to popular impression, James Watt did not invent the steam engine. Important parts of the engine—the boiler, the cylinder, and the piston—had been invented before he was born, and crude engines had been employed for a long time in pumping water. Indeed, Watt's interest in the steam engine seems to have been awakened first during the winter of 1763-1764, when, as an instrument maker in Glasgow, he was called upon to repair the model of a steam engine which had been invented sixty years before by an ingenious mechanic named Newcomen. Watt, however, was a brilliant and industrious experimenter, and, building upon the work of Newcomen and other men, he was able to make the steam engine a practical machine for furnishing power to the new factories. In 1785 the steam engine was first applied to run spinning machinery in a factory in Nottinghamshire. Arkwright adopted it in 1790, and by the end of the century steam engines were becoming as common as wind and water mills.

England was the first country to develop the modern use of machinery for manufacturing. It was not until after establishment of peace in 1815 that the Industrial Revolution really began in France. Napoleon endeavored to foster and protect French industries and stimulate the employment of machinery in manufacturing; but in spite of his best efforts, French industry remained in a backward state. On the eve of his downfall there was only one small steam engine employed in French industry—at a cotton factory in Alsace; but by 1847 France had nearly five thousand steam engines with a capacity of sixty thousand horse power. Germany was also much behind England.

The consumption of raw cotton was multiplied fivefold in thirty years, and in 1847 there were over one hundred thousand spinning machines with three and a half million spindles at work. By 1848 France had many important manufacturing centers. Paris alone had three hundred and forty-two thousand working people, and other cities, such as Lyon, Marseille, Lille, Bordeaux, and Toulouse, had their great factories and whole quarters peopled by factory laborers. And the working class had begun by that time to form unions and organize strikes against their employers for the purpose of increasing wages and reducing the hours of labor.

Effects of the Factory System

Having seen how machinery was introduced into England in the latter part of the eighteenth century and how steam came to be utilized as a motive power, we have now to consider some of the important results of these inventions in changing the conditions under which people lived and worked. Up to this time the term "manufacture" still meant, as it did in the original Latin (*manu facere*) "to make by hand." Artisans carried on trades with their own tools in their own homes or in small shops, as the cobbler does to-day. Instead of working with hundreds of others in great factories and being entirely dependent upon his wages, a workman, in England at least, was often able to give some attention to a small garden plot, from which he derived a part of his support. This old method of manufacture is known as the domestic system. For example, the cutlers of Sheffield (already famous in Chaucer's day) lived in cottages with small plots of land around them, and in dull seasons, or to change their occupation, engaged in gardening.

The "factory system" put an end to all this. The workmen now had to live near their work; long rows of houses, without gardens or even grassplots, were hastily built around the factory buildings, and thus the ugly tenement districts of our cities came into existence.

This great revolution in the methods of manufacturing produced also a sharp distinction between two classes of men involved. There were, on the other hand, the *capitalists*—then called mill owners—who owned the buildings and all the mechanisms, and, on the other, the *workmen* whom they hired to operate the machines. The workingman necessarily became dependent upon the few who were rich enough to set up factories. He could no longer earn a livelihood in the old way by conducting a small shop to suit himself. The capitalist owned and controlled the necessary machinery, and so long as there were plenty of workmen seeking employment in order to earn their daily bread, the owner could fix a low wage and long hours. While an individual employee of special ability might himself become a capitalist, the ordinary workman would have to remain a workman.

The destruction of the domestic system of industry had also a depressing effect upon the work and the lives of women and children. In all except the heaviest of the mechanical industries, such as ironworking or shipbuilding, the introduction of simple machines tended greatly to increase the number of women and children employed compared with the men.[1] Before the invention of the steam engine, when the simple machines were worked by hand, children could be employed only in some of the minor processes, such as preparing the cotton for spinning. But in the modern factory, labor is largely confined to watching machines, piecing broken threads, and working levers, so that both women and children can be utilized as effectively as men, and much more cheaply.

Doubtless the women were by no means idle under the old system of domestic industry, but their tasks were varied and performed at home, whereas under the new system they must flock to the factory at the call of the whistle and labor monotonously at a speed set by the foreman. This led to many grave abuses which, as we shall see, the State has been called upon to remedy by factory legislation. These laws have served to save the women and children from some of the worst hardships, although a great deal still remains to be done.

The Industrial Revolution, in addition to changing the old methods of living, traveling, and working, gave an entirely new direction to European politics and to theories of government and industry. The two great classes created by the Industrial Revolution—namely, the business leaders and the working class—each entered politics on its own account, and each had a theory of government.

[1] For example, in the textile industry in England during the fifty years from 1841 to 1891, the number of males employed increased 53 per cent, and the number of females 222 per cent.

THE DAWN OF OUR AGE OF MACHINES

The business classes naturally disliked to be interfered with. They deemed it hazardous if not wicked to permit the government to regulate the prices of goods or their quality. Neither should it interfere with the employer and his workmen, except to protect either from violence; it should not fix the hours of work or the conditions in the factories. Prices, they maintained, would be kept down by competition among the manufacturers, and wages would be fixed by the supply and demand. Every one should have the greatest freedom to do what he was able to do. If he was a person of ability he would prosper; if he had no special ability he could only hope to get the wages that the employer found it advantageous to pay him.

This view, which was advanced in the middle of the eighteenth century by Turgot and Adam Smith, was accepted and defended by the so-called Manchester school, or British classical political economy. All the reasons for *laissez faire* and free trade, the iron law of wages, and the theory of rent were elaborated in a most convincing fashion. This attitude in its more unqualified expressions was natural enough before the horrid effects of the factory system began to afflict observers like Carlyle and Ruskin.

The great manufacturing cities, instead of being filled with happy and prosperous people, became the homes of a small number of successful industrial magnates who had grown rich as the owners and directors of the factories, and multitudes of poor working people with no other resources than their wages, which were often not enough to keep their families from starvation. Little children under nine years of age working from twelve to fifteen hours a day and women forced to leave their homes to tend the machines in the factories were now replacing the men workers. After their long day's work they returned to miserable tenements in which they were forced to live.

After the close of the Napoleonic wars as things got worse rather than better, there were increasing signs of discontent in England. This led to various attempts to improve matters. On the one hand there were those who hoped to secure reforms by extending the right to vote, in order that the working classes

PL. XXXIV. RICHARD ARKWRIGHT

PL. XXXV. KARL MARX

might be represented in Parliament and so have laws passed to remedy the worst evils at least. In this movement some of the wealthier class often joined, but the working people were naturally chiefly interested and they embodied their ideas of reform in a great "people's charter," which is described below in Chapter XXVI.

In addition to this attempt to secure reform by political action, the workingmen formed unions of their own in the various trades and industries, in order to protect themselves by dealing in a body with their employers. This trade-union movement is one of the most important things in modern times. It began in the early part of the nineteenth century.[1] At first the formation of unions was forbidden by English law, and it was regarded as a crime for workingmen to combine together to raise wages. Men were sentenced to imprisonment or deportation as convicts because they joined such "combinations," or unions. In 1824 Parliament repealed this harsh law, and trade-unions increased rapidly. They were hampered, however, by various restrictions, and even now, although they have spread widely all over the world, people are by no means agreed as to whether workingmen's unions are the best means of improving the conditions of the laboring classes.

A more thoroughgoing plan for permanently bettering the situation of the working people is what is known as *socialism*. As this has played a great rôle in the history of Europe during the past fifty years we must stop to examine the meaning of this word.

Origin of Socialism

The socialists agree in general that "the means of production" should belong to society and not be held as the private property of individuals. "The means of production" is a very vague phrase, and might include farms and gardens as well as

---

[1] The medieval craft guilds described in a previous chapter somewhat resembled modern labor unions, but they included both capitalists and laborers. Our labor unions did not grow out of the medieval guilds but were organized to meet conditions that resulted from the Industrial Revolution.

tools; but when the socialist uses it he is generally thinking of the *machines* which the Industrial Revolution has brought into the world and the factories and mines which house and keep them going as well as the railroads and steamships which carry their goods. In short, the main idea of the socialists is that the great industries which have arisen as a result of the Industrial Revolution should not be left in private hands. They claim that it is not right for rich individuals to own the mills upon which the workingman must depend for his living; that the attempt of labor unions to get higher wages does not offer more than a temporary relief, since the *system* is wrong which permits the wealthy to have such a control over the poor. The person who works for wages, say the socialists, is not free; he is a "wage slave" of his employer. The way to remedy this is to turn over the great industries of the capitalists to national, state, or local ownership, so that all shall have a share in the profits. This ideal state of society, which, they say, is sure to come in the future, they call the Coöperative Commonwealth.

The first socialists relied on the kind hearts of the capitalists to bring the change, once the situation was made clear. Of these early socialists the most attractive figure was Robert Owen, a rich British mill owner, who had much influence in England in the period of hard times after Waterloo. To him, probably, is due the word "socialism."

Modern socialists, however, regard these early socialists as dreamers and their methods as impracticable. They do not think that the rich will ever, from pure loving-kindness, give up their control over industries. So they turn to working people only, point out the great advantage to them of socialism, and call upon them to bring it about in the face of the opposition of the capitalists. They claim that wealth is produced by labor, for which capital but furnishes the opportunity, and that labor is justified in taking what it produces.[1]

---

[1] This does not mean that socialists would divide up all private property. Socialists claim only that there shall be no unearned wealth in private hands, controlling, as now, the industries of the country. Brain workers are also "workers."

ORIGIN OF SOCIALISM

The great teacher of this modern doctrine of socialism has been Karl Marx,[1] a German writer who lived most of his life in London. He was a learned man, trained in philosophy and political economy, and he came to the conclusion from a study of history that just as the middle class or capitalists [2] had replaced feudal nobles, so the working class would replace the capitalists in the future. By the working class he meant those who depend upon their work for a living. The introduction of the factory system had reduced the vast majority of artisans to a position in which the capitalist was able to dictate the conditions upon which this work should be done. Marx, in an eloquent appeal to them in 1847,[3] called upon the members of this "proletariat," "who have nothing to lose but their chains," to rise and seize the means of production themselves.

Marx later wrote a learned work called *Das Kapital* in which he sought to prove by a review of history that socialism was bound to prevail. This book has exercised a great influence on European socialists and has become a sort of workingman's Bible.

Modern, or "Marxian," socialism is therefore a movement of the working class. As such, it must be viewed as part of the history of democracy. Many socialists deprecate partial reforms so long as the conditions remain which make possible the control of the work of one man by another for the latter's benefit. They insist that the workers shall keep one aim clearly in mind and not be drawn into other political parties until the Coöperative Commonwealth is gained.

[1] Karl Marx was born in 1818 in Trèves, reared in an enlightened home, and educated at the universities of Bonn and Berlin. He had early decided upon the career of a university professor, but the boldness of his speech and his radical tendencies barred his way and consequently he entered journalism. His attacks on the Prussian government led to the suppression of his paper in 1843, and he soon migrated to Paris. He was, however, expelled from France, and after some wanderings he finally settled in London, where he studied and wrote until his death in 1883.

[2] The French term *bourgeoisie* is often used by socialists for this class.

[3] The *Communist Manifesto*, written jointly with Frederick Engels. Marx used the word "communism" to distinguish his plan from the socialism of Owen and the "dreamers" who looked to capitalists to help. This word is now applied to radical socialists, such as the Bolsheviki.

There is one other important element in socialism. It is international. It regards the cause of workers in different countries as a common cause against a common oppressor—capitalism. The development of the "International" will be spoken of later.

This is not the place to criticize that Mid-Victorian product, Marxian socialism, or any other kind of socialism. The object has been merely to recall a few salient traits of the overwhelming Industrial Revolution. Even what is reviewed here is too often neglected in the careless talk—especially of the enemies of socialism—which still goes on to-day. The question of radical industrial reform frequently develops the acerbity and reckless misrepresentation of the older religious disputes.

CHAPTER XXV

CREATION OF MODERN ITALY AND GERMANY: THE THIRD FRENCH REPUBLIC

Revolutions in 1848. Recovery of Austria. Founding of the Kingdom of Italy. Creation of the North German Federation. The Franco-Prussian War, 1870–1871. Italy Becomes a European Power. Development of the German Empire. The Third French Republic

Revolutions in 1848

WHEN Metternich heard of the February revolution of 1848 in France, he declared that "Europe finds herself to-day in the presence of a second 1793." But the aged Prince Clemens Wenzel Nepomuk Lothar von Metternich-Winneburg was wrong. His historic sense failed him. It was no longer necessary for France to promote liberal ideas by force of arms, as in 1793. For sixty years ideas of reform had been spreading in Europe, and by the year 1848 there were many representatives of democratic and national ideas from Berlin to Palermo. The Europe of 1848 was no longer the Europe of 1793.

The overthrow of Louis Philippe encouraged the opponents of Metternich in Germany, Austria, and Italy to attempt to make an end of his system at once and forever. In view of the important part that Austria had played in central Europe since the fall of Napoleon I, it was inevitable that she should appear the chief barrier to the attainment of national unity and liberal government in Italy and Germany. As ruler of Lombardy and Venetia she practically controlled Italy, and as presiding member of the German Confederation she had been able to keep even Prussia in line. It is not strange that Austria felt that she could make no concessions to the spirit of nationality, for the territories belonging to the house of Hapsburg, some twenty in number, were inhabited by four different races, —Germans, Slavs, Hungarians (Magyars), and Italians. The Slavs (especially the Bohemians) and the Hungarians longed for national independence, as well as the Italians.

[563]

On March 13 the populace of Vienna rose in revolt against their old-fashioned government. Metternich fled, and all his schemes for opposing reform appeared to have come to naught. Before the end of the month the helpless Austrian emperor had given his permission to the kingdoms of Hungary and Bohemia to draw up constitutions for themselves incorporating the longed-for reforms (equality of all classes in the matter of taxation, religious freedom, liberty of the press, and the rest), and providing that both countries should have a parliament of

THE VARIOUS RACES OF AUSTRIA-HUNGARY

their own, which should meet annually. The Austrian provinces were promised similar advantages. None of them, however, showed any desire to throw off their allegiance to the Austrian ruler.

The rising in northern Italy, on the contrary, was directed to that particular end. Immediately on the news of Metternich's fall the Milanese expelled the Austrian troops from their city, and soon Austria had evacuated a great part of Lombardy. The Venetians followed the lead of Milan and set up a republic once more. The Milanese, anticipating a struggle, appealed to Charles Albert, king of Sardinia, for aid. By this time a great part of Italy was in revolt. Constitutions were granted in Naples, Rome, Tuscany, and Piedmont by their rulers. The king of Sardinia was forced by public opinion to assume the leadership in the attempt to expel the interloping Austria and ultimately, perhaps, to found some sort of an Italian state which should satisfy the longings for national unity. The pope and even the Bourbon king of Naples were induced to consent to the arming and dispatch of troops in the cause of Italian freedom, and Italy began its first war for independence.

The crisis at home and the Italian war made it impossible for Austria to prevent the progress of revolution in Germany. So spontaneous was the movement, that before the fall of Metternich reform movements had begun in Baden, Württemberg, Bavaria, and Saxony. The opportunity seemed to have come, now that Austria was hopelessly embarrassed, to reorganize the German Confederation.

The king of Prussia, Frederick William IV (1840-1861), suddenly reversed his policy of obedience to Austria, and determined to take the lead in Germany. He agreed to summon an assembly to draw up a constitution for Prussia. Moreover, a great national assembly was convoked at Frankfurt to draft a new constitution for Germany.

By the end of March, 1848, the prospects of reform were bright indeed. Hungary and Bohemia had been guaranteed constitutional independence; the Austrian provinces awaited their promised constitutions; Lombardy and Venetia had declared their independence of Austria; four Italian states had obtained their longed-for constitutions, and all were ready for a war with Austria; Prussia was promised a constitution, and, lastly, the National Assembly at Frankfurt was about to prepare a constitution for a united Germany.

The moderate reformers who had gained these seeming victories had, however, only just reached the most difficult part of their task. They had two kinds of enemies, who abhorred each other but who effectually combined to undo the work of the moderates. These were, first, the conservative party, represented by Austria and the Italian rulers who had been forced most reluctantly to grant constitutions to their subjects; and, secondly, the radicals, who were not satisfied with the prospect of a liberal monarchy and desired a republican or socialistic form of government. While the princes were recovering from the astonishing humiliations of March, the radicals began to discredit the revolutionary movement and alienate public opinion by fantastic programmes and the murder of hostile ministers.

Although for the moment Austria's chief danger seemed to lie in Italy, which was the only one of her dependencies that had actually taken up arms against her, the Italians had been unable to drive out the Austrian army under the indomitable general, Radetzky. Charles Albert of Sardinia found himself almost unsupported by the other Italian states. The best allies of Austria were the absence of united action upon the part of the Italians, and the jealousy and indifference that they showed as soon as war had actually begun. The pope decided that his mission was one of peace and that he could not afford to join in a war against Austria, the stoutest supporter of the Roman Church. The king of Naples easily found a pretext for recalling the troops that public opinion had compelled him to send to the aid of the king of Sardinia. Charles Albert was defeated at Custozza, July 25, 1848, and compelled to sign a truce with Austria and withdraw his forces from Lombardy.

The Italian republicans, who had imputed to Charles Albert merely personal motives in his efforts to free Italy, now attempted to carry out their own programme. Florence, as well as Venice, proclaimed itself a republic. At Rome the liberal and enlightened Rossi, whom the pope had put at the head of affairs, was assassinated in November just as he was ready to promulgate his reforms. Pius IX fled from the city and put himself under the protection of the king of Naples. A constitutional assembly was then convoked by the revolutionists, and under the influence of Mazzini, in February, 1849, it declared the temporal power of the pope abolished and proclaimed the Roman republic.

Recovery of Austria

Meanwhile the conditions in Austria began to be favorable to a reëstablishment of the emperor's former influence. Race rivalry proved his friend in his Austrian domains just as republicanism tended to his ultimate advantage in Italy. The Czechs [1] in Bohemia hated the Germans in 1848, much as they had hated them in the time of Hus. The German part of the population naturally opposed the plan of making Bohemia practically independent of the government at Vienna, for it was to German Vienna that they were wont to look for protection against the enterprises of their Czechish fellow-countrymen. The Germans wanted to send delegates to the Frankfurt convention, and to maintain the union between Bohemia and the German states.

The Czechs determined to offset the movement toward German consolidation by a Pan-Slavic Congress, which should bring together the various discontented Slavic peoples comprised in the Austrian empire. To this assembly, which met in Prague in June, 1848, came delegates from the Czechs, Moravians, Slovaks, and Polish population in the north, and the Serbians and Croatians in the south. Its deliberations were interrupted by an insurrection that broke out among the people of Prague and gave the commander of the Austrian forces a sufficient excuse for intervening. He established a military government, and the prospect of independence for Bohemia vanished. This was Austria's first real victory.

The eastern and southern portion of the Hapsburg domains were not more homogeneous than the west and north. When a constitution was granted to Hungary it was inevitable that the races which the Hungarians (Magyars) had long dominated should begin to consider how they might gain the right to govern themselves. The Slavs inhabiting Carniola, Carinthia, Istria, Croatia, Slavonia, Bosnia, and Serbia had long medi-

[1] The Slavic inhabitants of Bohemia.

tated upon the possibility of a united Slavic kingdom in the south.[1] Both the Serbians and Croatians now revolted against Hungary, fearing that the establishment of Hungarian independence would put them at the mercy of the Magyars.

In October, 1848, the radical party rose in Vienna as it had in Paris after the deposition of Louis Philippe. The minister of war was brutally murdered and the emperor fled. The city was, however, besieged by the same commander who had put down the insurrection in Prague, and was forced to surrender. The imperial government was now in a position still further to strengthen itself. The emperor, a notoriously inefficient person, was forced to abdicate (December 2, 1848) in favor of his youthful nephew, Francis Joseph I, who ruled for sixty-eight years. Moreover, a new Metternich appeared in the person of Schwarzenberg.

A vigorous campaign was begun against Hungary, which, under the influence of the patriotic Kossuth, had deposed its Hapsburg king and declared itself an independent republic under the presidency of Kossuth. The Tsar placed his forces at the disposal of Francis Joseph, and with the aid of an army of one hundred and fifty thousand Russians, who marched in from the east, the Hungarians were compelled, by the middle of August, to surrender. Austria took terrible vengeance upon the rebels. Thousands were hanged, shot, and imprisoned, and many, including Kossuth, fled to the United States or elsewhere. But within a few years Hungary won its independence by peaceful measures, and it was able to assume the same footing as the western dominions of Francis Joseph in the dual federation of Austria-Hungary (1866).

It remained for Austria to reëstablish her prestige in Italy and in the German Confederation. In March, 1849, Charles Albert renewed the war which had been discontinued after the defeat at Custozza. The campaign lasted but five days and closed with his crushing and definitive defeat at Novara (March 23), which put an end to the hopes of Italian liberty for the time being. Charles Albert abdicated in favor of his

[1] This ambition was realized only after the World War in 1918.

son, Victor Emmanuel, who was destined before many years to become king of Italy.

After bringing the king of Sardinia to terms, Austria pushed southward, reëstablishing the old order as she went. The ephemeral Italian republics were unable to offer any effectual resistance. The former rulers were restored in Rome, Tuscany, and Venice, and the constitutions were swept away from one end of the peninsula to the other, except in Piedmont, the most important part of the king of Sardinia's realms. There Victor Emmanuel not only maintained the representative government introduced by his father, but, by summoning to his councils men known throughout Italy for their liberal sentiments, he prepared to lead Italy once more against her foreign oppressors.

In Germany, as elsewhere, Austria profited by the dissensions among her opponents. On May 18, 1848, the National Assembly, consisting of nearly six hundred representatives of the German people, had met at Frankfurt. It immediately began the consideration of a new constitution that should satisfy the popular longings for a great free German state, to be governed by and for the people. But what were to be the confines of this new German state? The confederation of 1815 did not include all the German inhabitants of Prussia, and did include the heterogeneous western possessions of Austria,— Bohemia and Moravia, for example, where a great part of the people were Slavs. There was no hesitation in deciding that all the Prussian territories should be admitted to the new union. As it appeared impossible to exclude Austria altogether, the Assembly agreed to include those parts of her territory which had belonged to the confederation formed in 1815. This decision rendered the task of founding a real German state practically impossible; for the new union was to include two great European powers who might at any moment become rivals, since Prussia would hardly consent to be led forever by Austria. So heterogeneous a union could only continue to be, as it had been, a loose confederation of practically independent princes.

[569]

In spite of her partiality for the old union, Austria could not prevent the Assembly from completing its new constitution. This provided that there should be a hereditary emperor at the head of the government, and that exalted office was tendered to the king of Prussia. Frederick William IV had been alienated from the liberal cause, which he had at first espoused, by an insurrection in Berlin. He was, moreover, timid and conservative at heart; he hated revolution and doubted if the National Assembly had any right to confer the imperial title. He also greatly respected Austria, and felt that a war with her, which was likely to ensue if he accepted the crown, would not only be dangerous to Prussia, since Francis Joseph could rely upon the assistance of the Tsar, but dishonorable as well, in Austria's present embarrassment. So he refused the honor of the imperial title and announced his rejection of the new constitution (April, 1849).

This decision rendered the year's work of the National Assembly fruitless, and its members gradually dispersed, with the exception of the radicals, who made a last desperate effort to found a republic. Austria now insisted upon the reëstablishment of the old diet, and nearly came to war with Prussia over the policy to be pursued. Hostilities were only averted by the ignominious submission of Prussia to the demands of Austria in 1851.

While the revolutions of 1848 seem futile enough when viewed from the standpoint of the hopes of March, they left some important indications of progress. The king of Prussia had granted his country a constitution, which, with some modifications, served Prussia down to the end of the World War. Piedmont also had obtained a constitution. The internal reforms, moreover, which these countries speedily introduced, prepared them to head once more, and this time with success, a movement for national unity.

It will be noted that the revolution of 1848 aimed to do more than the French Revolution of 1789. Not only was the national question everywhere an important one, but there were plans for the economic reorganization of society. It was no longer simply a matter of abolishing the remnants of feudalism and insuring equal rights to all and the participation of the more prosperous classes in the government. Those who lived by the labor of their hands and were employed in the vast industries that had developed with the application of steam machinery to manufacture also had their spokesmen. The relation of the state to the industrial classes, and of capital to labor, had become, as they still are, the great problems of modern times. In 1851 Austria had once more, in spite of the greatest obstacles, reëstablished the system of Metternich. But this victory was of short duration, and it was her last.

Founding of the Kingdom of Italy

Under Victor Emmanuel and his great minister, Cavour, Piedmont had rapidly developed into a modern state. It sent a contingent to the aid of the western powers in the Crimean War waged by France and England against Russia (1853-1856); [1] it developed its resources, military and economic, and at last found an ally to help it in a new attempt to expel Austria from Italy.

Napoleon III, like his far more distinguished uncle, was a usurper. He knew that he could not rely upon mere tradition, but must maintain his popularity by deeds that should redound to the glory of France. A war with Austria for the liberation of the Italians, who like the French were a Latin race, would be popular; especially if France could thereby add a bit of territory to her realms, and perhaps become the protector of the proposed Italian confederation. A conference was arranged between Napoleon and Cavour. Just what agreement was reached we do not know, but Napoleon apparently engaged to come to the aid of the king of Sardinia, should the latter find a pretense for going to war with Austria. Should they together succeed in expelling Austria from northern Italy, the king of Sardinia was to reward France by ceding to her Savoy and Nice, which both geographically and racially belonged to her.

By April, 1859, Victor Emmanuel had managed to provoke

[1] See below, pp. 653 ff.

a war with Austria. The French army promptly joined forces with the Piedmontese, defeated the Austrians at Magenta, and on June 8 Napoleon III and Victor Emmanuel entered Milan amid the rejoicings of the people. The Austrians managed the campaign very badly, and were again defeated at Solferino (June 24).

Suddenly Europe was astonished to hear that a truce had been concluded, and that the preliminaries of a peace had been arranged which left Venetia in Austria's hands, in spite of Napoleon III's boast that he would free Italy to the Adriatic. The French emperor was disgusted with the actualities of the war and had, moreover, begun to fear that, with the growing enthusiasm which was showing itself throughout the peninsula for Piedmont, there was danger that it might succeed in forming a national kingdom so strong as to need no French protector. By leaving Venetia in possession of Austria, and agreeing that Piedmont should only be increased by the incorporation of Lombardy and the little duchies of Parma and Modena, Napoleon III hoped to prevent the consolidation of Italy from proceeding too far.

He had, however, precipitated changes which he was powerless to check. Italy was now ready to fuse into a single state. Tuscany, as well as Modena and Parma, voted (March, 1860) to unite with Piedmont. Garibaldi, a famous republican leader, with his red-shirted followers, sailed for Sicily, where he assumed the dictatorship of the island in the name of Victor Emmanuel, "King of Italy." After expelling the troops of the king of Naples from Sicily, he crossed to the mainland, and early in September he entered Naples itself, just as the king fled from the capital.

Garibaldi now proposed to march on Rome and proclaim the kingdom of Italy from the Quirinal. This would have imperiled all the previous gains, for Napoleon III could not, in view of the strong Catholic sentiment in France, possibly permit the occupation of Rome and the destruction of the political independence of the pope. He agreed that Victor Emmanuel might annex the outlying papal possessions to the north and reëstablish a stable government in Naples instead of Garibaldi's dictatorship. But Rome, the imperial city, with the territory immediately surrounding it, must be left to its old master. Victor Emmanuel accordingly marched southward and occupied Naples (October). Its Bourbon king capitulated and in this way all southern Italy became a part of the kingdom of Italy.

MAP OF UNIFICATION OF ITALY

In February, 1861, the first Italian parliament was opened at Turin, and the slow process of really amalgamating the heterogeneous portions of the new kingdom began. Yet the joy of the Italians over the realization of their hopes of unity and national independence was tempered by the fact that Austria still held one of the most famous of the Italian provinces, and that Rome, which typified Italy's former grandeur, was not included in the new kingdom. Within a decade, however, both these districts became a part of the kingdom of Italy through the action of

Prussia. William I and his minister and adviser, Bismarck, were about to do for Germany what Victor Emmanuel and Cavour had accomplished for Italy.

Creation of the North German Federation

With the accession of William I in 1858,[1] a new era dawned for Prussia. A practical and vigorous man had come into power, whose great aim was to expel Austria from the German Confederation, and out of the remaining states to construct a firm union, under the leadership of Prussia, which should take its place among the most powerful of the states of Europe. He saw that war would come sooner or later, and his first business was to develop the military resources of his realms.

The German army, which was the outgrowth of the early reforms of William I, became so extraordinary a feature of later Europe that its organization merits attention. The war of independence against Napoleon in 1813 had led to the summoning of the nation to arms, and a law was passed in Prussia making military service a universal obligation of every healthy male citizen. The first thing that William I did was to increase the annual levy from forty to sixty thousand men and to see that all the soldiers remained in active service three years. They then passed into the reserve, according to the existing law, where for two years more they remained ready at any time to take up arms should it be necessary. William wished to increase the term of service in the reserve to four years. In this way the State would claim seven of the years of early manhood and have an effective army of four hundred thousand, which would permit it to dispense with the service of those who were approaching middle life. The lower house of the Prussian parliament refused, however, to make the necessary appropriations for increasing the strength of the army.

The king proceeded, nevertheless, with his plan, and in 1862 called to his side a Prussian statesman, Bismarck, who would carry out that plan. The new minister conceived a scheme for

[1] He ruled until 1861 as regent for his brother, Frederick William IV, who was incapacitated by disease.

laying Austria low and exalting Prussia, which he succeeded in accomplishing with startling precision. He could not, however, reveal it to the lower chamber; he would, indeed, scarcely hint its nature to the king himself. In defiance of the lower house and of the newspapers he carried on the strengthening of the army without formal appropriations, on the theory that the constitution had not provided for a deadlock between the upper and lower house and that consequently the king might exercise, in such a case, his former absolute power. For a time it seemed as if Prussia was returning to a pure despotism, for there was assuredly no more fundamental provision of the constitution than the right of the people to control the granting of the taxes. Yet Bismarck was eventually fully exonerated by public opinion in Prussia, for it was agreed that the end had amply justified the means.

Prussia now had a military force that appeared to justify the hope of victory should she undertake a war with her old rival. In order to bring about the expulsion of Austria from the confederation, Bismarck took advantage of a knotty problem that had been troubling Germany, and which was known as the Schleswig-Holstein affair. The provinces of Schleswig and Holstein, although inhabited partly by Germans, had for centuries belonged to the king of Denmark. They were allowed, however, to retain their provincial assemblies, and were not considered a part of Denmark any more than Hanover was a part of Great Britain in the last century.

In 1847, just when the growing idea of nationality was about to express itself in the Revolution of 1848, the king of Denmark proclaimed that he was going to make these German provinces an integral part of the Danish kingdom. This aroused great indignation throughout Germany, especially as Holstein was a member of the confederation. The controversy over the relation of these provinces to the Danish kingdom continued for nearly twenty years, until in 1863, the king of Denmark, in spite of the opposition of Prussia, incorporated Schleswig into his kingdom. In this situation Bismarck saw his opportunity.

Bismarck's first step was to invite Austria to coöperate with Prussia in settling the Schleswig-Holstein difficulty. As Denmark refused to make any concessions, the two powers declared war, defeated the Danish army, and forced the king of Denmark to cede Schleswig-Holstein to the rulers of Prussia and Austria jointly (October, 1864). They were to make such disposition of the provinces as they saw fit. There was now no trouble in picking a quarrel with Austria. Bismarck suggested that the duchies should be nominally independent, but that they should become practically a part of Prussia. This plan was of course indignantly rejected by Austria, and it was arranged that, pending an adjustment, Austria should govern Holstein, and Prussia should govern Schleswig.

Bismarck now obtained the secret assurance of Napoleon III that he would not interfere if Prussia and Italy should go to war with Austria. In April, 1866, Italy agreed that, should the king of Prussia take up arms during the following three months with the aim of re-forming the German union, it too would immediately declare war on Austria, with the hope, of course, of obtaining Venice. The relations between Austria and Prussia grew more and more strained, until finally in June, 1866, Austria induced the German diet to call out the forces of the confederation with a view to making war on Prussia. This act the representative of Prussia declared put an end to the existing union. He accordingly submitted to the diet Prussia's scheme for the fundamental reorganization of Germany and withdrew from the assembly.

On June 12 war was declared between Austria and Prussia. With the exception of Mecklenburg and the small states of the north, all Germany sided with Austria against Prussia. Bismarck immediately demanded of the rulers of the larger North German states—Hanover, Saxony, and Hesse-Cassel—that they stop their warlike preparations and agree to accept Prussia's plan of reform. On their refusal, Prussian troops immediately occupied these territories, and war actually began.

So effective was the organization of the Prussian army that, in spite of the suspicion and even hatred which the liberal party

Pl. xxxvi. Cavour

Pl. xxxvii. Bismarck

in Prussia entertained for the despotic Bismarck, all resistance on the part of the states of the north was promptly prevented, Austria was miserably defeated on July 3 in the decisive battle of Königgratz, or Sadowa, and within three weeks after the breaking off of diplomatic relations the war was practically over. Austria's influence was at an end, and Prussia had won the power to do with Germany as she pleased.

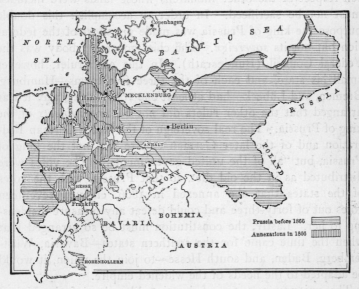

GERMAN STATES SEIZED BY PRUSSIA IN 1866

Prussia was aware that the larger states south of the river Main were not ripe for the union that she desired. She therefore organized a so-called North German Federation, which included all the states north of the Main. Prussia had seized the opportunity considerably to increase her own boundaries and round out her territory by annexing the North German states (with the exception of Saxony) that had refused to join her against Austria. Hanover, Hesse-Cassel, Nassau, and the free city of Frankfurt, along with the duchies of Schleswig and Holstein, all became Prussian.

Prussia, thus enlarged, summoned the lesser states about her to confer upon a constitution that should accomplish four ends. First, it must give all the people of the territory included in the new union, regardless of the particular state in which they lived, a voice in the government. A popular assembly satisfied this demand. Secondly, the predominating position of Prussia must be secured, but at the same time (thirdly) the self-respect of the other monarchs whose lands were included must not be sacrificed. In order to accomplish this double purpose the king of Prussia was made *president* of the federation but not its *sovereign*. The chief governing body was the Federal Council (Bundesrath). In this each ruler, however small his state, and each of the three free towns—Hamburg, Bremen, and Lübeck—had at least one vote; in this way it was arranged that the other rulers did not become *subjects* of the king of Prussia. The real sovereign of the North German Federation and of the later German empire was not the king of Prussia, but "all of the united governments." The votes were distributed as in the old diet, so that Prussia, with the votes of the states that she annexed in 1866, enjoyed seventeen votes out of forty-three and could defeat any measure displeasing to her. Lastly, the constitution must be so arranged that when the time came for the southern states—Bavaria, Württemberg, Baden, and south Hesse—to join the union, it would be adapted to the needs of the widened empire.

The union was a true federation like that of the United States, although its organization disregarded many of the rules which were observed in the organization of the American union. It was inevitable that a union spontaneously developed from a group of sovereign *monarchies*, with their traditions of absolutism, would be very different from one in which the members, like the states of the American union, had previously been governed by *republican* institutions.

The Franco-Prussian War, 1870–1871

No one was more chagrined by the abrupt termination of the war of 1866 and the victory of Prussia than Napoleon III.

He had hoped that both the combatants might be weakened by a long struggle and that at last he might have an opportunity to arbitrate and incidentally to gain something for France, as had happened after the Italian war. But Prussia came out of the conflict with greatly increased power and territory, while France had gained nothing. An effort of Napoleon's to get a foothold in Mexico had failed, owing to the recovery of the United States from the Civil War and their warning that they should regard his continued intervention there as a hostile act. His hopes of annexing Luxemburg as an offset for the gains that Prussia had made were also frustrated.

One course remained for the French emperor; namely, to permit himself to become involved in a war against the power which had especially roused the jealousy of France. The nominal pretext for hostilities was relatively unimportant. In 1869 Spain was without a king, and the crown was tendered to Leopold of Hohenzollern, a very distant relative of William I of Prussia. This greatly excited the people of Paris, for it seemed to them only an indirect way of bringing Spain under the influence of Prussia. The French minister of foreign affairs declared that the candidacy was an attempt to "reëstablish the empire of Charles V." In view of this opposition Leopold withdrew his acceptance of the Spanish crown early in July, 1870, and Europe believed the incident to be at an end. The French ministry, however, was not satisfied with this and demanded that the king of Prussia should pledge himself that the candidacy should never be renewed. This William refused to do. Bismarck did not hesitate to report the circumstances in the German newspapers in such a way that it appeared as if the French ambassador had insulted King William. The Parisians, on the other hand, received the impression that their ambassador had been affronted, and they demanded an immediate declaration of war—*à Berlin!*

Bismarck welcomed the war because he believed that it would force the South German states into a union under Prussia. On the other hand, the hostility which the South German states had hitherto shown toward Prussia encouraged Napoleon III to believe that so soon as the French troops should gain their first victory, Bavaria, Württemberg, and Baden would join him. This first French victory was never won. War had no sooner been declared than the Germans laid all jealousy aside and ranged themselves as a nation against a foreign power. The French army, moreover, was neither well equipped nor well commanded. The Germans hastened across the Rhine and within a few days were driving the French before them. In a series of bloody encounters about Metz one of the French armies was defeated and finally shut up within the fortifications of the town. Seven weeks had not elapsed after the beginning of the war before the Germans had captured a second French army and made a prisoner of the emperor himself in the great battle of Sedan, September 1, 1870.

The Germans then surrounded and laid siege to Paris. Napoleon III had been completely discredited by the disasters about Metz and at Sedan, and consequently the empire was abolished and France for the third time was declared a republic. In spite of the energy which the new government showed in arousing the French against the invaders, prolonged resistance was impossible. The capital surrendered January 28, 1871, and an armistice was arranged. Bismarck greatly humiliated France in drafting the treaty of peace by requiring the cession of two French provinces,—Alsace and northeastern Lorraine.[1] In this way France was cut off from the Rhine, and the crest of the Vosges Mountains was established as its boundary. The Germans exacted, further, an enormous indemnity for those days—five billion francs—and German troops were to occupy France till it was paid. The French people made personal sacrifices to hasten the payment of this indemnity in order that the

[1] Alsace had, with certain reservations,—especially as regarded Strasbourg and the other free towns,—been ceded to the French king by the Treaty of Westphalia (see above, p. 344). During the reign of Louis XIV all of Alsace had been annexed by France (1681). The duchy of Lorraine had upon the death of its last duke fallen to France in 1766. It had previously been regarded as a part of the Holy Roman Empire. The part of Lorraine demanded by Germany in 1871 included about one-third of the original duchy, in which was the fortified city of Metz.

country might be freed from the presence of the hated Prussians. The bitter feeling of the French for the Germans dates from this war, and the fate of Alsace-Lorraine was one of the crucial issues of the World War of 1914. Until 1919 a statue in Paris, representing the lost city of Strasbourg, was draped in mourning.

The war between France and Prussia in 1870, instead of hindering the development of Germany as Napoleon III had hoped it would, only served to consummate the work of 1866. The South German states,—Bavaria, Württemberg, Baden, and south Hesse,—having sent their troops to fight side by side with the Prussian forces, consented after their common victory over France to join the North German Federation. Surrounded by the German princes, William, King of Prussia and President of the North German Federation, was proclaimed German Emperor in the palace at Versailles, January, 1871. In this way the German Empire came into existence. With its powerful and victorious army and its chancellor, Bismarck, it immediately took a leading place among the western powers of Europe.

Immediately after the surrender of Paris the new French republican government had been called upon to subdue a terrible insurrection of the Parisian populace. The insurgents reëstablished the commune of the Reign of Terror, and rather than let Paris come again into the hands of the national government, they proposed to burn the city. When, after two months of disorder, their forces were completely routed in a series of bloody street fights, the city was actually set on fire; but only two important public buildings were destroyed,—the palace of the Tuileries and the city hall.

A National Assembly had been elected by the people in February, 1871, to make peace with Germany and to draw up a new constitution. Under this temporary government France gradually recovered from the terrible loss and demoralization caused by the war. There was much uncertainty for several years as to just what form the constitution would permanently take, for the largest party in the National Assembly was composed of those who favored the reëstablishment of a monarchy.[1] Those who advocated maintaining the republic prevailed, however, and in 1875 the assembly passed a series of laws organizing the government. These have since served France as a constitution.

Italy Becomes a European Power

The unification of Italy was completed, like that of Germany, by the Franco-Prussian War of 1870. After the war of 1866 Austria had ceded Venetia to Italy. Napoleon III had, however, sent French troops in 1867 to prevent Garibaldi from seizing Rome and the neighboring districts, which had been held by the head of the Catholic Church for more than a thousand years. In August, 1870, the reverses of the war compelled Napoleon to recall the French garrison from Rome, and the pope made little effort to defend his capital against the Italian army, which occupied it in September. The people of Rome voted by an overwhelming majority to join the kingdom of Italy; and the work of Victor Emmanuel and Cavour was consummated by transferring the capital to the Eternal City.

Although the papal possessions were declared a part of the kingdom of Italy, a law was passed which guaranteed to the pope the rank and privileges of a sovereign prince. He was to have his own ambassadors and court like the other European powers. No officer of the Italian government was to enter the Lateran or Vatican palaces upon any official mission. As head of the Church, the pope was to be entirely independent of the king of Italy, and the bishops were not required to take the oath of allegiance to the government. A sum of over six hun-

---

[1] The monarchical party naturally fell into two groups. One, the so-called *legitimists*, believed that the elder Bourbon line, to which Louis XVI and Charles X had belonged, should be restored in the person of the count of Chambord, a grandson of Charles X. The *Orleanists*, on the other hand, wished the grandson of Louis Philippe, the count of Paris, to be king. In 1873 the Orleanists agreed to help the count of Chambord to the throne as Henry V, but that prince frustrated the plan by refusing to accept the national colors,—red, white, and blue,—which had become so endeared to the nation that it appeared dangerous to exchange them for the white of the Bourbons. See table on page 546.

dred thousand dollars annually was also appropriated to aid the pope in defraying his expenses. The pope, however, refused to recognize the arrangement. He still regards himself as a prisoner, and the Italian government as a usurper who has robbed him of his possessions. He has never accepted the income assigned to him, and still maintains that the independence

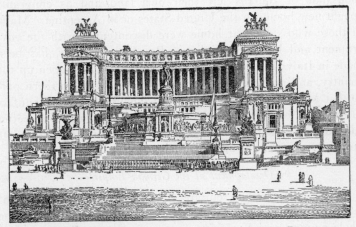

MONUMENT TO VICTOR EMMANUEL II, AT ROME

On the northwestern slope of the Capitoline Hill the Italians have erected the most imposing monument in Europe, to commemorate the unification of Italy. Its size is indicated in the picture by the relative size of people and buildings. A colossal statue of Victor Emmanuel adorns the center, while a vast colonnade surmounts the hill. The Forum of ancient Rome lies just behind it; but it faces in the opposite direction down a broad, busy street of the modern city, which is growing rapidly. Electric cars now connect the seven hills, and arc lights shine beside the Colosseum

which he formerly enjoyed as ruler of the Papal States is essential to the best interests of the head of a great international Church.

In order to maintain the dignity and security of her new position Italy rapidly increased her army and navy. Universal military service was introduced as in other European states, and modern warships were built. Then the Italians decided to seek colonies in Africa, and in 1887 sent an army into Abyssinia; but after fifteen years of intermittent warfare they were able to retain only a strip along the coast of the Red Sea. Later, in 1912, after a war with Turkey they took Tripoli on the south shore of the Mediterranean.

The cost of armaments reduced Italy almost to bankruptcy at times, and, as it was not a rich country, made the taxes excessive. Since these fell largely on the poor, hundreds of thousands of Italians left their own land and as emigrants sought new homes in the United States or in Argentina. Many of those who stayed at home were discontented with the government and became socialists. Progress, however, has been made in Italy; railroads were built by the State to open up the country, and manufactures have grown up in the northern part so that Milan and Turin are to-day among the great manufacturing cities of Europe. National schools are providing better education, although the peasants in the mountainous districts are still very ignorant and superstitious.

Development of the German Empire

In the new German empire Prussia occupied the dominating position. Her territory comprised nearly two-thirds of the whole empire, and her citizens amounted to nearly two-thirds of the entire population of Germany. The constitution of 1866 had been drawn up with the hope that the southern states would later become a part of the union; consequently little change was necessary when the empire was established. The head of the federation was the king of Prussia, who bore the title of German Emperor. According to the constitution the sovereignty was vested in the whole body of German rulers who were members of the union, all of whom sent their representatives to the Federal Council, or *Bundesrath*. Prussia's control of the Bundesrath was secured, however, by assigning her king a sufficient number of votes to enable him to defeat any measure he wished. Moreover, as German emperor (*Kaiser*) he enjoyed many powers exercised by an absolute monarch. He appointed and dismissed the chancellor, who was, next to the Kaiser, the highest official in the government. He commanded the unconditional obedience of all German soldiers and sailors and appointed the chief officers of the army and navy.

The German House of Representatives, or *Reichstag*, consisting of about four hundred members, was elected by universal male suffrage for a period of five years. The emperor might dissolve it, however, at any time with the consent of the Bundesrath, if it refused to pass the measures of his ministers.

The constitution gave the federal government power to regulate commerce, railways, telegraphs, and the currency. Under Bismarck, as chancellor, the old systems of the various states were subjected to uniform regulations. The bewildering variety of coins and paper money in the several states was done away with and the mark (normally worth about twenty-five cents) became the basis for the currency of the whole empire. A tariff system was introduced to encourage home industries by protecting the entire kingdom from foreign competition. The period was one of rapid development. Large manufacturing towns sprang up, railways were built, and industry made remarkable progress.

A new political party soon appeared, known as the Social Democratic Labor Party, which based its platform on the theories of Karl Marx. Socialism developed in Germany as elsewhere with the introduction of machinery and the growth of factories. Bismarck became alarmed, and in 1878 a law was passed to suppress socialistic agitation. In order to allay the discontent caused by the measure, the government undertook to introduce various socialistic measures of its own. The state gradually acquired the ownership of railways and mines until at the opening of the World War the national property was valued at about seven billion dollars with an income of about three hundred million dollars. The federal government also arranged a system of insurance for workingmen against sickness and accident, and required the employers to contribute to the expense. Similar laws later were passed to provide pensions in old age. These measures, however, failed to satisfy the socialists, for they claimed that this kind of "state" socialism did not really alter the conditions of labor for the workingmen or give them greater control of industry. Nevertheless, when, after the World War, Germany became a republic under socialist direction, Bismarck's work seemed a preparation for a quite unanticipated situation.

At the death of Kaiser William I in 1888 his grandson, the "Kaiser" of the World War, William II,[1] succeeded to the throne. Bismarck soon fell out with the arrogant new ruler and resigned in 1890. None of the chancellors appointed by William II, however, exhibited the capacity of the "iron chancellor," as Bismarck was called.

During the reign of William II (1888-1918) Germany increased rapidly in wealth and population. Vast new cities grew up; old ones were improved and laid out with great boulevards. German steamship lines, heavily subsidized by the government, developed rapidly, and their vessels were soon sailing on every sea. The farmers and manufacturers flourished, owing to the distant markets opened up by the new German merchant marine. Germany also sought colonies and got control of the large provinces of Togo and Cameroons in West Africa. She carved out a protectorate, called German Southwest Africa, far larger than the area of the German empire. Germans also established themselves in German East Africa. In 1897 they seized the port of Kiaochow in China and began to look about for still further colonial expansion. Few Germans, however, cared to emigrate to the new colonies, and they proved a costly luxury.

From a relatively poor country in 1871 Germany became by 1914 a rich and powerful nation with thriving industries at home and an almost unrivaled commerce abroad.

The Third French Republic

As one reviews the history of France since the establishment of the first republic in 1792, it appears as if revolutionary changes of government had been very frequent. As a matter

---

[1] William II's father, Frederick, lived for only a few months after the death of the old Kaiser. The new Kaiser was a grandson of Queen Victoria and spoke and wrote English excellently.

Pl. xxxviii. A View of Old Paris

Pl. xxxix. The Munition Works, Le Creusot, France

of fact, the various revolutions produced far less change in the system of government than is usually supposed. They neither called in question the main provisions of the Declaration of the Rights of Man drawn up in 1789, nor did they materially alter the system of administration which was established by Napoleon immediately after his accession in 1800. So long as the latter was retained, the civil rights and equality of all citizens secured, and the representatives of the nation permitted to control the ruler, it really made little difference whether France was called an empire, a constitutional monarchy, or a republic.

The president of the French republic is elected for seven years by the Senate and the Chamber of Deputies meeting together. The real head of the government, however, is the prime minister, who, with the other ministers, forms a cabinet, responsible to parliament as in England. The parliament of France differs from the Congress of the United States (and from the Parliament of Great Britain, in former days) in the way it works. Instead of two great parties, there are about ten groups of members, each representing certain ideas. A few monarchists still sit on the seats at the extreme right of the speaker's desk. Next to them sit the very conservative republicans. The largest group is that of the "radicals" or reformers, while at the left are the socialists representing the working classes.

The cabinet in order to remain in power must have the support of a majority in the Chamber of Deputies, as the house of representatives is called. This is elected every four years by universal male suffrage. When the cabinet loses the confidence of the Chamber of Deputies it resigns and the president appoints a new prime minister. It is his task to form a new cabinet whose policy is likely to win the favor of the Chamber and secure the support of a *bloc*. The Senate is elected for nine years by a more conservative system—one hundred members being elected every third year—and tends to be more conservative than the Chamber.

France under the third republic steadily increased in wealth, the French peasants being noted for their thrift and economy.

The savings of the French peasants enabled the great banks to lend money to other nations, particularly to Russia, so that Paris came to rival London and New York as a money center.

A system of national education was introduced. A public-school system was established, in which priests and members of religious orders were forbidden to teach, and the private schools which had been run mainly by religious orders were placed under strict government inspection. The government granted large sums of money to carry on its system of education and established normal schools for the training of teachers.

By the treaty or "Concordat" of 1801, between Napoleon and the pope, the bishops were appointed by the government and the salaries of all the clergy were paid by the State. The clergy, therefore,—naturally a very influential class because of their religious duties,—were in a sense government officials as well as clergymen. Many of the republicans had ceased to believe in what the Catholic Church taught, and finally a law was passed in 1905 to separate the Church and State in France. The government discontinued the contributions to the clergy, but placed the churches at the disposal of the priests. Moreover, in order to punish the clergy for refusing to accept the new arrangement, palaces of bishops and theological seminaries were turned into schools and hospitals. The Catholic Church in France is now dependent, as are all churches in America, upon the voluntary contributions of those who are interested in supporting the church and its institutions.

France also followed a policy of colonial expansion. The French had earlier conquered Algeria and made settlements on the western coast of Africa. After the Franco-Prussian War there was still greater activity and interest in gaining colonies. Before the World War in 1914 France had succeeded in carving out an empire in Africa many times her size, as Germany had done. The exports and imports from these colonies represented a business of millions of dollars. France also acquired in southern Asia a large territory lying between India and China, usually called French Indo-China.

CHAPTER XXVI

GREAT BRITAIN AND HER EMPIRE

The British Constitution. Reform of the Suffrage. The British Cabinet. General Reforms in England. The Irish Question. The British Empire: Canada and Australasia. The British Empire: Africa. British India

The British Constitution

IN the eighteenth century England seemed to have, in comparison with other countries, a model of free government. By the Bill of Rights (1689) the king was forbidden to make any new laws, or neglect any old ones, or lay any taxes, or keep a standing army without the consent of Parliament. He was not to interfere with freedom of speech, or refuse to receive respectful petitions from his subjects. Even the right that the king of England had formerly enjoyed of vetoing bills passed by Parliament fell into disuse and was exercised for the last time by Queen Anne in 1707. In short, the power of making laws was taken over by the English Parliament, at a time when continental countries were ruled by benevolent despots.

The English king could not arbitrarily arrest and punish his subjects. The Habeas Corpus Act of 1679 provided that any one who was arrested should be informed of the reason and should be speedily tried by a regular tribunal and dealt with according to the law of the land. In France, down to the Revolution, there were none of these restrictions placed upon the king, who could arrest his subjects on *lettres de cachet,* imprison them indefinitely without assigning a reason, and interfere in any suit and decide it as he chose.

The English had, therefore, won two important safeguards for their liberties—a parliament to make their laws, and a good system of courts of justice to see that the laws were properly carried out.[1] But in the nineteenth century it became

---

[1] The British constitution is an unwritten one and therefore can be readily changed if necessary, but the British have been, upon the whole, very slow to make any important changes.

apparent that there was great need of reform in both branches of the government.

Reform of the Suffrage

The reform of Parliament was the most pressing need, for Parliament had ceased to represent the nation at large and had become a council of wealthy landlords and nobles. This was due to two things. In the first place, there were the so-called "rotten boroughs." Such towns as had in earlier times sent their two representatives each to Parliament continued still to do so, regardless of the number of their inhabitants, and no new boroughs had been added to the list since the reign of Charles II.[1] On the other hand, towns which had developed under the influence of the Industrial Revolution, like Birmingham, Manchester, and Leeds, had no representatives at all.

In the second place, few persons had a right to vote even in the towns which were permitted to send representatives to the House of Commons. Many of the boroughs were owned outright by members of the House of Lords or others, who easily forced the few voters to choose any candidate they proposed.[2]

Bribery was prevalent and was fostered by the system of public balloting.[3] By long-established custom the price of a vote at Hull was two guineas (over ten dollars); at Stafford, seven.

The reform of the suffrage proved a very difficult matter. Those in control of the elections managed to prevent any change for years, in spite of the demands made not only by the working classes but by rich business men for the right to vote. Finally, in 1832, after two years of debate, a reform bill was forced through in spite of the firm opposition of the House of Lords.[4]

[1] Dunwich, which had been buried under the waters of the North Sea for two centuries, was duly represented, as well as the famous borough of Old Sarum, which was only a grassy mound where a town had once stood.

[2] A very cautious scholar of our own day estimates that not more than one-third of the representatives in the House of Commons were fairly chosen.

[3] Secret balloting was not established until 1872.

[4] The king gave permission to the prime minister "to create such a number of peers as will insure the passage of the bill." The Lords, afraid of such a wholesale change, yielded.

REFORM OF THE SUFFRAGE

According to its provisions fifty-six "rotten boroughs," each containing less than two thousand inhabitants, were entirely deprived of representation; thirty-two more, with less than four thousand inhabitants, lost one member each; and forty-three new boroughs were created with one or two members each, according to their respective populations. The suffrage was given in the towns to all citizens who owned or rented houses worth ten pounds a year (about fifty dollars), and to *renters* as well as *owners* of lands of a certain value in the country. In this way the shopkeepers and manufacturers and some of the more prosperous people in the country were given the right to vote; but nearly all workingmen and agricultural laborers were still excluded from the franchise.

The Reform Bill of 1832 was therefore not really a triumph for democracy. The disappointment among the poorer classes over their exclusion from the vote was great and widespread. The reformers at last agreed on pressing six demands, which they embodied in a *charter;* to wit: universal suffrage, vote by secret ballot, parliaments elected annually, payment of members of Parliament, abolition of property qualifications for members of Parliament, and equal electoral districts. This charter soon won thousands of adherents, to whom the name of "Chartists" was given. Great meetings and parades were held all over England; the charter was transformed into a petition for which, it was claimed, over a million signatures were obtained. This petition was presented to Parliament in 1839, only to be rejected by a large vote.

Despairing of securing reforms by peaceful means, some of the leaders began openly to advocate revolutionary violence, consequently rioting spread to such an extent that the government had to resort to extraordinary police measures to suppress it.

The Revolution of 1848 in France gave the signal for the last great outburst of Chartist enthusiasm. Owing to the hard times in that year thousands of workmen were unemployed, and the poor were roused to bitter hatred for a government that replied to demands for reform by calling out the police. Preparations were made to present another gigantic petition to the House of Commons, for which, it was claimed, six million names had been secured, and the Chartist leaders deter-

THE PARLIAMENT BUILDINGS, LONDON

This massive pile stands on the site of an old royal palace, between Westminster Abbey (which is not shown but is just across the street at the right) and the river Thames, which runs along the other side. The House of Commons met in the chapel of this palace—St. Stephen's—from the middle of the sixteenth century until 1834, when the palace was burned down, with the exception of the great hall with the plain roof in the foreground. The new building, completed in 1867, is richly ornamented. From its main tower, 340 feet high, a flag is flown by day when Parliament is in session, and by night a light shines over the clock tower, in which is hung the bell called Big Ben

mined to overawe Parliament by a march on London. This show of force was frustrated by the aged Duke of Wellington, then commander of the troops policing London. Parliament refused to take action, and the movement collapsed.

In spite of the failure of the Chartists the demand for a more democratic government spread, and finally, in 1867, the

House of Commons passed a reform bill which doubled the number of voters. In 1884 the Liberal party, under Gladstone, succeeded in further increasing the number by two millions. These various measures served to establish something approaching the manhood suffrage already common on the Continent, although many men were still excluded from voting, especially the unmarried laborers who, owing to the low rents in England, did not pay as much as ten pounds a year for unfurnished lodgings.

For twenty years the matter of the franchise excited little attention, for the Conservatives were in power and were satisfied to leave things alone. But when the Liberal party was again called to the helm, in 1906, it had to face not only the question of including more *men* among the voters but the much more novel demand that *women* also should be allowed to vote. The Industrial Revolution, by opening up new employments to women, had given them a certain kind of independence which they had never before had. During the latter part of the nineteenth century women were admitted to universities, and colleges began to be established for them as well as for men. These changes in women's education and occupation inevitably produced the demand that they be given the right to vote.

The struggle for woman suffrage in Great Britain lasted for years. Bill after bill was presented to the government, but Parliament refused to enfranchise the women. Finally a militant group of "suffragettes" resorted to various forms of violent demonstrations in order to force the government to yield to their demands. The final victory was undoubtedly hastened by the common experiences of men and women during the terrible years of the World War. In 1918 parliamentary suffrage was granted to all women over thirty years of age, and in December, 1919, they were declared eligible for any office, making their political status equal to that of men.

Before the war, in only five countries—New Zealand, Finland, Australia, Norway, and Sweden—did women possess the franchise. By the end of 1920 woman suffrage had been greatly extended, and women had the right to vote in Great Britain, Canada, British East Africa, Rhodesia, Denmark, Holland, Russia, Rumania, Serbia, Luxemburg, Germany, Austria, Hungary, and the United States; also in the new states, Poland, Esthonia, Lithuania, Latvia, Czechoslovakia, the Ukraine, and Palestine.

The British Cabinet

After the Civil War, in the seventeenth century, there grew up two great political parties in England: (1) the Tories,—in recent times called *Conservatives*,[1]—the successors of the Cavaliers (as the supporters of Charles I were named), who believed in defending the powers claimed by the king and the English Church; (2) the Whigs, or *Liberals,* the successors of the Roundhead, or parliamentary, party of Charles I's time, who were eager to get the government into the hands of the elected representatives of the people.[2]

The party which happens to have the majority of votes in the House of Commons assumes the right to manage the goverment of the country as long as it retains its majority. The leader of the party in power is accepted by the monarch as his prime minister, or premier. He and his associates form a cabinet, which for the time being is the real ruler of the British empire.

This device of cabinet government under a premier was put into operation in the time of George I, a German unable to speak English, who did not attend the meetings of his ministers. The little group of ministers constituting the cabinet got into the habit of holding its sessions and reaching its decisions without the presence of the king.

Since the House of Commons will not vote the money necessary to carry on the government after it has lost confidence in the cabinet, the cabinet has to resign as soon as it is convinced by the defeat of any of its measures that it no longer controls

---

[1] When Gladstone introduced his Home Rule Bill for Ireland in 1886, many Liberals who opposed it deserted to join the Conservatives, who have since sometimes been called *Unionists*.

[2] For the recent development of the Labor party see p. 725.

a majority of votes. The king then appoints the leader of the opposite party as premier and asks him to form a cabinet. It may happen, however, that the defeated cabinet believes that the country is on its side. In that case it will ask the king to dissolve Parliament and have a new election, with the hope that it will gain a majority in that way. So it is clear that the cabinet regards itself as responsible not merely to Parliament but to the nation at large.

As the members of the House of Commons are not elected for a definite term of years (though, according to a law passed in 1911, a new general election must be held *at least* every five years), that body may be dissolved at any time for the purpose of securing an expression of the popular will on any important issue. It is thus apparent that the British government is more sensitive to public opinion than are governments where the members of the legislatures are chosen for a definite term of years.[1]

General Reforms in England

In addition to the reforms in their Parliament the British have gradually altered their laws with a view to giving the people greater freedom and to improving their condition in important respects.

One of the most essential conditions of freedom is the right of free speech, free press, and liberty to meet for political discussions. Although during the eighteenth century English laws were less oppressive than those on the Continent, it was not until the middle of the nineteenth century that full liberty of

---

[1] The British sovereign is still crowned with traditional pomp; coins and proclamations still assert that he rules "by the grace of God"; and laws purport to be enacted "by the king's most excellent Majesty, by and with the advice and consent of the Commons in the present Parliament assembled in accordance with the provisions of the Parliament Act, 1911." But the monarch *reigns* rather than *rules;* he is still legally empowered to veto any bill passed by Parliament, but he never exercises this power. He has in reality only the right to be consulted, the right to encourage, and the right to warn. He cannot permanently oppose the wishes of the majority in Parliament, for should he venture to do so, Parliament could always bring him to terms by cutting off the appropriations necessary to conduct his government.

speech was attained. Now Britain is very proud of possessing this desirable institution of democracy.[1]

England was a country of religious freedom in the eighteenth century, but Catholics and those Protestants who disagreed with the State Church—namely, the Dissenters—were excluded from public offices. After long agitation this restriction was removed. In 1828 the old laws directed against Dissenters were repealed on condition that those seeking office should take an oath not to use their influence to injure or weaken the established Church of England. The following year the Catholics were put on the footing of other citizens by the passage of the Emancipation Act, which admitted them to both houses of Parliament and to almost all public offices upon condition that they would renounce their belief in the right of the pope to interfere in temporal matters, and would disclaim all intention of attacking the Protestant religion.

In the early part of the nineteenth century there was still a good deal of illiteracy in England. Since 1870 the government has been providing for the founding of free public schools, and as a result almost all Englishmen now learn to read and write. As newspapers may now be had for a cent, or two cents, almost every one who cares to do so is in a position to read them and to learn what is going on in the world.

The English criminal law was very harsh at the opening of the nineteenth century. There were no less than two hundred and fifty offenses for which the penalty of death was established. By a gradual process of abolishing one death sentence after another the long list of capital offenses was at last reduced, in 1861, to three.

In 1835, after a parliamentary investigation had revealed the horrible conditions of prisons, a law was passed providing for government inspection and the improvement of their administration. This marked the beginning of prison reform, which includes sanitary buildings, separation of the sexes, segrega-

---

[1] A striking illustration of the extent of this tolerance is the way the British police will protect from his audience an anarchist or a republican attacking the monarchy.

tion of the hardened criminals from the young offenders, and a more enlightened treatment of criminals generally, with a view to reforming them and protecting society rather than to wreaking vengeance upon them.

The cruelty of the criminal law had its origin in the Middle Ages, but with the coming of the Industrial Revolution, in the reign of George III, new forms of inhumanity had arisen. These were the result of the factory system, which brought untold misery to the working classes of England. Great factory buildings were hastily erected by men ignorant of the most elementary principles of sanitary science. Around the factories there sprang up long, dreary rows of grimy brick cottages where the workmen and their families were crowded together.

The introduction of steam-driven machinery had made possible the use of child labor on a large scale. The conditions of adult labor, save in the most skilled classes, were almost as wretched as those of child labor. Dangerous machinery was not properly safeguarded, and the working time was excessively prolonged. The misery of the poor is reflected in Mrs. Browning's poem "The Cry of the Children," in the bitter scorn which Carlyle poured out on the heads of the factory owners, and in the vivid word pictures of Dickens.

Finally, in 1833, Parliament, after much investigation, reduced the hours of child labor in cotton and woolen mills to nine a day, and in 1842 women and children were forbidden to work in the mines. It was not until 1847 that a bill was passed restricting the labor of women and children in all mills to ten hours per day exclusive of mealtime.

With this great victory for the reformers the general resistance to State interference was broken down, and year after year, through the long reign of Queen Victoria (1837-1901) and those of her successors, new measures were carried through Parliament, revising and supplementing earlier laws. To-day Great Britain does more than any other European country to protect the factory operatives.

[597]

England is famous for its free trade, while almost all other countries *protect* their manufacturers by a tariff imposing customs duties on most articles imported from foreign countries. England believed heartily in protection and shipping laws until about the middle of the nineteenth century, when English man-

WILLIAM EWART GLADSTONE

ufacturers decided that they could compete with the world on a free-trade basis. First, all duties on grain (the Corn Laws) were abolished, and then, between 1852 and 1867, all navigation laws and protective duties were done away with. In recent years there has been a growing agitation in favor of deserting free trade and of restoring protective duties, on the ground that British goods have to pay duties when they reach foreign lands where protective tariffs are in force.

Pl. xl. Gladstone Addressing the House of Commons

Pl. xli. Lloyd George

The Conservatives—or, as they were called for a time, the Unionists—were (except for a short period) in power for twenty years, from 1886 to 1906, and interest in general reform seemed to have died out in England. But in 1906 a general election took place, and the Liberals, reënforced by a new labor party and the Irish Nationalists, came into control of the House of Commons. A new period of reform then began, which continued until the outbreak of the World War.

The parties in power agreed that something must be done to relieve the poverty in which it was found that a great part of the population lived. Bills were introduced providing help for those injured in factories; for pensions for aged workmen no longer able to earn a livelihood; for diminishing the evils of sweatshops, where people worked for absurdly low wages; for securing work for the unemployed; for providing meals for poor school children; and for properly housing the less well-to-do and so getting rid of slums.

In 1908 Asquith became prime minister and David Lloyd George became Chancellor of the Exchequer, in charge of the nation's finances. In April, 1909, Lloyd George made his famous budget speech, in which he declared that if the reforms were to be carried out, a great deal of money would be necessary. More taxes must be collected, but from those best able to pay them, not from the poor. Every one should make his contribution according to his ability. So he advocated that the income tax should be increased on incomes above $25,000, that it should be lighter on earned than on unearned incomes; that those holding land in the neighborhood of cities with a view to a rise in value and those who happened to have mineral deposits under their property should share their profit with the government; that automobiles, and gasoline for their use, should pay a heavier tax. Lastly, that the tax on large inheritances, already heavy, should be increased.

He said in closing: "I am told that no chancellor of the exchequer has ever been called on to impose such heavy taxes in a time of peace. This is a war budget. It is for raising money to wage implacable warfare against poverty and squalidness. I cannot help hoping and believing that before this generation has passed away we shall have advanced a great step toward that good time when poverty, and wretchedness and human degradation, which always follow in its camp, will be as remote to the people of this country as the wolves which once infested its forests." [1]

The budget advocated by Lloyd George passed the House of Commons but was indignantly rejected by the House of

MODEL HOUSES FOR BRITISH WORKINGMEN

One of the most noticeable changes in the condition of the working people is the erection of pleasant homes, like these, in place of the tenements in slums. England has done much in this line, as have also other European countries [2]

Lords. Parliament was dissolved and a new election was held, to show that the voters were on the side of the ministry. Then the Lords yielded; but the Liberals had been so exasperated at their opposition that, by the Parliament Act of 1911, they took

[1] It will be noticed that Lloyd George and his supporters, before imposing taxes, not only asked how much a man had but how he got his income. Those who worked their lands or conducted mines or factories were to be treated with more consideration than those who owed their incomes to the efforts of others. In this way they introduced a new principle of taxation, which was vigorously denounced by the Conservatives as revolutionary and socialistic.

[2] A recent British law places vacant land, especially near cities, at the disposal of those who will cultivate it in garden plots, at very low rental. The horrible poverty of the middle of the last century has been very much lessened by these devices of the reforming government, aided by national prosperity.

away the power of the Lords to interfere effectively in future with the will of the people as expressed in the elections.[1]

One of the chief features of Lloyd George's programme of social reform—following Germany's lead—was a National Insurance bill which should provide against sickness, disability for work, and unemployment. One part of this law required the compulsory insurance of nearly all employees. The payments for the insurance were to be made by the employer, the worker, and the State, each contributing a certain part. The Liberal party was able to force the bill through, and it became a law. It was at first very unpopular, however; the employers disliked the additional burden, the workmen and servants did not like to have their wages taken for the benefit of others, and the doctors resented the terms upon which they had to treat the sick under the new law. But when the payments began to be made the dissatisfaction died down.

The Irish Question

Among the most serious problems that have constantly agitated Parliament during the past century is the Irish question. As early as the time of Henry II (1154-1189) Ireland began to be invaded by the English, who seized lands from which they enjoyed the revenue. There were constant rebellions, and under James I a revolt in the province of Ulster furnished an opportunity for the English government to confiscate a large area in northern Ireland. With the hope of raising a generation of Irish people more loyal to England, James encouraged Scotch colonists who were Protestants to settle in Ulster—the so-called Scotch Irish. The Irish revolted later under Cromwell. They

[1] According to the terms of this important act any bill relating to raising taxes or making appropriations, which the House of Commons passes and sends up to the House of Lords at least one month before the close of a session, may become a law even if the House of Lords fails to ratify it. Other bills passed by the Commons at *three* successive sessions and rejected by the Lords may also be presented to the king for his signature and become laws in spite of their rejection by the upper house. In this way control of the financial policy of the government is practically taken out of the hands of the House of Lords, and in the case of all other laws the House of Commons is able, by using a little patience and by waiting two years, to do what it pleases without regard to the sentiments of the peers.

were cruelly punished, and more estates were confiscated. In 1688 the Irish sided with the Catholic king, James II, and were again subdued and more land was taken.

Most of the English landlords, who got possession of these estates, lived in England. In the nineteenth century millions of pounds yearly were drained away from Ireland to pay absentee landlords, who rarely set foot in that country and took little or no interest in their tenants beyond the collection of their rents. If the tenants did not pay or could not pay, they were speedily evicted from their cottages and lands. It was estimated, in 1847, that about one-third of the entire rental of Ireland was paid to absentee landlords.

Throughout large portions of Ireland the peasants were constantly on the verge of starvation. They were deprived of nearly all incentive to improve their little holdings, because they were liable to be evicted and lose the results of their labors. Whenever there was a failure of the potato crop, on which from one-third to one-half the population depended for food, there were scenes of misery in Ireland which defy description. This was the case in the "Black Year of Forty-Seven," when the potato crop failed almost entirely and thousands died of starvation in spite of the relief afforded by the government. It was in the midst of this terrible famine that the stream of emigration began to flow toward America. Within half a century four million emigrants left the shores of Ireland for other countries, principally the United States, taking with them their bitter resentment against England.

When England became Protestant she attempted to convert Ireland, but the Irish remained faithful to the pope and the Roman Catholic Church. The English then set up their own Church in Ireland, drove out the Catholic priests, and substituted for them clergymen of the Church of England. Although the Protestants in Ireland numbered only one in ten of the population, the Catholics were forced to support the English churchmen by paying tithes from their scanty incomes. When Catholics were admitted to Parliament, in 1829, they set to work to get rid of the old system, and in 1869, after a long struggle of a generation, the English Church was disestablished in Ireland and the tithes abolished.

After gaining this important point the Irish members in Parliament, under the leadership of Parnell, forced the Irish land question on the attention of Parliament. From 1881 to 1903 a series of acts was passed securing the Irish peasants a fair rent and advancing them money to buy their holdings, if they wished, on condition that they would pay back the money in installments to the government.

Besides demanding that they be given fair treatment in the matter of religion and land the Irish leaders have clamored unceasingly for Home Rule. Until 1801 Ireland had maintained a separate parliament of her own; but in that year the English government determined to suppress it because it enjoyed a larger degree of independence than was deemed compatible with the security of English rule. The Act of Union of 1801, abolishing the Irish parliament, provided that Ireland should be represented by one hundred members in the House of Commons and, in the House of Lords, by twenty-eight peers chosen by the Irish nobles. This Act of Union was really forced upon the Irish by gross bribery of members of their parliament, and consequently the Irish patriots resented it. Accordingly they at once began agitating for Home Rule, that is, for a parliament of their own, in which they might legislate on their own affairs instead of being forced to rely upon the British Parliament, where the English and the Scotch had an overwhelming majority.

In 1882 a decided impetus to the movement was given by the shocking murder of Lord Frederick Cavendish and Thomas Burke, the undersecretary for Ireland, in Phœnix Park, Dublin. This deed convinced the Liberal statesman Gladstone that nothing short of Home Rule could solve the perennial Irish problem. Accordingly, in 1886, he introduced a Home Rule bill in Parliament providing for a separate parliament in Dublin. The bill was opposed by Conservatives and some Liberals on the ground that it threatened the unity of the empire. It was defeated, as was also a later bill, introduced in 1893.

For some years after this the issue was not an active one, partly because of the improved conditions which resulted, in Ireland, from the land laws. But in 1910 the purchase of land was brought to a standstill through some difficulty in the financial provisions of the bill. Renewed agitation for Home Rule followed almost immediately, but this time the question was far more difficult than before, owing to the division among the Irish themselves. There were now not only those who sought Home Rule and those who preferred to remain under the jurisdiction of the British Parliament,—notably Ulster,—but in addition a growing *republican* group who would not be satisfied with anything short of entire separation from Great Britain. This party of ardent patriots called themselves Sinn Fein (we ourselves). They were eager to revive the Gaelic language and culture and to establish an independent Irish republic.

For the following ten years Ireland found itself in a condition of violence and confusion bordering upon downright civil war. Ulster refused to listen to any suggestions of uniting with the south of Ireland, and collected arms to resist by force any attempt to make her do so. Her protest was based upon the long-standing animosity between Protestants (who constituted a slight majority in Ulster) and Catholics and the fear that separation from Great Britain would endanger her business prosperity. The republican party in the other parts of Ireland continued to grow in strength and audacity, and during the World War entered into negotiations with Germany. This was deemed treasonable by the British government, and a number of Sinn Fein conspirators were executed in 1916. This event tended to strengthen the republican party through sympathy for the Irish "martyrs." In January, 1919, the republicans proclaimed the independence of Ireland, and an Irish legislative body, the Dail Eireann, was created. It chose as president of the new republic Eamonn de Valera, a college professor. The new government was not recognized by Great Britain, and there followed two years of assassinations, imprisonments, executions, and vicious fighting between the Irish troops and the so-called "Black and Tans" sent over by the British to maintain order. For a time all attempts to reëstablish peace seemed fruitless.

At length a conference with the more moderate Irish republicans was arranged by Lloyd George; this met in London and worked out a form of Irish freedom. Article I of the treaty concluded in December, 1921, reads: "Ireland shall have the same constitutional status in the community of nations known as the British Empire as the Dominion of Canada, the Commonwealth of Australia, the Dominion of New Zealand, and the Union of South Africa, with a Parliament having powers to make laws for the peace, order, and good government of Ireland, and an executive responsible to that Parliament, and shall be styled and known as the Irish Free State." The new government was set up at Dublin, and the Irish Free State was admitted to the League of Nations.

Ulster refused to join with the south and is permitted to have its own "Government of Northern Ireland." The more extreme republicans continued to fight for the complete independence of Ireland, but it was hard to convince the British that it would be safe to have a power to the west which might make common cause with their enemies should war come. Ireland at last had Home Rule, but she was neither wholly unified nor completely independent.

The British Empire: Canada and Australasia

The kingdom of Great Britain and Northern Ireland and the Irish Free State form but a very small part of the vast empire now under British dominion. Scattered throughout Asia, Africa, America, Australia, and Oceania, the imperial territory covers nearly one-fourth of the inhabited portions of the earth, and one-quarter of the peoples of the world owe allegiance to the British sovereign. This great commonwealth of nations, composed of peoples of diverse race and language, and of every degree of civilization from the savage to the most highly cultivated, has been built up by occupation, conquest, or agreement, since the overseas discoveries of the seventeenth

[605]

century, with the assistance of an unequaled fleet of war and merchant vessels. To her supremacy on the sea Britain owes the unrivaled extent of her empire. Her widely distributed realms fall into three categories: (1) The self-governing dominions,—Canada, Newfoundland, Australia, New Zealand, South Africa, and the Irish Free State,—which enjoy complete independence within the empire; (2) India; (3) all the rest of the British colonies, dependencies, and mandates, some of which exercise a measure of self-government, while others are entirely administered by the crown and are known as Crown Colonies. We turn first to the self-governing dominions, the oldest of which is Canada.

When the British took Canada from the French in 1760, there were but a quarter of a million inhabitants of English extraction. On the eve of the American Revolution Parliament passed the Quebec Act (1774). In an age of intolerance it recognized the Catholic faith and left the French inhabitants their laws and customs. Many loyalists (called Tories) fled to Canada during the American Revolution, and peopled what are now called the Maritime Provinces and Ontario. This influx of English-speaking people led to the creation of two provinces, Ontario and Quebec, the one inhabited by English settlers, the other by the older French colonists. Both supported the mother country in the War of 1812. When, a quarter of a century later, discontent and even rebellion developed, the British government sent over the wise Lord Durham to investigate the sources of trouble. His report, made in 1840,— called the Magna Charta of the Colonies,—strongly advocated self-government for the British colonies. It marks a turning point in the policy of Great Britain toward her possessions beyond the sea. Thereafter all colonies were accorded the widest liberty that could be reconciled with the maintenance of the empire. The two provinces were united under one government responsible to the people.

This was an important step in the direction of the Canadian federation, which was organized a few years later. By the British North America Act of 1867, Ontario, Quebec, New

Brunswick, and Nova Scotia were united to form the Dominion of Canada, with the provision that the remaining provinces and territories might be admitted later. This federation was given a constitution, providing for a governor-general representing the sovereign of England; a Senate, the members of which are appointed for life by the governor-general; and a House of Commons, which is the real governing body, elected by popular vote. The new plan of federation went into effect on July 1, 1867—a day which is celebrated as the Canadian national holiday, like the Fourth of July in the United States.

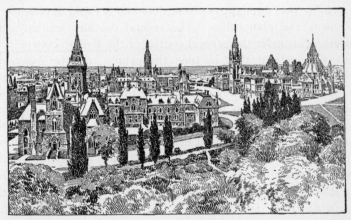

THE PARLIAMENT BUILDINGS, OTTAWA

Parliament Hill is beautifully situated beside the Ottawa River. The main building was burned, February, 1916

The Dominion of Canada has spread westward and northward. The rights of the old Hudson's Bay Company were purchased in 1869. The provinces of Manitoba and British Columbia were admitted to the union, 1870-1871. In 1905 the vast regions of Alberta and Saskatchewan were added. Railroads were built and projected, and the population, which was little over half a million in 1820, had in a century increased to eight millions. The Canadians have shown little tendency to join the great republic to the south of them and still look to Great Britain as their chief economic ally. Canada forms a distinct nation in spite of her membership in the British Empire.[1]

Australia and Tasmania are together somewhat larger than the United States. Before the coming of the English late in the eighteenth century they were inhabited by a scanty population of aborigines in a low state of civilization. In 1770 Captain Cook, a distinguished navigator, had taken possession of this scarcely known continent in the name of the British sovereign. For a time England used this distant land as a place to which she deported lawbreakers. The discovery of gold in 1851 brought many settlers and a rapid development of towns and plantations. The several colonies secured self-government under the general control of the British crown.

It was natural that in time the people of these colonies, speaking the same language and having the same institutions, should seek a closer union. The question of a federation was long discussed, and at last, in 1891, a general convention composed of delegates from all the states drafted a federal constitution, which was submitted to the people for their ratification. In 1900 the British Parliament passed an act founding the Commonwealth of Australia on the basis of this draft. The six states—New South Wales, Tasmania, Victoria, Queensland, South Australia, and Western Australia—are now formed into a union similar to that of the United States. The king is represented by a governor-general; the federal parliament is composed of two houses,—a Senate, consisting of six senators from each state, and a House of Representatives, chosen in the same way as in the United States.

To the southeast of Australia, twelve hundred miles away, lie the islands of New Zealand, to which English pioneers began to go in the early part of the nineteenth century. In 1840 the English concluded a treaty with the native Maoris,

---

[1] Newfoundland and Labrador, with a population of a little over 260,-000, form a self-governing colony and are not a part of the Dominion of Canada. The government is conducted by a governor, a legislative council, and a legislative assembly.

by which the latter were assigned a definite reservation of lands on condition that they would recognize Queen Victoria as their sovereign. The English settlers established the city of Auckland on North Island, and twenty-five years later New Zealand became a separate colony, with the seat of government at Wellington.

New Zealand, during the closing decade of the nineteenth century, became famous for its experiments in social reform. Organized labor rose to great power in politics and carried through a number of measures conceived in the interest of workingmen. Special courts were established to settle disputes between employers and their workmen.

The colony of Victoria vied with New Zealand in respect to social reform. The government attempted to stop "sweating" in the poorly paid industries, and public boards composed of employers and workmen were established for the purpose of fixing the minimum wages and standards of work, so that these matters were no longer arranged by private bargaining between individuals. The system of secret voting which originated in Australia—the so-called "Australian ballot"—is a reform which has already spread beyond Australasia and is in use both in England and in the United States.

The British Empire: Africa

Cape Colony, a Dutch settlement in South Africa, was turned over to Great Britain at the Congress of Vienna. The Dutch farmers (Boers, as they are commonly called) were an independent class, strongly attached to their customs, including slavery, and were greatly incensed by the regulations introduced by British officials. The more enterprising Boers moved northward and eastward into what was later called Natal and Transvaal. They fought the warlike savages and took possession of vast areas of farming and grazing land. The British pressed after, but concluded that it was not worth while to try to control the Dutch beyond the Vaal River, so they guaranteed them the right to manage their own affairs without interference (1852). Two years later a region south of the Vaal, the Orange Free State, was also recognized as a practically independent colony of Boers.

In 1885 the discovery of gold in Transvaal attracted thousands of miners, speculators, and adventurers, who soon outnumbered the Boers. These foreign newcomers (Uitlanders) were largely British. They wished to run the government in their own interests and planned an uprising to upset the constitution. Transvaal, under its president, Paul Kruger, formed an alliance with the Orange Free State, collected arms and supplies, and prepared to defend itself against British encroachments.

The British now began to claim that the Boers would not be satisfied until they had control of all the British possessions in South Africa. The Boers, with more reason as it seemed to the rest of the world, declared that Great Britain was trying to find an excuse for annexing the two republics which the Dutch farmers had built up in the wilderness after a long fight with the native savages. Finally, in 1899, the weak Transvaal and the Orange Free State boldly declared war on England. The Boers made a brave fight, and the British managed the war badly. Many Englishmen thought it a shame to be fighting Paul Kruger and his fellow farmers, but although the general sentiment throughout the world was heartily in favor of the Boers, none of the foreign powers intervened. The British, after some smarting defeats, soon won the war and annexed the two Boer republics.

With her victory over the brave farmers Great Britain reversed her former policy of harassing them and extended to them all the freedom enjoyed by her other colonies. In 1910 a Union of South Africa was organized on the model of the Canadian and Australian federations.

When war broke out between Great Britain and Germany, in 1914, the Germans expected all the Boers to rise against Britain, but they were disappointed. There was only a small revolt, which was easily suppressed. The prime minister of the Union of South Africa, General Botha, who had been the best Boer general in the war against Great Britain fifteen years before, not only frustrated the uprising of his old comrades but conquered German Southwest Africa for the British empire. In addition, South African troops invaded German East Africa and fought on the main battle line in France. General Smuts, another Boer commander, was prominent in the peace conference and showed much wisdom in his recommendations. The British look with much natural pride upon this tribute to their wisdom in granting freedom and self-government to the Boers.[1]

In addition to the Union of South Africa, Great Britain has three enormous provinces in Africa occupied almost entirely by negroes. Lying to the north is the Bechuanaland protectorate, inhabited by peaceful native tribes. Beyond Bechuanaland and the Transvaal is Rhodesia, which was acquired through the British South Africa Company by two annexations in 1888 and 1898 and, with subsequent additions, brought under the protection of the British government. On the east coast, extending inland to the great lakes at the source of the Nile, lies the valuable grazing land of British East Africa. It is of especial importance as controlling the southern approach to the Sudan and Egypt, which are so important to Great Britain.

In addition to these colonies in Africa, British Somaliland, on the Strait of Bab-el-Mandeb, was secured in 1884 in connection with the establishment of the British power in Egypt. Along the west coast Great Britain has five centers—Gambia, Sierra Leone, the Gold Coast, Lagos, and Nigeria—the beginnings of which date back to the time of Queen Elizabeth, when the English were ravaging the coast for slaves to carry to the New World. The British are now making atonement for the past by helping the natives to become civilized, sending physicians to fight tropical diseases, and governing well.

Several railways have been built in South Africa, one running through the whole country from Cape Town to the north-

---

[1] There are about six millions of people in the Union of South Africa, but a large portion of these are colored. The white population, including both those of British and those of Dutch descent, do not equal in number the inhabitants of Philadelphia.

ern border of Rhodesia. There was once much talk of an "all British line from the Cape to Cairo" across Africa, but the extension of the Belgian Congo Free State on the northwest, and especially of German East Africa on the northeast, blocked this plan. The hope was revived, however, by the victory over the Germans during the World War. At the close of the conflict German East Africa was handed over to Great Britain under the so-called "mandatory system," and German Southwest Africa was transferred to the Union of South Africa.

British India

India occupies a unique position in the British empire. Four-fifths of the colonial subjects of the king of England live in this peninsula, and are alien in race, language, and tradition to the mother country. The East India Company, a purely business organization, secured the original foothold for the English in India, and as early as 1686 declared its intention to "establish such a policy of civil and military power and create and secure such a large revenue as may be the foundation of a large, well-grounded, sure English dominion in India for all time to come." In Clive's time the company succeeded in supplanting the French and extending its control into the central portion of the peninsula and partially conquering Bengal. The company steadily increased its wealth and power, and, as its charter permitted, it maintained itself much like an aggressive state, with its host of officials and its troops, which it did not hesitate to employ in its constant conflicts with native rulers.[1]

The scandalous stories which reached London of the graft and the despotic behavior of its officials led Parliament, in 1784, to assume the control of political matters and leave only the business interests in the hands of the company. British control was extended on all sorts of pretenses and encouraged by the constant rivalry of the native princes. During the nineteenth century almost all of northern India and Burma were brought into the power of the British.

[1] See above, p. 411.

PL. XLII. COLLINS STREET, MELBOURNE, AUSTRALIA

Pl. xliii.   Street of the Three Gateways, Ahmedabad, India

Great Britain's conquests naturally caused great bitterness among the native princes who lost their thrones, and among the Mohammedans, who hated the Christians. In 1857 occurred the terrible revolt of the sepoys,—Indian troops serving under British officers. The sepoys mutinied at Delhi and massacred the English inhabitants of the city; the inhabitants of Lucknow rose against the foreigners, and at Cawnpore a thousand British men, women, and children were cruelly massacred. Many of the sepoys remained loyal, however, and the British armies were soon able to put down the mutiny.

After the suppression of the sepoy rebellion the Parliament of Great Britain revolutionized the government of India. The administration of the peninsula was finally taken entirely out of the hands of the East India Company, which had directed it for more than two hundred and fifty years. It was vested in the British sovereign (1858), to be exercised under parliamentary control. On January 1, 1877, Queen Victoria was proclaimed empress of India amid an illustrious gathering of Indian princes and British officials. King George V, as emperor of India, now rules over more than three hundred millions of Indian subjects inhabiting a domain embracing about 1,800,000 square miles. The Secretary of State for India is responsible for Indian affairs, while the actual administration in India is headed by a viceroy appointed by the British government.

The construction of railway lines has been pushed forward with great rapidity, so that the vast interior might be quickly reached by troops and an outlet opened for its crops of cotton, rice, wheat, indigo, and tobacco. Cotton mills are rising by the tombs of ancient kings, cities are increasing rapidly in population, and the foreign trade by sea has multiplied twentyfold in the past seventy years. About eight hundred newspapers, printed in twenty-two languages, including Burmese, Sanskrit, and Persian, are published; educational institutions have been provided for nearly five million students.

During the World War, Indian princes and troops came to the aid of Great Britain, but at the same time there were strong movements for the independence of India, or at least for self-government. Many Indian agitators were arrested and imprisoned or executed; mass meetings were broken up or fired upon by British forces.

In December, 1919, Parliament passed the Government of India Act, which, according to the Secretary of State, although it did not pretend to give the Indians a permanent constitution, provided a beginning in the gradual development of self-governing institutions in India. It put into the hands of the people certain matters of government, and reserved to the British other matters, to be given over as the people were prepared to assume responsibility. While the moderates accepted the new constitution, the extreme Nationalists, under the leadership of Mr. M. K. Gandhi, denounced it as utterly inadequate and insisted upon India's right to immediate self-government.

The Indians are thus divided among themselves. Almost all the native princes favor British rule, while millions of the people have been faithful to their adored Gandhi—whom they regard as a "holy man"—in his policy of "non-coöperation." This programme of passive resistance included the boycott of British goods and British schools and courts and the refusal to accept any office or position, civil or military, under the British government. The carrying out of this plan, together with famine and the high cost of food, resulted in rebellions and general disorder throughout the country. These were accompanied by increasing severity on the part of the judges for cases of sedition. In March, 1922, Gandhi was arrested and sentenced to six years' imprisonment, but was released in two years on account of ill health. Even before his arrest a group of Nationalists differed from Gandhi in their belief that in accepting positions in the legislative bodies Indians would have greater opportunities of making their demands felt. This Swa-raj (self-rule) party was, in 1924, indorsed by Gandhi, who admitted that his methods had not been successful and recommended that non-coöperation be given up except for the refusal to buy foreign cloth. Even the Liberal party, which had been more favorable than the moderate Nationalists to British policy, now demanded the status of a dominion for India.

CHAPTER XXVII

THE EXPANSION OF EUROPEAN INFLUENCE IN THE NINETEENTH CENTURY

International Trade and Competition: Imperialism. European Interference in China and Japan. Rivalry of Japan and Russia. Partition of Africa. The United States and Latin America

International Trade and Competition: Imperialism

AS a result of the Industrial Revolution, Europe became a busy world of shops and factories, which produced much more than Europeans could use. So new markets were constantly sought in distant parts of the world. The trade with the East, which, as we have seen, led to the discovery of America, had grown in the nineteenth century to an enormous extent, scattering the wares of England, Germany, France, and Italy through China and India and the islands of the Pacific. The eagerness to secure world trade is one of the great facts of modern history, for it led the European nations to plant new colonies and to try to monopolize markets in Asia and Africa and wherever else they could. This business rivalry fostered jealousies and conflicts between the European states and was one of the causes of the World War.

The prodigious expansion of commerce was made possible by the discovery that steam could be used to carry goods cheaply and speedily to all parts of the earth. Steamships and railways have made the world one great market place.

The problem of applying steam to propel ships had long occupied inventors, but the honor of making the steamship a success commercially belongs to Robert Fulton. In the spring of 1807 he launched his *Clermont* at New York, and in the autumn of that year the "new water monster" made its first trip to Albany. Transoceanic steam navigation began in 1819 with the voyage of the steamer *Savannah* from Savannah to Liverpool, which took twenty-five days, sails being used to help the engine. The *Great Western*, which startled the world in 1838 by steaming from Bristol to New York in fifteen days and ten hours, was a ship of 1,378 tons, 212 feet long, with a daily consumption of 36 tons of coal.[1] A commercial map of the world to-day shows that the globe is crossed in every direction by definite routes which are followed by innumerable freight and passenger steamers plying regularly from one port to another, and few of all these thousands of ships are as small as the famous *Great Western*.

The East and the West have been brought much nearer together by the piercing of the Isthmus of Suez, which formerly

THE "SAVANNAH"

barred the way from the Mediterranean Sea to the Indian Ocean. This enterprise was carried out under the direction of the French engineer Ferdinand de Lesseps. After ten years of work the canal was opened to traffic in November, 1869.

The construction of a canal through the Isthmus of Panama was undertaken later, in 1881, by a French company organized by De Lesseps; but the company failed, and in 1902 the Congress of the United States authorized the President to pur-

[1] Compare this with the *Lusitania*, which had a tonnage of 32,500 tons and engines of 68,000 horse power, was 785 feet long, and carried a supply of over 5,000 tons of coal for its journey across the Atlantic, which lasted less than five days. Later vessels of over 50,000 tons have been constructed.

chase for forty million dollars the property in which the French investors had sunk so much money. Arrangements with the republic of Colombia for the construction of the canal by the United States having come to naught, the state of Panama, through which the line of the proposed canal passed, seceded from Colombia in 1903, and its independence was immediately recognized by President Roosevelt. A treaty in regard to the canal zone was then duly concluded with the new republic, and after some delays, the work of the French company was resumed by the United States and was practically completed in 1915.

Just as the huge modern steamship has taken the place of the schooner for the rapid trade of the world, so, on land, the merchandise which used to be dragged by means of horses and oxen or carried in slow canal boats is being transported in long trains of capacious cars, each of which holds as much as fifteen or twenty large wagons. The story of the locomotive, like that of the spinning machine or steam engine, is the history of many experiments and their final combination by a successful inventor, George Stephenson.

In 1814 Stephenson built a small locomotive which was used at the mines; and in 1825, with the authorization of Parliament, he opened between Stockton and Darlington, in the northern part of England, a line for the conveyance of passengers and freight. A road between Liverpool and Manchester was formally opened in 1830. The locomotive used weighed about seven tons and ran at an average speed of thirteen miles an hour—a small affair when compared with the giant locomotive of our day, weighing a hundred tons and running fifty or sixty miles an hour. Within fifteen years trains were running regularly between Liverpool, Manchester, Birmingham, and London, and at the close of the century Great Britain had twenty-two thousand miles of railway carrying over a billion passengers annually.

The first railway in France was opened in 1828, and the first in Germany in 1835. Europe is now bound together by a network of over two hundred thousand miles of railway,

[617]

and before the World War railway construction was advancing rapidly in Africa and Asia, preparing cheap transportation for the products of Western mills and mines. As we shall see, the Trans-Siberian road connected Europe overland with the Pacific, and Russia also pushed lines southward toward Persia and Afghanistan. British India has over thirty-five thousand miles of railway, and the importance of the new roads in China and Turkey became so great as to involve rival European nations, each of which wished to control them.

Quite as essential to the world market as railway and steamship lines are the easy and inexpensive means of communication afforded by the post, telephone, telegraph, and cable. The English "penny post" is now so commonplace as no longer to excite wonder, but to men of Frederick the Great's time it would have seemed impossible. In England, until 1839, the postage on an ordinary letter was a shilling for a short distance. In that year a reform measure long advocated by Rowland Hill was passed, establishing a uniform penny post throughout Great Britain. Other European countries followed the example of Great Britain in reducing postage, and before long a letter could be sent almost anywhere in the world for five cents.

Still more wonderful is the development of the telegraph system. Cables have been laid under the ocean, connecting all countries. Distant and obscure places in Africa and Asia have been brought into close touch with one another and with Europe. China now has lines connecting all the important cities of the republic and affording direct overland communication between Peking and Paris. In October, 1907, Marconi established regular communication across the Atlantic by means of the wireless system of telegraphy discovered some years before, and now the wireless telephone can carry the voice from Washington to Paris.

The Industrial Revolution which enabled Europe to produce far more goods than it could sell in its own markets, and the rapid transportation which permitted producers to distribute their commodities over the whole surface of the globe, combined to produce a keen competition for foreign markets, as we have seen. The European nations secured the control of practically all the territory occupied by less progressive peoples in Africa and Asia, and introduced Western ideas of business into China and Japan, where steamships now ply the navigable rivers and railroads are being rapidly built.

The process of colonization and of Westernizing the Oriental peoples was further hastened by European and American capitalists, who invested in railroads, mines, and oil wells in backward countries. At the opening of the twentieth century Great Britain alone had about ten billion dollars invested abroad; one-fifth of the Russian industrial enterprises were financed by foreigners, who were also to a considerable extent constructing the railroads in China. The Germans supplied the money for large banking concerns in Brazil, Buenos Aires, and Valparaiso, which in turn stimulated industry and the construction of railways in South America.

These two great forces—manufacturers seeking markets for their goods and men of wealth seeking investment—affected the foreign and commercial relations of every important European country. They explain why the great manufacturing nations embarked on a policy of so-called *imperialism,* which means the business of adding distant territories for the purpose of controlling their products, getting the trade with the natives, and investing money in the development of natural resources. Sometimes this imperialism took the form of outright annexation; again, it assumed the form of a "protectorate," which proclaimed the intention of taking advantage of a country's resources without undertaking the full responsibility of governing it. Sometimes imperialism went no farther than the securing of concessions or privileges in undeveloped countries, such as foreigners obtained in China or citizens of the United States in Mexico.

The way for imperialism was smoothed by the missionaries. No sooner was a new country brought to the attention of Europeans than missionaries flocked thither along with the traders and soldiers.

Missionaries have not only spread the knowledge of the Christian religion, but have also carried with them modern scientific ideas and modern inventions. They have reduced to writing the languages of peoples previously ignorant of the existence of an alphabet. Their physicians have introduced scientific methods of treating the sick, and their schools have given an education to millions who without them would have been left in complete barbarism. Finally, they have encouraged thousands of Japanese, Chinese, and representatives of other peoples to visit Europe and America and thus prepare themselves to become apostles of Western ideas among their fellows. The missionaries have also created a demand for Western goods and opened the way for trade.

European Interference in China and Japan

The relations of Europe to China extend back into ancient times. Some of the Roman emperors, including Marcus Aurelius, sent embassies to the Chinese monarchs, and in the Middle Ages some missionaries labored to introduce Christianity into China. It was not, however, until after the opening of the water route around the Cape of Good Hope that European trade with China became important. Early in the sixteenth century, Portuguese merchants appeared in Chinese harbors, offering Western merchandise in exchange for tea and silks. In 1557 the Portuguese rented a bit of land at Macao, off Canton—a post which they hold to-day.

The Chinese, however, did not welcome foreign interference. Their officials looked upon the European merchants as barbarians. Nevertheless, Dutch and English merchants flocked to Canton, which was the sole port at which the Chinese emperor permitted regular commerce to be carried on with foreign countries.

When, in 1839, the Chinese government tried to put a stop to the opium trade (carried on with great profit by English merchants), and informed the British government that the traffic would have to be given up, the so-called Opium War broke out.

The British, of course, with their modern means of warfare, were speedily victorious, and the Chinese were forced to agree, in the Treaty of Nanking, to pay a heavy indemnity, to cede to the British the island of Hongkong, which lies at the mouth of the Canton River, and to open to foreign commerce four ports, including Shanghai, on the same terms as those that they held for Canton. The United States, taking advantage of this war, secured similar commercial privileges in 1844.

From the Opium War to the present date China has been troubled with foreign invasions. Napoleon III, supported by the English, waged war on China in 1858 and compelled the Chinese government to open new ports to European trade, including Tientsin, which was dangerously near the capital, Peking. But it was not only the distant Europeans who longed to get control of Chinese trade. There was a neighboring business rival, Japan.

To the northeast of China lies a long group of islands which, if they lay off the eastern coast of North America, would extend from Maine to Georgia. This archipelago, comprising four main islands and some four thousand smaller ones, is the center of the Japanese empire. Before the middle of the nineteenth century Japan was still almost completely isolated from the rest of the world; but now, through a series of extraordinary events, she has become one of the conspicuous members of the family of nations. Her people, who are somewhat more numerous than the inhabitants of the British Isles, resemble the Chinese in appearance and owe to China the beginnings of their culture and their art.

During the sixteenth century Dutch and English traders carried on some business in Japan, but they, as well as the missionaries, became disliked and were all driven out. For nearly two centuries Japan cut herself off almost entirely from the outer world. In 1853 and 1854 Commodore Perry entered the Bay of Tokio (Yedo) with a small fleet but sufficient to induce the Japanese to conclude a treaty opening two ports to American ships. Soon other powers obtained the right to trade with Japan. The Japanese decided that they must acquaint themselves with European science and inventions if they hoped to protect themselves against European encroachments. In 1871 feudalism was abolished, serfdom was done away with, and the army and navy were rapidly remodeled on a European pattern. In 1889 a constitution was established providing for a parliament. Factories were built, several thousand miles of railroad were constructed, and Japan was pretty thoroughly modernized within a generation.

Japan, having become a manufacturing country, wished to extend her trade and was specially anxious to get control of the neighboring Korea, which was claimed by China. The Japanese easily defeated the Chinese in a short war (1894-1895). Korea was declared independent (which practically meant opening it up to Japan). Russia, however, intervened, to discourage the Japanese from getting a foothold on the mainland, by inducing China to permit her to build a railroad across Manchuria and to lease Port Arthur to her. This port she fortified and connected by rail with the Trans-Siberian Railroad.

Meanwhile the Germans found an excuse for strengthening themselves in the same region. A German missionary having been murdered in the province of Shantung, which lies just opposite Korea, a German squadron appeared in Kiaochow Bay, in November, 1897, landed a force of marines, and raised the German flag. As a compensation for the murder of the missionary, Germany demanded a long lease of the town of Kiaochow on the Shantung peninsula, with the right to build railways in the region and to work mines. Upon acquiring Kiaochow the Germans built harbors and constructed forts, military barracks, and machine shops. In short, a German town sprang up on the Chinese coast, which, with its defenses, was designed to form a base for further extension of Germany's sphere of influence.

Great Britain, learning of the negotiations, sent a fleet northward from Hongkong to the Gulf of Chihli (or Pechili) and forced China to lease to her Weihaiwei, just between the recent acquisitions of Germany and Russia.

PL. XLIV. THE HEXAGONAL TEMPLE OF KIOTO

PL. XLV. AVENUE OF STONE LANTERNS IN UYENO PARK, TOKYO

Great Britain, moreover, believed it to be for her interest to be on good terms with Japan, and in 1902 an offensive and defensive alliance—the Anglo-Japanese Treaty—was concluded between the two powers, binding each to assist the other in case a third party joined in a conflict in which either was involved. For example, England, under the provisions, would have to aid Japan in a war with Russia, should France or Germany intervene on Russia's side.

The foreigners were by no means content with establishing trading posts in China; they longed to develop the neglected natural resources of the empire, to open up communication by railroads and steamships, and to Westernize the Orientals, in order that business might be carried on more easily with them and new opportunities be found for making money for Western investors.

The Chinese at first opposed the building of railroads, but several thousand miles of track were laid and many other lines planned. Telegraphs and post offices of the European type were established. In 1898, after the war with Japan over Korea, China began to remodel her army and to send students to foreign universities. These changes aroused the violent opposition of a party known as the "Boxers," who hated the missionaries and business men from the Western countries. They declared that the new ideas would ruin China and that the European powers would tear China to pieces if given a chance.

In June, 1900, the Boxers killed the German ambassador, besieged the Europeans in Peking, and appeared to be on the point of massacring them all. The foreign powers—Japan, Russia, Great Britain, the United States, France, and Germany—immediately collected a joint army which fought its way from the coast to Peking and brought relief to their imperiled fellow countrymen in the Chinese capital. The European troops looted the palace of the Chinese emperor, and China was forced to pay an indemnity of three hundred and twenty millions of dollars and pledged herself to suppress the Boxers and every society that was opposed to the presence of foreigners.

After the trouble in Peking was over, the Chinese government took up the matter of reforms once more, and in 1906 a proclamation was issued promising that a Chinese parliament should be established and the old system of absolute rule abandoned forever.

Rivalry of Japan and Russia

Scarcely had the Boxer rising been put down when it became apparent that Japan and Russia were drifting into war. Russia refused to evacuate Manchuria, a province of China, and insisted on getting a hold in Korea, even sending Cossacks to build forts there. Japan declared that Russia had repeatedly promised to withdraw her troops from Manchuria and had agreed that Korea should be independent. As the Tsar's government gave the Japanese no satisfaction, they boldly went to war with Russia in February, 1904.

Japan was well prepared for war and was, moreover, within easy reach of the field of conflict. The Russian government, on the contrary, was corrupt and inefficient and was already engaged in a terrible struggle with the Russian people.[1] The eastern boundary of European Russia lay three thousand miles from Port Arthur, and the only means of communication was the single line of lightly constructed railroad that stretched across Siberia to the Pacific.

The Japanese laid siege to Port Arthur, and for months the world watched in suspense the deadly attacks which the Japanese made upon the Russian fortress. On January 1, 1905, after a siege of seven months, Port Arthur surrendered.

Russia, meanwhile, dispatched its Baltic squadron to the Orient. It arrived in May in the straits of Korea, where Admiral Togo was waiting for it. The Tsar's fleet was practically annihilated in a few hours, with terrible loss of life, while the Japanese came out of the conflict almost unscathed.

Lest the war should drag on indefinitely, President Roosevelt, acting under the provisions of a Hague Convention, took measures which brought about a peace. The conference

[1] See following chapter.

between the representatives of Japan and Russia was held at Portsmouth, New Hampshire, and on September 5 the Treaty of Portsmouth was signed. This recognized the Japanese influence as paramount in Korea, which, however, was to remain independent.[1] Both the Japanese and the Russians were to evacuate Manchuria; the Japanese were, nevertheless, given the rights in the Liaotung peninsula and Port Arthur which Russia had formerly enjoyed.

Thus this conflict produced by the rivalry of the European powers in the East was brought to an end, but the resources of China and the fact that it had not yet organized a strong army or navy encouraged foreign powers to continue their interference in Chinese affairs. Nevertheless, China was changing rapidly as Japan had formerly done. Students returning home from Western countries determined to overthrow the Manchu (or Manchurian) dynasty, which had ruled for two hundred and sixty-seven years, and their corrupt officials. After a short struggle they forced the court, on February 12, 1912, to declare the abdication of the boy-emperor then on the throne, and the creation of a republic.

The president of the new republic, Yuan Shih-kai, although he posed as a revolutionist, really believed that a monarchy was the best form of government for China, and he longed to become the successor of the old Manchu dynasty. He soon fell out with the National Convention over the powers that were to be enjoyed by the president; and the radicals, realizing their mistake, attempted to bring about a second revolution. When this revolt failed, however, Yuan Shih-kai proceeded to make himself dictator and to work toward reëstablishing the monarchy. He appointed military governors (tuchuns) over the provinces to assist him in keeping the country under his control. After his death (June, 1916) the tuchuns began to fight among themselves for supremacy, and the new president and parliament were entirely in their power.

---

[1] The Japanese did not leave Korea independent. They immediately took control of the administration, and, finally, by the treaty of August 23, 1910, Korea was annexed to the Japanese empire.

Serious dissension arose among the various political factions in Peking over the entrance of China into the World War, and when parliament refused to declare war against Germany it was illegally dissolved. This led to violent protest on the part of the radicals in the south and to the secession of Canton. Under the leadership of Dr. Sun Yat-sen, a distinguished man of European education, an independent government was set up in southern China which was to follow more constitutional methods, and members of the dissolved parliament hastened to Canton; but no real settlement was reached.

It is very difficult to follow the confused history of China since the establishment of the so-called republic. The country has been at the mercy of rival military chieftains, who have carried on incessant warfare and intrigue to gain power for themselves and their parties. Brigands have overrun the land and made the life of foreigner and of native unsafe. Although the parliament has been assembled from time to time at Peking, it has usually dispersed in disorder. In 1922 one of the generals, Wu Pei-fu, won a victory over his rivals, and in 1923 he set up his candidate as president. It seemed as if order were to be restored; but the parliament broke up, again without a constitution. The next year Wu Pei-fu was overthrown by his enemies, and a group of generals combined to form a unified government with Tuan Chi-jui as president. This move was approved by Dr. Sun Yat-sen. The numerous parties seemed for the moment to have been reduced to two, which differed in their conception of what the government should be. Wu Pei-fu favored a strong central militaristic government, while the opposing party preferred a loose federation with more responsibility in the provinces.

About 1900 China seemed to be entering on a new period of industrial activity and progress. Machinery was introduced, mills and factories rapidly increased, plans for improved transportation were made, and the natural resources of the country were to be developed. This beginning has been checked by constant civil war and by the intervention of foreigners who have striven to obtain control of the rich op-

PL. XLVI. THE GREAT WALL OF SOUTHERN CHINA

Pl. xlvii.   Yuan Shih-kai, First President of the Chinese
Republic, and His Secretary

portunities for business. Foreign business men, especially the Japanese, have advanced large sums of money toward new enterprises, and, when China has been unable to meet her obligations, have obtained mortgages and the control of the industry.

While the mass of the population still cling to the ideas and customs of their forefathers, Western civilization has begun to influence the younger generation, who tend to break away from the authority and tradition of the past, much to the horror of the older generation. A modern system of education was introduced about 1905; but the country was kept bankrupt by military expenses, and there were no funds for the development of the new type of instruction.

Partition of Africa

The last great region to attract the attention of Europeans looking for trade was Africa. Little was known of the interior before 1870. Between 1850 and 1880 many explorers braved the torrid heat and the dangers from disease, savages, and wild beasts, to discover the sources of the Nile and to trace the courses of the Zambezi and the upper Congo rivers. Of these Livingstone and Stanley are best known.

Stanley's famous journey through the heart of "Darkest Africa" naturally aroused the intense interest of all the European powers, and within ten years after his triumphant return to Marseille in 1878 almost the whole surface of Africa had been divided among the European powers or marked out into "spheres of influence."

France has almost the whole of the northwestern shoulder of the continent, from the mouth of the Congo to Tunis. To be sure, a large part of this claim is only desert land. On the east coast of Africa, France controls French Somaliland. The French also hold the island of Madagascar.

Between 1884 and 1890 Germany acquired four considerable areas of African territory,—Togoland, the Cameroons, German Southwest Africa, and German East Africa,—which together included nearly a million square miles. The Ger-

[627]

mans attempted to develop these regions by building railways and schools and by expending enormous sums in other ways, but the wars with the natives and the failure to develop much commerce left the experiment one of doubtful value.

Wedged in between German East Africa and the French Congo is the Belgian Congo. In 1876 King Leopold of Belgium organized a company to explore this region; later he announced that he regarded himself as the ruler of the vast territories of the company. The conduct of this company illustrates the way in which the European invaders were tempted to force the natives to work. The savage natives, accustomed to a free life in the jungle, hated laying railroad ties, collecting rubber juice, and draining swamps for Belgian business men. The company therefore required native chiefs to furnish a certain number of workmen, and on their failure to supply the demand their villages were often burned. The company also required the natives to deliver a certain quantity of rubber each year; failure to comply with these demands was cruelly punished. Protests in Europe and America led the Belgian ministry, in 1908, to assume complete ownership of this territory, heretofore called the Congo Free State, which now took the name of the Belgian Congo.

South Africa, as has already been explained, had fallen to the English. They also gained important territories on the east coast running inland to the great lakes of Africa. But more important, in some ways, was their control over Egypt, which they enjoyed until the end of the World War. That ancient seat of civilization had been conquered by the Arabs in the seventh century, and in 1517 it fell under Turkish control. Shortly after Nelson and the English had frustrated the attempt of Bonaparte to bring Egypt under French rule a military adventurer from Albania, Mehemet Ali, compelled the Sultan, in 1805, to recognize him as governor of Egypt. He built up an army and a fleet, and not only brought all Egypt under his sway but established himself at Khartum, where he could control the Sudan, or region of the upper Nile. Before his death, in 1849, he had induced the Sultan to recognize his heirs as rightful rulers, Khedives, of Egypt.

The importance of Egypt to the Western powers was very much increased by the construction of the Suez Canal, begun in 1859, for both Port Said on the Mediterranean and Suez on the Red Sea are Egyptian ports. The English were able to get a foothold in Egypt through the improvidence of the Egyptian ruler Ismail I, who came to the throne in 1863. By reckless extravagance Ismail involved his country in a heavy debt, which forced him to sell a block of his canal shares to the British government. Still badly in debt, however, Ismail was forced by his English and French creditors to let them oversee his financial administration. This foreign intervention aroused discontent in Egypt, and in 1882 the natives revolted, demanding "Egypt for the Egyptians." Inasmuch as France declined to join in suppressing the rebellion, England undertook it alone, and after putting down the uprising assumed a temporary occupation of the country and the supervision of the army and finances of Egypt. The British continued their "temporary" occupation until shortly after the opening of the World War of 1914, when they assumed a protectorate over Egypt.

Soon after the British occupation of Egypt, trouble arose in the Sudan, where a revolt against the Khedive's government was organized under the leadership of Mohammed Ahmed, who claimed to be the Messiah and won great numbers of fanatical followers, who called him El Mahdi, "The Leader." General Gordon was in charge of the British garrison at Khartum. Here he was besieged by the followers of the Mahdi in 1885, and after a memorable defense fell a victim of their fury. This disaster was avenged twelve years later, when, in 1897-1898, the Sudan was reconquered and the city of Khartum was taken by the British under General Kitchener.

During the British occupation of Egypt the progress of the country was unquestioned; industry and commerce developed steadily, public works were constructed, and financial order was reëstablished under the supervision of the British agent,

[629]

whose word was law. A large dam was built across the Nile at Aswan to control the irrigation. There was strict honesty in the government, and Egypt had never, in all its long history, been so prosperous.

Nevertheless there was a growing feeling among the Egyptians that their country should be ruled by their own people and not by the British. During the years following the close of the World War, the Nationalist party under the able leadership of Zaghlul Pasha made vigorous efforts to force Great Britain to terminate its protectorate. Disorder and uprisings became so serious that finally, in 1922, the British acknowledged the independence of Egypt. The British reserved the right, however, to protect their own and foreign interests in Egypt, and so retained some control over the new government. Sultan Ahmed Fuad Pasha was made king of Egypt. The Egyptian constitution establishes a hereditary monarchy and provides for a Senate partly chosen by the king, partly elected, and a Chamber of Deputies elected by universal suffrage. It also provides for free and compulsory education.

The Nationalists, however, vigorously protested against the restrictions which Great Britain had placed on Egyptian sovereignty. In September, 1924, Zaghlul Pasha, then Egyptian premier, presented to Ramsay MacDonald, the British premier, a demand that he withdraw all British troops, officials, and advisers from Egypt and the Sudan, that Britain's control over Egypt's foreign affairs should cease, and that the Suez Canal should be placed under international control. The inevitable refusal of these demands by the British led to a great Nationalist demonstration during which General Stack, sirdar of the Egyptian army and governor-general of the Sudan, was murdered. The British seized this opportunity to present a harsh ultimatum in which they reaffirmed all their claims to control Egyptian policy, and required the payment of a fine of £500,000 as an indemnity for the murder of their general. They demanded the recall of all Egyptian troops from the Sudan and gave notice that they proposed to extend their irrigation of the Sudan as far as they saw fit. As this enterprise threatened to deflect the headwaters of the Nile and to decrease Egypt's own water supply, the Egyptians felt this to be an even more terrifying grievance than the restrictions on their sovereignty. The Egyptian parliament appealed to the League of Nations, which refused to take up the matter. The British claimed the Sudan, and pronounced the question a "domestic" one, outside the jurisdiction of the League.

The United States and Latin America

In striking contrast to the other powers of Europe, occupied with colonial expansion, stand the two countries which in the era of discovery led them all in enterprise and achievement—Spain and Portugal.[1] Spain, who once could boast that the sun never set on her empire, had been in decline since the days of Philip II. After losing her colonies on the American continents in the early nineteenth century she made no further gains in the other parts of the world to offset her losses.

In the meantime there was rising to predominance in North America a nation that was destined to deal the final blow to the Spanish empire. In the universal search for trade American business men were in no respect behind their European competitors. The natural resources of the United States and the skill of the American people placed that country among the first industrial and commercial powers of the whole world. In 1878 a coaling station was secured in the Samoan Islands, and later one of the islands was brought under the United States flag. In 1898 the Hawaiian Islands were annexed. In that same year came the clash between the United States and Spain, which put an end to Spanish dominion in the New World.

In 1895 the last of many Cuban insurrections against Spain broke out, and sympathy was immediately manifested in the

[1] Portugal, who lost her greatest possession, Brazil, about the same time that Spain lost her South American colonies, still retains considerable stretches of Africa, as a glance at the map will show, but her holdings in Asia are reduced to the posts of Macao in China and Goa in India. In foreign affairs she has been closely allied with England. In 1910 the monarchy was overthrown and Portugal became a republic.

United States. In February, 1898, the battleship *Maine* was mysteriously blown up in the harbor of Havana, where it had been sent in American interest. Although the cause of this disaster could not be discovered, the United States, maintaining that the conditions in Cuba were intolerable, declared war on Spain in April. The war was brief, for the American forces were everywhere victorious. Cuba was declared independent, and Spain ceded Porto Rico and the Philippines to the United States. The following year the Caroline Islands were transferred to Germany, and thus the territory of Spain was reduced to the Spanish peninsula, a few islands, and her small holdings in Africa.

Many forces conspired to extend the influence of the United States into Mexico, Central America and South America, and the Caribbean. In general the Latin-American peoples were formed from an amalgamation of native and European races, both inexperienced in the art of self-government. Their countries were rich in natural resources but backward in industries. They needed capital to develop their business, and foreign enterprise to start their factories and their railways. As they were near neighbors, the United States could not avoid taking an interest in their affairs. A Pan-American Congress, composed of delegates from the nineteen republics of America, met in Washington in 1889 to discuss mutual interests. A bureau of American republics, later called the Pan-American Union, was founded in Washington, and a handsome building was erected to house it.

The large population and the vast resources of the Latin-American countries promise to make them a very important factor in the history of the future. The cultivation of friendly relations between the United States and the countries to the south is one of the chief tasks of the American government.

CHAPTER XXVIII

RUSSIA AND THE NEAR EASTERN QUESTION

*Russia under Alexander I and Nicholas I. The Emancipation of the
Serfs: Terrorism. Industrial Development in Russia. Struggle for
Liberty under Nicholas II. Emergence of Serbia and Greece.
The Crimean War, 1854–1856. Disappearance of Turkey
in Europe. The Balkan Wars, 1912–1913*

Russia under Alexander I and Nicholas I

DURING the nineteenth century Russia came steadily into
ever closer relations with western Europe. Although
still a backward country in many respects, she was
engaged in slowly modernizing—that is, "Westernizing," herself. The works of some of her writers are widely read in
foreign lands, especially those of Leo Tolstoy, Chekhov, and
Turgeniev. The music of Rubinstein, Tschaikowsky, and Rim-
ski-Korsakov is as highly esteemed in London and New York
as in Moscow. Even in the field of science such names as that
of Mendelyeev, the chemist, and of Metchnikoff, the biologist,
are well known to their fellow workers in Germany, France,
England, and America. In 1917 the great social revolution in
Russia based on the gospel of a Western economic prophet—
Marx—roused the keen interest of the whole world.

When, in 1815, Tsar Alexander I returned to St. Petersburg
after the close of the Congress of Vienna, he could view his
position and achievements with pride. He had participated
in Napoleon's overthrow, and had succeeded in uniting the
rulers of western Europe in that Holy Alliance which he had
so much at heart. He was the undisputed and autocratic
ruler of more than half the entire continent of Europe, not
to speak of the vast reaches of northern Asia which lay beneath
his scepter.

Under Alexander's dominion there were many races and
peoples, differing in customs, language, and religion—Finns,
Germans, Poles, Jews, Tartars, Armenians, Georgians, and
Mongols. The Russians themselves, it is true, had colonized
the southern plains of European Russia and had spread north-

[633]

eastward, even into Siberia. They made up a large proportion of the population of the empire, and their language was everywhere taught in the schools and used by the officials. The people of the grand duchy of Finland, speaking Swedish and Finnish, resented their incorporation with Russia; and the Poles, recalling the time when their kingdom far outshone the petty duchy of Moscow among the European powers, still hoped that some day the kingdom of Poland might form an independent nation with its own language and constitution.[1]

In the time of Alexander I the Russians had not yet begun to flock to the cities, which were small and ill built compared with those of western Europe. The great mass of the population still lived in the country, and most of the peasants were serfs, as ignorant and wretched as those of France or England in the twelfth century.

Alexander I had inherited, as "Autocrat of all the Russias," a despotic power over his subjects as absolute as that to which Louis XIV laid claim. He could appoint or dismiss his ministers, and order the arrest, imprisonment, exile, or execution of any one he chose, without consulting or giving an account to any living being. Even the Russian national Church was under his personal control.

During his early years Alexander entertained liberal ideas, but after his return from the Congress of Vienna he began to dismiss his liberal advisers. He became as apprehensive of revolution as his friend Metternich, and threw himself into the arms of the "Old Russian" party, which obstinately opposed the introduction of all Western ideas. The Tsar was soon denouncing liberalism as a frightful illusion which threatened the whole social order. He permitted his officials to do all they could to stamp out the ideas which he had himself formerly done so much to encourage. The censorship of

[1] The Cossacks, or light cavalry, who constituted so conspicuous a feature of the Russian army, were originally nomadic horsemen on the southern and eastern frontiers, composed mainly of adventurous Russians with some admixture of other peoples. Certain districts were assigned to them by the government—on the lower Don near the Black Sea, the Urals, and elsewhere—in return for military service.

the press put an end to the liberal periodicals which had sprung up, and professors in the universities were dismissed for teaching modern science. The attraction of the new ideas was, however, so strong that the Tsar could not prevent some of his more enlightened subjects from following eagerly the course of the revolutionary movements in western Europe and reading the new books dealing with scientific discoveries and questions of political and social reform.

Alexander I died suddenly on December 1, 1825. The revolutionary societies seized this opportunity to organize a revolt known as the "Decembrist conspiracy." But the movement was badly organized; a few charges of grapeshot brought the insurgents to terms, and some of the leaders were hanged.

Nicholas I, Alexander's successor, never forgot the rebellion which inaugurated his reign, and he proved one of the most despotic of all the long list of autocratic rulers. His arbitrary measures speedily produced a revolt in Poland. Russian troops were stationed there in great numbers, Russian officials forced their way into the government offices, and the petitions of the Polish diet were contemptuously ignored by the Tsar. Secret societies then began to promote a movement for the reëstablishment of the ancient Polish republic, which Catherine II and her fellow monarchs had destroyed (see above, pp. 395 ff.). Late in 1830 an uprising occurred in Warsaw; the insurgents secured control of the city, drove out the Russian officials, organized a provisional government, and, appealing to the European powers for aid, proclaimed the independence of Poland, January 25, 1831.

The Tsar's armies were soon able to crush the rebellion, and when Poland lay prostrate at his feet, Nicholas gave no quarter. He revoked the constitution, abolished the diet, and suppressed the national flag. To all intents and purposes Poland became henceforth merely a Russian province, governed, like the rest of the empire, from St. Petersburg.[1]

---

[1] Thirty years later, in 1863, the Poles made another desperate attempt to free themselves from the yoke of Russia, but without success.

Nicholas I sincerely believed that Russia could only be saved from the "decay" of religion and government, which he believed to be taking place in western Europe, by maintaining autocracy, for this alone was strong enough to make head against the destructive ideas which some of his subjects mistook for enlightenment. The Russian-Greek Church and all its beliefs must be defended, and the Russian nation preserved as a separate and superior people who should maintain forever the noble beliefs and institutions of the past. The Russians were converted to Christianity by missionaries from Constantinople, the religious capital of the Eastern, or Greek, Church, which had gradually drifted away from the Latin, or Roman Catholic, Church in the seventh and eighth centuries. For many centuries the Russian Church remained in close relations with the patriarch of Constantinople, but after that city fell into the hands of the Mohammedan Turks it occurred to the Russian rulers that the Tsars must be the divinely appointed successors of the Eastern emperors. Old Rome, on the Tiber, and new Rome, on the Bosporus, had both fallen on account of their sins. Russia thus became the "third Rome," and the Tsar the head of all true Christians who accepted the only orthodox faith—that of the Greek Church. Under Peter the Great the Russian Church was brought completely under the control of the government. Certainly a great many of his advisers were well content with the system, and his army of officials were loath to recommend reform.

Accordingly the Tsar adopted strong measures to check the growth of liberalism. The officials bestirred themselves to prevent in every way the admission of Western ideas into Russia. Books on religion and science were carefully examined by the police or by the clergy, and foreign works containing references to politics were confiscated or the objectionable pages blotted out by the censors. The government officials did not hesitate freely to open private letters committed to the post. It may be said that, except for a few short intervals of freedom, this whole system was continued down to the time of the World War.

The Emancipation of the Serfs: Terrorism

In 1854 the efforts of Russia to increase her influence in Turkey led to a war with France and England. The Russians were defeated, and their strong fortress of Sevastopol, in the Crimea, was captured by the allies (see below). Nicholas I died in the midst of the reverses of the Crimean War, leaving to his son, Alexander II, the responsibility of coming to terms with the enemy, and then, if possible, strengthening Russia by reducing the disgraceful political corruption and bribery which had been revealed by the war and by improving the lot of the people at large, who lived in poverty and degradation.

Nearly one half of the Tsar's subjects were serfs, whose bondage and wretched lives seemed to present an insurmountable barrier to general progress and prosperity. The landlord commonly reserved a portion of his estate for himself and turned over to his serfs barely enough to enable them to keep body and soul together. They usually spent three days in the week cultivating their lord's fields. He was their judge as well as their master and could flog them at will. Indeed, the Russian serfs were practically slaves and were viewed as scarcely more than beasts of burden.

From time to time the serfs, infuriated by the hard conditions thus imposed upon them, revolted against their lords. During the reign of Catherine the Great a general uprising had taken place and was put down only with terrible bloodshed and cruelty. Under Nicholas I more than five hundred riots had occurred, and these seemed to increase rather than decrease, notwithstanding the vigilance of the police and the severity of the government.

Alexander II, fearful lest the peasants should again attempt to win their liberty by force, decided that the government must undertake the difficult task of freeing forty millions of his subjects from serfdom. After much discussion he issued an emancipation proclamation, March 3, 1861, on the eve of

[637]

the great Civil War which was to put an end to negro slavery in the United States.

In his anxiety to prevent any loss to the landowners, who constituted the ruling class in the Russian government, the Tsar did his work in a very half-hearted manner. It is true the government deprived the former lord of his right to force the peasants to work for him and pay him the old dues; he could no longer flog them or command them to marry against their will; but the peasants still remained bound to the land,

RUSSIAN PEASANT'S HOME

for they were not permitted to leave their villages without a government pass. The landlords surrendered a portion of their estates to the peasants, but this did not become the property of *individual* owners, but of the *village community* as a whole. The land assigned to each village was to be redistributed periodically among the various families of the community, so that, aside from his hut and garden, no peasant could lay claim permanently to any particular plot of land.

The Russian government dealt very generously with the landlords. It not only agreed that the peasants should be

required to pay for such land as their former masters turned over to them, but commonly fixed the price at an amount far greater than the real value of the land—a price which the government paid and proposed to collect from the serfs in installments.

His new "freedom" seemed to the peasant little better than that of a convict condemned to hard labor in the penitentiary. Indeed, he sometimes refused to be "freed" when he learned of the hard bargain which the government proposed to drive with him. There were hundreds of riots while the readjustments were taking place, which were sternly suppressed by the government. The peasants were compelled by force of arms to accept their "liberty" and pay the land tax which emancipation imposed upon them.

Naturally, if the people in a given community increased, the size of the individual allotments inevitably decreased, and with that the chances of earning a livelihood. More than fifty years after the "freeing" of the serfs the peasant had, on the average, scarcely half as much land as that originally assigned to him. Even though he lived constantly on the verge of starvation he fell far behind in the payment of his taxes. In 1904 the Tsar, in a moment of forced generosity, canceled the arrears, which the peasants, in any case, could never have paid. A little later the Tsar issued an order permitting the peasants to leave their particular village and seek employment elsewhere. They might, on the other hand, become *owners* of their allotments. This led to the practical abolition of the ancient *mir,* or village community,[1] and left millions of peasants as tenants of great landlords and sometimes as owners of their holdings. All these bitter ancient grudges of the Russian peasants explain the ruthless way in which they dispossessed the hated landlords as soon as the Bolshevik revolution in 1917 afforded them a chance.

In spite of freeing the serfs, Alexander II regarded the reformers with the utmost suspicion and began to arrest the

[1] These village communities had long existed in Russia, since the lords had usually found it convenient to have the village redistribute the land from time to time among the serfs as the number of inhabitants changed.

more active among them. The prisons were soon crowded, and hundreds were banished to Siberia. The Tsar and his police seemed to be the avowed enemies of all progress, and any one who advanced a new idea was punished as if he had committed a murder. The peaceful preparation of the people for representative government could not go on so long as the police were arresting men for forming debating clubs. It seemed to the more ardent reformers that there was no course open to them but to declare war on the government as a body of cruel, corrupt tyrants who would keep Russia in darkness forever. They argued that the atrocious acts of the officials must be exposed, the government intimidated, and the eyes of the world opened to the horrors of the situation by startling acts of violence. So some of the reformers became *terrorists*, not because they were depraved men or loved bloodshed, but because they were convinced that there was no other way to save their beloved land from the fearful oppression under which it groaned.

The government fought terrorism with terrorism. In 1879 sixteen suspected revolutionists were hanged and scores sent to the dungeons of St. Petersburg or the mines of Siberia. The terrorists, on their part, retaliated by attacks on the Tsar and his government. Attempts were made to blow up a special train on which the Tsar was traveling, and, in another effort to kill him, the Winter Palace in St. Petersburg was wrecked by a revolutionist disguised as a carpenter.

In short, the efforts of the Tsar's officials to check the revolutionists proved vain, and the minister to whom the Tsar had given almost dictatorial powers to suppress the agitation finally saw that the government must make some concessions in order to pacify its enemies; so he advised Alexander II to grant a species of constitution, in which he should agree to convoke an assembly elected by the people and thereafter ask its opinion and counsel before making new and important laws. The Tsar finally consented, but it was too late. On the afternoon when he gave his assent to the plan he was assassinated as he was driving to his palace (March, 1881).

The reign of Alexander II had not been entirely given up to internal reforms and repression, however. In 1877 Russia was again at war with Turkey, aiding the "south Slavs"—Serbians, Montenegrins, and Bulgarians—in their attempt to free themselves from Turkish control. Successful in arms, Russia was, however, obliged to relinquish most of her gains and those of her allies by a congress of the European powers held at Berlin in 1878 (see below).

While the body of the murdered Tsar, Alexander II, was still lying in state, the executive committee of the revolutionists issued a warning to his son and successor, Alexander III, threatening him with the evils to come if he did not yield to their demand for representative government, freedom of speech and of the press, and the right to meet for the discussion of political questions. The new Tsar was not, however, moved by the appeal, and the police redoubled their activity. The plans of reform were repudiated, and the autocracy settled back into its usual despotic habits. The terrorists realized that, for the time being, they could gain nothing by further acts of violence. It was clear that the people at large were not yet ready for a revolution.

The reign of Alexander III (1881-1894) was a period of quiet, during which little progress seemed to be made. The people suffered the oppression of the government officials without active opposition. Their occasional protests were answered by imprisonment, flogging, or exile, for Alexander III and his intimate advisers believed quite as firmly and religiously in autocracy as Nicholas I had done. Freedom and liberalism, they agreed, could only serve to destroy a nation. All ideas of democracy which had produced revolutions in western Europe must be kept out at all cost.

Industrial Development in Russia

It became more and more difficult, however, to keep Russia "frozen," for during the last quarter of the nineteenth century the spread of democratic ideas had been hastened by the coming of the steam engine, the factory, and the locomotive, all of which served to unsettle the humdrum agricultural life which the great majority of the people had led for centuries. In spite of her mineral resources Russia had lagged far behind her Western neighbors in the use of machinery. She had little capital and no adequate means of transportation across the vast stretches of country that separated her chief towns, and the governing classes had no taste for manufacturing enterprises.

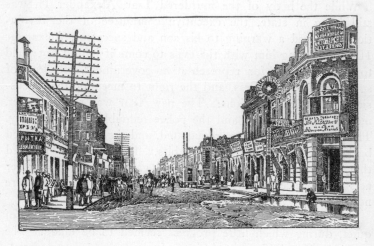

HARBIN, A CITY ON THE TRANS-SIBERIAN RAILWAY

Cities have sprung up along the great Russian railway just as they did along the transcontinental lines in the United States or Canada. This Western-looking town is northeast of Peking, in the farming country of Manchuria; nominally a part of the Chinese republic but in reality held by Russia

The liberation of the serfs, with all its drawbacks, favored the growth of factories, for the peasants were sometimes permitted to leave their villages for the manufacturing centers which were gradually growing up. The value of the products of the chief industries doubled between 1887 and 1897, and the number of people employed in them increased from one million and a quarter to over two millions.

Along with this business development went the construction of great railway lines, built largely by the government with money borrowed from capitalists in western Europe. Some of the railroads were constructed chiefly for political and military purposes, but others were designed to connect the great factory centers. Railway building was first seriously undertaken in Russia after the disasters of the Crimean War, when the soldiers suffered cruel hardships in consequence of the difficulty of obtaining supplies. By 1878 upward of eight thousand miles had been built, connecting the capital with the frontiers of European Russia. In 1885 the railway advance toward the frontiers of India [1] was begun, and within a short time Afghanistan was reached and communication opened to the borders of China. Important lines were also built in the region between the Black Sea and the Caspian.

The greatest of all railway undertakings was the Trans-Siberian road, which was rendered necessary for the transportation of soldiers and military supplies to the eastern boundary of the empire. Communication was established between St. Petersburg and the Pacific in 1900, and a branch line from Harbin southward to Port Arthur was soon finished. Before the World War one could travel in comfort, with few changes of cars, from Havre to Vladivostok, *via* Paris, Cologne, Berlin,

---

[1] The expansion of Russia to the southeast was very rapid. In 1846 the southern boundary ran along the lower edge of the Aral Sea. In 1863 Russia, claiming that the Turkestan tribesmen pillaged caravans and harried her frontiers, sent forces which captured the cities of Turkestan, Chemkent, and Tashkent, and two years later organized the region into the new province of Russian Turkestan. Shortly afterward the Ameer of Bokhara declared war on the Tsar, only to have the Russians occupy the ancient city of Samarkand and later establish a protectorate over Bokhara, which brought them to the borders of Afghanistan. In 1872 the Khan of Khiva was reduced to vassalage. During the following years (1873-1886) the regions to the south, about Merv, down to the borders of Persia and Afghanistan, were gradually annexed. In 1876 the province of Khokand on the boundary of the Chinese empire was seized and transformed into the province of Ferghana. By securing railway concessions and making loans to the Shah the Russians became powerful in Persia, and thus all along their southeastern frontiers they struggled for predominance against British influence. In 1907 the British and Russian governments came to a settlement in regard to their spheres of influence in Persia.

Warsaw, Moscow, Irkutsk on Lake Baikal, and Harbin, a distance of seventy-three hundred miles. In addition to the main line some important branches were built, and more planned. By means of these the vast plains of central Asia may, before long, be peopled as the plains of America have been.

Struggle for Liberty under Nicholas II

When Nicholas II succeeded his father, Alexander III, in 1894, he was but twenty-six years old, and there was some reason to hope that he would face the problems of this new industrial Russia in a progressive spirit. He had had an opportunity in his travels to become somewhat familiar with the governments of western Europe, and one of his first acts was to order the imprisonment of the prefect of police of St. Petersburg for annoying the correspondents of foreign newspapers. Nicholas, however, quickly dispelled any illusions which his more liberal subjects entertained. "Let it be understood by all," he declared, "that I shall employ all my powers in the best interests of the people, but the principle of autocracy will be sustained by me as firmly and unswervingly as it was by my never-to-be-forgotten father."

The censorship of the press was made stricter than ever, one decree alone adding two hundred books to the already long list of those which the government condemned.[1] The distinguished historian Professor Milyoukoff was dismissed from the University of Moscow on the ground of his "generally noxious tendencies," and other teachers were warned not to talk about government.

Nowhere did the Tsar show his desire for absolute control more clearly than in his dealings with Finland. When Alexander I had annexed that country, in 1809, he had permitted it to retain its own diet and pass its own laws, although it of course recognized the Tsar, under the title of Grand Duke, as its ruler. The Finns cherished their independence and have

---

[1] Among the books which the government prohibited in public libraries were the Russian translations of Mill's *Political Economy*, Green's *History of the English People*, and Bryce's *American Commonwealth*.

in recent times shown themselves one of the most progressive peoples of Europe. In 1899, however, Nicholas began a harsh and determined *Russification* of Finland. He sent heartless officials, like Plehve, to represent him and crush out all opposition to his changes. So far as possible he undertook to substitute the Russian language for the Finnish.

Finally, on June 17, 1904, the Russian governor of Finland was assassinated by the son of one of the senators, who then killed himself, leaving a letter in which he explained that he had acted alone and with the simple purpose of forcing on the Tsar's attention the atrocities of his officials. A year later the Tsar, under the influence of revolution at home and disaster abroad, consented to restore to Finland all her former rights.

We must now trace the history of the terrible struggle between the Russian people and their despotic government, which began openly in 1904. In 1902 an unpopular minister of the interior had been assassinated, and the Tsar had appointed a still more unpopular man in his place, namely, Plehve, who was notorious for his success in hunting down those who criticized the government and for the vigor with which he had carried on the Russification of Finland.

Plehve connived at the persecution of those among the Tsar's subjects who ventured to disagree with the doctrines of the Russian official Church, to which every Russian was supposed to belong. The Jews suffered especially. In 1903 there were massacres at Kishinev and elsewhere which horrified the Western world and drove hundreds of thousands of Jews to foreign lands, especially to the United States. There are good reasons for believing that Plehve actually arranged these massacres. At all events he continued to tolerate them until a bomb put an end to his career in the summer of 1904.

Plehve was mistaken, however, in his belief that all the trouble came from a handful of deluded fanatics. Among those who detested the cruel and corrupt government which he represented were the professional men, the university professors, the enlightened merchants and manufacturers, and the public-spirited nobility. These were not at first organized into a distinct party, but in time they came to be known as the *Constitutional Democrats.* They hoped that a parliament elected by the people might be established. They demanded freedom of speech and of the press, the right to hold public meetings to discuss public questions, and the abolition of the secret police system and of arbitrary imprisonment and religious persecutions.

In the towns a socialistic party had been growing up which advocated the theories of the Western prophet of socialism, Karl Marx (p. 561). It desired all the reforms advocated by the Constitutional Democrats just described, but looked forward to the time when the workingmen would become so numerous and powerful that they could seize the government offices and assume the management of lands, mines, and factories, which should thereafter be used for the benefit of all rather than for the small class of rich men who then owned them. Unlike the reformers next to be described, these socialists did not believe in terrorism or in murderous attacks upon unpopular government officials.

In contrast with these were those Russian agitators—forerunners of the Bolsheviki—who belonged to the Socialist Revolutionary party, which was well organized and was responsible for the chief acts of violence during the years of the revolution. They maintained that it was right to make war upon the government, which was oppressing them and extorting money from the people to fill the pockets of dishonest officeholders. Its members selected their victims from the most notoriously cruel among the officials, and after a victim had been killed they usually published a list of the offenses which cost him his life. Lists of those selected for assassination were also prepared, after careful consideration, by their executive committee.

The more the Tsar sought to stamp out all protest against the autocracy, the more its enemies increased, and at last, in 1904, the open revolution may be said to have begun. On February 5 of that year a war began with Japan (see above,

Pl. xlviii. Tsar Nicholas II at the Opening of the First
Duma

Berlin 15/5 1905

Dearest Nicky.

The widow of old Prince Antoine
Radziwill, Princess Marie, is going to Petersburg;
to beg for your approval of her late husband's
will. Prince Antoine was not only a cherished
& trusted servant of my deceased Grandfather
as his Adjutant & different general, but also
a faithful & beloved personal friend to him
as well as to my late beloved father & to me.
His winning ways & his gay nature and his friends
wherever he was, & Your Grandfather & father
have both always cherished him. His
whereas the intimate long-life friend of my
late mother, & has been made testator by
her husband for his will. The whole future
of her children & family rests on the fact
of your kind approval of the will, & I venture

preparation & even learnt your language
& will in no way be of any hindrance to
your Generals, as he is a quiet man, as the
army is large & powerful I think that it also
not matter if he goes, so to venture again to ask
that you can permit him to go &
with success for bothering you with all these
matters but they are little strayed betweenwork
& best love to Alix
I remain
Give Your most affte = Warm & friend
Willy.

PL. XLIX. OPENING AND CLOSE OF A "WILLY AND NICKY" LETTER

p. 624) which was caused by Russia's encroachments in Korea and her evident intention of permanently depriving China of Manchuria. The liberals attributed the conflict to bad management on the part of the Tsar's officials and declared it to be inhuman and contrary to the interests of the people. Whatever the cause, disaster was the outcome. The Japanese defeated the Russians in Manchuria in a series of terrific conflicts. The Russian fleets in the East were annihilated, and on January 1, 1905, Port Arthur fell, after one of the most terrible sieges on record.

The war produced a stagnation of commerce and industry, and strikes became common. At the same time the crops failed, and the starving peasants burned and sacked the houses and barns of the nobles. It became known that the government officials had been stealing money that should have gone to strengthen and equip the armies; rifles had been paid for that had never been delivered, supplies bought which never reached the suffering soldiers, and—most scandalous of all—high Russian dignitaries had even misappropriated the funds of the Red Cross Society for aiding the wounded.

On January 22, 1905, a fearful event occurred. The workingmen of St. Petersburg had sent a petition to the Tsar and had informed him that on Sunday they would march to the palace humbly to pray to him in person to consider their sufferings, since they had no faith in his officials or ministers. When Sunday morning came, masses of men, women, and children, wholly unarmed, attempted to approach the Winter Palace in the pathetic hope that the "Little Father," as they called the Tsar, would listen to their woes. Instead, the Cossacks tried to disperse them with their whips, and then the troops which guarded the palace shot and cut down hundreds and wounded thousands in a conflict which continued through the day. "Red Sunday" was, however, only the most impressive of many similar experiences which the citizens had with the brutal methods of the Tsar's police.

Finally the Tsar so far yielded to the pressure of public opinion that on August 19 he promised to summon a *Duma,* or council, which should meet not later than January, 1906. It was to represent all Russia, but to have no further power than that of giving the ruler advice in making the laws, for the Tsar refused to give up his old autocratic prerogatives.

This was a bitter disappointment to even the most moderate liberals. It was pointed out that both the workingmen and the professional men were excluded by the regulations from voting. A more effective measure in bringing the Tsar and his advisers to terms was a great general strike in the interest

THE WINTER PALACE, ST. PETERSBURG
The massacre took place just in front of the palace

of reform which began late in October. All the railroads stopped running; in all the great towns the shops, except those that dealt in provisions, were closed; gas and electricity were no longer furnished; the law courts ceased their duties; and even the apothecaries refused to prepare prescriptions until reforms should be granted.

The situation soon became intolerable, and on October 29 the Tsar announced that he had ordered the "government" to grant the people freedom of conscience, speech, and association, and to permit the classes which had been excluded in his first edict to vote for members of the Duma. Lastly, he agreed "to establish an immutable rule that no law can come into force without the approval of the Duma."

The elections for the Duma took place in March and April, 1906, and, in spite of the activity of the police, resulted in an overwhelming majority for the Constitutional Democrats. The deputies to the Duma assembled in no humble frame of mind. Like the members of the Estates General in 1789, they felt that they had the nation behind them. They listened stonily to the Tsar's remarks at the opening session, and it was clear from the first that they would not agree with their monarch any better than the French deputies had agreed with Louis XVI and his courtiers.

The Tsar's ministers would not coöperate with the Duma in any important measures of reform, and on July 21 Nicholas II declared that he was "cruelly disappointed" because the deputies had not confined themselves to their proper duties and had commented upon many matters which belonged to him. He accordingly dissolved the Duma, as he had a perfect right to do, and fixed March 5, 1907, as the date for the meeting of a new Duma.

In August the revolutionists made an unsuccessful attempt to blow up the Tsar's chief minister in his country house, and continued to assassinate governors and police officials. The "Black Hundreds," on the other hand, murdered Jews and liberals, while the government established courts-martial to insure the speedy trial and immediate execution of revolutionists. In the months of September and October, 1906, these courts summarily condemned three hundred persons to be shot or hanged. During the whole year some nine thousand persons were killed or wounded for political reasons.

A terrible famine was afflicting the land at the end of the year, and it was discovered that a member of the Tsar's ministry had been stealing the money appropriated to furnish grain to the dying peasants. An observer who had traveled eight hundred miles through the famine-stricken district reported that he did not find a single village where the peasants had food enough for themselves or their cattle. In some places the peasants were reduced to eating bark and the straw used for their thatch roofs.

In October, 1906, the decree was issued permitting the peasants to leave their particular village community and join another or to seek employment elsewhere. On November 25 the peasants were empowered to become owners of their allotments, and all redemption dues were remitted. This constituted the first step toward a practical abolition of the system of common ownership by village communities, described above, which was finally achieved by a law of June 27, 1910. It was the beginning of the great social changes in Russia, which were greatly hastened by the Bolshevik revolution that followed the World War.

The Tsar continued to summon the Duma regularly, but so arranged the system of voting for its members that only the conservative classes of the nation were represented, and his officials did all they could to keep out liberal deputies. In spite of this the fourth Duma, elected in 1912, showed much independence in opposing the oppressive rule of the Tsar's ministers. Although parliamentary government was by no means won in Russia, many important reforms were achieved. The Tsar, however, continued to retain the title of "Autocrat of all the Russias," and his officials went on persecuting those who ventured to criticize the government, until the revolution of March, 1917, deprived them of all power (see below).

Emergence of Serbia and Greece

The relations of the western European states with Russia as well as among themselves have been deeply affected since the opening of the nineteenth century by the so-called near-Eastern question. This was the great problem of what was to become of southeastern Europe, which had been overwhelmed by the Turks in the fourteenth and fifteenth centuries. The Balkan peninsula is inhabited to a considerable extent by Slavs; and Russia claimed to have some fraternal solicitude for their welfare as well as to be the natural protector of adherents to their form of Christianity, the Greek Orthodox church, which was the State church of Russia. An event in the Balkan peninsula touched off the fuse that ignited the conflagration of the World War; consequently none of us can be indifferent to the strange history and complexities of the Balkan situation.

Austria had long been a next-door neighbor of the Turks, but by the year 1700 the Mohammedans had been driven out of Hungary. This country came under the rule of the house of Hapsburg, which ardently desired to extend its control farther into Turkish territory. In 1774 Catherine the Great had secured the Crimea and so got a footing for Russia on the Black Sea which was extended by Alexander I, who won Bessarabia (also on the Black Sea). But so far Russia has never been able to win its longed-for goal, Constantinople, which remains to this day the prized conquest of the Turks, although after the World War it ceased to be the capital of their empire.

Shortly after the Congress of Vienna the Serbians, who had for a number of years been in revolt against the Turks, were able to establish their practical independence (1817), and Serbia, with Belgrade as its capital, became a principality tributary to Turkey. This was the first of a series of Balkan states which emerged, during the nineteenth century, from beneath the Mohammedan inundation. In the later Middle Ages Serbia had been a considerable power, and its people had never forgotten their former glory as an independent and aggressive state.

The next Balkan state to gain its independence was Greece, whose long conflict against Turkish despotism aroused throughout Europe the sympathy of all who appreciated the glories of ancient Greece. The inhabitants of the land of Plato, Aristotle, and Demosthenes were, it is true, scarcely to be regarded as descendants of the Greeks, and the language they spoke differed in many respects from the ancient tongue. At the opening of the nineteenth century, however, the national spirit once more awoke in Greece, and able writers made modern

Greek a literary language and employed it in stirring appeals to the patriotism of their fellow countrymen.

In 1821 an insurrection broke out in Morea, as the ancient Peloponnesus is now called. The movement spread through the peninsula; the atrocities of the Turk were rivaled by those of the Greeks, and thousands of Mohammedans—men, women, and children—were slaughtered. On January 27, 1822, the Greek National Assembly issued a proclamation of independence.

To Metternich this revolt seemed only another illustration of the dangers of revolution, but the liberals throughout Europe enthusiastically sympathized with the Greek uprising, since it was carried on in the name of national liberty. Intellectual men in England, France, Germany, and the United States held meetings to express sympathy for the cause, while to the ardent Christian it seemed a righteous war against the Mohammedans. Soldiers and supplies poured into Greece. Indeed, the Greeks could scarcely have freed themselves had the European powers refused to intervene.

It is needless to follow the long negotiations between the various European courts in connection with Greek affairs. In 1827 Great Britain, France, and Russia signed a treaty at London providing for a joint adjustment of the difficulty, on the ground that it was necessary to put an end to the sanguinary struggle which left Greece and the adjacent islands a prey "to all the disasters of anarchy, and daily causes fresh impediments to the commerce of Europe." The Porte—that is, the Turkish government—having refused to accept the mediation of the allies, their combined fleets destroyed that of the Sultan at Navarino in October, 1827. Thereupon the Porte declared a "holy war" on the unbelievers, especially the Russians. But the latter were prepared to push the war with vigor, and they not only actively promoted the freedom of Greece but forced the Sultan to grant practical independence to the Danubian principalities of Wallachia and Moldavia, which came thereby under Russian influence and later were united into the kingdom of Rumania. Turkey was no longer able to oppose the wishes of the allies, and in 1832 Greece became an independent state, choosing for its king Prince Otto of Bavaria.

The Crimean War, 1854–1856

A fresh excuse for interfering in Turkish affairs was afforded the Tsar two decades later. Complaints reached him that Christian pilgrims were not permitted by the Turks (who had long been in possession of the Holy Land and Jerusalem) freely to visit the places made sacred by their associations with the life of Jesus. Russia seemed the natural protector of those, at least, who adhered to her own form of Christianity, and the Russian ambassador rudely demanded that the Porte should grant the Tsar a protectorate over all the Christians in Turkey.

When news of this situation reached Paris, Napoleon III, who had recently become emperor and was anxious to take a hand in European affairs, declared that France, by virtue of earlier treaties with the Porte, enjoyed the right to protect Catholic Christians. He found an ally in Great Britain, who feared that if Russia took Constantinople it would command the route to India, and he accordingly advised the Sultan not to accede to Russia's demands. When the Tsar's troops marched into the Turkish dominions, France and Great Britain came to the Sultan's assistance and in 1854 declared war upon Russia.

The Crimean War, which followed, owes its name to the fact that the operations of the allies against Russia culminated in the long and bloody siege of Sevastopol, in the southern part of the Crimean peninsula. Every victory won by the allies was dearly bought. The British soldiers suffered at first in consequence of the inefficiency of the home government in sending them the necessary supplies. The Russians, however, were disheartened by the sufferings of their own soldiers, the inefficiency and corruption of their officials, and the final loss of the mighty fortress of Sevastopol. They saw, moreover, that their near neighbor, Austria, was about to join their enemies.

The new Tsar, Alexander II, therefore consented, in 1856, to the terms of a treaty drawn up at Paris.[1]

This treaty recognized the independence of the Ottoman Empire and guaranteed its territorial integrity. The "Sublime Porte" was also included within the scope of the international law of Europe, from which it had hitherto been excluded as an alien in religion and government. The other powers agreed not to interfere further with the domestic affairs of Turkey. The Black Sea was declared neutral territory and its waters were thrown open to merchant ships of all nations, but no warships were to pass through the Bosporus or Dardanelles. In short, Turkey was preserved and strengthened by the intervention of the powers as a bulwark against Russian encroachment in the Balkan peninsula; but, although the Sultan made liberal promises, nothing was really done to reform the Turkish administration or to make the lot of the Christian subjects more secure.

Disappearance of Turkey in Europe

Some idea of the situation of the people under the Sultan's rule may be derived from the report of an English traveler (Mr. Arthur Evans) in 1875. In the Turkish provinces of Bosnia and Herzegovina he found that outside the large towns, where European consuls were present, there was no proper safeguard for the honor, property, or lives of the Christians. The Sultan's taxes fell principally on the peasants, in the form of a tenth of their produce. It was a common custom for the collectors (who were often not Mohammedans but brutal Christians) to require the peasant to pay the tax in cash before the harvesting of the ripe crop, and if he could not meet the charges, the taxgatherer simply said, "Then your harvest shall rot on the ground till you pay it."

In 1874 a failure of crops aggravated the intolerable conditions, and an insurrection broke out in Bosnia and Herze-

---

[1] It will be remembered that Sardinia had joined the allies against Russia, and in this way forced the powers to admit it to the deliberations at Paris, where Cavour seized the opportunity to plead the cause of Italy.

govina which set the whole Balkan peninsula aflame. The Bulgarians around Philippopolis, incited to hopes of independence by the events in the regions to the west of them, assassinated some of the Turkish officials and gave the Ottoman government a pretext for cruel measures of suppression which involved the death of thousands of Bulgarians.

While the European powers were exchanging futile diplomatic notes on the situation, Serbia and Montenegro declared war on the Sultan, and the Christians in the Balkan region made a frantic appeal to the West for immediate help. A good deal naturally depended on the position taken by Great Britain, which was in alliance with Turkey. Gladstone, then leader of the Liberals, urged his countrymen to break the old alliance between Great Britain and the Turks, who had so long been dreaded by the western Europeans. But Gladstone's party was not in power, and Lord Beaconsfield was fearful that British encouragement to the Slavic rebels in the Sultan's dominions would only result in their becoming independent and allying themselves with Great Britain's enemy, Russia. The British believed that in the interest of their trade they must continue to resist any movement which might destroy the power of the Sultan, who was not so likely as a European power, such as Russia or Austria, to hamper their Eastern commerce.

The negotiations of the powers having come to nothing, Russia determined, in 1877, to act alone. Her declaration of war was shortly followed by Russian victories, and in 1878 a Russian army entered Adrianople—which was equivalent to an announcement to the world that the dominion of the Ottomans in Europe had come to an end. Great Britain protested, but the Sultan was forced to sign the Treaty of San Stefano with the Tsar and to recognize the complete independence of Serbia, Montenegro, and Rumania. In 1862 the so-called Danubian provinces of Moldavia and Wallachia had formed a voluntary union under the name "Rumania." In 1866 the Rumanians chose for their ruler a German prince, Charles of Hohenzollern-Sigmaringen, who, in 1881, was proclaimed king of Rumania, as Carol I. He died in 1914 and was succeeded by his nephew Ferdinand. As for Bulgaria, it was made an independent state except for the payment of tribute to the Sultan.

Great Britain and Austria naturally had serious objections to the Treaty of San Stefano, which increased the influence of Russia in the Balkans. They therefore forced Tsar Alexader II to submit the whole matter to the consideration of a general European congress at Berlin, where, after prolonged and stormy sessions, the powers agreed that Serbia, Rumania, and little Montenegro should be entirely independent and that Bulgaria should also be independent except for the payment of a tribute to the Sultan. The Tsar was permitted to annex a district to the east of the Black Sea, including the towns of Batum and Kars. The provinces of Bosnia and Herzegovina were to be occupied and administered by Austria-Hungary. This proved an important decision, as we shall see later.

The territorial settlement at Berlin, like that at Vienna half a century before, disregarded many national aspirations. The Bulgarians (who looked back to their independence before the coming of the Turks) were especially disappointed with the arrangement, for, instead of being united in one state, as they had hoped, only the region between the Danube and the Balkan Mountains, with some slight additions, was recognized as the principality of Bulgaria. Those Bulgarians dwelling just south of the Balkan range in the province of Eastern Rumelia were still subjects of the Sultan, although under a Christian governor-general. As for Macedonia and the region about Adrianople, where there were also many Bulgarians, it was left under the direct administration of Turkish officials.

Under the terms of the treaty the inhabitants of the Bulgarian principality proceeded to frame a constitution and chose, as their prince, Alexander of Battenberg (succeeded by Ferdinand of Coburg in 1886). They adopted as their watchword "Bulgaria for the Bulgarians," and took the first step toward the reunion of their race by quietly occupying the region to the south—Eastern Rumelia. At length, in 1908, they refused

[656]

to pay the Sultan's tribute and took their place among the independent nations of the world.

In 1897 Greece risked a war with Turkey, with the hope of increasing her realms, but was defeated. Turkey was of course anxious at all costs to hold onto the remnant of her once large dominion in Europe left her by the Congress of Berlin. She still held Macedonia and Albania. The European powers were well aware of the local massacres, assassinations, and robberies going on in Macedonia, but they dreaded the general war which might develop if any attempt were made to take the region away from Turkey and divide it among the independent Balkan states of Serbia, Bulgaria, and Greece, all of which laid claim to it as rightfully theirs. Nevertheless, in 1908, thirty years after the unsatisfactory settlement at Berlin, a series of events began which in six years precipitated the World War.

During the opening years of the twentieth century there developed in Turkey a small party of reformers, known as Young Turks, who were especially strong in the army, where as officers they had to study the ideas and methods of Western nations. In 1908 a so-called "Committee of Union and Progress" was formed in the Turkish port of Salonika. In July this committee declared that Turkey must have a constitution and that the reformers would march on Constantinople if the Sultan did not yield. The aged Sultan, Abdul Hamid, did not feel himself in a position to oppose the movement, and so at last even Turkey got something that passed for a constitution. The election of representatives to the Turkish parliament took place, and the assembly was opened by the Sultan with great pomp in December, 1908.

Bulgaria immediately seized the occasion to declare itself entirely independent of Turkey. Next Austria proclaimed the annexation of Bosnia and Herzegovina, the two Slavic provinces of Turkey which she had been managing ever since the settlement at the Congress of Berlin. She set to work to Germanize them as completely as possible and suppress all tendencies to join their Slavic relatives in Serbia. A glance at the map will show how important these provinces were for Austria, since they connected her other main possessions with Dalmatia and her ports on the Adriatic.

In September, 1911, the troubles of the new Turkish government were multiplied, for Italy declared war on Turkey, on the ground that Italian subjects in Tripoli were not properly treated. All Europe protested against this "high-handed" action by Italy; but Italy replied that she was merely following the example set by other countries—protecting the lives and property of her citizens by annexing a country beset by chronic disorders. Turkey was no match for Italy. There was not a great deal of fighting, but Italy took possession of such portions of Tripoli as she could hold with her troops and also captured the island of Rhodes. The Young Turks did not feel that they could face the unpopularity of surrendering the regions occupied by Italy, but after the war had dragged on for a year they were forced, in October, 1912, by the oncoming of a new Balkan war, to cede Tripoli, reserving only a vague Turkish suzerainty. Italy continued to hold Rhodes too.

The Balkan Wars, 1912–1913

Venizelos, the statesman who had been reorganizing Greece with the ability of a Cavour, secretly arranged an alliance with Bulgaria, Serbia, and little Montenegro for a war with Turkey, which began in October, 1912. The Turkish army disappointed every one, and the Bulgarians were able in a few days to defeat it, invest the important fortress of Adrianople, and drive the Turkish forces back close to Constantinople. The Greeks advanced into Macedonia and Thrace, and the Montenegrin and Serbian army defeated the Turkish army sent against them and attacked Albania.

Austria now began to get very nervous lest the Serbians should establish themselves on the Adriatic. She forbade Serbia to hold the port of Durazzo. Had Russia been inclined to support Serbia at that moment, the World War would probably have broken out at the end of 1912 instead of two years later. Serbia, however, backed down. A truce was arranged,

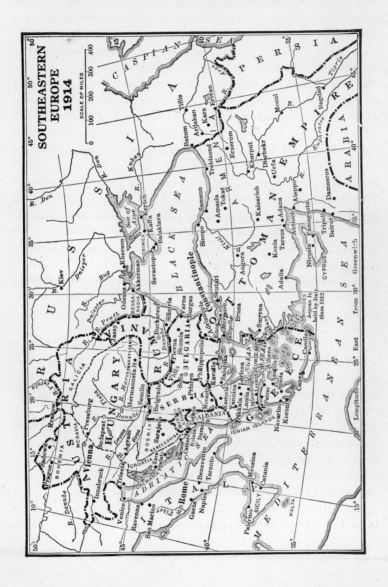

SOUTHEASTERN
EUROPE
1914

SCALE OF MILES
0   100   200   300   400

and representatives of the Balkan states and of Turkey met in London to see if peace could be arranged. The powers advised Turkey to give up everything in Europe except Constantinople and the region immediately to the west. The Young Turks decided, however, to fight a little longer, and the war was resumed in January. Everything went against them, and in May preliminaries of peace were signed in London in which Turkey turned over Macedonia and Crete to the Balkan allies.

But Serbia, Bulgaria, and Greece were all jealous of one another, and the division of the booty led immediately to Bulgaria's turning around to wage war on Greece and Serbia. There was a month of frightful war (July, 1913), and then the Bulgarians, defeated on all sides,—for even the Turks recovered Adrianople and the Rumanians invaded Bulgaria from the east,—agreed to consider peace, and delegates met in Bucharest, the capital of Rumania.

The treaties concluded at Bucharest between the Balkan kingdoms disposed of practically all of Turkey's possessions in Europe. The Sultan was left with Constantinople and a small area to the west, including the important fortress of Adrianople. The great powers, particularly Austria, had insisted that Albania should be made an independent state, so as to prevent Serbia's getting a port on the Adriatic. The rest of the former Turkish possessions were divided among Greece, Serbia, Bulgaria, and Montenegro. Greece got the important port of Salonika and the island of Crete, as well as a considerable area in Macedonia. Bulgaria was extended to the Ægean Sea on the south. Serbia was nearly doubled in area, and Montenegro as well.

The Balkan wars revived all the old bitter rivalry between Austria-Hungary and Russia and led immediately to a general European conflict unprecedented in the annals of history.

CHAPTER XXIX

THE WORLD WAR

*The Race for Armaments. Movements for Peace: The Hague Conferences.
Matters of Dispute: National Rivalries. Foretastes of the War.
Outbreak of the World War. Course of the War, 1914–1916.
Submarines and Blockades. The United States Enters
the War, 1917. The Russian Revolution. The
Tide Turns: End of the War*

The Race for Armaments

IN August, 1914, the most gigantic and destructive war in the
history of Europe began. Never before had millions and
millions of men been carefully trained to be ready at a
moment's notice to march against the enemy; never before had
armies been supplied with such deadly weapons; never before
had any war, however serious, so disturbed the affairs of the
whole globe. To most people the war came as a horrible surprise. They could not believe that the European governments
would dare take the fearful responsibility of entering a conflict
which they knew would involve untold woe and destruction.
Nevertheless the war came, and since it is the most important
single event of its kind in the whole history of Europe and perhaps of the world, we must endeavor to see how it came about
and what were the great questions involved.

After Germany defeated France in 1870-1871, nearly fifty
years passed without any of the Western powers coming to
blows with one another. They all felt, however, that they
must increase their military strength, and each year they spent
vast sums to train and equip soldiers and to build warships.
All the European powers except Great Britain adopted the
Prussian plan of building up an army by requiring all able-
bodied young men that the government could afford to train,
to enter the army for two or three years, after which they
were sent into the reserve to be ready in case of war. A large
number of permanent officers were maintained to see that the
military education of the soldiers was properly conducted, and
a vast amount had to be spent on rifles, cannon, and other

arms, which were being constantly improved and rendered more and more deadly.

The result of this competition in armaments was a tremendous increase in the size of the European armies and a fearful burden of taxation, which the people had to bear. When the war opened, Germany and France had each over four millions of men in their armies, Russia six or seven millions, Austria-Hungary over two and a half millions. Great Britain's forces, on the other hand, numbered less than two hundred thousand, only a few of whom were kept in Europe, since her army, like that of the United States, was recruited by voluntary enlistment and not built up by national conscription.[1]

Great Britain, however, relied for her protection upon her unrivaled navy, which she had maintained at a strength equal to that of any two other powers. There were two reasons for this great navy. England had a much larger population than it was possible to feed from her own farms, and so had to import most of her food. Her manufactures also depended largely upon her commerce. If, therefore, England were defeated at sea, she would be utterly overcome.

Other nations, however, were not willing to grant this supremacy of Great Britain on the ocean. They resented her ability to secure and maintain such widely scattered dominions, and were as anxious as the British to capture distant markets for their business men and to protect their trade by fleets. Germany finally became the most dangerous rival of England. Kaiser William II was, from the first, interested in the navy; twenty years before the war he declared that Germany's future lay upon the ocean. So in 1897 a bill was passed for the development of the German navy, which was built up so rapidly that the British began to fear for their supremacy at sea and began to increase the number and size of their ships. Other nations followed Great Britain's example. To the crushing cost of armies European nations now added the cost of

[1] As a result of the World War, Great Britain introduced universal compulsory military service (conscription), May, 1916.

navies, in which the rapid progress of invention made battle-ships almost worthless if they were but a few years old.

Movements for Peace: The Hague Conferences

The enormous cost of armaments, combined with the increasing horror at the thought of a war in which so many millions would be fighting, provided with such terrible weapons as mod-

THE PEACE PALACE AT THE HAGUE, HOLLAND

In August, 1913 (just a year before the war), this magnificent building was inaugurated as a center for the peaceful settlement of international disputes. Mr. Carnegie contributed $1,500,000 to pay for it

ern science supplies, led many earnest people to try to prevent war altogether. Their efforts proved fruitless in 1914, but no one can say that they have been entirely in vain.

The first notable movement toward arranging for a lessening of armaments originated with the Tsar, Nicholas II, when in 1898 he proposed a great conference of the powers at The Hague to discuss the problem. Unlike the Congress of Vienna or that of Berlin, this Peace Conference of 1899 did not meet to bring a war to a close; it came together in a time of European peace to consider how the existing peace might be maintained and military expenditures reduced.

The Hague Conference did nothing to limit armaments. It is significant in view of later events that Germany strongly opposed any such action. In spite of German opposition, however, the conference did establish a permanent Court of Arbitration, to which difficulties arising between nations "involving neither honor nor vital interests" might be submitted. But there was no way of compelling a nation to submit its grievances, and those very subjects that were most likely to lead to war were excluded from consideration. At the second Hague Conference, held in 1907, the limitation of armaments was advocated by Great Britain; but again Germany and Austria caused a postponement of any action on the question. Certain rules were established, however, in regard to the laying of mines, the bombardment of unfortified towns, and the rights of neutrals in war. Unfortunately, little or no attention was paid to these limitations after the war began.

Within a decade after the first Hague Conference more than one hundred and thirty treaties were made between nations, tending toward maintaining peace by voluntary arbitration. International societies and congresses were, moreover, steadily increasing in number, and it was generally recognized that peoples of different nationalities had innumerable common interests which they should help one another to promote.

Matters of Dispute: National Rivalries

The principal underlying conditions which made the World War possible have been suggested in earlier chapters—on the one hand "imperialism," and on the other the "Near-Eastern Question." We have seen how the nations of Europe began in the latter part of the nineteenth century, as rivals for the world's trade, to seize colonies and trading posts in Africa and Asia, and we have also seen how they stood eyeing one another suspiciously, to see which was to profit most from the decline of Turkey. Now we must see how these rivalries, which for almost fifty years had somehow been adjusted peacefully, were allowed, in the summer of 1914, to burst out into war.

First, let us recall the exploration and partition of Africa. France had taken most of the Mediterranean shore, and in so doing had stirred, at different times, the rivalry of Italy, England, and Germany. Its province of Algeria, conquered in 1830 and thoroughly subdued in 1870-1874, had two native states as neighbors—Tunis and Morocco. Claiming that the Tunisian tribesmen were raiding the border, France had conquered Tunis in 1881 and thus forestalled Italy, which had intended to take the site of ancient Carthage for itself. This threw Italy into the hands of Bismarck, and it joined Germany and Austria in the Triple Alliance.

France and Great Britain fell out when Great Britain got financial control in Egypt, for this was bitterly resented by the French. After the British under General Kitchener had conquered the Sudan in 1898, at the cost of many lives, a French explorer, Colonel Marchand, crossed the heart of Africa from the west and planted the French tricolor at Fashoda, in the upper Sudan, before Kitchener could arrive there. When word of this reached Paris and London, war seemed inevitable, and it would have come had not the French given way. The "Fashoda incident" created a very strained situation between France and England.

This was all changed, however, inside of four years. King Edward VII, who had succeeded to the British throne upon the death of his mother, Victoria, in 1901, was personally fond of France, and the French, of him. Skillful statesmen made the most of this friendly feeling, and in 1904 France and England came to an understanding—*entente cordiale*—concerning all their outstanding sources of quarrel. This *Entente,* as it is generally called, turned out to be one of the most important events in history. France was to recognize recent British interests in Egypt, and England those of France in Morocco, which France had begun to penetrate from the Algerian border. The *Entente* was hailed with great satisfaction on both sides of the Channel.

In 1902 England had also reënforced herself by an alliance with Japan.[1] She now came to terms with her ancient rival Russia. The Tsar's armies had been gradually penetrating nearer and nearer to India, and a conflict with the British seemed likely to come at any moment. In 1907, however, the two powers settled their dispute by each carving out a "sphere of influence" in Persia, where their industrial interests had conflicted. That is to say, they limited their control to a certain portion of the country and agreed not to interfere with each other. These two great powers were by no means naturally friendly, for the British hated the Russian autocracy, and London was a place of refuge for Russian revolutionists. The Russian government, on the other hand, disliked the English ideas of liberty. .

Foretastes of War

One great power had been rather noticeably left out of this circle of friends—Germany. The Germans thought that the alliances and *ententes* which Edward had encouraged were formed with designs hostile to the Triple Alliance of the Central Powers—Germany, Austria, and Italy,—and resolved, if possible, to break them up. In 1905, therefore, Germany, supported by Austria, objected to the agreement between England and France by which the latter was to have a free hand in Morocco. Germany claimed to have interests there too, and the Kaiser spoke in such a way as to bring on a general "war scare." France agreed to the conference at Algeciras, which gave the French police power in Morocco but guaranteed the latter's independence. By exercising this police power France, at the end of five years, had left little of the "independence" guaranteed to Morocco. So in 1911 Germany sent a cruiser to Agadir, on the coast of Morocco, as a warning to

---

[1] According to this alliance England was to support Japan if attacked by a third power. The alliance was therefore strictly limited, but was developed in 1905, after the Russo-Japanese War, into a mutually defensive alliance to safeguard the integrity of eastern Asia and India. Japan immediately followed England into war with Germany, 1914. "England" here and elsewhere usually means "Great Britain."

the French to change their policy. War was narrowly averted. France gave up territory on the Congo to Germany in order to be allowed a free hand in Morocco.

The Agadir incident alarmed statesmen in England as well. Every one saw how near Europe had come to the brink of war. Imperialists in Germany said the incident had been a failure for Germany, since France still held Morocco, and they demanded stronger action in future. Imperialists in France and England, angered at the bold way in which Germany had apparently tried to humble them before the world, were bitter because Germany got any satisfaction at all. The result was that all nations increased their warlike preparations.

Although war between Germany and England and France over the occupation of Morocco was avoided in 1911, another great danger appeared in the strained relations in southeastern Europe. Austria had been permitted by the Congress of Berlin (1878) to occupy the Turkish provinces of Bosnia and Herzegovina. Austria governed these provinces well for the next thirty years, while the rest of Turkey continued to suffer from misrule. When the Turkish revolution took place in 1908, however, and there seemed to be some chance of a new and strong Turkey, Austria determined to prevent Bosnia and Herzegovina from ever being reunited with it, and so boldly annexed them to the Austro-Hungarian empire.

The neighboring state of Serbia was alarmed and indignant at this, since the annexed provinces were peopled with southern Slavs, and the Serbians had cherished the ambition of uniting with them and the Montenegrins in a new south Slavonic state, which would reach from the Danube to the Adriatic. Russia also was angered; but when Germany, Austria's ally, declared that it would support Austria, with arms if need be, Russia, which had not yet recovered from the war with Japan and its own revolutions at home, found itself unable to take a hand in the Balkans. So war between the great powers was again averted for the time being; but the situation made plain the terrible danger that lurked in the Balkan rivalries, which were finally to plunge the whole world into an unparalleled conflict.

The annexation of Bosnia to Austria was in another respect very serious for Serbia. It shut her off from the sea and made her dependent upon her enemy across the Danube for a market for her farm products. As a result of the Balkan wars (1912-1913) Serbia all but reached the Adriatic through Albania. Again Austria interfered and had an independent prince set up in Albania to shut Serbia in. The Serbians now hated Austria as bitterly as they had Turkey. Serbia had nearly doubled her territory, however, and there was every probability that she would undertake to carry out her former plan of uniting the discontented southern Slavs in the neighboring provinces of Austria-Hungary—Bosnia, Croatia, and Slavonia. Germany was in hearty sympathy with the plans of Austria, while Russia was supposed to be ready to support Serbia and the southern Slavs—the distant kinsmen of the Russians.

Germany now expressed grave fears that Russia would dominate the Balkan regions and perhaps seize Constantinople. This would put an end to a cherished plan of Germany—a railroad from Berlin to Bagdad and the Persian Gulf, which would control an enormous trade with the Orient. Germany had already obtained a "concession" from Turkey to build this road, which was well under way when Serbia, through whose territory the trains from Germany must pass, became a danger.

The year 1913, therefore, brought renewed activity in military "preparedness." Germany took the lead by increasing its standing army, and the Reichstag voted about a billion marks for unusual military expenses (June, 1913). France replied by increasing the term of active service in the army from two to three years. Russia made heavy appropriations, and General Joffre, the French commander in chief, was called in to make suggestions in regard to reorganizing the Russian army. German military experts were permitted to train the troops of Turkey. Austria-Hungary strengthened herself with improved artillery; Great Britain devoted large sums to her navy; and even Belgium introduced universal military service on the ground that Germany had been constructing railroad tracks up to her borders, which could be explained only by her purpose to pass through Belgium when the fight began.

Outbreak of the World War

On June 28, 1914, occurred the event which served as a pretext for war. Archduke Francis Ferdinand, heir to the throne of Austria-Hungary, and his wife were assassinated while upon a visit to Bosnia. The Serbian government had warned the archduke not to go there, because it was afraid that hot-headed pro-Serbian conspirators might attempt an assassination. Austria nevertheless asserted that Serbia had favored such conspiracies and was therefore responsible for the crime. It allowed a month to pass, however, before making formal protest.

On July 23 Austria sent Serbia, not a protest, but an ultimatum. It gave Serbia forty-eight hours in which to agree to suppress anti-Austrian propaganda in press, schools, or by societies; to dismiss from the army or civil office anyone obnoxious to Austria; and to allow Austrian officials to sit in Serbian courts in order to bring the guilty to justice. Serbia agreed to all these humiliating conditions except the last, and offered to refer even that to the Hague Tribunal. This Austria refused to do; she was bent on reducing Serbia's power, which she believed to be a deadly menace to the very existence of Austria-Hungary. The decision to invade Serbia was loudly cheered by the Vienna crowds.

The last week of July, 1914, was perhaps the most momentous in the world's history. The Kaiser and his advisers wished to see Serbia punished and weakened, and they gave Austria a sort of "blank check" to go ahead and deal with her neighbor as harshly as she wished. There was great danger, however, that Russia would not stand by and see Serbia subdued by Austria. This danger was apparent to the British foreign minister, Sir Edward Grey, who, with the coöperation of the other chief powers, made an effort to induce Germany to warn instead of continuing to encourage Austria. But the German foreign office was reluctant to interfere with Austria's revenge. The German chancellor did finally expostulate with the government at Vienna, but it was too late. Germany's military leaders seem to have felt that war was inevitable, that they were ready for war, no matter on how large a scale, and they well knew that Russia and France had not finished their preparations.

As soon as Austria declared war on Serbia, July 28, Russia began rapidly to mobilize, and Germany, claiming this to be an attack on her, declared war on Russia, August 1. On the same day she demanded of France, Russia's ally, what she proposed to do. The French government replied that France would take such action as her interests might require; whereupon Germany declared war on France, August 3. But Germany was in such a hurry to strike first that her troops were marching on France a day before war was declared. On August 2 they occupied the neutral country of Luxemburg, in spite of the protests of its ruler. Germany issued an ultimatum to Belgium, giving her twelve hours, from 7 P.M. to 7 A.M., to decide whether she would permit the German troops to cross the little kingdom on their way to France. If she consented, Germany promised to respect her territory and people; if she refused, Germany would treat her as an enemy. The Belgian government replied to the German demand with great firmness and dignity, urging that her neutrality had been guaranteed by the powers, including Prussia, and that she should resist any attempt to violate it.

It was almost inevitable that Great Britain, as an ally of France, should be drawn into the conflict. On August 1 the German ambassador asked whether England would remain neutral if Germany promised not to violate Belgian territory, and urged the British to state the conditions of their neutrality, including a guarantee of the neutrality of France, but this suggestion was firmly rejected. On August 2 the British cabinet informed France that the British fleet would give all protection possible if a hostile German fleet came into the Channel or North Sea.

Two days later, learning that German troops were making their way into Belgium, Sir Edward Grey sent an ultimatum to Germany demanding assurances within twelve hours that she would respect Belgian neutrality. The German chancellor replied that military necessity required that the German armies cross Belgium. He told the British ambassador in Berlin that England ought not to enter the war just for the sake of "a scrap of paper." This contemptuous reference to the solemn treaties by which the European powers had guaranteed the neutrality of Belgium stirred the indignation of the entire outside world. It was the invasion of Belgium which aroused public feeling in Great Britain and served to array its people solidly behind the government when, on August 4, 1914, it declared war on Germany.

We have already learned enough of the wars, rivalries, suspicions, secret arrangements, and military preparations of the various European powers to see that, as an English historian puts it, "the Old World had degenerated into a powder magazine, in which the dropping of a lighted match, whether by accident or design, was almost certain to produce a conflagration." It is a mistake to imagine that the conflict took the diplomats and military commanders by surprise, because, as we have seen, they had been getting ready for war for years. Bismarck had said that a world war was sure to come and that it would begin in eastern Europe. Each country thought it was in the right and was taking measures for its own protection and honor. Germany and Austria were in great fear of the Slavic peril—that is, of Russia and her support of the outlying Slavic peoples, especially the Serbians. Germany was afraid of France and France of Germany. The British could not bear the prospect of a German fleet in the North Sea attacking France nor of a German occupation of Belgium.

Japan speedily declared war on Germany, and early in November Turkey decided to join the Central Powers. So within three months Germany, Austria-Hungary, and Turkey were pitted against Serbia, Russia, France, Belgium, Great Britain, Montenegro, and Japan. Italy declared herself neutral and not bound to help Austria and Germany, since in the Triple Alliance of 1882 she had pledged her aid only in case they were attacked; she considered that they were now the aggressors and that she was consequently free to keep out of the struggle.

When the great powers of Europe found themselves involved in a general war, the issue between Austria and Serbia sank into the background. The popular conviction among the Allies was that Germany—even the Kaiser personally—was responsible for the war. The Germans, on the other hand, were convinced that they were defending the fatherland against a great conspiracy to crush German civilization. They were threatened by a Slavic invasion from the east which they had long feared; France, they believed, was planning to avenge the humiliation of 1870; Great Britain's hostility they ascribed to her bitter resentment over Germany's growing prosperity and commercial power. Indeed, it was on England chiefly that the Germans centered their hatred, accusing her of being responsible for the war.

Course of the War, 1914–1916

The vast German army advanced on France in three divisions, one through Belgium, one through Luxemburg (also a neutral state) down into Champagne, and the third from Metz toward Nancy. The Belgians offered a determined resistance to the advance of the northern division and hindered it for ten days—a delay of vital importance to the French. But the heavy German guns proved too much for the forts around Liège, which were soon battered to pieces, and Brussels was occupied by the enemy, August 20. The French, reënforced by British troops hastily dispatched across the Channel, made their first stand around Namur. This famous fortress, however, immediately collapsed under the fire of the German siege guns, and the French and British rapidly retreated southward. The western division of the German army had come within twenty-five miles of Paris by September 1. The headquarters of the French government were moved to Bordeaux, and the

PL. L. MARSHAL JOFFRE

PL. LI. WHAT IT WAS LIKE TO BE FIGHTING AT THE FRONT

capital prepared for a siege. The victory of the French, however, in the famous battle of the Marne, under the leadership of General Joffre, put an end to the immediate danger of the Germans' occupying Paris. They were compelled to retreat a little way and took up a position on a line of hills running from Soissons to Reims. Here they were able to intrench themselves before the French and British could drive them farther back.

After the Germans had given up their first hope of surprising Paris, they proceeded to overrun Belgium. They captured Antwerp, October 10, and conquered the whole country, except a tiny corner southwest of Ostend. It was their hope to push on to Calais and occupy this port nearest to England as a base of attack against the British Isles, but they were checked at the Yser River. They treated the Belgians as a conquered people, exacted huge tributes, partially burned the city of Louvain, brutally executed many civilians, and seized any machinery or supplies they desired. This treatment of a peaceful little neighbor, whose safety from invasion they themselves had solemnly guaranteed, did more to rouse the anger of the rest of the world than any other act of the German government.

Thus the first three months of the war saw the Germans in practically complete possession of Belgium and Luxemburg, together with a broad strip of northeastern France, filled with prosperous manufacturing towns, farms and vineyards, and invaluable coal and iron mines. The Germans were ordered to do all they could to destroy the machinery in the factories, cut down the fruit trees, and wreck the mines, so as to disable and impoverish France in every way possible.

The lines established after the battle of the Marne and the check on the Yser did not change greatly in four years, in spite of the constant fighting and the sacrifice of hundreds of thousands of men on both sides. The Germans were not able to push very much farther into France, and the Allied forces were almost equally unsuccessful in their repeated attempts, at terrible sacrifice of life, to force the Germans more than a few miles back. Both sides "dug themselves in," and trench warfare went on almost incessantly, with the aid of machine guns, shells, and huge cannon. Airplanes flew hither and thither, observing the enemy's positions and operations and dropping bombs. Poisonous gases and liquid fire, introduced by Germany, added their horrors to the situation.

On the Eastern Front the Russians at first advanced far more rapidly than had been expected. They succeeded in invading East Prussia, but were soon driven out by the German general, Hindenburg, and his army. They made their main attack on the Austrians in Galicia, but were forced to withdraw, owing to the operations of the German and Austrian armies in Poland. During the winter of 1915 the Russians made fierce attempts to pass the Carpathians and invade Austria-Hungary. They failed, however, on account of lack of supplies, and hundreds of thousands of lives were sacrificed in vain. In August, 1915, Russia was forced to surrender Warsaw and other large Polish towns to the Germans, who pushed on beyond Poland and occupied Courland, Livonia, and Esthonia.

In November, 1914, the Teutonic allies had been reënforced by Turkey. The Sultan issued a call to all faithful Mohammedans to wage a holy war on the enemies of Islam. But, contrary to the hopes of Germany, there was no general rising of the Mohammedans in India and Egypt against the British rule. Great Britain seized the opportunity to declare Egypt altogether independent of Turkey, December, 1914, and established a new ruler, who was given the title of Sultan of Egypt and accepted a British protectorate over his country. The British invaded Mesopotamia, and finally captured the ancient old city of Bagdad, in March, 1917. The British also forced back the Turkish army in Palestine and succeeded in capturing the holy city of Jerusalem, in December, 1917.

An attempt made by the British and French in 1915 to take Constantinople proved, however, a terrible failure. In April of that year their forces, greatly strengthened by contingents from Australia and New Zealand, who had come to the Mediter-

ranean by way of the Red Sea, tried to force their way up the
Dardanelles. The Turks defended themselves with such success that the Allies, in spite of the sacrifice of a hundred thousand men, killed and wounded, were unable to hold their positions on the peninsula of Gallipoli, where they had secured a
footing.

In May, 1915, Italy finally decided that she could no longer
remain out of the war. It seemed that the opportunity had
come to win "Italia Irredenta,"—those portions of the Italian
people still unredeemed from Austrian rule who live around
Trent, in Istria and the great seaport of Trieste, and along the
Dalmatian coast. So this added another "front" which the
Central Powers had to defend.

The line-up at the opening of the second year of the war
consisted of the Central Powers—Germany, Austria-Hungary,
and Turkey—opposed to Russia, France, Italy, Great Britain
(including Canadians, Australians, New Zealanders, South
Africans, and East Indian troops, all ready to shed their blood
in the cause of the British empire), Belgium, Serbia, Japan,
and the tiny countries of Montenegro and San Marino,—
twelve belligerents in all, scattered over the whole globe. But
the war was not destined to stop at this point. Hundreds of
millions of people who were at that time still neutral later took
up arms against Germany and her allies.

Submarines and Blockades

It was the conflict on the sea that raised the chief problems
for the world at large. At the beginning of the war many
people supposed that there would soon be a great and perhaps
decisive naval engagement between the German and British
fleets, but no such thing happened.[1] The Germans kept their
dreadnaughts safe in their harbors, protected by cruisers and
mines. The German merchant ships took shelter at home or
in neutral ports. So German commerce was soon cut off alto-

[1] On May 31, 1916, a portion of the German fleet ventured out of the
Baltic and fell in with a strong detachment of the British fleet. After a
few hours the mist, smoke, and darkness put an end to the fight, and no
decision was reached.

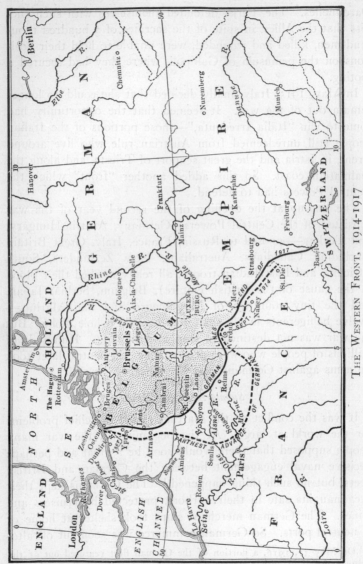

THE WESTERN FRONT, 1914–1917

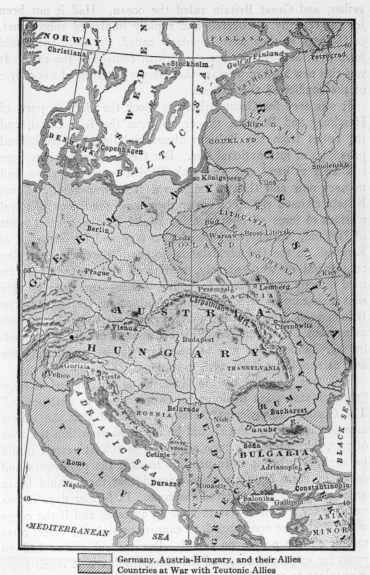

Germany, Austria-Hungary, and their Allies
Countries at War with Teutonic Allies

THE EASTERN FRONT, 1914–1917

gether, and Great Britain ruled the ocean. Had it not been for the recently discovered and rapidly improved submarines, or U-boats, as they were popularly called, the Germans would have been helpless against the British control of the seas. It was this new kind of warfare that largely determined the course of the conflict of the nations.

It was easy for Great Britain to block the German ports of Hamburg and Bremen, the egress from the Kiel Canal, and the outlet from the Baltic without violating the established principles of international law. But German submarines were still able to steal out and sink British merchant ships and manage now and then to torpedo a great war vessel. Great Britain claimed the right under these new conditions of naval warfare to force all neutral ships bound for the neutral ports of Holland, Norway, and Sweden to stop and be inspected at Kirkwall, in the Orkney Islands, to see if they were carrying contraband of war—namely, munitions and materials to be used directly or indirectly for military ends—and to make sure that their cargoes were not really destined for Germany. The British soon declared that all shipments of foodstuffs to Germany would be deemed absolute contraband of war, since feeding her fighting men was as necessary for her continuing the war as supplying them with munitions.

This was regarded by the Germans as an obvious attempt "through starvation to doom an entire nation to destruction." The German government thereupon declared that the waters around the British Isles should be regarded as within the zone of war, that inside this zone all enemy merchant vessels would be sunk, whether it were possible to save the passengers and crews or not. Neutrals were warned that they would be in great danger if they entered the zone. In former days it was possible for a man-of-war to hold up a vessel, and if the cargo was found to be contraband, to capture or sink the vessel after taking off the people on board. But the submarine had no room for extra persons, and the Germans found it much more convenient to torpedo vessels without even the warning necessary to enable the passengers and crew to take to the lifeboats.

In February, 1915, German submarines began to sink not only enemy vessels but neutral ones as well, sometimes giving the people on board warning, but often not. The most terrible example of the ruthlessness of the U-boats was the sinking,

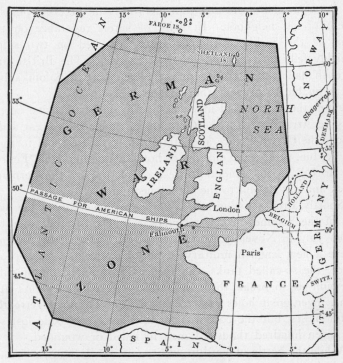

GERMAN WAR ZONE OF FEBRUARY 1, 1917

Late in the year 1917 and early in 1918 the German government extended the barred zone so as to include the islands off the coast of Africa, Madeira, the Cape Verde Islands, and the Azores, in order to cut the routes between Europe and South America

without warning, of the great liner *Lusitania*, May 7, 1915, involving the loss of nearly twelve hundred men, women, and children, including over a hundred American citizens. This act aroused the greatest horror and indignation not only in

[679]

England and the United States but throughout the rest of the world.

The Germans, who had succeeded in forcing back the Russians in Galicia, now undertook the invasion of Serbia. This encouraged Serbia's bitter enemy, Bulgaria, to declare in favor of the Central Powers and join vigorously in the cruel punishment of her neighbor. In spite of heroic resistance on the part of the Serbians, their country, attacked on two sides, quickly fell into the hands of their enemies. The British and French had landed troops at the Greek port of Salonika but were unable to prevent the disaster.

After the British had made a slightly successful drive northeast of Arras, in 1915, the Germans got together a great army under the Crown Prince and attempted to take the old fortress of Verdun. But after months of horrible fighting, from February to July, 1916, General Joffre was able to push the Germans back and put an end to the threatened danger.[1]

Shortly after, the long-talked-of Anglo-French drive, the battle of the Somme, began, which was fought for four months, from July to November, 1916, east and northeast of Amiens. Here a new English military invention made its first appearance, the so-called tanks—huge, heavily armored motor cars, so built as to break through barbed-wire entanglements and crawl over great holes and trenches. The Germans retreated a few miles, but the cost was terrible, since each side lost six or seven hundred thousand men in killed or wounded.

While the battle of Verdun was raging, the Italians, who had made but little progress against the strong Austrian fortifications, were suddenly pushed back by a great Austrian drive in May, 1916. By the middle of June they had not only lost the little they had gained but had been forced to evacuate some of their own territory. At this point the Russians, in spite of the loss of Poland, attacked Austria once more and again

---

[1] For a time Great Britain tried to increase its army by voluntary enlistments, and on the whole succeeded very well. But after much discussion and opposition she introduced (May, 1916) a system of universal compulsory military service, which included all able-bodied men between the ages of eighteen and forty-one (later, fifty).

threatened to press into Hungary. Austria had to give way in Italy in order to defend her Galician boundary, and the Italians were able not only to regain what they had lost but to advance somewhat on their way, as they hoped, to Trieste.

The brief success of the Russians encouraged Rumania to join in the war on the side of the Allies, who seemed to be getting the better of the Central Powers. She invaded Transylvania, which she had long claimed as properly hers. The Germans, notwithstanding the pressure on the Somme, immediately sent two of their best generals and with the help of the Bulgarians attacked Rumania from the west and south. In December, 1916, they captured Bucharest, the capital, and soon about two-thirds of Rumania was in possession of her enemies, and the Germans could supplement their supplies from her rich fields of grain and abundant oil wells.

For the first time in the history of war men were able to fly high above the contending forces, making observations and engaging in aërial battles. Airplanes are now among the essentials of war, and they bring new horrors in their train. The Germans made repeated air raids on England, apparently with the foolish notion that they would be able to intimidate the people. They first used the huge dirigible balloons called Zeppelins, but these were later replaced by airplanes of various kinds. They killed two or three thousand English civilians— men, women, and children—in town and country, and destroyed some property. Without accomplishing any important military aims the Germans increased their reputation for needless brutality and led the British, for the safety of their unfortified towns, to make reprisals. British and French airmen dropped bombs on the more accessible German towns, Freiburg, Karlsruhe, and Mannheim, and many military places.

The United States Enters the War, 1917

Early in the year 1917 Germany's submarine policy and reckless sinking of neutral ships finally involved her in war with a new antagonist, the great and powerful republic across the Atlantic. When the war broke out, President Wilson declared that the government would observe strict neutrality, and he urged American citizens to avoid taking sides in a conflict that did not directly concern them. But it was impossible to remain indifferent when such tremendous events were being reported day by day. The German newspapers in the United States eagerly defended the Central Powers and laid the responsibility for the war at England's door. On the other hand, the great body of the American people were deeply shocked by the invasion of Belgium, by the burning of Louvain, and by the needless destruction of Reims Cathedral by German guns. They disliked the arrogant talk of the Kaiser, and they felt a quick sympathy for France, who had lent essential aid in the American Revolution. Those of English descent naturally found themselves drawn to the side of Great Britain in the great struggle, while those of German descent sympathized with their fatherland.

As time went on President Wilson dispatched note after note to Germany, expostulating against the merciless and indiscriminate way in which the submarines sent vessels to the bottom,—not only British ships, like the *Lusitania,* carrying American passengers, but American ships and those of other neutral nations. There was often no warning until the torpedo actually struck the ship, and not sufficient time even to take to the lifeboats and face the hazards of a troubled sea. The anger of the American people as a whole against Germany became hotter and hotter, and President Wilson began to be denounced for tolerating diplomatic relations with the German imperial government, even though, in September, 1916, the Germans promised to reform their submarine policy.

In December, 1916, after the Central Powers had occupied Poland, Serbia, and Rumania, and Germany seemed victorious on all hands, she made proposals for peace. She suggested that the belligerents send representatives to some point in a neutral country to consider the terms of settlement. President Wilson seized this occasion to try to get both sides to state their aims and the terms on which they would bring the war to a close. The Allies refused to negotiate with Germany

at the height of her military successes, and the Germans declared that this threw the responsibility for the continuance of the war on the Allies. The war continued, and the United States was speedily drawn into the awful conflict.

At the very moment when the German government was exhibiting an apparent interest in President Wilson's efforts to bring about peace the German military leaders were planning a new and still more ruthless use of their submarines than they had hitherto made.

In January, 1917, Great Britain, in order completely to cut off supplies from Germany, extended the area which she declared to be in a state of blockade. Germany then proclaimed to the world that in order to make head against "British tyranny" and England's alleged plan to starve Germany she proposed to establish a vast barred zone extending far to the west of Great Britain, in which sea traffic with England would be prevented by every available means. In this way she flattered herself that England, who receives much of her food from distant regions, would soon be reduced to starvation and the war brought to a speedy end. One of the most irritating features of Germany's plan was that a narrow lane was to be left, through which the United States was to be permitted to send one ship a week provided it was painted with bright stripes of color and carried no contraband. By these measures Germany reserved a vast area of the high seas for her murderous enterprises, utterly regardless of every recognized right of neutral nations.

On February 1, 1917, the Germans opened their unrestricted submarine warfare in this great barred zone, and many vessels were sunk. On February 3 President Wilson broke off diplomatic relations with the German government. The sinkings went on, and popular opinion was more and more aroused against Germany.

It was finally apparent that war was inevitable. President Wilson summoned a special session of Congress and on April 2, 1917, read a memorable address to its members in which he said that Germany had to all intents and purposes declared

war on the United States. "Our object," he maintained, "is to vindicate the principles of peace and justice in the life of the world, as against selfish and autocratic power." The free and self-governed peoples of the world must combine, he urged, "to make the world safe for democracy," for otherwise no permanent peace is possible. He proposed that the United States should fight side by side with Germany's enemies and aid them with liberal loans. Both Houses of Congress approved by large majorities the proposed resolution that the United States had been forced into war. Provisions were made for borrowing vast sums; old forms of taxation were greatly increased and many new ones added. In May, 1917, conscription was introduced, and all able-bodied men between the ages of twenty-one and thirty-one were declared liable to military service. Preparations were made for training great bodies of troops to be sent across the Atlantic to aid the cause of the Allies, and measures were taken for building ships to replace those destroyed by German submarines.

One result of the entrance of the United States into the war was a great increase in the number of Germany's enemies during the year 1917. Cuba and Panama immediately followed the example set by the great North American republic. After much internal turmoil and dissension, Greece, under the influence of Venizelos, finally joined the Allies; in the latter half of the year Siam, Liberia, China and Brazil proclaimed war on Germany. The war had become literally a world conflict. The governments of nearly a billion and a half of the earth's population were involved in the amazing struggle. Thirteen hundred and forty millions of peoples were committed by their rulers to the side of the Allies, and the countries included in the Central European alliance had a total population of about one hundred and sixty millions. So nearly seven-eighths of the population of the globe were nominally at war, and of these nine-tenths were arrayed against one-tenth, led by Prussia. Of course the vast population of India and China, which greatly swelled these figures, had little or no part in the active prosecution of the war; and by the end of 1917, after the Rus-

sian revolution had destroyed the old government, that country, with its millions of inhabitants, could no longer be reckoned an active factor.

As for the countries which remained neutral, they included a population of perhaps one hundred and ninety millions) Holland, Switzerland, Denmark, Norway, and Sweden were far too close to Germany to risk breaking with her, although it would seem that many of their people disapproved of her conduct. Spain and a number of Latin-American states, including Mexico and Chile, held aloof. But no country could escape the burdens and afflictions of a war of such magnitude. Real neutrality was almost impossible. Everywhere taxes and prices rose, supplies were cut off, and business was greatly interrupted.

The Russian Revolution

In March, 1917, one of the chief belligerent countries, Russia, underwent such a great internal change as greatly to modify the course of the war and the problem of peace. We must now consider the astonishing revolution which led to the overthrow of the old Russian despotism and the retirement of Russia from the war.

The world conflict had hardly opened before it revealed the corruption, the weakness, the inefficiency,—indeed, in some cases, the treason,—of the Tsar's court and his imperial officials. The millions of Russian troops who perished in the trenches of the Eastern Front in vain endeavors to advance into Germany and Austria-Hungary or to stem the tide of German invasion were ill supported by their government. The Duma became unmanageable, and in December, 1916, it passed a resolution declaring that "dark forces" were paralyzing the government and betraying the nation's interests. The Tsar then proceeded to dismiss the liberals from the government and replace them by the most unpopular tyrannical officials he could find. He seemed to be declaring war on every liberal movement and reverting to the methods of Nicholas I. There was a distressing scarcity of food in the cities and a growing repugnance to the continuance of the war.

Bread riots broke out in Petrograd [1] in March, 1917, but the troops refused to fire on the people, and the Tsar's government found itself helpless. When ordered to adjourn, the Duma defied the Tsar and called for the establishment of a provisional government. The Tsar, hastening back to Petrograd from the front, was stopped by representatives of the new provisional government on March 15, 1917, and induced to sign his own and his son's abdication in favor of his brother, Grand Duke Michael. But Michael refused the honor unless it were authorized by a constitutional assembly; this amounted to an abdication of the Romanoffs, who had ruled Russia for more than three centuries. There was no longer any such thing in the world as "the autocrat of all the Russias." The Tsar's relatives renounced their rights, his high officials were imprisoned in the very fortress of Peter and Paul where they had sent so many revolutionists, and political prisoners in Russia and Siberia received the joyous tidings that they were free. The world viewed with astonishment this abrupt and complete collapse of the ancient system of tyranny.

A revolutionary cabinet was formed of men of moderate views on the whole, but Alexander Kerensky, a socialist and representative of the Workingmen's and Soldiers' Council, was made minister of justice. The new cabinet declared itself in favor of many reforms, such as liberty of speech and of the press; the right to strike; the substitution of militia for the old police; universal suffrage, including that of women. But the more extreme socialists were not content, and demanded an immediate peace on the ground of "no annexations, no indemnities, and self-determination." The failure of the government to heed their demand caused uprisings in Petrograd and much disorder among the soldiers. Through their Council of Workingmen's and Soldiers' Delegates the socialists began to exercise great power. By July, 1917, all the more moderate

[1] The new Slavic name given to St. Petersburg at the opening of the war.

members of the provisional government had been forced out and their places taken by socialists. A desperate attempt to lead the flagging Russian troops forward to victory against the Austrians failed utterly and was followed by further uprisings on the part of the radicals.

At length the storm which had long been gathering broke. Early in the revolution a Council of Workingmen's and Soldiers' deputies, or *soviet,* had been set up in Petrograd and had begun to dispute the authority of the Duma. All over Russia similar soviets, or councils of workmen, soldiers, and peasants, were instituted. Finally, in November, two leaders, Lenin and Trotzky, who had returned from exile, supported by soldiers and soviets overturned the Kerensky government and founded instead a "dictatorship of the proletariat." The faction which engineered this enterprise was known as the Bolsheviki, or "majority men," a term given to them when they constituted a majority of the Russian socialists.

The Bolsheviki proceeded at once to abolish private property in land and capital and institute a "communist system." They denounced the war as an "imperialist struggle for trade and territory," and they called upon the warring powers to join them in a peace conference. Receiving no replies, they opened the Russian archives and published secret treaties, drawn up by the European powers before and during the war, which showed up the selfish aims of the old-fashioned diplomacy.

Then, late in December, the Bolsheviki opened peace negotiations with the Central Powers at Brest-Litovsk, on the eastern Polish boundary. Meanwhile Finland and the Ukraine, which comprises a great part of southern Russia, declared themselves independent, and established governments of their own. So on March 3, 1918, the representatives of the Bolsheviki concluded a peace with the Central Powers in which they agreed to "evacuate" the Ukraine and Finland, and surrendered Poland, Lithuania, Courland, Livonia, and certain districts in the Caucasus, all of which were to exercise the right of establishing such government as they pleased. Shortly after, the capital of Russia was transferred from Petrograd to

Moscow. The result of this peace was that Russia was dismembered and all the western and southern regions were, for the time being, under the strong influence of the Germans. (For a further account of Russian conditions see next chapter.)

The Tide Turns: End of the War

In addition to the increase in Germany's enemies the chief military events of 1917 were the following: In March the Germans decided to shorten their lines on the Western Front from Noyon on the south to Arras on the north. They withdrew, devastating the land as they went, and the French and British were able to reoccupy about one-eighth of the French territory that the enemy had held so long. The Germans were disturbed by fierce attacks while establishing their new line of defense, but in spite of great sacrifices on the part of the French and British, and of the Canadians, who fought with special heroism, this "Hindenburg" line was so well fortified that it held, and with slight exceptions continued to hold during the year. Attempts to take the important mining town of Lens and the city of Cambrai were not successful for another year, but the terrible slaughter went on and tens of thousands were killed every week.

On March 21, 1918, the Germans began a great drive on the Western Front with the hope of gaining a decisive victory and forcing the Allies to sue for peace. Germany was in a hurry, for she knew that her U-boat warfare was not reducing England to starvation, that the United States troops were beginning to arrive in ever-increasing numbers, and that the German plans for getting supplies from Russia were meeting with little success. Moreover, the German people were suffering all sorts of bitter hardships and might at any time begin to complain that the final victory which the Kaiser had been promising from the first, and the hope of which had sustained them, was too long in coming.

For some days the Germans were victorious and were able to push back the British almost to Amiens; but the French rushed to the aid of their allies, the drive was checked, and

[688]

Amiens, with its important railroad connections, was saved. No previous conflict of the war had been so terrible as this, and it is estimated that over four hundred thousand men were killed, wounded, or captured. The Germans, however, regained only the devastated territory from which they had retired a year before, and their fierce efforts to advance farther failed.

The grave danger in which the Allies found themselves finally convinced them that their safety lay in putting all their forces—French, British, Italian, and the newly arriving troops from America—under a single commander-in-chief. It was agreed that the French general Ferdinand Foch (appointed March 28, 1918) was the most likely to lead them all to victory; and this confidence in his skill and character was justified. Almost immediately matters began to mend.

Every one knew that the Germans would soon make a second drive somewhere on the long front of one hundred and fifty miles, but at what point the Allies could only conjecture. The new blow came April 9, when the Kaiser's armies attempted to break through the British defenses between Arras and Ypres, with the intention of reaching Calais and the English Channel. The suspense was tense for a time, but after retreating a few miles the British made a stand and were ordered by their commanders to die, if necessary, at their posts. This checked the second effort of the Germans to break through. In the latter part of May the German armies attempted a third great attack, this time in the direction of Paris. They took Soissons and Château-Thierry, which brought them within about forty miles of the French capital. In June they made a feeble effort to extend to the south the strip of territory gained in the first drive. Here they were opposed for the first time by the American troops, who fought with great bravery and ardor.

The first contingent of United States troops had arrived in France in June, 1917, under the command of General Pershing, who had a long and honorable record as a military commander. In his younger days he had fought Indians in the

West; he served in the Spanish-American War and later subdued the fierce Moros in the Philippine Islands.

By the first of July, 1918, about a million American troops had reached France and were either participating actively in the fighting or being rapidly and efficiently trained. They had taken their first town by the end of May, 1918, and gained great distinction for themselves by coöperating with the French in frustrating the German attempt to break through at Château-Thierry. Northwest of that town they forced back, early in June, the picked troops of the Kaiser sent against them.

During the following weeks the Germans lost tens of thousands of men in minor engagements and finally, on July 15, 1918, made a last great effort to take Reims and force their way to Paris, but this drive was speedily turned into a retreat. During the following month the combined efforts of the French and Americans served to drive the Germans far back from the Marne and put an end to their hopes of advancing on Paris. The French general Mangin warmly praised the valor of the Americans during these "splendid" days when it was his privilege to fight with them "for the deliverance of the world." Then the British began an offensive on the Somme, east and south of Amiens. By the end of September the Germans had been pressed back to the old Hindenburg line; this was even pierced at some points, and the Allied troops were within a few miles of the Lorraine boundary.

The American troops in France, numbering slightly over two million men before the armistice was signed, on November 11, 1918, were scattered along the whole Western Front, and it is estimated that nearly one million four hundred thousand actually took part in the fearful struggle against the Germans.[1] It is impossible to mention here all the battles in which they fought valiantly, side by side with the French or British, as the hosts of the enemy were rapidly pushed back. In the middle of September the Americans distinguished themselves

[1] The United States proposed to have at least four million men in France by June 30, 1919. The limits of the draft were extended so as to include all able-bodied men between the ages of eighteen and forty-five.

PL. LII. GENERAL PERSHING

PL. LIII. MARSHAL FOCH

by taking the St. Mihiel salient and bringing their lines within range of the guns of the great German fortress of Metz. Reënforcing the British, they performed prodigies of valor in the capture of the St. Quentin canal tunnel far to the north, where thousands of lives were sacrificed. In the Argonne Forest, and especially in the capture of Sedan, on November 7, the United States troops played a conspicuous part. In the months from June to November, 1918, the battle casualties of the American expeditionary forces—killed, wounded, missing, and prisoners—amounted to about three hundred thousand.

On the other fronts the fortunes of war were turning in favor of the Allies. Germany, instead of being able to get supplies from demoralized Russia, met resistance at every point. The people of the Ukraine resented her domination and began to look to the Allies to assist them in forming their new republic. In Finland civil war raged between the "White Guard" (Nationalist) and the "Red Guard" (Bolshevik), while British and American troops on the Murman coast to the north coöperated with the anti-Bolsheviki to oppose the extremists then in power.

At Vladivostok, far away across Siberia, British, Japanese, and American forces landed with the object of working westward through Siberia and, as they hoped, restoring order. Among the enemies of the Bolsheviki was a Czechoslovak army, composed of former Austrian subjects, who had deserted to fight in Russia for the Allies.

As a part of the great forward movement organized by General Foch, the combined Serbian, Greek, British, and French forces in the Balkans once more became active in Serbia and rapidly pushed back the Bulgarians, who, with the help of the Germans and Austrians, had overrun the country three years before. Neither Germany nor Austria was in a position to send aid to their ally, and on September 29, 1918, the Bulgarians threw up their hands and asked for an armistice. This was granted on condition of absolute surrender. The defection of Bulgaria proved decisive, and it was clear that Turkey could not keep up the fight when cut off from her Western allies, and that Austria-Hungary, who had spent the best of her strength and was now open to invasion through Bulgaria, must soon yield.

Turkey was the next to give up the fight. In Palestine General Allenby followed up the capture of Jerusalem (December, 1917) by relentless pursuit of the Turkish armies. The British and French speedily conquered Syria, taking the great towns of Damascus and Beirut, and the Syrians could now celebrate their final deliverance from centuries of subjection to the Turks. The Turkish army in Mesopotamia was also captured by the British. So Turkey was quickly forced to follow Bulgaria's example, and accepted the terms of surrender imposed by the Allies (October 31).

Thus the loudly heralded "peace drive" of the Germans had turned into a hasty retreat on the Western Front, and their Eastern allies had dropped away. The oncoming troops from the United States, steadily streaming across the Atlantic, brought new hope to the Allies; for the Americans were fresh and brave and full of enthusiasm, and they were backed by a great and rich country, which had thrown its well-nigh inexhaustible resources on the side of the war-weary Allies in their fight against the Central Powers.

The Germans began to see that they had been grossly deceived by their leaders. The ruthless use of the U-boats had not succeeded in subduing England, but it had aroused this new and mighty enemy across the Atlantic, whose armies found themselves able to cross the ocean in spite of Germany's submarines. The Germans had forced shameful treaties upon the former Russian provinces with the purpose of making the poor, discouraged, and famine-stricken people help support the German armies. This plan failed to relieve German distress; her commerce was ruined, her people starving, her national debt tremendous, and she had no hope of forcing her enemies to pay the bills. She was deserted by both her Eastern allies. Austria-Hungary alone continued feebly to support her against a world coalition brought together in common hostility toward her policy and aims.

But even Austria-Hungary was fast giving way. Torn by internal dissension and the threatened revolt of her subject nationalities, disheartened by scarcity of food and by the reverses on the Western Front, she sent a note to President Wilson, October 7, requesting that an armistice be considered. By the end of the month her armies were retreating before the Italians, who in a second battle on the Piave not only swept the Austrians out of northern Italy but quickly occupied Trent and the great seaport of Trieste. On November 3 Austria-Hungary unconditionally surrendered, accepting the severe terms that the Allies imposed on her.

But Austria-Hungary had already disappeared from the map of Europe. The republic of the northern Slavs, Czechoslovakia, had been proclaimed, and the southern Slavs, or Jugoslavs, no longer recognized their former connection with Austria and Hungary. Hungary itself was in revolt. Under these circumstances the Hapsburg ruler of Austria-Hungary resigned all share in the government, November 11.

Germany herself was on the verge of dissolution, as it proved. Early in October it seemed to have become apparent to her military rulers that there was no possibility of stopping the victorious advance of the Allies, and the imperial chancellor opened a correspondence (transmitted through the Swiss minister) with President Wilson in regard to an armistice. She expressed her willingness to "make peace on the basis of President Wilson's Fourteen Points." In an address on January 8, 1918, President Wilson had outlined a program of world peace which embodied fourteen principles which he regarded as essential. President Wilson made it plain that the Allies would not stop their advance except on condition that Germany surrender, and on such terms that she could not possibly renew the war. "For," the President added, in his third note, "the nations of the world do not and cannot trust the word of those who have hitherto been the masters of German policy." [1]

[1] The Fourteen Points included freedom of the seas in peace and war, the removal of economic barriers and the reduction of armaments, the restoration of Belgium, and the formation of an association of nations for the purpose of insuring the independence of small as well as large nations.

The German War Council, including the Kaiser and crown prince, made a vain effort to save the old system. General Ludendorff, who had command of the German armies, was sent off, and the Allies were informed that far-reaching changes in the government had been undertaken which assured the people a complete control not only over the government but over the military power (October 27).

Soon the German government began to deal directly with Marshal Foch in its eagerness to secure an armistice at any cost, for a great social revolution was imminent. Moreover, the Allied forces were closing in on Germany all along the line from the North Sea to the Swiss boundary, and the Germans were retreating with enormous losses of men and supplies. On November 9, to the astonishment of the world, it was announced that His Majesty, Emperor William II, had abdicated. He soon fled to Holland, and the glory of the Hohenzollerns was a thing of the past. The king of Bavaria had been forced off his throne the day before, and all the monarchies which had composed the German Empire were speedily turned into republics. On November 10 a revolution took place in Berlin, and a socialist leader, Friedrich Ebert, assumed the duties of chancellor with the consent of the previous chancellor and all the secretaries of state. Even Prussia had become a republic overnight. The German empire of Bismarck and William I was no more.

Meanwhile negotiations in regard to an armistice were in progress. Representatives of the German government made their way across the lines and met Marshal Foch, November 8, and received the terms which the Allies had drawn up.

The Germans were required to evacuate within fifteen days all the territory they had occupied,—Belgium, northeastern France, Luxemburg, and Alsace-Lorraine. Moreover, the German forces were to retire beyond the eastern bank of the Rhine, and that portion of Germany which lies west of the river was to be occupied by troops of the Allies. All German troops in territories formerly belonging to Austria-Hungary, Rumania, Turkey, and Russia were to be immediately withdrawn. Germany was to hand over her war vessels, submarines, and vast supplies of war material, and put her railroads and all means of communication on the left bank of the Rhine at the disposal of the Allies. She was to free all war prisoners, and restore the money and securities taken from Belgium. Moreover, the blockade of Germany was to be continued throughout the Peace Conference. These and other provisions were designed to make any renewal of the war on Germany's part absolutely impossible. Hard as were the terms, the Germans accepted them promptly, and on November 11 the armistice was signed at Réthondes, in the forest of Compiègne. The World War was now at an end. The Germans, however, believed that in the end they would secure a fair peace based on the Fourteen Points.

It is estimated that during the World War nearly sixty million men were mobilized. Of these nearly eight million were killed in battle and over eighteen million wounded. Of those who recovered perhaps a quarter or more were permanently mutilated or crippled. The loss among the civilian populations was tremendous, owing to famine, disease, and massacres, amounting to perhaps seventeen million lives.

The national debts of the nations participating in the war were in the case of the Central Powers raised from about five to forty-four billions of dollars, and in the case of the Allies from twenty-one to eighty-six. Five thousand six hundred and twenty-two British merchant ships were sunk, nearly half of them with their crews on board. The French Chamber of Deputies calculated that the damage done by the Germans in northern France amounted to almost thirteen billions of dollars. These figures give some hint of the really unimaginable cost of the conflict in life and treasure.

CHAPTER XXX

EUROPE SINCE THE WORLD WAR

The Treaty of Versailles. The League of Nations. Changes in the Map of Europe. The League of Nations: Plans to Abolish War. New Experiments in Government

The Treaty of Versailles

THE Allies selected Paris and the neighboring Versailles as the meeting place for their representatives, who convened in January, 1919, to settle the terms of peace.

Five great powers—Great Britain, France, the United States, Italy, and Japan—organized the conference and took the leading part in all the discussions and in the final decisions at Versailles. There were delegates from the British dominions—Canada, Australia, New Zealand, and South Africa—and also from India; from Brazil and eleven others of the Latin-American republics; from Belgium, Serbia, Greece, and Rumania; from the new states of Poland, Czechoslovakia, and Hejaz; from the republic of China, Siam, and the African state of Liberia. So thirty-two states, scattered all over the globe, had their representatives on hand to take part in, or at least to watch, the momentous proceedings.

Germany, Russia, and the powers that had remained neutral were excluded from the conference.

In spite of the protests of the lesser powers the representatives of France, Great Britain, and the United States, namely, Clemenceau, Lloyd George, and President Wilson,—popularly known as "The Big Three,"—met in secret council and made all the important decisions. They urged that their nations had really borne the chief responsibility of winning the war, and further that it was impossible, in view of the conflicting interests of many of the powers, to accomplish the tremendous work of the conference in a large assembly with public meetings.

A draft of the peace treaty was presented to the delegates on May 5, 1919, and after considerable discussion was accepted by them. By the terms of the treaty Germany was reduced in size, for she was required to give up Alsace-Lorraine to France, and to cede a great part of her provinces of Posen and West Prussia to the Polish republic. Other smaller territories were to be permitted to join Poland on the one hand, or Denmark on the other, if their people so voted. The important port of Danzig was to be a free city. Germany was to surrender all her colonies. Those in Africa were turned over to Great Britain or France as "mandatories," to be administered under the authority of the League of Nations. Her possessions in the Pacific were assigned either to Australia or to Japan. In order permanently to weaken Germany as a military power she was required to surrender a great part of her navy and all her airships and submarines. Her army was never to exceed one hundred thousand men, and compulsory military service was abolished. Great limitations were placed on the manufacture and buying of arms and munitions. The Allies were to occupy the west bank of the Rhine until the terms of the treaty should be carried out.

The most difficult question of the treaty was to determine the amount of *reparations* which the Allies were to demand as their bill for the damage which the Germans had done during the war. This was to be decided by a Reparations Commission of the Allies, which was to report two years later as to how much Germany could and should pay. Germany was required to make an initial payment of some five billions of dollars. She was to build ships for the Allies, to replace those that she had sunk. She was to deliver large quantities of coal to France as payment for the destruction of French coal mines. Various British, Italian, and American economic experts foresaw that the terms of the treaty would be very difficult to carry out and would hinder the financial recovery of Europe. This proved to be the case.

When the Germans learned the terms of the treaty, they denounced it as revengeful and ruinous to their country. They sent long protests to the conference, maintaining that the treaty violated President Wilson's Fourteen Points, and that the failure to fix a definite sum for the final bill of reparations would mean slavery for them, while the immediate payments proposed by the Allies exceeded all the wealth that Germany possessed. They asserted that even if they were forced to sign the treaty, its obligations could never be fulfilled. They also refused to acknowledge their sole responsibility for the war.

Nevertheless, the attempts of the Germans to secure any considerable modification of the terms of the treaty were futile. On June 28, 1919, their representatives reluctantly signed the document in the historic palace of Versailles, where, in 1871, the German empire had been proclaimed.

The League of Nations

The first section of the treaty with Germany is devoted to the Covenant of the League of Nations, one of the most significant documents in history. President Wilson never deviated from his plan for incorporating the League as the leading provision in the treaty of peace, so firmly did he believe that such an association of nations was the only effective guaranty against the recurrence of wars. The League was to be composed of those fully self-governing states and colonies that should be able to give effective guaranties of their intention to observe its obligations. In the beginning, however, Germany and her allies were temporarily excluded, and Russia and Mexico were not to be invited to join until they had established thoroughly stable governments. The League was to have its permanent offices and staff at Geneva, and was to be organized with an *Assembly* in which each of the members, including the British dominions, should have one vote, and a *Council* made up of the representatives of the five great powers (the United States, Great Britain, France, Italy, and Japan), to which others might later be added, and of four states to be selected from time to time by the Assembly. The Assembly and Council were to meet at stated intervals, the Council at least once a year. All important decisions were to require a *unanimous* vote.

Any war or threat of war, or any matter affecting the peace of the world, is declared in the Covenant a matter of concern to the whole League. Members of the League agree to sub-

Pl. liv. Signing of the Treaty of Peace in the Hall of Mirrors at Versailles, June, 1919

Pl. LV. Celebration in Strasbourg of the Return of Peace
and the Reunion of Alsace with France

mit any dispute which might lead to war either to arbitration or to investigation by the Council or Assembly. If they submit the dispute to *arbitration*, they pledge themselves to carry out the award made and not to resort to war. If they submit the dispute to inquiry, the Council or Assembly must fully investigate the matter and, within six months after the submission of the dispute, make a report and recommendations in regard to it. Should the report and recommendations be unanimously agreed to by all the powers except those which are parties to the dispute, the latter agree not to go to war in the matter. If, on the other hand, the recommendations should not prove unanimous, the parties to the dispute pledge themselves in no case to resort to war for three months after the report is made.

Should any member resort to war in disregard of these agreements, it is deemed to have committed an act of war against all the governments and states which are members of the League, and the latter agree to sever all trade and financial relations with the offending state and to prohibit all intercourse between its citizens and their own. The members of the League also undertake (Article X) to respect and preserve as against external aggression the territorial integrity and political independence of one another.

The Covenant of the League provides also for the establishment of a permanent Court of International Justice,—or World Court, as it is often called,—to hear and determine any dispute of an international character. The Council of the League is to prepare plans for the reduction of armaments and to control the manufacture of munitions and implements of war. All treaties are to be registered with the League and made public.

Certain territories inhabited by backward peoples formerly belonging to the Central Powers—parts of the Turkish empire, of Central and Southwest Africa, and of the southern Pacific islands—are declared to be under the guardianship of the League. By a system of so-called *mandates* the guardianship of such peoples is to be intrusted to "advanced" nations, as *mandatories,* which are to seek to promote their well-being and development. The governments acting as mandatories are to report annually to the League.

Under the general supervision of the League of Nations the treaty establishes also a very important International Labor Bureau, on the ground that "the well-being, physical, moral, and intellectual, of the industrial wage-earners is of supreme international importance." This labor bureau is designed to improve working conditions throughout the world and to secure fair conditions of labor for men, women, and children.

Although President Wilson was its chief promoter, there was much difference of opinion in the United States as to the wisdom of joining the League of Nations. Many felt that in so doing the United States would sacrifice some of its sovereignty and would risk becoming involved in "entangling alliances."

On the other hand, there was an important group who claimed that the United States could not stand aloof. Ex-President Taft, for instance, said: "The argument that to enter this covenant is a departure from the time-honored policy of avoiding entangling alliances with Europe is an argument that is blind to the changing circumstances in our present situation. The war itself ended that policy. . . . We were driven into it because, with the dependence of all the world upon our resources of food, raw material, and manufacture, with our closeness, under modern conditions of transportation and communication, to Europe, it was impossible for us to maintain the theory of an isolation that in fact did not exist. It will be equally impossible for us to keep out of another general European war. We are, therefore, just as much interested in stopping such a war as if we were in Europe."

When the treaty was submitted to the United States Senate for ratification, most of the Republican senators declared that various amendments and reservations were needed, especially in the case of the League of Nations. The chief objections raised were that Article X might involve the United States in war over European territorial disputes in which it had no interest; that it might be forced into war without the consent of

Congress; that the Monroe Doctrine was not secured; that the British empire had five votes, since its various members—Canada, Australia, New Zealand, and South Africa—were assigned each a vote; that the United States would sacrifice its sovereignty by entering the League and might not be able to control immigration, the tariff, and other matters.

After prolonged and bitter discussions the treaty was sent back to the President in March, 1920, unapproved, and the United States remained outside the League of Nations.

The adoption or rejection of the Treaty of Versailles (including the Covenant of the League of Nations) was an issue in the presidential election of 1920. The Republican party, which opposed ratification, was victorious and elected its candidate, Warren G. Harding. On July 2, 1921, President Harding signed a joint resolution of Congress declaring that war between Germany and the United States was at an end. Six weeks later a brief treaty was signed in Berlin by which the Germans agreed to give the United States all rights and advantages included in the Treaty of Versailles, except those specially excluded at the wish of the United States.

Changes in the Map of Europe

The dissolution of the ancient Austrian empire was one of the most striking results of the war. As the great conflict came to a close, the northern Slavs, the Czechs, formed themselves into the republic of Czechoslovakia; the southern Slavs, into the kingdom of Jugoslavia; and Hungary, much reduced in size, became an independent state. Austria itself was converted into a small republic, with an area less than that of Ireland. Charles I, the successor of old Francis Joseph (who died in 1916), was unable to maintain himself as ruler either of Austria or of Hungary, and died in exile in 1922. Thus the rôle of the Hapsburgs, which had continued in European history for six centuries, was brought to an end.

Austria, which had been the center of the empire, now that most of her former sources of revenue were cut off, found herself in a sad plight. Bankrupt, with no means of meeting the cost of her new government, she was unable to carry on the thorough reorganization necessary if she was to continue to exist as a republic.

After a three years' struggle against starvation and revolution, with her currency reduced to one-fifteen-thousandth part of its previous value and with no prospect of improvement, the League of Nations devised a means by which she obtained a loan of a hundred and thirty-five million dollars, guaranteed

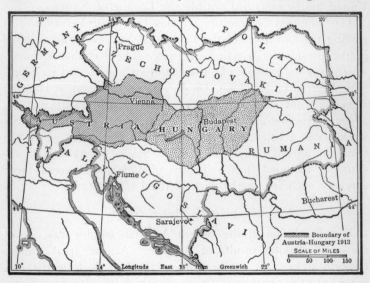

THE AUSTRIAN REPUBLIC AND THE HUNGARIAN MONARCHY

by Western European governments. In collaboration with the Austrian government a committee of the League undertook to rehabilitate the distracted state. Her financial affairs were straightened out, her currency stabilized, and her income made equal to her expenditures.

In Hungary a very transient republic was established under the presidency of Count Karolyi, a statesman who, himself a great landowner, was eager to have the vast estates of Hungary divided among the peasants. His government was overthrown by a communist revolution, which was speedily succeeded by a counter revolution, in which (March, 1920) Admiral Horthy came into power as "regent" and frustrated all attempts to carry out much-needed reforms. Hungary, unlike Austria, remained nominally a monarchy with a vacant throne.

In 1923 Hungary applied to the League for aid in restoring her financial situation. The Council appointed a committee which, having studied the situation, arranged a reconstruction loan. The financial affairs of Hungary have been administered by a commissioner-general, Jeremiah Smith, Jr., of Boston, working in coöperation with the League. In 1926 Mr. Smith finished his work, having succeeded in balancing the budget of Hungary.

The most prosperous of the "succession states" of Austria-Hungary was the republic of Czechoslovakia, composed of the old kingdom of Bohemia, Moravia and Silesia, and Slovakia. The Czechs and Slovaks constitute about 60 per cent of the population, while there are three and a half million Germans and a mil-

JUGOSLAVIA, THE KINGDOM OF THE SERBS, CROATS, AND SLOVENES

lion Hungarians and members of other minor racial groups. The Germans formed a separate party in parliament and insisted on using their own language. The old hostility between Germans and Slavs continued under the new government.

The brief career of Jugoslavia; "the kingdom of the Serbs, Croats, and Slovenes," has not been so fortunate as that of her sister state to the north. Although the movement for the union of these southern Slavs is an old one, there has been difficulty in amalgamating so many different peoples—Serbs, Croats, Slovenes, Dalmatians, Bosnians, Herzegovinians, and Montenegrins—into a harmonious state. While of the same race, they have been separated for many centuries and differ widely in their social, political, and religious ideas and in their education. All elements combined, however, under the new king, Alexander. In addition to their difficulties at home, the Jugoslavs had a good deal of trouble with Italy, which insisted upon keeping Fiume and the neighboring region, inhabited by many Italians and serving as an outlet to the sea. This matter was finally settled by giving Fiume to Italy, and the neighboring port of Baros to Jugoslavia.

The greatest of the Slavic lands except Russia was the restored Poland. She was unhappily so intent on adding territory which she claimed belonged to her by "historic right" that she was soon at war with Czechoslovakia, Russia, the Ukraine, and Lithuania. The war with Russia (1919-1920) was particularly serious, and ended with a victory for the Poles. Russia ceded a considerable part of White Russia to Poland, and the Ukraine was forced resentfully to give up her claims to eastern Galicia. The result was that Poland, with the help of France, became a large country with a bare majority of Poles, the rest of the population being made up of Germans, Lithuanians, White Russians, and Ukrainians, in addition to a large Jewish element.

In Russia, Trotzky, the communist leader, organized a powerful "Red Army" to put down the attempts to overthrow the Bolsheviki. The counter-revolutionists, under the command of generals like Kolchak, Denikin, and Wrangel, were encouraged by the Allies to undertake several campaigns in Siberia and Russia against the Soviet government; but in this fierce civil war the Bolsheviki were victorious and remained in power.

Four former provinces of the Russian empire are now numbered among the free and sovereign nations of the world. Finland, which had been an independent duchy under the Tsar as its duke, had long opposed the attempts of the Russian government to reduce its rights. With the fall of Nicholas II it naturally seized the opportunity to secure its entire independence. The other three neighboring provinces,—Esthonia, Latvia, and Lithuania,—which had suffered for centuries from the intrigues and invasions of their more powerful neighbors, were able to secure recognition as independent republics and along with Finland were admitted to the League of Nations.

Turning now to the Balkan peninsula, we have seen that the western portions had been consolidated into the Jugoslavic kingdom, with the Serbian monarch as its ruler. The Allies punished Bulgaria, Serbia's old enemy on the east, by transferring to Jugoslavia certain border regions and cutting off Bulgaria from the Ægean Sea by depriving her of western Thrace. Moreover, they awarded to Rumania the rich farm lands of the upper Dobrudja between the Danube and the Black Sea. In spite of these losses and her reparation payments Bulgaria recovered rapidly, owing partly to the sturdy peasants, who own the lands they cultivate, and partly to the freedom from military expense, and the peaceful utilization in reconstruction work of the small army which the Allies permitted Bulgaria to maintain.

Although Rumania was overwhelmed by the Germans, she nevertheless emerged from the war with an area twice the size of the former kingdom. With the concurrence of the Allies she annexed Bessarabia, which had belonged to Russia since 1812; Bukowina, which had belonged to Austria; Transylvania and other portions of Hungary. Greater Rumania now included Rumanians, Serbians, Hungarians, Russians, Bulgarians, and Turks. In order to keep her hold on all these alien peoples, the parliament voted a number of reforms. These included universal suffrage and a redistribution of the land. Large estates were divided up, and part of the land was assigned to the peasants, who were to pay a portion of the cost while the state paid the rest. Citizenship was granted to native-born Jews.

The possessions of the Ottoman Empire in Europe had, as a result of the Balkan wars (1912-1913), been reduced to Constantinople and a little patch, eastern Thrace, to the west. During the war, in various ways, Egypt, the Hejaz, Mesopotamia, Syria, and Palestine had altogether escaped from Turkish control. When the armistice was concluded, the Allies demanded that Turkey give up its chief seaport, Smyrna, as well as eastern Thrace, to the Greeks. This aroused a nationalist movement in Turkey under a vigorous leader, Mustapha Kemal Pasha, who made Angora, not Constantinople, the headquarters of the new government. The Nationalists refused to recognize the settlement which the Sultan made with the Allies. Kemal's army repulsed the Greeks, who had marched into Asia Minor from Smyrna. The Turkish Nationalists received a certain support from Italy and France, whose business men hoped to gain oil and trade concessions.

After the expulsion of the Greeks the Turkish Nationalists stood firmly for what they considered their rights. The Treaty of Lausanne (July, 1923) with the Allies recognized Turkey's possession of Smyrna, Constantinople, and eastern Thrace. The Dardanelles, however, were to be open to the ships of all nations. The Nationalists then forced the Sultan to leave Constantinople, and established, in October, 1923, a Turkish republic, with its capital at Angora. A few months later the members of the house of Osman, which had ruled the Turks for seven centuries, were exiled and went the way of the Hohenzollerns, Hapsburgs, and Romanoffs. The caliphate was abolished on the ground that the Turks repudiated the ancient combination of religion and politics and that the Moslems no longer needed an intermediary between themselves and Allah.

Although the Greeks had entered the World War late, they kept on fighting the Turks after its close, with the hope of getting Smyrna and eastern Thrace. The Allies, who for a time had encouraged these aggressions, finally thought best to make terms with the new Turkish government at Angora. The Greeks seem to have attributed their military failure to their sovereign and to his ministers, several of whom were executed. In March, 1924, monarchy was abolished and a republic set up.

When, in 1815, a great congress of diplomats assembled at Vienna to rearrange the map of Europe, their chief ambition was to restore the old régime and place once more on their thrones the monarchs who were "legitimately" entitled to rule. They determined ruthlessly to suppress any uprisings on the part of reformers who wished to secure constitutions or checks on the powers of their lawful sovereigns, or who dreamed of uniting kindred peoples into national states. But in spite of all these precautions the reformers gradually succeeded in adding, during the nineteenth century, no less than seven new independent constitutional national states to the family of European nations—Serbia, Greece, Belgium, the German empire, the Kingdom of Italy, Rumania, and Bulgaria.

A hundred years later, at Versailles, the representatives of the great powers undertook once more to remake the map of Europe. At this conference, however, Austria no longer dictated to a vanquished France, but victorious France to a defeated and divided Austria; thus "Time brings in his revenges." Metternich, Talleyrand, and Alexander were gone, but Clemenceau, Lloyd George, and the Italian statesman Orlando were there; and since, in the meantime, European history had grown into world history, there was also the representative from the great republic across the Atlantic, whose armies had now for the first time fought on the battlefields of Europe. These diplomats no longer placed their faith in kings and emperors, but in government by the people, and welcomed the establishment of republics in place of the ancient monarchies. Moreover, they believed in what they called the right of nations to self-determination. The political reconstruction of Europe since 1918 is largely the result of these two ideas of government,—democracy and self-determination,—which would have stood for revolution and ruin to the conservative gentlemen at the Congress of Vienna.

The most startling changes in the map of Europe are those which have taken place in central and eastern Europe, where the proud dynasties of the Hohenzollerns, Hapsburgs, and Romanoffs have disappeared and their empires have become republics in the hands of socialist and communist leaders. Hardly less astonishing is the disappearance of the ancient Ottoman empire and the appearance, in its place, of the republic of Turkey. Seven new republics (Finland, Esthonia, Lithuania, Latvia, White Russia, Ukraine, and Transcaucasia) have been formed from the western and southern fringe of the Tsar's realms; while the larger part of the Hapsburgs' territory (Austria-Hungary) has been taken to restore Poland, to enlarge Italy, Rumania, and Jugoslavia, and to make the new republic of Czechoslovakia.

The League of Nations: Plans to Abolish War

One of the most difficult questions which continued to perplex Europe was that of the indemnity to be paid by Germany. This was fixed at about fifty-six billions of dollars (February, 1921), but the German government replied that it was absolutely impossible for it to meet such a demand even in annual installments extending over forty-two years. Great Britain was in favor of compromise, but French and Belgian troops invaded (January, 1923) the industrial region of Germany beyond the Rhine, especially the cities along the Ruhr valley, in order to collect from Germany on the spot. The Germans resisted, and the plan was economically a failure. The following autumn the German government agreed to submit the question of the indemnity to an international tribunal to determine how much was to be paid and in what manner.

In November, 1923, the Reparations Commission therefore voted to name two committees of experts to determine (1) the means of improving Germany's financial situation at home and (2) the amount of German wealth which had been sent abroad and how it could be recovered. General Charles G. Dawes, the former Director of the Budget of the United States, was made chairman of the first committee, and the former chancellor of the British exchequer, Reginald McKenna, chairman of the second. The most helpful contribution to the settlement of this long and perplexing question was made by these committees of experts, who handed in their reports in April, 1924. The French, British, and German governments promptly expressed their approval of the reports, and the Germans indicated their willingness to abide by their provisions. The total sum for reparations was not, however, fixed.

The fact that the United States government refused to join the League of Nations did not prevent efforts on the part of the government to reduce the expense and danger of armaments. A conference of foreign governments was invited by President Harding to meet in Washington in November, 1921. Delegates were sent by the British Empire, China, France, Italy, Japan, Belgium, the Netherlands, and Portugal. The chief maritime powers—Great Britain, the United States, France, Italy, and Japan—agreed to cease building new warships for a period of ten years and to maintain a ratio on the part of Great Britain, the United States, and Japan of five-five-three. The powers also agreed not to interfere in China by seeking special advantages and concessions.

According to the provisions of the Versailles Treaty the League of Nations was organized and in November, 1920, held its first session at Geneva. At this meeting there were present the representatives of forty-two nations which had enrolled in the League. Since that time the membership has grown to fifty-five.[1] Regular meetings of the Council and Assembly have been held, while numerous committees and commissions have been engaged in investigating special problems and preparing technical reports.

The League has promoted peace in Europe in several ways. In the first place, it has been able to avert serious trouble between its members by settling a number of political controversies arising over conflicting claims to territory. War between Italy and Greece and between Greece and Bulgaria was fended off by the intervention of the League. Relief work for refugees from war-devastated areas has been carried on on a large scale by its commissions, and aid and advice in financial reconstruction have been given, notably to Austria and Hungary. Permanent auxiliary departments for the prolonged study of important questions have been organized. These departments are of two kinds; technical bodies dealing with

[1] At the opening of 1926 the League's membership included all Europe except Germany and Russia; all North and South America except the United States, Mexico, and Ecuador; and, including the mandates, it embraced all Asia except Turkey and Afghanistan, and all Africa except Egypt. The Locarno treaties provided for Germany's entrance into the League.

finance and economics, transit and health; advisory committees occupied with military questions, disarmament, mandates,
traffic in women and children, opium, and intellectual coöperation. In addition, two related but practically independent
bodies have been established—the International Labor Organization and the Permanent Court of International Justice.

One of the most notable accomplishments of the League has
been the establishing of the Permanent Court of International
Justice provided for by Article 14 of the Covenant. In February, 1920, the Council appointed a committee of jurists of international reputation to draw up a plan for the proposed
court.[1] This committee prepared a draft-statute which with
some amendments was approved by the Assembly in December of the same year. The statute was then embodied in a
protocol, or treaty, which was to be signed by nations wishing
to become members of the Court and was left open for the
signature of those countries which later decided to join. When
the Assembly met the following year (December, 1921), twenty-eight countries had ratified the Treaty, which then went into
effect. The Court held its first session at The Hague, January 30, 1922. By the end of 1924 the Court had enrolled
forty-eight members.

The statute states that the Permanent Court of International Justice is established in addition to the Court of Arbitration organized by the Conventions of The Hague of 1899 and
1907. That the Court is to be composed of a body of independent judges of high moral character who possess the qualifications required in their respective countries for appointment
to the highest judicial offices, or as professional experts of
recognized competence in international law.

The Court is to consist of fifteen members: eleven judges
and four deputy judges. The members of the Court are elected
by the Assembly and the Council from a list of persons nominated by the national groups in the Court of Arbitration; in

---

[1] Among the members of this committee was Mr. Elihu Root, former
Secretary of State, who acted in a *personal* capacity and not as the *official*
representative of the United States.

cases of members of the League of Nations not represented in the Court of Arbitration, the list of candidates is to be drawn up by a committee appointed by the government. Members of the Court are elected for nine years and may be reëlected. The seat of the Court is to be at The Hague. Unless otherwise provided, an annual session of the Court shall be held beginning on June 15 and continuing as long as is deemed necessary to finish the cases on the list.

"The jurisdiction of the Court comprises all cases which the parties refer to it and all matters specially provided for in treaties and conventions in force." An acceptance of the jurisdiction of the Court is, in general, voluntary, but by signing an optional clause members may also agree to accept the Court's jurisdiction as obligatory in all disputes concerning (1) the interpretation of a treaty; (2) any question of international law; (3) the existence of any fact which, if established, would constitute a breach of an international obligation; (4) the nature or extent of the reparation to be made for the breach of an international obligation.

Of the forty-eight states which have joined the World Court twenty-three have accepted the obligatory jurisdiction of the Court.

The first serious discussions of an international court took place at the Hague conferences. The nations, however, wished to retain their complete independence and to submit only such questions as they saw fit. They refused to consider seriously compulsory arbitration. The result was—as earlier pointed out —the founding of the Hague Court of Arbitration, which consisted of a list of judges chosen by the nations meeting at the conferences, from which a tribunal was to be selected for each case that came up. The Court was established at The Hague and was presented with a handsome building called the Peace Palace, the gift of Mr. Andrew Carnegie. The Hague Court of Arbitration differs from the World Court (also established at The Hague) in a number of fundamental points. The Hague Court is a court of *arbitration* which seeks to adjust disputes through compromise. The World Court, on the other hand, is a court of law whose decisions and advisory opinions are based on legal rules. The Hague Court lacks continuity in its work, since its judges change from time to time. The World Court, composed of judges who devote all their attention to the Court, promises by its continued practice to build up a new body of international law.[1]

From the first many Americans wished the United States to become a member of the World Court, whether they believed it wise to enter the League or not. On February 24, 1923, President Harding proposed the acceptance of the Protocol by the United States, but with the following reservations formulated by Secretary Hughes: That the United States should not become involved in any legal relation with the League of Nations or assume any obligations under its Covenant: That the United States should participate in the election of judges: That the United States should pay a fair proportion of the expenses of the Court: That the Statute of the Court should not be amended without the consent of the United States.

Late in 1925 President Coolidge indorsed the Court, and following this the question of the entry of the United States was warmly debated in Congress. On January 27, 1926, the Senate ratified the Protocol with substantially the same reservations as had been made by Secretary Hughes. An additional reservation states that the Court is not to render an advisory opinion "touching any dispute or question in which the United States has or claims an interest" without the consent of the United States. Further, the signature of the United States is not to be affixed to the Protocol until the other members of the Court have accepted these reservations as "a part and a condition of the adherence by the United States."

The most difficult problem which the League has had to face is the question of disarmament. Any attempt to persuade a nation to reduce the military forces on which it has

---

[1] Among the judges who were chosen for the World Court in September, 1921, was Professor John Bassett Moore, a distinguished American authority on international law.

been wont to depend for protection arouses all the old-time fears and suspicions and is met with strong opposition. This is not due to perversity but to a feeling that it is not safe to do so. The third Assembly of the League recognized the principle that the two problems of *disarmament* and *security* were inseparable; it is not possible to expect a nation which is in danger of attack to reduce its armaments without falling back upon some guaranty of security, such as the promise, in the Covenant, of help if attacked (Art. 16). The Hague conferences called for the purpose of disarmament failed, and the Washington Conference of 1921, although it established a set ratio of strength for naval forces, did not regulate land armaments and failed to do more than denounce the most effective method of destruction—chemical warfare.

These obvious difficulties have led to the consideration of other solutions, such as compulsory arbitration and the *outlawing* of war. A number of plans have been brought before the League. In 1924 a Draft Treaty of Mutual Assistance (based on plans of Lord Cecil and French experts), which was drawn up by the Temporary Mixed Commission of the League, composed of civilian and military members, was accepted by some members of the League but rejected by others. Its main features were that it *declared aggressive war a crime.* The signatories were to assist the victims of "aggressive" war and were also to reduce their armaments in proportion to the security offered by the treaty. But "aggressive" was not defined!

An alternative plan, known as the "American plan," was drawn up by an unofficial committee of Americans and became an official document of the League. The great contribution of this plan was its *definition of an aggressor* as one who goes to war without obeying a summons to an appropriate international tribunal, or without accepting the unanimous decision of the Council. The plan also called for international inspection of armaments and for recurring conferences on disarmament in which outsiders (for instance, the United States) could join. These two plans became the basis for the

Geneva Protocol of the Assembly of 1924, which outlawed aggressive war and plainly stated that a nation is an aggressor when it refuses the alternatives for war. Aggressive war was for the first time in history officially declared to be a crime; and although defense is regarded as legitimate, it is not to be based on the individual judgment of one party to a controversy. The Protocol called upon the members of the League to come to the assistance of a nation that is attacked. The states decide in what ways they will assist, having due regard to geographical position and peculiar situation. At the Council meeting in March, 1925, the British government announced that although it sympathized with the objects in view, it could not accept the Protocol, because a *general* obligation to assist the victim of aggression put too heavy a burden upon a world empire so long as the United States was not included in the League. It urged that a more satisfactory solution would be to supplement the Covenant by making special arrangements to meet special needs; those nations whose differences might lead to war should be brought together by means of treaties framed with the sole object of maintaining between them an unbroken peace.[1]

Following along the general lines of the British proposal, a conference of the representatives of Germany, France, Belgium, Great Britain, Italy, Poland, and Czechoslovakia met at Locarno on October 5, 1925, for a discussion of the great question of security, which had agitated the Western nations ever since the World War. The signing, on October 16, of a Treaty of Mutual Guaranty between Germany, Belgium, France, Great Britain, and Italy (commonly called the Security Pact) and six other treaties brought this unusual conference to a happy close. For the first time since the war Germany became a party to an international undertaking for

[1] This whole matter is made very clear by Professor James T. Shotwell in *International Conciliation*, No. 208, March, 1925. Professor Shotwell was chairman and one of the most influential members of the committee which was responsible for the "American plan." This had a considerable influence upon later plans for peace.

the maintenance of peace, and was received on a friendly footing with the other nations in a common enterprise.

By the terms of the Security Pact the signatories guarantee to maintain the frontiers between Germany and Belgium, and Germany and France, as provided in the Treaty of Versailles and to observe Articles 42 and 43 of the Treaty concerning the demilitarized zone.[1] Germany and Belgium, and Germany and France, pledge themselves not to attack one another or to invade one another's territory or to resort to war against one another. The right of "legitimate defense," however, is reserved in the case of a violation of the Security Pact or of Articles 42 and 43 of the Treaty, and also the right to act in accordance with the decision of the League. Germany and France, as well as Germany and Belgium, agree to settle peacefully all questions arising between them. In case of conflicting rights they promise to submit the matter to judicial decision and comply with such decision. Other questions are to be brought before a conciliation commission. If the proposals of this commission are not accepted, the question is to be submitted to the Council of the League for settlement. In case of the violation of the present Treaty or of Article 42 and 43, the matter is to be brought immediately before the Council of the League. If the Council is satisfied that a violation has been committed, the powers signatory to the Treaty promise to come immediately to the aid of the party against whom the wrong is committed.

In case of a *flagrant* aggression, such as actual invasion, the signatory powers promise to come *immediately* to the aid of the party attacked. Even then both parties agree to accept the decision of the Council of the League if all the other countries are unanimous. Article 5 deals with aggression not flagrant and is therefore the kernel of the Treaty if it is to

[1] Articles 42 and 43 of the Treaty of Versailles establish a demilitarized zone between France and Germany on the right bank of the Rhine extending fifty kilometers from the bank of the river. Germany may not construct or maintain fortifications on the left bank or on the right bank west of the demilitarized zone, and may not maintain armed forces or engage in military maneuvers or mobilize in this area.

prevent war. It applies the definition of the "American plan," making the test of aggression the refusal to accept the decision of courts for legal matters or conciliation tribunals for other controversies. Thus the very principles which the Geneva Protocol attempted to extend to all nations are here accepted in western Europe at least.

The arbitration treaties between Germany and France, Germany and Belgium, Germany and Poland, and Germany and

MAP OF THE PEACE ZONE

Czechoslovakia, which form a part of the Locarno settlement, provide that all disputes between these nations which cannot be settled by the usual methods of diplomacy may be submitted to an arbitral tribunal or to the Permanent Court of International Justice. Before resort is made to arbitral procedure the dispute may, by agreement, be brought before a permanent international commission styled the Permanent Conciliation Commission. This commission, which in each case is to be appointed within three months after the Treaty has entered into force, shall be composed of five members, two of them chosen from the respective nationals of the powers directly concerned, and the three remaining chosen by agreement from the nationals of other powers. The special task of this commission is to gather information and elucidate the questions in dispute, and to endeavor to bring the parties to an agreement. The commission shall draw up a report of its labors, which must be completed within six months.

Two further treaties were signed between France and Poland and between France and Czechoslovakia, who agree reciprocally to aid one another if, in case of a violation of the Security Pact, they are attacked by Germany.

The Locarno treaties mark a great advance in international relations and are regarded by some as the beginning of a series of such conventions which may break down old barriers between nations and perhaps lead eventually to something like a federation of states of Europe. However this may be, the Locarno settlement is unique in many ways. In the first place, the Security Pact is notable for its simplicity and directness and for making no concessions to "national honor." The signatories pledge themselves to coöperate to maintain peace rather than to establish, as of old, a defensive alliance against a real or an imaginary enemy. This is not a secret treaty to preserve the "balance of power," but a frank and published agreement to "seek peace and pursue it." Furthermore, the parties chiefly concerned associate with themselves other nations as guarantors to see that their contracts are kept. Above all, they voluntarily promise to submit their future disputes to a third party—a commission, a court, or a council—and to abide by the decision of this body.

One of the provisions of the Covenant of the League requires that all treaties made between members must be registered at the League; otherwise they shall be invalid. Over a thousand treaties and conventions have so far been deposited at Geneva, where they can be examined by all. "Public diplomacy" is furthered by the frequent meetings of statesmen in Geneva, and their deliberations, instead of being filed away in various foreign offices, as formerly, are reported by the daily papers all over the world. In this way information is furnished upon topics hitherto not generally understood. All this works for the education of public opinion and for the promotion of peaceful adjustment and of a widespread sentiment against resorting to war.

New Experiments in Government

The World War resulted in the creating of a number of new states and in the transformation of old ones. Almost without exception the new form of government was republican. Germany became a very democratic republic, under the control of moderate socialists, and all the states which compose that federation did away with their kings and princes. The old aristocratic upper houses, composed of nobles and appointees of the sovereign, have greatly declined in importance, even in Great Britain. Everywhere there has been a tendency to give the working classes more influence and to make the ministry responsible to the people, as in Great Britain.

In the earlier portions of this book something has been said of the sad state of the farming classes from the days of the Roman Empire down to the abolition of serfdom in Prussia and Russia. Although every human being is dependent on the farmer for food, the agricultural class has been badly treated through the ages and is not in a favorable position for defending itself against the extortions of landlords, middlemen, and financiers. After the war the peasants of Bulgaria issued a sort of declaration of rights, a "Green Manifesto," in which they call attention to the fact that those who farm the land have "everywhere and always been compelled to submit to unjust and evil treatment." They propose an international union of the peasants, so that their voices, "too long silent, shall be heard."

Since *socialists* of various kinds, moderate and radical, have become a very important element in European politics, it is now possible to make a fairly clear distinction in Europe between the socialists who do not believe in violence but in peaceful readjustment and those who stand boldly for a war of the workers, or proletariat, on the capitalists, or bourgeoisie. If we call the reformers who oppose violent revolution moderate socialists, and those who believe in a *class* struggle between capitalists and workers extreme socialists, or, rather, "communists," we have a grouping corresponding to the facts.

[718]

NEW EXPERIMENTS IN GOVERNMENT

For example, the British Labor ministry was peacefully socialistic, the German government was, after the establishment of the republic, controlled by moderate socialists, while Russia was, after the war, under the sway of real communists.

The socialists have usually maintained that the revolution which they advocate in government, business, and trade is not limited to this nation or that, but is to be a great *international* reform affecting workingmen regardless of the country in which they happen to live; hence the war cry "Workers of the world, unite!" In 1864 Karl Marx had helped form an international organization of those interested in the spread of socialism. This "First International" was discredited by the violent action of the Paris Communists in 1871 and finally disappeared. A "Second International" was founded in the 'eighties and is still in existence.

This was not radical enough to please the extreme party, and in 1918 a "Third International" was organized in Moscow under the auspices of the Bolsheviki. This has adherents in many European countries. The leaders in Russia belonged to it, and one of the chief reasons why the United States persistently refused to recognize the Russian government was the fact that it was identified with the avowed attempt to overturn the whole business system of other countries.

Some account of the history of Russia under its Tsars has been given in previous chapters. We have seen how the liberal leaders who tried to introduce Western ideas and secure a constitution were cruelly persecuted by the government officials. With the deposition of the house of Romanoff and the victory of the extreme socialists, which came before the end of the World War, an extraordinary experiment in communism was begun in Russia, which has been going on since 1917. Under the leadership of Lenin the Bolsheviki made an attempt to carry out a complete social and economic revolution by which the *laboring classes* should be given control not only of the government but of the land and factories and business in general, which were to be managed thereafter in the interests of the workmen and peasants. The peasants were authorized to take the estates of the great landowners and even the land of the *richer* peasants. Factories, banks, and mines were taken over by the nation, to be used for the benefit of the proletariat. The older government was replaced by a system of *soviets,* or councils, elected by groups of workers in the various factories, trades, and occupations, and by the farmers. There were local and provincial soviets, and these elected representatives to the all-Russian Congress at Moscow.

Naturally these revolutionary changes aroused bitter opposition. In order to stifle this the Bolsheviki suppressed many forms of freedom and resorted to cruel imprisonment and killing of their enemies—a method with which they had long been familiar under the despotic rule of the Tsar. The leaders of the Bolsheviki claimed that these terrible measures were only temporary, but were necessary to carry out the revolution against the opposition of its many enemies within and without Russia.

An assembly was elected late in 1917 to draw up a new constitution for Russia, but the Bolshevik leaders found that it would not accept their ideas and were able to dissolve it. In July, 1918, an all-Russian Congress of Soviets, which took the place of a national parliament or congress, proclaimed a constitution for the Russian Socialist Soviet Republic. Russia was declared to be a federation of "free nations," any one of which might retire from the union if it so desired. In 1924 the Russian federation included Russia proper, White Russia, Ukraine, the Transcaucasian Soviet Republic, and the Far-Eastern Republic, established in Siberia.

The constitution provided that the power in the State shall belong entirely to "the toiling masses," and shall be exercised through their representatives in the soviets. "The Russian Socialist Federated Soviet Republic considers work the duty of every citizen of the Republic, and proclaims as its motto: 'He shall not eat who does not work.'" Only "workers" may vote; consequently no one may vote or hold office who hires labor to increase his income, or who lives on his capital without doing any work, or who is a private merchant, broker, clergy-man, or monk.

Private property in land is abolished; the land is to be nationalized and distributed among the farmers according to their ability to till it, and the former owners shall receive no compensation. All forests and treasures of the earth are declared national property. Arrangements are to be made for transferring the ownership of all factories, mills, mines, rail-ways, and the like to the Soviet Republic. Banks and all financial operations are to be taken over by the workers' and peasants' government.

Finally, "for the purpose of securing the working class in the possession of complete power, and in order to eliminate all possibility of restoring the power of the exploiters, it is decreed that all toilers be armed, and that a Socialistic Red Army be organized and the propertied class disarmed."

While the Russian Soviet Republic denounced the old kind of wars for additional territory and colonies, it declared a new kind of world war on capitalistic industry and trade of all kinds. It proposed to fight for the "victory of socialism in all lands." The representatives of extreme socialism or com-munism of the Russian type made attempts, especially in Hungary, Italy, and Germany, to introduce the soviet control of manufacture and trade. In Budapest and Munich the com munists were actually in power for a short time. They were, however, suppressed in both cases. All over central Europe there were abortive attempts on the part of labor leaders to seize factories and set up "workers' councils" on the model of the Russian soviets.

The efforts of the workingmen in Italy under the influence of communist agitators to take possession of the factories in Milan, Turin, and other manufacturing cities led to a remark-able alteration in the Italian government. A new party called the *Fascisti* appeared, to oppose any overthrow of the usual business methods, but this party of order, as not uncommonly happens, was quite ready to exercise violence itself. The *Fascisti* developed a sort of vague ideal "Fascism" (*Fascismo*) about which they talk, as in the United States one speaks of "Americanism." The new party found a vigorous leader in Mussolini, who with his supporters became in 1923 the dictator of Italy. He got complete control of the Italian parliament and gained the confidence of the king. In the elections early in 1924 his party had votes enough to continue him in power. He chose a ministry of capable men and straightened out the badly demoralized finances. As time went on Mussolini showed signs of arrogance and a tendency to despotism which recalled the example set by Napoleon. The Fascisti were accused of maltreating their enemies, suppressing the freedom of the press, and censoring the news in a manner much like that of the Bolsheviki. Yet no one questioned that the new party had hastened the reconstruction of Italy, ruthless as may have been its methods. The panic that spread among timid and conservative people in regard to the Bolshevik danger made even harsh measures seem justifiable.

As for Germany, there was a sharp conflict in Berlin between the extreme socialists, Sparticides, and the moderate socialists (headed by President Ebert), who found themselves in the majority after the flight of the Kaiser. It must be remembered that Bismarck had opposed socialism by socialistic measures, so the country was prepared for this change of régime, although the monarchists remained an important element in the political situation. A republican constitution was drawn up at Weimar early in 1919. It was thoroughly democratic, but scarcely more socialistic than Bismarck's programme. Germany had to be weaned from its long monarchical traditions, but was already familiar with state ownership in many forms and with government alleviation of poverty and sickness.

The republic retained the old name of *Das Deutsche Reich*, for *Reich* means "realm" as well as "empire." Both men and women over twenty years of age were given the right to vote. The men had long enjoyed the right to fight at even an earlier age. The *Reichstag* represents the German people; the *Reichsrat* the German states, all of which must be republics in order to be members of the federation. The old predominance of

A Registered Letter from Germany

The Julius Tower, Spandau, Germany

Pl. LVI

PL. LVII. VON HINDENBURG

Prussia is abolished, for no state may have more than two fifths of the votes. Prussia gave itself a new constitution in November, 1920, which provided that "the sovereignty of the States resides in the whole people"—no longer in a monarch. All attacks both of communists and of the old-fashioned royalists, who did not hesitate to resort to assassination, were successfully resisted by the new government.

We have seen in a previous chapter the peculiar way in which the British Parliament is arranged so as to respond to the views of the voters. From 1895 to 1905 the Conservative (or Unionist) party controlled the ministry. From 1905 to 1915 the Liberal party was in power and succeeded in enacting some of the laws advocated by Lloyd George and in reducing the ancient influence of the House of Lords and admitting a considerable number of women to the franchise. Then the great responsibilities involved in carrying on the war led to a *coalition* between the Liberals and Conservatives, which lasted down to the armistice. A general election held in 1918 secured the coalition 467 seats, over two-thirds of them belonging to the Conservatives. But Lloyd George, who remained prime minister, had done his work; the coalition fell apart, the cabinet resigned and was replaced by a Conservative leader. Then the Conservatives decided to "go to the country" by having a new election, November, 1922, in which they came off very well. Owing to the creation of the parliament of the Irish Free State the number of members in the House of Commons had been reduced from 707 to 615. Of these seats the Conservatives won 344—well over half; the Liberals won only 114 seats, while the Labor party secured 142 members. Being second in numbers, the Labor party became for the first time the recognized "opposition" party in Parliament.

The history of the labor movement in Great Britain is complicated. A great many of those interested in improving the condition of the workingmen have relied on the formation of trade unions,—combinations of employees to make better terms in regard to wages, hours of labor, and conditions of work than could be made by single workers looking for a job. One may, of course, belong to a labor union without being in any way socialistic. That is to say, he may accept our present methods of business and only ask that the workers be treated better. The labor unions have become powerful in Great Britain and have done their part in improving conditions.

After the war, conditions favored a rapid increase of the Labor party in Parliament. In December, 1923, the prime minister, Mr. Stanley Baldwin, determined to have a general election on the ground that some form of protection should be introduced to remedy the depression in business and the consequent widespread unemployment. This challenge to Free Trade, the historic doctrine of the Liberal party, resulted in arousing the Liberals to array themselves against the Conservatives along with the Labor party, and swept the Labor party into office. The Conservatives were reduced to 258 seats, while Labor rose to 191. Mr. Baldwin saw that he should not have the support of the House and recommended to the king that the opposition be asked to form a ministry. Accordingly, January, 1924, Ramsay MacDonald, the most conspicuous leader of the Labor party, was invited by the king to form a cabinet.

In choosing his cabinet Mr. MacDonald did all he could to remove the fear of a radical break with the past. His appointment of such men as Lord Parmoor, Arthur Henderson, J. R. Clynes, Viscount Haldane, Philip Snowden, Sidney Webb, and Lord Olivier showed that the prime minister was eager to have able representatives of all classes who shared the conviction that the government should exist in the interest of the people as a whole. The Labor party had attached to its ranks not only socialists but many thoughtful persons who believed that the old Liberal party was not thoroughgoing enough in its methods to wage war on poverty and to meet the very serious problems which had arisen since the close of the World War.

Mr. MacDonald realized from the first that although his party was in *office* it was not in *power*, since it was dependent on the support of the Liberals to maintain a majority vote.

tember, 1924. One of the most interesting features of the general election was the virtual disappearance of the Liberal party. Many Liberals, coming to the support of the Conservatives, deserted their own party, and the result was that the Liberals retained only forty seats. The new Conservative ministry showed an active interest in promoting friendly relations among the European states and were justly proud of the part they played in achieving the Locarno settlement.

A British publicist writes: "The year that has just closed [1924] will be a landmark in the history of British politics. In its first months it witnessed the consummation to which the democratic movement had been advancing for centuries. Executive power, which had descended from king to barons, and from barons to knights of the shire, and so on, with the extension of the parliamentary institution, to the landed aristocracy, to the professional classes, and to the middle classes, had at last passed to Labor—to the manual worker, the miner from the coal pit, the engine driver from the train, the carpenter from the bench, the laborer from the docks."

This in itself was a serious handicap in securing any independent legislation. The government had not only to please the various groups within the Labor party but to win the approval of the Liberals as well. In spite of these difficulties the government was able to maintain itself in office about eight months.

It is universally conceded that its most notable achievement was in the fields of finance and of foreign affairs. Mr. Snowden, the chancellor of the exchequer, presented a budget which was regarded as a masterpiece of sound finance and wise statesmanship. Mr. MacDonald, acting as his own foreign secretary, introduced a new note into European diplomacy. With great simplicity, tact, and candor he addressed himself to the serious task of restoring confidence between the exhausted nations of Europe. The problem of Russia received careful consideration, and the Soviet government was recognized. Better relations were established between France and Great Britain, while fresh hope was brought into international affairs by his successful handling of the Dawes plan.

Opposition to the government was aroused on the part of both Liberals and Conservatives in regard to a proposed Anglo-Russian treaty which included a loan to that country, guaranteed by the British government. Realizing that the Liberals were unlikely to support him, Mr. MacDonald chose a less important issue as a test of his power,—the so-called Campbell case. The editor of a communist weekly had been arrested for the publication of an article deemed seditious, but the attorney-general decided to withdraw the case. This action the Conservatives viewed as an interference with the course of justice and as due to pressure from the extreme element in the Labor party. A demand for an investigation into the matter Mr. MacDonald regarded as the equivalent of a vote of "lack of confidence" in his government, and recommended that the king dissolve Parliament. The issue of the campaign turned on the hazards of socialistic government *versus* "security," and the Conservatives received a huge majority of votes.

Mr. Stanley Baldwin was again appointed premier, in Sep-

PL. LVIII. RAMSAY MACDONALD

Pl. lix. Naples Biological Station

CHAPTER XXXI

THE PRESENT TREND OF HUMAN AFFAIRS

The Importance of Being Historically Minded. The Present Drift of Human Affairs.

The Importance of Being Historically Minded.

THE object of this volume has not been primarily to explain merely how things used to be. It has had an ulterior ambition. As indicated in the first chapter, its aim is to answer the question whence have come our own prevailing ideas, institutions, and ideals rather than what were those of our predecessors. We have been reviewing things as they once were in order the more clearly to perceive how they now are. This is the only kind of history that matters much, and it is gradually coming to be recognized as a new and precious device for increasing intelligence and insight.

Various roads to truth have been followed since man began consciously to seek it. The Hebrew prophets called upon their God, and began their messages with the imperative claim, "Thus saith the Lord." In India much reliance was placed upon silent meditation and the inward revelations of the holy man. In ancient Athens Socrates led lively discussions in the market place and all comers were invited to take a hand in reconsidering and revising current beliefs. The medieval professors busied themselves interpreting revered and unquestioned authorities—the Bible, Aristotle, the Church fathers—and bringing them into ingenious order and harmony by the deft application of formal logic.

In the early part of the seventeenth century, scarcely more than three hundred years ago, a few leading thinkers began to denounce the older ways of looking for truth as mistaken and barren, at least so far as the study of natural processes was concerned. They believed that a vast amount might be found out about the world, and what was needed was more knowledge. They no longer put their trust in revelation, authority, passive meditation, or mere discussion, so long as no measures were taken to discover how things really were. They had little trouble in showing that the older conceptions of nature, transmitted to them in revered books, were ignorant surmises which could not stand the test of careful observation and experiment. They began the arduous task of supplanting beliefs long unquestioned by newer conceptions, which frequently aroused the suspicion and hostility of the older type of philosopher and theologian.

Of the development of the modern scientific attitude something has been said in an earlier chapter. We cannot trace here the progress of discovery and practical invention since the eighteenth century. It is a difficult theme with troublesome technical complications. We are familiar with its many startling results. No other line of human development explains so many of the peculiarities of our present Western civilization, its unprecedented resources, prospects, possibilities, and problems. The modern scientific method of seeking knowledge has in short proved itself fruitful beyond the wildest dreams of those who first advocated it, and its future progress, should conditions remain favorable, outruns all calculation.

Scientific research is based on the assumption that the older methods of seeking truth about man's world and man himself were so defective that they led to fundamental errors. Their chief defect was the failure to take the requisite pains to find out how things really are and how they work. Just reading old books, thinking and talking, were not enough—natural objects and processes had to be examined with the most scrupulous care in order to discover their nature and operations. This was the way to add to human knowledge. Besides observation, there must be refined measuring and analysis. There must be experimentation; new and artificial conditions and methods of "control" had to be devised, since mere observation of what happens to come under one's eyes is not sufficient.

Lastly, special apparatus had to be invented to enhance the delicacy of our senses and enable scientific men to take note of objects and changes imperceptible to the naked eye. As early as the thirteenth century it was discovered that a convex crystal or bit of glass would magnify objects. Early in the seventeenth century the telescope was contrived and, feeble as it was at first, it served to overthrow the ideas of both ancient and medieval authorities in regard to the whole structure of the universe. A few decades later the microscope began to be employed with astonishing results. It revealed a whole new world of plants and animals. In the nineteenth century combinations of lenses were introduced which permitted the observer to see things only a hundredth of an inch in diameter almost as clearly as if they were a foot or so across. In this way a vast number of species of single-celled animals, protozoa, and minute plants, could be observed. These constitute the game and pasturage of the sea, on which fish and other larger aquatic creatures are absolutely dependent. In the latter part of the nineteenth century bacteria, so tiny that even fair-sized ones look like ghostly specks when magnified a thousand diameters, began to play a great part in medical science and agriculture. The tissues of animals and plants could be studied, as well as the activity of the blood cells, the structure of tumors, the presence and nature of bacterial infections. Without the microscope none of these achievements would have been possible—and the ancients had no microscopes.

In chemistry both of earthly and heavenly things the spectroscope has served greatly to increase human insight. The camera with its sensitive plates can reveal millions of stars which cannot be seen directly through the most powerful telescope. Then, very recently, electrical apparatus has been applied to the investigation of the atom and in many other ways.

Scientific men are few, and it takes a vast amount of patience and time to learn to use the requisite apparatus with skill, and to make and verify one's observations. For most of us it is much easier to accept the beliefs in which we were reared and supplement them now and then by an article which we happen to read in a newspaper or magazine about the wonders of science. But all of us can see the effects of scientific discovery in the various every-day conveniences which we now enjoy and of which our grandfathers had never heard. So the scientist now revolutionizes human existence and habits far more profoundly than politicians and clergymen, who aspire to conduct our public and private lives.

In addition to the various ways of seeking information already mentioned, including the newer scientific methods, another very important one was added in the nineteenth century. This was the historical or developmental consideration of what we find around us. It was first used by geologists, paleontologists, and biologists, and only later by students of human beliefs, customs, and institutions. The present complexion of the globe, with its various mountains, valleys, lakes, and salty oceans, its igneous and metamorphic rocks, its deep beds of sandstone and limestone and chalk, and, above all, the fossils of ancient forms of animal and plant life, could only be explained by considering the history of our planet. The Christian theologians had believed it to be scarcely more than 5,000 years old, and a chronology based upon this assumption was incorporated into the authorized English version of the Bible, and gained great currency. All existing species of animals and plants, as well as the sun and stars, were supposed to have been created within a week, and mankind to have had its origin in the Garden of Eden, fully equipped with language and the ability to name the beasts of the fields and the fowls of the air and cultivate the garden and enjoy its fruits.

This set of ideas began in the first half of the nineteenth century to be questioned by geologists and paleontologists. Gradually these substituted another which traced the history of the world back millions and hundreds of millions of years in order to give time for all the slow processes of stratification which they observed. Darwin maintained that species of animals and plants came and went—that there were to-day new ones and old ones and vestiges of altogether extinct species and genera and families. He tried to explain this long history of organic life by the struggle for existence, variation, and the survival of those fittest to make head against the multiform dangers of existence.

Various traces of human workmanship, especially stone implements, began to be discovered, and these indicated that tool-making creatures had been on the earth for a half million or a million years, and that earlier human beings, to judge from their skulls, were inferior in capacity to men of to-day. It is now assumed by most persons of scientific training that the human race has an ancestry which if carried back for enough would merge into that of the higher mammals, especially into that of the Primates and monkeys. All these momentous conclusions, which so deeply affect our present attitude toward the human species, are the result of historical research, not of a study of the various races of the earth as we now find them.

The biologists began to realize that their insight into the peculiarities of a plant or animal could be vastly increased by taking account of how the organism had come about—that is, by studying its history and that of its ancestors. The human body, for instance, is far more explicable in many respects when viewed historically than "as is." The atrophied muscles for moving our ears and those which once wagged an ancestral tail, together with certain maladjustments which came from getting on our hind legs, become plain enough if we look back far enough. Anatomy to-day tends to run off into embryology and even into protozoölogy, for our life is dependent upon the amœba-like white blood corpuscles which swim through our arteries and veins and cluster by the hundreds of millions in our tissues.

It turns out, then, that it was, curiously enough, the students of nature rather than historians who first appreciated the tremendous advantage of finding out how things had come about in order to comprehend the more fully how they are. But the students of nature did more. They furnished a new setting for human history. They have shown that man is part and parcel of the vast realm of living creatures and shares with them the exquisite responsibility of being alive. They also suggest the starting point from which we may reckon the beginnings of the unique human experiment which we call civilization. Its advance is to be measured by the degree in which it transcends the possibilities of our animal progenitors and all our animal relatives. An individual chimpanzee can be taught by patient trainers to do many human-like things—such as drinking out of a cup, riding a bicycle, and smoking a cigarette. But if he returned to the jungle and his own folk he would not be able to interest them in these innovations. Man alone, owing to certain unique physical peculiarities, into which we cannot go here, has been able to take up, apply, and gradually accumulate the inventions and ideas of those rare fumblers who came from time to time upon some new notion.

Gradually the historical study of individual men and women is coming to be recognized as highly essential, especially if they suffer from some emotional aberration. A new type of psychologists, the "behaviorists," are casting much light upon the life of adults by considering the reactions and development of babies and children. It is astonishing how much their discoveries contribute to an understanding of the conduct and feelings of maturity. Some day this kind of investigation may revolutionize our ethical ideals and our methods of social control—hitherto very disappointing in their operation.

We are pretty well accustomed to the idea that a great deal is being found out of late about the world and even about human beings. Physicists have discovered dead matter to be electrical charges in an amazing state of agitation; biologists reveal every day something astonishing about the ways of life; psychologists, about the play of the emotions. Knowledge certainly comes in rapidly enough, but Wisdom tarries. Life seems to be rather more of a mess now than ever before. At least, our poets and best story-writers and dramatists present it full of bewilderment and frustration. Still, there is usually the implication that a great many of our disappointments and woes are gratuitous and unnecessary, the result of tragic stupidity and want of insight, rather than the fatal dictates of the gods. We ask pitifully, "What keeps us back, when so many undreamed-of possibilities are opening before us?" The older longing to be "good," with the hope of making all things right, is giving way to the suspicion that intelligence is what we most need.

This suspicion is reflected in a great number of books which have been coming out since that most imposing stupidity—the World War—to show how badly we think. Formerly only a few philosophers wondered about thinking; now all of us are invited to consider why we manage our growing resources of information and insight so ineffectively as regards reducing friction with our fellows and maintaining peace in our own bosoms.

It is evident enough that our thinking and feelings do not change so readily as our circumstances, and cannot as yet keep pace with our knowledge at its present rate of increase. We continue to think of new things in old ways. Our sentiments teem with embarrassing anachronisms of which we are usually quite unconscious. Both old and new elements enter into all life's perplexities. The old, as we shall see, always enjoys the right of way. It is as yet rarely summoned to prove its case. The old is at bottom a habit; the new an adventure. And habit is so much more safe and comfortable to most of us most of the time than adventure! The new attracts attention and comment by reason of its freshness. The old, by reason of its familiarity, is commonly merely taken for granted. Nevertheless, since almost all things are as they are because they have been as they have been, their secret lies in the past. Our present problems cannot be understood by just looking them in the face. We have to ask how they arose—in trenchant slang, "How did we get that way?"

Notwithstanding our sprightly criticisms, we are far more old-fashioned than we realize. Old habits of thought yield very reluctantly to new. This is not astonishing when we consider that it has taken perhaps a half million years to inch along as far as we have gone. Ancient ways of thought and action become terrible nuisances long before they can be discarded.

The old drags us down like a chronic disease—and its nature has hitherto been badly diagnosed.

This is obviously but one aspect of man's fate. The old is the indispensable foundation of the new. Without it no advance in knowledge and human improvement would be possible. Father Time is the benefactor to whom we literally owe everything, but he is exceedingly jealous of his established scheme of things. Wisdom will come as we learn to recognize vividly our abject dependence upon him and at the same time invent more ingenious ways than those hitherto discovered for exposing and overcoming his inveterate prejudices.

How instructive is our annual symbolism as we reach December 31. The old year makes his bow to the newborn and totters off to the grave. Within a twelvemonth the baby goes the way of his hoary predecessor. We cannot start anew on January 1 or any other day. This truth historians dignify by the term "Continuity of History." We are sadly familiar with this disagreeable fact, but rarely appreciate its essentiality in all profitable thinking about human troubles.

It is easy enough to illustrate our unconscious debts to the past. Our knowledge and various dexterities, our prejudices and conceits, our scruples and obligations, are very seldom of our own making. They are historical products handed down to us, frequently from remote periods and alien peoples.

Let us consider the historical implications of this volume. It is printed on paper invented by the Chinese early in the Christian era and introduced into Europe in the twelfth and thirteenth centuries. The letters were devisd by the Phœnicians, adopted by the previously illiterate Greeks, modified by the Romans, and altered, so far as the "lower case" is concerned, by the medieval scribes. The capital letters are still the same that we find in ancient Roman inscriptions. The language is based upcn a western German tongue used by the Teutonic invaders of England in the fifth century. It was later given added range and sophistication by the admixture of Latin and Norman-French words. English colonists brought it to this country, and it remains almost the same as when Jamestown and Plymouth were founded. Shakespeare and Francis Bacon could have understood this book as it appears to-day, just as we can read the authorized version of the Bible prepared under their dread monarch, James I. Printing was a Dutch and German innovation made nearly five hundred years ago. The month of August, in which I happen to be writing, is called after the Emperor Augustus, who added a day taken from February to make his month as long as the preceding one dedicated to Julius Cæsar. The year of Our Lord 1926 represents a method of reckoning time initiated by the ancient Egyptians, improved by Julius Cæsar, connected with the birth of Christ by Dionysius Exiguus in the sixth century, and readjusted by Pope Gregory XIII. These are but a few of the ways we unconsciously perpetuate the past. But they are enough to depreciate the stock of the hundred-per-cent American to a point where it would have to be reckoned in thirty-seconds of one per cent. *The continuity of history* is an inexorable fact. It is generally recognized by all who deal with the past. It means that in the great majority of cases one generation goes on doing and believing what the previous one did and believed. It is not true that there is nothing new under the sun. But the new prevails gradually and partially and, compared with the traditional, bulks much less even to-day than is usually believed. As examples, the Protestants in Luther's time agreed with the adherents of the older Catholic faith in most respects, and still do from the standpoint of an outside observer, such as a Japanese Buddhist. The radicals of the French Reign of Terror were in the main unconsciously conservative, as are the Bolsheviki. We still adhere to a division of the day into twelve hours, as established by the Babylonians, and of the circle into three hundred and sixty parts. The efforts to reform the calendar or get rid of primitive inches, feet, furlongs, grains, pennyweights, and the rest meet an opposition in this country which no recommendation of the convenient French revolutionary metric system can at present overcome. Our mile is based on the thousand paces of a Roman legionary.

One who undertook half a million of years ago to guess how man would turn out when he got civilization well under way might be puzzled by the outcome. He would have been a very shrewd prophet indeed to have foreseen that, being a sort of ex-animal, man would tend to sanctify the habits he happened to acquire. The other animals presumably just obey their habits without attempting to justify them or give them a fine name. One of the great obstacles to a free reconsideration of the details of our human plight is our tendency to regard familiar notions as "sacred"—that is, too assured to be questioned except by the perverse and wicked. This word to the student of human sentiment is redolent of ancient, musty misapprehensions. It recalls a primitive and savage setting-off of purity and impurity, cleanness and uncleanness. The French retain the double meaning of the word in their *sacré,* which means at once "blessed" and "damned." Blessed is he who agrees with me and let others be damned. When we realize that this and that notion of ours is "sacred," we may be sure that, as Mr. William Trotter has emphasized in his *Instinct of the Herd,* it is a childish impression which we have never carefully scrutinized.

The young Arab chants the Koran in a Cairo mosque; the Japanese mother trips through the red gate of a Shinto temple to rub her ailing baby on a stone fox; the old-fashioned Chinese student conned Confucius's *Analects;* and Mr. Bryan read his Bible. Their ways were different, but to the critical onlooker each had exactly the same reason for his particular confidence. Each takes for granted the habits of the group in which he happens to be reared and these are sanctified for him. This is Truth for the multitude and for the conspicuously good and respectable of all ages and climes.

The claim to immunity from criticism on the ground of sacredness is by no means confined to religious controversy; it now includes the current system of business, governmental organization, and the family. It is one of the important obstacles in the way of free discussion and readapting our habits so as to bring them into accord with increasing knowledge and new conditions.

All advancement in intelligence and insight depends upon our ability to call in question and reconsider what we have previously taken for granted. Ordinary prejudices and carelessly formed convictions are so numerous in all human beings that the urgence and shortness of life hardly permit any one, even the most alert, to summon all of them before the judgment seat. We might aspire, however, to become conscious of our sacred prejudices. If we could but be induced to trace back their history and analyze their hold on us we should at the same time free ourselves from the dread of looking into their authenticity in the light of new knowledge and experience.

Our problems, as we have seen, are ofttimes inherited, and can best be met by fuller knowledge of their origin and development. The State, as we now know it, is a sort of reincarnation of the ancient chieftain and his entourage. Our religious beliefs are ostensibly Semitic, derived from a pastoral people and dwellers in Syrian villages and small towns. Our education still perpetuates the medieval or classical conceptions. Our standards in the relations of men and women still smack of the ascetic theories of virtue of the days of Saint Augustine, and our theories of business, as Veblen points out, hark back to the eighteenth century. In the discussion of a relatively new issue—the teaching of evolutionary hypotheses—and of a very recent question—the entrance of the United States into the League of Nations—we find the sacredness of Biblical anthropology and the authoritative utterances of Washington invoked. A proper understanding of the past would show the irrelevance of this type of argument. Precedent, however venerable, must be reinspected before it is accepted. Indeed, the more venerable it is the more suspicious should we become that it is an anachronism, originating in times and under conditions far removed from our own. When reverence for the past encroaches upon our meditations and decisions we are admitting an ancient but highly dangerous mischief-maker, so far as honest analysis and planning are concerned.

Now history might be so studied as to undermine prejudice—which means that of which we are quite sure without giving it any proper attention—and especially the savage survival of "sacredness."

History would thus become the sovereign solvent of prejudice and the necessary preliminary to readjustments and reforms. It is a sort of *aqua regia* which loosens up things and gives our thinking its necessary freedom. Nowadays all expert physicians in dealing with physical and mental dislocations always ask, "How did he get that way?" They are not content to take what they can see without wondering how it came about. Our social, political, economic, and educational diseases must be dealt with in the same way.

It is a fundamental and hopeful discovery, to be ranked among the great inventions of mankind, that we do not necessarily learn much about a situation from what is sometimes called a scientific method of dealing with it. We can fill a big book with statistical tables and imposing graphs, but so long as we do not ask how we got into the fix we miss the main point. When in the seventeenth century almost all educated men, doctors, theologians, jurists, professors, believed in witchcraft, one might have prepared questionnaires and surveys to seek out and record the incidence of witchcraft, the frequency of the devil's "sabbaths," the technique of getting up a chimney on a broom or three-legged stool; the per cent of witches who sank when they were cast into the water, the average location of the devil's mark. But all this would hardly have forwarded the disappearance of the delusion. Witchcraft was, it is true, supported by history, but by history in the old sense. One might cite the terrible command "thou shalt not suffer a witch to live"; the instance of the witch of Endor, and the tales in Apuleius. But none of these had anything to do with the manner in which the superstition had come about.

What a chastening effect it might have on an ardent Marxian socialist to realize that Marx's theories were a mid-Victorian product, the counterpart of the classical, Manchester, school of defenders of things as they were! What effect would it have on the worshipers of our Federal Constitution, who would have every school child believe it a sacred and inspired document, to read the Madison Papers, realize the groping, the compromises, the British and French influences that went into the patching together of that important state paper? For an opponent of the entrance of the United States into the League of Nations it might not be a bad thing to see how exactly his arguments resemble those of the opponents of our Federal

Constitution when it was submitted to the various States for ratification.

Those who "believe in" the Bible might believe in it in so much less intolerant and hampering a fashion if they but knew the history of the Hebrew religious anthology comprising contributions extending through a thousand years. The late Professor Morris Jastrow has in his *Gentle Cynic* given a gracious account of the origin of the Book of Ecclesiastes and illustrated the methods of sacred writers of yore. The basis of the little treatise as we have it was a description of the vanity of human life. All things are full of weariness unutterable, the "eye is not satisfied with seeing, nor the ear filled with hearing." Man hath no preëminence above the beasts. They all go speedily to the same place. Get what you can but remember that "there is no work, nor device, nor knowledge, nor wisdom in the grave whither thou goest." This gloomy picture was later toned down by the interpolations of a more hopeful editor. Then, since the little book (written perhaps in the time of Alexander the Great or later) had been ascribed to Solomon (who had died some five hundred years before it was composed), a third writer adds a few proverbs to which it was supposed that wise king had been addicted. If one is reluctant to accept the conclusions reported by Professor Jastrow he may consult a little book by George Foot Moore on *The Literature of the Old Testament,* which is a sketch of the various ways the books of the Bible were built up. The history of the New Testament is equally enlightening.

These few instances must suffice as illustrations of the way in which fuller knowledge of how a thing came about may alter our attitude toward it.

The Present Trend of Human Affairs

The writer explained in the first introductory chapter that, as the years went on, history had come to seem to him a more and more vital matter; that it should not be regarded primarily as an accumulation of information about the past, but as a means for cultivating intellectual freedom and sagacity. This precious historical-mindedness, so essential to estimating man's plight, has hitherto been rare even among historians. It is a realization of how things come about that is the important thing. It opens our eyes wider upon matters as they now stand and at the same time suggests more ingenious ways of forwarding their improvement than we are likely to discover without its aid. The past loses its sacredness and we are no longer its slave. We become free to reconsider and even to neglect its dictates when we realize their often quite stupid origin and their thoughtless transmission to us.

But taking history in the usual sense—that is as a record of the past doings, conditions, institutions, feelings, and faiths of mankind—are there not certain instructive trends to be observed in human affairs? Does not the recollection of man's former conduct yield important hints of the drift of human change to-day? Are there not valuable conclusions to be drawn from the ways things have gone which make clearer the ways they are now going and are likely to continue to go? This is not a new question by any means, but we have reached a stage of thought and knowledge which makes it wise to reopen it with the hope of finding better answers.

In the eighteenth century, to go back no farther, the German poet, Herder, turned aside to establish certain "laws" of history, which should form a sort of human parallel to those laws of nature that were beginning to impress even poets. As time went on came Hegel with his *Philosophy of History* which claimed that each distinguished civilization of the past represented à stage in the development of the World Spirit, which was evidently becoming more and more noble-minded and sophisticated through the ages and was utilizing the genius of the German peoples to exemplify its highest achievements up to date. More recently Benedetto Croce had again traced the story of the "Spirit."

The "philosophy" of history, as represented by these and many less notable writers, is held in abhorrence by those who engage in, or at least revere at a distance, historical research. They are convinced that those who have philosophized most

confidently about history had no more than superficial and anti-
quated information about the past, and that they were inevitably rearing their majestic structures on misapprehensions.
Toil and patience are necessary to collect and present such
facts as may be discovered about the policy of an ancient king,
or even the origin and effects of a single one of his edicts. I
have on my desk the history of a mathematical manual used
for centuries in medieval schools, the *Introduction to Arithmetic* by Nichomachus of Gerasa (who lived in the first or second
century). The account of the life and philosophy of the author,
his authorities, the complicated story of the manuscripts of the
work, and the explanations of the many commentators who
have, through the ages, sought to interpret it fill about two
hundred large pages, with hundreds of footnotes giving references to the sources. This is an instance of how much trouble
it is to find out about one popular old textbook. The late Professor Thomas Francis Carter, dead ere his prime, spent years
collecting information on the invention of paper and printing
in China and its spread westward. Our present civilization is
based on paper and printing, and hitherto we have had very
sketchy and erroneous ideas as to how its foundation was laid
in the early Christian era in a remote and often ignorantly
despised country.

It is no great trick for one so minded to stake out a claim
in historical hinterlands and to work so hard and find so much
that those seeking the soul of history in a handful of out-of-date
manuals and books of reference appear to him wholly negligible
if not absurd.

Yet making full allowance for what is still undiscovered and
not likely ever to be known, and for all that is tucked away in
nooks and corners where it escapes even assiduous students of
the past, is there not after all an astonishing amount of historical information available which will in all probability never be
seriously revised? It seems to me that there is.

The search for "laws" of history appears, however, to be
premature, perhaps vain. I prefer the word "tendencies" or,
better, the "drift" of affairs; these are vaguer terms than "laws"

and better suit the groping and provisional nature of our conjectures. Perhaps the continuity of man's experiences, which has been so constantly insisted upon in the previous pages, may be deemed a "law" and the only one.

In the interpretation of what is now known and is being learned two great changes are in progress, but scarcely as yet beyond their beginnings. One is the growth of historical-mindedness which will enable future writers to give history far more importance than hitherto in the useful enlargement of our memories by showing not so much how things were as how they came about. The second is the appreciation of the current discoveries in regard to man's nature contributed by biologists and psychologists and reënforced by anthropologists.

To offer a single example—the rulers, heroes, sages, saints, and conspicuous rogues of the past are now being reckoned with as human beings rather than as historical celebrities. They had mental and bodily disorders and dislocations even as we have. These must be taken account of in our historical explanations. Gibbon relates with evident pleasure various anecdotes which had for him the gamy relish of indecency. To the historian who possesses some little acquaintance with abnormal psychology, the pornographic becomes scientific. We are now in a much better position to estimate Nero or Theodosia than was Gibbon; even godly men like Luther and Calvin bear looking into.

An Australian physician has recently shown that Joan of Arc was a tomboy before she was a saint, that the black pox which afflicted Henry VIII played a great part in English history during his reign and down to the present; that the hardened arteries of Charles V had their importance in European history; that the manifold disorders of James I and the distaste of Frederick the Great for bathing are by no means negligible in estimating their careers.

This is but an instance of how the increasing knowledge of man tends to modify our estimates of his conduct in the past. He is not a very ingenious or independent creature and the fears some harbor of an inordinate development of individualism seem gratuitous. He usually quietly borrows rather than invents. He is a perpetuator rather than an innovator. As historical and anthropological investigations go on this fact becomes more and more securely established. Each people in any age owes a great part of what it has and thinks to older and very often remote peoples. The "diffusionists" among the anthropologists such as Elliot Smith and the late Doctor Rivers point out many astonishing instances of the migration of inventions and customs. They feel that it is so hard for anything new to be found out and get adopted that it is safest to assume that innovations are imported rather than that they arise independently. This sense of indebtedness might, as Mr. Wells urges, become an important moral sentiment in forwarding a real brotherhood of man. It is a special aspect of the continuity of history which our blustering patriots and nationalists are too ignorant to realize.

In modern times there is the steady prevailing of democracy. Politically this has exhibited itself in the right extended to all men and women to participate nominally in the selection of their governmental representatives. There are some impressive indications that the notions of free government held by nineteenth-century liberals may be superseded before the end of the twentieth. But the right to vote is but a by-product of a far-reaching tendency toward social equalization and uniformity. There is socialism, "equal opportunity for all," "social justice," mass production, and its agent, advertising. Business men find it natural to talk in terms of "service" and social responsibility. Underlying these manifestations of democracy are the public school, the ability to read, and the whirling printing presses.

The somewhat unsteady enlargement of liberty is associated with the previous tendency. This statement will cause some complicated reflections in many minds. It is true that the grosser forms of slavery and serfdom have gone, and their disappearance is impressive. Moreover, since the French Declaration of the Rights of Man in 1789, most national constitutions have proclaimed various kinds of freedoms; and we like to think of the United States as begotten in Liberty. Just now, however, there seems to be a sort of revulsion against personal freedom, not only in Russia and Italy, but in the United States. In this land of liberty we have many "defense" leagues; conscription and the Lusk laws are still fresh in our minds. The Ku Klux and the Fundamentalists are busy securing to every one the imprescriptible right to believe what one's ignorant neighbors believe. Aldous Huxley has wisely said that liberty is something not *given* but *taken*. This is likely to remain true. Genuine tolerance demands a degree of intelligence which outruns that which even exceptionally sophisticated persons possess to-day. There are, nevertheless, various modern circumstances which tend to promote liberty and self-determination.

I should be inclined to substitute for "freedom" quite another word, namely "possibility." Our age, owing to all sorts of novel devices for disintegrating routine and tempting invitations to escape from it, offers us more choices than ever before. Mrs. Grundy finds it impossible to be ubiquitous in a large city. Even in smaller communities she cannot listen in on every telephone conversation in a public booth or chase every runabout or flivver. It is not her fault; circumstances have got too much for her. Like Chaucer's widow, she is "somdel stope in age" and not spry enough to keep up with newer and more ingenious ways of eluding her virtuous attempts to make everything right and proper. And then the psychoanalyst says things about her motives which quite upset her. She is no longer so sure of herself.

Modern conditions and possibilities and the multiplication of options are producing an emancipation far more fundamental than the mere legal freeing of slaves and serfs. A full half of the race, the women, are tempted into occupations and varied activities which were closed to their grandmothers or did not exist a generation or so ago. Formerly, according to both earthly and heavenly law, husbands were encouraged to think that they owned their wives and children. "The family" and "marriage" have been a good many different kinds of things in the past and they promise to undergo new changes as time goes on. This will not be due to the prevailing of wickedness, as the clergy would have us believe, but to an altered situation.

The children too are involved. Modern psychologists think of a child as far older at six than was formerly believed. Bertrand Russell in his new book on *Education and the Good Life* holds that "character" is pretty completely developed at that age. The effect of modern social and economic conditions on the views and relations of boys and girls is explained, on the basis of long and intimate experience with the actual facts in a large city, by Judge Lindsey, in his *Revolt of Modern Youth*.

There is a tendency toward the decrease of gratuitous and ruthless cruelty and the widening of human sympathy and kindliness. We do not publicly impale or eviscerate or burn or decapitate or break on the wheel the enemies of God, the king, and society, as formerly. And only when a holy war comes on do we blow them to pieces. On our breakfast table we find piled up appeals to help relieve the sufferings of the sick, destitute, and erring. Being prone to explain changes in human practices and moods by taking into account altering conditions, I suspect that the fact that we are so squeezed together nowadays makes it impossible for us to be so indifferent to our neighbor as once we were. This accounts for some new decencies and seeming understandings. Disease is now known to be transmissible and to come from an infected fellow creature rather than from either God or the devil. Black and white, Jew and Gentile, Oriental and Occidental have to snatch the same seats and hang to the same straps in the New York subways. This foments a sort of enforced brotherhood of unavoidable competition and interlocking misfortunes. This does not mean that I underrate the unmistakable increase in benevolence; I am only explaining that it now rests on a more solid foundation than that of mere exhortation to love our neighbor as ourselves. If "love" should be interpreted "understand" it would become a scientific ambition with most revolutionary consequences.

But there is certainly a very sour and ugly strain in men, women, and children which, given the right stimulus, will under many pious disguises express itself in cruelty of word and deed. Even gentle souls will suddenly become acrid and exhibit a ferocity which is a correlative of their successful repressions. Fear and jealousy and envy are in their hearts as in those of the more openly inhumane. Many of the most successful films have their scenes of torture, their voluptuousness of cruelty. "Sadism" is a rather new word for a class of very common and inveterate reactions of human beings. Every day brings illustrations of it in the newspapers. We are, however, making progress through a fuller understanding of this horrid element in human nature.

One of the most important of modern trends, as must have become fully apparent to the reader, is that toward secularization, or the reduction of human affairs to earthly standards. There are no longer many kings by the grace of God. The Treaty of Vienna in the early part of the nineteenth century was concluded in the name of the Holy Trinity; that of Versailles, a hundred years later, invokes no celestial benediction upon its stupidities. Education has to a great extent escaped from the control of the churches; ecclesiastical courts, which, before the French Revolution, settled a wide range of cases, have largely disappeared. Legislative assemblies may still be opened with prayer, but rarer and rarer are the appeals made to the Bible by lawgivers.

The belief in supernatural beings still prevails, and openly to question the existence of God is still unusual and shocking. But Satan and his hosts are becoming mere shadows of their former selves. Their malignant rôle as tempters, storm raisers, and disease producers is pretty much played out in our Western World.

The so-called free thinkers of the eighteenth century held that a belief in a future life of rewards or punishments for the deeds done in the flesh was essential to maintain the morality of the multitude; otherwise men and women would cast off all restraint and obey the impulses of the moment. Whether confidence in the survival of our personalities beyond the grave is declining I do not know. It has been reënforced in recent years by what are known as "psychic" phenomena. At any rate, much less is said about the terrible alternative between heaven and hell, and morality is gradually being shifted on to a new and, what seems to me, a firmer basis, namely that *it pays,* in this world as well as in the next, if such there be. But morality itself is assuming a different guise from that familiar to the moralists of past days.

Whether the growing knowledge of man's nature and origin and of the resources of the world in which he lives will ultimately destroy the old and spontaneous belief in supernatural beings it is impossible to say. The increasing possibilities of our earthly existence and the disturbance of long-established routine in thought and action conspire to give this mortal life an ever-enlarging and absorbing interest. Nor is this interest necessarily "materialistic," as is sometimes hastily inferred by the "spiritual." It may bring with it quite as noble aspirations as any preached in the past.

The bringing together of all the peoples of the earth is a very new thing under the sun. The daily news is, with trivial exceptions, common to the whole globe. President Wilson could talk to the world at large with as much ease and more assurance than he could address the Senate. All this suggests a unification of mankind impossible in the past which may take the form of unprecedented coöperation or of rivalries and struggles which will make earlier wars look like feeble forecasts of what is to come.

Were there space here I think that I could make out a fair case for the guess that the World War which began in 1914 may prove to be the last of its species. We are at least gradually coming to see that "war" has become an old name for a new thing, as amply exemplified in the last great instance. The extension of conscription coerced the most gentle and unwarlike into the lines; non-combatants, however far from the scene of battle, were, as never before, subject to sudden death and mutilation; the nations' whole economic systems suffered unprecedented derangement and imminent bankruptcy. And more impressive still is the assurance that all is ready to

[747]

intensify these horrors should another general conflict occur. Consequently war never before appeared to so many as not only a crime, but, what is much more important, a most atrocious farce.

To judge from the way in which witchcraft, slavery, and active religious persecution disappeared—all ancient and sanctified and seemingly *permanent* human institutions—the doom of war may possibly be near at hand. At any rate the forces making against war are far more potent than ever before. It may be that we shall need one more lesson. Perhaps if New York, London, Paris, Berlin, and Rome could be shattered by means now in hand and their peaceful inhabitants suffocated, it might bring the rest of mankind into a chastened frame of mind suitable to an honest reconsideration of the implications of war as now practiced.

Man was originally an utterly improvident animal. He had no inclination to store up provisions like a squirrel. He was no more frugal than a horse. An empty maw was his chief incentive to activity. He spent a great part of his life wandering about in search of something to eat. His leisure was the lethargy following a good gorge. His only form of "investment" was bringing down a sufficiently large animal to outrun the appetites of himself and his hungry companions. What the socialists call the exploiter and capitalist is the modern representative and successor of a long line of inventors who have taught men frugality in some degree and made possible active leisure as over against savage apathy. Were the ingenuities of these inventors done away with, human life would be reduced once more to that of the raccoon—saving his honor. Viewed in the light of man's history, our present system of industrial organization based upon an ever-enlarging mechanism of credit is one of the most astounding inventions. With all its defects it holds great promise for the further liberation of mankind from ancient and hitherto unavoidable hazards. As yet it is an experiment the results of which cannot be foreseen. It has produced socialism and may very well before long discredit it both in theory and in practice. The lot of the overwhelming mass of mankind has always been miserable; our present industrial and financial system did not create poverty and over-work; it has somewhat alleviated them already, and is likely to be utilized, with various mollifications and changes of attitude, in their further reduction.

These historical memories must suffice, for there is not space for more. They seem to me to suggest an attitude toward general and individual betterment very different from what most of us have been brought up on. The fundamental fact is that almost all leaders of humanity still feel that the new should not only rest, as it inevitably must, on the old, but that it must be in unquestioned subjection to sanctified tradition. The International Eucharistic Congress held in Chicago in 1926 is an instance of this. Modern methods of transportation and publicity were utilized to republish, amid gorgeous ancient pageantry and popular acclaim, one of the fundamental doctrines of the Medieval Church.

The world is, however, assuredly turning out to be a very different place from what it was conceived to be in the Middle Ages; human possibilities have expanded beyond belief, and man himself as well as his heaven and earth has little resemblance to the pictures of him which have been furnished by his moral guides. *Is not the moral overrating of the past our besetting danger?* We have the great task before us of gradually replacing archaic aspirations, abhorrences, tastes, and scruples by others which shall conform more closely to the actual facts as now understood and the actual conditions in which we live. Otherwise, our struggles toward the good life must perforce be feeble, hesitant, and ineffective, as indeed we find them to be.

To become historical-minded is to attain intellectual and moral majority.

INDEX

*"Index-learning turns no student pale
Yet holds the eel of science by the tail"*
—POPE: Dunciad

INDEX

Austria, origin of, 260; in eighteenth century, 369 ff.; after 1815, 530; in 1848, 565 f.; war with Prussia, in 1866, 576 f.; union with Hungary (1867–1918), 568; relations with Serbia, 657 f., 669; dissolution of, 693, 701; republic of, 701. *See* Hungary, World War
Avignon, 278 ff.

Babylonian Captivity, 278 ff.
Bacon, Francis, 349, 353
Bacon, Roger, 210
Bacteria, 729
Bæda. *See* Venerable Bede
Bagdad, 79; railway to, 668; in World War, 674
Balance of power, 309, 406
Baldwin, king of Jerusalem, 142, 144
Baldwin, Stanley, 723 ff.
Baliol, John, 247
Balkans, conditions in the, 650 ff.; wars in the, 658 ff.
Baltic States, 704 ff.
Bannockburn, battle of, 248
Baptists, 365
"Barbarians, Laws of the," 46
Barbarossa. *See* Frederick I
Bards, Welsh, 245
Basilica, the, 53
Bastille, fall of the, 469
Batavian Republic, 504 f.
Battering-rams, 102 f.
Bavaria, 510, 537, 581, 694
Bayeux tapestry, 231 f.
Becket, Thomas, 235 f.
Bechuanaland, 611
Belgian Congo, 628
Belgium (Austrian Netherlands), recognized as independent kingdom, 549 f.; neutrality of, violated by German invasion in 1914, 671; in the World War, 673
Benedictine order, 64 and note
Berlin, Congress of 1878, 641, 656
Berlin Decree, 514
Bessarabia, 705
Bible, 26 ff., Luther's translation of the, 298; English translation of the, 312; King James version of the, 353
Bill of Rights, 367 f., 589
Biology, 731 f.
Bishop of Rome, early claims of, 56 and note; leading position of, 58 f, 154 f. *See* Popes

Bismarck, 574 f., 585 f., 722
Black death, 251
"Black and Tans," 605
Black pox, 266 note
Black Sea, 387; neutrality of, 651
Blanc, Louis, 548
Blockade, in the Napoleonic Wars, 509, 514, 515 note; in the World War, 678, 683
Boer War (1899–1902), 610
Bohemia, 86 f., 271, 340 f., 383, 563, 565, 567, 569, 703
Boleyn, Anne, 309 ff., 313
Bologna, University of, 206
Bolsheviki, 687, 691, 719 ff.
Bonaparte, Joseph, 511, 517 f.
Bonaparte, Louis, 511, 519 note
Bonaparte, Napoleon. *See* Napoleon
Boniface, St., apostle to the Germans, 71 f.
Boniface VIII, Pope, 275 ff.
Books in Middle Ages, 212 ff.; censorship of, 368 f., 636, 644 and note
Borodino, battle of, 520 f.
Bosnia and Herzegovina, 654, 656 f., 667, 703
Botha, General, 610
Bourbon, House of, 257, 329 f., 546
Bourbons, Spanish, 379 f.
Bourgeoisie, 556 f., 561 and note, 718
Boxer Rebellion, 623
Brandenburg, elector of, 271, 388 ff.
Brazil, 693 note
Bremen, 86, 173
Brest-Litovsk, 687
Britain conquered by the Angles and the Saxons, 69 f.
British East Africa. *See* East Africa, British
British Empire, 408, 605 ff., 628 ff.
Bruce, Robert, 247 f.
Brumaire, 500
Bubonic plague, 251
Bucharest, Treaty of, 660, 681
Bulgaria, 656 ff., 680, 691 f., 705
Bundesrat, powers of, 584
Burgundians, 35, 41, 46; number of entering the Empire, 46
Burgundy, 254, 258, 268, 377
Buttress, 180 ff.

Cabinet, British, 594 f.
Cable, Atlantic, 618
Cahiers, 465
Calais, 255
Calendar, 734

INDEX

Caliph, title of, 77

Caliphate, transferred from Medina to Damascus, 77; transferred to Bagdad 77 ff.; abolished, 706

Calonne, 462

Calvin, 307 f., 327 ff.

Cameroons, 586, 627

Campbell case, 725

Campo-Formio, Treaty of, 495

Canada, France and England rivals in settlement of, 409 f., 414; ceded to England, 412; the Dominion of, created, 606 ff.

Canon law, 153 note

Canossa, 129 and note

Cape-to-Cairo railway, 612

Cape Colony, 609

Capitalism, 557, 718, 748

Capitularies, 90

Carbonari, the, 541

Cardinals, origin of, 125 and note

Carlsbad Resolutions, 536 f.

Carnot, 489

Carolingian line, 82 note

Carter, Thomas Francis, 272 note, 741

Cartwright, 552

Cassiodorus, treatises of, on the liberal arts and sciences, 35 f.

Castles, medieval, 100 ff.

Cathedrals, 178 ff.

Catherine II of Russia, 387, 651

Catherine of Aragon, 309 f.

Catherine of Medici, 328 ff.

Catholic Church. *See* Church, Clergy

Catholic emancipation in England, 596

Catholic League, 342 f.

Cavaliers, 358 f.

Cavour, 571, 582

Celts, 69; in Britain, 70

Chalcedon, act of the council of, 58

Chalons, battle of, 33

Charlemagne, 83 ff.; disruption of empire of, 94

Charles I of England, 353 ff.

Charles II of England, 364 ff., 377

Charles VIII of France invades Italy, 264 ff.

Charles IX of France, 328 f.

Charles X of France, 545. *See also* Artois, count of

Charles V, Emperor, 259, 263 ff., 293 f., 322

Charles I of Austria, 693, 701

Charles XII of Sweden, 387

Charles Albert of Sardinia, 565 f., 568 f.

Charles Martel, 80, 82

Charter, French, of 1814, 544

Charter, Great, 241 ff.

Charters, town, 169

Chartists, 591 ff.

Chartres, cathedral of, 183

Château-Thierry, 689

Chaucer, 197

Chemistry, 204, 729

Child labor, 557, 597

China, relations with Europe, 586, 620 ff.; reforms in, 625 ff.; republic of (1912), 625 ff.; and World War, 626. *See also* Korea, Manchuria

Chino-Japanese War (1894–1895), 622

Chivalry, 199 ff.

Chosen. *See* Korea

Christianity, 58 note, rise of, 23 ff., 26; promises of, 18, 52; contrast with paganism, 28 f., 51

Chrysoloras, 209

Church, under Roman Empire, 24 ff., 53 ff.; sources of power of, 51 ff.; relation of, to the civil government, 54 f.; in time of Charlemagne, 81, 91 f.; property of, 120 ff.; character and organization of medieval, 152 ff.; relation of, to State, 274 ff.; break-up of medieval, 273 f., 280 ff.; discontent with, in Germany, 282; in France before the Revolution, 450; attacked by Voltaire, 441 f.; property of, confiscated by the National Assemby, 474; secularization of lands, 503 f.; separation from State in France, 505 f., 588. *See* Clergy, Popes

Church of England, 310 f., 334 f.; disestablished in Ireland, 495, 502, 602 f.

Cisalpine Republic, 495, 502

City of God, The, Augustine's, 31, 84

City-states, 184 ff.

Civil war in England, 358 f.

Civilization, progress of, 5 ff.; diffusion of Western European, 728

Clement VII, Pope, 280

Clergy, position of, in Middle Ages, 123 f., 157 f.; in France before the Revolution, 450; Civil Constitution of the, in France, 475 f.; nonjuring, in France, 476 f., 481, 505 f. *See also* Marriage

[753]

INDEX

INDEX

German Empire, formation of, 581
Germanic languages, origin of, 45, 195
Germans, 8 f., objects of, in invading
the Empire, 30; number of, invading the Empire, 44 f.; fusion of,
with the Romans, 22, 41, 46; character of early, 42, 47; conversion of,
71 ff.
Germany, 119 ff.; division of, into
small states, 137, 260, 270; universities of, 206 ff.; in the sixteenth
century, 270 ff.; religious division
of, 301; after the Thirty Years'
War, 344 ff.; territorial reorganization of, in 1803, 503 f.; condition
of, in 1814, 530; effects of Napoleonic Era in, 533 f.; in 1848,
565; unification of, 574 ff., 581;
under the Empire (1871–1918), 584;
constitution of, 584 f.; colonial ex-
pansion of, 586, 622, 627 f.; and the
Near East, 667 f.; republic of 1918
in, 694, 722, provisions of the
Treaty of Versailles imposed on,
696 f. See also Holy Roman Em-
pire, World War
Ghiberti, 218
Gibbon, Edward, 722
Gibraltar, 381
Girondists, 486 ff.
Gladstone, 593, 594 note, 603, 721
Godfrey of Bouillon, 142
Goethe, 4
Golden Bull, 114
Gordon, General, 629
Gothic architecture, 178 ff.
Gothic sculpture, 183 f.
Granada, the Alhambra at, 81, fall of,
87
"Grand Remonstrance," 358
Gravitation, discovery of universal,
801
Great Britain, 405, after 1688, 404 ff.;
colonies of, in North America,
409 f., 412, 414 ff.: settlements of,
in India, 410, 411 ff.: involved in
war with France (1793), 485; re-
news war with Napoleon, 508 f.;
constitutional government in,
589 ff.; extension of suffrage, 590 ff.;
political parties in, 594 f., 599,
723 f.; reforms of the nineteenth
century in, 595 ff.; the Irish question, 601 ff.; in the Far East,
620 ff., 666 and note; the Near
Eastern question, 656 f.; govern-

ment by the Labor party, 724 ff.
See also Britain, British empire,
World War
"Great schism," 192, 280
Greece, creation of the kingdom of,
549, 651 f.; war with Turkey (1897),
657; war with Turkey (1912), 658,
war with Bulgaria, 660; republic of,
706
Greek, study of, in the Middle Ages,
208.
Greek Church, tends to separate
from the Latin, 58; in Russia,
636, 645; in the Balkans, 650
Green, John Richard, 3
"Green Manifesto," 718
Gregory VII, Pope, 125 ff.
Gregory XI, Pope, 280
Gregory the Great, 60 ff.; writings
of, 61 f.; missionary work of, 62
f., 70
Gregory of Tours, 37, 39 f.
Grey, Sir Edward, 669
Grotius, 382
Guienne, 238
Guilds, in the Middle Ages, 171; of
teachers, 206; in eighteenth cen-
tury, 423 ff.
Guise, House of, 328 ff.
Gunpowder, 211
Gustavus Adolphus, 342 f.

Habeas Corpus Act, 589
Hague, peace conferences at the
(1899, 1907), 663 f., 711; per-
manent Court of Arbitration at,
663, 711
Hamburg, 173, 504
Hampden John, 355 f.
Hanover, electorate of, 405 note
Hanover, House of, 405; occupied
by Napoleon, 509; relations of,
with Prussia, 512, 576
Hanseatic League, 176 f.
Hanseatic towns, annexation of, to
France, 519
Hapsburg, House of, 259 ff., 393,
399, 519, 651; fall of, 701
Hapsburg, Rudolf of, king of Ger-
many, 137, 260
Hardenberg, Count, 534
Harding, President, 701, 712
Hargreaves, James, 552
Harold, earl of Wessex, 230 f.
Hastings, battle of, 230 f.
Hawaiian Islands, 631

INDEX

INDEX

fore 1806, 521; under the Third Republic, 587 f.; in Russia, 634, 637 ff.; in Turkey, 654; in Bulgaria, 718

Peasants' Revolt, 252 f., 279

Penance, 157

Peninsular War, 518

Permanent Court of Arbitration, 664, 711

Permanent Court of International Justice, 699, 710 ff.

Perry, Commodore, 621

Persecution in England, 316

Pershing, General, 689 f.

Persia, British and Russian spheres of influence in, 643 note, 666

Peter, St., regarded as first bishop of Rome, 56 and note

Peter the Great, 385 ff.

Peter the Hermit, 141

Petition of Right, 354

Petrarch, 209 and note

Petrograd, 386 and note, 686 and note, 687

Philip II of Spain, 315 f., 336

Philip Augustus, 148, 239 f.

Philip the Fair, 147, 247, 275 f.

Philip of Hesse, 304

Philippine Islands, 632

Piave, battle of the, 693

Piedmont, 543, 565, 569 ff., 571

Pilgrim Fathers, 357

Pippin the Short, 82

Pirates in the Middle Ages, 176

Pitt, the elder, 412

Pius IX, Pope, 543, 566

Plantagenets, 238 ff.

Plebiscite, 500 f.

Poitou, 240

Poland, partition of, 395 ff.; Napoleon's campaign in, 513; dispute over, at the Congress of Vienna, 530; revolts of 1830–1831 and 1863, 635 and note; reduced to Russian province, 635; in World War, 682; independence established, 687; war with Russia, Czechoslovakia, the Ukraine, and Lithuania (1919–1920), 704

Political economy, rise of, 445

Pope, 56; origin of the title of, 59; relation of, with Otto the Great, 119 f.; position of, in Middle Ages, 154 f.; position of, since 1870, 581 f.

Popes duties of the early, 60; origin of, the temporal power of, 56 ff. and notes; election of, 125; claims of, 125 f.; at Avignon, 278 ff.

Port Arthur, 683, 685 f., 712

Portcullis, 105

Porto Rico, 632

Portsmouth, Treaty of, 625

Portugal, explorations by Portuguese, 224, 409; colonies of, 631 and note

Posen ceded to Poland, 697

Postal system, 618

Praise of Folly, by Erasmus, 283

Prayer book, English, 315, 334

Prayer rugs, 74

Presbyterian Church, 307, 356

Press, censorship of: in England, 368 f., 434 f.; in the eighteenth century, 458; in France, 507, 547; in Germany, 536 f.; in Russia, 634 f., 644 and note

Pressburg, Treaty of, 510

Pretender, the Young, 406 f.

"Pride's Purge," 359

Priests, duties of, 156 f.

Prince of Wales, 245 f.

Printing, invention of, 212, 217 f., 734, 741

Prison reform, 596 f.

Proletariat, 718, 720

"Protestant," origin of term, 302 f.

Protestant Revolt, in Germany, 284 ff.; in Switzerland, 311 ff.; in England, 308 ff.

Protestantism, progress of, 304

Protocol for the pacific settlement of international disputes (1924), 714

Provencal, 198 and note

Provence, 258

Prussia, rise of kingdom of, 388 ff.; at war with France, 482, 484; acquires district on left bank of Rhine at Congress of Vienna, 531; at war with Napoleon, 512 f.; after 1814, 533 ff.; in 1848, 565; constitution granted to, 570; strengthening of army of, 574 f.; at war with Denmark (1864), 576 f.; at war with Austria (1866), 576 f.; at war with France (1870), 578 f.; predominating influence of, in the German Empire, 584

Puritans, 357 and note

Pyramids, battle of, 499

Psychology, modern, 732, 742

INDEX

Sadowa, battle of, 577
St. Bartholomew, Massacre of, 332
St. Benedict, Rule of, 64 f.
St. Bernard, 9, 147 f.
St. Boniface anoints Pippin, 82
St. Dominic, 163 f.
St. Francis, 161 ff.
St. Mihiel, 691
St. Peter's, rebuilding of, 285
St. Petersburg (Petrograd), founding of, 386 and note
St. Quentin, 691
Saint-Simon, 374
Saladin takes Jerusalem, 148
Salonika, 660, 680
Samoan Islands, 631
San Stefano, Treaty of, 655
Saracens, 145, 173
Sardinia, kingdom of, 495 note; in the Crimean War, 654 note. *See also* Piedmont
Savannah, the, 615
Savonarola, 265 f.
Savoy, France deprived of, 529
Saxons, settle in England, 69 f.; conquest of, by Charlemagne, 85; rebellion against Henry IV, 130.
Saxony, elector of, 271; question of, at the Congress of Vienna, 530 f.; member of North German Federation, 576 f.
Schleswig-Holstein affair, 575 f.
Scholasticism, 208; attack of Roger Bacon on, 210
"School of the palace," 92
Science, medieval, 202 ff.; methods of modern, 347 ff., 727 ff.; opposition to modern, 439
Scott, Reginald, 352
Scone, Stone of, 247
Scotch nation, language of, 246 f.; differs from English, 248
Scotland, 246 ff., 357, 360 ff.; Presbyterian Church in, 335; union with England, 404
"Secular clergy" defined, 65
Secularization, 746
Security Pact, 714 ff.
Sedan, battle of (1870), 580; capture of (1918), 691
Seas, freedom of the, 515 note
Self-determination, 707
Seljuk Turks, 139
Senlac, 230
Separatists, 356 f.
Sepoy Rebellion, 613

Serbia, 651; war with Turkey (1878), 655; independence recognized, 655 war with Turkey (1912), 658; relations with Austria, 657 f., 667 f., war with Bulgaria (1913), 660; relations with Russia, 667; in World War, 680, 691. *See* Jugoslavia
Serbs, Croats, and Slovenes, kingdom of the. *See* Jugoslavia
Serfdom, 105 ff., 419; disappearance of, 109; in England, 253, 419 f.; abolished in France, 470; in Prussia, 523; in Japan, 622; in Russia, 637 ff.
Sevastopol, siege of, 653
Seven Years' War, 393, 412 ff.
Seville, tower (Giralda) at, 80
Sèvres, Treaty of, 705 f.
Shakespeare, 353
Shantung, Germans in, 586, 622 f.
Ship Money, 355
Shires, 246
Shotwell, James T., 714 note
Sicilies, kingdom of the Two, 97, 135 f., 137, 151, 264 note, 322, 540, 572
Sidon, 144
Sigismund, Emperor, 387
Silesia, 392 ff., 703
Simkhovitch, V. G., 22 note
Simony, 123 f.
Sinn Fein, 604
Slavery, disappearance of, 743; in Roman Empire, 17 ff.
Slavonia, 668. *See also* Jugoslavia
Slavs, subdued by Charlemagne, 86; invasion of, 97, 99; settle Russia, 384; in the Balkans, 567 f., 650 ff., 668
Slovakia, 703. *See also* Czechoslovakia
Smith, Adam, 445
Smith, Elliot, 743
Smuts, General, 611
Smyrna, 706
Social Democratic party, in France, 548; in Germany, 585 f.; in Russia, 645 f., 686 f.
Socialism, 559 ff.; in Germany, 585 f.; in Russia, 645 f., 686 f.
Soil, depletion of, Roman, 22 and note
Solferino, battle of, 572
Somaliland, British, 611; French, 627
Somme, battle of the, 680
Song of Roland, 198 f.
Sorbonne, 327
South Africa, 609 ff.; creation of